INTIMATE MATTERS

Intimate Matters

A HISTORY OF SEXUALITY IN AMERICA

John D'Emilio and Estelle B. Freedman

PERENNIAL LIBRARY

Harper & Row, Publishers, New York
Cambridge, Philadelphia, San Francisco, London
Mexico City, São Paulo, Singapore, Sydney

A hardcover edition of this book was published in 1988 by Harper & Row, Publishers.

First PERENNIAL LIBRARY edition published 1989.

Library of Congress Cataloging-in-Publication Data

D'Emilio, John
  Intimate matters.

  "Perennial Library"
  Bibliography: p.
  Includes index.
  1. Sex customs—United States—History. I. Freedman, Estelle B., 1947–.II. Title.
HQ18.U5D45 1989   306.7'0973   87-45608
ISBN 0-06-091550-1 (pbk.)

89 90 91 92 93 FG 10 9 8 7 6 5 4 3 2 1

for Jim and for Susan

Contents

Illustrations appear following pages 108 and 274.

Acknowledgments

IN the course of writing this book, we have incurred numerous debts. The list of colleagues and friends who have read the manuscript in various stages of composition and have offered invaluable criticisms is long. We thank Allan Bérubé, Albert Camarillo, Clay Carson, Antonia Castañeda, Carl Degler, Mary Felstiner, Bert Hansen, Margo Horn, Susan Krieger, Mary Beth Norton, Jim Oleson, Elizabeth Pleck, Deborah Rhode, Ellen Rothman, Mary Ryan, Katherine Stern, and Jack Winkler for reading drafts of chapters. Nancy Cott, William Chafe, Lisa Duggan, Emily Honig, Jonathan Katz, Elaine Tyler May, and Sharon Thompson gave us useful comments on the entire manuscript. We are also grateful to a series of able graduate research assistants who greatly facilitated our work: Allida Black, Phil Ethington, Meg Johnson, Sue Lynn, Peggy Pascoe, Julie Reuben, and Mary Wood. David Lubin offered helpful advice on visual sources. Martin Duberman, Noralee Frankel, Elaine Tyler May, Mary Beth Norton, Elizabeth Pleck, and Laurel Ulrich generously shared sources from their own research.

The staffs of the libraries at Stanford University and the University of North Carolina at Greensboro have been extremely helpful in tracking down obscure references. Those at the Kinsey Institute for Research in Sex, Reproduction, and Gender at Bloomington and the Arthur and Elizabeth Schlesinger Library at Radcliffe College made research visits there efficient and profitable. A summer fellowship from the UNCG Excellence Foundation, a semester's freedom from teaching, and a fellowship for the Study of Modern Society and Values from the American Council of Learned Societies provided John D'Emilio time and money necessary for completing this book. Fellowships from the American Association of University Women and the Stanford Humanities Center gave Estelle Freedman a critical year during which to work on the book. A Pew Foundation Grant from Stanford University provided funds for travel and research; a faculty grant from the Program in Feminist Studies at Stanford made possible bibliographical assistance. The Academic Computer Center at UNCG and Instructional Research and Information Systems at Stanford gave us valuable instruction, funds, and equipment for preparing the manuscript. The students in our courses on the history of sexuality have encouraged us greatly, while the history club of UNCG, the faculty at UNCG's Residential College, and the Stanford Humanities Center provided forums in which some of these ideas could be presented.

Finally, Jim Oleson and Susan Krieger each tolerated with grace and humor the endless disruptions in daily life that sharing a home with an obsessive author unfortunately entails. We thank them, and each other, for the intellectual and emotional support that made this book possible.

Introduction

In olden days a glimpse of stocking,
Was looked on as something shocking,
But now, God knows,
Anything goes.
Anything Goes, 1934

WHEN Cole Porter wrote these lyrics more than half a century ago, he was reflecting the common-sense perceptions of denizens of New York's sophisticated nightlife. Freud, flappers, petting parties, Hollywood scandals, even the crusade of Margaret Sanger for easy access to birth control, all pointed to the same conclusion: the sexual mores of the times seemed infinitely freer than those of bygone eras. H. L. Mencken's stereotypical Puritan, tortured by "the haunting fear that someone, somewhere, may be happy," was finally, and firmly, buried. The Puritans' straight-laced prudish successors, the Victorians, so uncomfortable with the erotic that they hid the nakedness of classical statuary beneath fig leaves, had also passed from the scene. In their place were the liberated moderns of the post–World War I decades, the young men and women who danced the Charleston, discarded the heavy corsets and starched collars of their parents' generation, enjoyed double entendres, and appreciated the pleasures of intimate, erotic companionship. From the perspective of Cole Porter's audience, the history of sexuality in America was a story of progress triumphant. The ignorance and suffering caused by past repression had given way to the freedom and expressiveness of an enlightened present.

As readers of this volume will quickly discover, *Intimate Matters* recounts a very different kind of story. The history of American sexuality told in the following pages is not one of progress from repression to liberation, ignorance to wisdom, or enslavement to freedom. Indeed, the poles of freedom and repression are not the organizing principles of our work. Rather, we have constructed an interpretation of American sexual history that shows how, over the last three and a half centuries, the meaning and place of sexuality in American life have changed: from a family-centered, reproductive sexual system in the colonial era; to a romantic, intimate, yet conflicted sexuality in nineteenth-century marriage; to a commercialized sexuality in the modern period, when sexual relations are expected to provide personal identity and individual happiness, apart from reproduction. We argue, in short, that sexuality has been continually reshaped by the changing nature of the economy, the family, and politics.

We have been prompted to write this book, and to depart from past orthodoxy about the contours of America's sexual past, in part because of our own historical experiences. Coming of age during the 1960s, we witnessed firsthand the resurgence of feminism as well as the rise of gay liberation. Both movements focused national attention on issues of sexuality, sharply challenging common assumptions about the "naturalness" of gender and sexuality. Partisans of each cause argued that the cultural construction of gender and sexuality served political ends, namely, to keep women and homosexuals subordinate to men and heterosexuals. Their analysis raised intriguing possibilities: if what these movements claimed was true for the present, then the study of the past might offer insight into how contemporary sexuality took shape and how sexuality as an expression of power had changed over time.

Simultaneously, the academic world we entered in the 1970s offered a favorable intellectual climate for historians interested in the study of sexuality. In the first half of the twentieth century, the study of sexuality had taken place largely within the fields of medicine, psychology, and biology, as typified by the work of Freud and Kinsey. Scholars who concentrated on individual bodies and psyches tended to ask questions about whether sexual behavior was normal or pathological. After World War II, building on the work of anthropologists such as Margaret Mead, social scientists gradually recast sexuality as a subject embedded in social structure and cultural forms. Authors such as John Gagnon and William Simon explored the relationship between sexuality and other forms of social interaction, adding a measure of cultural relativism to the study of sex.[1]

Meanwhile, a renewal of interest in social history emphasized the study of everyday life, or the private side of history. Borrowing methods from the social sciences, historians explored intimate aspects of individual, family, and community life, including birth, adolescence, courtship, marriage, divorce, and death. By the 1970s, the resurgence of feminism and social history combined in the burgeoning field of women's history, an academic endeavor with strong ties to a political movement for gender equality. Feminist historians helped spark a moderate explosion of literature about sexuality in the past. Their insight that sexual relations are a significant source of inequality between men and women has made an understanding of sexual history critical to the larger project of social history. Together, historians of the family and of women introduced new intellectual paradigms and historical sources to expand our understanding of the sexual behavior, values, and politics of Americans in the past. By now, the field of sexual history has grown so large that only specialists can keep up with all the monographs and articles written each year on topics such as abortion, contraception, prostitution, courtship, venereal disease, and homosexuality.[2]

This new literature on the history of sexuality has begun to challenge older, stereotypical views of Puritans, Victorians, and liberated moderns. For one, Puritans and Victorians have been distinguished from each other more clearly. As Edmund Morgan pointed out over forty years ago, Puritans were more interested in sex and more egalitarian about male and female sexual expression than we previously thought. More recently, scholars have revised the older picture of the Victorians. One school argues that repression characterized official ideology, but just beneath the surface of society lay a teeming, sexually active underground. Another argument holds that repression did not characterize even the ideology. Rather, in the view of scholars such as Carl Degler and Peter Gay, middle-class Victorians accepted sexual pleasures, as long as they occurred within the sanctuary of marriage. Finally, one can interpret the work of Michel Foucault to suggest that Victorians were actually obsessed with sexuality, elaborating on its meanings and creating new categories of sexual deviance and identity. For the modern period, new research refines the notion of a sexual revolution. Some scholars push its origins backward in time, before the 1960s or even the 1920s; others question whether a sexual revolution ever occurred, arguing that modern sexual ideas simply restated nineteenth-century concerns about family stability. In this view, birth control, for instance, did not challenge the existing order but merely gained acceptance as a means to strengthen marriage through family planning.[3]

The above description does, admittedly, oversimplify the new sexual history, some of which attempts to construct entirely new frameworks of understanding. Foucault rejected what he called the "repressive hypothesis" as the organizing principle for the study of sexuality in the West since the seventeenth century, and instead viewed sex as an expression of complex, dynamic power relations in society. Some feminist historians, such as Linda Gordon, Carroll Smith-Rosenberg, and Judith Walkowitz, who begin with gender as a primary category of social analysis, have understood sexuality in terms of shifting power relationships between men and women and have explored as well the symbolic role of sexuality in the historical creation of gender.[4]

Despite these and other exceptions, it seems to us that implicit in much of the new history of sexuality is the same underlying set of questions that created the older stereotypes with which we began: Was sexuality repressed or not? Did Puritans and Victorians enjoy sexual relations? Has society made sexual progress in the last three hundred years? One problem with this approach is that questions of repression and enjoyment are themselves present-minded. They rest upon a contemporary belief—based perhaps on popular conceptions of Freudian thought—that physical sexual pleasure, or satisfaction, is critical to human happiness. They often also assume that sexuality is a fixed essence that resides within the individual and, unless interfered with by society, reaches its proper, fullest expression. This essentialist framework overlooks the different meanings that sexuality may have had in the past and the way it has been historically constructed. It also ignores the many relationships sexuality has to other, nonsexual aspects of culture, especially its grounding in economic change and its role in maintaining systems of social inequality. A second problem in the new literature on sexual history is that most studies thus far have been highly specialized, revising only a small piece of the total picture. Thus we know a good deal about the legal history of abortion, the political movement for birth control, the demography of marital fertility, and the changing content of marital advice manuals, but we have no coherent picture of how these parts relate to each other and how the whole relates to the larger story of American history.

For these reasons, we have attempted to translate this new body of scholarly work into a synthetic, interpretive narrative that will, we hope, engage the interest of both scholars and general readers. Our discussion draws on our own research, but also relies heavily on the labors of many colleagues in social history, as a glance at the endnotes will quickly reveal. The sources upon which we have built our interpretation are diverse, ranging from medical texts and social-scientific surveys to personal memoirs, legal cases, and popular music. Since firsthand accounts of past sexual experience are rare, we draw heavily upon the few sources that are available, indicating when we believe these sources are representative and when they are atypical. We have tried to be as inclusive as possible, presenting the history of sexuality with an awareness of gender, class, racial, ethnic, and regional variations. Yet we cannot fully escape the limits of the field, which has tended to tell us more about women than about men (one of the few areas of history where this is true), more about whites than about other racial groups, and more about the native-born middle class than about the experiences of immigrants and the working class.

Moreover, some of the sources that we and other historians have employed—court records, vice investigations by reformers, medical cases, and survey research—represent members of the white middle class peering into or exercising control over the experiences of others. In mining these materials for clues about the past, we have taken care to separate content from judgments, a risky business to say the least. We are also aware that because of the strong tradition of public reticence about sexuality in our culture, many of the sources that may eventually enlighten us have yet to be used by scholars. In some cases, sexual content has been censored from published or unpublished personal papers by family members who wish to protect the privacy of their ancestors. In other cases, scholars have simply overlooked the clues to sexual history that exist in sources that are available because of lack of interest in the subject.[5] We hope that one effect of this volume will be to help unearth both kinds of untapped sources by encouraging the recognition that sexuality is both an intriguing and a legitimate subject of historical inquiry.

In organizing our research, we immediately found ourselves dissatisfied with one distinction drawn in some of the literature—the opposition between sexual ideology ("what ought to be") and sexual behavior ("what was"). It seems to us that this dichotomy assumes too simple and direct a relationship, as well as an opposition, between what individuals believe and what they do. It also can obscure important topics of inquiry. To avoid these problems, we have chosen to explore three subjects that most concern us, each of which incorporates evidence of behavior and ideology: sexual meanings, sexual regulation, and sexual politics. In the chapters that follow we show how each of these has changed over the course of our history. Here we want to explain briefly what questions we ask about each and the direction our overall interpretation takes.

First, by looking at sexual meanings, we make historical the problem of defining sexuality. Sexuality has been associated with a range of human activities and values: the procreation of children, the attainment of physical pleasure (eroticism), recreation or sport, personal intimacy, spiritual transcendence, or power over others. These and other meanings coexist throughout the period of this study, but certain associations prevail at different times, depending on the larger social forces that shape an era. To understand the meanings that sexuality has at any given time, we ask a number of historical questions. What was the language of sexuality—were the terms and metaphors religious, medical, romantic, or commercial? In what kinds of sources did references to sexuality appear—secular or sacred, personal or public? In which social institutions was sexual experience typically located—marriage, the market, the media?

Our chapters articulate many answers to these questions, but, in brief, we argue that the dominant meaning of sexuality has changed during our history from a primary association with reproduction within families to a primary association with emotional intimacy and physical pleasure for individuals. In the colonial era, the dominant language of sexuality was reproductive, and the appropriate locus for sexual activity was in courtship or marriage. In the nineteenth century, an emergent middle class emphasized sexuality as a means to personal intimacy, at the same time that it reduced sharply its rate of reproduction. Gradually, commercial growth brought sex into the marketplace, especially for working-class women and for men of all classes. By the twentieth century, when the individual had replaced the family as the primary economic unit, the tie between sexuality and reproduction weakened further. Influenced by psychology as well as by the growing power of the media, both men and women began to adopt personal happiness as a primary goal of sexual relations.

Various groups within society experienced these changes in different ways. The separation of sexuality and reproduction, and the gradual emergence of individual pleasure as a primary sexual goal, had divergent meanings for each gender. Women remained more closely linked to reproduction, while men experienced greater sexual autonomy apart from the family and simultaneously greater responsibility for sexual self-control. In addition, the concept of "dominant sexual meanings" usually refers to the beliefs and experiences of members of the white middle class. Their beliefs were dominant not only in the sense of being widespread, through an expanding published discourse, but also because sexual meanings enforced emerging racial and class hierarchies. Thus European settlers attempted to justify their superiority over native peoples in terms of a need to civilize sexual savages, and whites imposed on blacks an image of a beastlike sexuality to justify both the rape of black women and the lynching of black men. Similarly, portrayals of workers as promiscuous and depraved helped define middle-class moral superiority in the nineteenth century.

Although images of sexual depravity served to strengthen class and race hierarchies, there were also real cultural differences between white middle-class Americans and workers, immigrants, and blacks. Afro-American culture was in fact more tolerant of sexual relations outside of marriage, even as blacks valued long-term monogamous unions. In addition, sexual meanings changed at a varying pace. Immigrant and black reproductive rates fell later than those of native-born whites. Whatever the differences in sexual values and the timing of change, however, the dominant sexual meanings—those emanating from the white middle class—strongly affected the ways that other groups were seen and, indeed, saw themselves.

The second concern of this book is how systems of sexual regulation have changed. By sexual regulation we mean the way a society channels sexuality into acceptable social institutions. Who has authority for determining what is normal and what is deviant: clergy, doctors, legislators? By what means have social rules about sexual behavior been enforced: church discipline, courts, external peer pressure, internalized control?

When we began our study, we suspected that the agents of sexual regulation had changed from the church in the seventeenth century, to the medical profession in the nineteenth century, to the state in the twentieth century.

After surveying the historical evidence, we discovered a more complex pattern. In early America, a unitary system of sexual regulation that involved family, church, and state rested upon a consensus about the primacy of familial, reproductive sexuality. Those who challenged the reproductive norm could expect severe, often public, punishment and the pressure to repent. But those who confessed and sincerely repented were welcomed back as members in good standing of church and state. From the late eighteenth to the late nineteenth centuries, an era of extensive economic and geographic mobility, the role of both the church and the state in sexual regulation diminished. This process left the family—which increasingly meant women—with the task of creating self-regulating sexual beings, both male and female. The medical profession played an important role in fostering the objective of sexual self-control, as did voluntary associations that hoped to reform sexuality along with other aspects of American culture. In the late nineteenth century, each of these groups—women, doctors, and sexual reformers—argued that the state ought to play a larger role in regulating personal morality. The twentieth century has witnessed an intense conflict over the ways in which state power can appropriately be used to do so.[6] At the same time, modern American culture has regulated sexuality in both overt and subtle ways. The media, for instance, are saturated with sexual images that promise free choice but in fact channel individuals toward particular visions of sexual happiness, often closely linked to the purchase of consumer products.

Systems of sexual regulation, like sexual meanings, have correlated strongly with other forms of social regulation, especially those related to race, class, and gender. Women's role in sexual regulation has varied throughout our history, from responsibility shared with men in preindustrial communities, to a specialized female moral authority in the nineteenth-century middle class, to a weakened role in formal sexual regulation in the twentieth century. Even as middle-class reformers have claimed authority over sexual regulation, members of black and immigrant communities have created unique internal systems of morality, as in the case of the black church, or of immigrants maintaining preindustrial patterns of community control over sexual behavior. However diverse the systems of sexual regulation, white, middle-class, and Protestant authorities have tended to maintain formal authority over sexual morality, whether through the control of religion, medicine, or law.

The third topic we address, sexual politics, relates closely to the changing nature of sexual regulation, especially the competition between interest groups that attempt to reshape dominant sexual meanings. In the nineteenth century, for example, women led movements for moral reform and social purity, wishing to impose a single standard of morality (chastity before marriage and fidelity within it) upon both men and women; doctors attempted to criminalize abortion; anarchist free lovers opposed all state intervention in personal and sexual relations. Censors like Anthony Comstock—the chief proponent of the laws to limit circulation of "obscene" materials, such as birth control information, through the postal service—wanted to use the power of the state to limit public sexual discussion. Since the mid-twentieth century, sexual politics have emerged on a national scale, not only from the forces of sexual "liberation"— namely, the feminist and gay-rights movements—but also from the conservative politics of the New Right's Moral Majority.

We have found that three critical patterns recur in the history of sexual politics in America. First, political movements that attempt to change sexual ideas and practices seem to flourish when an older system is in disarray and a new one forming. For example, in the nineteenth century, the reproductive system of the colonial period fragmented as sexual meanings moved simultaneously into the private realm of personal identity and the public realm of commerce, exacerbating the gap between male and female, working-class and middle-class values. In response to these changes, women, doctors, free lovers, and censors began to battle over the meaning and regulation of sexuality. Again, by the 1960s, the so-called sexual revolution brought to the surface and tried to extend beyond marriage long-term shifts toward the acceptance of sexual pleasure as a critical aspect of personal happiness, a trend we refer to as sexual liberalism. These changes set the stage for political struggles over sexuality that pitted various liberationists against moral conservatives. In each period, some groups tried to extend a newly emergent system further, perhaps to its logical extreme. Thus the anarchist free lovers of the nineteenth century took romantic ideas about the importance of love in sexual relations to the extreme of substituting love, rather than marriage, as the precondition for sex. Other groups, however, resisted the new system and attempted to restore elements of an earlier one. Thus the contemporary New Right holds up an older model of familial, reproductive sexuality in an era when sexuality is no longer limited to the family.

A second pattern of sexual politics reveals a consistent relationship to inequalities of gender. Even more than its relationship to class and race, sexual politics arise from efforts of male authorities to define female sexuality and of women either to resist such definition or to counter through efforts to reshape sexual values and practices. The attitudes of the predominantly male medical profession toward female sexuality, as well as the organization of women in moral reform, social purity, anti-prostitution, and later movements against sexual violence all point to ways in which sexuality has been a primary battlefield in a struggle to insure or combat gender inequality.

Third, the politics of sexuality responds to both real and symbolic issues. Sex is easily attached to other social concerns, especially those related to impurity and disorder, and it often evokes highly irrational responses. The crusade against commercialized prostitution illustrates this process. It attacked a real social problem that had serious consequences for women's lives and for public health. At the same time, opponents of prostitution tapped deeper symbolic associations when, in order to justify nativist fears of immigrants, they claimed that foreign women filled the ranks of prostitutes. Similarly, when southern whites lynched black men for raping white women, the charges usually stemmed not from any sexual assault, but because of economic and political competition between blacks and whites. Yet the highly charged issue of interracial sex proved very effective in establishing a new method of racial control—the fear of lynching—in the turn-of-the-century South. Similarly, rape, homosexuality, and sexually transmitted diseases have all become symbolic, as well as real, targets of political movements, especially at times of particular stress in American society.

In the following pages, the history of sexual meanings, regulation, and politics are placed within a chronological framework that reflects main currents of American social and economic life. We attempt to periodize sexual history, yet it is important to keep in mind that we are not trying to draw strict chronological boundaries, nor do we wish to suggest that a new sexual system replaces an older one at a given moment. Rather, the process is one of layering, in which certain motifs dominate sexual discourse in a given era; later they remain influential but are joined and gradually overwhelmed when another set of concerns takes precedence.

In Part I, "The Reproductive Matrix," we explore the centrality of marriage and procreation to the preindustrial sexual system. The first chapter begins with cultural diversity during the era of settlement, when English men and women confronted native Americans and the wilderness, and when unique sexual patterns characterized the northern and southern colonies. In Chapter 2, by exploring both the life cycle of the family and the regulation of deviance, we explain how the family-centered sexual system was recreated throughout the mature North American colonies. The seeds of change during the era of commercial growth and revolutionary politics in the eighteenth century, the subject of Chapter 3, provides a hint of the ways sexual life would later expand beyond the familial system of the colonial era.

The title of Part II, "Divided Passions," refers to the fragmentation of sexual meanings along lines of gender, race, and class, as well as to the split between the intensely private passions of the middle-class family and the increasingly public world of commercialized sex. Chapter 4 looks at the family, where control over fertility coexisted with the middle-class idealization of marital sex as a means to personal intimacy. It emphasizes the difficulties of achieving this new ideal, given the unique social worlds occupied by men and women. Racial diversity and the role of sexuality in maintaining white supremacy is treated separately in Chapter 5, while Chapter 6 looks closely at the expanding opportunities for sex outside the family—in utopian communities, same-sex relationships, and the urban world of sexual commerce. In Chapter 7 we analyze political responses to the movement of sexuality outside the family and into the marketplace, including cooperation and conflict between clergy, women, doctors, and radical free lovers.

In Part III, "Toward a New Sexual Order," we examine the transition to recognizably modern forms of sexuality. Chapter 8 explores the challenges to middle-class respectability posed by conflicting male and female values within marriage, innovations in the sexual marketplace, new forms of intimate relationships among college-educated women, and the public sexuality of working-class youth. In the early twentieth century these tensions exploded into the political sphere, with movements against venereal disease, prostitution, and interracial sex—the subjects of Chapter 9. In Chapter 10, we present the ideas and the movements, including Freudianism and the birth control crusade of Margaret Sanger, that most clearly rejected nineteenth-century middle-class assumptions and that consequently helped usher in a new sexual era.

The final part, "The Rise and Fall of Sexual Liberalism," describes the dominant sexual system of the mid-twentieth century and the recent assaults upon it. Chapter 11 analyzes the contraceptive revolution, the patterns of sexual expressiveness that evolved among youth, and conjugal experience in an era that emphasized the importance of sexual satisfaction for a happy marriage. In Chapter 12, we look at new sexual boundaries, namely, the expansion of heterosexuality in the marketplace and the public realm, intensified penalties against homosexual behavior, and the reshaping of sexuality as a mechanism of racial control. Chapter 13 examines various "sexual revolutions"—those of urban middle-class singles, radical youth, feminists, and gay liberationists—and the impact that they had on sexual liberalism. Chapter 14 presents the dimensions of change from the mid-1960s to the early 1980s, a period that saw a major shift in patterns of sexual behavior and values. The final chapter assesses the political reaction spawned by rapid change as well as the rethinking provoked by the AIDS epidemic.

At the very least, we want the drama and novelty of the story that follows to capture the interest of our readers. But we also hope to reveal through our interpretation the ways that historical forces continually reshape our sexuality, and the ways that individuals and groups have acted to alter the contours of sexual history.

PART I
THE REPRODUCTIVE MATRIX,
1600–1800

CHAPTER 1

Cultural Diversity in the Era of Settlement

IN 1625, the English adventurer Thomas Morton established a plantation in the New England colony of Plymouth that soon proved to be the antithesis of the Pilgrim vision of life in the New World. Most migrants to early New England sought to create godly communities built upon the centrality of the family, a well-ordered and stable "little commonwealth." In contrast, the men and women who joined Thomas Morton at "Merry Mount" engaged in "profane and dissolute living," including sexual relations outside of marriage. In addition, while most European settlers expressed shock at the sexual habits of the native tribes and tried to convert them to what they believed to be a superior Christian morality, Morton and his followers welcomed Indians to Merry Mount and openly had sexual relations with them. In a further affront to Pilgrim values, Morton revived the pagan May Day festivities, complete with the erotically charged maypole. Merry Mount proved so threatening to the Pilgrims' vision of social order that in 1628 they deported Morton back to England. When he later returned to Massachusetts Bay Colony, the Puritan authorities there imprisoned him under such severe conditions—he was kept in irons, without adequate food and clothing, for a year—that Morton died soon after his release.[1] Libertinism, paganism, and sexual relations with the Indians clearly had no place within the Puritan scheme, based as it was upon reestablishing the Christian family in the wilderness.

Thomas Morton was a mere thorn in the side of Pilgrim and Puritan leaders, but during the seventeenth century, these English colonists faced more serious challenges to their goal of creating stable family life and implementing the values of marital, reproductive sexuality. First, the varied sexual practices of the native peoples of North America, which both fascinated and disturbed the settlers, offered possible alternatives to European traditions. Second, and more challenging, demographic conditions in the New World strongly affected family life. Climate and settlement patterns facilitated the reestablishment of a family-centered sexual life in New England but delayed it in the Chesapeake colonies of Maryland and Virginia. Only after several generations did social conditions in these two regions converge to the point that one may speak of a reproductive sexual system throughout the colonies. Thus, to understand the sexual values colonists brought with them and the obstacles to adopting them, it is important to begin this history by exploring the European, and especially English, influence on America, the native American cultures that confronted European migrants, and the regional variations that shaped diverse sexual systems in the seventeenth century.

From England to America

The men and women who migrated from Europe to the English colonies brought with them a set of beliefs about sexuality shaped by the Protestant Reformation. Along with other cultures influenced by Protestantism, the English rejected the Catholic condemnation of carnal desires that had required celibacy of priests and associated all sexual expression—even in marriage—with the fall from grace. The idea that marriage was acceptable primarily as a way to channel lust and prevent sexual sin gave way to a belief that marital love, as well as the need to produce children, could justify sexual intercourse. At the same time, by placing a new emphasis on the importance of sexuality within marriage, Protestantism distinguished more clearly between proper sexual expression—that which led to reproduction—and sexual transgressions—acts that occurred outside of marriage and for purposes other than reproduction.

The Protestant attitude toward sexuality rested upon a larger system of beliefs about the family. Just as Reformation ideas emphasized the importance of the individual, so too did Protestantism encourage a heightened sense of the family as a discrete unit. Once deeply embedded within kinship and community networks, the nuclear family that emerged in this period stood as an independent entity, a "little commonwealth" ruled by its own patriarch, and mirroring the political unit of the state. Courtship and marriage within the middle and upper classes continued to hinge largely upon property alliances. According to the Duchess of Newcastle, for example, love was "a disease" with which she "never was infected." For other social groups, however, love became one element in the choice of a mate. Once wed, husbands and wives were encouraged to learn to love each other, a significant departure from an older ideal of extramarital and unrequited courtly love. Affectionate relations ideally bound husband and wife together, and parents to their children.[2]

Within this context of affectionate relations, marital sexuality assumed new meanings in early modern Protestant cultures. Sex became a duty that husband and wife owed to one another; it also could be a means of enhancing the marriage. Nonetheless, pleasure alone did not justify sexual union, which remained closely tied to procreation. The Protestant churches advised moderation in the frequency of marital sex and condemned sex outside of marriage. As in the past, church and society dealt more harshly with women who engaged in pre- or extramarital sexuality than with male transgressors, for female chastity and fidelity assured men of the legitimacy of their children.[3]

In addition to religious opinion, early modern medical views of sexuality emphasized the importance of reproduction, while they stressed as well the legitimacy, even necessity, of physical sexual pleasure. According to sixteenth- and seventeenth-century English physicians, both men and women expected to experience pleasure during sexual intercourse. Indeed, a long-standing scientific and popular tradition held that female orgasm was necessary not only to maintain physical health but also to insure conception. As one midwifery text explained, the clitoris was the organ "which makes women lustful and take delight in copulation." Without it, they "would have no desire, nor delight, nor would they ever conceive." Like early modern religious writers, English medical authorities cautioned against the excessive practice of sexual intercourse, recommending moderation in marital relations.[4]

The regulation of sexual behavior reinforced the primacy of marital, reproductive sex and the need for the legitimacy of children. In practice, most English men and women remained chaste at least until betrothal. Sexual relations between engaged couples were tolerated because a subsequent marriage was virtually assured. Thus, between 1550 and 1750, the rate of "prenuptial" pregnancy—the birth of a child within eight months of marriage—ranged from ten to thirty percent in English marriages. In contrast, heavy penalties awaited the woman who gave birth to a child out of wedlock, for the economic burden of child support fell upon her community. Consequently, the rate of illegitimacy remained extremely low prior to 1750. The churches helped maintain these patterns by fining or excommunicating sexual transgressors, while public opinion reinforced community values by condemning extramarital sexuality.[5]

Once married, women of all classes could expect to bear children until menopause, and many women desired to do so. High infant and child mortality rates (up to twenty-five percent or more in some regions) encouraged frequent pregnancies in order to produce living heirs. When people did wish to limit family size, they usually delayed marriage; or, once wed, women might prolong breastfeeding and refrain from sex while nursing. Some couples may have used coitus interruptus (withdrawal), but outside of the aristocracy it was unlikely that many married couples used contraceptives. Members of the Puritan sect especially rejected this practice, not only in order to obey the biblical injunction to be fruitful and multiply, but also as a strategy to increase the population of their church. Folk remedies to prevent conception or abort unwanted pregnancies, ranging from laxatives and bloodletting to the use of pessaries, had long been known. But only in extramarital relationships—which the English both condemned and practiced—did women rely on these methods to limit conception or abort. For example, seventeenth-century prostitutes—a growing class in English cities at this time—used folk remedies to prevent pregnancy or to treat venereal disease, while unmarried female servants who became pregnant might resort to herbal remedies or infanticide. Among married middle class couples, however, women did not begin to control their fertility until after the seventeenth century.[6]

As English men and women migrated to North America in the early seventeenth century, they brought with them these sexual beliefs and practices. Motivated primarily by the desire to improve their economic positions, or in some cases in order to establish a purer church, the English colonists founded permanent settlements in North America, beginning around the Chesapeake Bay after 1607, throughout New England after 1620, and, after the 1660s, in the Carolinas and the middle colonies of Pennsylvania and New York, where they mingled with a variety of non-English settlers. Innovative in their willingness to strike out in an unknown territory, most English settlers had a conservative vision: the reestablishment of traditional patterns of family and community life in the colonies.

Cultural Conflict: Native American Indians and Europeans

The English colonists who settled on the Atlantic seaboard in the seventeenth century immediately came into contact with North American Indian tribes who had long populated the continent. Native American sexual customs varied widely, from the Penobscots of New England and the Cherokees of the Southeast to the tribes dwelling west of the Mississippi River, such as the Plains Indians or the Pueblos. In every region in which Europeans and Indians came into contact, however, the Europeans, applying the standards of the Christian tradition, judged the sexual lives of the native peoples as savage, in contrast to their own "civilized" customs. Thus Spanish and French missionaries attempted to eradicate "devilish" practices, such as polygamy and cross-dressing, and condemned the "heathen friskiness" of the natives.[7] Elaborating on the differences between native sexual customs and their own provided one basis for the Europeans' sense of cultural superiority over the Indians. It also served to justify efforts to convert the native population to Christianity, whether to the Protestantism of East Coast settlers or to the Catholicism of the Spanish and French in Florida, Louisiana, or northern Mexico. In each region, however, Indians resisted the efforts of Europeans to enforce Western sexual standards, particularly the imposition of monogamous marriage on those tribes that practiced polygamy. At the same time, some colonists, such as the followers of Thomas Morton at Merry Mount, rejected their own heritage and adopted Indian customs.[8]

To some extent, Europeans accurately perceived that native American sexual customs differed from their own. For instance, most native peoples did not associate either nudity or sexuality with sin. Although sexuality might be embedded within a spiritual context—as in the case of puberty rituals, menstrual seclusion, or the visionary call to cross-dress—sexual intercourse and reproductive functions rarely evoked shame or guilt for Indian men or women. Many native American tribes accepted premarital intercourse, polygamy, or institutionalized homosexuality, all practices proscribed by European church and state. In certain tribes, women, like men, could exercise considerable choice in their selection of sexual partners, and children grew up with few restrictions on sexual experimentation, which might range from masturbation to sexual play between same-sex or opposite-sex partners. The existence of a category of men who dressed and lived as women, and more rarely of women who dressed and lived as men, astounded Europeans. Even more alarming was the realization that these *berdache* (from the French term for a sodomite) could be "as much esteem'd as the bravest and hailest men in the country." To the Europeans, the acceptance of men who practiced "the execrable, unnatural abuse of their bodies" and who performed women's tasks, led to "a corruption of morals past all expression."[9]

As this last comment reveals, the fact that Indians had so much personal choice in sexual matters disturbed Europeans greatly. Missionaries claimed that "Impurity and immorality, even gross sensuality and unnatural vice flourish" among the native peoples. Reflecting the English emphasis on reproductive sexuality, one observer speculated that the extent of their "Intemperance" made Indian women "unfitt to the office of Increase." It distressed Englishmen like John Smith when young Indian women welcomed him to their tribe by offering to spend the night with him. Those Indians who converted to Christianity were urged to obey the Seventh Commandment, cover their bodies with European clothing, and partition their wigwams so that children could not easily observe "what nature is ashamed of."[10] Catholic priests in New France and northern Mexico, as well as Protestant missionaries in New England, attempted to impose monogamous marriage, encountering strong resistance when they did. One Jesuit missionary told a Montagnais Indian that "it was not honorable for a woman to love any one else except her husband," for such sexual practices meant that a man "was not sure that his son . . . was his son." Unmoved by this argument, the man's reply suggested how larger cultural differences underlay the sexual conflict of Europeans and Indians. "You French people love only your own children," he explained, "but we all love all the children of our tribe."[11]

For all the differences between them, Europeans may have distorted the contrasts with Indians in order to affirm their right of conquest. In practice the English settlers and the Indians had more similarities within their sexual systems than Europeans cared to recognize. True, New England Indians typically condoned premarital sexuality, with marriages often confirmed after the birth of a first child, while the English condemned premarital sex. Yet many courting couples in England did in fact have sexual relations, marrying after pregnancy but as long before childbirth as possible. Like the English, most North American Indians rarely used either contraception or abortion, although, as in Europe, herbal methods were known and occasionally applied. (Some tribes, such as the Cherokees, did practice abortion and infanticide, practices that Christian missionaries later attempted to eliminate.) Like many English families, New England Indian couples controlled family size by breast-feeding infants for at least two years and by proscribing marital intercourse during nursing. Native peoples tended to wean children later than Europeans, though, and they condoned the husband who had extramarital sexual relations during the two- to five-year nursing period. Otherwise, however, exclusive unions were typical among many New England and southeastern tribes. "Single fornication they count no sin," Puritan Roger Williams observed of New England Indians, "but after Mareage . . . then they count it h[e]inous for either of them to be false."[12]

Perhaps the most striking contrast between English and Indian sexual systems was the relative absence of sexual conflict among native Americans, due in part to their different cultural attitudes toward both property and sexuality. Indians easily resolved marital discord by simply separating and forming new unions, without penalty, stigma, or property settlements. In cultures in which one could not "own" another person's sexuality, prostitution—the sale of sex—did not exist prior to the arrival of European settlers. Rape—the theft of sex—only rarely occurred, and it was one of the few sexual acts forbidden by Indian cultures. Contrary to their fears about suffering sexual brutality at the hands of savages, English women captured during the colonial-era Indian wars noted with relief that native American men did not assault them sexually. "I have been in the midst of those roaring lions and savage bears," wrote Mary Rowlandson about her captivity by New England Indians. "[B]y night and day, alone & in company, sleeping all sorts together, and yet not one of them ever offered me the least abuse of unchastity to me in word or action." In contrast, the Spanish settlers justified the rape of Indian women as a right of conquest and expected sexual service from female captives of war. In the South, only in the nineteenth century, after a period of close contact with white settlers, did the Cherokee Nation find it necessary to enact laws punishing rapists.[13]

Regional Diversity: New England and the Chesapeake

For the English settlers, pointing out the contrasts between their own sexual customs and those of the Indians may have been reassuring. Newcomers to a vast, unknown wilderness, the immigrants needed to remind themselves that they represented "civilization" and that they were capable of reestablishing the social patterns of their homelands. Whether they would succeed in this task of reconstruction was, in the earliest years of settlement, in doubt. Until the 1660s, colonial demographic patterns were in such flux that it was not yet clear whether the English system could be recreated. In all regions of settlement, for example, the sex ratio—the proportion of men to women—was higher than in England; with fewer women than men, how would traditional family life develop? In addition, the colonists faced an abundance of land but a shortage of laborers. Who would provide the work force to establish productive communities?

The initial answers to these questions differed for the two major areas of early settlement, New England and the Chesapeake. In the former, patterns of settlement facilitated the reestablishment of the family-centered sexual life of England. Indeed, because of its religious, utopian nature, early New England society deviated from the English pattern by creating an excess of order, based on an ideal of extreme social cohesiveness and the practice of close surveillance of personal morality. In contrast, the seventeenth-century Chesapeake faced an excess of social disorder, the result in part of highly unstable family life and a dispersed population. A comparison of New England and the Chesapeake in the seventeenth century illustrates the ways in which ideology, demography, and the economy combine to shape sexual practices. Although the two regions would, by the end of the seventeenth century, resemble each other more closely, for several generations their sexual histories provide a lesson in contrast.

Distinctive motives for settlement, types of migrants, and systems of labor lay at the heart of these regional variations. Although all colonists shared a desire for economic improvement, particularly the ability to acquire land in the New World, many New England migrants had strong religious motives as well. Puritans hoped to establish close-knit, "godly" communities, centered upon family and church, that would purify the Protestant church and create a standard of moral order for the rest of the world. New Englanders tended to arrive in families and come from fairly homogeneous social backgrounds, primarily the middling classes of farmers and artisans. In contrast, those who migrated to the Chesapeake colonies of Maryland and Virginia had more varied origins, ranging from the gentry to servants. These migrants brought no overriding moral mission, arrived more frequently as individuals, and settled on scattered farms and plantations rather than in towns. Men far outnumbered women, and a significant number of settlers were indentured servants who sold their labor for four to seven years to repay the cost of their passage. After 1670, as more African slaves were imported to the colonies, the northern and southern labor systems diverged further. Although every colony had some slaves, in New England slavery failed to take root. By the early eighteenth century, however, it had supplanted indentured servitude as the major source of labor in the South.

One important consequence of these different settlement patterns was a much higher sex ratio in the southern than in the northern colonies. In New England, where so many people arrived in families, the sex ratio during the first generation of settlement was approximately three men to two women, while in the Chesapeake, men outnumbered women by four to one. As a result, during the seventeenth century, family formation was much easier in New England. Young people married in their early twenties and, given the low mortality rates that resulted from a healthy environment, reproduction rates soared. In the Chesapeake, however, the shortage of women delayed family formation, while high mortality rates prevented the rapid population growth that would otherwise have produced more even sex ratios. In addition, since indentured servants could not wed until they had fulfilled their labor contracts, the childbearing years of many women were curtailed by late marriage.[14]

The more balanced sex ratio in most of New England not only created higher fertility rates; it also helped channel sexuality into marriage. In contrast, because the skewed ratio in the Chesapeake delayed or prevented marital sexual relations, pre- and extramarital sexuality seem to have been more common. Premarital pregnancy rates provide one good example of the difference. In early New England, under one-tenth of all brides were pregnant when they married. Among the immigrant population of the Chesapeake, however, up to one-third of all brides would give birth within less than nine months of their wedding day, a rate more than two times that of the English parishes from which settlers came.[15]

Family stability in New England communities helped parents enforce an ideal of marital, reproductive sexuality. In the Chesapeake, the large number of single migrants and the high mortality rates, which created many orphans, made it more difficult to control youthful sexual activity. The sex ratio itself also contributed to this disparity. Single women in the southern colonies were in such high demand as wives that they may have been less concerned about guarding their virginity than women in England or the Puritan settlements. Even women who bore illegitimate children might marry respectably in this region. In 1657, for example, Jane Palldin bore a child by a married planter in Maryland; within two years, she had wed. Similarly, Lucie Stratton named Arthur Turner as the father of her bastard, but she refused to marry him because she believed that "hee was a Lustfull man a very lustfull man and that shee never could bee quiett for him." "Why Lucie," Turner allegedly replied, acknowledging his paternity, "Who was most lustful, you or I? . . . You came to my Bed, . . . and putt your hands under the cloaths, and took mee by the private parts." Whoever initiated their sexual relations, Lucie Stratton felt confident enough of marriage to reject Turner.[16]

The sex ratio may have influenced extramarital sexuality as well. Knowing that they could easily remarry, Chesapeake-area women could be tempted by the advances of men other than their spouses, while husbands might well suspect that single men had designs upon their wives. Although adultery occurred in New England too, the abundance of unattached men meant that southern women had more opportunities for contact with single men, such as laborers, neighbors, or the business partners of their husbands. For example, Robert and Dorothy Holt had lived together with Edward Hudson in Maryland. Dorothy's "heart was Soe hardened" against her husband, Robert, that she swore she "would never darken his door again." She began to live openly with Hudson, "lyeing in bed together," until the court arrested and punished the adulterers.[17]

In the Chesapeake, as in New England, church and court prosecuted sinners, levying fines on or whipping those who fornicated, committed adultery, sodomy, or rape, or bore bastards. But New Englanders monitored sexual crimes more extensively and more systematically than did residents of the southern colonies. A racially and socially homogeneous population, common religious values, and the geographical proximity of the New England towns facilitated the social control of personal behavior. In Puritan theology, the entire community had responsibility for upholding morality, for as Puritan minister Cotton Mather warned, "Heinous breaches of the seventh Commandment" could bring the judgment of Sodom upon all of New England. Moreover, individuals could not easily engage in illicit sex without being noticed in the close-knit towns. The law confirmed the importance of sexual morality. By enacting the death penalty for adultery, sodomy, and rape, the colony of Massachusetts Bay equated these acts with other capital offenses such as treason, murder, and witchcraft. Although capital punishment rarely, in fact, took place, in an extraordinary case, such as that of Mary Latham, it did. This eighteen-year-old woman had confessed to adultery with twelve men and to calling her elderly husband a cuckold. In 1645 the Massachusetts court ordered her to be executed by hanging.[18]

Although settlers in the southern colonies shared the sexual values of other English colonists and passed laws to punish sexual crimes, the laws were less extensive and colonial authorities did not prosecute offenders as vigorously. Living on dispersed farms and plantations made it more difficult to monitor their neighbors' personal lives. In some backcountry areas, where clergy were in short supply, people simply accepted consensual unions, with or without marriage, and did not condemn the births of illegitimate children.[19] Occasionally even the courts seemed to tolerate sexual offenses. When Richard Owens sold the contract for his servant Anne Gould to Joseph Wicks, he first "did make use of her body" and infected her with "the ffrench [sic] Pox"—venereal disease. The court, ignoring his sexual crime, found Owens guilty of defrauding Wicks and merely ordered him to provide a new servant. In blatant cases, however, Chesapeake-area courts inflicted harsh penalties. Captain William Mitchell, an influential Marylander who served on the governor's council, not only impregnated Mrs. Susan Warren and gave her a "physic" to abort the child, but he also "lived in fornication" with his pretended wife, Joan Toaste. Even so, the first charge filed against Mitchell by the Maryland attorney was that he "professed himself to be a Atheist" and openly mocked "all Religion." For his crimes, Mitchell had to pay the steep fine of five thousand pounds of tobacco, court charges, and a bond for good behavior, and to resign from the council.[20]

The distinctive labor systems of North and South also influenced the extent to which each region recreated the English sexual system. In the South, indentured servitude formed a large group of young people who could not marry. Young female servants were especially vulnerable to unwanted sexual advances by their masters or other men. Throughout the colonies, courts heard charges against masters for "violating" a female servant, making "forcible attempts" on her chastity, exhibiting "lewd behavior," or attempting rape. In seventeenth-century New England, for example, one-third of the victims of rape were female servants, a group that comprised only ten percent of the area's population.[21] Because Maryland, Virginia, and Carolina society depended on indentured servants, the opportunity for sexual exploitation was much greater. Virginia servant Margaret Connor charged that her master attempted to "prostitute her body to him, which he Dayly Practices to the other Servant Woman belonging to him." The court accepted her charge and forced her master to provide a cash bond to secure his good behavior. Less severe sexual abuse occurred on a daily basis. "I sent for the wench to clean my room," William Byrd of Virginia reported in his diary, "and when I came

[in] I kissed her and felt her, for which God forgive me."[22]

Servitude magnified the possibility of bastardy as well. Prior to 1750, illegitimacy rates throughout the colonies remained quite low, at about one to three percent of all births. In the seventeenth-century Chesapeake, however, as many as one in five female indentured servants gave birth to bastard children. Even when female servants engaged willingly in sexual relations, they could not marry without the permission of their masters, and many bore children. Along with the standard whipping or fine, a female servant who became pregnant had to add a year of service to her contract in order to make up for time lost during pregnancy and childbirth. In Maryland, after 1658, if a female servant identified the father of her bastard, the court might force him to pay for her lost time, and if he had promised marriage, he would be ordered to fulfill his commitment.[23]

After 1670, slavery began to supplant indentured servitude in the South. The growth of slavery further distinguished the southern from the northern and middle colonies. Although slaves could be found in all areas, they remained a small minority outside of the South, where slavery provided the primary agricultural labor force by the eighteenth century. Slavery contributed to the diversity of sexual systems in the southern colonies. It ultimately led to elaborate efforts to differentiate whites from blacks in sexual terms and to contain interracial sex.

The sex ratios of Africans imported as slaves, like those of early white settlers, influenced their family and sexual life in the Chesapeake. For several generations, the importation of Africans, rather than natural population growth, fueled the slave system. Because many more male than female Africans arrived and were scattered on small farms, they could not easily form families. Birth rates among slaves remained low throughout the seventeenth century, in part because African women delayed conception by nursing their children for up to three years, which was longer than did most English settlers, and possibly because the adjustment to enslavement kept black women in a state of depression. In addition, high infant mortality prevented the African population from reproducing itself. In the absence of families and without property considerations, and given their African cultural background, the sexual norms of slaves differed from those of whites. For example, some of the early slaves accepted polygamy, and many did not condemn premarital intercourse.[24]

The meeting of Europeans and Africans in the New World created possibilities for interracial sexual relations and, before long, gave rise to legal efforts to prevent these unions. The shortage of white women encouraged some southern men to take black wives or mistresses. In the earliest colonial statutes—such as a 1662 Virginia law—fornication between blacks and whites brought more severe penalties than similar acts between whites. The law did not yet forbid interracial marriage, which seems to have been tolerated during the early years of settlement. Only after slavery became entrenched during the late seventeenth century did southern legislatures ban marriage between blacks and whites. Illicit unions persisted, however; mulattoes accounted for over one-fifth of the children born out of wedlock in Virginia at the turn of the century.[25]

By the early eighteenth century, white demographic and social patterns in New England and the Chesapeake were converging in ways that influenced sexual life in the colonies. By 1700, a sex ratio of approximately three men to two women made family formation easier in the Chesapeake, while the decline of white indentured servitude removed other obstacles to early marriage. For both reasons, reproductive rates increased. White married women in the Chesapeake, as in New England, now raised seven or eight children.[26] By the mid-eighteenth century, the Afro-American population began to reproduce itself too. Lower mortality, higher birth rates, and the evolution of an Afro-American family structure all contributed to this process. As sex ratios evened out, it became easier to marry, and slaves tended to form stable, monogamous unions. In addition, breastfeeding practices came to resemble the one- to two-year European pattern, rather than the longer African custom, thus encouraging more frequent conception and higher fertility. By the end of the eighteenth century, married Afro-American women in the Chesapeake region bore an average of six children.[27] Meanwhile, New England communities lost some of the characteristics that had produced an excess of order. As small towns grew in population and grown children moved further away from parental homes, community control over sexuality became less effective. As early as the 1680s, Puritan clergy lamented the decline in godly living and church membership. By the early eighteenth century, New England churches echoed with jeremiads that fornication, "a shameful sin," was "much increasing among us, to the great dishonor of Godde."[28]

Two significant regional distinctions persisted, however, as the colonies matured in the eighteenth century. First, New Englanders remained more vigorous in their efforts to regulate individual morality than did their neighbors in the southern or middle colonies. Second, the slave system, along with the sexual tensions surrounding interracial unions, clearly differentiated the southern colonies, foreshadowing an even greater divergence in sexual systems in the next century. Regional differences notwithstanding, by the early eighteenth century, sexual practice and sexual meaning were clearly situated within marriage, and the goal of sexuality was procreation.

CHAPTER 2

Family Life and the Regulation of Deviance

IN 1650, young Samuel Terry of Springfield, Massachusetts distressed his neighbors when, during the Sabbath sermon, he stood outside the meeting-house "chafing his yard to provoak lust." Several lashes on the back may have dissuaded him from masturbating in public again, but in 1661 Samuel Terry endured another punishment for sexual misconduct. Now married, his bride of five months gave birth to their first child, clear evidence that the pair had indulged in premarital intercourse. A four-pound fine was not the last Terry would pay for defying the moral standards of his community. In 1673 the court fined Terry and eight other men who had performed an "immodest and beastly" play. Despite this history of sexual offenses, however, a sinner like Samuel Terry could command respect among his peers. Terry not only served as a town constable, but, in addition, the court entrusted him with the custody of another man's infant son.[1] In short, as long as he accepted punishment for his transgressions, Samuel Terry remained a citizen in good standing.

The case of Samuel Terry allows us to refine the stereotype of the American colonists as prudish, ascetic, and antisexual. This view has enjoyed so much popularity in modern America that the term *puritanical* has come to mean sexually repressive. Not all colonists were Puritans, those nonconforming, largely middle-class English men and women who attempted to establish a community of saints in seventeenth-century New England. Members of the Anglican and Quaker churches, and migrants from the Netherlands, Germany, and northern Ireland settled in the southern and middle colonies, especially during the eighteenth century. Even among the Puritans and their Yankee descendants, sexuality exhibited more complexity than modern assumptions about their repressiveness suggest.

An accurate portrait of sexuality in the colonial era both incorporates and challenges the puritanical stereotype. Early Americans did indeed pay close attention to the sexual behavior of individuals, as the case of Samuel Terry and numerous church and court records confirm. They did so, however, not in order to squelch sexual expression, but rather to channel it into what they considered to be its proper setting and purpose: as a duty and a joy within marriage, and for the purpose of procreation. Both religious beliefs and economic interests supported this family-centered sexual system. A close look at sexuality in colonial America reveals that, despite gender differences in the meaning of sexuality, for both women and men the organizing principle of sexual relations was reproduction. An examination of, first, the family and, second, the treatment of deviance illustrates the main contours of this reproductive matrix from the mid-seventeenth to the mid-eighteenth centuries.

Sexuality in the Family Life Cycle

Despite initial regional variations, the family quickly became the central economic unit in every American colony. As in other preindustrial societies, the family both produced and consumed almost all goods and services. Reproduction and production went hand in hand, for family survival in an agricultural economy depended on the labor of children, both in the fields and in the household. Moreover, English inheritance practices supported parental authority, for fathers bequeathed to their sons the land that was necessary for establishing new families. For all of these reasons, colonial laws and customs strongly supported family formation. New England colonies forbade "solitary living" in order to insure that everyone resided within a family, either their own or, as in the case of servants and apprentices, in another household. Even in colonies without such laws, economic survival demanded family living. Thus the life of the individual was integrally connected with that of the family. To understand the meaning and practice of sexuality in colonial America, then, we look first at the life cycle of the individual within the family, beginning with attempts to socialize children to channel sexual desire toward marriage, and turning next to the experiences of courtship, marriage, and childbearing.

A young person growing up in colonial America learned about sexuality from two primary sources: observation within the family and moral instruction from parent and church. A small minority of colonists were also exposed to medical advice literature published in London and reprinted in America during the eighteenth century. Although these various sources of information might conflict on specific points, overall they transmitted the expectation that sexuality within marriage, aimed toward reproduction, would become a part of normal adult life.

Childhood observation of sexual activity is common in agricultural societies, and all regions remained agricultural throughout the colonial period. "Procreation was everywhere, in the barnyard as well as in the house," one historian has written of seventeenth-century New England.[2] Colonial laws against bestiality, and scattered prosecutions for buggery with farm animals, attest to one influence of the barnyard. In Connecticut, for example, a man confessed to having had sexual relations with a variety of animals since the age of ten; Massachusetts executed several teenage boys for buggery. Sexual relations with animals required harsh punishment, for colonists believed that these unions could have reproductive consequences. The mating of humans and animals, they feared, would produce monstrous offspring. For this reason, colonists insisted on punishing not only the man but also the beast, who might bear such monsters. Thus William Hacketts, "found in buggery with a cow, upon the Lord's day," had to witness the execution of the cow before his own hanging took place. Sixteen-year-old Thomas Grazer of Plymouth confessed to buggery "with a mare, a cow, two goats, five sheep, two calves and a turkey." The court ordered a lineup of sheep at which Grazer identified his sexual partners, who were "killed before his face," and then "he himself was executed."[3] Although executions were rare, sexual observation or experimentation with animals was no doubt as widespread in colonial America as in other agricultural societies.

Children also learned about sex in the home. The small size of colonial dwellings allowed children quite early in their lives to hear or see sexual activity among adults. Although curtains might isolate the parental bed, all family members commonly slept in the same room, especially during winters, when a single fireplace provided the heat. Thus a four-year-old girl reported to a servant that she saw a man "lay on the bed with her mamma," and heard him instruct the mother to "lay up higher." Furthermore, the practice of sharing beds exposed some young people to adult sexuality. In one home, three adults and a child were sleeping together when one of the men unbuttoned his breeches and had "carnal knowledge" with a female bedmate. One woman got into bed with her children, and when a man joined them, her daughter recalled, the mother instructed the children to "lie further or else shee would kick us out of bed." Even couples who sought greater privacy had difficulty finding it, for loosely constructed houses allowed neighbors and kin to observe what happened behind closed doors.[4]

Whatever they observed, children learned early on that sexual behavior ought to be limited to marriage. The harsh language directed at those who defied this model provided one kind of moral lesson. Neighbors cursed women with epithets such as whore, adulteress, slut, or "brasen-faced bawd." While women's illicit sexual relations evoked scorn, for men the equivalent slander was to be accused of cuckoldry, that is, ignorance or tolerance of a wife's infidelity. For example, a Massachusetts woman hurled a slanderous comment at a couple, claiming that "the wife was a whore and that shee had severall children by other men, and that Cuckoldlay old Rogue her husband owned [acknowledged] them." In an extreme insult, a Maryland man declared that "Mis [Alice] Hatches Cunt would make Souse Enough for all the doogs in the Toune." In at least one instance, a man was ridiculed for monitoring too closely the sexual morality of women. In 1664, after an investigation into a morals case near the town of Concord, Massachusetts, neighbors posted a satiric verse outside the meetinghouse charging "cunstable" Thomas Pinion of unseemly behavior. To keep Pinion from prying further, one verse read: "If natures purll bag does burn / Then quickly send for they pinion. / If sick though art and like to die / Get pinon to fuck thee quickly."[5] Such scornful or satiric speech encouraged youth and adults alike to limit sexuality to the marriage bed.

Formal moral teaching confirmed what popular speech implied. Clergy and lawmakers warned that sex ought to be limited to marriage and aimed at procreation rather than mere physical gratification. Ministers throughout the colonies invoked biblical injunctions against extramarital and nonprocreative sexual acts, while colonial statutes in both New England and the Chesapeake outlawed fornication, rape, sodomy, adultery, and sometimes incest, prescribing corporal or capital punishment, fines, and, in some cases, banishment for sexual transgressors. Together these moral authorities attempted to socialize youth to channel sexual desires toward marriage.

The best-known of the colonial authorities, the New England Puritan clergy, were extremists among Protestants on issues of church doctrine and sexual morality. These ministers left abundant evidence that they considered sexuality itself "uncleane," and lust a danger to body and soul. Spiritual leaders such as Thomas Shephard and Cotton Mather advised youth and adults alike to avoid sexual stimulation and to control the desires that "lie lurking in thy heart." As Mather wrote, extramarital sexuality would "bloodily Disturb the Frame of our Bodies, and Exhaust and Poison the Spirits, in our Bodies, until an Incurable Consumption at last, shall cut us down, Out of Time." Puritan clergy emphasized marriage as the only suitable outlet for sexual desire and warned against both masturbation and premarital sex. Their ideas reflected age-old gender distinctions about proper sexual behavior. To young women they directed a particular message about the importance of chastity. According to Mather, it was scandalous for a woman to exhibit "sensual lusts, wantonness and impurity, boldness and rudeness, in Look, Word or Gesture." New England ministers chastised women for wearing immodest dress and blamed them for enticing men into sexual sin.[6] Men, considered more rational and better able to control their passions than women, were raised with warnings to resist their carnal desires by concentrating on their love of God.

Puritan clergy, however, were not the only moral authorities in early America. Youths growing up in the middle colonies or the Chesapeake might be exposed to the religious advice of Quaker and Anglican ministers or Catholic priests. Equally important, both secular advice and the model of adults around them influenced the sexual values of the young. Although all adults agreed on an ideal of marital, reproductive sex, some permitted greater acceptance of sexual desire than did the early Puritans. Describing early American childrearing practices, historian Philip Greven identified three categories of Protestant "temperaments," each of which had a different attitude toward sexuality. Unlike Puritan "evangelicals," who emphasized the suppression of lust, "moderate Protestants" placed less emphasis on sexual control. Thus John Adams acknowledged to his children that he was "of an amorous disposition," even as he assured them that he had sired no illegitimate offspring. A third temperament allowed the open expression of sexual desires and approximated the European libertine ideal, represented by three young rakes who frequented New York coffeehouses and indulged in a "good deal of polite smutt then went out whoring." This "genteel" model, which appeared more frequently after 1740, characterized many upper-class southern men, such as William Byrd of Virginia, whose diary recorded numerous sexual conquests. Even though church and court in this region upheld the ideal of marital, reproductive sexuality, young white males of the planter class learned that they did not necessarily have to exert sexual control around female servants and slaves.[7]

Although church and court remained the most important sources of sexual standards, in the eighteenth century a limited medical advice literature appeared in America. It is impossible to know whether these books about reproduction and sexuality were read by youth, but if so, young men were far more likely than young women to have access to them, for women's literacy rates lagged behind those of men. Only a few gynecological or marital advice texts could be found in early America, including *The Oeconomy of Love* (1736) and *The Art of Preserving Health* (1744), both reprinted from British editions. The eighteenth-century anti-masturbation tract *Onania* had only two or three editions in America.[8]

Aristotle's Masterpiece, first published in London in 1684, did become highly popular in America. Largely a compendium of reproductive lore, *Aristotle's Masterpiece* also contained a prescriptive message about sexuality. It repeated early modern English beliefs that sexual pleasure for both male and female was not only desirable but also necessary for conception. That reproduction was the primary goal of sexuality recurred as a theme throughout its

various editions. Offering no information about contraception, the book
stressed means to insure conception. It admonished couples to chain the
imagination to melodious airs, rather than to sadness, during intercourse, and
to avoid withdrawal too soon after "they have done what nature requires," lest
they lose "the fruit of the labor." Moreover, the language of *Aristotle's Masterpiece* underscored the association of pleasure and procreation. Thus an explanation of sexual desire stated that "nature has implanted in every creature a
mutual desire of copulation, for the increase and propagation of its kind."[9]

It is difficult to know to what extent colonial youth internalized either
religious or medical views about sexuality. Most personal testimony about
youthful sexual feelings comes from Puritan clergy, who were most likely to
have left introspective written accounts and to have accepted the evangelical
view that emphasized the suppression of lust. In their diaries, young Puritan
men recorded their efforts to contain the desires that rose up in them and to
subordinate sexual desire to the love of God. Michael Wigglesworth's diary
recounted his dismay over frequent "unresistable torments of carnal lusts"—
masturbation and seminal emissions—that were provoked when he read,
dreamed, or felt "fond affection" for his pupils at Harvard College. He prayed
to God to deliver him from his lusts: "The last night some filthiness in a vile
dream escaped me for which I loathe myself and desire to abase myself before
my God." Only marriage, Wigglesworth concluded, could save him from
temptation. Similarly, Cotton Mather prayed and fasted for fear that as "a
Young Man in my single *Estate*" he might fall into "lascivious violations of
the *Seventh Commandment.*" Although no such personal accounts exist for
young women, one kind of evidence, conversion narratives recorded during the
religious revivals of the mid-eighteenth century, suggests that New England
women who joined the church accepted the evangelical view of sexuality.
Women, even more than men, interpreted their past sinfulness in sexual terms.
References to improper dress signified mere wastefulness in men's narratives
but represented "Harlotry" in women's accounts.[10]

Not all young people were as devout as the clergy and the newly converted.
Court records attest to the sexual escapades of those youths who, rather than
struggling against their lusts in private, attempted to express them in public.
Recall Samuel Terry of Springfield, whose first sexual offense involved public
masturbation. Similarly, a group of "sundrie youthes" in New Haven "committed much wickedness in a filthy corrupting way one with another"—so
filthy, in fact, that the court refused to record the acts. In Middlesex County,
Massachusetts, a "girl and youth" partied until two in the morning one
Thanksgiving by singing dirty songs. Harvard students often engaged in
"youthful lusts, speculative wantonness and secret filthiness," according to
Thomas Shepard, Jr., who warned his son that "there are and will be such in

every scholastic society, for the most part, as will teach you how to be filthy." One group of Harvard students, for example, spent their evenings drinking, singing, and dancing with Negroes and maids, for which several were fined or whipped. Furthermore, servants in all colonies defied proscriptions on premarital sex. Indentured servant Elizabeth Storkey committed fornication and adultery in Virginia. In Massachusetts, a female servant confessed to fornicating with two men "when all in the house were in bed" and a black maid and servant held secret rendezvous in the attic of the home in which she worked.[11]

For those young people who accepted the primacy of marital sexuality, courtship provided a transitional period in which they might begin to express their sexual desires. In the colonial system of courtship, parents did not arrange marriages. Nonetheless, parental opinion played a large role in the selection or approval of a future spouse, for as long as sons expected to inherit land from their fathers, they tended to heed parental advice. Furthermore, although a young man courted the daughter, he proposed marriage to her parents. According to a popular British advice book available in the colonies, "Children are so much the goods, the possessions of their Parents, that they cannot without a kind of theft, give away themselves without the allowance of those that have the right in them." Thus, for example, William Byrd of Virginia spoke first to Lucy Parkes's father about marrying her, and in turn Byrd threatened to disown his own daughter if she married a particular gentleman who did not meet with his approval.[12]

Within the confines of parental approval, formal courtship between young men and women took place unhampered by the supervision of a chaperon but often in public view. In New England, courtship included visits by a young man to a young woman's home or meetings after church. In the Chesapeake, within the planter class, family connections played an important role in introducing couples. Young people met at social affairs such as barbecues, dances, and, in the late eighteenth century, elaborate balls. When a couple did form, their choice rested largely upon a sense of compatibility rather than on notions of romantic love. Couples hoped to develop loving relationships, and courtship gave them an opportunity to begin the process.[13]

That courting couples sought to explore their sexual desires is clear from their efforts to circumvent community surveillance. During warm weather a couple might wander off into the barn or fields in search of the privacy unobtainable in small colonial homes. According to one moralist, during harvest time, with its abundant opportunities for outdoor meetings, New England youth were filled "with folly and lewdness." In 1644, a New England couple left a party but were soon "seen upon the ground together, a little from the house." The cold winters necessitated greater ingenuity. One daring young man crept through the window of his beloved's home, only to wind up in court charged with "incivility and immodesty" for courting without her parents' consent. Some young men tried to exploit opportunities for premarital sexual encounters. After three years of courting Elizabeth Gary of Maryland, Robert Hawood cornered her in a garden and forced her "to yield to lie with him" in an attempt to ruin her for any man but himself.[14]

In the eighteenth century, and probably earlier, courting couples in New England and the middle colonies had the opportunity for physical intimacy with parental approval through the custom of bundling. This practice, which had antecedents among Welsh, Dutch, and German peasants, allowed a couple to spend the night together in bed as long as they remained fully clothed or, in some cases, kept a "bundling board" between them. Bundling served the needs of suitors who traveled long distances and called in small houses that offered neither privacy nor much heat. Parents and youth shared the expectation that sexual intercourse would not take place, but if it did, and pregnancy resulted, the couple would certainly marry.[15]

The treatment of premarital pregnancy suggests that, as in England, engagement might include the right to have sexual intercourse. As one young woman explained, "He promised marriage or I never would have yielded." As long as a couple's sexual relations were channeled toward marriage, colonial society could forgive them. Although church and civil authorities officially condemned fornication and prosecuted offenders, they showed greater leniency toward betrothed couples. In addition, in both New England and the Chesapeake, those who had sex and then married could remain respectable members of the community as long as they participated in the rituals of punishment affirming that marriage provided the only appropriate locus for sexual relations.[16]

Fornication carried heavy penalties, including fines, whipping, or both. In Maryland, where laws were less likely to be enforced, unmarried couples who had sex could receive up to twenty lashes and be fined as much as five hundred pounds of tobacco. In Plymouth Colony, civil penalties for fornication included a ten-pound fine—reduced to only fifty shillings for a betrothed couple—several lashes on the back, or both. Throughout New England, a fine of nine lashes awaited both parents of a child born too soon after marriage. Thus, when Lawrence Clenton and Mary Woodin of Massachusetts confessed to fornication, he was sentenced to be severely whipped and fined forty shillings plus court fees, and she too received a whipping and a fine.[17]

Prenuptial pregnancy rates varied by region and over time. The high rates of up to thirty percent of all brides for the mid-seventeenth-century Chesapeake declined in the eighteenth century, while the low ten-percent rate of early New England rose significantly during the same period. There is little data for the middle colonies, but in one eighteenth-century community, Germantown, Pennsylvania, one-fourth of all first births occurred under nine months after marriage, a pattern that reflected in part the premarital pregnancy rates in the settlers' German homeland.[18]

Through confession and repentance, colonial society offered a means of clearing the stigma associated with premarital pregnancy. In New England, couples whom the church court found guilty of fornication had to repent publicly before their child could be baptized. They stood before their congregation, confessed to premarital sex, and often wept, as did a Plymouth woman who in 1689 "manifested much sorrow and heavyness by words and tears." Having confessed, and if truly repentant, sinners were welcomed back into good standing in the church. Even in Maryland, where there was less church discipline, marriage and repentance could reduce the punishment. In 1663, for example, Thomas Hynson, Jr., came into court "very sorrowfull" for having committed fornication with Ann Gaine. Since Hynson had "now made her his Lawfull Wife," the magistrate ordered no fine or whipping, but merely suspended him from sitting in the county court for a year and a day. His wife, Ann, later appeared in court, as ordered. For "submissively tendering her selfe . . . and Acknowlidgeing her faulte with Extreame Sorrow," the court remitted her punishment.[19] That Thomas Hynson, Jr., could resume his seat at the county court after a year and a day reflects the ease with which Chesapeake society reintegrated sinners. Similarly, New Englanders accepted the penitent fully. Like Samuel Terry, who became a Springfield town constable, New England men convicted of fornication later served as town clerks, selectmen, and even as representatives to the General Court. Women convicted of fornication could marry and join the church.[20] In contrast, those who refused to undergo public confession could be excommunicated from their congregation.

Whatever ambivalence colonists had toward premarital sexual relations, they agreed that husbands and wives ought to have sex. For New England Puritans, conjugal union was a duty; if unfulfilled, the neglected spouse might be tempted to commit adultery. So important was marital sex that a bride could leave a marriage if her husband proved to be impotent. At least one church excommunicated a husband because he denied conjugal relations to his wife for two years. Sexual attraction was valued within marriage only in moderation, however, and sexual intercourse as an act necessary to propagate the family. The Puritans admonished married couples not to allow their affections for one another to compete with their love for God. Cotton Mather warned of the "Inexpressible *Uncleannesses* in the married State," including "*Inordinate Affection.*" Michael Wigglesworth decided to marry as a way of channeling his lusts, but then feared that his conjugal relations were excessive.

"Lord, forgive my intemperance in the use of marriage," he prayed.[21] Some authorities believed that too-frequent marital sex could be physically danger-ous as well as impious, warning that "satiaty gluts the Womb and renders it unfit for its office."[22]

In spite of these fears of sexual excess, affectionate and even passionate relations developed between husbands and wives. The Puritan Edward Taylor valued spiritual union with his savior over physical union in marriage, yet he wrote of his relationship with his wife as "the True-Love knot, more Sweet than Spice." Similarly, John Winthrop wrote to his "sweet wife," Margaret, that her "love is such to me and so great is the bond between us." "I Kisse and love Thee," he closed, "with the Kindest affection." The correspondence between married couples in the southern colonies included expressions of affection and desire. "How is it possible for me to live without my only Joy & comfort?" wrote the southerner Thomas Jones to his wife, Elizabeth, in 1728. Margaret Parlor wrote to her husband that she longed to go to bed with him, while Theodore Bland, Jr., assured his "dearest Patsy" that on his return she would feel her "husband's lips flowing with love and affection warmth."[23]

Explicit discussions of physical relations in marriage were much less com-mon than references to affection, and so we have few clues about the nature of marital sex. Mary Knight of Massachusetts threw some light on the subject when she forgave her lover for having climaxed too soon. "That is no strange thing," she said, "for my Husband has done so often when he has been gone a few Nights."[24] Her admission suggests both an ideal of mutual pleasure and the difficulty of achieving it. We know that couples sometimes had sex during pregnancy, for women cautioned their husbands to be gentle at such times. The Virginian William Byrd had sex with his wife, Lucy, during her frequent pregnancies, even in the later months. Byrd's "secret diary" provides a rare, though probably atypical, record of marital intimacy among southern planters. Lucy and William Byrd quarreled often, and sexual union provided an impor-tant means of resolving their differences. According to Byrd's accounts of his sexual prowess, both husband and wife enjoyed these unions. "I gave my wife a powerful flourish and gave her great ecstasy and refreshment," he wrote in 1711. Another time, after a quarrel, the couple reconciled with a "flourish" performed on the billiard table.[25] Unfortunately, Lucy Parkes Byrd did not record her version of these events.

Sexual complaints from both husbands and wives appeared in divorce cases heard in New England in the eighteenth century. Dissatisfaction did not necessarily result from physical disappointment but rather when one partner believed that the other had stepped outside the bounds of the marital, repro-ductive sexual system. The Puritan Benjamen Keayne sought a divorce be-cause of "the insatiable desire and lust" of his wife, Sara, whom he accused of adultery and of exposing him to "the french pox," or venereal disease. Abigail Bailey, mother of ten, filed for divorce after her husband not only had sexual relations with a servant but also began to "court" their eldest daughter. The importance of maintaining marriage, despite sexual conflicts, is illustrated by the case of Stephen Temple's wife. Although she went to court to accuse her husband of sexually violating their fourteen-year-old daughter, Mrs. Temple did not seek a divorce. Rather, she wanted to force her husband to change his behavior. When he apologized and promised to reform, the couple reconciled.[26]

Whether sexuality was a source of comfort or conflict, married couples engaged in intercourse with the knowledge and hope that it would lead to children. Among free, white colonists, the availability of land and the need for laborers in the New World encouraged reproduction. They welcomed the birth of a child and, within most families, had little reason to think about preventing conception. For Puritans, theological principles supported the emphasis on procreation, including the biblical injunction to "be fruitful and multiply" and the view that childbearing was woman's "calling." So important was reproduction to marriage that failure to participate in marital sexual relations could be grounds for divorce. A Plymouth wife testified in a 1686 divorce case that her husband was "always unable to perform the act of generation."[27] Her choice of a reproductive term to describe male impotence reflected the understanding that the duty to engage in marital relations meant the duty to procreate, and not simply to provide mutual comfort. For similar reasons, a woman who was past her childbearing years was less likely to gain a divorce on the grounds of her husband's impotence.[28]

The need to produce children, along with the risk that a child would not live to adulthood, required that married women endure repeated pregnancies. In addition to the risk of death in childbirth—which in some regions of the colonies accounted for as many as twenty percent of maternal deaths—the physical labors of pregnancy, childbirth, and nursing preoccupied married women. For good reason, women feared childbirth, or in one woman's terms, "the Dreaded apperation."[29] Mary Clap, who bore six children and buried four before she died at the age of twenty-four, recognized that "Bearing tending and Burying Children was Hard work." At the same time, however, most women assumed that childbearing was their natural "calling." Mary Clap believed "it was the work she was made for and what god in his providence Had Called Her to." After six childless years of marriage, the Puritan poet Anne Bradstreet expressed a longing for pregnancy: "It please God," she wrote, "to keep me a long time without a child, which was a great grief to me and cost me many prayers and tears before I obtained one." Bradstreet knew that lying-in carried the possibility that she would "see not half my day's that's due." She herself

survived the births of eight children, seven of whom outlived her. Less fortunate was her daughter-in-law Mercy Bradstreet, who lost three infants and
died herself after childbirth at the age of twenty-eight. After each of these
deaths, Anne Bradstreet wrote not only of her grief, but also of her resignation
to God's will. She consoled herself that the dead "with thy Saviour art in
endless bliss."[30]

Although colonists knew about contraceptive methods such as withdrawal
or prolonged nursing, demographic evidence from New England and Pennsylvania reveals that few married women limited family size. Women commonly
spaced pregnancies by breastfeeding their infants for a year, during which time
many couples refrained from intercourse. Throughout the colonies, however,
other means to impede conception or terminate pregnancy were rarely employed. Women turned to folk remedies and fertility medicines to encourage
conception and avoid miscarriage rather than to avoid pregnancy.[31] Contraceptive practice could lead to divorce, as in the case of Abigail Emery, who
in 1710 complained that her husband practiced the "abominable" sin of Onan
(withdrawal) because "he feared the charge of children." The Plymouth Pilgrims banished an adulterous minister not only because he "satisfied his lust"
on women, but because he did so while he "endeavored to hinder conception."
Cases of attempted abortion usually involved illicit lovers, not married couples. "When a single woman," Margaret Lakes later confessed, she "used
means to destroy the fruit of her body to conceal her sin and shame." Elizabeth
Robins of Maryland confessed that she had twice taken savin, an abortifacient;
her husband suspected that she had an incestuous relationship with her
brother.[32] In contrast, married couples had little motive to prevent or terminate
pregnancy.

Once sex ratios had balanced in the late seventeenth century, this emphasis on reproduction contributed to the rapid increase of the colonial population, which doubled itself every generation. Natural increase, rather than
immigration, accounted for this remarkable growth rate. A lower average
marriage age than was prevalent in England allowed native-born women to
begin childbearing early; many bore a child every two to three years, an
interval determined in part by breastfeeding practices. Some white women
had as many as ten pregnancies and bore up to eight live children. They
could expect from three to seven of these to survive. Completed families
could include from six to eight children.[33] In the eighteenth century, early
marriage and high fertility contributed to population growth in the South as
well, and among the planter class, women bore as many as seven to eight
children, of whom five to six survived into adulthood. Slave fertility rates
also rose by the mid-eighteenth century. Married black women bore an average of six children. Their lower fertility rates no doubt resulted from the

poorer health and more strenuous labor performed by slaves.[34]

The high fertility rates of the colonial period, along with qualitative evidence about both religious beliefs and personal behavior, all point toward the importance of marital, reproductive sexuality in early America. Over the course of the life cycle, youths expected to marry and couples expected to engage in mutually pleasurable marital sex that would lead to procreation. The goals of reproduction and sexual pleasure did not necessarily clash, as long as they were combined within marriage. Even premarital intercourse could be accommodated if a couple wed and affirmed that marriage was the rightful place for sexual relations. When the primacy of marital, reproductive sexuality was challenged, however, colonists took strong steps to maintain their sexual institutions.

Regulating the Boundaries: The Treatment of Deviance

Although colonial society upheld an ideal of marital, reproductive sexuality, and many individuals attempted to put it into practice, a significant minority deviated from the norm when they committed adultery, sodomy, incest, or rape, or when women bore bastard children. Church and court records reveal the extensive efforts colonists made to identify, outlaw, and punish such practices. New Englanders enforced their laws against sexual deviance more thoroughly, but all English colonists inherited a legacy in which the state played a role in the regulation of personal life. From the founding of each colony, community members, churches, and the courts mobilized to impose sanctions in response to sexual offenses—that is, sexual relations that took place outside of marriage and, especially in the South, those that threatened the racial dominance of whites over blacks. In doing so, they revealed the extent of community involvement in the sexual lives of others.

Through their response to sexual transgressions, colonists reaffirmed the boundaries of acceptable behavior. Courts in New England and the Chesapeake typically sentenced offenders to some form of public humiliation, such as whipping at the post or sitting in the stocks. Thus a Maryland court sent Agnes Taylor to the whipping post to receive twelve lashes "in the Publicke Vew of the People" for having borne a bastard child. Hugh Davis of Virginia was whipped "before an assembly of Negroes and others for . . . defiling his body in lying with a negro."[35] In New England, public confession and repentance both restored the individual to the congregation and at the same time confirmed the propriety of sexual rules. When someone was convicted of a capital crime, such as rape or infanticide, clergy preached execution sermons, elaborating on the wages of sexual sin and the need to resist temptation. The regulation of deviance served the larger function of reminding the community at large that sexuality belonged within marriage, for the purpose of producing legitimate children.

The gender of offenders shaped the treatment of deviance. Sodomy and rape were men's crimes. Although adultery, fornication, and bastardy involved couples, women in both northern and southern colonies were more likely than men to be prosecuted and convicted for these sexual offenses.[36] The fact that pregnancy made a woman's participation in these acts apparent helps account for the disparity. In addition, Western culture had traditionally feared the sexual voraciousness of women. As the "weaker vessell," woman supposedly had less mastery over her passions and had to be carefully controlled. Penalties also differed. Men more often had to pay fines and court costs, while women, who had less access to property, had to accept whipping. Despite these distinctions, both women and men participated fully in the regulation of deviance. Both kept a close watch on neighbors and testified in court about illicit activities; both faced fines, whipping, public humiliation, or execution; both could repent and be reinstated in the community.

For men and women, laws against extramarital sexuality carried harsh penalties. Even behaviors that might lead to sex outside marriage required punishment. The relatively minor offense of being a "person of Lude Life and conversation" earned a fine of fifty pounds sterling in Virginia, while one man paid twenty pounds for "profainly" drinking and dancing with a married woman. In 1631, Massachusetts enacted the death penalty for adultery—a crime defined as sexual relations between a man and a married woman. (Sex between a married man and a single woman, or between a single man and woman, would have been charged as fornication.) Most other colonies adopted the death penalty for adultery, although it was rarely enforced. After 1660, New England courts usually imposed fines of ten to twenty pounds, along with public whipping or the wearing of the letters *AD* on a garment or burned onto the forehead. In 1736, Thomas Clarke of Dorchester, Massachusetts, had to choose between a five-pound fine or ten stripes for having "in a wanton and Lascivious Manner had the use and Carnal Knowledge of the Body of Susannah the Wife of Joseph Browne . . . with her consent." Maryland law condemned adultery whether the man or woman was married. Southern courts often sentenced whipping and sometimes used the threat of banishment to punish adulterers; they might also require a bond of up to one hundred pounds sterling to prevent an adulterous couple from seeing each other.[37]

In some cases, adultery could lead to divorce, separation, or violence. In New England, over half the divorce cases in the seventeenth century cited adultery as a cause. One woman sought a divorce when her husband acknowledged "that he had Rog[e]red other women and meant to Roger Every Likely Woman He Could and as many as would Let Him."[38] Husbands sometimes physically attacked adulterous partners. After Stephen Willey found his wife, Abigail, in bed with one man and saw her sitting on the lap of another, he struck her and threatened to kill her.[39]

The regulation of adultery, like all forms of nonmarital sexuality, depended upon the extensive involvement of community members in each other's lives. Intrusiveness characterized the attitude toward sexuality, especially in the closely knit settlements of New England, where individuals could not easily engage in illicit sexual activities without being noticed.[40] Among Puritans, each community member had responsibility for upholding the morality of all lest God punish the group as a whole. Acting on these precepts, Clement Coldom of Gloucester, Massachusetts, "heaved the door off the hinges" to see what his neighbor John Pearce was doing with "the widow Stannard" at night. So clear was the responsibility of family and neighbors to help regulate sexuality that a New England father who allowed his son to live with an unmarried woman was charged as an "accessory to fornication."[41] Even without the Puritan religious obligation to oversee the behavior of others, men and women in other colonies testified about the sexual crimes of neighbors, illustrating an acceptance of intrusiveness in what would later come to be considered purely private matters.

The testimony of observant neighbors was essential for convicting adulterers in court. In Maryland, for example, several people witnessed John Nevill having sexual relations with Susan Attcheson, a married woman; they testified that they had seen her hand in his breeches and his "in Susan's placket" (a slit in her skirt). The court fined Nevill and ordered Attcheson whipped. When Susanna Kennett and John Tully of Virginia heard snoring in the next room, they stood on a hogshead of tobacco and peered over the wall to see that "Richard Jones Laye snoring in her plackett and Mary West put her hand in his Codpis." Kennett then pried loose a board to observe Mary West "with her Coates upp above her middle and Richard Jones with his Breeches down Lying upon her." In 1732, a New England woman testified to having "look'ed in at a hole in the End of the house," where she saw her neighbor's wife and another man "on the bed in the act of Adultery." Similarly, a widowed lodger testified in the 1760s that he "heard a Man and woman discoursing in the Chamber over the Room" and looked in to find the mistress of the house having sex with a male friend.[42]

In addition to testifying in court, neighbors zealously guarded moral standards in the community. The comments of two Massachusetts women who observed a man "in Act of Copulation" attest to the sense of community responsibility for regulating morality. Interrupting the act, the women asked "if he was not Ashamed to Act so when he had a Wife at home." An incident in Maryland further suggests how even in a less settled area, the community could mobilize against adultery. Several travelers lodged overnight at the residence of Captain Fleet, who became "verie angerie" when he realized that one lodger, Mr. Carline, was committing adultery on the premises. Fleet had the couple turned out-of-doors. The court subsequently banished Carline for disowning his wife; when he tried to return home, Carline's neighbors would not allow him to show his face. Finally, in the fishing town of Marblehead, Massachusetts, neighbors wielding clubs attacked the home of William Beale, whose wife, Martha, was suspect for having a previous marriage annulled and an intimate relationship with a servant. "Come out, you cuckolly cur," they called to William, "we are come to beat thee. Thou livest in adultery."[43]

Because they so clearly defied the norm of reproductive sexuality, the crimes of sodomy, buggery, and bestiality carried the death penalty. As the founder of Massachusetts Bay Colony, John Winthrop, explained in the case of William Plaine, who was executed for sodomy and corrupting youths "by masturbations," these acts were "dreadful" because they "tended to the frustrating of the ordinance of marriage and the hindering [of] the generation of mankind." The narrow legal definition of sodomy, which required proof of penetration, along with the requirement of two witnesses for capital punishment, limited the application of the death penalty. At least five men were executed for sodomy or buggery during the seventeenth century—one by the Spanish in Florida, one in Virginia, one in New Haven, and two in New York. No one was executed for sodomy in the eighteenth century, but men convicted of "sodomitical acts," such as "spending their seed upon one another," received severe and repeated whipping, burning with a hot iron, or banishment. As in other morals cases, the higher the status of the accused, the less likely was severe punishment. Despite his thirty-year history of attempted sodomy with servants and neighbors, the wealthy Nicholas Sension of Connecticut merely had his estate held as bond to insure his future good behavior.[44]

It is important to note that the crime of sodomy was not equivalent to the modern concept of homosexuality. Sodomy referred to "unnatural"—that is, nonprocreative—sexual acts, which could be performed between two men, a man and an animal (technically considered buggery or bestiality), or between a man and a woman. When a Maryland woman sued her husband for divorce, charging that he had committed "diverse inhumane usages and beastly crimes," she could have meant anal intercourse in marriage or with another man. Although the term *sodomy* was not applied to sexual relations between women, one colony, New Haven, listed among its capital offenses women's acts "against nature." The few surviving cases that refer to "lewd behavior" between women record punishments of whipping or admonishments, rather than execution. In 1642, for example, a Massachusetts court severely whipped a servant and fined her for "unseemly practices btwixt her and another maid."[45]

Unlike many native American tribes in which the male *berdache* might live as a woman and marry a man, colonial society had no permanent cultural category for those who engaged in sexual relations with members of their own gender. Like other sinners, women or men who were punished for unnatural sexual acts did not acquire a lifetime identity as "homosexuals," and they could be reintegrated into the fold. In 1732, for example, Ebenezer Knight of Marblehead confessed and repented "a long series of Uncleanness with Mankind." His church suspended Knight, but after he returned from a six-year sojourn in Boston, the congregation reinstated him.[46]

As in the case of sodomy, conviction for rape carried the death penalty, but lesser punishments usually applied. Rape was the only sexual offense that did not involve consensual acts, and much of the testimony by a rape victim and the required witnesses focused on proving that the woman did not consent to the act. Accounts of rape and attempted rape emphasize the extent to which women resisted their assailants. Nonetheless, conviction and sentencing patterns disclose a reluctance to prosecute men fully for this crime. Out of seventy-two rape accusations in seventeenth-century New England, only six resulted in executions, though more than half the men were convicted. That Massachusetts courts were more likely to convict when a child or a married woman had been raped suggests that single, adult women were often perceived as willing sexual partners. The rape of a daughter or wife could be seen as an attack on the "property" of a father or husband, rather than a crime against the woman herself. Indeed, the death penalty for rape applied only if a woman was married, engaged, or under the age of ten.[47]

The disposition of rape cases depended strongly upon the status of both victim and assailant. Men of higher social standing—farm owners and artisans, for example—were less likely to be brought to trial for rape or attempted rape, while lower-class and nonwhite men accused of rape could expect harsher treatment by the courts. In 1685, a servant convicted of attempted rape upon a married woman received the severe punishment of thirty-five lashes. In eighteenth-century Massachusetts, three of the five executions for rape involved blacks or Indians, even though nonwhite men represented only fourteen percent of those accused of rape. The other two executed were white laborers.[48] The harshest penalties for sexual assault applied to blacks who attacked white women. In New York, a free black convicted of two attempted rapes of white women was burned alive. Another free black in Virginia received twenty-nine lashes, an hour in the pillory, and a sentence of temporary servitude for attempted assault on a seven-year-old white girl. In several colonies, the laws prescribed castration for blacks who attempted to rape white women.[49]

Neighbors were especially important as witnesses in rape cases, for it was incumbent upon the victim to call out in order to notify others of an attack; otherwise, the court might consider her a willing partner. When Elizabeth Goodell of Salem accused her brother-in-law of frequent "assaults" and "affronts," her neighbors stated that she should have called out for help. Even nine-year-old Ruth Parsons testified that she had cried out when Edward Sanders forcibly abused her by "enteringe her body with his pisseinge place (as shee called it)," but no one was near the house to hear her, except "little children wch he put out of doores."[50] In some cases, women were punished for not having called out when assaulted. When a victim of unwanted sexual advances was afraid to call out or press charges, neighbors might step in to bring the case to light. The testimony of other members of the community was also important in determining whether a rape had actually occurred. Midwives and other women who examined the victims of assault helped the court determine whether to prosecute for rape or a lesser charge.[51] As in the response to adultery, the entire community mobilized to ferret out those who engaged in sexual acts outside of marriage.

Bastardy, like adultery, sodomy, and rape, threatened the centrality of marital, reproductive sexuality, but it also posed a particularly troubling economic problem for the colonists: who would provide for children born out of wedlock in a society in which the family was the central economic unit? Lest the cost fall upon other members of the community, colonies passed bastardy laws, patterned upon English antecedents, that severely punished the parents of bastards and attempted to hold the purported father responsible for the child's care. In order to establish paternity, midwives questioned an unmarried woman during labor, "the time of her travell [travail]," when they believed she would be incapable of lying about the father's identity. The court then accused the father and meted out punishment to both parents in the form of fines or whipping, along with an effort to enforce marriage. Maryland courts, for example, doled out thirty-nine lashes to parents of bastards, while Connecticut courts sentenced five pounds and ten stripes of the lash. By the mid-eighteenth century, many courts ceased to punish the parents for their sexual transgressions and concentrated entirely on obtaining support for the child. It was then left to the churches to enforce morality and try to pressure the parents of bastards into marrying.[52]

The mechanism by which colonists attempted to determine paternity was extremely vulnerable to manipulation by either the mother or the father of a bastard. For one, no matter how coercive they might be, midwives could not always force an unwilling mother—like Nathaniel Hawthorne's fictional Hester Prynne—to reveal the name of her child's father. The Quakers, as an added sanction, disowned from their church congregations a woman who did not name the father. Or, a woman might calculatingly decide to follow the course of the servant Elizabeth Wells, who told another servant that "[i]f shee should bee with child shee would bee sure to lay it un to won who was rich enough abell to mayntayne it weather it wear his or no." A pattern of false paternity accusations is revealed by another woman, who wrote to her illicit lover: "der loue [love] . . . i am a child by you and i will ether kil it or lay it to an other . . . I have had many children and none [of the fathers] have none of them [to support]."[53]

At the same time, fathers could refuse to acknowledge paternity. The wealthy George Hammond of Maine, cited by Lydia Spinney as father of her child, refuted the charge and would not pay child support. Some men attempted to deny responsibility by claiming that the mother had been promiscuous; others claimed economic inability to support a child. In New Amsterdam, Geleyn Verplank admitted "to have had carnal conversation" with Geertruyd Wingres, but he denied that he promised to marry her and failed to pay the lying-in charges and child maintenance ordered by the court.[54] John Harrington denied paternity in a 1771 bastardy case by claiming that he could not possibly be the father of the child. In the process, he inadvertently revealed what was probably the predominant method for avoiding conception: "I f——d her once," he admitted, "but I minded my pullbacks. I sware I did not get it." The court did not share his faith in *coitus interruptus,* and Harrington was convicted.[55]

The female servant could have an especially hard time sustaining a paternity charge. If a man denied her claim, she had to produce witnesses to support her in court. If a free man, and particularly a master, denied paternity, the court might well accept his word over that of a servant. In Maryland, servant Jane Palldin bore an illegitimate child by her married master, John Norton. Afraid of the consequences of revealing the father, she first claimed that a stranger "gott her with Child." Indeed, after she confessed the truth, Norton's wife "began to raile at her" and a brawl broke out among the three of them.[56] Masters could abuse the law by impregnating a servant and enjoying not only sexual privilege but an extra year of servitude as well. To prevent this practice, courts began to remove female servants from households if their masters allowed them to become pregnant.[57]

Despite the difficulties of enforcement, colonial society did maintain a low rate of illegitimacy. Historical demographer Robert Wells has estimated that prior to 1750, between one and three percent of all births occurred outside of marriage. The seventeenth-century Chesapeake, with its large number of indentured servants, had a much higher rate, while some regions had even lower ones. In the middle colonies, Quaker congregations recorded no bastardy cases until 1780, and in Germantown, Pennsylvania, illegitimate children accounted

for under one percent of all colonial-era baptismal certificates. Persistent regional variation is clear from the ratios of illegitimate births per thousand live
births at the beginning of the eighteenth century. These ranged from a low of
one in a New York Dutch Reformed church, to between thirteen and eighteen
in several Connecticut, Massachusetts, and Virginia counties, to a high of
twenty-six in one Maryland county.[58]

Both the stigma and the cost of bearing an illegitimate child led some
unwed mothers, whether free or servant, to commit infanticide. In Massachusetts, Grace, a "Negro single woman servant," murdered her bastard son in
1692, and Elizabeth Emerson, an unwed mother who lived with her parents,
buried her illegitimate children in the garden. Lucy Stratton of Maryland
received thirty lashes for having "unnaturally dried up her milk," a neglectful
action that the court believed had put her infant's life in danger.[59] Because
unwed mothers, attempting to avoid prosecution, sometimes claimed that their
children had been stillborn or had died of natural causes, colonial, like English,
law assumed maternal guilt if a bastard child was found dead. Therefore it was
a crime to conceal the death of a bastard child. Widespread concern about
infanticide led the colonies by the eighteenth century to enact laws providing
that unless sworn witnesses could testify that a child was stillborn, the mother
of a dead bastard was presumed to be guilty of murder. Nonetheless, New
England courts charged only thirty-two women with infanticide in the seventeenth century. Although the overall indictment rate was over twice as high
in the Chesapeake, conviction rates were lower in the South. As in other
criminal prosecutions, black servants and slaves had a higher conviction rate
than all whites, free or servant.[60]

Even though infanticide rates remained low throughout the colonies, this
crime provided a particularly frightening symbol of the wages of sexual sin.
Since so many infanticide victims were newborn bastard children, the crime
represented the ultimate destructiveness wrought by illicit sexual union. The
clergy did not miss the opportunity to bring this message home to their flock.
As Cotton Mather expounded in his sermon on the execution of Sarah Smith,
who had murdered her newborn infant, "an *Unchaste Life*" had brought Smith
to the gallows, for the "*Fires of Lust*" had baked her heart into "Insensible
Hardness."[61] Lust, unchecked, could lead not only to illegitimacy, but worse,
to the death of both child and sinner as well.

In the late seventeenth century, the prohibition of interracial sex and
marriage emerged as an additional sexual boundary. In the early years of
settlement, before slavery became entrenched, interracial unions, though unpopular, did not necessarily elicit harsh punishment. In cases of fornication,
adultery, or bastardy, the offenders received punishments similar to those

white couples endured. In 1640, for example, a Virginia gentleman had "to do penance in church . . . for getting a negroe woman with child," while the woman received a whipping—not an extraordinary punishment.[62] In many areas of the South, the white sex ratio remained so unbalanced that white men sometimes sought black mates in the absence of white women. By the late seventeenth century, however, the white sex ratio began to even out. More importantly, large numbers of Africans were being imported as slaves, and slavery began to supplant indentured servitude as the major source of labor. Colonial assemblies soon enacted an array of statutes—including laws punishing interracial sexual relations—to strengthen the race line by reinforcing the unequal status of blacks and whites.

As with native American Indians, sexual stereotyping provided one means by which the English colonists justified their domination of Africans. English colonists brought to America a set of stereotypes that differentiated Europeans from Africans by assigning to the latter a sexual nature that was more sensual, aggressive, and beastlike than that of whites. Influenced by the Elizabethan image of "the lusty Moor," colonists accepted the notion that Africans were "lewd, lascivious and wanton people." With the growing reliance on slavery, colonists drew upon these English stereotypes to help justify their economic and social control of blacks. Not only their dark color, but also their allegedly animal-like sexuality, whites argued, proved that blacks were of a different breed than whites; it was thus "natural" that the two races should not mix, and that whites should dominate blacks. Throughout the American colonies, a caste system based on race took hold by the eighteenth century. From New Englander Samuel Sewall to Virginian Thomas Jefferson, white colonists, regardless of their views on slavery, opposed interracial mixing. But in the southern colonies, where slavery grew in economic importance, the racial boundary became more deeply institutionalized.[63] Individuals who transgressed this racial boundary challenged not only a set of cultural values but also the basis of an emerging system of racial control.

As African slaves came to dominate the labor force, slavery required legal support. Colonial legislatures acted to outlaw and penalize individuals who practiced what would later be termed miscegenation. Legislation to regulate interracial unions first appeared in the 1660s. The Virginia legislature in 1662 doubled the fines for fornication in the case of interracial couples, and in 1691 it outlawed "that abominable mixture" of interracial union, ordering banishment from the colony for any white man or woman who married or fornicated with a Negro, mulatto, or Indian. In 1705, the Assembly strengthened the law by ordering six months' imprisonment and a ten-pound fine for interracial marriage or fornication, and fined the minister who performed an interracial marriage ten thousand pounds of tobacco. Maryland banned such marriages in 1664, ordering a white woman who married a slave to serve her husband's master. Between 1705 and 1750, all of the southern colonies, as well as Pennsylvania and Massachusetts, passed laws prohibiting interracial marriages and any other "unnatural and inordinate Copulations" between whites and blacks. Discriminatory treatment of interracial children further supported the institution of slavery. Delaware enacted heavier fines in interracial than white bastardy cases, and the 1664 Maryland anti-miscegenation law defined the children of mixed marriages as slaves. In most colonies, bastard children of mixed unions had to spend up to thirty-one years in servitude.[64]

The laws against miscegenation did not entirely prevent the formation of interracial unions. Where French, Spanish, and West Indian influences remained strong, as in Louisiana and coastal South Carolina, the taboos on amalgamation were weaker, and interracial unions might be discussed in public. In all of the English colonies, however, some forms of miscegenation persisted. In New England, where few blacks lived and slavery failed to take root, some interracial marriages survived social and legal proscription. More typical, however, were illicit unions formed between southern whites and blacks. Male planters, by virtue of their class, were not bound by the prohibitions against interracial sex. Thus relationships between white planters and black women often formed. Some southern men acknowledged these unions when they manumitted or left property to their mulatto children.[65]

In addition to ongoing interracial relations, brief sexual encounters took place frequently in the South. As a Boston traveler to South Carolina observed in 1773, "The enjoyment of a negro or mulatto woman is spoken of as quite a common thing." Given the prevailing stereotype of African sensuality, white men assumed that black women were willing to have sexual relationships with them. In fact, female slaves had little choice about whether to respond to white men's sexual advances, whatever their actual desires. Interracial unions between white women and black men were least frequent and usually confined to the rural backcountry of the South, where the status difference between poor whites and slaves was narrower. One Maryland husband banished his wife from his sight and refused financial responsibility for her because she "polluted my Bed, by taking to her in my stead, her own Negro slave, by whom she hath a child." As in this case, a woman's adultery with a slave or free black male might lead to divorce.[66]

Probably the rarest form of interracial union, but the most symbolically charged, was the rape of a white woman by a black man. So frightening was the specter of this inversion of the racial hierarchy that colonial legislatures devised a uniquely American criminal penalty, castration, as a means of deterrence. Laws in Pennsylvania, New Jersey, and Virginia allowed castration for blacks who attempted to rape white women. Even when this literally emasculating punishment was dropped from other criminal codes, it could still be applied in cases of assaults on white women by slaves. That assaults on black women provoked no such reaction confirms the racial character of this legislation. At least one eighteenth-century Virginia slave was formally sentenced to castration. Blacks convicted of rape were usually hanged.[67] Nonetheless, the law set a precedent that could be followed by extralegal means. Thus in 1718, when a white man in Connecticut observed a black man lying with a white woman, he attacked the black and castrated him. Whites particularly feared that when slaves revolted against their masters, as they did on several occasions during the eighteenth century, the men would assault white women to retaliate for white assaults on black women. However, there is no evidence that black men sexually assaulted white women during the slave uprisings of the colonial period.[68]

White attitudes toward interracial sexual relations reflected complex psychological, economic, and legal dynamics. That white men of the planter class could have casual sexual relations with slave women, but reserved the most brutal corporal punishment for black men who slept with white women, clearly illustrates the ways that sexual rules reinforced a system of racial dominance. That enormous scorn was heaped upon a white woman who had sex with a black man—even if they were married—while black women were expected to service the sexual needs of white men, reveals the combined forces of gender and racial hierarchy. As Winthrop Jordan has convincingly argued, white men desired sexual union with blacks, but given their culture's aversion to racial mixing they refused to acknowledge that desire and those unions. Thus white men projected sexual desire onto black women, viewing them as lustful and available, and onto black men, fearing them as potential rapists. Finally, white men refused to acknowledge the products of interracial union by systematically relegating mulatto children to the status of slaves. Unlike Spanish and Portuguese colonies, with their elaborate racial hierarchies in which mulatto children were often considered to be free rather than enslaved, the English colonies allowed no gradation of color. They condemned the child of mixed unions to the status of slave.[69] The different sex ratios of Latin and North American colonies contributed to this divergent practice, but so did the colonists' psychological conflicts about interracial union. "Sexual intimacy," Jordan has written of the white man, "strikingly symbolized a union he wished to avoid. If he could not restrain his sexual nature, he could at least reject its fruits and thus solace himself that he had done no harm. . . . By classifying the mulatto as a Negro he was in effect denying that intermixture had occurred at all."[70]

The regulation of deviance in the American colonies, from the mid-seventeenth to the mid-eighteenth centuries, helped to enforce the system of marital, reproductive sexuality and to maintain white dominance over blacks. Just as the socialization of youth channeled sexuality into marriage, so too did church, court, and community join forces to identify sexual crime and publicly affirm the proper place of sex. Selective enforcement led to the prosecution of more women than men, and to lesser penalties for free, white, and wealthier individuals. For all colonists, however, a clear message surrounded the public pronouncements about sexual crime: the family provided the only acceptable outlet for sex, with the primary goal of producing legitimate children.

Paralleling the growth of colonial society and the decline of Puritanism, the regulation of morality changed over time. In the eighteenth century, the sexual boundary between white and black intensified. In contrast, the enforcement of marital, reproductive sexuality among whites lessened. Even New Englanders, with their religious obligation to create a godly community, meted out fewer, and less severe, punishments for adultery, sodomy, rape, and infanticide in the eighteenth century. The middle and southern colonies traditionally had lower rates of enforcement for morals offenses, but there, too, convictions declined after 1720. As white colonists turned their attention to the pursuit of the secular goal of a prosperous community, sexual transgressions elicited less public concern, while state regulation of morality weakened. After 1750, even more rapid social changes would begin to transform the American family and with it sexual norms and their regulation.

CHAPTER 3

Seeds of Change

IN 1793, a mob of several hundred working men took to the streets of New York City, attacking brothels and gentlemen's residences. The riot protested the acquittal of Harry Bedlow, who had been charged with the rape of a seventeen-year-old seamstress named Lanah Sawyer. The two had met on the streets of New York and had "walked out" together on several evenings before Bedlow took Sawyer to a "bawdy house," where they had a sexual "connection." Testimony at his trial centered on whether Bedlow—who posed as "Lawyer Smith"—had forced an innocent working woman to have sex with him, or if she had done so from "desire of gratifying her passions," knowing full well that when a working girl walked out at night with a gentlemen, it inevitably led to illicit sex.[1] The case itself highlighted both the possibilities for sexual encounters between strangers in late-eighteenth-century cities and the ambiguity of social rules governing such relationships. The riot that followed Bedlow's acquittal revealed deep popular discontent about the lack of regulation of sexual morality by the state, as well as the class antagonisms that could erupt from the sexual exploitation of working women by gentlemen. Above all, the seduction or rape of Lanah Sawyer suggested the extent to which both sexual relations and their social regulation had begun to move beyond the traditional networks of family and community life by the end of the eighteenth century.

The family-centered sexual life of the colonies had been undergoing subtle but important transformations for several generations in response to the economic, social, and political maturation of the colonies. Commercialized agriculture, in which crops grown for cash were traded within regional markets, replaced the self-sufficient subsistence farms of the early settlements. By mid-century, a few port towns, such as Boston, Charleston, and Philadelphia, housed a bustling maritime trade. These economic developments undermined the patterns of stable community life which had largely regulated sexual morality. In seaport cities, a more mobile and heterogeneous population mingled in a more highly stratified society, marked by extremes of poverty and wealth. In farming areas, young couples increasingly established their homes in outlying areas, where land was available, beyond the reach of family, church, and traditional community surveillance. Population pressures on the land undermined the powers that fathers once exercised over the young by virtue of their control over inheritable lands. As a consequence, individual choice, rather than parental or state control, became more important, whether in courtship, marriage, or the treatment of sexual deviance.

New concepts within religion and politics also affected sexuality. Beginning in the 1740s, the religious revival known as the Great Awakening encouraged individuals to take responsibility for their own actions, and state regulation of morality diminished. After the Revolutionary War, the gradual disestablishment of the Protestant churches further weakened the bond between state and church and, consequently, the moral authority of the churches. Finally, at a time when "the pursuit of happiness" became a political ideal, individual pleasure, and not simply the duty to procreate or to give comfort to one's spouse, came to be valued as a goal of sexual relations.

A brief glance at European intellectual and social history provides an important context for sexual change in the American colonies and the new nation. In Europe, Enlightenment ideas about the relationship of the individual to society, along with the decline of the traditional patriarchal family, encouraged new sexual beliefs. In the seventeenth century, English Puritans had been suspicious of bodily pleasure and associated sensuality with the biblical fall from grace. Strict community control was therefore necessary to prevent the sins of the flesh from undermining the godliness of the community. In contrast, Enlightenment writers of the eighteenth century elevated all that was related to nature, including sexuality, as good and desirable. Influenced by an intellectual climate that emphasized the pursuit of individual happiness, many European writers stressed that sexual relations provided a healthy means to this ideal. One logical extreme of this position was the practice of sexual libertinism, or the pursuit of pure pleasure unbounded by social responsibilities. Only a small group of elite males could emulate this ideal, such as the rakes and seducers who shared their stories of sexual exploits in the London coffeehouses of the late eighteenth century. For others, nonetheless, the introduction of personal pleasure as a goal placed a new, more positive value upon sexuality. In America, for example, Benjamin Franklin, who had been exposed to European ideas, referred to sexual intercourse as "a virtuous Action."[2]

At the same time, new scientific accounts of the functioning of the human reproductive system reconceptualized sexuality as something distinct from procreation. As European scientists learned about the role of the sperm and egg in creating an embryo, they helped undermine the older belief that pleasure was a precondition to conception and made possible the separation of sexual intercourse as an act and reproduction as a goal. Significantly, the new medical literature attached special cultural meanings to the physiological differences between men and women. Elaborate metaphors of the active male sperm and the passive female egg employed scientific knowledge to transform sexual values.[3] Just as Enlightenment views about individual happiness applied primarily to men, so too did medical ideas increasingly differentiate by gender, encouraging men, but not women, to seek sexual pleasure. Indeed, a new ideal of female "passionlessness" emerged in Anglo-American culture in the late eighteenth century, and biological arguments supported its contention that women had desires that were more maternal than sexual.

Coincident with this ideological reconstruction of sexuality came subtle shifts in English family life. By the late eighteenth century the ideal of affective relationships within the family had become more widespread. Most couples now recognized that the mutual rights and obligations of spouses included emotional and sexual pleasure. At the same time, although lust and love remained suspect as motives for marriage, young people could increasingly choose their own mates, regardless of parental opinion. Gradually, love was becoming a respectable basis for marriage choice, encouraging a new view of marriage in which the affections of husband and wife were as important as their economic and reproductive obligations to each other.[4]

Further evidence from English history suggests that individual choice played a larger role in sexual life. After a long period of relatively low premarital pregnancy rates, the incidence of "early births" nearly doubled in eighteenth-century England. Illegitimacy rates rose even more sharply, from under one percent of all births in the early seventeenth century to six percent in the 1780s. Together these figures suggest a breakdown in traditional sexual restraints during courtship and a decline in the pattern of premarital intercourse followed by marriage. A hint of the loosening of the tie between reproduction and sexuality in marriage appeared in the century after 1675, when members of the British upper classes began to practice contraception.[5] As survival rates for children improved, women could bear fewer children. When this happened, sexual relations within marriage might increasingly serve other than reproductive purposes. In short, in eighteenth-century England—the source for most American immigrants and ideas—science, social thought, and family life all reflected a belief in more freedom of individual choice in sexual relations.

From courtship through marriage and divorce, and in the regulation of deviance, American patterns also point toward a new constellation in which individual attraction and fulfillment gained importance in sexual relations. Along with adopting an ideal of affective unions, Americans experienced a decline in parental power over marriage choice, increased rates of premarital pregnancy and illegitimacy, and the beginnings of conscious family limitation. In addition, the late eighteenth century witnessed an overall decline in state regulation of morality and a shift in concerns from private to public moral transgressions. In the process, male and female experiences of sexuality came to differ more deeply than in the past, and women's greater sexual vulnerability contributed to the emergence of new, more highly gendered ideas about sexuality.

Love and Marriage

The nature of courtship in late-eighteenth-century America illustrates many of these themes. After midcentury, courting couples in all English colonies began to employ the language of romantic love, expressing passion in their correspondence and exploring intimate emotions, rather than mere property arrangements, when they planned for marriage. Open expressions of sentiment replaced the religious language of earlier couples. One southern gentleman, St. George Tucker, encouraged such expressions: "If the Ardor of my Affections . . . inspire you with a Tender Sentiment," he wrote to his beloved, then "suppress not the Emotion." By the late eighteenth century, many American women viewed affection as a precondition for engagement. According to Mary Stevenson, "an union without affection is the most deplorable situation a woman can be in." After 1800, historian Ellen Rothman has explained, "the state of one's heart" would dominate letters written between courting couples.[6]

Colonists also spoke more openly about the physical component of courtship. In the 1760s, for example, when a storm prevented John Adams from visiting Abigail Smith, Adams wrote that the forced separation was "perhaps blessed," for when brought into "striking distance," their magnetic attraction for each other might have led to "Itches, Aches, Agues and Repentance." A young suitor in North Carolina welcomed the opportunity for such attractions when he pleaded to take liberties with his beloved: "Let not your chiefest glory be immurd in the nice casket of a Madenhead," he wrote. Expectations of physical intimacy also appeared when a young man lamented to an absent friend that there was "not much corting in Spencertown. I have not Staid with wone Since you left the Place but I will a Sabady-night and will hump them for you."[7]

A new emphasis on the physical attractiveness of women accompanied the introduction of sentimental language and sexual references in courtship. According to Laurel Ulrich, the female ideal shifted from one of meekness and spirituality to one of beauty and sexual appeal. After the 1730s, she has noted, American portraiture began to idealize the young, full-bosomed, small-waisted and raven-haired woman, as opposed to the practical helpmeet of an earlier generation.[8] Both language and art thus pointed the way toward new criteria for the selection of mates, based on personal taste and emotions rather than practical and familial concerns.

Sons and daughters not only chose mates with less attention to property and family considerations, but some young people even disregarded parental opinion altogether. Operating within a political climate that decried tyranny and exulted the rights of the individual, some children married over parental objections while others failed to inform their parents at all. In 1760, William Byrd III told his mother of his wedding after the fact. "Good God," she cried out, "is my Son married and never acquainted me with it!" Other parents reacted more calmly to the new style of individual choice. As one father explained in 1757, "all marriages [ought] to be entirely from the choice of each party."[9] More often, however, parents and children who lived during this transitional period were likely to be in conflict over the relative roles of the family and the individual in choosing a marriage partner.

One means by which young people could exert some control over marriage was to force the issue by announcing a premarital pregnancy. Indeed, premarital pregnancy rates rose so sharply in late-eighteenth-century America that some historians view the change as signaling a "revolt of the young" against familial controls over marriage and sexuality.[10] Although premarital pregnancy continued to be socially scorned, increasing numbers of young women became pregnant before marriage. In some parts of New England, as many as one-third of all brides were pregnant in the late eighteenth century, compared to under ten percent in the seventeenth century.[11] These rates approached those of the early Chesapeake settlement during the initial period of social and familial instability.

Increased premarital pregnancy reflected not only an effort to control marriage choice, but also a breakdown of the traditional familial and community regulation of sexuality. With greater geographical mobility and the growth of commercial towns in the late eighteenth century, and in light of the social disruptions brought on by years of warfare, the relatively stable communities of the early colonial period could not survive intact. As transients appeared in seaport towns or when families dispersed during wartime, individuals could no longer be held accountable for their personal behavior. As a result, in both New England and the Chesapeake, the incidence of bastardy rose during this period.[12]

Although some historians have viewed the breakdown of traditional controls over sexuality as a step toward personal autonomy for women, much evidence suggests that in fact many young women, and especially those of the lower classes, became more sexually vulnerable during this period. On city streets, women endured both verbal and physical harassment. One account of New York City portrayed young men using obscene language and crude gestures as women passed: "If she essays to proceed by the wall, they instantly veer that way, and defeat her intention. In this manner she is often obliged to pass and repass several times in front of the line, each one making his impertinent remarks on her as she tried to get forward—'An Angel, by H——s!' 'Dam'd fine girl, by go——d!' 'Where do you lodge, my dear?' " That women who walked alone on city streets were considered fair game for the advances of men became clear in the trial of Harry Bedlow. His lawyer asked how a working woman could "imagine that a man of his situation would pay her any attention . . . unless with a view of promoting illicit commerce?"[13] Other rape cases attest to the vulnerability of women. At the same time, popular culture included frequent references to the problem of women who were seduced and ruined by men. In New England magazines of the last quarter of the eighteenth century, both fiction and nonfiction writers sympathized with women who, through force or ignorance, had illicit sexual relations. Similarly, popular ballads published in American almanacs after 1799 frequently spoke of women seduced and ruined by men. At least some women complained when they learned of these seductions, as did a New England woman who wrote to a friend about a girl who had "fallen victim to the baseness of those who call themselves the Lords of the Creation."[14]

Women, who had long been both constrained and protected by community enforcement of moral codes, faced new risks in consensual sexual relationships. It was now harder to insure that premarital intercourse would lead to marriage in the event of pregnancy. Then, too, because the once-favorable sex ratios had reversed themselves, women had more difficulty marrying or remarrying, especially in older settled areas like New England. At the same time, women had few alternatives to marriage, since it was virtually impossible to be economically self-supporting. As marriage and premarital virtue took on greater significance for most women, the prospects of abandonment by a lover or of illegitimate birth became even more problematic.

For these reasons, women themselves and society in general voiced greater concern about women's ability to maintain their sexual virtue and displayed increasing suspicion about expressions of female passion. In Europe and America, moralists now stressed the need for women, especially, to resist sexual desire and to maintain their chastity. These anxieties spoke to the real problem of female sexual vulnerability at a time of changing community standards. They also gave voice to deeper fears about the expression of passion. The formation of a republican government intensified fears that strong passions would undermine the virtue of the citizenry. Patriots like Thomas Jefferson and Benjamin Rush called on Americans to exercise moderation in all things, including sex, to resist the dissipation that, they believed, weakened European governments. In this setting women could serve as a convenient symbol for the irrational and the uncontrollable in all people. Social and political concerns thus combined to create a new accent on female purity at the close of the eighteenth century, pointing the way toward the further specialization of sexual values by gender in the nineteenth century.[15]

Historian Nancy Cott has identified three sources of this new Anglo-American ideal of female "passionlessness," the belief that women have less innate sexual desire than men. In the eighteenth century, middle-class British moralists elevated the concept of female virtue as part of an attack on aristocratic libertinism; in their views, female chastity provided a model for both sexes. At the same time, upper-class etiquette manuals read in England and America stressed the importance of female modesty, though they did not necessarily deny women's sexual desires. Then, at the beginning of the nineteenth century, evangelical Protestants called on women to act as a source of moral reform, implying that women were naturally more virtuous, more modest, more chaste than men. According to Cott, "Passionlessness was on the other side of the coin which paid, so to speak, for women's admission to moral equality." In contrast to the older image of Eve the temptress, a new ideal of female moral superiority gradually came to dominate prescriptive literature addressed to middle- and upper-class women.[16]

In the late eighteenth century, female chastity did not yet presume an absence of sexual desire. Virtue could be attained through self-control; it was not necessarily innate or biologically determined. Advice literature at the turn of the century embodied a malleable concept of female passion. According to a book published in America in 1807, women felt love most strongly, and "other passions more feebly." More gentle than men, women could conceal their sentiments, so that they would grow weaker, while men, "at all times bold and extravagant with impunity, give to their passions what tone they please." The same manual suggested that women could manipulate their passions in order to enhance marital sex, as the following "Advice to Married Ladies" illustrates:

> Use the man that you wed like your fav'rite guitar,
> Tho' music in both, they are both apt to jar;

> How tuneful and soft from a delicate touch,
> Not handled too roughly, nor play'd on too much![17]

As late as the 1830s, sexual advice literature continued to draw upon the older image of the voluptuous woman and the necessity that she achieve orgasm in order to conceive. Thus the 1831 edition of *Aristotle's Masterpiece* attributed desire for "venereal embraces" to fourteen-year-old virgins who indulged in spicy foods. Women were "more or less fond of men's embrace," the text explained, depending on the "greatness or smallness" of the clitoris, an organ which could "stir up lust and give delight in copulation, for without this the fair sex neither desire nuptial embrace nor have pleasure in them, nor conceive by them."[18] Only later did ideas about female sexuality completely reverse traditional notions by claiming an absence, rather than excess, of desire on the part of women; even then, older views persisted within popular culture and medical literature. Moreover, the idea of innate female virtue, or of sexual passionlessness, applied primarily to native-born, middle-class women; working-class, immigrant, and black women continued to be seen as sexually passionate, and thus sexually available. If passionlessness emerged in part in response to greater female sexual vulnerability, it resolved the problem for only a select group of American women.

While the advice literature about passionlessness applied to a literate, urban middle class, the controversy over bundling that erupted after 1750 reflected how tensions over female sexual vulnerability affected rural people from lower and middling families. Among these groups, bundling had been widespread. The practice rested upon the assumption that courting couples either refrained from sexual intercourse when they stayed together overnight, or that they would marry if pregnancy did occur. As premarital pregnancy and illegitimacy increased and familial controls over young people declined, some authorities began to attack bundling as a symbol of immorality. In the 1750s, a few towns had attempted to prohibit it, but without much success. In the 1770s, a renewed attack came from New England clergymen who preached that bundling was "unchristian," much to the dismay of young women and their mothers, who saw nothing wrong with the practice.[19] For several years, critics and defenders of bundling voiced their opinions.

The popular debate on bundling offers a glimpse into the changing meaning of sexuality at a moment when sexual attraction and sexual experience were gaining in importance within American society. The new view of courtship appeared in the verses and songs composed by opponents of bundling, who could not believe that a young couple spending the night in bed together would be able to resist sexual temptation. "A New Bundling Song," published in a 1785 almanac, satirized the claims to chastity during bundling:

A bundling couple went to bed,
With all their clothes from foot to head,
That the defence might seem complete,
Each one was wrapped in a sheet.

But O! this bundling's such a witch,
The man of her did catch the itch,
And so provoked was the wretch,
That she of him a bastard catch'd.

In contrast, traditionalists who argued for the practicality and safety of bundling waged a counterattack on the morality of nonbundlers:

Cate, Nance and Sue proved just and true,
Tho' bundling did practice;
But Ruth beguil'd and proved with child,
Who bundling did dispise.

Whores will be whores, and on the floor
Where many has been laid,
To set and smoke and ashes poke,
Wont keep awake a maid.

Bastards are not at all times got
In feather beds we know;
The strumpet's oath convinces both
Oft times it is not so.[20]

Two themes recur on both sides of this popular debate. First, the publication of these verses attests to the fact that premarital sexual desire had become a subject of public discourse, not in the form of condemnatory sermons, but rather in relatively lighthearted jesting that referred to strumpets, whores, and bastards as social, rather than moral, problems. Second, all observers recognized that young couples could find ways to satisfy their desires if they chose. In short, the sexual component of courtship was in clearer public view than in the past. According to opponents of bundling, an earlier period of innocent courtship had passed, and more effective controls over premarital sexuality would have to be found to replace bundling. In fact, the practice of bundling did decline after the late eighteenth century, except in rural areas of New England and Pennsylvania, where it persisted well into the nineteenth century.[21]

Not only courtship but marital practices as well suggest the changing meaning of sexuality in late-eighteenth-century America. As in England, there is evidence that a small minority of couples practiced family limitation during this period. The records of the Society of Friends reveal that during and after the Revolutionary War, the number of children born per family declined significantly. Because the reduction in family size cannot be explained fully by either an increase in age at marriage or a decrease in the length of marriages, it is likely that Quakers were practicing some form of family limitation. In Philadelphia, with a large Quaker population, apothecaries sold syringes that could be used for contraceptive purposes. Historians speculate that sometime after 1780, other married couples also began to use contraceptive methods. These included the traditional practices of prolonged breastfeeding, which delayed conception, and *coitus interruptus.* In 1794, a popular almanac proclaimed that hundreds of women echoed the cry of the biblical Rachel: "give me no more children, or else I die." For those who did not wait for their prayers to be answered, contraceptive practice represented a new willingness to make family size a matter of choice, rather than a fate determined by God. At the same time, it suggested that sexual pleasure, apart from reproduction, could become more important to at least some married couples.[22]

The dissolution of marriage, by divorce or desertion, provides further evidence of the new importance placed upon sexual relations in the late eighteenth century. In some colonies, such as Connecticut and Massachusetts, liberalized statutes led to more frequent divorce cases. Before the Revolutionary era, the few divorce cases that reached the courts centered on economic complaints, such as charges of desertion or lack of support, especially on the part of abandoned wives. Prior to 1765, Massachusetts divorce petitions never mentioned loss of conjugal affection as a reason for dissolving a marriage. After 1770, however, concerns about affection made their first appearance in divorce records. Ten percent of Massachusetts petitions complained about husbands who "lost all affection" or "ceased to cherish" their wives. The fact that more people sued for divorce may reflect a general belief that as marriage became a matter of personal choice—a social contract and not simply a financial arrangement—the dissolution of marriages that failed to become "affectional unions" seemed more reasonable. If love was required to create a marriage, the loss of affection might justify its end.[23] Formal divorce, however, remained rare throughout the century. Those who could not afford to divorce could desert an undesirable spouse. According to announcements published in the Boston press in the latter part of the century, women who tired of their husbands simply ran away. In 1769, for example, William Chambers proclaimed the desertion of his wife Susannah, who had permitted "other men to frequent my house and cohabits with them."[24] Changing ideals of marriage, along with the anonymity of the city, allowed a few women, and men, to seek pleasure outside of marriage, and to get away with it.

Morality in Flux

The regulation of deviance was also changing, especially where heterogeneous towns replaced small, rural settlements, and where the goal of commercial success supplanted that of salvation. Social stratification contributed to the problem. In cities such as Boston and Philadelphia, it was difficult to scrutinize the private lives of a small but troubling underclass of transients. Moreover, with the post-Revolutionary disestablishment of the churches, state regulation of morality declined noticeably. Legislatures and courts had once responded to the clergy's jeremiads about moral laxity by passing and enforcing laws that punished sexual relations outside of marriage. Now, however, courts less frequently enforced morals laws and showed more concern about the economic implications of illicit sexual activity.

Responses to illegitimacy, fornication, and rape illustrate these changes. In the seventeenth century, laws against bastardy had been couched in terms of the punishment of sin and the protection of the family. During the eighteenth century, however, bastardy came to be treated more as an economic than a moral problem. According to Robert Wells, "governments in the American colonies gradually lost interest in prosecuting sexual sinners so long as the children of sin were financially cared for." Similarly, the state less frequently prosecuted fornication and rape. In Virginia, for example, the number of morals cases heard in the courts peaked in the 1720s and then declined sharply; in New England after 1775, courts convicted fewer attempted rapists than in the past, and they tended to convict for the lesser charge of assault rather than rape. Indictments for infanticide decreased as well, and after 1775 infanticide laws were relaxed to require proof of live birth for conviction. Thus, with the formation of state and local governments during and after the Revolution, and the gradual separation of church from civil authority—a process that extended into the 1830s—the prosecution of sexual offenses lost the central place it had held in early colonial society.[25]

Even in the churches, moral regulation no longer took the same form. In the seventeenth century, all sex outside marriage was subject to action as fornication. In the eighteenth century, however, churches continued to punish adultery but not necessarily all fornication between single men and women. In addition, the rituals of confession and readmission to the community of the godly had less meaning for those who lived in the late eighteenth century. By the 1790s, the public confession of sin was being replaced by written confessions.[26] Many communities abolished their church courts entirely. With the loss of community involvement in the moral affairs of individuals, it was left to the family to regulate the morality of its own members. Eventually, the individual would be expected to act on internalized, rather than externally enforced, sexual controls.

The more frequent appearance of prostitutes in eighteenth-century American cities attests to the breakdown of community regulation of morality. In the seventeenth century, seaport towns such as Boston and New Amsterdam had some prostitutes in their midst. Boston courts charged Alice Thomas with allowing men and women the "opportunity to commit carnall wickedness," and a 1673 Massachusetts law prescribed whipping and hard labor for a "Baud, whore or vile person." The public sale of sexual services remained quite limited, however. In 1720, William Byrd failed in his attempt to find a prostitute in Williamsburg, Virginia. The residents of Massachusetts had so little concern about prostitution that Cotton Mather was unable to mobilize support for his proposed Society for the Suppression of Disorders, modeled on English organizations that opposed brothels.[27]

By the 1750s, however, the growth of maritime trade, the transiency of urban life, and the social dislocations of the French and Indian Wars encouraged prostitution. When soldiers congregated in cities such as Boston and New York, female camp followers soon arrived to minister to the needs of the men. Women provided food or washed clothing, and some sold their bodies. Widowed or impoverished women who remained in the cities after the war might take to walking the streets or working in the bawdy houses that appeared in Boston, Philadelphia, Newport, and Charleston. In addition to streetwalkers, some women, such as Hannah Dilley of Boston, operated from their homes. In 1753, at the age of sixty, this artisan's wife was convicted of using her home "for Letchery Fornication." She permitted persons "not of good Behavior or Fame" to "carnally lye with Whores, which the said Hannah then and there procured for them." Along waterfront areas, where transients, vagrants, and prostitutes intermingled with sailors, servants, and slaves, taverns often served as fronts for "disorderly houses." Areas such as Philadelphia's "Hell Town" were considered "little better than Nurseries of Vice and Debauchery." In other districts, travelers might encounter prostitutes at the local tavern, an institution decried by John Adams "for extinguishing virtuous Love and changing it into filthiness and brutal Debauch." By the end of the century, New York City brothels rented rooms to both white and black women who brought customers there, while laborers, sailors, prostitutes, and runaway wives drank together in "bawdy houses" where "dancing, kissing, cursing and swearing" took place nightly.[28]

For the first time, urban men could easily locate prostitutes if they tried. Benjamin Franklin claimed that women walking the streets would "expose themselves to sale at the highest bidder." As a young man traveling by boat to New York, Franklin himself was approached by two young women who turned out to be "a couple of Strumpets." His fears that frequent "Intrigues with low women" may have endangered his health imply that Franklin took advantage of these opportunities.[29] For other men, the resurgence of camp following during the Revolutionary War exposed them to opportunities for illicit sex.

Outside of a few cities, prostitution had not really become widespread, yet the specter it presented of unbridled sexual license provoked popular response, especially from respectable laborers, merchants, and professionals. In 1753, the New York courts ordered raids on "Houses of Ill Repute," with whipping and banishment for some of the "Ladies of Pleasure." On several occasions, citizens voiced strong opposition to the brothels and even took to the streets to do so. In 1766, the New York *Gazette* criticized the colonial government for not wiping out "receptacles or nests of villany." In both New York and Boston, angry mobs attacked brothels. They allowed one to burn and "Routed the Whores" at another. Similarly, in 1772 Philadelphia citizens called for the suppression of houses of ill fame. Thus the bawdy house seemed a logical target for the New York City mob that rioted in 1793 after the acquittal of Lanah Sawyer's seducer.[30]

These attacks on brothels reveal the symbolic power that prostitution had begun to acquire in the late eighteenth century. Prostitutes provided a reminder of the increasing class stratification that occurred in late-eighteenth-century cities, for they came from the newly formed ranks of urban poor. In addition, the appearance of prostitutes symbolized larger changes in the meaning of sexuality as it began to move outside of the private sphere of the family and away from its reproductive moorings. Prostitution did not go unnoticed as a threat to social order at a time when, on the one hand, family and community controls over morality weakened and, on the other hand, republicanism proclaimed that individual virtue was an essential condition for political well-being.

By the end of the eighteenth century, the family-centered, reproductive sexual system remained powerful throughout most of American society, but new sexual meanings were clearly emerging. As in England, ideas about sexuality, changing family structure, and the commercialization of the economy all laid the groundwork for a transformation in sexual values. In contrast to an earlier emphasis on the reproductive meaning of sexual relations, an affectionate, sometimes passionate, language now appeared in discussions of courtship, and individual choice became more important in all sexual relations. Meanwhile the first signs of family limitation evinced a weakening of the association between sexuality and reproduction. The decline of traditional church and state controls over morality lifted earlier restraints on nonmarital sex, as rising illegitimacy rates suggest. But illegitimacy also reflected the increasing vulnerability of women, who could no longer assume that pregnancy would lead to marriage. The maintenance of female virtue had become more problematic for most women. For the middle classes, a new model of sexual virtue had begun to form. Among the poor, cities may have created opportunities to sell sexual favors, but at the cost of periodic harassment of all women and extreme social stigma attached to those who sold their bodies. For most Americans, however, the possibilities of buying or selling sex in the marketplace had simply not yet appeared. Despite the threats to the organization of sexuality within the family, the trends first evident in the late eighteenth century would not fully affect the majority of American families for several generations. In the meantime, a new sexual system would transform the reproductive society of early America.

Although preindustrial America seems at first glance a unique and distant era, several themes that characterized its sexual history recur in different form in subsequent periods. First, throughout the seventeenth and eighteenth centuries, reproduction held a central place within the constellation of meanings associated with sexuality, more so than it would at any later time. Yet the relationship between reproduction and sexuality would remain critical throughout American history, even as sexual behavior increasingly took on new, nonprocreative meanings. Second, despite the relatively egalitarian attitudes toward male and female sexuality among colonists, gender clearly made a difference in the ways individuals experienced sexuality and the ways society regulated it. By the close of the colonial period, sex was becoming more highly differentiated along gender lines, as it would continue to be for over a century. Third, for most of the colonial era, sexuality was not really a private matter, for family and community drew few boundaries between the sexual concerns of individuals and those of the group. This legacy of community regulation of morality lasted long after privacy became a central sexual value for most Americans. Finally, the use of sex as a form of domination—by race, especially, but increasingly by gender and class—took shape in the seventeenth century and continued throughout American history. In short, the heritage of the preindustrial era influenced sexual history long after the colonies had become the United States and the preindustrial economy gave way to industrializing America.

PART II

DIVIDED PASSIONS, 1780–1900

CHAPTER 4

Within the Family

AT the end of the nineteenth century, Clelia D. Mosher, a physician and college professor, began to survey her women patients, asking them to describe their sexual and reproductive lives. Although most of the forty-five respondents to her questionnaire came of age in the latter part of the century, a handful had been born before 1850. Thanks to Mosher's scientific curiosity, historians have a small but intriguing sample of middle-class, married women's sexual histories that allows some tentative comparison across the generations. Two cases, in particular, highlight major themes in the transformation of sexuality within the family over the course of the nineteenth century.

The sexual relations of Mr. and Mrs. "B."—who were born in antebellum rural America—seemed as rooted to reproduction as those of their Puritan ancestors. Mrs. B. experienced twelve pregnancies over twenty-eight years of marriage. Although she miscarried six times, she bore six surviving children. Reproduction, Mrs. B. told Dr. Mosher, was the highest purpose of intercourse, although individual health also warranted marital sex. Few efforts were made to limit family size; occasionally, Mr. B. practiced withdrawal. Although Mr. B.'s attitude toward sexual intercourse was not recorded, Mrs. B. stated that she found it agreeable when she was "not too tired," and when she desired it she "always" experienced orgasm. At other times, however, she could have "blotted [it] out and never missed it." In short, apart from its reproductive purpose, sex was neither extremely important nor particularly problematic.

Married in the 1880s, Mr. and Mrs. "C." also believed that reproduction was a main purpose of sex. After eight years of marriage, however, they had only one child, who died at birth. Reproductive control seemed important to this couple, as did the intimacy fostered by sexual relations. At the beginning of their marriage, the C.'s slept in separate beds. Within less than a year, however, they spent their nights together, engaging in intercourse once or twice a month at times when Mrs. C. was less likely to conceive. The couple desired and enjoyed sex, and Mrs. C. "almost invariably" experienced orgasms which resulted in "absolute physical harmony." In this marriage, neither reproduction nor physical necessity alone justified intercourse. According to Mrs. C., sex was "only warranted as an expression of true and passionate love."[1]

These two marital histories make visible and concrete the changes in American sexual life over the course of the nineteenth century. Although older patterns persisted in rural, immigrant, and working-class families, the reproductive moorings of sexual experience gradually gave way to a new constellation of meanings, in which both love and intimacy became increasingly important. Within the family, two related developments contributed to this transformation. First, married couples increasingly exercised control over fertility, and in doing so, they began to loosen the tight link between reproduction and sexuality. Second, during courtship and in marriage, sexuality came to be more deeply associated with the emotion of love and the quest for interpersonal intimacy. These changes affected men and women in different ways. Women remained closely tied to the physical labors of pregnancy, childbearing, and childrearing. In addition, a new system of gender relations emerged in the nineteenth century in which middle-class women lost their association with lust and instead were invested with the quality of innate purity. As a result of these gender differences, sex became a powerful arena of conflict, as well as closeness, within marriage.

Major economic and social change helped account for these new patterns of sexual life. During the century that followed the War of Independence, new technologies of transportation and communication, the growth of commerce and industry, and the continual process of westward expansion reshaped the entire fabric of daily life. Beginning soon after the Revolution, a regional market economy gradually replaced the local, self-sufficient farms of the colonial period. Except for the South—where slave labor and plantation agriculture prevailed—towns rapidly grew into cities in the decades after 1820. Meanwhile, families moved west and individual fortunes rose and fell during the boom-bust cycles of the burgeoning northern economy. Industrialization accelerated during and after the Civil War, creating both a class of owners and professionals and a class of skilled and unskilled laborers. Record numbers of immigrants, not only from England but from Ireland and Germany as well, swelled the work force. As industrialization intensified divisions of class, of race, and of region, sexuality became a highly charged source of both comfort and conflict.

Not surprisingly, the fluidity that characterized nineteenth-century American society bred a strong desire to maintain social order in the midst of change. But older methods, such as church discipline and community surveillance, no longer operated in this period of economic and geographic growth. Americans came to rely more heavily on the family as a source of social stability, and within the family they elaborated unique roles for men and women.

The family itself was evolving from the patriarchal model of the "little commonwealth" to what historians have since termed the era of the "separate sexual spheres." In the new market economy, men commonly left their homes to seek their fortunes in the public sphere of paid labor. Most women remained in the private, or domestic, sphere, where they continued to perform their unpaid reproductive and household labors. Although the two spheres were interdependent, distinctive social worlds evolved around the separate work spaces of men and women. In the public sphere, white men could earn wages, vote, enter local or national politics, and venture on their own to new regions, such as the West. An ideal of the self-made man, conquering nature and acquiring wealth, pervaded the masculine world. Within the middle class, gentlemen learned to control their sexual appetites in order to succeed. In nineteenth-century thought, sexual control helped differentiate the middle class from the working class, and whites from other races. Men also learned that a double standard of morality condoned their sexual transgressions. In contrast, women had neither the property and political rights, nor the freedom of movement enjoyed by white men. For the middle class, an elaborate ideal of femininity emphasized innate sexual purity as a means of controlling male excess and stressed women's domestic and maternal roles. Women who did not achieve the ideal of purity were considered to have "fallen" into a lower class. If poor, they might even be arrested for committing such "crimes against chastity" as "lewd and lascivious behavior."[2]

The starting point for understanding how these economic and social changes affected sexuality is the family, the traditional locus of sexual practice and meaning. This chapter first explores the historical problem of reproductive control, a phenomenon that laid the basis for the separation of sexuality and reproduction within the family. It then turns to the growing importance of love, intimacy, and the erotic within courtship and marriage, the different meanings each had for women and men, and the conflicts engendered by the disparity between the ideal of sexual harmony and the reality of family life.

Reproductive Control

In the late eighteenth century, the first signs of decline in marital fertility rates foreshadowed the dramatic transformation that occurred in marital sexuality during the nineteenth century. White reproductive rates illustrate this change. In 1800, a married couple had an average of slightly over seven children. A generation later, in 1825, the marital fertility rate had fallen to under six children. By 1850, married women were bearing on an average only 5.42 children, and by 1880, only 4.24. Throughout this period, as childbearing decreased, both male and female life expectancy increased. Thus, childbearing and childrearing were occupying an increasingly smaller proportion of an adult woman's life.[3]

These overall rates mask regional, racial, and ethnic differences. The drop in marital fertility began with the northern middle class; ultimately it extended to all groups within the society, but at varying times. Fertility declined in both rural and urban areas, but higher birth rates persisted in frontier communities during early periods of settlement. In the southern states, where white women married at a younger age and large families were desired to produce heirs, birth rates remained high. Black slaves bore large numbers of children, as well, in part because their owners encouraged reproduction in order to increase their valuable human property. In the North, among immigrant families such as the Irish and Germans who flocked to the United States after the 1840s, fertility remained higher than among native-born whites. Nevertheless, family size for these groups often declined in the second generation. Given the higher rates in these rural and immigrant families, a very steep decline among urban middle-class families accounts for much of the overall decline in white marital fertility.[4]

A constellation of motives created the trend toward smaller families. Economic interest encouraged some families to have fewer children. According to historical demographers, the major determinant of fertility in the early nineteenth century was the availability of land in a given area. That is, if families thought that there was sufficient land for the next generation to establish an economic foothold, they were less likely to limit family size. Those who moved away from self-sufficient family farms into commercial agriculture, or later into industry, no longer had land to pass on to children. Children who were once an economic asset as farm laborers now required a greater economic investment by parents in order to train them for skilled jobs. Cultural factors dovetailed with economic concerns. For white, native-born couples, family limitation became an effective strategy for maintaining middle-class status and aspiring toward higher social mobility. Family limitation also reflected changing religious beliefs, especially a new willingness on the part of individuals to take their futures into their own hands, rather than accepting that the will of God must prevail. Finally, the decline in marital fertility may have evidenced the growing power of women in the domestic sphere, where they insisted on limiting births, either to free themselves from burdensome reproductive labors or to wield control over sexuality. While women did have a unique physical interest in controlling fertility, their husbands also had economic reasons for limiting family size. Thus, a combination of women's and men's interests may have motivated family limitation.[5]

As important as the question of why family size declined is the question of how reproductive control took place. Abundant historical evidence suggests that nineteenth-century Americans turned to contraception and abortion in order to limit their families. Marital advice literature that urged continence in sexual relations complemented these efforts at fertility control. Both contraception and continence helped reshape sexual meanings. Contraceptive use forced couples to think of sexual intercourse as something other than a reproductive act. Marital advice literature frequently emphasized the power of sexual desire, even as it called for sexual self-control. Through both methods, married couples not only reduced fertility but also became more self-conscious about their sexual lives.

In the name of preserving women's health and producing happier marriages and healthier children, nineteenth-century Americans both learned about and practiced a variety of forms of family limitation.[6] It is difficult to know which method, of the several available, most couples used. The one most often recommended was simply abstaining from sexual relations. Some authors of marital advice literature believed that it was only acceptable to limit offspring if conjugal chastity was the means. Couples who agreed with this message slept or even lived separately to avoid intercourse. Others limited sex to those occasions when they desired to have children. It is likely that the most commonly used method was *coitus interruptus,* in which a man withdrew his penis before orgasm and ejaculated outside of his partner's body. Withdrawal had the advantage that it cost nothing, required no preparation, and allowed at least some sexual pleasure. But it also required rather delicate timing and it could interfere with the orgasm of either partner. As one man who used withdrawal lamented in his diary, "I fooled [withdrew] so that I could not get my gun off."[7] Moreover, many doctors opposed the practice as unhealthful or sinful.

Between the 1830s and the 1870s, information about contraceptive devices circulated widely. Books on the subject enjoyed impressive publication records. In 1831, utopian socialist Robert Dale Owen published *Moral Physiology,* which remained in print for over forty years. In 1832, Dr. Charles Knowlton's *Fruits of Philosophy; or the Private Companion of Young Married People* appeared; it remained in circulation through a tenth edition in 1877. Dr. Frederick Hollick's *The Marriage Guide,* first published in 1850, entered its three hundredth edition by 1875. In the intervening years, at least a dozen other texts advised couples on contraceptive methods, including the popular *Medical Common Sense* by Dr. Edward Bliss Foote (1858), which had sold over

250,000 copies by 1900. Meanwhile, itinerant lecturers, such as Alfred Hall and Sarah Bleslee Chase, popularized contraception among small-town audiences to whom they spoke about physiology and health. Sometimes they also peddled folk medicines to be used in douching or to induce miscarriage. Finally, circulars advertised various contraceptives. According to one doctor, who wrote in 1867, "There is scarcely a young lady in New England—and probably it is so throughout the land—whose marriage [was] announced in the paper" who did not receive a printed circular with information on contraceptive "instrumentalities."[8]

These published guides, itinerant lecturers, and circulars provided information about a variety of contraceptive methods. Owen favored withdrawal, but he discussed as well the vaginal sponge and French *baudrache,* or condom, then made from animal skin or membrane or from oiled silk. Knowlton and Hollick recommended postcoital vaginal douching, while Foote described both condoms and cervical caps. These latter barrier methods became increasingly popular over the course of the century. In 1846 a diaphragm was patented under the title "The Wife's Protector." Pessaries, which were sold in drugstores to help correct prolapsed (fallen) uterus, came in over a hundred varieties—wood, cotton, and sponge. By the late nineteenth century, devices made of India rubber could be used like vaginal diaphragms, while rubber condoms joined the contraceptive market. Even books that recommended the "natural mode," or rhythm, included detailed information on sponges, condoms, and syringes for douching.[9]

Not only middle-class readers of marital advice guides had access to contraceptive information. Advertisements in newspapers and almanacs reached a wider audience, especially in cities, while declining prices made contraceptives available for workers as well as members of the middle class. In the 1830s, newspapers carried ads for "female syringes" and chemicals to use with them, such as alum or sulphates of zinc or iron. An 1861 New York *Times* advertisement revealed that Dr. Power's French Preventives (condoms) sold for five dollars per dozen. By the 1870s, the price of these and other contraceptives had fallen, so that most couples could afford to purchase condoms for six to twelve cents each, diaphragms for a dollar, or syringes for forty cents.[10]

By the 1870s, contraceptive use seemed to be growing so rapidly that some Americans organized to oppose its spread. Concerned about declining birth rates, they supported legislation to curtail the circulation of contraceptive information. In 1873, the U.S. Congress passed the so-called Comstock law, named for its supporter, Anthony Comstock, which outlawed the circulation of contraceptive information and devices through the U.S. mails. The Comstock Act, however, must be understood as a response to increased contraceptive usage and not necessarily as an effective deterrent to family limitation.

Even after the bill passed, Americans continued to learn about contraception through medical journals, sympathetic physicians and pharmacists, and veiled advertisements in newspapers. In 1890, for example, the *Police Gazette* carried ads for "Gent's latest improved rubber Protectors" and "Ladies' patent shields."[11] Equally important, individuals of both sexes passed their knowledge along to friends and younger siblings.

Women had particularly good reason to share contraceptive knowledge, for they faced the physical risks of repeated pregnancy. Female friends and relatives on the midwestern frontier kept alive a repertoire of folk remedies, such as drinking gunpowder or eating dried chicken gizzards. Other women told of new contraceptive devices in letters. In 1876, for example, Mary Hallock Foote wrote to her lifelong friend Helena Gilder about "a sure way of limiting one's family." Foote advised her friend to have her husband "go to a physician and get shields of some kind. They are to be had also at some druggists. It sounds perfectly revolting," she added, "but one must face anything rather than the inevitable result of Nature's methods."[12] (By "Nature's methods," she may have been referring to the rhythm method, which was so misunderstood that nineteenth-century doctors inadvertently advised women to refrain from sex during the last half of their menstrual cycle, when they were safe, and encouraged them to engage in intercourse immediately after ovulation, which put them at risk of pregnancy.) Similarly, Rose Williams wrote to her newlywed friend Allettie Mosher in 1885 about "a sure prevenative [*sic*]." At first she jokingly suggested that her friend "sleep in one bed and your Man in another," but added that "I don't see any one that does." In a serious vein Williams continued:

> Well now the thing we [use] (when I say *we* I mean us girls) is a thing: but it hasn't always been *sure* as you know but that was our own carelessness for it is we have been sure. I do not know whether you can get them out there. They are called Pessairre or female prevenative if you don't want to ask for a "pisser" just ask for a female prevenative. They cost one dollar when Sis got hers it was before any of us went to Dak[ota]. She paid five dollars for it. The Directions are with it.[13]

Some correspondents were less explicit about methods, such as a Texas woman who responded to a letter from her pregnant sister: "Am I *free* yet? Yes!! No more babies for me. . . . But I must not exult too much I might be *caught* yet; but I'll try not." In another family communication, Alice Belknap hinted to a sister who had just miscarried that it was possible to avoid pregnancy, suggesting that she would help her if asked. And Lizzie Nesbett, who traveled to the West in the 1860s, wrote home to a female cousin about the vaginal sponge, while she vowed to keep breastfeeding her own baby in order to "ward off some danger" of pregnancy.[14]

Middle-class men and women also communicated, either discreetly or directly, about ways to prevent conception. In 1861, Lester Ward took a copy of Frederick Hollick's marriage guide on a walk with his fiancée, Lizzie Vought; too embarrassed to discuss the subject, he left her alone with the book long enough for her to absorb its lessons. Married couples collaborated in efforts to postpone or prevent childbearing. In 1860, James Cormany recorded in his diary the outcome of a discussion with his wife, Rachel, who hoped to prevent conception more than he did. "Wife and I had a long talk on childbearing—we differ on some points, but sweetly agree to disagree, and avoid any risks by continued abstinence &c., &c." Whether "&c." meant rhythm, a contraceptive device, or simply more abstinence is unclear. Lizzie Nesbett also prevailed in her desires to avoid constant childbearing. In 1864 she wrote to her husband that the "doom" of having a child every other year would be worse than "solitary confinement in prison." Rather than forgo sexual inter- course, however, she urged him to procure "preventives" and wrote instruct- ing him: "don't start home without a good quantity of pulverized Ergot and as good a syringe as you can find, Richardson's No. 1 that I described to you long ago is the best I know of."[15]

Even when married couples did attempt to limit family size, they were not always consistent, nor were they necessarily successful. In an analysis of the sexual and reproductive record found in the diary of Mary Pierce Poor, historian Janet Brodie detected cycles of uncontrolled fertility alternating with those of successful contraception. Poor's relief at the arrival of her menses, as well as comments in letters to her husband, reveal her strong desire to control reproduction. Yet in her twenty-one-year reproductive history, Mary Pierce Poor bore seven children and had two miscarriages. For years at a time the Poors regularly engaged in intercourse but managed to avoid pregnancy. At other times, children arrived in rapid succession. Other married couples only sporadically used contraception, as did Mr. and Mrs. "B.", who "sometimes" relied on withdrawal and had six children. Another couple tried to use rhythm, which didn't work, and then tried a hot syringe; the wife conceived six times during their twenty-seven years of marriage. A mother of eight, married for thirty-eight years, explained that her first two children were "by choice," thanks to a "Goodyear Rubber Ring." When health problems precluded use of the diaphragm, she conceived another six children "by chance." A diary entry by Mabel Loomis Todd recorded how she and her husband, David, attempted to prevent conception at the beginning of their marriage, in 1879. They used withdrawal or a rhythm method to "restrain ourselves from the fullness of our intercourse at all times except from fourteen days after my sickness ceased, until three before the next time." She also rose after inter- course to allow "the precious fluid" to escape. To the Todds' surprise, this practice resulted in the birth of their only child.[16]

When contraception failed, women might attempt to induce miscarriage themselves or to seek abortions. In the early nineteenth century, and in rural areas for many later generations, herbal and home remedies for terminating unwanted pregnancies continued to be passed on through oral tradition. Native American healers and midwives prescribed roots or herbs known to induce abortion. At midcentury, black women in Texas employed indigo or a mixture of calomel and turpentine to "unfix," or miscarry, while midwestern women rubbed gunpowder on their breasts and drank tea made of rusty-nail water. Printed information about elixirs and drugs that induced miscarriage appeared in home medical manuals. The 1808 edition of Samuel K. Jennings's *The Married Ladies Companion* offered remedies for missed menstrual periods, including bleeding from the foot, hot baths, and cathartics such as calomel and aloes. Other advice for unblocking "obstructed menses" included jumping, exercise, and douching. Following these prescriptions, Jennie Scott of Pittsburgh repeatedly jumped off a ladder to try to abort. One young woman "dreading her second labor," a doctor reported in 1870, "procured the fresh roots of rue," which she boiled and drank. After "[d]readful pain in the stomach . . . she aborted forty eight hours later." Many women resorted to drinking tea brewed from the leaves of the tansy plant. Emma Beeks, an unmarried black servant, steeped wild tansy in whiskey and borax in an unsuccessful effort to miscarry.[17]

Surgical procedures, such as the use of a probe by a doctor or by a pregnant woman herself, were available but dangerous. When tansy failed, Emma Beeks used a sharp instrument that punctured her vaginal wall; she died of infection. In 1861, one doctor acknowledged that he had performed three hundred abortions with instruments, an operation that cost, according to advertisements, between ten and one hundred dollars. For approximately eight dollars, a woman could buy a silver probe with instructions for relieving "female complaints." One widow who became pregnant induced abortion by using a sharp wooden implement inserted into her uterus; another woman claimed to have self-aborted twenty-one times, the last of which proved fatal.[18]

Abortion, like contraception, found a growing commercial market due to the spread of both the patent-medicine industry and newspaper advertising. By the 1860s, over twenty-five different chemical abortifacients—aloes, iron, and other cathartic powders—could be located through newspaper ads, postal circulars, and pharmacies. Ranging in price from one to ten dollars, the abortifacients promised, more or less explicitly, to end pregnancy. The New York *Herald* advertised "infallible French Female Pills" and powders from Madame Restell—New York City's most notorious abortionist—to aid "married ladies whose health forbids too rapid increase of family." A doctor's cure for "interrupted menstruation," advertised in the New York *Times,* explained that "there is one condition of the female system in which the pills cannot be taken, without producing a peculiar result. The condition referred to is pregnancy—the result miscarriage." In 1865, one upstate New York doctor claimed to have sold as many as twenty thousand boxes of a "female monthly pill."[19]

Despite its increasing visibility in newspapers, abortion remained a personal secret about which few nineteenth-century women spoke or wrote. Their silence reflects, in part, the sense of privacy that middle-class women felt about sexuality, but it suggests as well that they felt less comfortable about abortion than they did about contraception. After bearing two children and aborting twice, an anonymous married woman wrote in the 1840s that "abortion was most repulsive to every feeling of my nature . . . and at times rendered me an object of loathing to myself." Toward the end of the century, women's rights activists wrote publicly in opposition to contraception and abortion because they believed that these practices encouraged men's sexual license. But the many women who procured abortifacients and underwent surgical procedures left few records of their motivations or of the personal consequences of their decisions.[20]

According to the limited sources that describe who chose to abort and why, northern white women, both working-class and middle-class, single and married, sought abortions. One drama, that of the young, unmarried working woman seduced by her employer, recurred throughout the century. A typical case appeared in Philadelphia court records for 1839. A twenty-year-old mill worker, engaged to be married, took a job as a domestic servant in the home of her supervisor. Seduced by her employer, she became pregnant, broke her engagement, sought an abortion, and died of complications after the operation. Similarly, in 1858 Miss Olive Ash worked as a servant for a Vermont farmer, by whom she became pregnant. Her employer agreed to pay one hundred dollars to a Dr. Howard, whose three surgical operations proved fatal to Miss Ash. In 1859, sixteen-year-old mill worker Marty Kirkpatrick of Patterson, New Jersey, accepted her employer's offers of clothing and became pregnant by him. Despite the abortifacients he procured, she gave birth and died. In a variation on this theme, Susan Hays, madame of a Maryland brothel, performed abortions whenever the prostitutes in her house became pregnant.[21]

By the 1860s, the clientele for abortions was expanding to include married, middle-class women who wished to limit family size. Sue Dickinson, the wife of poet Emily Dickinson's brother Austin, underwent four abortions after she had borne one child. She no doubt found this remedy distasteful, for she later attempted to refuse her husband intercourse in order to avoid pregnancy and, presumably, any further abortions. Throughout the country, couples attempted self-induced abortions. A married woman told a California divorce court that with the help of her husband she had miscarried on four occasions by injecting water into her uterus. Similarly, a Wisconsin midwife's recollections of the 1880s included the story of a married couple who used hot saltwater injections to try to get rid of an unwanted fetus.[22]

In the South, where both abortion and contraception were strongly condemned, white women rarely mentioned these practices in their personal papers. In exceptional circumstances, such as wartime, southern couples might resort to abortion. A Confederate general, for example, sent his wife abortifacients procured from his camp surgeon.[23] Black midwives knew how to use roots and seeds of tansy, rue, or cotton to induce miscarriage, but they faced the fate of being sold down the river for helping slave women to abort. In addition, although blacks did not condone indiscriminate sexual relations, the slave community accepted rather than stigmatized children born outside of marriage. Thus slaves had one less reason than white women to seek abortions. Black fertility rates remained high until the end of the nineteenth century. As an 1860 medical report explained, most abortions among slaves occurred spontaneously, as a result of overwork or undernourishment, rather than by choice.[24]

Although few women left records of their abortion experiences, other sources suggest that the incidence of abortion increased significantly in the nineteenth century. Estimates by reformers show that between 1800 and 1830, one abortion occurred for every twenty-five to thirty live births. By the 1850s, the proportion had increased to as many as one abortion per every five to six live births. Some doctors pointed to higher rates of stillbirths as proof that more women were using abortifacients. It is possible that abortion began to supplant infanticide as a last resort for women who could not raise children. In at least one city, infanticide rates decreased markedly during the late nineteenth century.[25] Many doctors attributed the increase in abortions to married women who wished to limit family size, rather than to the traditional clients, unmarried women seeking to avoid the stigma of illegitimate birth. As one professor of medicine explained in 1857, abortion now involved not only those "who have been deceived and ensnared by the seducer" but also "the virtuous and the intelligent wife and mother." A report issued by the Michigan Board of Health in 1878 estimated that one-third of all pregnancies in that state ended in abortion, and that seventy to eighty percent were secured by "prosperous and otherwise respectable married women."[26]

In the early nineteenth century, neither doctors, women, nor judges necessarily condemned these practices as long as they were performed within the early months of pregnancy. According to the prevalent doctrine of "quickening," life did not begin until a woman felt the fetus move within her, usually after about three months. Laws enacted between 1820 and 1840 to regulate abortion retained the quickening doctrine and attempted to protect women from unwanted abortion, rather than to prosecute them. Even when the state did prosecute for illegal abortion, the courts remained tolerant, as was the case in Massachusetts, where not one conviction resulted from the thirty-two abortion trials held between 1849 and 1857. Between 1860 and 1890, however, forty states and territories enacted antiabortion statutes, many of which rejected the quickening doctrine, placed limitations on advertisements, and helped transfer legal authority for abortion from women to doctors.[27] The new antiabortion laws, like the Comstock Act, placed obstacles in the way of controlling reproduction, but women and married couples attempted to overcome them. As in the case of contraceptive information, abortifacients and abortionists continued to be known through informal channels. Criminalization may have raised the price of abortion, however, making it more difficult for working-class women to resort to it. In addition, the courts did not enforce the new laws very strictly. Juries tended to be sympathetic toward defendants, and unless a woman herself filed a complaint or died as a result of an abortion, it was difficult to convict.[28] Finally, for all women, criminalization made abortion more physically dangerous than in the past by forcing it into the hands of the least reputable medical practitioners.

The evidence of contraceptive use and the growing visibility of abortion in mid-nineteenth-century America helps to explain the decline in white marital fertility rates and the especially steep decline among educated, urban, and northern families. The use of contraception and abortion attests to the conscious desire to limit family size within these groups. Many married couples clearly sought ways to maintain sexual relations even as they sought to reduce fertility. By encouraging sex apart from reproduction, contraception paved the way for sexuality itself to take on new meanings, in both ideal and in practice.

The Quest for Sexual Health

Contraceptive efforts to limit family size were complemented in the middle class by a new system of sexual regulation that evolved in the nineteenth century. Older means of maintaining common sexual values no longer operated effectively in a mobile and industrializing society. Parental power, and particularly fathers' control over their children through the dispensation of property, had been eroding since the mid-eighteenth century. Nor did traditional church discipline retain its power to shame individuals into conformity to the sexual values of the congregation, although ministers continued to offer sexual advice throughout the century. In addition, the state no longer backed up church discipline, as it had in early America. The new laws formulated by the American state and federal governments took a laissez-faire attitude toward the regulation of the family in general and of sexuality in particular. In the early nineteenth century, property rather than morals offenses preoccupied legislatures and courts. Bastardy, for example, became a private rather than public offense.[29] Working-class and immigrant communities continued to exert strong neighborhood and church influence over individual morality, but in the middle class, the task of sexual regulation fell largely to the family, and especially to women. At the same time, increasing secularization and the rise of the medical profession began to shift authority over sexuality from clergy to doctors. Doctors and women agreed that individuals should internalize control over sexuality.

New ideas about sexuality reached Americans in part because a growing publishing industry catered to the tastes of an increasingly literate population. A prolific sexual advice literature—written by both men and women, physicians and lay health reformers—inundated Americans with the message that bodily well-being required that individuals exercise some measure of control over their sexual desires. Influenced by the idea that the body constituted a closed energy system, whose resources were depleted by each use, these authors argued that sexual indulgence could be dangerous to physical health. According to Benjamin Rush, the leading physician at the beginning of the nineteenth century, the sexual appetite, "when excessive, becomes a disease of both the body and mind." The results could include "seminal weakness, impotence . . . pulmonary consumption, hypochondriasis, loss of memory . . . and death."[30] Doctors attempted to inculcate habits of continence in young men and women to avoid these ills. For those who internalized this message, continence could contribute to efforts to control reproduction by limiting the frequency of sexual intercourse within marriage. At the same time, the advice literature called attention to the importance of sexuality in personal life, often elevating it as a powerful force imbued with possibilities for heightened marital intimacy and even spiritual transcendence.

Two sets of sexual advice literature—one directed at men and one at women—originated in the 1830s as part of a health reform movement that was symptomatic of the quest for physical, as well as spiritual, perfection. The republication of guides to sexual health—such as William Alcott's *Young Man's Guide* (1833; it went through twenty-one editions by 1850), Russell Trall's *Sexual Physiology* (reprinted twenty-eight times between 1866 and 1881), and Alice Stockham's *Tokology: A Book for Every Woman* (1883, with forty-five editions by 1897)—revealed how hungry Americans were for instruction about the meaning of sexuality.[31] Lay reformers and professional physicians alike provided a variety of ideals, ranging from abstinence from all but reproductive sex to moderate sex in marriage that left both partners physically fulfilled.

The growing popularity of medical advice literature, much of it concerned with sexuality, reflected in part a new attitude toward disease and death within the middle class. Rather than simply accepting God's will, these Americans increasingly wished to improve their chances of survival and their well-being during their lifetimes. Health reformers promised a means to physical salvation and tapped concrete fears about physical vulnerability, for both men and women worried about the mysterious forces of cholera, which swept through American cities. In addition, venereal disease, which was increasing at epidemic rates, could neither be cured nor, in women, clearly detected.[32] Young women faced the particular fear of being "ruined" by sexual seduction, since parents and clergy no longer had the authority to enforce marriage in the event of premarital pregnancy. And even when death did not occur, women suffered the costs of childbearing, whether in illicit or licit relationships.

Men had specific reasons to seek advice, for despite their greater personal and sexual autonomy, they faced new economic insecurity in the competitive marketplace, which ruined as many fortunes as it made. Therefore young men welcomed guides to self-improvement, including the health reform literature that promised to contribute to individual success. Authors of this self-help literature constantly held up the virtues of thrift and industry, along with the call for sexual self-control. As Dr. John Cowan explained, male continence was critical both for physical well-being and economic success. "Especially should the continent man exercise and train his will power," Cowan wrote, "for the doing of this not only enables him to lead a continent life, but it as surely guides to success in all business undertakings."[33]

Much of the self-help and medical advice literature directed at young men concentrated on the dangers of masturbation and how to control it. The theory that masturbation caused disease and insanity, introduced in the eighteenth century, gained popularity in nineteenth-century America. Benjamin Rush made this point in *Diseases of the Mind* (1812), in which he advised men to avoid masturbation by "close application of the mind to business, or study of any kind."[34] Health reformer Sylvester Graham's 1834 lectures on "Chastity" also condemned masturbation and called for self-restraint to avoid it. Graham recommended cold baths, fresh air, and bland foods (including the cracker that bears his name) to remove unnecessary physical stimulation that might lead to sexual excitement. Similarly, the Reverend John Todd's 1835 *Student's Manual,* a highly popular guide for the self-made man, urged young men to overcome the "secret vice" of masturbation because each loss of sperm depleted the total energy system, leaving fewer resources for productive labor.[35]

What has been called the "new chastity message" of these nineteenth-century writers differed from earlier proscriptions on masturbation. In the colonial period, the practice was taboo simply because it was nonprocreative. Eighteenth-century European writers introduced the theme that masturbation could destroy both body and mind, but they contrasted the dangers of masturbation with the healthfulness of marital sex. Now, however, certain reformers, such as Graham and Todd, argued that *all* sexual excitement was physically dangerous. Graham condemned any excessive "venereal indulgence," even within marriage, and considered all lust to be unnatural.[36] Todd also feared that intercourse with women, like masturbation, robbed men of their physical powers. Self-control, then, had to be asserted both before and after marriage. This view appeared, for example, in an 1835 article in the *Boston Medical and Surgical Journal.* The author professed that ejaculation "should be made but sparingly," for "sturdy manhood . . . loses its energy and bends under too frequent expenditure of this important secretion." Other authorities advised separate beds to prevent husbands and wives from temptation. In the late nineteenth century, the views of Todd and Graham found expression in the work of reformers such as John Kellogg, who incorporated health reform and continence at his Battle Creek Sanitarium, where bland food, such as his cereals, prevailed.[37]

Despite extremists such as Graham and Kellogg, most health reformers and medical writers who supported male continence did not reject sexual pleasure completely. Rather, they attempted to train men to exert self-control and channel their desires toward procreative, marital relations. In his midcentury talks to boys, for example, John Ware stressed that marital relations were "the essential element of human happiness and human progress." Improper sexual expression, however, and worst of all "the solitary indulgence," led to disease, social stigma, and tainted offspring. Similarly, Dr. Andrew J. Ingersoll opposed contraception, for he believed that "every thought or deed in opposition to having children is a sin against the soul, and is productive of disease." At the same time, however, Ingersoll encouraged married couples to "yield" to complete sexual enjoyment in the procreative act. He opposed the view that sex was mere animal passion and praised it as a transcendent spiritual state that brought a couple closer to God. By the late Victorian period, medical writers increasingly spoke of sexuality as an important means for enhancing the spiritual unity of husband and wife. An 1882 text illustrated this theme quite clearly: "The sexual relationship is among the most important uses of married life; it vivifies the affection for each other, as nothing else in the world can, and is a powerful reminder of their mutual obligation to each other and to the community in which they live."[38]

The advice literature directed to women also combined the views that sexual expression had to be controlled and that sexual relations could enrich marriage. For women, even more than for men, however, nineteenth-century health literature represented a significant departure from earlier ideas about sexuality. In a reversal of the traditional western European view that woman— like Eve, the temptress—embodied carnal desire, late-eighteenth- and early-nineteenth-century moralists suggested that women had fewer sexual desires than did men. Their lusts lay dormant, to be awakened, perhaps, by their husbands. The British physician William Acton, who was widely read in America, best expressed this view. According to Acton, "the majority of women (happily for society) are not very much troubled with sexual feelings of any kind. . . . Love of home, of children, and of domestic duties are the only passions they feel." Or, as an American writer paraphrased him in 1875, the majority of women "are innocent of the faintest ray of sexual pleasure." Women writers championed the theory of woman's lesser passion and her role in controlling men's sexual urges. Eliza Duffey explained in *What Women Should Know* (1873) that "the passions of men are much stronger and more easily inflamed" than those of women. Woman's maternal instincts, she later wrote, were stronger than her sexual desires. As one woman reformer explained, "The purity of women is the everlasting barrier against which the tides of man's sensual nature surge."[39]

The new ideal of sexually pure womanhood created an antithetical model: the so-called fallen woman who defied female nature or failed to resist men's advances. In popular culture, seduction could be literally deadly. American folk songs, unlike earlier British ballads that tended to celebrate women's sexual independence, stressed the sexual vulnerability of women. Those who were seduced by men would ultimately die, often at the hands of their lovers. One Vermont ballad, "Pearl Bryan," closed with a typical cautionary moral:

> Young ladies, now take warning
> Since you find young men unjust.
> It may be your own best lover's hand;
> You know not whom to trust.
>
> Pearl Bryan died away from home
> And in that lovely spot.
> My God, my God, believe it girls,
> Don't let this be your lot.[40]

Prescriptive literature reiterated the message. In the past, as long as she repented, the woman who once sinned—like a male transgressor—could be reintegrated into the community. Now, however, because woman allegedly occupied a higher moral plane than man, her fall was so great that it tainted her for life. "Even as woman is supremely virtuous," a novelist explained, she became, "when once fallen, the vilest of her sex."[41] The extreme social stigma attached to the fallen woman helped enforce the ideal of female purity.

Just as middle-class men had reason to embrace the ideal of self-control, many middle-class women accepted the view that women lacked innate sexual desire. For one, it provided a means of elevating women to spiritual equality with men. In addition, purity could be a useful tool with which women could gain leverage in sexual relations, for it provided them with grounds for refusing unwanted sex. Pointing to the ideal of male continence for her husband, the allegedly asexual wife could achieve control over reproduction by limiting marital sex to periods in which she might wish to become pregnant.[42]

Even within the advice literature, however, purity rarely took the extreme form that Acton defined, and the older knowledge of women's sexual capacity coexisted with the theory of lesser desire. For example, the *Young Married Lady's Private Medical Guide,* translated from the French and published in Boston in 1853, taught women that the "principal use of the clitoris is, unquestionably, to contribute a large share, and perhaps the greater part of the pleasure and gratification which the female experiences, from sexual intercourse." Some advice literature told men to cultivate their wives' pleasure through gentle, moderate sexual relations. Furthermore, when health reformers advised parents to channel their daughters' thoughts away from "vicious habits," such as touching their genitals or reading romantic novels, they recognized that if left to their own devices, women's natural sexual desires could easily be stimulated. An abundant anti-masturbation literature, aimed at women "of all classes," contradicted the notion of innate purity.[43]

For some doctors, the problem was not so much one of female asexuality as of marital incompatibility. In the 1860s, the American physician George Naphey wrote that frigidity was a defect, rather than a virtue, in women. Other doctors recommended ways that husbands might learn to satisfy their wives. A late-Victorian writer, C. A. Greene, advised husbands that "a careful retarding of [the conjugal act] will, after a little time, lead to reciprocal enjoyment."[44] Elizabeth Blackwell, the first woman to earn a medical degree in the United States, wrote about the "immense power of sexual attraction felt by women" and argued that in healthy women, uninjured by too-frequent childbearing, "increasing physical satisfaction attaches to the ultimate physical expression of love." In attempting to define sexual passion in terms of personal intimacy, Blackwell hinted at a difference between male and female experience: "It is the profound attraction of one nature to the other which makes passion; and delight in kiss and caress—the love touch is physical sexual expression as much as the special act of the male."[45] Ideally, Blackwell implied, both men and women could experience sexual pleasure, with or without procreative sexual intercourse.

Sexual advice literature does not tell us much about how people acted, but it does reveal the system of ideas against which they measured their behavior. When read carefully, the medical and health reform literature holds important clues not only to middle-class ideals, but also to the impressive decline in marital fertility rates in nineteenth-century America. For those who did internalize the messages of male self-control and female purity, marital continence may well have been used to reduce fertility, either as the sole means of avoiding pregnancy or in combination with periods of contraceptive use. Eliza Duffey, for example, supported both contraception and continence. Equally important, because the advice literature encouraged greater personal attention to and responsibility for sexual control, it may have prepared couples to practice contraception. Control could mean resisting sexual desires, but it also implied a management of sexuality. When women and men took charge of sexual decisionmaking, they learned habits that could be applied to reproductive decisionmaking as well.

Medical advice, then, did not necessarily seek to "repress" sexual desire. Rather, it attempted to shift sexual control from traditional external community pressures to individual will, or self-control. In the process, some men and women exposed to this literature did internalize sexual controls. Others may have been introduced to the very practices the texts proscribed. As an adolescent, for example, Caroline Healey of Boston was shocked to learn about masturbation when she read a pamphlet condemning the "Solitary vice." She addressed the author in a journal entry: "Your pamphlet will instill ideas—I dare not name," and could inspire sexual indulgence by those who "fear to seek [it] any other way."[46] Above all, nineteenth-century medical advice literature reveals how important sexuality was becoming in the building of individual character. Properly channeled, the experts claimed, sexual relations promised to contribute to individual health, marital intimacy, and even spiritual joy.

Taken together, the evidence of contraceptive practice and medical advice suggests the ways that sexual meanings were changing over the course of the nineteenth century. The use of contraception and abortion attests to the conscious desire to limit family size, especially among white, educated, urban, and northern families. When these married couples engaged in sex, they often did so with the knowledge, or at least the hope, that the act would have no reproductive consequences. Thus sex might become more closely associated with the goals of romantic or spiritual union, and even of a physically pleasurable, or erotic, experience. The medical advice literature, though contradictory on the propriety of contraception, supported these new meanings by stressing the importance of sex within marriage and the intimacy that it could bring to husband and wife. Even the emphasis on individual sexual control heightened personal awareness of sexuality as an important force, one that men and women had to be conscious of in order to use appropriately. At the same time, the medical advice literature reveals that men and women brought different sexual values to marriage. As a result, both sexual love and sexual conflict intensified within marriage during the nineteenth century.

Sexual Love and Sexual Conflict

As nineteenth-century Americans began to reduce fertility and internalize sexual regulation, they also incorporated a romantic attitude toward marriage. Since the mid-eighteenth century, marriage had become more important as a union based on love and affection. Even so, financial considerations remained important. Within the upper class, such as southern planter families, marriage involved the transfer of significant property. As a working class emerged in the nineteenth century, laboring men and women pooled their labor power for family survival. In the middle class, however, an ideal of romantic love also began to influence the decision to wed. The romantic ideal, in which love bound a couple together, also encouraged expectations that marriage would involve a new level of personal intimacy, along with requiring the traditional duty between spouses. This goal could prove elusive, however, for it emerged at the very time that greater distance separated the idealized spheres of middle-class women and men. Husbands and wives sought to bridge the gulf through marital relations, but the task was not an easy one, since love and sex meant something at once similar and different for men and women. Both, for example, experienced a gradual separation of sexuality from its traditional justification as a means for procreation, but this transition was more problematic for women, who remained centrally involved in reproduction.

The evolution of courtship provides important evidence for the view that personal intimacy became more important and more problematic during the nineteenth century. Between the 1780s and the 1820s, courtship took place within the settings of rural family life. In this sexually integrated world, young men and women formed friendships while they worked, attended church, or participated in mixed-gender social groups. Premarital sexual activity—possibly encouraged by the eighteenth-century practice of bundling—was reflected in the high rates of pregnancy at marriage: at the end of the eighteenth century, thirty percent of all brides gave birth within eight and a half months of marriage.[47] In rural and frontier areas, these older patterns persisted well into the nineteenth century. In the South, among small farmers, young people courted after church or at revival meetings. As a Confederate soldier wrote to a friend, "right to me about the big meating and how you in joyed your self and how menny girls you Sqese." In the West, community events, such as holiday and harvest celebrations, facilitated courtship. On the mining frontier, couples gathered in groups, with little privacy, as Alf Doten recorded in his diary:

> About a dozen couples in all assembled—Surprise party—Jolly girls—Jolly time—
> One of the pleasantist parties I ever attended—music & singing—... Ever so much
> kissing—most I ever saw— ... left 11 ½ [P.M.]—Saw the girls home.[48]

Courtship continued to take place in public among urban working-class youth, as well. At the beginning of the century, young men and women met and flirted openly on the public beaches near New York City, or they took Sunday boat trips and carriage rides. Groups of women "walked out" together on Broadway and the Bowery, flirting with the young men they encountered and then pairing off in couples. By the 1830s, anticipating the later development of an urban youth culture, women who worked in factories or as seamstresses joined the "Bowery Boys," young working men who were the "dandies of the day." These "Bowery Gals" wore bright-colored clothing that accentuated their figures, and they walked with "a swing of mischief and defiance." According to historian Christine Stansell, working-class youth used the time that had been "freed up from domestic obligations and family discipline" to pursue "sexual and commercial pleasures" with the wages they earned. They met at ice-cream parlors, dance halls, or at the Bowery Theatre, apart from the watchful eyes of kin. At least until the Civil War, Stansell maintains, working-class youth accepted sex between engaged couples.[49]

The working class joked openly about the flirtations of unmarried men and women, even as reticence increasingly characterized middle-class sexual etiquette. At theaters and, later in the century, music halls, they enjoyed performers who defied middle-class advice about controlling sexual desires. Songs like "Isn't He a Tease" and "Only in Fun"—sung nightly by Adah Richmonds during the 1870s—delighted in rousing the passions:

> Each afternoon dressed in the fashion
> I promenade out in the street
> O'er everything else I've a passion
> To flirt with the gents whom I meet.
> Of course it is wrong you are saying
> And tell me it should not be done
> It is only a game I am playing
> And it's only, just only in fun.[50]

Flirtations were not, however, always "only in fun," for the outings of working-class youth involved new risks for women. As Lanah Sawyer learned a generation earlier, seduction or rape might befall a woman who paired off with the wrong man on urban streets. More than one Bowery Gal met a similar fate. In 1842, for example, Ann Murphy walked out on a Saturday night and was raped by a man whom she asked for directions.[51] Even a betrothed woman, if she became pregnant, might find herself abandoned rather than wed, since neither parents nor clergy intervened to the extent they had in the past.

In contrast to the continuing public courtship of rural and working-class youth, in which young people openly pursued pleasure, between the 1820s and the 1880s middle-class courtship became an intensely private affair. One of the few settings in which young middle-class men and women met outside of the boundaries of their separate spheres, courtship involved a delicate ritual, a sharing of hearts that only gradually overcame middle-class reticence about sexuality. During courtship and once engaged, couples exchanged personal confidences, baring their souls and exposing their weaknesses to each other. The specialization of rooms within middle-class homes facilitated this privatization. Unlike colonial-era dwellings, in which the entire family gathered around the hearth, the Victorian home had separate rooms for dining, sitting, and sleeping. The parlor became a space where a young woman and her suitor could visit uninterrupted, with the expectation that they would behave properly. At the same time, community involvement in courtship decreased in importance. In a more mobile and heterogeneous society, neighbors could not oversee courtship as before, and church and state had fewer points of interference, as evinced by the removal of laws that required the public posting of banns before marriage. Finally, the language of romantic love increasingly entered the vocabulary of courting couples. Rather than choosing a mate whom one might come to love through marriage, middle-class youth now expected to "fall in love" before agreeing to marry. Newly available romantic novels of this period encouraged such hopes, while correspondence between couples stressed the importance of love in the decision to wed and openly expressed loving feelings once an engagement occurred. The legal grounds for breach-of-promise suits incorporated these new emotional ideals. Formerly, when an engagement was broken, the plaintiff sued on the basis of property damage; in the early nineteenth century, the grounds expanded to include emotional loss, as well.[52]

The betrothal of Samuel Cormany and Rachel Bowman in 1859 illustrates the importance of both emotional intimacy and romantic language within middle-class courtship. On the night of his proposal, Samuel recorded in his diary, he and Rachel had "such a blending of hearts. . . . Spontaneously we flowed together." Then he asked her to marry him. "She said 'Yes!' and rested her head upon my bosom as never before—thus the Rubicon was crossed." Having pledged their love, the courtship became more intense and more private. At their next meeting, he greeted her as "My Darling," and they embraced "with such a kiss of rapture." Now when Samuel came to visit, Rachel's family tactfully withdrew from the parlor. "[L]eft to ourselves," he wrote, "and a joyful time we had til 2 Ock—when we lovingly retired—each to our rooms."[53]

Romantic language and expectations of personal intimacy did not necessarily lead to sexual intercourse during courtship, even though it intensified erotic sensibilities. Declining premarital pregnancy rates—which dropped from twenty percent of marriages in the 1830s to ten percent in the 1850s—suggest that many middle-class courting couples internalized sexual restraint, at the least removing intercourse from the realm of acceptable premarital sexual acts. Two examples from the 1830s illustrate how romantic love and sexual control could combine to heighten erotic consciousness while avoiding sexual intercourse. In 1837, abolitionists Angelina Grimke and Theodore Weld became engaged. Love, they told each other, was the real purpose of marriage; sex was merely a necessity for procreation. Weld had been impressed by Sylvester Graham's gospel of physical self-control. He explained in a letter to Grimke that when they met, he struggled to control his passions and even left the room in order to "keep an extinguisher" on the expression of his strong feelings. In so doing, Weld communicated both his lust and his determination to master it. Another engaged couple, Nathaniel Hawthorne and Sophia Peabody, confided their mutual yearning for physical intimacy in highly romantic, even spiritual, terms. "Dove, come to my bosom," Hawthorne wrote to her while imagining that she was next to him in bed. "How many sweet words I should breathe into your ear in the quiet night—how many holy kisses would I press upon your lips." Despite these fantasies, this couple, like many of their generation, postponed the act of coitus until after marriage, and even then they confirmed that sex was not simply a physical pleasure, but "a spiritual joy" and "a wondrous instrument . . . for the purposes of the heart."[54]

Later in the century, other courting couples sought to satisfy both erotic and romantic longings. By the 1860s, more explicit discussions of sexual experience appeared in the diaries and letters of engaged couples, indicating a possible expansion of premarital sex among middle-class couples. The courtship of Lester Ward and Lizzie Vought progressed from hand holding and kisses on the face to kisses on the mouth and on "her sweet breasts." Troubled by having taken "too many liberties," the couple vowed to stop their late-night erotic sessions. Several months later, however, Ward recorded in his diary that "she received me in her arms of tenderness and pressed me to her form of honey, and our lips touched and our souls entered Paradise together. . . . That evening and that night we experienced the joys of love and tasted the felicity which belongs to married life alone." Similarly, in the 1870s, Mabel Loomis and her fiancé David Todd exulted in their passionate embraces and their ability to arouse each other. "Mabel will remember with pleasure the new sensation I caused her this evening," David confided to his diary. "Well, I couldn't help it," Mabel wrote in hers. "I woke up the next morning very happy though, and feeling not at all condemned."[55]

Mabel Todd's somewhat defensive comment about her sexual activity reflects a pattern in middle-class women's accounts of premarital intercourse. Despite the cultural taboos on female passion, many women did express sexual desire. At the same time, however, women seemed more reluctant, more ambivalent, and more regretful about premarital sexual experimentation than did men. Some women no doubt accepted the theory that men had stronger sexual desires than women. Harriet Beecher, for instance, loved her fiancé Calvin Stowe quite intensely, but she claimed that she simply did not feel "the pulsation" that tempted men to indulge in sexual intercourse. Other women feared the ruined reputation that could accompany loss of virginity. For a middle-class woman, even the suspicion that she had fallen by having sex before marriage could ruin her future chances of matrimony. A suitor who discovered that his fiancé was not a virgin had grounds to break the engagement, and a husband could file for divorce if he learned that his wife had been unchaste before marriage. Thus Rachel Bowman, engaged to Samuel Cormany, worried about her reputation when she heard that a young man she knew had been accused of fathering a bastard child. "I fear it will injure me some," she wrote in her diary. "Although I never once went with him alone, still I was in his company."[56]

Given the greater physical risk of pregnancy and the cultural emphasis on female purity, it is not surprising that women's personal accounts of premarital sex differed from men's. For women brought up with little information about sex, premarital erotic play was largely a man's game, to be taught to them by partners who had to elicit women's hidden passions. Thus in 1853, when Will Adkinson courted Lu Burlingame in an Indiana town, he tried to "draw out" her passions and convince her that women could feel sexual desire. She, however, believed that sexuality could not be enjoyed outside of the goal of motherhood. "I learned to hunger for your tender words and caress," she confessed, "but I never wanted extremes." She resisted his pressures to have intercourse and eventually became repulsed by sexual passion. Annie Cox did have coitus with her fiancé, but she "detested" herself afterward and resolved to resist in the future. Her partner's desire for intercourse seemed natural enough to Cox, but her duty was to prevent it from overpowering her: "I failed in the full possession of my reason and judgement thus giving strength to your desire and weakening my better nature." Despite misgivings, other women appreciated their sexual initiation by men. After their first sexual intimacy, for example, Mary Butterfield told her fiancé that she wanted to hide her face in some corner and that she could not "resign all the feelings which nature and education have fixed in my mind" about the importance of female purity. Nonetheless, she felt happy to have pleased her lover and wrote: "You have lifted a veil which concealed from me many beautiful paths of happiness and which taught me joys and blessings I had never dreamed of."[57] For women like Butterfield, male instruction revealed the pleasures of sex, but the fears of defying female norms lingered.

Whether sexual intimacy began during courtship or not, marriage provided a legitimate arena for sexual exploration. In the working class, the end of courtship marked a shift to a "practical household arrangement based on reciprocal obligations." Sex led to babies, and it might mean pleasure for husband or wife, but it did not necessarily lead to greater intimacy. For one, the individual couple continued to be connected to a public world through neighbors and kin who knew a great deal about the couple's intimate life, especially in the urban tenement districts. As Stansell explains, the neighborhood was "an alternative court, judge and jury" that helped regulate marital sex, intervening, for example, if adultery or family violence threatened to disrupt a union.[58] Moreover, for the working class, the struggle to make a living dominated daily life; as in the past, a couple's economic, rather than romantic, partnership largely determined the success of a marriage. For the middle class, in which men ideally provided financial security for dependent wives and children, the new concept of marriage as a romantic union created strong aspirations for satisfying personal, and sexual, relations within the privatized realm of the family. Some middle-class couples were able to achieve sexual harmony, even physical bliss, within their marriages. For others, however, sexuality became a source of marital stress, in part because of the different meanings it held for women and for men.

Historians know more about the qualitative experience of marital sexuality than about its frequency. Only a handful of sources record frequencies, ranging from once a month to six times a week.[59] Many couples left no record of their sexual feelings, but those who did documented the presence of desire within marriage. According to diaries and the correspondence of couples during periods of separation, both men and women felt longing for sexual union and expressed their desires to their mates. During the Civil War, for example, when many married couples endured long separations, an Iowa frontierswoman wrote to her husband that she dreamed of him nightly. "Do you ever wish you had me for a bedfellow?" she asked. "I have wished you were here more than once when I would get ready for bed. But I feel in hopes [sic] that we can have that privilege before long, don't you?" When a short leave from the army allowed a visit between Samuel and Rachel Cormany, he recorded in his diary that they "didn't sleep much last night," for the "reunion so buoyed up our affections, that we had a great deal of loving to do."[60]

The desire of husbands and wives for sexual union became apparent in circumstances other than wartime separation and reunion. In 1835, for example, a southern couple discreetly employed the word *home* as a code for sexual intercourse in their correspondence: "Your anticipations of Home," wrote the wife to her absent husband, "are not greater than mine are and you will find on your return how mutual have been our feelings." Joseph and Laura Lyman wrote more explicitly about their feelings during a separation: "I anticipate unspeakable delight in your embrace," he wrote, while imagining her "caressing hands" and "voluptuous touch." Laura Lyman returned in kind: "How I long to see you . . . I'll drain your coffers dry next Saturday I assure you." Finally, in an unusually explicit diary of her erotic life, Mabel Loomis Todd recorded her joy in marital and extramarital lovemaking. In a passage written in 1879, while she was pregnant, Todd articulated how sexuality could be tied to the goals of both marital intimacy and physical pleasure:

> The night brought us very near to each other. The physical effect of our close communion was unlike anything I ever experienced—it was enjoyment, and yet it was hard for me to feel the same kind of intensity as before—it was a thrilling sort of breathlessness—but at last it came—the same beautiful climax of feeling I knew so well.[61]

In short, both men and women expressed their desire for sexual intimacy and their experience of erotic pleasure in marriage, often in romantic and spiritualized terms.

At the same time, however, expectations of sexual intimacy could intensify conflict between husbands and wives. This was especially so given the unequal balance of economic and political resources within nineteenth-century marriages. Under the law, a woman was the sexual property of her husband; that is, she had a duty to have intercourse with him. Although marital rape was gradually recognized as a form of cruelty, it was not a crime. A Virginia court was sympathetic to Robert Latham when Fannie Latham "denied him access to her bed"; he won both a divorce and custody of their children. Moreover, a woman had few means by which she could support herself outside of marriage, so she had reason to remain in her husband's favor. Equally important, men and women had grown up with different understandings of their sexuality. Despite the prescriptive literature that recommended male continence, a persistent double standard acknowledged men's "natural" lust and their need for sexual gratification. Despite the availability of contraception, sexual activity continued to mean, for women, the possibility of pregnancy and childbearing. Although her husband welcomed another child, Mary Pierce Poor breathed a sigh of relief when she miscarried, and she referred to a later pregnancy as a "lot to be borne."[62] Not surprisingly, then, when sexual discord emerged within marriages, in the working class or the middle class, it often took the form of a struggle between men's desire for sex and women's concerns about health and maternity.

Evidence of this conflict in male and female ideals about sexuality can be gleaned from the responses given by several middle-class married women to Dr. Clelia Mosher. The seven women born in the early nineteenth century all agreed that reproduction was a major purpose of sexual relations; two added that sex was necessary only for men's pleasure, while four considered sex important for pleasure, love, or the bond between husband and wife. When asked whether sex was a necessity, however, most of these women believed it was so only for a man; a woman could "do without." Half of these women expressed sexual desires and found sex agreeable, at least "at times," but more telling was the fact that even those who felt no desire participated in regular sexual relations. One woman who found sex "usually a nuisance" and "never cared much for it" nonetheless engaged in marital intercourse twice a week and sometimes nightly, presumably to please or comply with her husband.[63] When read within the context of other evidence, this small sample raises the possibility that for women, sexuality retained its close association with reproduction, even as love and pleasure became sexual goals. For men, however, the separation of sexuality and reproduction, along with an emphasis on physical pleasure, seems to have proceeded more smoothly.

The conflict between male and female sexual expectations in marriage was especially pronounced among divorcing couples. Throughout the nineteenth century, divorce cases reveal, men complained when they were not sexually gratified in marriage. For example, men rather than women usually instituted divorce proceedings on the grounds of impotence, reversing an older pattern of women's dissatisfaction when male impotence prevented reproduction.[64] In contrast, historian Elaine Tyler May has concluded, "women complained of sexual abuse, not frustration," when they filed for divorce. Not untypical was the middle-class wife who accused her husband of having "a gross, brutal and lustful nature, which he does not control." Other women agreed that men's lust endangered the health of wives by requiring too-frequent intercourse. In 1869, a California woman complained that her husband compelled her to have intercourse when she was in ill health. Similarly, in 1880, another woman testified that her husband wanted sex "day and night."[65]

Extreme cases of sexual abuse in marriage also appeared in divorce records. In 1867, Nancy Jane Hicks told an Arizona court that her husband, William, "commenced and continued abusing me. . . . While I was pregnant and near childbirth [he] would insist on having carnal connection with me, and when I would refuse he would sometimes hold me by force until he accomplished his purpose, and at other times he would kick me . . . until I had blue spots over my body." In New Jersey, Abigail English complained that her husband insisted on regular sexual intercourse, even though a uterine disease, contracted after bearing three children within five years, made intercourse painful for her. After submitting to intercourse twice a night, and bruised from his use of physical force, Mrs. English left her husband and filed for divorce. "I cannot control myself," her husband explained to the court. Although she initially won her suit on the grounds of extreme cruelty, an appeals court reversed the decision. The judges accepted a doctor's testimony that "a large proportion of married women assent [to intercourse] under exactly those conditions" of ill health, and the court accepted her husband's promise to reform his behavior.[66]

Despite such conflicts, married women did not necessarily reject sexuality. Significantly, neither Nancy Hicks nor Abigail English argued that they had no desire for sexual relations. Rather, they wished to limit sex during ill health or pregnancy. Occasionally, women did complain of insufficient sex within marriage. In an exceptional case, Annie Court of Arizona ran away from her husband; a friend repeated Mrs. Court's reasons at the divorce hearing: Despite her husband's "teasing her by his caresses and kissings exciting her womanly passions . . . he had never cohabited with her and could not." She claimed that her husband "was no man [and] that she might as well sleep with a woman." However, most women who complained that their husbands neglected marital sexuality stressed their desire for children rather than their desire for physical pleasure.[67]

Conflict over sex, or simply the desire to avoid pregnancy, drove both men and women to seek separations. At one extreme, some women chose to avoid sexual intimacy altogether by living apart from their husbands. In the 1860s, a group of women in Belton, Texas, substituted female community for heterosexual intimacy. Their leader, Mrs. Martha McWhirter, had ceased to have sexual relations with her husband after they fought over his behavior toward a female servant. Over the next few decades, other married women joined McWhirter to found the all-female Sanctificationist religion, whose members embraced celibacy as a central creed. On a less formal basis, other middle-class women postponed both sex and pregnancy by living apart from their husbands during some of the year. Drawing upon family and friendship ties formed within the female sphere, they visited relatives or tended to their health at one of the water-cure spas that dotted the northern states. At these hydropathic retreats, women could enjoy the sensual pleasures of mineral baths, nurture their female friendships, and temporarily avoid conception. Within the working class, long-term separation occurred as well. Among the Irish, for example, marital conflict often led men to seek work apart from their families, or simply to desert them.[68]

Adultery provided another response to marital dissatisfaction. For men, the double standard allowed extramarital relationships to develop without necessarily disrupting marriage. Indeed, under certain circumstances, even the most loving husbands could be tempted to commit adultery and expect to be forgiven by their wives. Thus did Samuel Cormany "transgress" while separated from his wife during the Civil War. After weeks of praying and thinking of his wife in order to resist the temptation to sin, he finally yielded to readily available southern prostitutes. On his return, Samuel confessed to his wife, Rachel, and prayed to Jesus to help restore their family. His diary recorded "the peace, the joy, the rest" that the couple shared after his confession; Rachel's diary recorded a heart "almost broken": "It takes all the powers of my mind and soul to bear up under this my greatest of sorrows so as to hide the anguish of my heart." She forgave him, and he promised that no further "missteps" would occur.[69]

It is highly unlikely that Samuel Cormany would have forgiven such a transgression by his wife, Rachel. Because of the double standard and the chance of pregnancy, adultery was much more risky and more costly for women than for men. Even suspicion of adultery could lead to physical assault by a jealous husband. A New York laborer so feared that his wife would find another man while he left town to seek work that he returned home and in a drunken rage killed her. If a husband did in fact discover a wife's infidelity, it could lead to divorce, social ostracism, and a loss of custody over her children. In 1843, the Louisiana Supreme Court gave child custody to the husband of an adulterous wife, even though he had abused her and murdered her lover. One wife, divorced for adultery, wrote in a suicide note to her husband: "I have been a faithful and true wife, and now you have driven me on to this cold world, without any money, and but a few friends, and you say for me to lead the life of a fancy woman." A study of divorce suits in California found that women were twice as likely as their spouses to be accused of adultery and twice as likely to be found guilty than were men. This disparity was no doubt due to women's acceptance of male infidelity, rather than the frequency of female adultery. So serious was the stigma of infidelity that a false accusation of adultery could be grounds for a wife to divorce her husband.[70]

Despite the risks, adultery provided opportunities for intimacy apart from marriage and reproductive responsibility. In early American communities, neighbors had regularly intruded into extramarital relationships. In some working-class and immigrant neighborhoods, this practice continued. Thus outside the wedding party of a Brooklyn minister who had been accused of adultery, an Irish mob harassed the participants and guests with a chorus of "groans, yells, and hootings" accompanied by "cow horns, marrow bones and cleavers . . . and thunder mugs." In the privatized middle class, however, as long as discretion prevailed, a couple might engage in adultery without arousing public response. Mabel Loomis Todd, who so passionately embraced her husband, David, both before and during their marriage, turned with equal ardor to her married neighbor, Austin Dickinson, in an affair that defied the marital norms of the quiet college town of Amherst for almost fifteen years. Todd and Dickinson enjoyed frequent bedroom trysts in Mabel's house while her husband was out. When he returned home, David Todd obligingly whistled a familiar tune to warn the adulterous couple that their time together must end. "Their affair was secret," historian Peter Gay has explained, "but it was a secret that everyone shared." As long as the pair expressed their love in coded, private letters, and behind locked doors, they could maintain a public facade of respectability. Mabel Todd knew, too, that her husband was not "what might be called a monogamous animal," but by unspoken agreement, neither one publicized the liaisons of the other.[71]

The Todd-Dickinson affair may have been extreme among the middle class for its intensity and longevity, but adulterous relationships were formed throughout the country, in all classes. In the rural California town of Woodside, a married woman asserted her sexual desires in discreetly coded letters to her lover. Translated, they read: "When I see you again, perhaps I might find the way up your trowser leg . . . I wish you was here tonight. . . . [I]f you was here, I suppose we should do some tall fucking." Bachelor Alf Doten of Nevada used similar language to record in his diary the sexual pleasures of his secret affair with his married landlady, providing one of the few descriptions of foreplay and sexual variations for the time:

> Sept. 10. 1867. Evening at home. . . . Me and my love had thus far one hundred good square fucks—the best fucking on the face of the earth—Heavenly.

> Oct. 13, 1867. I came home at 9 this evening and me and my love went to bed and had one of our best fucking matches—we felt each others cocks all we pleased and then she got on and fucked me bully and I lying on my back—got my gun off in that position for the second time in my life—

Only rarely, and usually within the working class, did women publicly admit to extramarital relationships, perhaps because working-class women had less to lose in terms of property or public reputation. Anna Anderson of California, sued for divorce by her husband for committing adultery, "declared her intention to commit it in the future"; Susan Delashmutt told the court that she "prefers to live in adultery . . . than to live in lawful wedlock" with her husband.[72] For the most part, however, the quest for love and pleasure outside marriage remained private.

The evidence from harmonious spouses, divorcing couples, and adulterous lovers all points toward an ideal of sexual pleasure that coexisted with the search for sexual control. Three patterns stand out that differentiate nine-teenth-century sexual life from the past. First, both women and men had become more self-conscious about sexuality as a personal choice and not simply a reproductive responsibility. When sex no longer fell under the regula-tion of a larger community, each individual had to decide whether to engage in premarital sex or not, whether to have frequent or infrequent marital intercourse, and whether to yield to or resist the temptation to commit adul-tery. Second, especially within the middle class, sexual desires had become increasingly fused with a romantic quest for emotional intimacy and even spiritual union. The use of language—a "blending of hearts," "holy kisses," "spiritual joy," when "souls entered Paradise" along "beautiful paths of happi-ness" to new "joys and blessings"—contrasted with the frankly physical and reproductive terms in which earlier Americans had spoken of sexuality. Ex-tramarital relations also echoed with "rapture" and "communion with beloved ones." The exultation of pure physical pleasure—"tall fucking" and the "best fucking matches"—typically appeared within the working class or in rural and frontier areas. Finally, although women and men shared in both the intensifi-cation of sexuality as a form of interpersonal intimacy and the separation of sexuality from reproduction, gender made an important difference in the ways they experienced these changes. The separate spheres of the middle class, the emphasis on female purity, the double standard, and woman's reproductive role all made the transformation of sexuality more problematic for women. Although they did so in different ways, however, both women and men con-tributed to the long-term transition of sexuality within the family, from the context of reproduction to the realm of romantic love and physical passion.

CHAPTER 5

Race and Sexuality

ELIZA GRAYSON was a Mississippi slave whose husband died while fighting in the Union army. In 1893 she applied to the federal government for a widow's pension. In order to determine the legitimacy of her claim, a special examiner took depositions from Mrs. Grayson and a neighbor. The interrogation, conducted by Julius Lemkowitz of the Pension Office, disclosed much about racial differences in sexual practices and attitudes. It also revealed the power whites had to pass judgment on the morality of people of other races.

"Elisha Grayson and I were Mr. Montgomery's slaves before the war," Eliza Grayson told the examiner. "We were married by Jerry Benjaman some time before the war; I cannot say when." "Who is Jerry Benjaman? . . . Was he a preacher?" Lemkowitz inquired. "He was no preacher; but being the head man on the plantation and a member of the church he married me and Elisha." "Whose permission did you get to marry? . . . Could Jerry Benjaman read and write?" They had their master's permission, she answered, and the headman was literate. The Graysons' first son had died three months after birth, but a second son, Spencer, survived. "How many children have you had before your marriage to Elisha Grayson, and who is their father?" "I had one by my master's son, Frank Montgomery," Mrs. Grayson stated, without further comment. "After the birth of that child" and before marriage, the examiner continued, "have you lived or cohabited with any man?" "No sir," she assured him. "I never lived with any man after that until I took up with Elisha Grayson." "How long after your marriage to Elisha Grayson was Spencer born?" "I do not know," Mrs. Grayson replied, "but we did not 'get' him till after our marriage." Hadn't she cohabited with Elijah Hall, a married man, before Elisha enlisted? "No, sir." Only several years after her husband left the plantation did she "commence cohabiting" with Elijah Hall. "I was a faithful wife as long as Elisha Grayson was at home." In answer to a query about her other children, Eliza Grayson listed four with Hall's last name, and of the remaining two, she explained, "I have had to do with several men and I cannot say really who their fathers are." Since the birth of her last child by Hall, over ten years ago, she swore "that no man has ever touched me." The inquiry closed with the question, "By whom can you prove that your first child was by your master's son?" "By Hanson Clay, if he is living."[1]

From youth to old age, Eliza Grayson's sexual life was shaped by two worlds, that of black slaves and that of white authorities. Within the slave community, she was no doubt a respectable woman. Serial monogamy and frequent childbearing characterized her life, like that of most slave women. Interactions with whites, however, transformed Mrs. Grayson from a wife and mother into a loose woman. Presumably raped by her master's son, the ambiguous phrase "I have had to do" suggests that forced sexual relations may have led to the births of two more of her seven surviving children. Under slavery, white masters assumed Eliza Grayson to be sexually available to them. In freedom, a white government interpreted her history as one of illegitimacy and infidelity. The final requirement that Eliza Grayson prove her own rape reveals how little whites were willing to acknowledge their own role in a system of racial and sexual exploitation. For blacks, as for Indians and Mexicans, this story of sexual stereotyping, sexual difference, and sexual abuse recurred throughout the nineteenth century.

Ever since the seventeenth century, European migrants to America had merged racial and sexual ideology in order to differentiate themselves from Indians and blacks, to strengthen the mechanisms of social control over slaves, and to justify the appropriation of Indian and Mexican lands through the destruction of native peoples and their cultures. In the nineteenth century, sexuality continued to serve as a powerful means by which white Americans maintained dominance over people of other races. Both scientific and popular thought supported the view that whites were civilized and rational, while members of other races were savage, irrational, and sensual. These animalistic elements posed a particular threat to middle-class Americans, who sought to maintain social stability during rapid economic change and to insure that a virtuous citizenry would fulfill the dream of republicanism. At a time when middle-class morality rested heavily upon a belief in the purity of women in the home, stereotypes of immoral women of other races contributed to the belief in white superiority. In addition, whites feared the specter of racial amalgamation, believing that it would debase whites to the status of other races. Thus Thomas Jefferson favored the removal of blacks to avoid racial mixing, for "their amalgamation with the other colour produces a degradation to which no lover of his country, no lover of excellence in the human character, can innocently consent." The belief in white moral superiority surfaced in relation to all racial and ethnic groups—whether the Chinese in California, who were considered a "depraved class," or the Irish in eastern cities, who were portrayed as an animalistic race with a "love for vicious excitement."[2] Indians, Mexicans, and blacks elicited the most extensive commentaries, in part because of the nature of their contact with whites. Patterns differed, but in each region the belief that white sexual customs were more civilized, along with the assumption that Indian, Mexican, and black women were sexually available to white men, supported white supremacist attitudes and justified social control of other races.

Cultural Conflict in the West and Southwest

The interplay of racial and sexual ideology can be seen clearly in the attitudes of whites who moved into and annexed western and southwestern territories. Encountering native American Indians whose sexual practices differed from their own, whites condemned them as sexually debased. As in the colonial period, the tolerance for cross-dressing and sodomy among some Indians evoked strong censure. One observer cited the *berdache* as "another illustration of the strange capacities which the California Indians develop for doing morbid and abnormal things." In other tribes, the idea of a bride price, or paying a young woman's family in order to marry her, shocked many Anglo-Americans, who condemned the practice as symptomatic of "a loose state of morals." Europeans and Americans also expressed horror at the practices of polygamy and premarital sex among Indian tribes. In the case of the Plains Indians, for example, whites wrote that polygamy demeaned women. In fact, women in these tribes enjoyed a fairly high status, and polygamy, often the product of an unbalanced sex ratio after wartime losses, offered women the benefit of sharing domestic work with other wives. Polygamous marriage also lessened the reproductive labors of each wife; among the Lakota, for example, plural wives bore an average of six children, monogamous wives an average of eight children. Missionaries to various Indian tribes failed to recognize the advantages of this practice and demanded that Indian converts adhere to strict monogamy.[3]

At the same time that whites condemned the sexual habits of Indians for degrading women, their own accounts objectified native American women in sexual terms. The image of the good Indian—the beautiful, pure princess who saved white men, as did Pocahontas—gave way in the nineteenth century to the image of the savage and promiscuous squaw. Cowboy lore in particular elaborated on the theme of the Indian whore, who "lays on her back in a cowboy shack, and lets cowboys poke her in the crack." Even more refined observers, such as authors of travel accounts or pioneer journals, referred to "dirty little squaws" who slept with or married white men. According to one white woman, intermarriage with Indians was a "shame and disgrace to our country."[4]

Similarly, Americans used sexual imagery to criticize the Mexicans they encountered in the areas that would later become California, New Mexico, and Arizona. White travelers described residents of northern Mexico as "debased in all moral sense." One writer claimed that all "darker colored" races were "inferior and syphillitic." Mexican women received particular censure. As Richard Henry Dana wrote in *Two Years Before the Mast*, "the women have but little virtue," and their morals were "none of the best."[5] White stereotypes rested upon misinterpretations of native cultures. For example, white settlers and Protestant missionaries expected courtship to take place in private and young people to act with extreme decorum. Just as in Eastern cities they found the behavior of working-class youth disturbing, when they observed Mexicans courting in public, celebrating festivals in the streets, and dancing without restraint, they labeled the women "vicious" and disparaged their "low virtue." Similarly, eastern settlers, revealing the ways that white cultural standards of physical privacy had evolved since the colonial era, expressed shock at the sight of women suckling their infants in public.[6]

These judgmental newcomers failed to appreciate the unique sexual system that had evolved in the Southwest, a combination of Spanish-Mediterranean and indigenous Indian practices. Before the growth of commerce in the mid-nineteenth century and the influx of Protestants after the Mexican-American War, Anglo-American notions of internalized sexual controls had not penetrated this region. In the traditional preindustrial culture of the area, the Catholic church and the family played important roles in the regulation of morality and the maintenance of individual and familial honor. As in the seventeenth-century English colonies, the family insisted that marriage occur when premarital sex led to pregnancy, and some young couples used premarital sex to win approval for a union not arranged by their parents. In addition, neighbors made public accusations or spread rumors about anyone whose behavior deviated from community standards. A young woman who had illicit sexual relations might have her braids snipped off as a form of public humiliation. When an anonymous rumor maligned her virtue, Maria Francisca Martinez found it impossible to marry in her hometown. Moreover, it was illegal to tolerate sexual immorality among one's kin. In 1836, for example, Luis Rael went to jail for allowing a female relative to commit adultery with a married man.[7]

Cultural misunderstanding also arose when sexual values in the Southwest differed from those evolving in the rest of North America. Catholics, like

Protestants, emphasized the importance of female purity, and they maintained a double standard that allowed men to indulge in pre- or extramarital sexual relations. However, no ideal of passionlessness emerged among the Mexicans. Women could both have and express their sexual desires, as long as they did not betray the honor of their families. As in the seventeenth-century colonies, both men and women might be tempted by pre- or extramarital relations, and church and community attempted to keep both sexes in line. At a time when reticence characterized white middle-class culture, Mexicans openly expressed sensuality. Thus dancing in public was not in itself offensive. A love poem published in 1858 spoke freely of male and female desire:

> I want to gaze at your rising bosom
> Showing the agitation within your soul.
> And I want to see your colored cheeks
> When you awaken with divine calm.
>
> . . . .
>
> By your side in the silent country side
> I want to look at your purple aurora.
> I want to see, by your side
> In the repose of the night,
> The seductive moon.[8]

For the most part, external controls kept sexual desire from threatening community stability. Only rarely did individuals defy accepted standards. In an extreme case, for example, a woman defended her right to have extramarital relations. In 1844, Juana Lopes's Anglo husband, testifying to the Santa Fe court, complained of rumors that "adulterers knock on the window when they want my wife to go out." Lopes retorted that "it is my ass, I control it, and I'll give it to whomever I want." The judge's plea for reformation no doubt went unheeded.[9]

Despite the acceptance of sexual desire, in the northern Mexican region marriage continued to be based on economic rather than romantic considerations, and parents continued to play an important, though gradually declining, part in their children's decisions to wed. Marital separation was also likely to be an economic matter. For example, Barbara Roybal complained to the Santa Fe court that her husband had affairs and beat her, but she was more interested in obtaining alimony in order to feed her children than in regaining his affections. Economic factors also influenced the acceptance among Mexicans of "free unions," which constituted between five and thirty percent of all Mexican marriages in midcentury California and the Southwest. Adopting Spanish and Indian customs, those who could not afford a wedding or who lived far from a local priest simply established households and lived as husband and wife. The children of these unions, recorded in church documents as *hijo* or *hija natural*, did not bear the stigma of illegitimacy. To Anglo eyes, however, both parents and children were deemed immoral.[10]

Whatever distaste white Americans had for Mexican and Indian sexual customs, some migrants formed interracial unions when they came into contact with natives. The nature of these unions differed, depending on white attitudes, the sex ratio during each period of contact, and the changing proportion of whites in the region. Overall, three patterns of interracial sexual relations formed: the assimilation of whites via marriage into Indian or Mexican society; the assimilation of Indian and Mexican women via marriage into Anglo society; and white sexual dominance, whether through physical violence or through efforts to obliterate "uncivilized" Indian and Mexican sexual practices.

The assimilation of whites took place in areas where a small number of white men settled near Indians or Mexicans. Typically the earliest white male migrants, such as trappers, traders, miners, and sailors, sought wives of another race because they had no women of their own to marry. These marriages provided an important form of economic alliance between white men and the groups among whom they lived. Some men used them to acquire land or trading rights, and some deserted their wives when they had nothing more to gain. Others expressed sexual attraction for native women. One white settler found "the Eve-like and scanty garments" worn by Indian women both a "little astonishing" and "really graceful, easy—ay, becoming."[11]

During the early period of white migration, men tended to assimilate into the cultures of their native wives, and their children retained their mothers' racial identity. In 1850, for example, half of the small group of white men in Santa Fe lived with Mexican women, whose culture predominated. Some men adopted the local custom of forming free unions with Mexican or Indian women. In other parts of the West, "squaw men" lived with or married according to native practice, such as French traders who sometimes took several wives. Among the northern and southern California Indians, there were many mixed households. These included informal, or free, unions, in which white men acknowledged the children as their own. Less frequently, white women assimilated through intermarriage. A long tradition of women who married their Indian captors provides one example. More unusual was the experience of a New England teacher, Elaine Goodale, who married an Indian physician with whom she worked on a Sioux reservation in the 1880s.[12]

As more white men and women migrated west, the pattern of intermarriage and assimilation changed. Men who married Indian or Mexican wives now expected them to conform to Anglo customs, and their children no longer retained the racial identity of their mothers. In the southeastern states, where intermarriage of white men and Cherokee women accounted for one-fourth of Cherokee marriages, children were taught to observe the legal and sexual rules of white, rather than Indian, society. In addition, whites increasingly defined themselves as racially superior to Cherokees and began to oppose intermarriage. Similarly, after 1848, when white families migrated to the territories annexed after the Mexican-American War, racial barriers to intermarriage arose. Not only did the white sex ratio even out, but as Mexican-Americans became the minority, Americans drew on long-standing stereotypes to label them both racially and sexually inferior. Intermarriage persisted, but now when white men married Mexican women, they brought their children up as whites.[13] After the American conquest of California, white men who married Mexican women attempted to transform the earlier image of immoral Mexicans into that of "aristocratic, virtuous Spanish ladies," despite the fact that the women they wed were neither Spanish nor aristocratic. Historian Antonia Castañeda argues that this shift in stereotype was part of an effort to assimilate Californian women into Anglo-American society. At the same time, it drew a distinction between "good" (Spanish and assimilable) and "bad" (Mexican and unassimilable) women, with the latter usually depicted as prostitutes. In creating this distinction, whites rewrote their genealogies in an effort to purify their bloodlines and deny their Mexican heritage. The distinction was not necessarily effective, for in many western communities, the terms "Spanish woman" or "senorita" remained synonymous with "prostitute."[14]

A third category of sexual interaction evolved when whites invaded native territory and claimed the right to control the sexuality of individual women or of a whole culture. In the nineteenth century, this pattern was typically one of American dominance over Indians or Mexicans, but it had antecedents in the Spanish treatment of Indians in the Southwest. One means by which Spaniards had subjugated local Indians was rape. As a Spanish man explained, "only with lascivious treatment are Indian women conquered." Seventeenth-century Pueblo Indians had petitioned the Spanish government because soldiers so often forced Indian women to have sex. Some Indians also complained against the Catholic clergy, and at least one priest was accused of raping Indian servants. In a different form of sexual imperialism, the Catholic church tried to force Indians to give up their sexual practices. For example, the church opposed polygamy, and friars physically punished Pueblos who continued this custom. The Spanish also attempted to suppress the cross-dressing *berdaches* among those Indians who were brought under the influence of the missions.[15]

When white Americans became the conquerors in western territories, they too claimed sexual access to native women and tried to obliterate Indian and Mexican sexual customs. Warfare with western Indian tribes justified, for white soldiers, the rape of Indian women. During the Bear Flag Revolt in California, John C. Frémont ordered a Mexican prisoner to deliver her young Indian maid to the officers' barracks. "By resorting to artifices," Rosalia Vallego de Lessee recalled, "I managed to save the unhappy girl from the fate decreed to her by the lawless band." Other Indian women were less fortunate. After winning a battle in 1869, Lieutenant Colonel George Armstrong Custer allegedly invited his officers to "avail themselves of the services of a captured squaw," while he selected a Cheyenne woman named Monasetah for himself. The absence of Anglo women at frontier military garrisons encouraged enlisted men to seduce or bribe Indians to become prostitutes. Some army officers were known to keep "favorite squaws," or mistresses, and several were court-martialed for their involvements with Mexican or Indian prostitutes.[16]

In the predominantly male mining areas of California, where local Indian tribes had been decimated by disease and impoverishment, sexual contact between white men and Indian women usually took the form of rape, and sometimes paid prostitution. Miners seeking temporary sexual outlets assumed the availability of local Indian women. The fact that most of these women did not cover their breasts gave miners the false impression that they had no modesty or were promiscuous. Miners also knew that they could act with impunity, since white men could not be convicted of rape, or of any crime, based on the testimony of an Indian. Together, these white stereotypes and legal privileges made Indian women highly vulnerable to sexual attack. In 1850, for example, three Indian women were "bedevilled and tormented" by white men. Some white miners offered food or money to buy Indian women's sexual favors, but as a California newspaper reported in 1858, if men failed to "obtain a squaw by fair means, [they would] not hesitate to use foul." White men were known "to drag off" Indian women as if they were literally fair game. As one settler recorded after a hunting trip, he had bagged, "all told, two grizzlys one Antlope and a digger squaw este noche." Indians resisted white men's assaults, either through retaliatory raids or individual effort. During a California military expedition in 1850, a settler approached "a comely squaw hidden in the brush" and tried to force her to go with him; the woman's response left him "more glad to escape with his life from the clutch of a she bear, than he was to get away from her." Other women fled to the mountains to escape pursuit by drunken white men in search of sexual partners. For those unable to avoid the assaults, the birth of a mixed-blood child often resulted.[17]

Other white settlers and Protestant missionaries in the West—and throughout the world, as well—attempted to impose the sexual values of the northern middle classes upon native peoples. In California, for example, female missionaries condemned polygamous marriage among the Chinese who immigrated at midcentury and sought to convert them to the ideal of the

Christian, nuclear family. Elsewhere, missionaries called for intervention in the lives of Indians on the grounds that young people too easily engaged in premarital sexual relations, women learned to be sexually assertive, or married couples performed varieties of sexual acts. They defined these Indians as pagans who had to be converted to the "missionary" position—man on top, woman on bottom—and taught to repress their "uncivilized" sexual practices. Among the Hopi Indians of the Southwest, for example, those who converted to Christianity could no longer attend the ritual snake dance, where male cross-dressing, adultery, and bestiality could be observed publicly. Missionaries urged Indians to adopt the nuclear family and the separate spheres of middle-class Americans. They tried to wipe out the practice of polygamy among the Cherokee and encouraged both Cherokee and Seneca to confine women to domestic pursuits. Indian boarding schools attempted to achieve these goals by teaching girls the values of domesticity and purity.[18]

The pattern of imposing middle-class American sexual values upon Indian and Mexican communities persisted throughout the nineteenth century. During this period, however, interaction between whites and Indians remained fairly limited, in part because large areas of the West continued to be sparsely populated. More importantly, the prevailing reservation policy insured large-scale racial separation by relegating Indians to lands where whites did not expect to settle. Even after the reservation policy officially ended with the Dawes Act of 1887, many Indians remained on reservations, and whites (other than soldiers, missionaries, or Indian agents) had little to do with native Americans. After the conquest of California and the Southwest, the Mexican population diminished as white Americans seeking land and gold came to dominate these regions demographically, economically, and politically. Here, too, racial segregation increased as the earliest Mexican-American barrios formed in the late nineteenth century and Mexicans became marginalized in isolated communities. Most white Americans took little notice of sexual practices among minority peoples who were removed from their view, although they retained the stereotypes of women of color as sexually available and likely to be prostitutes.

Master and Slave

The institution of slavery conditioned sexual as well as racial relations in the South in ways that differed from both the North and the West. White supremacist ideology characterized all regions. Northerners, for example, stereotyped free blacks as immoral, outlawed interracial marriages, and segregated their schools because of a fear of racial "amalgamation."[19] Unlike northerners, who lived in racially segregated cities with very few blacks, and in contrast to those inhabiting the West, where geographical distance separated whites from Indians and Mexicans, southerners lived in close proximity to the majority of blacks. For southern whites and blacks, slavery and the culture that supported it generated a unique moral system.

White southern sexual norms differed from those of the North in large part because of slavery. The concentration of southern resources on slave labor and plantation agriculture prevented the development of the urban, commercial, and industrial economy that gave rise to social—and sexual—transformation in the northern states. In contrast to the separate spheres of northern middle-class families, the southern planter family remained a patriarchy in which a man ruled over the women, children, and slaves within his household. Parents continued to influence marital choice, courtship remained public rather than private, and fertility rates showed very little decline. Although bonds of love developed within marriage, during courtship economic considerations continued to be significant, and men expected to exercise sexual freedom with women slaves.[20]

Although both northerners and southerners idealized white female purity, the demand for self-control—by men or women—rarely appeared in the slave states. Rather, familial surveillance over female virtue prevailed. The presence of slavery heightened planter insistence on protecting white women, and their family line, from the specter of interracial union. Greater regulation of women's sexuality was matched by greater sexual privilege for white men. Slavery provided abundant opportunity for white men to exercise sexual license. Especially within the planter class, relations with black women provided white men with both a sexual outlet and a means of maintaining racial dominance.

For white women, the effects of this system could be sexually stultifying. As early as 1809, a northern visitor noted the impact of slavery on white women's sexuality. The "dull, frigid insipidity, and reserve" of southern women, he claimed, was one of the worst "curses slavery has brought on the Southern States." A slave recollection supported this observation that the availability of black women as men's sexual partners destroyed the sexual relations of white men and women. After discovering that her husband had sex with black women, Mistress Mary Reynolds "don't never have no more children, and she ain't so cordial with the Massa."[21] Another reason for southern women's sexual reserve was the strict controls placed upon them. A belief in women's moral weakness, rather than moral superiority, necessitated standards that made courtship, for example, less private and more supervised than in the North. Both elaborate social rules and the geographical isolation of plantations limited opportunities for intimacy during courtship. Chaperons escorted unmarried young women to balls or on visits, restricting premarital sexual exploration and reminding women that property and family connections were as important as romance in the selection of mates. As in the North, the woman who "fell" from the standard of female purity—as evidenced by the birth of an illegitimate child—paid extremely high social costs. The unwed mother Rachel Warrenton, for example, was considered "lost to everything that is dear to women."[22] Even worse was the fall from racial purity, for a white woman's sexual relations with a black man challenged the basic hierarchy of southern society.

Strict controls on women's sexuality persisted after marriage. Married women in the South might have chaperons when they traveled, lest their reputations be tainted. An extreme double standard condemned any woman who engaged in extramarital sexual relations. She risked personal disgrace, violent physical punishment by her husband, divorce, and the loss of her children. Furthermore, although married women of the planter class did develop loving relationships with their husbands, their sexual lives remained, for the most part, associated with procreation and the duty to produce heirs. As a result, southern women were less likely to limit family size and more vulnerable to condemnation if they attempted to do so. They continued to bear the full physical costs of repeated pregnancies and childrearing—up to seven children in a planter-class family—at a time when their northern sisters were beginning to reduce these labors.[23]

In contrast to the exaggerated protection of white women's virtue and the containment of female sexuality within marital, reproductive relations, southern white men of the planter class enjoyed extreme sexual privilege. Most southern moralists condoned white men's gratification of lust, as long as they did so discreetly with poor white or black women. Polite society condemned the public discussion of illicit sex, but men's private writings reveal a good deal of comfort with the expression of pure sexual desire, unrelated to love or intimacy. One college youth recorded in his diary how he sought black or white women when his "cock stood as furious as a studs," and another young man told a friend where to find girls and how to avoid "the Damn's clap." As in the eighteenth century, a single or married gentleman could engage in such "wenching" (or casual, recreational sex) without shame or tarnish to his reputation. One planter defended his own wide-ranging sexual activities in a diary entry: "the very greatest men . . . have been addicted to loose indulgences with women . . . Webster and Clay are notorious for it and President Harrison got his wife's niece by child." Men's affairs were so institutionalized that southerners had a special term—the "gander months"—that referred to the late months of pregnancy, when husbands typically sought sex outside of marriage. Defenders of the southern system, such as William Gilmore Simms, argued that the planter's ability to have sex with his female slaves provided a safety valve that protected the virtue of white women.[24] Critics of this view, such as a Louisiana planter who sent his sons north to be educated, lamented that there was "no possibility of their being brought up in decency at home." One southern mother warned her son not to adopt "the vile and bad habits of men. . . . The more I see and know men," she confessed, "the more I dislike them and think they are a vile set of animals."[25]

South Carolina politician James Henry Hammond illustrated the sexual privilege enjoyed by men of the planter class, as well as the effect of their behavior on white women. Governor of the state during the 1840s, Hammond not only had sex with female slaves, but he also engaged (in his words) in "everything short of direct sexual intercourse" with his four teenage nieces, the daughters of politician Wade Hampton II. Over a period of two years Hammond kissed and fondled the girls and pressed against their "most secret and sacred regions." When one of his nieces informed her father of these episodes, Hampton tried to ostracize his brother-in-law from polite society and ruin his political career. At first, the revelation of Hammond's incestuous relationships seemed to damage his social and political prestige. It also temporarily estranged his wife. However, Hammond recovered from the setback and went on to serve in the U.S. Senate. In contrast, the reputations of the four nieces were ruined by the scandal. As one observer explained, "no man who valued his standing could marry one of the Hampton girls." They all remained single. Hammond showed no contrition; in his diary he blamed the girls for "permitting my hands to stray unchecked" and for not "shrinking" from his touch. He showed as little concern for the feelings of his wife, with whom he never discussed the affair, and whose coldness he found unjust. While separated from her, Hammond had a relationship with a female slave, justifying the liaison on the grounds that his wife could not fulfill the "great craving of my nature."[26]

The double standard for southern men and women may have been less extreme among yeoman farmers and poorer whites. Although the evidence for these groups is scanty, scattered incidents suggest that female sexual expression could occur more easily outside of planter society. An 1833 divorce case cited the wife of an "illiterate yeoman" who engaged in adulterous sex with several different men "in broad daylight." When caught in the act, the woman rejoined with language as bold as that of Juana Lopes of Sante Fe: "My ass is my own and I will do as I please with it." Poor and servant white women occasionally crossed the racial barrier to cohabit or have sex with black men. One married woman who bore a black child explained to her white husband that "she saw no more harm in a white woman's having a black child than in a white man's having one, though the latter was more frequent."[27] Although many southern women shared her knowledge about the prevalence of miscegenation between white men and black women, very few dared to act on the logic of her defense.

Among slaves, about whom there has been much more research, sexual values both resembled and differed from those of the white planter class. According to historian Herbert Gutman, whites perpetrated a myth of unrestricted black sexuality, explaining it either as the product of inherent racial tendencies toward licentiousness (the southern view) or as the product of the institution of slavery, which denied black people the right to legal marriage and thus the restraint on passion that marriage provided (the northern abolitionist view). Both groups, Gutman argues, failed to see the unique Afro-American family system that evolved under slavery and within which slaves adhered to a moral code that differed from that of whites.[28] In many ways, the slave community resembled certain preindustrial and peasant societies. Premarital sex might occur without stigma; most adults married and maintained stable unions when possible; and sexuality and reproduction remained closely linked, with little tension between the goals of pleasure and procreation and little thought to family limitation. At the same time, however, slavery complicated this picture immensely. The inability to wed legally, the separation of partners by sale or by residence on separate plantations, and the ultimate ownership of women's bodies by white masters rather than by black husbands or wives all forced slaves to balance their own desires with the demands of their masters.

Courtship provides a good illustration of the ways that slaves maintained their own sexual system even as they were continuously influenced by bondage itself and by the whites with whom they came in contact. Among whites, the taboo on premarital intercourse rested largely upon the need to establish legitimate heirs and to maintain female purity before marriage. These considerations had little relevance for slaves, who were themselves property rather than property owners and who could not marry in law. For these and other reasons, slaves did not have arranged marriages. Although parents might be consulted, individual attraction could be a major consideration in courtship. In addition, slaves did not condemn premarital intercourse, and many adolescent girls had sexual relations. No special stigma attached to the young woman who bore an "outside" child, that is, one born outside of marriage. According to one set of plantation records, up to twenty percent of all slave mothers had one or more children before marriage. Although this premarital pregnancy rate far exceeded that of the planter class, it probably resembled that of poor southern whites. A slave named Violet illustrated the common pattern of premarital pregnancy followed by marriage. Violet had several children before she settled down with a man whom she married two years later, and then only after she had assured herself that he accepted her children. Such trial, or "make-out," marriages seemed advantageous to the white mistress Mary Boykin Chestnut, who wrote in her diary that slave women "have a chance here that women have nowhere else. They can redeem themselves—the 'impropers' can. They can marry decently, and nothing is remembered against these colored ladies." Most members of her class, however, condemned the practice as immoral.[29]

The acceptance of premarital sex did not imply indiscriminate sexual relations. Rather, blacks, like whites, expected to form stable, monogamous unions. A woman who bore several "outside" children, for example, eventually settled down with one man for a long-term marriage. In addition, blacks regulated moral standards within the slave community. Like white settlers in the colonial period, some slaves preferred to marry before the birth of a child. Eliza Grayson had borne a child to her master's son; later she married Elisha Grayson and gave birth to a son who was not conceived until after their marriage. As one man reminisced about slave morality: "If you fooled up a girl with an arm full of you, you had to take care of her." Similarly, if a young woman seemed too sexually active, traditional sanctions might be imposed to restrain her. In Georgia, where slaves held especially strong views about female chastity, one community employed an African custom of "drumming" a banjo to control such women: "Den everybody know an dat girl sho better change her ways." Finally, the myth of slave promiscuity is belied by the facts that slaves had no prostitution and very little venereal disease within their communities.[30]

Aside from engaging in premarital sexual activity, slaves also participated in courtship rituals when they sought to marry a particular mate. Although slaves had little leisure time and few private meeting places, they carried on courtships that could last up to a year. Initial meetings took place at holiday parties, dances, or at church services, and courtship continued during formal visits. For some slaves, marriage preceded sexual relations, as was the case for Jim, who proposed before the first kiss, and only after asking permission of his intended wife's mother.[31] It was common to seek parental approval for marriage, and it was uncommon for slaves to choose spouses from among their own blood relatives. Although some slaves spoke of love as a basis for marriage, one historian has concluded that "for every marriage that was anchored in romantic love there was probably one that grew out of pragmatic consideration."[32]

In addition to adhering to the customs of their own community, slaves had to obtain the consent of their masters to court women from other plantations (since a pass was needed to travel alone) and to marry. Former slave Camilla Jackson recalled that Dr. Hoyle, a Georgia planter, allowed his slaves to chose their own mates, as long as they came from the plantations of his friends and not from his own. A suitor, armed with pass, went to call on Sundays, courting in the presence of the woman's parents. When the couple married, Dr. Hoyle provided a wedding feast and a white preacher to perform the ceremony. Underlying such benevolence was the control that masters exercised over slave courtship. For example, as another ex-slave from Georgia explained, "If the woman wasn't willing, a good, hard-working hand could always get the master to make the girl marry him—whether or no, willy nilly." When Rose Williams's master sent her to live with Rufus, she complained to her mistress, who explained, in Rose's words: "Yous am de portly gal and Rufus am de portly man. De massa wants yu-uns fer to bring forth portly chillen." Rose stayed with Rufus until emancipation, when she left him. Not all women slaves complied with their masters' commands, however. As Violet explained when refusing several mates chosen by her owner, "No, Misses, I can't take one ob dem, 'cause I don't lub' em." She succeeded in choosing her own partner.[33]

As the property of their masters, slaves did not have the legal right to contract marriage, but they nonetheless performed marriage rituals ranging from jumping over a broomstick to Christian wedding ceremonies performed by black or white preachers, along with festive celebrations in the slave quarters. Once married, a couple had little privacy. If they came from the same plantation, a young couple usually shared a separate area of a crowded slave cabin. If theirs was a "broad marriage," in which husband and wife lived on separate plantations, the husband would usually get a pass to visit on Saturday nights.[34] As a former slave from South Carolina recalled, her father "had to git a pass to come to see Mammy. He slipped in and out 'nough of times to have four chillun." If the couple was sold apart, each was likely to remarry.[35]

Despite these obstacles to traditional family life, most slaves participated in long-term, monogamous marriages. Slaves and masters jointly supported the ideal of monogamy. Some masters, like a Florida planter, "never interfered in their connubial or domestic affairs, but let them regulate these after their own manner," but others attempted to impose monogamy on slaves. Thus an Alabama owner whipped those slaves who violated "the right of husband and wife and such other immorality."[36] Regardless of their owners' efforts, slaves regulated marriage through their own traditional mechanisms of group pressure and church discipline. As did preindustrial white congregations, black churches punished adultery by suspending sinners from church membership. In addition, either partner might leave a marriage if he or she suspected adultery, for no disgrace fell upon those who "divorced."[37]

Reproduction, like courtship and marriage, meant different things to masters and slaves. For the former, children represented property; for the latter, family. Slave fertility rates, like those of southern white women, remained high during the first half of the nineteenth century, for both owners and slaves encouraged reproduction.[38] Owners had a financial interest in slaves producing children and openly encouraged "breeding." Women known as breeders brought higher prices on the slave market and might enjoy special privileges, such as a job in the master's house rather than in the fields. Male slaves known as "bucks" also brought higher prices and had special privileges, as the former slave John Cole recalled: "If a hand were noted for raising up strong black bucks . . . he would be sent out as a species of circuit-rider to the other plantations . . . [and] there he would be 'married off' again—time and again. This was thrifty and saved any actual purchase of new stock." More typically, some owners offered incentives to reproduction, such as a new pig for each child born to a family, a new dress for each surviving infant, or Saturdays off for mothers of six children.[39]

The extent of planter breeding, however, has probably been exaggerated, for slaves bore children for their own reasons and not simply at the bequest of their masters. As Angela Davis has suggested, the creation of families gave slave women an arena of personal meaning denied them in the productive labor they performed for their owners. Thus slaves, like most preindustrial peoples, valued motherhood and did little to interfere with it. Within marriage, children were usually welcomed, and those born outside of marriage attracted no stigma. Planters did complain when they suspected that women slaves tried to avoid childbearing, and some slave women clearly did prevent conception or abort through the use of herbs. At least one "barren" slave proved capable of bearing children after emancipation. On the whole, however, slaves did not attempt to limit family size. Like southern whites, and unlike increasing numbers of northerners, the southern slave family maintained a close link between sexuality and reproduction.[40]

Interracial Sex in the South

In the South, as in the West, the mingling of races led to interracial sexual relations, but slavery restricted the possibilities for permanent unions and encouraged the pattern of white dominance. It is difficult to know the precise extent of sexual relations between white masters and black slaves, but the percentage of mulattoes among southern blacks provides a clue. Among free blacks in southern cities in 1860, close to forty percent were of mixed blood; for urban slaves, the proportion was twenty percent; and for rural slaves, it was only ten percent. Some historians cite these figures to argue that whites rarely had sex with blacks, since ninety-five percent of southern blacks were rural slaves.[41] From another perspective they suggest that children of mixed unions were more likely to be freed. Furthermore, in comparison to the large number of rural slaves, there were only a few white men who had access to them; thus, even if all planter-class men had sex with slaves, the mulatto population could have been as low as ten percent.

Whatever the actual extent of interracial sex, it is important to recognize that these unions did not simply involve powerless black victims subject to the total domination of white masters. Incidents of brutal rape and sadistic beatings of slave women, popularized in nineteenth-century abolitionist literature, did in fact take place. But when abolitionists emphasized these acts in the cause of opposing slavery, they often overlooked the ability of slaves to resist or circumvent the sexual advances of their masters. (They also attributed to slavery a form of sexual exploitation that occurred in the free-labor society of the North, where prostitution grew visibly by midcentury and working women had to contend with the sexual advances of their employers.) To characterize interracial sex purely in terms of the victimization of black women would be a distortion. Not only did black women resist sexual assault successfully, but in addition, sincerely affectionate unions sometimes formed between white men and black women. As in the colonial era, white men's access to black women continued to provide a critical link between the economic need of masters to reproduce their human property and their psychological need to dominate both blacks and women. At the same time, however, this volatile intersection of sex and race encompassed a range of relationships—from rape to informal marriages—some of which could challenge as well as support the status quo.

Both law and social thought encouraged white men to assume sexual access to female slaves. By legal definition, a slave could not be raped, since she was the property of her master. According to popular white opinion, black women had strong passions and always desired sexual relations. As a result, owners and overseers often approached slave women, expecting or commanding sexual relations to satisfy their own physical desires or confirm their superior status. Some men used brute force or the threat of severe whipping or sale to overcome women's resistance. As a Georgia slave explained to a white mistress, "When he make me follow him into de bush, what use me tell him no? He have strength to make me." One owner fathered children by many of his female slaves by beating reluctant partners, and other masters also resorted to whippings if slaves resisted their advances. A former slave recalled how a South Carolina master prevented the intervention of other slaves. He would tell a young female slave, "You go yonder and shell corn in de crib. He's de marster so she have to go. Then he send others to work some other place, then he go to the crib. He did dis to my very aunt and she had a mulatto boy." Male as well as female slaves suffered sexual humiliation from these assaults, as did a husband whose master told him "to go outside and wait 'til he do what he want to do" with the slave's wife.[42]

Despite the enormous power of slave owners to force women to have sex with them, the stories of women's resistance testify to the influence that slaves could at times exert over whites. Martha Bradley, an Alabama field-worker, took her hoe and knocked down an overseer when he "come 'roun and say sumpin' to me he had no bisness say." A cook named Sukie refused her master's order to take off her dress. When he tore it off, a former slave reminisced, "dat black gal got mad. She took an' punch ole Marsa . . . an' den she give him a shove an' push his hindparts down in de hot pot o' soap." In retaliation, however, the master sold Sukie to slave traders. Other women avoided being alone with seductive white men. One maid evaded the sexual advances of her master, first by taking her children to sleep with her and nailing up the windows of her house, and then by threatening to holler when he managed to enter during the night. Blacks and occasionally white women helped prevent masters from cornering female slaves. Finally, white men who raped black women might have to confront a husband's anger and efforts to defend his wife. In at least one case a male slave killed a master who raped his wife, even though he knew that he would die for his act.[43]

Although the rape of a female slave was probably the most common form of interracial sex, other types of unions also existed. Many white men took black mistresses, visiting them regularly in their quarters or setting up a special residence for the purpose of sexual relations. Occasionally, white men brought their black mistresses into their own homes, enraging the wives who were forced by propriety to remain silent. Some single men lived with concubines, referring to their mistresses as "housekeepers." In a rare case, Richard Johnson lived openly with Julia Chinn and acknowledged their two children, but they were condemned by planter society. Another interracial couple who married were run out of town for their act. More typical was the experience of the slave Louisa Picket, who was purchased as a concubine. "Mr. Williams told me what he bought me for soon as we started for New Orleans," she recalled. "He said if I behave myself he'd treat me well; but if not, he'd whip me almost to death." During his lifetime Williams never acknowledged their sexual relationship or their offspring, but in his will he freed Picket and their four children.[44]

For those men who preferred light-skinned women as concubines, a "fancy trade" in women operated in New Orleans and Charleston. Interracial patterns in the lower South resembled those of the West Indies, where sexual mingling took place to a much greater extent. Both slave and free black women in Louisiana participated in forms of concubinage. A fancy girl could bring in more than twice the price of a prime field hand and would enjoy a less taxing life, as well. Freeborn light-skinned women contracted sexual relations with white men through a system known as *plaçage*. A white gentleman usually met one of these free black women at a Louisiana quadroon ball and then courted her, making a formal arrangement to support her and their children for a period of several years to a lifetime.[45] The concubine might be able to use her sexuality to negotiate an economic partnership with a white man. Sex could thus become one of the few areas of economic exchange open to black women. Whatever leverage they may have achieved, however, the bartering of sexuality reinforced notions of sexual availability that would haunt black women long after slavery ended. In addition, the open concubinage of New Orleans left a legacy of a multiracial society that represented the worst fears of whites, who opposed any mixing of the races.

Aside from open concubinage, more discreet long-term unions between white men and black women involved both economic negotiation and sincere affection. The former slave "Linda Brent" recalled that at age fifteen, she constantly evaded her master's unwanted sexual advances in order to preserve her purity and self-respect, but when another white man appealed to her, she agreed to have sex with him. Contrasting the two sexual possibilities, she explained that "[i]t seems less degrading to give one's self, than to submit to compulsion. There is something akin to freedom in having a lover who has no control over you, except that which he gives by kindness and attachment."[46] When white men emancipated their mistresses and mulatto children in their wills they implied that more than mere physical exploitation characterized these relationships. The Virginia planter Ralph Quarles, who held antislavery views, made his slave Lucy the mistress of his household and treated their four children as his own, educating and eventually emancipating them. In Georgia, South Carolina, and Mississippi, prominent white planters left wills directing the emancipation of their slave mistresses and children. In 1854, Elijah Willis of South Carolina attempted to free his slave mistress and her children, four of whom were his own, by taking them to Ohio. Similarly, a Louisiana slave owner took his slave and their children first to Ohio and then to Texas, where they lived as man and wife. Another master willed money to the slave who had become his "adopted wife."[47] These arrangements proved vulnerable to the whim of relatives, however. Elijah Willis died during the journey north, and his family contested his will by suggesting that he was insane to have allowed a black woman to act as the mistress of his household. Henry Grimke's will asked that his slave mistress, Nancy Weston, and her children be treated as members of the family, but his heirs disregarded his wishes and treated them as servants.[48]

As in the colonial period, the least frequent—or least frequently acknowledged—interracial relationship was that between a white woman and a black man. Women of the yeoman or poor white classes had sexual relations with and married mulatto men. Frequent references in court records to black children born of white mothers attest to these unions. In New Orleans, where police sent white women to jail for one- to six-month terms for having sex with black men, the law was less strictly applied to lower-class women. The extent of illicit sex between women of the planter class and black slaves is not well documented. One Virginia wife lived for six years "in open adultery with a negro man," and some planters' wives gave birth to light-skinned mulatto children.[49] An observer believed that the daughters of small planters and other white women who came into regular contact with slaves did in fact have sexual relations with them and may even have "compelled some of the men to have something to do with them."[50] Because unions of planter-class white women and black men so inverted the southern racial and sexual hierarchy, an intriguing historical silence masks their frequency and dynamics.

Reconstruction: Sex and Social Control

The emancipation of the slaves and the era of Reconstruction presented both new opportunities and new challenges to the struggle of southern blacks to achieve some degree of sexual freedom. On the one hand, emancipation enabled former slaves to enjoy the privileges of legal marriage, to reunite long-separated families, and to escape the paternalistic control their former owners had exercised over courtship, marriage, and parenthood. On the other hand, the dismantling of slavery initiated a new and terrifying era in southern race relations in which sexuality became one of the central means of reasserting white social control over blacks.

The postwar South witnessed widespread family formation and re-formation among blacks. Some southern states automatically validated slave marriages after emancipation, while others required formal registration. In both cases, slaves eagerly legitimated their unions, holding mass-marriage ceremonies and individual weddings. As one couple explained, they "didn't know if de first marriage was good or not," so they held a formal wedding. In 1866, over nine thousand couples registered their marriages in a seventeen-county area of North Carolina, indicating the eagerness of former slaves to affirm their unions. For those who had been separated, some of whom had remarried, family reconstitution could be wrought with emotion. A literate couple, separated by sale during slavery, corresponded gingerly about the possibility of reunion after one had taken a new mate. Anticipating her former husband's return, Willie Ann Grey wrote to him in romantic terms: "I know that I have lived with you and loved you then and love you still. Every time I hear from you my love grows strong."[51]

Both black ministers and the northern teachers and missionaries who came to the South during Reconstruction preached the sexual values of premarital chastity and monogamous marriage. Some blacks embraced these views, along with the ideal of the middle-class separate spheres and the importance of female purity. Like free blacks in the North who aspired to middle-class respectability, postwar southern freedmen associated "race progress" with the values of chastity and fidelity. Many adopted the dominant ideology. They sought to defend black women's honor and establish stable families. As in the northern states, the large majority of black families in the postbellum South consisted of male-headed, two-parent households. At the same time, however, older black sexual practices persisted long after emancipation. According to late-nineteenth-century census reports, for example, southern blacks continued to practice premarital intercourse and to accept the birth of children before marriage.[52]

The Civil War benefited blacks by allowing the legitimation of families, but it also set the stage for a sexual battleground that would rage long past Reconstruction. As Herbert Gutman has written, "Military occupation and emancipation unsettled the exploitative sexual ties" of slavery. Black women's vulnerability to sexual abuse by whites did not disappear with the eradication of slavery. For one, northern soldiers who shared southerners' assumptions about the sexual passions of black women both raped black women and girls and took black concubines. In addition, during Reconstruction southerners unleashed their rage against freed slaves by sexually assaulting black women. Whites, arguing that black men lusted after white women, also used the specter of black sexual violence against whites to terrorize black men and ultimately to justify lynching.

Both poor and "upstanding" white men responded to the granting of political rights to black men by attacking black women. In Louisiana, for example, two well-known white men broke into Martha Kemp's home in the middle of the night and attempted to have sex with her and another woman. When Kemp explained that she was "a woman of the church and did not do such things," the men hit her and threatened to shoot her. In another Louisiana case, the son of a white employer raped the daughter of a black worker, while in Texas four white men raped the daughter of a black man. During the Memphis race riot in 1866, whites attacked and killed black people, burned their homes, robbed and gang raped former slaves, raped several other black women at gunpoint, and attempted to rape a black child. In 1871, Harriet Smirl, wife of a black radical Republican in Columbia, South Carolina, told a congressional committee of her ordeal. Ku Klux Klan members had beaten her husband and later returned when she was alone in the house. They spit in her face, threw dirt in her eyes, told her to make her husband vote Democratic, and then gang raped her. When black men responded to these outrages and attempted to protect black women from the sexual assaults of white men, they became subject to physical attack themselves. In at least one case, a white sheriff authorized the public, sadistic beating of a black man who had tried to protect his wife's virtue.[53]

White men's violent response to emancipation represented one part of a wider quest by southern whites to replace slavery with a new system of social control over blacks. Once the absolute white dominance inherent in ownership no longer operated, whatever paternalism may have existed under slavery quickly became extinct. Now that blacks posed the threat of becoming social and political equals, whites sought new ways to maintain racial supremacy. Sexuality became a "weapon of terror" with which to intimidate blacks and keep them from assuming social equality with whites. But sexuality was not simply another weapon alongside lynching, arson, and outright murder. Sexual domination had particular meanings for southern whites, not only because of the access white men had to black women under slavery, but also because the demise of slavery reopened the troubling question of the status of children born of interracial unions. Who would they be now that slavery no longer made them the property of white owners? What, indeed, would happen to the concept of white supremacy if social and sexual mixture took place among free blacks and whites?

Historian Leon Litwack has suggested that the fear of racial mixture, outside of a system of white dominance, underlay the opposition to integration that so pervaded the South in the late nineteenth century. Although explicitly a means to prevent the races from associating in public accommodations, the institutionalization of segregation in the late-nineteenth-century South rested upon a deep-seated fear that social mixing would lead to sexual mixing. As one southerner explained, "if we have intermarriage we shall degenerate; we shall become a race of mulattoes; we shall be another Mexico; we shall be ruled out from the family of white nations. Sir, it is a matter of life and death with the Southern people to keep their blood pure." Although white men fully expected to continue to have sexual access to black women, they refused to consider the possibility that white women marry black men or that the children of interracial unions be recognized as legitimate heirs of whites. The fear of mixing led southern states to pass new laws to prevent interracial marriage during the 1860s, and the term *miscegenation* first appeared in these laws.[54]

During the brief period in which they had a political voice in southern state governments, black men attempted to reform the laws governing interracial sex to extend legal protection to black women who had sexual relations with white men and to their mulatto children. Blacks hoped to make white fathers responsible for their bastard children and to outlaw the system of concubinage by forcing legal marriage upon cohabiting interracial couples. Similarly, black women exerted pressure to legitimize interracial unions. At least one quadroon mistress threatened to deny her services to a planter unless he married her. In the words of a northern observer, Mississippi concubines "not only kicked against the pricks, they actually began to wear armor against them." In New Orleans, black concubines married their white partners in the decade after the

Civil War, and a small number of black men married white women. Elsewhere, black women brought paternity suits against the white fathers of their children.[55]

In the long run, however, blacks failed to legalize interracial sexual relations and to protect black women within them. Bastardy laws passed by Reconstruction legislatures were later repealed, and none of the legal reforms of concubinage passed. Rather, southern state legislatures outlawed interracial marriage, while courts and vigilantes prosecuted those who defied the ban. White men who slept with black women continued to escape criticism. Indeed, when black women were no longer the property of only a small number of white men, they became sexually available to all white men. As a result, the number of mulattoes increased after emancipation. But black men who courted or married white women could, along with their female partners, expect trouble, foreshadowing the lynch law that soon emerged throughout the South. In Alabama, for example, a black man went to jail and paid a steep fine for proposing to marry a white woman in 1867; a decade later a white woman spent two years in prison for marrying a black man. When a former slave courted a "yaller woman" in Mississippi, a white man delivered a beating to enforce his warning that even a mulatto was off limits.[56] Thus, in the post-Reconstruction South, as in the West, whites asserted sexual dominance as one means of insuring political and economic dominance over members of other races.

Attitudes toward interracial sex reflected larger social dynamics in nineteenth-century America. In an era of rapid change, marked by anxiety about the maintenance of social order, the northern middle class clung to ideals of family stability, female purity, and male self-control. When members of this group encountered people of other races, whose sexual patterns differed from their own, their reactions were both extreme and ambivalent. For one, whites stereotyped other groups as negative images of their own ideals. By labeling them sexual savages, whites reassured themselves that their own race was indeed the civilized one it aspired to be. Distancing themselves from the sexuality of other races served instrumental, as well as symbolic, purposes. By characterizing other races as, at best, remote sexual pagans and, at worst, sexual monsters in pursuit of white women, whites could manipulate the sexual fears of their own culture in order to justify the conquest of Indians, Mexicans, and blacks. In the latter case, southerners invoked the specter of miscegenation to support their efforts to deny freed black people full citizenship and to create a racially segregated society based on a rule of terror. Thus, despite missionary efforts at conversion, white Americans had an investment in maintaining the differences between themselves and people of other races.

Given their own unique traditions, the preindustrial economic patterns they maintained, and the ambivalence of white "civilizers," it is not surprising that other racial groups maintained their own distinctive sexual customs throughout the nineteenth century. Whites influenced the patterns of sexual life wherever they had contact, but middle-class morality did not supplant older sexual traditions. Outside of the white middle class, for instance, neither reticence nor privacy characterized the treatment of sexuality. In addition, many Indians, Mexicans, and blacks accepted consensual unions, and they did not necessarily stigmatize children born outside of marriage as "illegitimate." Traditional church and community sanctions, rather than the internalized individual controls of the middle class, maintained sexual norms in these groups. Fertility rates remained high, and as in preindustrial societies, reproduction, love, and erotic desire coexisted within marriage.

Throughout much of the nineteenth century, the meaning of sexuality for white middle-class Americans balanced uncomfortably between the reproductive moorings of the past and the romantic and erotic leanings of the present, between female control and male license, between private passion and public reticence. No wonder that the sexuality of minority races became a foil against which whites redefined themselves. Alternative sexual systems threatened the precarious balance of white sexuality. Even more threatening was the challenge from within their own culture, as sexuality moved beyond the family and into the public sphere.

1. A Massachusetts fornication case: "The Jurors for our Sovereign Lord the King having upon their Oath presented that Phinehas Parker of Groton in the County of Middlesex Gentleman and Mehitabel Flanders of Contoocuck in the Province of New hampshire Single Woman and Sempster on the last Day of November AD 1748 at Groton aforesaid carnally knew each other, had carnal Knowledge of each other's Bodies & committed the Crime of Fornication together in evil Example to others against the Peace of our Said Lord the King and the Law of this Province in that Case made and provided. . . ." Parker pleaded guilty and was fined five pounds and costs. (Courtesy of the Commonwealth of Massachusetts Archives.)

2–3. Native American Indian culture included explicit representations of sexual acts, such as this Cherokee stone pipe, portraying oral and anal sex between humans and animals, and this Hopi katcina doll with an erect phallus. Missionaries attempted to suppress native art and religious ceremonies that offended Christian sensibilities. (Pipe courtesy Museum of the American Indian, Heye Foundation, New York; Doll courtesy of Carnegie Museum, Division of Anthropology, Pittsburgh.)

4. Frontispiece and title page from the 1788 American edition of *Aristotle's Master-piece,* the most popular printed source of reproductive and sexual lore in the colonies. The illustration reflects contemporary beliefs that parents could influence the outcome of birth by their moods or thoughts during conception. (Courtesy of the Rare Books Division, Library of Congress.)

CONSTITUTION
Of the SOCIETY *for the* SUPPRESSION *of*
Vice and Immorality.

WE the Subfcribers, Inhabitants of the Borough of Wilmington, and its Neighbourhood, taking into our ferious confideration, the awful prevalence of Vice and Immorality, at the prefent time; and being impreffed with a fenfe of the duty, which we conceive to be incumbent on ourfelves and others; do hereby agree to affociate, for the purpofe of aiding the civil Authority of the State of Delaware—the Burgeffes of Wilmington, and other Magiftrates and Officers of New-Caftle County—in bringing to conviction Offenders againft the Laws which at prefent exift, or may hereafter be enacted, for the fuppreffion of Vice and Immorality. We alfo engage, that we will ufe our influence and exertions, to fupprefs practices fo evil in their nature, and deftructive in their confequences, by endeavouring to reftrain the young and inconfiderate by our *example and advice*, and to effect the reformation of the *Obftinate* and *Refractory*, by bringing them under the power of thofe Laws, which they may be found guilty of violating. We further agree, that we will earneftly endeavour by all *Conftitutional means*, to obtain from the Legiflature of the State of Delaware, and from the Corporation of the Borough of Wilmington, the enacting of fuch further Laws, as may be found neceffary to promote the objects of this Affociation.

Among the Vices which are at prefent prevalent, we confider the prophanation of the Lord's Day, or the Firft Day of the Week, by numerous claffes of Citizens, particularly by the young and rifing generation—perfons retailing Liquors contrary to the Laws of this State—keeping Tippling-Houfes and other Houfes of ill-fame—gambling-Houfes—riotous or disorderly affemblages of perfons, all prophane curfing and fwearing, and taking the name of God in vain—as demanding our ferious attention.

In order to purfue the objects for which we affociate, depending on *Divine Affiftance* for fuccefs, we agree to be governed by the following Rules—which however, may be amended, altered, or repealed by a majority of *Two Thirds* of the whole number of members of the Society—But fpecial notice fhall be given at leaft *Ten Days* before the meeting, at which it is intended that any fuch alterations fhall be made.

5. Although brothels had been rare in the colonial period, by the late eighteenth century, citizens in cities such as Wilmington, Delaware, decried the prevalence of vice, including houses of ill-fame, and organized to suppress them. (Courtesy of the Historical Society of Delaware.)

7. This comic "Toby jug," possibly intended to mock the British, illustrates the incorporation of explicit, phallic humor in the popular culture of the early nineteenth century. (Courtesy of the Kinsey Institute for Research in Sex, Gender and Reproduction.)

6. An enterprising engraver transformed these pennies into sexual jokes during the 1840s, defying the growing trend toward reticence. (Courtesy of the Kinsey Institute for Research in Sex, Gender and Reproduction.)

THE FEMALE ABORTIONIST.

8. From the 1840s through the 1870s, New York newspapers condemned the notorious Madame Restell, who provided thousands of abortions to married and single women. An infant-devouring monster replaces her womb in this drawing of "The Female Abortionist" in *The Police Gazette*.

9. Advertisements for contraceptives, such as "Rubber Goods," and abortifacients —as well as remedies for venereal disease—could be found in nineteenth-century newspapers, even after the passage of the Comstock Laws in 1873.

10. Although Indians did not sexually assault white women during the wars of the colonial period, American artists frequently depicted savage warriors ravishing innocent women. (Courtesy of the Massachusetts Historical Society.)

11. Critiques of slavery often emphasized violations of female modesty as well as physical brutality. Like the representations of Indian attacks, exposés of sexual assault against women slaves may have been intended to titillate viewers. (Courtesy of the Schomburg Collection, New York Public Library.)

12. This 1834 northern critique of "family amalgamation" showed an unlikely scene in which a planter and his family casually accepted an interracial child at the table. (Courtesy of the Print Division, Library of Congress.)

13. In nineteenth-century cities, working-class men and women met and courted at dance halls, some of which catered to sailors and waterfront laborers.

14. The growth of prostitution in the mid-nineteenth century evoked social comment in the *Police Gazette,* which compared a female procurer to "the gaudy spider spreading her webs for the flies who make her loathsome trade profitable." Above, gentlemen cavort with prostitutes in "Gotham's Palaces of Sin."

H-r furniture is of the most costly, and the decorations and upholstering will vie with any we have seen. Her lady boarders are courteous, pretty and accommodating. The hostess is a lady of pleasing manners, sociable, and well understand the art of entertaining visitors. The wines are the best the market affords, selected from the best brands, and cannot be surpassed. In fact, she seeks nothing but the pleasure of her visitors. We know of no better house to recommend strangers and others to, than this.

MRS. EVERETT,
No. 158 Laurens St.

This is a quiet, safe and respectable house, and altogether on the assignation order, and conducted on true Southern principles. She accommodates a few charming and beautiful lady boarders, who are from the sunny South, and equal to any of its class in the city. The proprietress strictly superintends the operations of her household, which is always in perfect order. The beautiful senoritas are quite accomplished, sociable and agreeable, and pattern after the much admired landlady. Gentlemen visitors from the South and West, are confidently recommended to this pleasant, quiet and safe abode. The landlady possesses all the charming mannerisms which so highly characterize that soothing clime. The very best wines constantly kept on hand, and selected from the best brands the market affords.

MISS CLARA GORDON,
No. 119 Mercer St.

We cannot too highly recommend this house, the lady herself is a perfect venus: beautiful, entertaining and supremely seductive. Her aids-decamp are really charming and irresistible, and altogether honest and honorable. Miss G. is a great belle, and her mansion is patronized by Southern merchants and planters principally. She is highly accomplished, skilful and prudent, and sees her visitors are well entertained. Good Wines of the most elaborate brands, constantly on hand; and in all, a finer resort cannot be found in the city.

MISS THOMPSON.
No. 75 Mercer st.

This lady keeps one of the largest and most magnificiently furnished mansions in the central part of the city. She has spared no expense in fitting up this establishment—which is furnished, and decorated in the most superb style. The hostess is a great favorite, and always happy to see her friends and visitors. She accommodates a number of handsome lady boarders, who are agreeable and accomplished. We recommend visitors and others to give them a call, and partake of the good things of this life.

MISS MARY TEMPLE,
No. 122 Green st.

This is an elegantly fitted up mansion, conveni-

15. This 1859 published guide to houses of prostitution in America's large cities described in detail what various brothels offered. (Courtesy of the New-York Historical Society.)

16. "A Chinese Bangio, San Francisco," in the 1880s. Young Chinese contract laborers served as prostitutes on the West Coast. (Courtesy of the Amon Carter Museum, Fort Worth, Texas.)

17. With its typical sensationalism, *The Police Gazette* alleged "obscene orgies and pernicious teachings of the patriarch Noyes among the novices of his saintly sect" at the Oneida, New York, utopian community.

18. The flamboyant Victoria Woodhull brought the issue of free love into the open in the 1870s. Thomas Nast satirized the various protagonists in *Harper's Weekly* in 1872. A wife saddled with children and a drunken husband tells the "satanic" Woodhull, "I'd rather travel the hardest path of matrimony than follow your footsteps." (Courtesy of the New York Historical Society.)

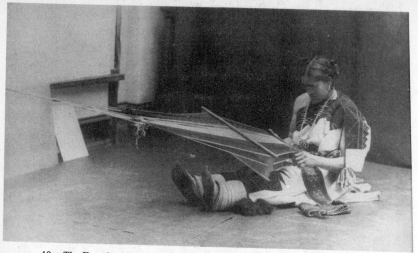

19. The French settlers applied the term "berdache," derived from a word for buggery, to American Indian men who dressed and worked as women. Here We-Wa, a Zuni man, performs women's work in 1879. (Courtesy of the National Archives.)

A SECRET FOR YEARS.

Luisa Matson Masqueraded as a Man.

HER SEX REVEALED IN JAIL.

A Strange Story of Her Career Told to the Officials.

THEY ARE INCLINED TO DOUBT IT.

Sho Says She Came From Australia—Onco Engaged to Marry a Young Lady Who Had Money.

Milton B. Matson.

20. In California, Luisa Matson adopted a male identity in order to earn money and court other women, a practice frequently reported in newspapers of the late nineteenth century. (Courtesy of the Bancroft Library, University of California, Berkeley.)

21 and 22.   These drawings from a New Orleans newspaper in the 1890s suggest a heightened awareness of the erotic possibilities in same-sex relationships. (Courtesy of the Tulane University Library.)

23. In the late nineteenth century, reproductions of *Nymphs and Satyr* (1873), by the French artist Adolph William Bouguereau, hung over the bars of men's saloons throughout the country. (Courtesy of the Sterling and Francine Clark Art Institute, Williamstown, Massachusetts.)

24. *Cupid and Psyche* (1843), William Page's depiction of the classical myth of sexual and romantic union, may be the most erotic painting in nineteenth-century America. The National Academy of Art refused to exhibit it because of its nudity. (Courtesy of the M.H. de Young Memorial Museum, San Francisco.)

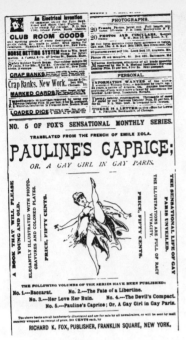
25.   The growth of sexual commerce included advertisements for mail-order obscene pictures and racy stories, which censorship laws attempted to suppress.

26.   As part of its social purity crusade, the Women's Christian Temperance Union in 1896 prevented "Bacchante," by sculptor Frederick William MacMonnies, from being exhibited at the Boston Public Library. (Courtesy of the Metropolitan Museum of Art.)

27.   By 1915, Anthony Comstock's campaign against obscenity appeared ludicrous to this cartoonist for *The Masses,* a radical magazine that championed the new morality of sexual freedom.

Drawn by Robert Hunt.

"Your Honor, this woman gave birth to a naked child!"

28. Accompanied by her children, a mother offers support to Margaret Sanger, whose 1916 trial for illegally dispensing contraceptives at a birth control clinic in Brooklyn brought the new movement publicity. (Courtesy of the Print Division, Library of Congress.)

29. For many Southern rural families in the early twentieth century, sexuality was still closely tied to reproduction. (Courtesy of Walter Rosenblum.)

30.   In 1905, artist John Sloan espied this scene in a New York tenement. A working-class couple playfully embraces as their child watches. (Courtesy of Helen Farr Sloan.)

31.   Young working girls flocked to the commercialized amusements available in early twentieth-century cities. Here Sloan depicts them enjoying such penny pleasures as "Girls in Their Night Gowns," and "Those Naughty Girls." (Courtesy of Helen Farr Sloan.)

32. While the controversy over higher education for women in the late nineteenth century focused on the damage of study to the reproductive system, this pamphlet sensationalized the effect of college on female morals.

33–34. In one illustration from white slavery tracts, 1910, a dark, predatory dragon symbolized the danger that young women faced in the big city. In the other, a panderer entices a hesitant woman to enter a dance hall. The sign for "Hotel Rooms By Day" suggests the proximity of opportunities for illicit sex. (Courtesy of Special Collections, University of North Carolina–Greensboro.)

CHAPTER 6

Outside the Family

IN 1885, twenty-seven-year-old Frederick Ryman lived alone in Catskill, New York, where he wrote poetry and letters to the editor, lived off a small inheritance, and fancied himself a latter-day Byron. Although Ryman's poetry earned neither fame nor fortune, he left a rich historical legacy in his extensive diaries, which provide a rare personal account of male sexual experience during the nineteenth century. Ryman was by no means a typical American man. An atheist, he espoused free-love doctrines, passionately loved the poetry of Walt Whitman, and championed women's rights to equal education and employment. Nonetheless, the adventures he recorded at length in his diaries disclose a sexual subculture that Ryman shared with other single men and women of his era.

One crisp Sunday morning in February 1885, Fred Ryman set out for the nearby city of Hudson to visit Claude Macy, a close male friend about whom he wrote, "I can truly say I *love.*" But on this visit, a man's love was not his object. "I told Claude plump and plain that I had come up to Hudson for some horizontal happiness," Ryman later recorded in his diary. In the past the young writer had sought sexual pleasure with one of the "mistresses" he courted; at least once he had invited a young woman he did not know to his room for the night and was shocked when she expected him to pay for her company. But this excursion, Ryman reminisced, was "the first time in my life that I ever took a Vigil of Venus in a regular Villa of Venus and it is the second time I ever gave any woman money as a direct payment for pleasure." He later justified this violation of his free-love principles in economic terms:

> I was simply suffering for something and I felt as if I should go crazy if I did not get it soon & I don't know but it is cheaper and more fun to pay a professional than

it is to fool around with these d——d nonentities who cackle so much about virtue. This only cost me $2.00 & I had $5.00 worth of fun I can swear.

Ryman eased his remaining doubts about the propriety of going to a prostitute by referring to a physiological need to ejaculate. In contemporary slang, he revealed a number of methods men might use to achieve this goal, implying a hierarchy among them.

Perhaps I was wrong to go but "a stiff prick has no conscience" as the proverb says, & I believe I would have gone crazy almost if I had not gone to her or to some other similar lady. It is one of four things suck shuck buck or fuck & I'll be G——d d——d if I don't propose to fuck as long as I feel such a pressing of my vital fluid as I do now & d——n a man who will do either of the other three things [i.e., fellatio, masturbation, or sodomy].

When Fred and Claude arrived at Sue Best's brothel on this Sunday morning, "a lovely little blonde" who looked about eighteen years old greeted them "in a very cordial manner." Soon Ryman was "upstairs and in bed with the same little charmer and enjoying a vigil of Venus with her." He described her as a physical object and rated her sexual skills highly, despite behavior that he found unusual:

She had the plumpest & firmest legs and arms I ever saw on any woman I think. Her breasts were rather flabby but her arms & legs were as solid almost as a horse's four legs are next to the body. She played her part well though I usually prefer to have a woman lie perfectly quiet when I am enjoying a vigil. This "playing up" is not agreeable to me but she was truly one of the finest little armfulls of feminine voluptuousness I ever yet laid on the top of. She was not splendidly formed but she was voluptuous & quite gracious & being a blond was the kind of girl I could love I think to a certain extent.

Later that night, alone in his room, Ryman wrote a lengthy poem to the young prostitute, who called herself Lillie Costello. Aside from describing the sexual acts of the day, the verses emphasized Ryman's respect for the woman he had hired and so enjoyed:

> My Dear Little Lillie Costello
> I met you and crammed you today
> And I would I might be your best fellow
> So I with you often could play
>
> . . . .
>
> Today for the first time I met you
> And played with your pussy so cute

And Lillie if e'er I forget you
Then I am a crank & galoot.

. . . .

But Lillie you treated me kindly
Your price I paid freely & more
I'll say that I will not now blindly
Forget this & call you a "whore"

You're but like myself you need money
For food & for fun & for clothes

. . . .

Ryman went on to recall the "gush" of his orgasms, his postcoital bliss, and the kisses he placed on "lips covered with hair." He concluded by pledging his intentions toward Lillie: both "To Cram you again" and "to remain your true friend."[1]

Whether Fred Ryman fulfilled his promise is not known, but he did continue to enjoy a variety of erotic pleasures with women until he married several years later. As with other single men of his era, his sexual relations had begun neither in courtship nor in marriage, but in the growing opportunities for sex outside the family.

In colonial society, marriage had provided the only appropriate locus for sexual activity, and throughout the nineteenth century it remained the most common and acceptable sexual relationship. But as young men like Frederick Ryman discovered, opportunities for sexual expression gradually expanded. For one, small groups of individuals openly challenged marital sexuality when they espoused free love or joined utopian communities that offered alternatives to monogamous sexual relations ranging from celibacy to polygamy and group marriage. For some men and women, same-sex relationships developed outside the family, often mirroring patterns of romantic union in marriage. Sexuality also moved into the world of commerce. Expanding upon the limited sexual commerce of late-eighteenth-century cities, American entrepreneurs began to trade in sexual fantasy and sexual experience. They found a small market for their wares among men of all classes, especially single men who lived apart from families. At the same time, a growing class of working women found that the "wages of sin" paid more highly than did other forms of labor. At first, these expanding arenas for sexual expression enjoyed a degree of tolerance, for they were protected by the laissez-faire attitude toward morality and commerce. By the end of the century, however, sex outside the family had come to loom as a significant threat to the primacy of marital, reproductive sexuality, a threat that would not go unchallenged.

Utopian Alternatives

The utopian communities that sprang up from the late eighteenth through the mid-nineteenth centuries embodied both an older American quest for perfection and a more recent longing to recreate small-scale, homogeneous communities at a time of rapid urban and commercial growth. Many of these groups, including the free lovers, Shakers, Mormons, and Oneidans, experimented with alternative sexual systems. The sexual views of these utopians varied widely, but they shared a central concern about the proper way to regulate sexual impulses. In the more mobile and heterogeneous social world of the nineteenth century, the surveillance of individual sinners was no longer possible, nor could the ritual of confession, repentance, and reintegration into the community take place. For most Americans, the family had to suffice to train the young in sexual self-control. Mothers, aided by an extensive advice literature, taught their children moral values. Utopians, however, did not find these familial mechanisms sufficient. From the 1820s through the 1860s, these sexual dissidents created elaborate alternatives to the family. Although some free lovers found inspiration in the political legacy of the Revolutionary era, which emphasized individual rights and the pursuit of happiness, most utopians developed their sexual alternatives within the context of a religious movement for moral perfectionism.

The perfectionist spirit that swept American religious life in the early nineteenth century strongly influenced utopian sexual alternatives. A revival movement known as the Second Great Awakening incorporated into American culture a millenarian theology that encouraged men and women to approximate spiritual perfection. The revival inspired not only numerous reform movements—from temperance to abolitionism—but also the formation of separatist communities, or "backwoods utopias." Thousands of men and women left their homes to join these communitarian experiments. Some came in quest of spiritual perfection. Others, dissatisfied with the social order of industrializing America, sought alternatives to the burgeoning capitalist economy, rejecting private ownership for communitarian systems, and sometimes reviving agriculture or crafts in place of industrial labor.

Just as they sought alternatives to the religious and economic organization of American society, many utopians practiced forms of sexual perfectionism. Free lovers, Shakers, Mormons, and Oneidans each elaborated alternatives to the nuclear family and monogamous marital sexuality. Free lovers embraced the idea of individualism, extending it to its logical extreme and elevating love and desire, rather than reproduction, as the basis for sexual union. Mormons, in contrast, turned back to biblical models of the patriarchal family, reproductive sexuality, and strict community regulation. Shakers and Oneidans grappled with the troubling potential of the erotic by demanding extreme self-control along with community surveillance of sexuality. Thus, at its borders, utopians illuminated the tensions that pervaded the nineteenth-century sexual landscape: What was the place of intimacy and the erotic, when reproduction became less important as a goal of sexual relations? And who should regulate sexuality, the individual or the society?

Free love referred not to promiscuity—or sex with multiple partners—but to the belief that love, rather than marriage, should be the precondition for sexual relations. With intellectual origins in eighteenth-century libertarian views, its first American proponent, Frances Wright, was an ardent freethinker who opposed organized religion, slavery, and marriage. A Scottish orphan with independent wealth, close friend of Lafayette and of the utopian socialist Robert Owen, Wright emigrated to the United States in the 1820s. She first aroused controversy when, after visiting Owen's New Harmony utopia, she decided to establish her own, interracial, community. To encourage the emancipation of slaves by proving that they could become free laborers and equal citizens, Wright bought several blacks and set them to work alongside whites at Nashoba, Tennessee. An interracial abolitionist community would itself have offended the majority of Americans, northern or southern, but Wright had even more radical intentions. She had come to the conclusion that only the amalgamation of the races would resolve the conflicts inherent in a biracial society. As her sister explained to Nashoba's slaves, "we consider the proper basis of the sexual intercourse to be the unconstrained and unrestrained choice of both parties." Therefore, the Nashoba community permitted interracial sexual relations, regardless of marital ties, and such unions occasionally formed.

When orthodox abolitionists learned of these practices, they dissociated themselves from Wright and condemned her in their publications. In response, Wright formulated one of the earliest defenses of free love to appear in America. She based her theory on the belief that individuals who mutually desired sexual union should be constrained neither by marital status nor by race. In her vision, sex could be a key to human happiness, but society kept it from becoming so. Writing in 1827, when the middle class had begun to embrace female purity, Wright affirmed sexual passion as "the best source of human happiness" and criticized public opinion and social institutions for warping this naturally "noble" instinct. In reaction to the growing public reticence about sexuality, Wright initiated a century-long free-love attack on sexual silences. "[I]gnorant laws, ignorant prejudices, ignorant codes of morals," she wrote, condemned "one portion of the female sex to vicious excess, another to as vicious restraint, . . . and generally the whole of the male sex to debasing licentiousness, if not to loathsome brutality."[2] Only the free expression of sexual passion would undermine these powerful constraints that subverted its positive force.

The vehemence of the press's attacks on her, even after the Nashoba experiment had failed miserably, suggests how deeply Wright threatened basic principles of antebellum American society: the sanctity of marriage and family, the moral guardianship of women, and the superiority of the white race. One writer called her the "priestess of Beelzebub" and another proclaimed in 1829 that Fanny Wright "contemns and discards altogether the marriage contract and in effect recommends transforming this glorious world . . . into one vast immeasurable brothel; and concludes by anticipating the blending of the black and white population, as the social millenium."[3] At a time when women simply did not speak at public gatherings, Wright defied the ideology of the separate spheres and drew large crowds to her lectures. In response, angry mobs threatened to disrupt the meetings; during an 1838 speaking tour, violent riots followed her talks. No matter which reform Wright supported, whether universal public education or a decentralized banking system, the charge of free love was invoked to discredit her, and for years when women spoke in public, critics hurled the accusation of "Fanny Wrightism," intimating sexual immorality.

Her political opponents could not silence Frances Wright, but the weight of public opinion took a huge toll on her personal life. Despite her libertarian views, Wright could not bring herself to bear a child out of wedlock, and so she compromised her principles and in 1831 married the man who had impregnated her. As a result, until her death in 1852, Wright spent much of her energy struggling in private against the very marital constraints that she had publicly opposed. These efforts drained Wright, who had no political allies to support her. She soon deteriorated into a lonely and ineffective figure.

Ironically, at the time of her death, a free-love movement that might have championed Frances Wright was emerging within anarchist and utopian circles. Anarchists opposed on principle any state regulation of personal life. In contrast to middle-class culture, and unlike members of the recently established women's rights movement, the anarchists did not shy away from the public discussion of sexuality.[4] Elaborating on the romantic ideal that linked sexuality to love, anarchist writers such as Marx Edgeworth Lazarus and Stephen Pearl Andrews attacked the "sexual slavery" of women who were forced to bear children in "loveless marriages." The title of Lazarus's 1852 tract *Love vs. Marriage* embodied the free-love message that emerged at midcentury. Just as the state thwarted the individual, so did the "legalized prostitution" of marriage oppress women and suppress love. Anarchists believed that a just society had to be based upon freely chosen personal relationships. In the words of one free lover—later jailed for putting his beliefs into practice—marriage was "the head and cornerstone of the temple of injustice, darkness, disease, death, and all the countless ills that afflict us."[5] Free love was the first step to their cure.

During the 1850s, small groups of men and women who shared the belief that "passional attraction" rather than legal marriage should bind individuals together gathered to discuss or practice free love. Some met in New York City at Stephen Pearl Andrews's Broadway salon, known as "The Grand Order of Recreation." In 1855, however, sensationalist newspaper accounts of the salon compared it to a brothel and accused the members of practicing "barbarism." As a result, police raided the club and arrested its members, who were later acquitted. In the meantime, Andrews and other anarchists practiced free love at two short-lived utopian communities: Modern Times, on Long Island, and Berlin Heights, near Cleveland, Ohio.[6]

Two Modern Times participants, Mary Gove Nichols and Thomas Low Nichols, carried the free-love message even further than these separatist experiments, championing the free-love critique of both marriage and of uncontrolled sexuality. The author of anti-masturbation and women's health tracts in the 1840s, Mary Gove had once run a "Grahamite" boardinghouse that incorporated the health reformer's dietary principles. She also embraced dress reform, opposing the tight-laced corsets then in vogue for women. Gove became personally interested in free love when she herself left an abusive husband and later formed free unions with more congenial men. Eventually she married Thomas Low Nichols, a hydropathic physician. The couple ran a water-cure institute and published journals sympathetic to free love. Their popular books *Esoteric Anthropology* (1853) and *Marriage: Its History, Character and Results* (1854) elaborated the free-love claim that marriage was a form of prostitution that encouraged libertinism. They also founded their own free-love community, Memnonia, near Yellow Springs, Ohio, which lasted for a year. Although the pair ultimately toned down their sexual advice, converted to Catholicism, and embraced middle-class respectability, at midcentury they tried to popularize the free-love alternative to marriage.[7]

The Nicholses marriage guides called for free choice of sexual partners, insisted on a woman's right to choose when to have children, and advocated birth control. In addition, they stressed two points that would recur throughout late-nineteenth-century free-love literature. First, they employed eugenic arguments to justify free-love practices. Echoing the hereditarian ideas of nineteenth-century science, they claimed that children born of freely chosen unions would have biological advantages over those conceived by force; the latter, they believed, would be more susceptible to the "diseases" of masturbation, insanity, and criminality. Second, like other utopians, the Nicholses sought to balance their belief in individual sexual freedom with the need for individual restraint. Defending free lovers from the charges of promiscuity so often leveled against them, they insisted that sexual union should take place only when love was present *and* procreation desired. Mary Gove Nichols, embracing a romantic ideal of sexuality as spiritual union, wrote that most women desired sex only under these circumstances. Thomas Low Nichols suggested that women had the capacity for greater sexual pleasure than did men; nonetheless, he recommended only monthly intercourse, for procreative purposes, between monogamous free-love partners.[8]

By midcentury, free love had emerged as a radical means of resolving the conflict between the sexual freedom demanded by the ideal of individualism and the self-control thought to be required by the necessities of social order. While free-love advocates placed sexuality at the center of their political discourse, other utopian groups, founded primarily upon religious or economic principles, also struggled with the dilemmas posed by the transformation of sexuality in the nineteenth century. Of the dozens of communitarian experiments established in the United States, three groups—the Shakers, the Mormons, and the Oneidans—offer an especially revealing perspective on the sexual discontents of American society. Each sect established a distinctive alternative to the norm of monogamous, marital sexuality. Shakers chose celibacy; Mormons practiced polygamy, and the followers of John Humphrey Noyes at the Oneida community engaged in "complex marriage." In each experiment, these utopians sought a new balance between the erotic and reproductive meanings of sexuality and between individual and community regulation of both sex and reproduction.

The Shaker religion had been founded in the eighteenth century by Ann Lee, an English Quaker whose four children all died in infancy. In addition to her traumatic reproductive history, a series of religious visions helped convince Ann Lee that sexual relations were the basis of all evil. Between her arrival in America in 1774 and her death in 1784, she preached celibacy to her followers, who gathered in rural communitarian settlements based on plain living. In the 1790s, her successors drew new members into several Shaker "families," and during the religious revivals of the Second Great Awakening, membership expanded. By 1860, six thousand Shakers lived in eighteen villages in upstate New York and the old Northwest.[9]

The Shakers adopted the Christian view that the shameful curse of sexuality resulted when Eve yielded to the serpent, who "infused into her mind the filthy passion of *lust.*" Like Christian monastics, Shakers believed in transcending physical lust in order to live the life of the spirit. Unlike the monastics, however, Shakers resided in sexually integrated communities. Although men and women had separate quarters and were forbidden to speak or walk together, they nonetheless saw each other regularly at work, meals, and worship. To overcome the temptation of carnal desire, the Shakers demanded extreme self-control. "And when ye are together, and in any way begin to feel your natures excited," their rules explained, "withdraw immediately from each other's presence, and war against that filthy spirit." Significantly, Shakers supplemented individual restraints with community controls. During the 1840s, for example, Shakers established minute regulations for monitoring physical behavior. Children could not bathe unattended, "lest they tempt each other"; animals could not be kept as pets, lest their copulations invite imitation or participation; brothers and sisters in the extended Shaker family could not even pass on the stairs, so women stepped aside to let men proceed. Through careful surveillance, members attempted to prevent masturbation, homosexuality, bestiality, and, indeed, any physical touching between men and women.[10]

The Shakers abolished reproductive sexuality by instituting celibacy, but they did not necessarily eliminate eroticism from their midst. In fact, the Shaker way of life—including the elaborate rules concerning sexual propriety—may well have focused attention upon the erotic. Shaker religious practices spiritualized physical desire through rituals such as individual trances and group dances. Women, especially, enjoyed physical release during spiritual visions, when they rolled and fell on the ground as if possessed. Although men and women could not touch during the ritual dance, they could be "moved by the spirit" to step, jump, clap, cry out, and twirl convulsively. One observer thought that the dancing "neutralized the desire for coition." In contrast, it may have served as an acceptable form of erotic release, experienced by the individual but in the presence of the community and in the name of the spirit.[11]

While the Shakers proscribed reproduction, the Mormons glorified procreation as the sole aim of sexuality. Mormon founder Joseph Smith had introduced plural marriage in 1843, and his successor, Brigham Young, publicly revealed polygamy as a Mormon principle in 1852. Polygamy allowed men to take additional wives but strictly forbade women to engage in any pre- or extramarital relations. In practice, only a small proportion of the male leadership—perhaps under one-fourth—could afford to keep more than one wife.[12] Nevertheless, the American public perceived the already unpopular sect as, above all, composed of sexual infidels. Concerned Protestant missionaries and women writers attempted to emancipate plural wives from their alleged sexual slavery. The author of *Apples of Sodom,* one of dozens of antipolygamy novels written by Protestant women, claimed that the "accursed system" made "*brutes* and *tyrants* of men." "This vile doctrine," claimed another exposé of polygamy, "has destroyed the peace of happy, inoffensive neighborhoods, and seduced many a virtuous and respectable woman into vices from which there is no redemption." From the 1860s through the 1880s, the federal government prosecuted Mormons who engaged in polygamy.[13]

Despite the Mormons' public image of sexual depravity, they were, in fact, sexually conservative. Their ideas reached back to preindustrial times and drew as well upon biblical notions of patriarchy. Polygamy, in essence, extended the traditional patriarchal family beyond the boundaries of one household. Just as southern men took slave mistresses and northern men visited prostitutes, Mormon men affirmed male dominance when they took additional mates, a privilege unavailable to women. Unlike the northern middle classes, for whom marital intimacy and reproductive control became increasingly important during the nineteenth century, the Mormons rejected romantic love, intense courtship, and contraception. Sexuality had one purpose—procreation. Polygamy maximized opportunities for reproduction by using every available woman in the primary role of childbearer. Equally important, Mormon theology required earthly bodies in order to baptize the souls of one's ancestors *in absentia.* The man who fathered many children gained prestige because he enabled past relatives to be saved.[14]

Mormons recognized sexual desire in both men and women, but they opposed its expression outside of reproductive sex. The leadership forbade masturbation and premarital sex, as well as contraception. As in the seventeenth century, adultery was a capital offense. The colonies had ceased to enforce this punishment, but among Mormons, some men and women were in fact executed for adultery. Miscegenation, bestiality, and incest were also capital crimes. In 1857, Henry Jones, who "had previously been emasculated on a charge of bestiality," was accused of incest, a crime for which both he and his mother died. To prevent these illicit practices and to achieve spiritual perfection, the Mormons demanded that men master their own flesh. They believed that women lacked the ability to control their passions, so men had to supervise them, channeling women toward reproductive sexual relations within single or plural marriages. Despite women's efforts to subvert it, this system of male control proved extremely effective. Premarital pregnancies did occur, but less frequently than in what Mormons called the "gentile" world; wives did attempt to space births by late weaning, but reproductive rates remained high. The community as a whole valued propagation and male control and continued to do so even after the Mormon church withdrew approval for polygamy in 1890.[15]

Perhaps the most elaborate alternative sexual system of the nineteenth century was the "sexual communism" developed by John Humphrey Noyes and practiced by his followers in Putney, Vermont (1846–1848), and after their expulsion, in Oneida, New York (1848–1879). Noyes attempted to place not only property but also sexuality and reproduction under communal control.

In addition, he designed a unique means of controlling reproduction while exploring the erotic possibilities of sexuality.

As in the case of Ann Lee, personal crisis partly inspired Noyes to experiment with an alternative sexual system. His wife, Harriet, had survived four stillbirths, and like other nineteenth-century couples, the Noyeses wished to avoid both unwanted children and the physical burdens women endured during repeated pregnancies. Unlike the Shakers, however, Noyes did not control reproduction by eliminating sexual intercourse, nor did he sanction contraception. Borrowing a distinction from the popular pseudo-science of phrenology, Noyes urged the avoidance of "propagative" sex in favor of the pursuit of "amative" sex. His followers did so through the practice of a form of male continence known as *coitus reservatus*. Like *coitus interruptus*, or withdrawal, it involved male self-control, but instead of withdrawing and ejaculating outside of a woman's body, the man withdrew and did not ejaculate. In Noyes's words, this practice allowed a couple "the most essential freedom of love, and at the same time avoid[ed] undesired procreation and all the other evils incident to male incontinence." The method required enormous self-control on the part of men, for which they were trained from puberty, but it seemed to work: Oneida's birth rate remained low, and there were few accidental pregnancies among Noyes's followers.[16]

Theoretically, amative love could flourish at Oneida, enhancing the "fellowship" between men and women. But Noyes carefully differentiated his system from mere licentiousness. Erotic pleasure was acceptable only within an ideology of extreme male self-control. Oneidans, like Mormons, incorporated traditional western European views of man as the superior being who controlled his bodily instincts; woman, the weaker vessel, succumbed to sexual desire. Unlike Mormons, Noyes encouraged women to succumb, even to experience multiple orgasms. Oneidans could engage in extensive foreplay, positional variations, and oral sex to achieve this goal. The favored position was "wife on side—upper thigh bent—husband enters from the rear, they play manually with each others [*sic*] genitals." A doctor claimed that "women were particularly satisfied by the long play," while men "prided themselves on bringing women to climax."[17]

Equally challenging to nineteenth-century notions of sexual propriety was the Oneidan institution of "complex marriage." Through this practice, Noyes hoped to subordinate individual, or selfish, love to the social good of the community. Noyes disapproved of the romantic concept of "falling in love" and condemned flirtation and courtship. Since love should be able to develop between any man and woman of the community, all were married to each other. A man could ask to have sex with any woman—and a woman could refuse, though not initiate. Nevertheless, the community as a whole played a large role in shaping individual sexual relations. At mutual criticism sessions, members attempted to break up exclusive romances and pressured women to accept certain partners. To avoid accidental pregnancies, the community encouraged young men who were not yet experienced in *coitus reservatus* to mate with postmenopausal women. Through a system of eugenic breeding called stirpiculture, Noyes and the elders of the community determined which matings could include propagative sex. Like sexuality, childrearing was communal.[18]

Compared to the dozens of short-lived utopias, the Oneida community persisted for an impressive thirty-one years, with over three hundred members residing there in the 1870s. In that decade, however, the younger generation began to lose interest in Noyes's system, and the strains of communal sex and childrearing took their toll on older members. In 1879, a conflict over complex marriage sent Noyes into exile, and the remaining members of the community restored monogamous marriage.

Despite his loss of power at Oneida, Noyes remained influential. His theory of coitus reservatus captured the imagination of the next generation of radical sexual theorists, who would elaborate variations on his system of erotic pleasure combined with control over orgasm and reproduction. Noyes's vision had an impact beyond this sexual fringe, as well. In 1872, for example, a respectable newspaper editor, influenced by Noyes, articulated a new sexual ethic that reversed the earlier emphasis on reproductive sexuality. As David Goodman Croly explained, "It is the brutal and inferior morality which simply allows the sexes to come together for purposes of propagation; and the higher, the human civilized morality which allows intercourse without reference to propagation."[19] Extreme at the time, the elevation of sexual relations, apart from reproduction, would be incorporated during the twentieth century into the sexual ideals of American society.

Free lovers, Shakers, Mormons, and Oneidans stood apart from the dominant society, yet they mirrored its sexual concerns when they sought alternative resolutions to the tensions between erotic and procreative sexuality and between individual and social control over sexuality. Free lovers exalted individual moral responsibility and justified sex on the basis of love. Other utopians emphasized self-control but instituted extensive community controls as well. Close surveillance kept Shakers in line; Oneidans employed mutual criticism and stirpiculture; and Mormons elevated polygamy to a social duty and achieved some eugenic control by requiring church approval for men's choice of wives. In these ways the utopians attempted to keep sexuality a communal issue, as it had been during an earlier historical era. At the same time, the utopians' ideas revealed the fears shared by other nineteenth-century Americans that the pursuit of pure erotic pleasure would place the individual beyond the control of the community. For some, communitarian alternatives provided a means to allay those fears. Most Americans, however, chose to remain within the dominant society, where opportunities for individual choice and sexual pleasure expanded.

Same-Sex Intimacy

The alternatives proposed by utopians expanded the range of acceptable sexual practices beyond familial, reproductive relationships. But utopians, like the society from which they came, condemned as unnatural or immoral any sexual relations that took place between members of the same gender. Despite this universal disapproval, several kinds of same-sex relationships, some of them sexual, flourished in the nineteenth century. The unique social worlds inhabited by middle-class men and women encouraged intimate relationships, especially between women who were socialized to view themselves as more spiritual than men and to value the separate female sphere.[20] For both women and men, a cult of friendship fostered romantic feelings and may have sheltered sexual practices. Outside of this largely middle-class arena of romantic friendship, a variety of same-sex relationships formed where men or women lived in isolation from the opposite sex, in mining or cowboy towns, for example, or in female academies. Within these settings, romantic friendships coexisted with sexual relationships, overlapping at times. Although they differed in formal structure from courtship and marriage, intimate relationships between members of the same sex often mirrored the underlying themes in nineteenth-century family life. In them, women and men expressed passionate longings for emotional, spiritual, and physical intimacy, without the traditional association of sexuality and reproduction.

The overlap of the romantic, erotic, and physical has made it difficult to define these relationships, especially in light of the way sexual meanings have changed in the twentieth century. The modern terms *homosexuality* and *heterosexuality* do not apply to an era that had not yet articulated these distinctions. Only in the late nineteenth century did European and American medical writers apply these categories and stigmatize some same-sex relationships as a form of sexual perversion. Until the 1880s, most romantic friendships were thought to be devoid of sexual content. Thus a woman or man could write of affectionate desire for a loved one of the same gender without causing an eyebrow to be raised.

Just as contemporary observers assumed these relationships to be asexual, so have many historians. Given the stigma attached to same-sex love in the twentieth century, some writers have taken great pains to deny even the possibility of homosexual contact in nineteenth-century friendships. The de-

scendants and biographers of well-known figures, such as Emily Dickinson or
Walt Whitman, insist that the terms of loving endearment expressed by these
writers for their same-sex friends by no means implied sexual longing.[21] The
dearth of direct evidence about all sexual relations compounds the problem of
definition. Even though letters and diaries only rarely mention genital contact,
the birth of children provides a confirmation of heterosexual intercourse. The
absence of procreative evidence, and the fact that few people left direct records
of homosexual acts, could mean either that the acts did not occur or simply
that they were not recorded. The condemnation of the practice at the end of
the century provides a clue that it indeed existed. At the same time, however,
this censure may have silenced the mention of same-sex intimacy within
sources of the past.

However difficult it may be to know whether sexual—that is, genital—
relations characterized particular same-sex friendships, it is clear that the
meaning of same-sex love gradually changed over the course of the nineteenth
century. Colonial Americans had no concept of homosexuality as a personal
condition or identity. Rather, individual acts of sodomy (anal sex between
men) or buggery (sex with animals) were considered sins to be punished and
for which a man could repent. The laws almost always applied to men, not
women, because they typically referred to the unnatural spilling of seed, the
biblical sin of Onan. Nineteenth-century Americans continued to condemn
sodomy, a term which they used to refer not only to anal sex between men but
also to various nonprocreative sexual acts, including masturbation and oral
sex. Over the course of the century, new meanings were attached to these
terms. At first, the language of religion remained prominent in discussions of
sodomy. For example, an 1810 Maryland court indictment for sodomy stated
that the defendant had been "moved and seduced by the instigation of the
Devil." But gradually legal concerns replaced religious ones. After the American Revolution, the phrase "crimes against nature" increasingly appeared in
statutes, implying that acts of sodomy offended a natural order rather than the
will of God. By the end of the century, physicians employed a medical language, referring to sodomy not as a sin or a spiritual failing, but rather as a
disease and a manifestation of a bodily or mental condition. During the 1880s,
the labels "congenital inversion" and "perversion" were applied not only to
male sexual acts, but to sexual or romantic unions between women, as well as
those between men.[22]

Underlying these redefinitions were growing possibilities for sexual relations between members of the same gender. Within the working class, men and
women who lived outside of traditional families formed same-sex partnerships
for economic or sexual reasons, or for both. Within the middle class, romantic
friendships fostered both spiritual and physical intimacy that might become

sexual. For men, more than for women, same-sex relationships often crossed class boundaries. For both sexes, these relationships formed unselfconsciously. Not until the last quarter of the century did those who engaged in same-sex relationships find it necessary to hide or deny their passionate attachments.

The first model of same-sex relationship, that of sexual or romantic partnerships outside the familial model, was most readily available to white wage-earning men. For them, the industrializing economy offered opportunities to explore sexuality outside of marriage, whether on city streets or in the separate sphere of all male activity. The ability to purchase goods and services allowed men to live beyond familial controls, while the city provided anonymity for their actions. Wage-earning men who lived in urban boardinghouses could bring other men to their rooms for the night or longer. In 1846, two New York men who had met in church lived together for three months, engaging in nightly "carnal intercourse."[23] During the 1860s, poet Walt Whitman frequently brought home young working-class men whom he met in New York, Brooklyn, and Washington, D.C. "City of orgies, walks and joys," he called Manhattan. The city's "frequent and swift flash of eyes offering me love" repaid the poet's effort:

> Saturday night Mike Ellis . . . took him home to 150 37th Street . . . *Dan'l Spencer* . . . slept with me Sept 3d . . . Theodore M. Carr . . . came to the house with me . . . *David Wilson*—night of Oct 11, '62, walking up from Middagh—slept with me . . . October 9, 1863, Jerry Taylor . . . slept with me last night weather soft, cool enough, warm enough, heavenly.[24]

Another writer also benefited from urban anonymity. In 1866, Horatio Alger was run out of his pulpit in a small Massachusetts town for the "revolting crime of unnatural familiarity with boys." Alger moved to New York City, where he could avoid censure for his pederastic interest in the young men of the streets, about whom he wrote in his popular novels.[25]

At a time when the state was not heavily involved in the regulation of morality, urban police did not vigorously prosecute consensual sodomy. Between 1796 and 1873, for example, New York City courts issued only twenty-two indictments for sodomy, and these usually involved the use of force or a disparity in the men's ages. Thus in 1857, George Mason was arrested for committing sodomy with boys aged eleven to fourteen. Not until the end of the century did New York law criminalize "consenting to sodomy." By then Americans had been alerted to the phenomenon of homosexuality, for as the opportunities for same-sex relationships grew, the first signs of a visible, urban homosexual subculture appeared, along with strong condemnation of homosexuality by medical writers.[26]

In addition to the cities, wherever young, single men congregated—as soldiers, prisoners, or cowboys—the possibility for same-sex relationships increased. During the Civil War, for example, when Walt Whitman served as a nurse, he formed deep attachments to the young Union and rebel soldiers he tended. "I believe no men ever loved each other as I and some of these poor wounded, sick and dying men love each other," he wrote. Before he left at night he kissed the "poor boys." Of a nineteen-year-old southern captain, he declared "our affection is quite an affair, quite romantic—sometimes when I lean over to say I am going, he puts his arm round my neck, draws my face down, &c." Similarly, a Confederate general developed a strong attachment to his adjutant, a young man who shared the officer's "labours during the day and his blankets at night." In the navy, accounts of flogging for homosexual activity attest to the opportunities for sex on board ships. After the 1820s, the growth of the American prison system created further possibilities for situational homosexuality. Convicts testified that strong attachments often developed between older and younger prisoners, who shared their possessions, their meals, and their beds. Other prisoners recalled being forced to engage in sex against their will.[27]

The West provided extensive opportunities for male-male intimacy. Some men were drawn to the frontier because of their attractions to men. All men were thought to have strong innate lusts, and the absence of women may have channeled these desires to other men. Cowboy lore suggests that both long-term attachments and temporary sexual unions could form in the wild West. Upon the death of his partner, for example, one cowboy wrote a poem declaring that the two had loved "in the way men do," that is, an unspoken love truer than "any woman's kiss could be." A limerick jokingly insinuated that older cowboys occasionally initiated younger men sexually: "Young cowboys had a great fear / That old studs once filled with beer / Completely addle' / They'd throw on a saddle, And ride them on the rear." At least one territorial court case reveals that cowboys attempted to hire younger men to spend the night with them. In the frontier army, where soldiers often purchased the services of female prostitutes, some men clearly sought male partners as well. At Fort Meade, in the Dakota Territory, a Mrs. Nash first married one soldier, and when her husband was transferred, she married another man. After her death, "Mrs." Nash's identity as a man was discovered.[28]

Working-class women also found that adopting the identity of the opposite gender could expand their sexual opportunities. Most women did not share men's ability to support themselves outside of the family. Thus when working-class women sought to establish same-sex relationships, they often did so by adopting men's clothing and "passing" as men in order to earn wages and marry other women. In the 1850s, for example, Lucy Ann Lobdell left her husband in upstate New York and passed as a man in order to support herself. "I made up my mind to dress in men's attire to seek labor," she explained, and to earn "men's wages." Later, she became the Reverend Joseph Lobdell and set up house with Maria Perry, living for ten years as man and wife. In the 1870s, a French immigrant, Jeanne Bonnet, was frequently arrested by San Francisco police for wearing men's clothing. Reporters called her a "man-hater" and described her as having "short cropped hair, an unwomanly voice, and a masculine face which harmonized excellently with her customary suit of boys' clothes." Bonnet visited brothels as a male customer and fell in love with prostitute Blanche Buneau, whom she convinced to leave her trade. In 1876, an angry pimp murdered Bonnet while she lay in Buneau's bed. Across the country in New York City, a woman took the name Murray Hall and began to dress as a man. She opened an employment bureau, settled down with the first of her two wives, and later adopted a daughter. Hall became influential in the Tammany Hall Democratic political machine and earned a reputation for drinking, playing poker, and being "sweet on women." Other stories of passing women appeared in newspapers throughout the country. The account of "Bill," a Missouri laborer who became secretary of the International Brotherhood of Boilermakers, typified the successful passing woman, who lived as men did and loved other women: "She drank . . . she swore, she courted girls, she worked hard as her fellows, she fished and camped, she even chewed tobacco."[29]

Within the middle class, a different kind of same-sex relationship formed in the separate spheres of men and women, where romantic friendship was an acceptable part of social life. In their own realm, for example, many women formed close attachments that could rival marital relationships in their personal intensity. White middle-class women found it particularly easy to form such ties, given the emphasis placed on their superior spiritual and nurturing qualities. Women's socialization, at home or in boarding schools, encouraged them to form bonds with other women, and many chose a special female friend in whom to confide. These youthful friendships often turned into lifelong relationships that survived both marriage and geographical separation. The friendship of Sarah Butler and Jeannie Field ripened at boarding school in the 1850s. After Sarah married they corresponded and visited each other. "Dear darling Sarah!" Jeannie wrote after a meeting, "How I love you and how happy I have been! You are the joy of my life." To send "a thousand kisses" did not seem strange for these lifelong friends.[30]

Within what historian Carroll Smith-Rosenberg has called the "female world of love and ritual," intensely emotional and even physical relationships could form. A woman novelist captured this unique female ardor in 1859 when she wrote:

> Women often love each other with as much fervor and excitement as they do men. When this is the case . . . the emotions awakened heave and swell through the whole

being as the tides swell the ocean. Freed from all the grosser elements of passion, as it exists between the sexes, it retains its energy, its abandonments, its flush, its eagerness, its palpitation, and its rapture. . . . The electricity of the one flashes and gleams through the other, to be returned not only in *degree* as between man and woman, but in *kind* as between precisely similar organizations.

Although the author, Margaret J. M. Sweat, contrasted same-sex love with the "grosser elements" of sexual relations in marriage, her main character described her relationships with women in extremely physical terms. "I have had my passionate attachments among women," she confessed, "which swept like whirlwinds over me, sometimes scorching me with a furnace-blast. . . . I have loved so intensely that the daily and nightly communion I have held with my beloved ones has not sufficed to slake my thirst for them, nor the lavishness of their love for me been able to satisfy the demands of my exacting nature."[31]

This fictional confession echoes the historical experiences of women. In 1852, for example, poet Emily Dickinson wrote to her absent beloved friend (and later sister-in-law) Sue Gilbert:

Susie, will you indeed come home next Saturday, and be my own again, and kiss me as you used to? . . . I hope for you so much, and feel so eager for you, feel that I *cannot* wait, feel that *now* I must have you—that the expectation once more to see your face again, makes me feel hot and feverish, and my heart beats so fast—[32]

Among women who attended college in the 1860s and 1870s, many formed intensely romantic relationships that paralleled heterosexual courtship. An 1873 letter described this process as "smashing":

When a Vassar girl takes a shine to another, she straightway enters upon a regular course of bouquet sendings, interspersed with tinted notes, mysterious packages of "Ridley's Mixed Candies," locks of hair perhaps, and many other tender tokens, until at last the object of her attentions is captured, the two become inseparable, and the aggressor is considered by her circle of acquaintances as—*smashed.*[33]

Physical intimacy—though not genital stimulation—among women was, to an extent, normative within Victorian culture. An 1860 advice book accepted the customs of girls holding hands, kissing, and caressing, explaining that these practices should be reserved for "hours of privacy, and never indulged in before gentlemen." In the early nineteenth century, few Americans associated women's physical closeness with sexuality, because female sexuality was at that time so closely linked with reproduction. Gradually, however, the separation of sexuality and reproduction made Americans more conscious of the erotic element of these friendships. In 1875, the anonymous author of *Satan in Society* decried the "enormous" extent of female masturbation and claimed that at schools for young ladies "the most intimate *liaisons* are formed under this specious pretext; the same bed often receives two friends."[34]

Women themselves clearly discovered the erotic possibilities between loving friends. Evidence from letters and diaries reveals that some friends longed for physical expressions of intimacy and spoke the language of courtship. In 1865, for example, a married woman wrote to her friend, the feminist orator Anna Dickinson:

> I want to look into your eyes and squeeze your "lily white hand," and pinch your ears *all,* for love of you darling. Four sweet letters I rec'd a day or two since and it made me very happy; oh! you do love me! . . . I have an irresistible desire all through this letter to make love to you.

In the language of the day, "to make love" implied a desire to court, not necessarily to touch, her beloved. Dickinson inspired this sentiment in other "suitors" as well. Over the next few years suffrage activist Susan B. Anthony wrote to Dickinson in a similar vein:

> Darling I can't tell you any where, but specially can't on paper how my spirit yearns for your safe and sure growth into all that is true and beautiful and noble and heroic. . . .Now when are you coming to New York—do let it be soon—I have *plain quarters*—at 44 bond St—*double bed*—and big enough and good enough to take you *in*— . . . I do so long for the scolding and pinched ears and every thing I know awaits me—what worlds of experience since I last snuggled the wee child in my long arms. . . . Your loving friend *Susan.* [35]

Such intense and erotic relationships could form between men as well, although fewer sources record their existence. In the antebellum period, writers and artists of the Transcendentalist movement formulated an ideal of romantic friendships in which two kindred spirits might develop deep and lasting attachments. Ralph Waldo Emerson's essay "On Friendship" idealized such relationships, and men exposed to these ideas emulated his model. Emerson himself had experienced a romantic attraction to a fellow student at Harvard in the 1820s. Herman Melville was another member of this literary circle who explored homoerotic themes. Melville dedicated *Moby Dick,* with its depiction of male "Bosom Friends," to his own dear friend, Nathaniel Hawthorne. But Walt Whitman served as the most important reference point for men who aspired to the ideals of "manly affection" and comradeship. Whitman used the phrenological term *adhesiveness* to describe the attraction of one man for another and the spiritual connection they could establish. "Adhesive love," or "fervid comradeship," he believed, was necessary to counterbalance and spiritualize "our materialistic and vulgar American democracy." In *Democratic Vistas* Whitman called for "threads of manly friendship, fond and loving, pure and sweet, strong and lifelong, carried to degrees hitherto unknown—"[36]

Whitman provides a good example of the filtering of middle-class romantic friendship across class lines. The poet shared much of his life with a series of younger, working-class companions. For several years he lived with Fred Vaughan, of whom he wrote, "I have found him who loves me, / as I him, in perfect love." In 1860, Vaughan heard Emerson lecture on friendship, and in a letter to Whitman he reported on the theme of the talk, "that a man whose heart was filled with a warm, ever enduring *not to be shaken by anything* Friendship was one to be set on one side apart from other men, and almost to be worshipped as a saint."[37]

Whitman described his love affairs with other young working men in highly spiritual terms. To a former soldier named Tom Sawyer he wrote: "Dear comrade, you must not forget me, for I never shall you. My love you have in life or death forever. . . . [M]y soul could never be entirely happy, even in the world to come, without you, dear comrade." Similarly, Whitman wrote to Peter Doyle, a young streetcar conductor he met in 1866, "Dear comrade, I think of you very often. My love for you is indestructible, & since that night & morning has returned more than before." Doyle recollected the moment of their initial attraction, on a streetcar in Washington, D.C.:

> He was the only passenger, it was a lonely night, so I thought I would go in and talk with him. Anyway, I went into the car. We were familiar at once—I put my hand on his knee—we understood. He did not get out at the end of the trip—in fact went all the way back with me.

The pair spent long hours together exploring the city, and when they were apart they exchanged intimate letters. In 1869, when Doyle was despondent from fear that he had contracted syphilis, Whitman wrote in tones as maternal as they were paternal:

> It seemed indeed to me, (for I will talk out plain to you, dearest comrade,) that the one I loved, and who had always been so manly and sensible, was gone. . . . My darling, if you are not well when I come back I will get a good room or two in some quiet place . . . and we will live together, and devote ourselves to the job of curing you.[38]

Whitman's life embodied the tension between romantic and sexual love among same-sex friends in the nineteenth century. He championed manly love as a form of intense, romantic friendship, yet at times, he struggled to suppress his erotic desires for men. "Depress the adhesive nature" he wrote in his notebook in 1870. "It is in excess—making life a torment / All this diseased, feverish disproportionate adhesiveness." Toward the end of his life, Whitman replied to questions from the British homosexual writer John Addington Symonds about the Calamus poems in *Leaves of Grass,* which contain highly homoerotic passages. Whitman insisted that he spoke only of the " 'adhesiveness' of comradeship" and not of "the 'amativeness' of sexual love," and he resented the "morbid inferences" Symonds had drawn about homosexuality. Yet a confidant reported that Whitman had contemplated Symond's questions: "Perhaps it means more or less than what I thought myself . . . [P]erhaps I don't know what it all means—perhaps never did know."[39]

By the 1880s, when he wrote to Symonds, Whitman's reluctance to be identified as a homosexual may have been due to the growing importance of the medical model of sexual disease. Previously, romantic friendships could be erotic in part because they were assumed to be sexually innocent. However, loving friends had begun to question whether their physical intimacies marked them as deviant. In 1886, for example, young Frederick Ryman described in his diary a night spent with a close male friend. After talking about their lives and loves, the two men went to bed, and Ryman's friend "put his arms around me & lay his head down by my right shoulder in the most loving way." In the morning they "kissed each other good bye." Ryman felt the need to make a significant distinction between these acts and "sex," adding that "there was no sexual sentiment on the part of either of us." As if to reassure himself that they had not crossed an unnamed boundary, he continued:

> I am certain that the thought of the least demonstration of unmanly & abnormal passion would have been as revolting to him as it is & ever has been to me, & yet I do love him & loved to hug & kiss him because of the goodness & genius I find in his mind. Christ kissed & embraced those whom he loved I believe & why shall I fear to do the same?[40]

Yet Ryman did fear being labeled sexually abnormal, as men and women of an earlier period did not. In the decade in which he wrote, American doctors, following the lead of Europeans, began to define same-sex relationships as perverse, and they debated methods for treating homosexuality as a diseased mental state. This shift in attitudes is evident in the case of Lucy Ann Lobdell, the passing woman from upstate New York. In 1855 Lobdell had safely published a brief narrative of her life as "the female hunter." By 1883, however, she had become the subject of a medical account of "sexual perversion." Lobdell spent the last decade of her life in an insane asylum, where Dr. P. M. Wise categorized her as a "Lesbian" and described her "paroxysmal attacks of erotomania." According to Wise, "It is reasonable to consider true sexual perversion as always a pathological condition and a peculiar manifestation of insanity."[41]

When the medical discourse on sexual perversion emerged at the end of the century, the possibilities for same-sex love had already expanded greatly. Wage labor, the ability to live apart from families, and the sociability of the separate sexual spheres had fostered romantic, spiritual, homoerotic, and sexual unions.

The medical labeling of same-sex intimacy as perverse conflated an entire range of relationships and stigmatized all of them as a single, sexually deviant personal identity. Same-sex relationships thus lost the innocence they had enjoyed during most of the nineteenth century. Nonetheless, these unions had expanded the opportunities for intimacy and sexuality apart from reproduction and the family. Both men and women would continue to engage in same-sex relations, but with greater self-consciousness about their sexual component.

Sexual Commerce

In addition to the emergence of new types of intimate relationships, the social spaces in which the expression of sexuality took place expanded over the course of the nineteenth century. Although the middle-class family valued sexual privacy and called for public reticence, within working-class neighborhoods, sex retained its public presence, and the growing world of commerce increasingly incorporated sexuality within its nexus. Beginning in port cities of the late eighteenth century, certain urban districts catered to sexual commerce. As these terrains grew, in defiance of middle-class reticence, contemporary observers labeled them the "underworld." Whether in eastern cities or on the frontier, wherever single men congregated they created a market for sexual services, ranging from titillation by erotic literature or the theater to physical access to prostitutes in dance halls and brothels. In the West, for example, comic almanacs of the early nineteenth century openly represented sexual desire; a generation later, dime novels provided vicarious sex and violence to both western and eastern readers. In cities throughout the country, legitimate commercial dance halls hired women to entice men to drink, while illicit sex occurred on the premises or in brothels and discreet assignation houses.

Dance halls appealed to a clientele of single men who worked either in cities or mining towns. By the 1850s these men could also entertain themselves at clubs that offered *tableaux vivants,* forerunners of the strip show. The Melodeon, a "concert saloon" on Broadway in New York City, featured "waiter girls" in short-skirted theatrical costumes who performed "Gaieties," served drinks, and sometimes joined customers at their tables. Women could also attend, and some of the working women who frequented the Bowery did so. Other establishments catered to specialized clientele. Near the New York waterfront, sailors and dock workers frequented dance houses named Neptune's Home and Snug Harbor, where they paid twenty cents a dance to waltz or polka with the prostitutes available there. At other dance houses, prizefighters brought their own women. Free blacks attended separate dance halls.[42]

The underworld was not simply a working-class phenomenon. It housed a variety of services catering to men of all classes. As one author explained in 1869, New York's underworld ranged from fashionable Fifth Avenue mansions, where wealthy men kept prostitutes, to Canal Street cigar stores that sold erotic pictures. In addition, the underworld provided the space for sexual mixing between classes, primarily when middle-class men purchased the sexual services of working-class women. Contemporary observers of the mid- to late nineteenth century also expressed concern about the opportunities for middle-class women to have illicit sexual encounters. "Women of high position and culture, no less than the unlettered shop girls," one author bemoaned, "resort to the houses of 'assignation.' " At these elegant urban or suburban restaurants, couples could rent rooms for prices ranging from fifty cents to ten dollars, suggesting a class mixture in the clientele. By 1866, a policeman claimed that New York had ninety-nine such houses, as well as seventy-seven concert saloons and over six hundred brothels.[43]

In addition to the lure of dance halls and houses of assignation, by midcentury sex for sale took the form of cheap "licentious" literature, or what would later be termed pornography. Prior to the 1840s, Americans could procure only limited reprints of erotic classics published in Europe, although the lurid anti-Catholic novel *Maria Monk* (1836), with its allegations of sex between nuns and priests, was a best-seller for a generation. The production of an indigenous American pornography began after 1846, when William Haynes, an Irish surgeon who immigrated to New York, took the money he had made by publishing *Fanny Hill* in the United States and reinvested it into the production of cheap erotic novels. Titles such as *Confessions of a Lady's Waiting Maid* (1848), *Amours of an American Adventurer in the New World and Old* (1865), and *The Merry Order of St. Bridget* (a flagellation novel, 1857) rolled off American presses.[44] At the same time, less-sexually-explicit but titillating western adventure literature, often featuring the seduction of helpless women, became increasingly available to a growing male market in cities of the North and West. In the 1850s, a flurry of editorials decried the "Satanic Literature" that could be purchased at railroad depots, steamboat docks, and in hotels. Significantly, the editorials did not call for censorship but rather invoked community pressure to cultivate purer literary tastes.[45]

The market for pornography expanded during the Civil War. The congregation of men in the army apart from families created a demand for sexual commerce and constituted an easy market for purveyors to target. The cheap fiction produced by William Haynes became "barracks favorites" during the war and encouraged increased production in the postwar years. According to one infantry officer, "obscene prints and photographs" were "quite commonly kept and exhibited by soldiers and even officers." Disturbed by the army's failure "to checkmate and suppress" the sale of these items, Captain M. G.

Tousley wrote directly to Commander in Chief Abraham Lincoln, enclosing as evidence a circular advertising "New Pictures for Bachelors." Tousley's vigilance has left a rare record of midcentury tastes in male fantasy. For twelve cents a piece or $1.20 a dozen, men could purchase twelve-by-fifteen-inch pictures, suitable for framing. Most of the advertised pictures placed the man in the role of voyeur observing groups of young women in various states of undress. In "Wood-Nymphs' Frolic," for example, girls "engaged in a rustic dance . . . in all the consciousness of innocence, caring little whether or not they are seen in their nude and interesting frolic." Less frequently the viewer could imagine himself in sexual command, selecting or seducing a woman. Significantly, the women depicted in these scenes—"Circassion Slaves" and an Indian maiden—were not white.[46]

Titillating pictures and literature continued to circulate during the late nineteenth century. In the newly popular pool halls, working-class men exchanged obscene postcards and books, while images of semiclothed women adorned the wall. Similarly, the all-male saloons often had paintings of nude women. The most famous was Adolphe William Bouguereau's *Nymphs and Satyr* (1877); copies of this French painting hung in many hotel bars.[47] Saloons offered a background of ribald music, to which men could drink, talk, and glance through the scandalous *Police Gazette*. This popular crime and sports newspaper, which often portrayed women of the "demimonde," carried ads for patent medicines promising to cure syphilis and gonorrhea or to enlarge "certain parts" of the body. It also advertised books such as *Pauline's Caprice*— "daringly unique in its spiciness" and complete with colored illustrations, it told the story of "a Young and Gay Girl's Life in the Whirlpool of Fast Parisian Gayety."[48]

Sexual commerce involved not only the vicarious pleasures of pictures, songs, and stories; men could also buy the services of prostitutes. On a small scale, prostitution had taken economic root in the late eighteenth century, but commercial and urban growth in the early industrial era created both an enlarged supply of prostitutes and a new demand for their services. The economic disruptions of early industrialization displaced poor women from traditional means of support, such as spinning. Domestic service was one of the few paid jobs that women could find, but most disliked the work. According to a thirteen-year-old girl whose income helped feed her family, she would rather sell her body for a shilling than become a scrubwoman. Servants not only earned low wages, they were also extremely vulnerable to the sexual advances of their employers. Furthermore, because of the new cultural emphasis on female purity, a young woman who was "ruined" by rape or seduction might have difficulty finding respectable work or a marriage partner. One young woman, seduced in 1835, first lived with her lover but decided to leave him in order to become a prostitute. Other working-class women engaged in casual prostitution. In New York City, for example, impoverished teenage girls combined petty thievery with streetwalking to support themselves. Some working-class women who "walked out" on city streets in search of amusements occasionally accepted money for sex. Thus fifteen-year-old Jane Groesbeck of New York went to the races, met a storekeeper, and earned five dollars for spending the night with him.[49] In short, sexual services became one of women's labors to be drawn outside of the home and into the public sphere of commerce.

At the same time, an expanded clientele for prostitutes filled the cities: men who lived unattached to families, earning money as laborers or clerks and enjoying the protections of urban anonymity. Gentlemen, too, could afford to take advantage of the availability of streetwalkers, justifying their behavior in the name of protecting the purity of women of their own class. At a time when male lust was thought to be natural, the availability of paid consorts, like that of black slaves in the South, provided an outlet that protected middle- and upper-class women from unwanted intercourse. The "pure" woman and the "fallen" woman represented two sides of the same sexual coin.

By the 1830s, prostitutes, though still few in number, were more visible on urban streets than they had been in the eighteenth century. In New York City, for example, a distinct class of prostitutes could be identified by their ankle-length skirts, bright-colored clothing, and painted faces—all fashions shunned by respectable women. In later decades, prostitutes adopted other symbols, such as cigarette smoking, to mark their status. Higher-paid prostitutes openly solicited customers on fashionable Broadway, a neighborhood that housed elegant brothels; lower-paid prostitutes congregated in the poorer Five Points district, and later on the "Arch Block" near Broome Street. At midcentury some brothels catered to specialized tastes, offering nude dancers or child prostitutes. Out-of-town visitors could purchase a "gentleman's guide" to help locate better houses and prostitutes. In the 1850s, Dr. William Sanger estimated that there were over six thousand prostitutes, or one for every sixty-four men, in New York City. Smaller cities had their brothels, as well. Between 1865 and 1883, forty madames in St. Paul, Minnesota, operated houses that lasted for eight to ten years each. San Francisco hosted a full range of establishments, from dance halls to brothels to elegant "parlor houses." One estimate claimed that Chicago had over five hundred brothels in 1860, and by the 1880s, a Philadelphia neighborhood included parlor houses, massage parlors, and dance halls.[50]

In the South, which became urbanized much later than the North, prostitution operated on a smaller scale. White men who seduced or raped black women had less need to purchase sex from prostitutes. Nonetheless, both married and single men did visit brothels in southern cities. In 1858, the mayor of Savannah estimated that his city had one prostitute for every thirty-nine men and that Norfolk had one per twenty-six men. Most southern prostitutes were white; in antebellum Petersburg, Virginia, for instance, no black women were among those arrested for "keeping a Bawdy House and House of bad fame." In New Orleans, foreign-born women and teenage girls, hard pressed to find jobs outside of domestic work, sold sexual services in ballrooms, coffeehouses, and brothels. They served a clientele of transient single men— sailors and river workers—as well as married family men.[51]

The Civil War facilitated the expansion of prostitution. Where men massed for training or battle, women congregated to profit from sexual labor. Union soldiers wrote home about the availability of prostitutes throughout the South, claiming to find "loose women on every hill and in every valley" and "plenty of whores" in the cities. One observer, testifying about the Union occupation of the South, claimed that he had "never been to any locality where the officers and the men, who were so disposed, did not sleep with all the women around." The incidence of venereal disease among soldiers—estimates range from eight to seventeen percent for the Union army as a whole—suggests one effect of wartime prostitution.[52]

The social disruption of the Civil War brought more women into prostitution. Some southern women no doubt turned to it out of destitution born of the destruction of homes and farms. Their attitude toward northern customers was revealed by a soldier stationed in Richmond, Virginia, shortly after its capture. The women "damnyankee us on the street in the daytime," he wrote home, "but at night the skirts come up for good yankee gold." Other women, such as those in Carlisle, Pennsylvania, who joined a drinking party of soldiers, engaged in sex less for profit than for adventure. "After much whiskey and dancing," a soldier recorded, "they shed most of their garments and offered to us their bottoms." Brothels proliferated as well during the war. Washington, D.C., allegedly had over four hundred "bawdy houses," including Mrs. Wolf's Den, Fort Sumter, and Unconditional Surrender; prostitutes honored General Hooker by naming the brothels lining Lafayette Square "Hooker Row." It is unclear whether they did so because he frequented the area or because he limited them to this section, but in any case the term "hooker" became slang for "prostitute."[53]

The settlement of the western territories contributed further to sexual commerce. During the early periods of settlement, heavily skewed sex ratios in cattle and mining towns created a demand for sex among single male settlers. Their demands, and their ready cash, in turn opened opportunities for madames and prostitutes. A western ballad captured the process: "First came the miners to work in the mine / Then came the ladies who lived on the line."

In some towns on the Comstock, Nevada, silver lode during the 1860s, prostitution was the largest occupational category for women working outside the home. One historian has estimated that twenty percent of all women in California during the decade after the gold rush were prostitutes, and that prostitutes outnumbered other women in early mining camps by a ratio of twenty-five to one. In Virginia City, Nevada, fifty prostitutes resided on one downtown street in 1880, and one of the many brothels, Cad Thompson's Brick House, had been in operation for seventeen years.[54]

The military presence in the West also attracted prostitutes. As during the Revolutionary War, female camp followers sometimes performed sexual as well as domestic labor for soldiers. Traders and soldiers also drew Indian women into prostitution, spreading venereal disease among Indians who lived near army posts in the Southwest. The demand for prostitutes to service soldiers encouraged the establishment of the only rural brothels in the country, the "hog farms" that sprang up near military forts. These ranches, often operated by a married couple, housed from three to twelve prostitutes, usually white but sometimes black women as well. Although the army officially condemned the ranches, soldiers kept them in business.[55]

On the West Coast, a distinctive system of sexual slavery involving Asian women developed during the late nineteenth century. Along with the importation of Chinese male laborers to work on the railroads during the 1860s, thousands of Chinese women came to the United States as prostitutes. Lured by promises of marriage in America, kidnapped, or sold by poverty-stricken families in China to become indentured servants, these young women signed papers to secure their passage, usually to San Francisco. Unable to pay their debts, they contracted to serve from four to six years of sexual labor. Most worked in the lowest form of brothel, the small "cribs," or rooms, that lined Chinatown's alleys. They serviced Chinese and white men for a small fee per customer. At the peak of importation during the 1870s, the census listed "prostitute" as the occupation of two-thirds of the thirty-five hundred Chinese women in California. Similarly, in the 1880s, Japanese sailors and brothel owners abducted women and brought them to the United States to become prostitutes. They served white, Chinese, and Japanese men in Seattle, San Francisco, and Los Angeles. In each case, Chinese and Japanese men profited from the sale of women and the operation of brothels, investing their money in the burgeoning Asian communities in these cities.[56]

In contrast to the tight male control over Asian prostitution, most white prostitutes seem to have operated independently or within brothels run by women. Men profited from prostitution—as landlords of brothels, owners of saloons and theaters, and police and politicians who received payoffs. Some women lived with or helped support a "sporting man" who controlled her earnings; in the late nineteenth century, some working-class boys began to pimp for prostitutes at gambling houses or as newsboys on the street.[57] But the role of the pimp who controlled one or more dependent prostitutes had not yet evolved. From streetwalker to madame, prostitution remained, for the most part, a female-dominated occupation.

Nineteenth-century social reformers frequently tried to explain the growth of prostitution in terms of the types of women who entered the trade. Dr. William Sanger, for example, noted that slightly over half of the two thousand New York City prostitutes he surveyed in the 1850s were foreign-born—the majority from Great Britain—and that three-fourths were under age twenty-five. Reluctant to consider female sexual desire as a motive for prostitution, Sanger emphasized alcohol and economic need, as his "case studies" indicate. Under the cause of "inclination" he included C.M. While still "virtuous" she had "visited dance-houses, where she became acquainted with prostitutes, who persuaded her that they led an easy, merry life; her inclination was the result of female persuasion." Another woman, E.C., had willingly entered the trade "in order to obtain intoxicating liquors." C.R.'s husband deserted her "because she drank to excess," and she too turned to prostitution "in order to obtain liquor." In sum, Sanger wrote, "in many of the cases, what is called willing prostitution is the sequel of some communication or circumstances which undermine the principles of virtue and arouse the latent passions." To illustrate the economic origins of prostitution, Sanger offered cases such as that of M.M., "a widow with one child" who "earned $1.50 per week as a tailoress." Another woman, a servant, "was taken sick while in a situation, spent all her money, and could get no employment when she recovered." Sanger quoted the words of M.T., who explained that she "had no work, no money, and no home." Other cases of poverty included a widow with three children who "could not obtain steady employment," and a German immigrant who "was robbed of all her money the very day she reached the shore."[58]

Subsequent studies both confirm and refine Sanger's profile of midcentury prostitutes as impoverished young women who were often foreign-born. Some had run away from home to escape parental controls, and some preferred prostitution to work in textile mills or as domestic servants. In New England, for example, Annie B. entered the mills at age ten, began drinking at age fifteen, and soon left home to become a prostitute. In the West, most prostitutes were under the age of thirty, and a significant minority had immigrated from France, Australia, Chile, Mexico, and Central America. In antebellum cities, Irish immigrants may have been overrepresented among prostitutes, largely because of their poverty. Only a small proportion of prostitutes, however, came from the poorest group, blacks. The experience of slavery may have influenced black women to reject the trade, and in the South men took rather than bought sex from female slaves. In addition, when blacks did become prostitutes, they tended to be arrested more frequently than whites.[59] Most women who stated their reasons for becoming prostitutes emphasized their need to earn a living. The comment of a Denver madame was representative: "I went into the sporting life for business reasons and for no other. It was a way for a woman in those days to make money, and I made it."[60] Prostitution attracted women because they had so few other means to support themselves. Despite the physical risks of pregnancy, venereal disease, violent death, or police harassment, prostitution seemed a logical choice when compared to the alternative of low-paid and often demeaning jobs as domestic servants.

Women who became madames of their own brothels could earn fortune and even fame. "Madame Moustache" (Eleanor Dumont) presided over a gambling house in Nevada City, California, after the gold rush; "La Tules" (Doña Gertrudis Barcelo) of Santa Fe, reputed to be a madame, was worth over ten thousand dollars in 1852; and an anonymous mulatto madame from Galveston, Texas, was immortalized in song as "The Yellow Rose of Texas." Ella Hill, who ran a brothel and dance hall in Amarillo, Texas, later retired to Wichita, where she operated a laundry that employed only former prostitutes. Julia Smith Bullette, a madame on the mining frontier, earned up to one thousand dollars a night during the heyday of Julia's Palace and became a respected local citizen. Her upward social mobility ended abruptly, however, when robbers slit her throat. Like Julia Smith, many rank-and-file prostitutes met violent ends: suicide and deaths related to abortion and drug use marked the toll that sexual labor extracted from these women. For every story of a socially mobile madame, many more could be told of a former prostitute who ended her life in the poorhouse.[61]

Little has been said about the men who purchased the sexual labor of prostitutes because the historical sources so rarely mention them. Except when they complained to the police after prostitutes had robbed them, men usually kept silent about their visits to brothels. The double standard may have condoned their sexual indulgences, but most men still did not draw attention to these adventures, at least not in print. Some married men frequented prostitutes. The diary of a North Carolina man recorded a visit to a brothel, where he ran into several married acquaintances. The primary market for sexual commerce, however, was most likely the unattached man of any background such as Fred Ryman, the Catskill, New York, poet. In California, a single man testified at a divorce trial that he had seen a married friend at a brothel. He disapproved of the man's behavior, but added, "I am not a married man, and go around considerable myself." Similarly, Alf Doten frequented prostitutes in Virginia City, Nevada, while he was a bachelor, recording in his diary the "jolly time" he had with his favorites. Once Doten married, however, he stopped visiting the brothels where he had once been a regular customer, and only returned occasionally for the sociability of a ball or show, but not necessarily for sex.[62] Married men could, of course, purchase sex from prostitutes, but for single men the practice seemed to be more socially acceptable.

At midcentury, in cities throughout the country and mining towns in the West, prostitution had become the most public form of sexuality in America. In the antebellum "walking city," it was hard to avoid noticing even the few women of the streets. At a time when most white women remained in the home, prostitutes, even more than other working-class women, moved outside the boundaries of the female sphere. They cruised public streets and met men at theaters, saloons, balls, and cigar stores. During wartime, they followed the troops to the battlefield. Despite occasional outbursts of popular violence against brothels and perfunctory arrests by the recently established urban police, city authorities mostly tolerated prostitutes as a "necessary evil." By the late nineteenth century, however, tolerance would give way to campaigns to regulate or eradicate the "social evil," as this visible symbol of the movement of sexuality from the private to the public sphere mobilized middle-class women into a political movement to control men's sexuality.

The movement of sexuality beyond marriage proceeded throughout the nineteenth century, whether in utopian communities, same-sex relationships, or sexual commerce. Individual mobility, especially for men, along with the individualist spirit of the age, loosened familial control over sex. At the same time, the capitalist economy drew sexuality out of the family and into the marketplace. In the first half of the century, American society remained relatively tolerant of these extra-familial forms of sexual expression as long as they were invisible. Utopians, for example, operated at a distance from mainstream social life; same-sex intimacy could be masked within romantic friendships; and sexual commerce took place largely in working-class or poor neighborhoods, out of sight of the middle class. Between the 1860s and the 1880s, however, social tolerance seemed to diminish. Fewer Americans formed utopian communities, and older groups experienced a decline in membership; in the case of the Mormons, long subject to persecution, the federal government launched a legal assault on their sexual practices. Free lovers would soon become targets for moral censors, as well. Some same-sex relationships were becoming more self-conscious about sexuality by the 1880s, as a medical model of perversion began to take form. Pornography and prostitution, despite public distaste for both, had been able to gain a foothold in nineteenth-century cities. In the late nineteenth century, however, sexual commerce provoked extreme public concern, and a variety of interest groups mobilized to regulate or abolish it. By the 1880s, in response to the movement of sexuality outside the family, sexual politics emerged in full force.

CHAPTER 7

Sexual Politics

IN 1874, Missouri state legislators witnessed a unique political spectacle staged to influence their morals and their votes. Four years earlier, the city of St. Louis had implemented the nation's first, and only, system of regulated prostitution. Under a law supported by doctors, public health officials licensed prostitutes and required them to pass a weekly inspection for venereal disease in order to receive a health certificate. The plan was anathema to Protestant clergymen and middle-class women, who believed that the state should uphold the single standard of morality—that is, chastity before marriage and fidelity within it—rather than institutionalize prostitution. To urge the legislature to abolish the St. Louis experiment, reformers obtained 100,000 signatures on anti-regulation petitions. The women and clergy then seized upon powerful symbols of vulnerable womanhood, and literally marched them to the state-house doors: A group of virgins of tender years, each clad in a pure white gown, conveyed the petitions in a white-ribboned wheelbarrow. Clergy, women reformers, and the innocent young girls deposited their political bounty at the legislature, culminating a crusade to rid the state of this threat to female purity and the sanctity of the family. The politicians answered their prayers by passing a bill that repealed the St. Louis experiment in state-regulated prostitution.[1]

Such organized efforts to reform sexual practices represented yet another expansion of sexuality beyond the family, into the world of politics. The increased visibility of sexuality in the public sphere disturbed middle-class Americans, especially middle-class women, who had been entrusted with the guardianship of the nation's morals. In response to the movement of sexuality outside the family, these women sought to retain their authority over sexuality by organizing moral reform and social purity crusades. In the process, women themselves contributed to the expansion of sexuality into the public arena. As they left the hallowed domestic sphere, women increasingly perceived sexuality as a political, and not simply a private, issue. Other sexual reformers responded as well. Doctors and vice crusaders such as Anthony Comstock opposed abortion, contraception, and the public expression of sexuality in art and literature. Their anti-vice crusades helped politicize sexuality by demanding greater state intervention in the regulation of morality. In contrast, sexual radicals of the anarchist free-love movement rejected any state involvement in personal matters. By the end of the century, diverse reformers—women, doctors, vice crusaders, and free lovers—engaged in heated debate over who should regulate sex: the individual, the family, or the state.

Moral Reform and Prostitution

The growing visibility of prostitution provoked the earliest sexual reform movement, which attempted to dismantle the dominant American view of prostitution deriving from the long-standing tradition of the double standard. Throughout most of Western culture, men had enjoyed the freedom to have sexual relations with mistresses or prostitutes; since female chastity maintained honor and legitimacy within the family, only women's transgressions were severely punished. At the same time, most men, and some women, viewed the prostitute as a marital safety-valve who allowed men to fulfill their supposedly greater sexual desires, sparing their wives from unwanted sex and pregnancy. Prostitution was, thus, a necessary evil.

For these reasons, and despite the social condemnation of the prostitute herself, laws that prohibited "nightwalking" or "keeping a house of ill repute" were only sporadically enforced. In some cities, such as Philadelphia, prostitution itself was not considered a crime at the opening of the century. Before the establishment of professional police forces, irate citizens occasionally attacked brothels, as they did during the whorehouse riots in eighteenth-century Boston and in Maine and Pennsylvania during the 1820s. But only when bawdy houses exceeded community standards did they invite attack, as was the case in New York City when a house that catered to interracial sex provoked mob action. As long as prostitutes and their customers remained relatively quiet, they might be tolerated. After 1830, with the increasing visibility of prostitutes and the organization of metropolitan police forces, streetwalkers risked periodic arrest for vagrancy or disorderly conduct. However, they usually returned to their trade after a short term in the jail or workhouse. Aside from infrequent raids on brothels—such as those in Chicago in 1857 and in Boston in 1858— legal toleration prevailed in most eastern cities and in the western mining and cattle towns to which prostitutes gravitated.[2]

In the 1830s, however, voluntary organizations composed of middle-class reformers began to call attention to prostitution as a social problem and demand a solution. Initiated by clergymen, a movement to oppose prostitution soon gathered support among Protestant women, whose antebellum campaigns for "moral reform" condemned not only prostitution but also the men who resorted to it. In the postwar decades, a broader movement, led by women but including men as well, demanded "social purity," that is, a single standard of morality for both sexes.

Middle-class Americans, and especially Protestant women, had many reasons to oppose prostitution. For one, all sexuality that took place outside of the family generated deep concerns about social order. In general, the "fallen woman" symbolized the fate of the familyless individual in the anonymous city. Sexual commerce also represented the extreme case of the separation of sexuality, not only from reproduction, but also from love and intimacy. For women, especially, prostitution defied the ideal of female chastity. It exposed the double standard and highlighted the disparity between the freedom of men and the dependence of women in economic and sexual life. But it did not merely symbolize deeper social dilemmas. Sexual commerce had in fact become more visible in the urban areas of the northern states and had spread as well in western towns and cities. Moreover, the prostitute evoked fears of disease at a time of recurrent and inexplicable cholera epidemics and a growing incidence of syphilis. Thus women had legitimate concerns about threats to the health and stability of their families.

Prostitution, in short, presented both a symbolic and a real social problem, but that does not explain sufficiently why groups mobilized to oppose it. Equally important, the attack on prostitution emanated from a particular social group at a particular historical moment. Antiprostitution originated where revivalism and commerce converged: in New York City and Boston, along the newly opened trade route of the Erie Canal in upstate New York—known as the "Burned Over District" because waves of revivalism passed through it—and among middle-class men and women. The response to prostitution, then, must be understood within the context of the perfectionism of the Second Great Awakening and the needs of a developing commercial class.

The religious revival brought into the Protestant churches tens of thousands of Americans who hoped to achieve salvation in this life. Women, who were overrepresented among the converts, believed in addition that it was the special mission of their sex to uphold the moral standards of society. Influenced by the revivals, men and women formed associations to espouse their faith and solve social problems that arose in growing cities. Supplementing earlier Bible and tract societies that aimed at converting "heathens"—both Indians and irreligious white settlers in the West—new voluntary associations formed to oppose intemperance, poverty, and slavery. Middle-class women founded urban missions that ministered to impoverished widows, orphans, and prisoners and tried to convert prostitutes to a purer life.

The response to prostitution took place not only during an era of revival and reform, but also of class formation, when artisanship gave way to an industrial working class, and an older merchant-professional class reconstituted as a commercial and manufacturing middle class. The new industrial economy required greater discipline on the part of both managers and workers. The northern middle class's strong commitment to moral order, in addition to its economic interest in encouraging sobriety and self-control, served as one means by which that class differentiated itself from other social groups. Rejecting the libertinism of the European aristocracy, middle-class factory owners, clergy, and doctors upheld the values of frugality and temperate personal habits. Indeed, their critique of slavery rested in part on a revulsion against what they viewed as sensual indulgence by southern whites. In addition, members of the northern middle class considered themselves more civilized than blacks, immigrants, and the poor, whom they stereotyped as sexually promiscuous. Among the newly forming working class, preindustrial practices, such as casual drinking at work and holiday carousing, persisted well into the nineteenth century. The opportunities for public drunkenness, profanity, and lascivious behavior at holiday celebrations dismayed middle-class employers, who led efforts to outlaw drinking, gambling, and "licentiousness." In Lynn, Massachusetts, for example, reformers both embraced middle-class reticence and attempted to discipline the work force when they imposed fines for profanity and abolished the election-day holidays at which public drinking and "lewd and lascivious behavior" had abounded.[3] Thus, even as the middle class idealized the internalization of sexual controls for themselves, they sought to reestablish external controls over workers and the poor.

Finally, organized opposition to prostitution appeared at a moment when the responsibility for morality was being transferred from one set of male professionals to another. In the past, clergy had primary control over personal morality. The declining authority of the clergy, and the reluctance of the state to regulate morality, left a vacuum that was eventually filled, for the most part, by doctors. In the interval, middle-class women emerged as a powerful interest group committed to the guardianship of the nation's morals and critical of the sexual privileges enjoyed by men. As doctors began to assert authority over sexual behavior as a matter of health, they sometimes clashed with women reformers. Prostitution provided a social issue about which each of these groups could articulate a sexual politics rooted in gender and class, in an effort to influence social policy.

In the 1820s, Protestant clergymen initiated an attack on licentiousness when they identified loose sexual conduct as a fearful blight afflicting American society. As one minister told an upstate New York congregation, the "loathsome monster—licentiousness—crawls, tracking the earth with his fetid slime and poisoning the atmosphere with his syphilitic breath." Despite the specific reference to venereal disease, his jeremiad evoked even deeper fears of contamination through the serpent, symbol for both evil and forbidden sexual desire. In addition to such preaching, Protestant reformers issued pamphlets and newspapers to spread their campaign against sexual license. In 1833, John McDowall warned in *McDowall's Journal* and the *Magdalen Report* that ten thousand depraved harlots threatened to corrupt innocent young men in New York City. Other clergy condemned "depraved women" who led astray inexperienced young men in the city.[4]

Middle-class Protestant women already involved in benevolent associations to help the poor, widowed, and orphaned soon recast the attack on licentiousness. Unlike male reformers, who usually portrayed the prostitute as a source of depravity and a threat to men's health, these women claimed sympathy with the prostitute. In the words of one New York reformer, "How, then, can we be pitiless toward the transgressions of the untaught, the unwarned, the neglected!" Adopting a model of female victimization, they argued that seduction by a licentious male led to many a woman's fall into prostitution. "It cannot be concealed," reformers wrote, "that the treachery of man, betraying the interests of . . . woman, is one of the principal causes, which furnishes the victims of licentiousness. Few, very few . . . have sought their wretched calling."[5] Rather than condemning the "fallen woman," female reformers promised to uplift her and restore her to true womanhood. In the name of gender solidarity, they launched an attack on male sexual privilege.

In 1834, New York City women who shared these views formed a Female Moral Reform Society. They hired McDowall and other missionaries to try to convert prostitutes in city jails and hospitals. Their agents also visited brothels, engaging in what historian Carroll Smith-Rosenberg has termed "pious harassment"—praying, singing, and writing down the names of customers. Women soon took over the leadership of moral reform. They edited a newspaper, *The Advocate of Moral Reform,* and traveled throughout the countryside organizing auxiliaries. By 1839, the American Female Moral Reform Society included several hundred associations.[6]

Female moral reformers thought they could transform fallen women into true women, whether prostitutes desired to change or not. To aid this task, Boston and New York women opened temporary homes where prostitutes could stay and where, the founders hoped, inmates would convert to Christianity. Similarly, from the 1840s through the 1860s, women prison reformers throughout the northern states opened halfway houses for released women prisoners, many of whom were prostitutes, in the belief that a woman's "help-ing hand" might prevent them from returning to the streets. As Boston moral reformers observed, however, it was "extremely difficult to persuade inmates of brothels to forsake their road to ruin." Most prostitutes did not think of themselves as fallen women, nor did they aspire to middle-class moral stan-dards. Rather, they often resisted reformers' efforts to make them leave the city, take up sewing, or become domestic servants. Yet these efforts persisted, in part because they served both real and symbolic functions for women reformers for whom the attack on prostitution was a permissible outlet to question men's authority, men's sexual conduct, and women's dependence on men.[7]

In addition to their attempts at proselytizing the fallen, female moral reformers waged a concerted attack upon men who seduced young women or visited brothels. Echoing male health reformers, women cautioned young men to restrain their sexual impulses, but they called for restraint not in the name of preserving men's health, but rather to oppose the injustice of the double standard. "Why should a female be trodden under foot and spurned from society and driven from a parent's roof, if she but fall into sin—while common consent allows the male to habituate himself to this vice, and treats him as not guilty," wrote New York women. The "deliberate destroyer of female inno-cence" deserved to be exposed rather than protected. In 1835, *The Advocate of Moral Reform* warned that it would publish the names of men who indulged in sex outside of marriage. Thus New York women would circumvent the protection afforded men by the anonymity of the city: "Young men in the country!" they cautioned, "beware what you do when you come into the city," for urban missionaries would reveal their names.[8]

In the countryside, as well, women organized to regain some of the control over sexual morality that they had lost during the transition to a more mobile and heterogeneous society. Historian Mary Ryan has found that in Oneida County, New York, factory and college towns drew a large population of young, single men and women who lived apart from family surveillance. The local Female Moral Reform Society devised numerous strategies to protect female chastity and oppose men's use of prostitution. They issued pamphlets and tracts to warn mothers of the dangers of licentiousness, and they at-tempted to ostracize male seducers from the community. Defying the taboo on women's public discussions of sexual matters, they revealed the names of adulterers, stopped men on the streets or in taverns, and visited employers who made sexual advances to their servants. One mother even followed her errant son into a brothel to demand that he return home![9]

In the course of their work in the female moral reform societies and related efforts, thousands of middle-class women transcended the limits of the female domestic sphere. Acting on their belief in female moral superiority, they seized sexual regulation as the prerogative of women. In doing so they transformed the informal female networks of the past into formal organizations that engaged in the world of public reform. A decade before the American women's rights movement began in 1848, they waged petition campaigns to convince state legislators to enact criminal penalties for seduction and adultery. After women had gathered thousands of signatures and won the support of liberal male reformers, such as New York *Tribune* editor Horace Greeley, the campaign succeeded in winning the passage of anti-seduction laws in New York and Massachusetts.[10]

In one sense, female moral reformers anticipated later activists who petitioned legislatures for property rights and suffrage after 1848. Although they did not espouse women's rights per se, moral reformers found ingenious ways to transcend the boundaries of the domestic sphere. They spoke in public, organized independently, and sought the passage of legislation. Ironically, to achieve some of their ends they turned to the state and to the very lawmaking bodies from which women were excluded. In another sense, however, moral reformers were as traditional as they were innovative. Although they believed that the once-fallen woman should not be condemned to a life of prostitution, they accepted fully the social value placed on female chastity. Few understood the different sexual culture of the working class, in which casual sex for pay might be tolerated. In response to women's greater sexual vulnerability in urban and industrial society, they attempted to confine sexuality to marriage by restoring some measure of traditional community control. For these women reformers, sexuality outside the family threatened the only identities available to them—that of wives and mothers. Prostitution, they feared, would destroy the base of their world, the family, by bringing into it the specter of disease and drawing out of it their sons, daughters, and husbands. Like other middle-class women, female moral reformers opposed sexuality that was unrelated to either reproduction or marital intimacy.

Medicine and Morality

Like other antebellum movements to perfect American society, moral reform declined after the 1850s, although middle-class Protestant women continued missionary work with prostitutes throughout the century. In the decades after the Civil War, however, a new spirit of "scientific charity" replaced the benevolence of earlier reforms, and doctors began to supplant clergymen as male authorities over sexual matters. To an extent, doctors filled the vacuum into which women had been drawn earlier. The medical profession soon became the second major group to mobilize sexual reform movements in

America, targeting both abortion and prostitution as professional concerns. On the latter issue, doctors' attitudes differed significantly from the moral reformers who had preceded them. By the 1870s, the medical response to prostitution would inspire a new generation of women reformers to join the political debate over the regulation of prostitution.

Doctors initiated sexual reform movements at a time when the medical profession hoped to improve its reputation. The American Medical Association (AMA), founded in 1847, hastened a process begun earlier in the century by which "regular" physicians drove out "irregular" competitors, including midwives, homeopaths, and bogus healers. Until the 1880s, when the germ theory of disease paved the way for progress against cholera, tuberculosis, and syphilis, physicians could do little to cure these nineteenth-century killers. In the meantime, however, doctors increased both their prestige and their public authority by claiming expertise in new areas, including public health and sexuality.

In the process of expanding their authority, some nineteenth-century doctors seemed to be waging a covert battle against women. New theories of reproductive science reinforced the concept of the separate sexual spheres by exaggerating the centrality of the womb to women's health. Particularly in the new specialization of gynecology, women were seen as merely reproductive beings, ideally confined to the home and to lives of repeated childbearing. As Dr. Horatio Storer wrote in 1871, woman was "what she is in health, in character, in her charms, alike of body, mind and soul because of her womb alone." Harvard physician E. H. Clarke argued in his 1873 book *Sex in Education* that women should not participate in higher education. Alarmed at the declining birth rates among educated, white middle-class women, Clarke reasoned that the energy women expended in studying depleted their reproductive capacities. Some nineteenth-century physicians, such as J. Marion Sims and Robert Battey, employed radical gynecological surgery, including female castration, to "correct" masturbation or other expressions of sexual passion. Similarly, women diagnosed as neurasthenic or insane sometimes had their ovaries removed on the grounds that the reproductive organs determined a woman's overall physical and mental health.[11]

In addition to their efforts through medical advice and private practice, doctors joined political movements to maintain the traditional reproductive framework of marital sexuality. Regular physicians opposed the irregulars who profited from the trade in contraception and abortion. One doctor wrote in outrage in 1867, claiming that married women received circulars "offering information and instrumentalities, and all needed facilities by which the laws of heaven with regard to the increase of the human family may be thwarted."[12] Obstetricians such as Horatio Storer and Augustus Gardner joined Anthony

Comstock's campaign to limit access to contraception, which culminated in the passage of the Comstock Act in 1873.

The medical response to abortion further suggests that doctors viewed women primarily as mothers. In the early nineteenth century, neither doctors, women, nor judges had necessarily condemned abortion as long as it was performed before "quickening," when the mother felt the fetus move within her at about three months. Antebellum laws retained the quickening doctrine and attempted to protect women from unwanted abortion, rather than to prosecute them. After 1860, in response to increasing alarm about the commercialization of abortion and its growing use by married women, doctors began to organize to outlaw abortion and place it under the strict regulation of the medical profession. Horatio Storer led a crusade to punish not only those who performed the operation but also the women who sought them. Unwilling mothers, Storer claimed, who selfishly sought "the pleasures of a summer's trips and amusements," used abortion to evade their maternal duties. Storer mobilized the fledgling American Medical Association, while newspapers such as the New York *Times* popularized his cause and began to ban ads for abortionists and abortifacients. As a result of these efforts, between 1860 and 1890, forty states and territories enacted anti-abortion statutes, many of which rejected the quickening doctrine, placed limitations on advertisements, and helped transfer legal authority for abortion from women to doctors.[13]

Members of the medical profession did not necessarily conspire to limit women to motherhood. Doctors acted independently, but upon widely shared values, when they upheld the legitimacy of the separate spheres. Further, not all doctors supported these efforts, while some women did, including those who opposed abortion and higher education. Some women sought radical gynecological surgery for themselves, whether because they believed the medical opinions or because the removal of womb or ovaries relieved them of the risk of pregnancy. Nonetheless, taken together, these medical constraints suggest that doctors may have gained authority at the expense of women. Just when middle-class women had begun to leave the home, whether as reformers or college students, doctors seemed eager to displace women from the public sphere and reaffirm female domestic and maternal roles.

That many doctors supported not only the separate spheres but also the double standard further indicates a conflict between the interests of women and doctors. Despite their efforts to contain middle-class women within the home and maintain the primacy of reproductive sexuality, the medical profession largely accepted prostitution as a necessary evil. Unlike female reformers of the antebellum decades, doctors at midcentury viewed prostitution not as a moral issue but as a public health problem. In the name of preventing venereal disease, they recommended a system of legalized, or regulated, prostitution that would be overseen by medical authorities. Given their inability to cure syphilis and gonorrhea, however, the plans for regulation represented a symbolic attack on disease that was aimed at prostitutes themselves.

Consciously modeled on the licensing of prostitutes in Paris, and akin to the Contagious Diseases Acts in England during the 1860s, the regulation of prostitution through medical inspection originated in the United States during the Civil War. In Nashville, Tennessee, for example, Union army officials had become concerned about the exposure of soldiers to venereal disease in the brothels that sprang up during wartime. Their first solution, shipping the city's prostitutes to Cincinnati, failed when most of the women simply returned. Next the army turned to regulation, setting up the medical inspection of prostitutes. Those found healthy received a license, while those infected with syphilis went to a special hospital that quickly filled with women. Similarly, the martial law imposed in Memphis in 1864 included a system of regulated prostitution. "All women . . . living in boarding houses, singly or as kept mistresses," had to "be registered and take out weekly certificates" attesting to their health.[14] The fees women paid for their licenses supported a hospital ward where prostitutes were treated for venereal disease. Regulation also restricted prostitutes from soliciting in public or offending respectable women on the streets. These military experiments, aimed at the preservation of soldiers' health rather than improving the lives of prostitutes, ended with the war.

Doctors and public health officials revived the idea of regulated prostitution when they encouraged municipalities to enact medical licensing as a public health measure. Dr. J. Marion Sims, prominent gynecologist and president of the American Medical Association, recommended that regulation become the norm in American cities. Other doctors supported his position, and several localities considered the idea. Between 1868 and 1877, the New York state legislature debated several bills to establish regulated prostitution. In 1870, St. Louis, Missouri, became the only postwar city to enact regulated prostitution.[15]

The idea of state-supported prostitution offended a variety of Americans. Most clergymen continued to see prostitution as a matter of sin rather than disease. Most women reformers considered prostitutes to be the victims of men's lust. In their view, state regulation of prostitution provided men with unlimited sexual access outside of marriage. Both clergy and suffragists knew about the work of Josephine Butler, the British reformer who successfully campaigned against the English Contagious Diseases Acts of the 1860s. Like the Civil War regulation of prostitution, the "C.D. Acts" operated in areas where soldiers or sailors congregated, incarcerating prostitutes in state "lock hospitals" if they were suspected of venereal infection, while their patrons suffered no penalties. Butler's coalition to defeat the C.D. Acts made prostitution a political issue that mobilized British working-class and suffrage leaders against regulation. It also led to the founding of an international Federation for the Abolition of State Regulated Prostitution, whose members alerted Americans to the threat of state-regulated vice.[16]

The British message reached a receptive audience in the United States. Middle-class American women were already sensitive to the double standard by which women, and not men, paid the penalties for illicit sex. They had opposed male sexual license since the antebellum moral reform campaigns. A new generation of educated women, such as doctors Elizabeth Blackwell and Caroline Winslow, argued that women should have responsibility for creating a single standard of sexual morality. In addition, male reformers, such as former abolitionist Aaron Macy Powell of New York, believed that state regulation of prostitution paralleled state sanctions of slavery in the antebellum South; prostitutes, like slaves, had to be delivered from their plight by a "new abolitionist" movement.

American suffragists also opposed regulated prostitution. Since 1848, women's rights activists had exposed inequalities between men and women, especially the denial of property and voting rights to women. In the postwar period, as more women entered the paid labor force but earned much less than men, suffragists developed a feminist interpretation of the prostitute as the ultimate victim of women's economic dependence. In her 1875 public lecture "Social Purity," woman suffrage leader Susan B. Anthony concluded that to prevent prostitution, women needed " 'fair play' in the world of work and self-support." Anthony also targeted men's intemperance in drink and sex: "There is no escape from the conclusion that, while woman's want of bread induces her to pursue this vice, man's love of the vice itself leads him there." Suffragists sympathized with women who became prostitutes, assuming that they had been victimized by men rather than having chosen their trade. As Anthony explained, "For every abandoned woman, there is always *one* abandoned man and oftener many more." Rather than institutionalizing this system of inequality through state regulation, suffragists wanted to eradicate prostitution.[17]

When doctors recommended that Americans adopt regulated prostitution, they sparked a counteroffensive much larger than their own initial efforts toward regulation. The suggestion that the state should officially recognize prostitution as a necessary evil struck a sensitive chord among clergymen, former abolitionists, and women's rights activists. Together they organized formidable resistance to legalized prostitution. In Missouri, clergy and women succeeded in overturning the St. Louis experiment in 1874. Susan B. Anthony convened women's meetings to explain the implications for women's rights of the proposed New York legislation to regulate prostitution. Opponents of regulation helped defeat each of the New York state bills. Similarly, Chicago women and clergymen formed a social purity society in 1870 to defeat regulated prostitution. The following year women's club members in Washington, D.C., called mass meetings and formed a committee for preventing the legalization of prostitution. In the West, women petitioned city councils and state legislatures to close down brothels and enforce vagrancy laws against prostitutes. The San Francisco Women's Suffrage Club opposed laws to legalize prostitution on the grounds that the laws provided an ineffective means of controlling venereal disease. Only a single standard of purity, they argued, could insure public health. By 1886, local social purity coalitions had effectively staved off state-regulated prostitution in America.[18]

The Politics of Social Purity

The battle over regulated prostitution inaugurated a sexual reform movement akin to antebellum moral reform but with more ambitious goals and wider impact. The social purity movement of the late nineteenth century incorporated many of the ideas of moral reform, especially the demand for a single sexual standard. From its local grass-roots origins within the anti-regulation efforts of the 1870s, social purity grew into a national, institutional, and more conservative mold by the 1890s. In the process, it helped transform American attitudes toward sexuality by making women's belief in a single sexual standard the dominant middle-class view. Like earlier moral reformers, and like conservative vice crusaders, social purity advocates resisted the movement of sexuality outside of the private sphere. At the same time, they launched a critique of marital sexuality and attempted to break through the conspiracy of silence regarding the public discussion of sex. Thus social purity unintentionally contributed to the movement of sexuality beyond the family.

The purity leadership included Protestant clergy, former abolitionists, and women's rights activists. Its membership drew heavily from the ranks of middle-class women who, in the late nineteenth century, became increasingly comfortable as activists in the public world of social reform. Unlike earlier moral reformers, who had been motivated primarily by religious enthusiasm, this later generation was influenced as well by the ideas of social Darwinism and by the growing women's rights movement. Furthermore, both white middle-class women and their male counterparts felt a sense of urgency about social reform during the last quarter of the century. The rapid pace of industrial and urban growth, as well as mass immigration from southern and eastern Europe, was transforming American social structure and politics. At one end, the newly wealthy created a world of conspicuous consumption; at the other, an industrial proletariat periodically threatened class war. In between, the middle class attempted to create a semblance of order suitable to their needs.

Earlier in the century, the ideal of the pure woman in her domestic sphere had helped stabilize the rapidly changing society. By the late nineteenth century, however, more and more women left the domestic sphere, entering the paid work force or attending college before marriage. Once married, the declining birth rates revealed, maternity was less central to women's lives. Some doctors tried to return women to the domestic sphere, but middle-class women organized to expand their maternal authority beyond the home, through movements for social purity and temperance. In order to protect the home and enforce their own vision of moral order, they became active in politics. Their attack on legalized prostitution eventually raised criticisms of marital sexuality, as well. Like free lovers and utopians, social purity activists grappled with the new meanings of marital sexuality, especially the relationship of sexuality and reproduction.

Opposition to prostitution united the various strains of the social purity movement. In place of regulated prostitution, purity activists believed in preventing women from "falling" into the trade and in penalizing men for corrupting women. During the late nineteenth century, they expanded efforts (initiated earlier by moral and prison reformers) to uplift prostitutes. Now, however, their goals shifted from conversion to prevention. Conversion had never reaped great rewards, largely because most prostitutes, who entered the trade as a means of support, defied the reform plan for rescuing sexual victims. Missionary outreach continued throughout the century, but it was most successful when women had in fact been forced into prostitution. In California, for example, Presbyterian women led by Donaldina Cameron established a home for escaped Chinese slave prostitutes that lasted from 1874 to 1939. Cameron and her co-workers literally rescued Chinese women from brothels, escorting them to a safe house and accompanying them to court to prevent their "owners" from enforcing labor contracts for sexual service. In contrast to this kind of rescue work, many women reformers now focused on reaching young working-class or immigrant women with social services that would prevent them from becoming prostitutes.

To counter the temptations of urban vice among the recently enlarged ranks of urban working women—mainly low-paid seamstresses, domestic servants, and factory operatives—reformers established clubs such as the Working Girls Society and the Women's Educational and Industrial Union, as well as supervised residences, or surrogate homes. Similarly, new agencies to help migrants or immigrants, such as Travellers Aid and the Young Women's Christian Association, hoped to prevent newly arrived young women from being approached by procurers or exploited by unscrupulous landlords and employers. For those who had "once sinned," reformers established homes for unwed mothers, such as the Florence Crittenden Homes or the Denver Cottage Home, that shielded women from an intolerant society and set them back on the course of virtue instead of the road to the brothel.[19]

In offering preventive or protective services, women reformers could be as condescending as they were "uplifting." They demanded that their clients adopt middle-class values of temperance and domesticity, and they did not encourage working women to view their sexuality in a positive light. Nevertheless, these reformers did challenge an earlier view of the fallen woman as an outcast. Moreover, they recognized that institutional inequalities of class and gender forced some women to sell their bodies. In a sense, through the social services they provided, women reformers attempted to give working women greater access to resources in a society in which these women were particularly vulnerable economically and sexually.

Even more important than reaching women was the task of converting men to the single standard. Rescue work saved only a small number, explained Dr. Caroline Winslow, president of the Washington Moral Education Society; women needed to look deeper into the origins of evil. Those who blamed women for prostitution missed the point, Ellen Battelle Dietrick wrote in the suffrage newspaper *The Woman's Journal.* "They are only dealing with one half of the problem so long as they utterly ignore the fact that the chief cause for 'fallen women' is fallen men." Suffragists Lucy Stone and Henry Blackwell wanted the law to punish men who procured women as prostitutes.[20]

The largest women's organization in nineteenth-century America, the Women's Christian Temperance Union (WCTU), mobilized to uplift men to women's sexual standards. Founded in 1874, the WCTU originated among small-town, midwestern women who took militant action to try to close saloons, which they viewed as a major threat to their homes. Drunken husbands, they believed, used up a family's income on liquor and often physically or sexually abused their wives and children. The attack on the saloon had symbolic meanings as well, for the saloon represented the innermost sanctuary of the male public sphere from which women were excluded. The antithesis of the home, the saloon fostered gambling, obscenity, and prostitution, all of which threatened women's moral purity. WCTU members engaged in political campaigns to achieve temperance in their localities. What began as a crusade for "home protection" soon turned into a larger campaign to give women greater political power in the society. Thus Frances Willard, an inspirational leader who became national president of the WCTU from 1879 until her death in 1898, championed woman suffrage, Populism, and "Christian Socialism" as well as temperance.

In 1885, the WCTU reflected the shift in the direction of antiprostitution sentiment when its Committee for Work with Fallen Women became the

Social Purity Division. In their quest to purify men, WCTU members rallied to the slogan "The White Life for Two," a reference to purity, but one that fit well with popular views about the superior morality of the white race. They launched a White Ribbon campaign, in which men who promised to remain sexually pure wore small white banners to help forge their new identities. The WCTU joined forces with male reformers within religious organizations. In 1885, Episcopal clergy established a branch of the British White Cross Society, a sex education campaign through which the church helped men resist sexual temptation. The WCTU adopted the White Cross crusade, and Frances Willard publicized it in national lectures and in the press. The Union cooperated as well with the Young Men's Christian Association, the Society of Friends, and the Seventh-Day Baptists to encourage men to join the White Cross.[21]

The WCTU, along with other social purity activists, also turned to the state to enforce its moral vision. In the 1880s, the purity movement called on states to raise the age at which a woman could legally consent to sexual relations. The legislation would make men who had sex with young women liable to prosecution for statutory rape, whether or not the women freely consented to intercourse. Age-of-consent legislation rested upon the belief that men initiated unwitting young women into sexual activity that led to prostitution. Its purpose was to deny men their youngest victims. Thus the social purity movement perpetuated the view that prostitutes had been victims of male deception, rather than freely choosing their trade. It effectively limited the sexual choices of working-class women as much as it protected them. But the legislation served the cause of social purity by calling attention to male sexual privilege. For these strategic and symbolic reasons, purity groups gathered signatures on petitions to state legislatures and to Congress to raise the age of consent. Between 1886 and 1895, the social purity campaign succeeded in raising the age of consent from as low as ten years in some states to between fourteen and eighteen years in twenty-nine states.[22]

Although the debate over prostitution inspired the social purity movement, women went on to attack all forms of male sexual privilege. The most radical theorists, such as suffrage leaders Susan B. Anthony and Elizabeth Cady Stanton, drew parallels between prostitution and marriage. In both institutions, women engaged in sexual relations in return for economic support. Marriage and divorce laws trapped women in unhappy relationships, they wrote, and made it impossible for them to escape from drunken or sexually abusive husbands. As remedies, Stanton called for more liberal divorce laws, while Anthony repeated her analysis that women had to become self-supporting in order to prevent unhappy marriages. In the meantime she recommended that women decline offers of marriage from "impure" men and refuse "to continue in the marital relation" if their husbands visited prostitutes or took mistresses. Even a moderate like Lucy Stone exposed sexual injustice within marriage. As editor of the *Woman's Journal,* she instituted a weekly catalogue of "crimes against women," including rape, incest, wife beating, and marital rape.[23]

Short of criticizing marriage as an institution, suffragists and social purity workers insisted that women should have more control over marital sexuality. Their key demand was "voluntary motherhood," or the right to say no to sex unless a woman wanted to become pregnant. Despite the increased use of contraception to limit family size, suffragists preferred voluntary motherhood to either contraception or abortion. They associated contraception with men's privilege to have sex outside of marriage, while abortion, they believed, unjustly burdened women with the costs of unwanted pregnancy. Influenced by Darwinian ideas about the improvement of the species, many believed that children who were conceived during voluntary intercourse would be healthier and more intelligent, while those conceived during unwanted intercourse might become criminals, idiots, or paupers. As suffragist Harriet Stanton Blatch explained in 1891, the "welcome" child—one whose mother chose to perform the labor necessary to proper upbringing—advanced the evolution of the race.[24]

Despite their rejection of "artificial" contraception and their belief that force, not choice, led women into prostitution, social purity workers did not necessarily deny female sexual pleasure. In their marital advice books, social purity leaders Elizabeth Blackwell, Eliza Duffey, and Alice Stockham each recognized women's desires, but they stressed that women could only enjoy intercourse if they truly wanted it. Blackwell termed unwanted marital intercourse a "grave social crime," but she challenged what she termed the "prevalent fallacy" that men had stronger sexual passions than women. In healthy women, uninjured by too-frequent childbirth, "increasing physical satisfaction attaches to the ultimate physical expression of love." Similarly, social purity advocate Ida Craddock encouraged married women not to submit to unwanted or unfulfilling intercourse, yet insisted that they could enjoy sexual relations. In "Right Marital Living" Craddock echoed the spiritualization of sexual relations so prevalent in the middle class:

> the nude embrace comes to be respected more and more, and finally reverenced, as a pure and beautiful approach to the sacred moment when husband and wife shall melt into one another's genital embrace, so that the twain shall be one flesh, and then, as of old, God will walk with the twain in the garden of bliss "in the cool of the day," when the heat of ill-regulated passion is no more.[25]

In short, social purity sought not to oppose all sexuality but rather to control male sexuality and to spiritualize marital relationships. In their approach to prostitution as well as to marital sexuality, women's rights activists concentrated on the problem of gender inequality, not necessarily on the dangers of sexuality itself.

The social purity view of sexuality must be interpreted in light of women's historical experience. The declining importance of reproduction as a part of sexual life had different meanings for men and women, creating for a time a gap between the extended privileges of men and the traditional responsibilities of women. Despite their shared experience of the heightened importance of sexual intimacy within courtship and marriage, women maintained a closer connection to reproduction, and men had greater access to sexuality beyond the family, without reproductive responsibilities. Not only did women continue to experience the physical consequences of pregnancy and childbirth, at a time when contraception did not always insure their avoidance, but women also continued to perform the social role of mothering. As Linda Gordon has argued, the insistence of women reformers that sexuality and reproduction remain linked served women's interests by preserving their traditional maternal authority when women still had little access to political or economic power outside the home.

Even as the social purity arguments resisted both the separation of sexuality and reproduction and the movement of sex outside the home, its program in fact provided a bridge from the past to the future. Gordon argues, for example, that voluntary motherhood was the first step in an ideological progression toward the acceptance of family limitation and, ultimately, of contraception.[26] In addition, social purity embraced the notion, growing among the middle class, that a romantic, even spiritual, bond should exist between husbands and wives. Fearing the economic and physical costs that women might pay as sexuality became less closely associated with reproduction, social purity theorists, like free lovers, accepted the positive value of the erotic only if love bound partners together.

Finally, women's rights and social purity advocates looked toward the future by rejecting middle-class reticence about discussing sex. Through a "moral education" movement, for example, nineteenth-century reformers issued the first call for sex education in America. Women, they argued, must teach children about sex, lest they learn incorrectly from other sources. As one writer exhorted mothers, "Show your sons and daughters the sanctities and the terrors of this awful power of sex, its capacities to bless or curse its owner." Both women and children needed moral education, Lucinda Chandler argued. For children, special education "to fit them for parenthood" would advance social purity, while women needed to be educated to know that they had the right to control their own person. From their exposés of the evils of prostitution to the "No Secrets" approach of the Moral Education Societies, social purity workers called for a public sexual discourse that, in contrast with the portrayal of sexuality in the male and working-class world of sexual commerce, emphasized love and reproductive responsibility rather than lust. Sex, they wanted children to learn, could be holy; in the absence of love and marriage, however, it defiled woman or man.[27]

By the 1890s, social purity had become a broad-based national movement that included suffragists, temperance workers, and clergy from every denomination. It had succeeded in its goals to the extent that doctors who had originally recommended legalized prostitution now accepted the view that the social evil should be abolished. By the time of the first National Purity Congress in 1893, the single standard had become the common ideal, although not necessarily the common practice, among middle-class Americans. Moreover, key political victories had been won. Cities and states had rejected regulated prostitution and raised the age of consent.

Yet the success of the social purity movement was in many ways illusory. Despite the defeat of regulation, prostitution continued to flourish in red-light districts, away from the view of the middle classes. The sanctity of the home was constantly belied by sweatshop conditions and tenement housing, as well as by a noticeable rise in the frequency of divorce. And even as the revivalistic fervor for social purity swelled, a renewed free-love movement took purity ideals to their uncomfortable yet logical extreme. Indeed, the last quarter of the nineteenth century witnessed an intense battle between those who sought to control sexuality by returning it to the private sphere of the family and those who sought to release it from social constraints.

Sex Wars: Obscenity and Free Speech in the Late Nineteenth Century

To some extent, all of the responses to prostitution, from moral reform to social purity, combined a vision of individual control over sexuality with a program of external regulation, whether by family, community, or the state. In the battle over obscenity, however, sharply opposing camps, one embracing individual and the other social control of sexuality, squared off against each other. The attack on obscenity, commandeered by Anthony Comstock, called for direct government involvement in the suppression of sexual expression in the public sphere and the confinement of sexuality to its reproductive function. In contrast, a small but vocal anarchist and free-love movement demanded that neither church nor state should limit the expression of sexual ideas and feelings; whether in private or in public, the regulation of sexual life should be solely a matter of individual choice.

The frequent skirmishes between these two armies of true believers—free lovers committed to exposing all sexual matters to the light of day, and vice crusaders determined to keep all such "obscenity" (that is, open discussion of sexuality and contraception) behind closed doors—portrayed dramatically a central problem of late-nineteenth-century sexual thought. Was sex best regulated by expanding or restricting its public discussion? In the late nineteenth century, the restrictive policy advocated by Comstock triumphed in most of the battles. By the early twentieth century, however, the expansive mode, supported by free lovers, suffragists, and sex educators, would win the war.

The initial impulse to suppress obscenity had originated at the same time as moral reform and from a common source. In 1834, New York City moral reformer John McDowall had invited several hundred clergymen to a display of obscene books and articles he had collected. At that time, however, New Yorkers were reluctant to join McDowall in a campaign against such literature. In fact, a New York grand jury investigating McDowall found that his exposés, "under the pretext of cautioning the young of both sexes against the temptation to criminal indulgence," were as offensive as the literature he condemned. Despite McDowall's efforts, Americans neither established a voluntary agency to parallel England's Society for the Suppression of Vice (founded in 1802), nor did they call for further state intervention against obscenity. In the antebellum era, Americans seemed to be more interested in individual purification through internalized control than in the public regulation of sexual expression.[28]

A commitment to freedom of the press, as well as the limited circulation of obscene publications, also forestalled a movement for censorship. Only rarely did the states express concern about the potential of art and literature to corrupt the morals of youth. In 1821, a Massachusetts court did sentence a bookdealer to six months in jail for selling the eighteenth-century English novel *Fanny Hill* to local farmers. But American courts heard very few obscenity cases between 1821 and 1870, and these concerned guides to marital sex (such as Charles Knowlton's *Fruits of Philosophy*) containing contraceptive information. Only four state legislatures enacted obscenity laws prior to the Civil War. The federal customs law of 1842 prohibited the importation of indecent and obscene prints and paintings, but it excluded printed matter from regulation.[29]

The growing reticence about sexuality among the middle class did affect American artists of the antebellum period. At a time when it was acceptable to depict the naked body in European art, those who exhibited in America learned that nudity and sexuality were highly controversial. When Adolphe Ulrich Wertmüller, a Swedish-born painter living in Delaware, exhibited his *Danäe and the Shower of Gold,* with its clear reference to sexual intercourse, an American critic commented that it was a scene "that public decorum requires to be shut out from the eye of day." Writing in 1812, the critic claimed that "no modest woman would venture to contemplate [it] in the presence of a man." (In fact, the gallery that exhibited the painting in New York set aside separate days for "ladies" to view it in private.) Similarly, the American press denounced as indecent French paintings that included nudes, even in biblical scenes, but the American public defied the critics and continued to pay admission fees to see condemned paintings. As artist Henry Inman wrote in 1833, "Crowds of both sexes sit together for hours gazing upon these very nude figures with delight."[30]

Nonetheless, American artists shied away from nude or sexual subject matter. At the advice of his father, for example, Rembrandt Peale gave up the depiction of nudes and turned his hand to portraiture. One of the few exceptions to the trend, the Transcendentalist painter William Page, was accused of violating "all modern delicacy" in his studies of Venus. In the 1840s, the National Academy refused Page's *Cupid and Psyche* because of its nudity, and some critics feared that the painting threatened to infest American culture with the decaying morals of decadent Europe. A close look at this work reveals how conflicted Americans were about sexuality and its public expression. The Greek statue that inspired Page had shown fully the nude figure of Cupid embracing a partially bare-breasted and scantily clothed Psyche. Compared to the original, Page's perspective, revealing only Psyche's bare back and the couple's entwined hands, seems modest, almost protective, while the idyllic setting places sensuality tamely within the natural world. Like other Americans, however, Page seemed ambivalent about the sensual, especially in his composition: the masking of her face, the tentative groping toward an embrace by his right hand, the contortion of her torso and their arms, the uncomfortable merging of two bodies into one indistinguishable unit. *Cupid and Psyche* was, undeniably, an erotic painting, perhaps the most explicitly so by any nineteenth-century American artist. Yet its representation of sexuality was not unequivocally positive, and its reception exposed a strong hostility to explorations of any sexual theme in American art.[31]

While high culture imposed self-censorship to limit the representation of sexuality, commercial culture respected no such bounds, especially after the 1860s. The Civil War encouraged the growth of sexual commerce in the form of both obscene literature and prostitution. After the war, cheaply produced and sexually titillating pulp novels, including dime novels for adults and half-dime or story papers for boys, could be mailed at new second-class postal rates.[32] Simultaneously, the presence of single men living outside family supervision in the cities provided both a market for sexual commerce and a disturbing reminder of the movement of sexuality from the private to the public spheres.

The expansion of sexually explicit popular literature was met by a new sexual reform movement, one more willing to turn to the state to support its goals. One reform agency, the New York City Young Men's Christian Association, instigated a postwar anti-obscenity crusade. In 1866, a YMCA report bemoaned the decline of paternalistic supervision over the morals of young workers. Employers no longer took notice of the "social and moral interests of young men." In urban boardinghouses, the "virtuous and the vicious" were thrown together; after work, young men frequented saloons and theaters, where they were likely to meet prostitutes or buy the cheap "vile newspapers" that the YMCA believed were "feeders for brothels."[33] The Association tried to redirect young men along the path to pure Christian living by providing alternative housing, reading, and recreation.

One YMCA member, Connecticut dry-goods salesman Anthony Comstock, adopted as his life's work the task of combating sex in print, art, or private correspondence. Story papers and pulp novels, he explained in *Traps for the Young* (1883), bred "vulgarity, profanity, loose ideas of life, impurity of thought and deed." Moreover, Comstock claimed, when impressionable youth read dime novels, they proceeded to act out their plots of seduction, theft, and murder. He implored parents to monitor their children's reading and boycott newsdealers who sold "these death-traps." Comstock's greatest concern, however, was the availability of "obscene literature" and articles through the mails. Only state action could defeat this threat to national morality.[34]

In 1872, Anthony Comstock began a crusade to strengthen anti-obscenity laws. With financial backing from the upper-class businessmen on the board of the YMCA, Comstock tirelessly lobbied state and federal legislatures. He also founded the New York Society for the Suppression of Vice to support his work. Through the Society, Comstock enforced existing obscenity laws; he seized and handed over to the police "bad books" and "articles made of rubber for immoral purposes, and used by both sexes."[35] Comstock's major political victory came in 1873, when the U.S. Congress passed, without debate, "An Act for the Suppression of Trade in, and Circulation of Obscene Literature and Articles of Immoral Use." This revision of the federal postal law forbade the mailing of obscene, lewd, lascivious, and indecent writing or advertisements, including articles that aided contraception or abortion.

Throughout the 1880s and 1890s, Congress strengthened the so-called Comstock law, and the courts upheld its constitutionality. Comstock himself supervised enforcement. As an unpaid U.S. postal inspector, he almost single-handedly prosecuted those who wrote, published, and sold literature or art that he considered obscene. In 1875 alone, his vigilance led to forty-seven arrests, twenty-eight convictions (aggregating thirty years in prison), and ninety-one hundred fines. That year the New York Society for the Suppression of Vice seized twelve hundred pounds of books and destroyed over twenty-nine thousand sexually explicit photos, songs, leaflets, rubber goods, and circulars. The objects of Comstock's attack ranged from penny postcards sold on the Bowery to fine arts exhibited in Fifth Avenue galleries depicting the nude body, from dime novels of seduction to Leo Tolstoy's *Kreutzer Sonata,* an 1889 novel that spoke openly of prostitution. The conviction rate under the Comstock Act—as high as ninety percent of those accused—attested to Comstock's boundless (some claimed prurient) interest in suppressing vice.[36]

Comstock could not have managed his campaign without broader public support. While he set about enforcing anti-obscenity postal statutes, the social purity and suffrage movements also voiced concerns about the danger of vicious literature. In 1883 the WCTU established a Department for the Suppression of Impure Literature. In the 1890s, local women successfully campaigned for the removal of a painting depicting a nude from the bar of a Cincinnati restaurant, and the WCTU kept the sculpture *Bacchante and Infant* from being displayed at the Boston Public Library.[37] Eventually, both the WCTU and the *Woman's Journal* became critical of Comstock's methods of intimidation and entrapment, and he in turn attacked the suffragists. In the meantime, however, Comstock had consolidated extensive support from wealthy urban businessmen who formed local societies to suppress vice. In Rochester, Providence, Detroit, Toledo, San Francisco, Portland, and Cincinnati, local elites organized chapters of the Society for the Suppression of Vice. A New England branch, founded in 1882, declared itself the Watch and Ward Society in 1891. Fueled by Comstock's Boston counterpart Godfrey Lowell Cabot (who privately wrote lascivious sexual fantasies in letters to his wife), the Watch and Ward succeeded in strengthening the Massachusetts anti-obscenity law to imprison publishers and to fine news dealers who sold any literature that might corrupt the morals of the young. By the end of the century, at least seven states had passed "Little Comstock Acts" to regulate newsstand sales of lascivious literature, and almost every state eventually joined their ranks. Meanwhile, respectable publishers imposed self-censorship to avoid conflict with the anti-vice societies.[38]

Two underlying themes characterized the anti-vice efforts to use the state to regulate sexual expression. First, sexuality had to be restored to the private sphere; therefore, any public expression of sexuality was considered, by definition, obscene. Second, lust was in itself dangerous; therefore Comstock and his allies attacked not only sexual literature sold for profit but also any dissenting medical or philosophical opinion that supported the belief that sexuality had other than reproductive purposes. Thus, even doctors paid heavy fines for publishing discussions of contraception or sex education. In 1874 Comstock arrested Dr. Edward Bliss Foote for including information about condoms and womb veils in his marital advice books. As a result of his conviction and fine, Foote deleted these methods from his text, even as he waged an attack on the Comstock laws. But the severest penalties awaited those radicals who, during the 1880s and 1890s, elaborated the anarchist and free-love theory of sexuality. Comstock hounded free lovers such as Victoria Woodhull, Ezra Heywood, Moses Harmon, and social purity writer Ida Craddock, imprisoning each for a time. Craddock, a spiritualist who had published a guide to marital sex for women, was one of several suicides that resulted from Comstock's ruthless pursuit (others included Madame Restell, the notorious New York city abortionist, and pornographer William Haynes). In a letter to the public, written before she took her life, Craddock accused Comstock of being a "sex pervert" and called for an exposé of his activities:

> Perhaps it may be that in my death more than in my life, the American people may be shocked into investigating the dreadful state of affairs which permits that unctuous sexual hypocrite, Anthony Comstock, to wax fat and arrogant, and to trample upon the liberties of the people, invading, in my own case, both my right to freedom of religion and to freedom of the press.[39]

Just why these radicals elicited so much of Comstock's rage requires a closer look at the late-nineteenth-century free-love movement, the antithesis of vice suppression. In many ways, the anarchist free-love philosophy formulated in the 1870s resembled social purity. Free lovers opposed prostitution, criticized male sexual dominance in marriage, and envisioned a society in which women would have greater equality with men. Some free-love advocates incorporated other social purity ideals, such as voluntary motherhood and the importance of male continence. Despite these similarities, free love differed fundamentally from social purity in that free lovers wanted to abolish the institution of marriage rather than reform it. In addition, some free lovers believed that erotic pleasure, with or without reproduction, was a valuable goal of sexual relations, but not apart from love.

As its proponents were quick to point out, free love did not mean sexual licentiousness. Rather, free love referred to the right of all men and women to choose sexual partners freely on the basis of mutual love and unconstrained by church, state, or public opinion. Despite their opposition to marriage, many free lovers had long monogamous unions; others practiced what has come to be called "serial monogamy," leaving one long-term partner only when another true love exerted its call. These practices had roots within both anarchist and spiritualist traditions. Many anarchists opposed marriage on the grounds that it represented an unjust intrusion of the state into personal life or because marriage laws made women the property of men. Spiritualists believed that the soul could transcend the boundaries of the material world and were therefore sympathetic to the anarchist critique of societal controls over the individual. Both groups opposed organized religion, which, they believed, supported the enslavement of women to men within the institution of marriage.

Although free love originated in the antebellum period, when Frances Wright and others created short-lived utopian communities, it reached a wider audience in the last quarter of the nineteenth century, when public lectures by Victoria Woodhull attracted national attention. As in the past, free love evoked fears that uncontrolled promiscuity would undermine the moral base of the society—the family. Now, in addition, Americans associated free love with anarchist politics. Especially after the Haymarket Riot of 1886, when seven anarchists were convicted of murder after a bomb exploded at a protest rally in Chicago, anarchism raised the specter of the violent overthrow of the government. As a result, newspaper editors, clergymen, and Comstock crusaded to suppress what they perceived to be a dangerous tendency. They ridiculed, ostracized, and imprisoned free lovers, who nonetheless continued to express their alternative sexual theory. Free lovers remained committed to breaking middle-class taboos on the public discussion of sexuality, the very taboos that Comstock was committed to enforcing. The stage was set for the sex wars of the late nineteenth century.

During the 1870s, Victoria Claflin Woodhull issued the clearest battle cry of the free-love–free-speech offensive. Woodhull's personal background prepared her for her later, infamous career. Raised in a spiritualist family, at age fifteen she married a doctor who turned out to be a drunkard. Woodhull abandoned her husband and supported herself as an itinerant spiritualist. In the 1860s, with the help of Cornelius Vanderbilt, she and her sister Tennessee Claflin became the first women stockbrokers on Wall Street. Woodhull remarried Colonel James Blood, whom she eventually left to marry a wealthy Englishman. First, however, she joined and was expelled from the Marxist International Workingmen's Association, ran for the presidency of the United States, and scandalized American society by publicizing her free-love doctrines.[40]

Woodhull derived her sexual theories from her own personal experience and from the philosophy of Stephen Pearl Andrews, whom she had met in New York. The central theme in her public lectures and articles of the early 1870s was that sexual consummation should only occur when a man and a woman loved each other; marriage restricted this ideal by allowing sex without love between husbands and wives and by preventing loving sex between those not married to each other. In addition to elevating individual sexual choice over the laws of marriage, Woodhull emphasized the positive value of sexuality and condemned marriage for stifling the liberating potential of sexual passion. Anticipating modern notions of the centrality of sex to personal identity, she declared that "[s]exuality is the physiological basis of character and must be preserved as its balance and perfection." To develop human sexuality, a young man or woman "should be taught all there is known about its uses and abuses, so that he or she shall not ignorantly drift upon the shoals whereon so many lives are wrecked." To charges that sexual desire was "vulgar," she responded as a romantic and a libertarian:

> What! Vulgar! The instinct that creates immortal souls vulgar! Who dare stand up amid Nature, all prolific and beautiful, whose pulses are ever bounding with the creative desire, and utter such sacrilege! Vulgar, indeed! Vulgar, rather, must be the mind that can conceive such blasphemy.[41]

Victoria Woodhull's public advocacy of free love might have been tolerated in the 1870s, when many Americans engaged in nonprocreative sex and sophisticated New Yorkers were well aware of the extent of adultery among them. But Woodhull went a step further and broke the conspiracy of silence that protected the middle classes from the contradictions in their sexual ideology. To highlight the hypocrisy of opposition to free love, she announced in public that the prominent Brooklyn minister Henry Ward Beecher was having an affair with a married parishioner, Elizabeth Tilton. Not only did the Beecher family and all of respectable society condemn her for the revelation, but an infuriated Anthony Comstock sent Woodhull to jail for publishing the details in *Woodhull and Claflin's Weekly*. She was ultimately acquitted, but after her marriage and emigration to England, Woodhull no longer spoke out on free love.

The controversy set off by Victoria Woodhull helped inspire a budding new generation of free lovers, including Ezra Heywood, who founded the New England Free Love League to provide a forum for Woodhull to address. An abolitionist, pacifist, and anarchist, Heywood published a free-love tract, *Cupid's Yokes* (1876), for which Anthony Comstock had him and his publisher jailed. Like earlier free lovers, Heywood considered marriage a form of prostitution. Although he accepted male continence, along with other methods of contraception, Heywood endorsed the ideas of the healthfulness of sexual passion, as did his wife, women's rights and free-love advocate Angela Tilton Heywood. Both Ezra and Angela Heywood believed that frank discussion of all sexual matters was critical to alleviating the sexual ills that seemed to pervade American society. Thus they named their journal *The Word*, and in it they employed direct language. As Angela explained,

> Such graceful terms as hearing, seeing, smelling, tasting, fucking, throbbing, kissing, and kin words, are telephone expressions, lighthouses of intercourse; . . . their aptness, euphony and serviceable persistence make it as impossible and undesirable to put them out of pure use as it would be to take oxygen out of air.

For such plain speaking, the Heywoods, too, incurred the wrath of Anthony Comstock, who twice convicted Ezra Heywood for printing obscenity. Ezra served three years at hard labor, while Angela supported their four children alone. Within a year of his release from prison, Ezra Heywood died, one of many martyrs of Comstock's crusades.[42]

The task of naming the sexual was carried on by Moses Harmon, a Virginia-born minister who converted to "free thought" in Kansas during the 1880s. Between 1883 and 1907, Harmon published *Lucifer, The Light Bearer,* a radical journal opposed to lynching, the Spanish-American War, and women's sexual slavery. *Lucifer* published biblical descriptions of sex, letters from women who complained about their husbands' sexual excesses, and even accounts of oral sex, which, like homosexuality, free lovers condemned as unnatural. Although Harmon shared the social purity–suffragist belief that women should have the right to say no to unwanted sex and motherhood, *Lucifer* was too sexually explicit for Anthony Comstock. In 1886, Comstock prosecuted Harmon for publishing a letter exposing the horrors of marital rape. Harmon served a prison term for his plain speaking; during his absence, Lois Waisbrooker, a women's rights supporter and spiritualist, edited the journal. Harmon's seventeen-year-old daughter, Lillian, also clashed with the law when she "married" Edwin Walker without the blessings of church or state. Publicized in *Lucifer,* their free-love ceremony led to the couple's arrest and imprisonment. Lillian Harmon later opposed the age-of-consent laws because they forced chastity upon young women.[43]

Although sexual radicals and some liberal supporters tried to stop Comstock, they were unsuccessful. Two organizations—the National Liberal League and the National Defense Association—publicly opposed Comstock, and Heywood's publisher gathered seventy thousand signatures on a petition to repeal the Comstock Act. The popular press frequently ridiculed Comstock, but they never undermined his political power. Comstock succeeded until his death in 1915 at least in part because his tactics of intimidation immobilized many critics. On a deeper level, Comstock could remain powerful because his crusade tapped both the fears and the longings of mainstream America. Even as middle-class men and women began to limit family size and value romantic union in marriage, they worried about the specter of sexuality unleashed from traditional controls. At a time when the middle class sought to establish social order in the face of rapid industrialization and immigration, the control of sexuality outside of the family seemed all the more pressing. Whatever new sexual meanings they may have embraced within the private realm of marriage, middle-class Americans increasingly insisted on limiting the public expression of sexual desire. Sex divorced from reproduction was simply too disturbing to unleash in public. Thus public reticence accompanied the private transformation of sexuality.

In addition to their battles against the suppression of sexuality, late-nineteenth-century free lovers engaged in an internal dialogue about the meaning of sexuality and its relationship to reproduction that mirrored broader, often unspoken social concerns. In the pages of *The Word* and *Lucifer*, and in their novels and political tracts, free lovers struggled with the problem of how to balance the increasing importance of erotic sexuality against the fear that it would lead to sexual chaos. The free-love response pointed in the direction of modern sexual ideas when it affirmed the positive value of the erotic, but its ties to the nineteenth-century theory of sexual control remained strong. Like John Humphrey Noyes's system of *coitus reservatus,* each of the major sexual alternatives endorsed by free lovers combined sexual pleasure with sexual restraint. In *Karezza* (1896), for example, Alice Stockham explained how both men and women could build stronger characters by engaging in sexual relations that stopped short of climax. Karezza, and other theories such as Alphaism, Dianism, and Zugassent's Discovery, differed in their recommended frequency of sexual intercourse, but they all claimed to enhance sexual pleasure by avoiding orgasm. Thus, each method allowed erotic sex to flourish while preventing procreation, and each combined individual sexual choice with individual sexual control. Although some free lovers accepted contraception, and in some cases abortion, they perceived homosexuality as an unnatural vice. As libertarians, they opposed the imprisonment of British writer Oscar Wilde, but their sexual radicalism pressed only to the boundaries of heterosexuality, and not beyond.[44]

Free love remained within the mainstream of nineteenth-century sexual thought in other ways as well. Despite its opposition to marriage, the free-love doctrine was rooted in a perfectionist notion of the family in which the "true love" of a man and woman would produce not only morally stronger characters but also biologically superior children. Free lovers, social purity advocates, suffragists, and some utopians combined this romantic vision with late-nineteenth-century Darwinian theories of natural selection to create what historian Hal Sears has termed "anarchist eugenics," the forerunner of the Progressive-era eugenics movement.[45] Edward Bliss Foote, Stephen Pearl Andrews, the Nicholses, Elmina Drake Slenker, as well as women's rights leader Elizabeth Cady Stanton and social scientist Lester Ward, all supported women's right to control reproduction on the grounds that women would select mates wisely and produce healthier, physically stronger, and morally superior offspring. By justifying free love in the name of race progress, they countered the charges of "race suicide" leveled against Anglo-Saxon women who chose to bear few children, but they did so by accepting the argument that racial purity was a major goal of sexual intercourse.

Anarchist eugenics reflected how closely the free-love vision resembled the sexual thought of the dominant society. Despite the persecution of free-love anarchists, their values were not entirely incompatible with those of most Americans. Indeed, by 1907, when *Lucifer* became the *American Journal of Eugenics,* free love had ceased to occupy the radical fringe. Its once-threatening message of sex education, birth control, and the romantic union of love and sexuality was about to become the dominant middle-class sexual ideology. Along the way, however, the central anarchist theme of individual freedom would be discarded, as church, state, and public opinion gradually joined in enforcing many of the sexual ideas for which nineteenth-century free lovers had been sent to prison.

The emergence of sexual politics in the late nineteenth century was one manifestation of the expansion of sexuality beyond marriage. Although sexuality continued to be rooted in marriage and reproduction, its meaning and its regulation had moved in two directions over the century. First, within the middle class, sexuality increasingly became a privatized, rather than communal, concern. As reproduction ceased to be the primary goal of sexual relations, romantic intimacy and erotic pleasure played larger roles in sexual relations, while an ideal of self-government and the internalization of sexual controls replaced the regulation of morality by church and state. Thus by midcentury, health reform, free-love, and utopian alternatives all emphasized the importance of the individual management of sexual impulses. At the same time, however, sexuality had begun to move into the public sphere. The market economy drew sexuality out of the home in many forms, including the sale of marital advice, advertisements for contraception and abortion, "obscene" literature, dance halls, and prostitution. The sexually segregated labor market also helped provide a supply of underpaid working women who served as prostitutes, especially for men who now lived apart from families. By the last quarter of the century, the ideal of privacy coexisted uncomfortably with the commercialization of sex, and the tension between the two influenced the regulation of sexuality.

At the beginning of the century, the communal regulation of the colonial era had been supplanted by the ideal of the self-regulating individual, operating in the free market of sex. Those who accepted the movement of sexuality into the marketplace—including publishers, prostitutes, and procurers—sought to profit, or at least to survive, from its sale. Many Americans, however, became uneasy over the prospect that the individual would not be self-regulating, or that the market in sexual commerce had become too visible and too powerful for individuals to resist its allure. Fears of uncontrolled sexuality tapped deep symbolic concerns. The rapid social changes wrought by industrialization triggered fears about Americans' ability to maintain social order. The middle class responded to these anxieties by emphasizing the centrality of female purity for family stability and by attempting to impose limits on the public expression of sexuality. To some extent, these efforts can be seen as a form of social control over the working class, for whom public expressions of and commerce in sexuality did not pose serious difficulties. In another sense, the theme of sexual control supported the American myth of a classless society characterized by expansive social mobility. Those who embraced the values of female purity and sexual reticence could aspire to middle-class status; in contrast, the failure to control one's sexual impulses explained economic failure. In this system, those who sought social control over sexuality—such as opponents of prostitution or obscene literature—saw themselves as agents of uplift, directing working-class women and men toward middle-class respectability.

The sexual reformers who sought to supplement internal controls with social controls over sexuality sometimes agreed and sometimes conflicted about the means of sexual regulation. The free-love ideal shored up individual men and women by removing all external constraints; utopian experiments balanced individual and community controls, placing more responsibility in the hands of men than of women; doctors too stressed male control of sexuality and accepted the double standard that constrained married women to motherhood but accepted prostitution as a necessary evil; female moral reform and social purity campaigns upheld a single standard of sexual behavior, targeted men of all classes as the root of prostitution, and, like free lovers, emphasized the spiritual bond of sexuality; vice crusaders reasserted the link between sex and reproduction, accepting, as did social purity adherents, state regulation of sexuality. The latter solution proved increasingly palatable to middle-class Americans. Despite their strong opposition to government interference in the workings of the economy, by the late nineteenth century many had come to support state regulation of sexuality. Their willingness to do so provides a measure of both their recognition that sexuality was moving irreversibly beyond the family and their commitment to resisting that movement.

PART III

TOWARD A NEW SEXUAL ORDER,

1880–1930

CHAPTER 8

"Civilized Morality" Under Stress

IN 1929, Katharine Bement Davis published a massive study, *Factors in the Sex Lives of Twenty-Two Hundred Women*.[1] The product of almost ten years of work, the book had a depth and breadth that made it unique for the times. Based on lengthy questionnaires completed by both married and single women, it covered virtually every facet of the erotic experience of her respondents. Childhood influences, expectations about conjugal relations, birth control practices, the frequency of intercourse, the relationship of desire to the menstrual cycle, factors related to happiness in marriage—all these as well as other topics came under her scrutiny. Beyond its specific findings, the study is notable for the dispassionate way in which Davis applied modern techniques of social science to the subject of sex. Gone was the reticence that characterized the nineteenth-century middle-class approach to sexual matters. Unlike Clelia Mosher, who never published her small study of female sexuality, Davis was bringing sex into the public sphere as a subject worthy of scientific exploration.

Davis's life made her uniquely appropriate to initiate such a study. A long and distinguished professional career had placed her in contact with a wide range of sexual value systems. The oldest of five children, she was born in 1860 in western New York, the site of decades of religious revivals and intense female moral reform efforts whose exploits she learned from her grandmother. After years of teaching high school, she attended Vassar, where the daughters of many middle-class families were preparing for careers that they would pursue to the exclusion of marriage. As a settlement-house worker in Philadelphia, Davis, along with other men and women of her class, observed at close hand the lives of blacks and European immigrants whose family forms and sexual mores were strangely different from her own upbringing. Later, in the role of superintendent of the Bedford Hills Reformatory for Women, she had to deal with working-class women incarcerated for prostitution and other morals offenses, and had to respond as well to the homosexual liaisons that frequently formed among inmates. Throughout her career Davis, who never married, found herself in close association with other female professionals whose lives often revolved around intimate relationships with other women.

Though Davis left little evidence to help us identify the motives behind her interest in sexuality, one can reasonably speculate that her awareness of sexual diversity in the American social landscape piqued her intellectual curiosity. By the early twentieth century, what Freud termed the "civilized morality" of the middle class was subject to intensifying pressures and diverse influences.[2] Among middle-class couples, extremely low fertility rates testified to the declining importance of procreation in conjugal relations, while the social purity movement was promoting an ethic of refined, tender passion between spouses. In many of these marriages the single standard of morality advocated by feminists and social purity crusaders had won acceptance. But the contrasting socialization of men and women continued to create tensions in the implementation of this ideal. Prostitution flourished as never before in large, commercialized red-light districts, placing the genteel morality of the middle-class home on tenuous foundations at best. At the same time, points of contact between middle-class and working-class culture were multiplying, as Davis's own life illustrated. Middle-class reformers were confronting norms that appeared sharply different from their own and seemed resistant to "uplift."

Meanwhile, between the 1880s and the First World War, the pace of economic and social change seemed to accelerate, transforming the context that had given rise to the civilized morality of the middle class. As growing numbers of working-class women left the home to work in factories, offices, and retail establishments, and as middle-class women entered college and pursued professional careers, the separate spheres that underlay nineteenth-century sexual codes disintegrated. Simultaneously, the economy moved beyond the stage of early industrialization, in which habits of thrift, sobriety, and personal asceticism had won plaudits. Instead, the emphasis in American life was shifting toward consumption, gratification, and pleasure. One result was that the commercialization of sex, previously an underground, illicit phenomenon, moved somewhat into the open, as entrepreneurs created institutions that encouraged erotic encounters. In the process, working-class forms of sexual interaction, previously beyond the ken of the middle class, were projected outward into society. Massive immigration from southern and eastern Europe, as well as the movement of blacks from the rural South to northern cities, aided this development by making these alternative cultures of sexuality far more visible. Having experienced directly two generations of rapid economic change, and having observed the divergent mores of America's social groupings, one can imagine Davis deciding to examine the sexual practices and meanings of women of her class. Moreover, the very fact of her study, initiated shortly after World War I, suggests that by the 1920s, erotic life was assuming a new, distinctive importance in the consciousness of some Americans.

This chapter describes some of the variety, tension, and change in American sexual patterns in the late nineteenth and early twentieth centuries. It looks first at the world of marriage, and then turns to two very different arenas, each affected by the economic transformations of the era, in which sexual meanings were assuming new configurations: the social milieu populated by the college-educated, unmarried "new woman," and the nighttime subculture of urban working-class youth. Three themes in particular stand out. First, within the middle class, gender differences were becoming sharper. While the ideals of social purity advocates had permeated the consciousness of women, men had ever easier access to a world of commercialized sex whose size dwarfed the more casual prostitution that had existed earlier in the century. Second, a flood of immigrants in the generation before World War I, as well as the growth of a native-born white and black urban working class, confronted middle-class sensibilities with patterns of family life and sexual mores that diverged dramatically from their own. Placed alongside the tensions within the middle class, this weakened the hegemony of middle-class ideals. Finally, the economic transformations of the era, particularly the movement of growing numbers of women beyond the domestic sphere, were opening new opportunities for nonprocreative, nonmarital forms of sexual behavior. Some middle-class women were withdrawing from men entirely, while young working-class women were creating new modes of heterosexual interaction. Together, this combination of diversity and change undermined the foundations of late-nineteenth-century civilized morality.

The World of Marriage

By the late nineteenth century the values of the social purity movement had permeated middle-class marriage. Nurtured by activists and sustained by the female world in which women were socialized, they promoted passion between spouses, but a passion tempered by female ideals of mutuality and spiritual union. At the same time, these marriages had to contend with the cultural assumption that men were by nature lustful, as well as with the influences that men who had access to prostitution brought to their domestic life. Although the gulf between male and female could be bridged, it also provided a source of tension and change.

The sexual practices of middle-class marriage at the turn of the century had clearly moved beyond a procreative framework. In 1900, the total fertility of white American women stood at an average of 3.54, or fifty percent below the level of a century earlier. Large as this decline was, it seriously underestimates the extent of the change experienced by the urban native-born middle class, since immigrants and rural women tended to bear more children than the average. One study of middle-class families found that for women born between 1846 and 1850, whose childbearing years ended in the 1890s, almost half of those with husbands in the professions or in business had two or less children. For a comparable group of wives born between 1866 and 1870 the small size of families was even more pronounced: in 1910, almost two-thirds had families of no more than two children. By the latter date, between fifteen and twenty percent of these couples remained childless. The percentage of large families also evinced a sharp decline. Among the older group of women, about a quarter had five or more offspring, while among the younger, the figure dropped to under ten percent.[3]

This dramatic fall in fertility is all the more remarkable when one recalls the context in which it occurred. By the end of the century, the physicians' campaign to criminalize abortion had succeeded, forcing the phenomenon into hiding. Congress had outlawed the dissemination of birth control information through the mails; many states restricted the sale or advertising of contraceptive devices; Comstock and company were waging a ceaseless battle to enforce these laws; and the threat of imprisonment had impelled many authors of marital advice literature to expunge discussions of contraception from their books. Large sectors of the medical profession were declaiming against artificial methods of limiting fertility. Birth control information had virtually been driven underground, yet middle-class couples were exhibiting extraordinary success in sharply curtailing the number of children they conceived. Although the age of marriage had risen in the latter part of the century, with the median age reaching 26.1 years for men and 22.0 years for women in 1890, the change was not significant enough to account for the drop in family size.[4] The waning of procreation as the inevitable outcome of married life seemed to defy the attempts of lawmakers and reformers to block access to birth control.

Such widespread and successful efforts among the middle class to curtail fertility spark intriguing questions about the place of sexual expression in the relationship of husbands and wives. Although it might seem to raise once again the old specter of stereotypical Victorians repressing their sexual desires in the interest of family limitation, more likely the fertility decline suggests that the social purity movement succeeded in shaping conjugal relations in an era when options for restricting fertility narrowed. The call for voluntary motherhood and a single standard of morality offered a method by which middle-class women could exert some control over childbearing. The sexual ideals that emanated from the movement—of a passion that was tender and refined and that respected female needs—could curtail male excess. At the same time, it might also permit the incorporation of some contraceptive practice into marriages to foster the spiritual union that women sought. The split between private behavior and public values so central to civilized morality allowed couples consciously to choose artificial methods of contraception even as some representatives of their class attacked it. The low fertility rates at the turn of the century demonstrate a sexual ethic in which a spiritualized intimacy and passion existed apart from procreative intent.

Two pioneering sex surveys provide a window into middle-class marriage. Their findings illustrate the extent to which sex had moved beyond its reproductive purpose and entered the realms of personal desire and intimacy by the turn of the century.[5] Katharine B. Davis studied one thousand women who had reached a marriageable age before World War I and three-quarters of whom were born before 1890. Seventy-four percent of the women in the Davis study practiced some form of contraception, while even larger proportions believed that its use was morally right and that reasons other than procreation justified sexual expression. Two-fifths of the women had intercourse more than twice a week, and four-fifths reported having sexual relations at least weekly. Forty percent acknowledged masturbating during childhood or adolescence, while others began the practice after marrying. Almost half of the women reported that they were "attracted" by their first experience of sex with their husbands, and many more came to enjoy conjugal relations after an initial period of adjustment. Finally, thirty percent of the women surveyed judged their sexual desires to be as strong as those of their spouses.

The results of Dr. Clelia Mosher's study are consistent with this portrait. Of the forty-five women she surveyed, eighty percent were born between 1850 and 1880. Approximately two-thirds of the women acknowledged feeling sexual desire, reported that intercourse was generally agreeable, and listed pleasure as a legitimate purpose of conjugal relations. An overwhelming majority said they experienced orgasm, with one-third reporting that they always or usually did. Eighty-four percent used at least one method of fertility control. Interestingly, despite the restricted access to contraceptive information and devices, a clear trend emerged over time toward adoption of artificial methods of limiting family size. Among the twenty oldest women—those born through 1862—thirty percent used the safe period of the menstrual cycle, forty percent practiced withdrawal, and forty percent employed some form of contraceptive device. For the twenty-five youngest women, the comparable figures were twenty percent for the safe period, twelve percent for withdrawal, and seventy-six percent for contraceptive devices. Finally, slightly over two-thirds of the women indicated that they continued to have intercourse even while pregnant.

At the same time, the women in these surveys could hardly be considered "sexual enthusiasts."[6] The responses of many, including some of those who acknowledged their own sexual desires and who found sex agreeable, were brimming with tension, confusion, and guilt. For the most part, they viewed sexuality as properly confined to the marital relationship. Three-fifths of the Davis respondents had not masturbated as children or adolescents, and half of those who did described the effects as "harmful." A mere seven percent had engaged in premarital intercourse, while four-fifths of the sample thought it was never justified for men or women. (Mosher did not even question her patients about the issue of premarital experience.) Less than half of those in each survey considered sex necessary for mental and physical health. Although most of the women acknowledged the legitimacy of sexual relations for non-procreative purposes, the overwhelming majority of Mosher's patients still considered reproduction to be the primary goal of sex. Even among those who accepted sex for the pleasure it brought, many also revealed deep ambivalence about erotic enjoyment. One woman who listed pleasure among the purposes of sex immediately qualified her answer with the phrase "but not necessarily a legitimate one." Another thought "pleasure is sufficient to warrant it," but then described her ideal as "to have no intercourse except for reproduction." A third believed that procreation was "the real purpose," and that sex had been "made pleasurable so it would be indulged in, to accomplish [the] purpose of reproduction." Now that she was past her childbearing years she defined her ideal frequency of intercourse as "never." Most women felt less sexual desire than their husbands, and in the Mosher study, many described their "ideal habit" as involving less sex than they had. As one woman born in 1878 told Mosher, she did not find sex agreeable, yet had intercourse two to three times a week because her "husband's pleasure demands it and therefore [she] prefers to want it herself."[7]

Ignorance about sex stands out in bold relief as a prominent cause of the ambivalence many women felt about sexual passion. The limited sphere in which many late-nineteenth-century women moved, as well as middle-class reticence about sexual matters, restricted their access to information. Over forty percent of the women in the Davis study and half of Mosher's respondents reported less than adequate instruction about sex before marriage. Even among women who claimed knowledge about sexual matters, the content of their learning hardly suggested an easy marital adjustment. As one woman in the Davis study proclaimed, and she was by no means unique, her mother "had taught me what to expect. The necessity of yielding to her husband's demands had been a great cross in her own life." A number of the women in the Mosher study cited Alice Stockham's *Tokology*, an advice manual overwhelmingly concerned with pregnancy, childbirth, and childrearing, as their chief source of information.[8] Fully a quarter of the Davis women reported that their initial experience of conjugal relations "repelled" them; Davis found a high correlation between lack of sexual instruction, distaste for sex, and unhappiness in marriage.

Absence of information and distorted teaching about sex spawned fears before marriage, and anger afterward, as women struggled to overcome their early socialization. Worries about pregnancy loomed large in the minds of many adolescents who believed that "kissing, sitting beside someone, . . . eating certain foods, [or] touching a boy's hand" might cause conception. One woman, happily married, reported that her mother informed her that "the doctor brought [babies] in his grip and they were once mossy stones in the brook." Reflecting back, she recalled that the "Immaculate Conception was never clearly understood, and it occurred to me that there might be a recurrence." Others complained that they were given "mere knowledge of facts" or euphemistic explanations "by means of birds and flowers," but no understanding of *"sex emotions."* As one woman put it, "my books left out the factor of passion. This was a surprise to me after marriage." Mothers in particular seemed so perverse in their teaching that Davis labeled them one of the more "unfortunate" sources of information. Yet, despite this, many women managed to leave behind their early instruction. "I think mother gave me an abnormal idea of men by her own sex attitude. . . . I thought most men must be beasts," said one woman, whose phrasing suggested that she had since learned differently.[9]

The impression that finally emerges from these surveys is that a small number of women approached sex eagerly, enthusiastically, and with great delight; a somewhat larger group experienced marital intercourse as difficult, painful, and unwanted; and finally, a clear majority found that sex, as social purity crusaders advocated, occupied an important, respected, but also limited place in their marital life. Properly restricted to marriage, it served procreative goals, yet not exclusively, since most employed contraceptive measures. Though not perceived as a necessity, intercourse was potentially a pleasure to be enjoyed, but only if experienced in moderation. "I consider this appetite as ranking with other natural appetites," said one woman, who preferred it "to be indulged legitimately and temperately." Repeatedly, women in the Mosher study referred to the "spiritual completeness" that sex engendered, while objecting to an unrestrained animal passion that inevitably would "degrade their best feelings toward each other." The foundation for this approach was a deeply held belief in mutuality, of husbands tailoring their passions in a way that was respectful of a wife's desires and concerns, and of wives willing to respond to the overtures of their mate. When this adaptation occurred and both could find a common ground, women spoke of the sexual side of marriage with satisfaction. "There is no experience on earth comparable to . . . the love and complete satisfaction of two perfectly mated people," said one woman after thirteen years of marriage. Another, the mother of eight children, simply wrote that after affectionate sex with her husband, "the next day filled with the joy of life."[10]

A woman's desire for mutuality meant, ultimately, that in sex, as in so many other aspects of married life, her happiness and security depended upon the character and behavior of her husband. As Davis reported,

> The comments of the women who were attracted [to sex in marriage] . . . emphasized the spiritual or emotional agreement—the "mental unity," as one puts it—which accompanied physical pleasure. Over and over again in this group are stressed the unselfishness, consideration, and self-control of the husband. Just the opposite qualities are most often emphasized in the [group that was repelled by sex]. . . . The wife ignorant, unprepared, shocked at the strength of her husband's passion; the husband unable to realize this, inconsiderate, uncontrolled; a long period of adjustment—and if this fails, unhappiness for both.[11]

Again and again, women in the Mosher survey specified mutuality as their ideal. "When acceptable to both," said one. "When desired by both," said another. "Everything to be absolutely mutual," responded a third. For some, the promise and fulfillment of mutuality was so great that they wrote lyrically when describing it. One woman who desired intercourse and found it agreeable, and who "almost invariably" reached orgasm, defined her ideal as "no habit at all, but the most sensitive regard of each member of the couple for the personal feeling and desires and health of the other. In fact, pure and tender *love*, wide awake to the whole of life, should dictate marriage relations." She penned these words after eight years of a marriage in which she and her husband indulged in intercourse once or twice a month. The tone of all her answers suggests that, in her husband, she had attained her ideal mate. On the other hand, another woman who also believed in mutuality and who described herself as "more alive mentally and physically" when she reached orgasm, had been badly disappointed by her husband's sexual demands. Throughout their sixteen-year marriage, she had acquiesced to intercourse more frequently than she cared to have it. The result was that she did not find sex agreeable and encapsulated male character by saying that "men have not been properly trained."[12]

Although her own experience in marriage makes this woman's judgment about men understandable, the deficiency did not lie in men's training as much as in the cultural prescriptions about male character. If the middle-class woman suffered from a tension between the inadequacy of her premarital instruction and the possibilities of the conjugal bed, her male counterpart found himself battered by the incompatibility of what he was told was his "natural" self and the ideals expected of a husband. Late-nineteenth-century commentators, both professional and lay, described men as assertive, aggressive, and impassioned, with a physiology and character that was, by nature, "more or less explosive."[13] Such untamed energy had value in the world of work, though even there a man of integrity might strive to master his most unruly impulses. But, in the home, as husband and father, man's nature served him poorly, and he was expected to exhibit self-control and restraint. In short, the middle-class man was a personality divided against itself.

The tensions embedded in late-nineteenth-century masculinity revealed themselves most clearly in the realm of sexuality. Here, the passions associated with manhood were perceived as almost bestial, scarcely capable of containment. Ironically, middle-class culture seemed to encourage this presumed physiological bent. As Dr. Alice Stockham described it in her sex education manual for women, "We teach the girl *repression,* the boy *expression,* not simply by word and book, but the lessons are graven into their very being by all the traditions, prejudices, and customs of society. . . . Physicians and physiologists teach, and most men and women believe: That sexual union is a *necessity* to man, while it is not to women." Social custom demanded that young men take the lead in courtship by expressing interest, devising trysts, and pursuing their beloveds. Yet such a role only magnified, as one young man ruefully acknowledged, a "strained condition of mind and body," making it difficult for men to respect the supposedly natural modesty of the opposite sex. These contradictory pulls on men could lead to confusion and guilt. "When I tried to tell you how I love you," wrote one man to his fiancée, "I thought I was a kind of criminal and felt just a little as though I were confessing some wrong I had done you." Explosive as his desires were thought to be by nature, the middle-class man knew that somehow he had to control them. "You have only to ask . . . that I recede from any given position or privilege, and I shall do so," a young man informed his sweetheart.[14] To the woman he courted and the one he eventually would marry, the civilized male ideally was to bring the most refined expressions of love.

In the battle that raged between the call of nature and the demands of civilized society, a man's own efforts at self-control received assistance from the women around him. Since the antebellum era, notions of proper womanhood had placed upon mothers the task of moral guardianship, of inculcating in the young purity of thought and action. Changes in American society in the last third of the nineteenth century made middle-class mothers especially prone to fulfill that responsibility toward their sons. The residential segregation of the middle class in the sprawling cities of the Gilded Age kept working fathers away from the home. Women, meanwhile, had fewer children to care for, and were yet to embark upon extensive extra-familial roles. The habits and values that these mothers might pass on to their sons could later make the difference between continence and indulgence. As one young man remarked to his fiancée, "my love for my wife can not be less strong or pure, because of the love I shall always have for my mother." Others looked to their intended brides to set limits upon their sexual propensities. "Help me fight myself—my worse self that has so long had the mastery," pleaded one man to his future bride. Another wrote, "you are the very incarnation of purity to me . . . and you shall help to cleanse me."[15] As the testimony of women in the Mosher and Davis surveys suggests, many late-nineteenth-century men, through their own efforts and the influence of the women close to them, shaped their sexual desires in ways that successfully combined chastity and passion.

However, males encountered other influences on their sexual development that ran counter to the dictates of civilized morality. The reticence that characterized middle-class mores meant that boys would often learn about sex not from parents or teachers, but from male peers. One study of about a thousand male college students who were born in the early to mid-1890s found that, on the average, boys had received their "first striking and permanent" impression of sex before the age of ten, from sources that the overwhelming majority of respondents labeled as "unwholesome." In most cases, the information came from another, somewhat older, boy, and a picture emerges of a transmission belt in which male youth taught each other surreptitiously. By contrast, two-thirds of the students did not receive any kind of formal sex instruction—from parents, educators, or specialized literature—until after the age of fourteen. By that time, as the author of the study remarked, the lesson was "six years too late," since most of the boys already had commenced sexual activity of some sort. Over three-fifths of the students reported masturbating, and more than a third had engaged in sexual intercourse by the time they were surveyed, figures that the author considered "very conservative."[16]

For most of these young men, their underground sexual learning did not represent a welcome alternative to repressive moral strictures, but rather a troublesome deviation from norms they valued. It created a preoccupation with the erotic such that one young man reported, "my sex ambitions run so high that often I could not control myself." Another confessed that he could think of "nothing but sexual indulgence and every girl that passed was thought of in a vulgar manner." The example of older boys gave one student "a wrong idea of manhood and led me to look upon women as merely to be used to satisfy one's passions." Time and again, respondents used words such as "vicious," "evil," "vulgar," and "degrading" to describe what they had learned, and the habits they had developed. Most of the young men viewed their sexual behavior as a problem, as a sign of moral weakness and a failure of manly self-control.[17]

The high incidence of intercourse among this group of young unmarried males immediately points to a major area of tension in turn-of-the-century sexual life. Large numbers of middle-class men were participating in sexual activities not shared by women of the same class who, overwhelmingly, entered marriage without the experience of coitus. By the early twentieth century, among the white native-born middle class, the gulf between the premarital sexual socialization of male and female had grown larger than ever, with important ramifications for marital adjustment. While women remained virginal and chaste, with desires that stopped short of coital expression, many men honored the ideal of continence only in the breech, and entered marriage sexually experienced.

Commercialized prostitution made this disparity of experience possible. By the end of the century, the casual streetwalking prostitution of an earlier era had long given way to a highly organized system of urban red-light districts. The success of feminists and purity reformers in the 1860s and 1870s in forestalling the legalization of prostitution did not obstruct brothels from operating in segregated vice districts with the connivance of police and municipal officials. In fact, social purity campaigns may have contributed to the creation of these districts by forcing prostitution beyond the view of middle-class women and into the working-class neighborhoods of immigrants and blacks. Investigations into the workings of the "social evil" found it to be a feature not only of major metropolitan areas such as New York and Chicago, but of smaller cities throughout the nation. Little Rock, Arkansas, for instance, reportedly had nineteen houses of prostitution, and Lancaster, Pennsylvania, twenty-seven. The districts were so much a fixture of the age that "sporting guides" and "blue books" were published to direct customers to them. The guide books told the price, location, and "services" of various brothels, identifying the ethnicity or the sexual practices of prostitutes with descriptions such as "Jew Louie" or "French Studio." The most enterprising madams kept track of patrons, sending them from time to time "announcements of change of address or a veiled suggestion as to the 'quality' of 'goods' on display." As the practice implied, sex for sale had become an integral feature of urban life, on a much larger scale than in the mid-nineteenth-century city where it originated.[18]

Prostitutes were available to serve the sexual needs of men of every class and ethnic background. Fifty-cent "crib houses" catered to casual laborers who sat on wooden benches waiting for a turn so quick that they barely took down their pants. One- and two-dollar joints might attract young clerks and other white-collar workers. Fancy parlor houses with ornate decor, racy music, and expensive liquor won the loyalty of the more economically privileged men. In these, the sexual transaction with a prostitute might be but one element in a long evening of ribaldry.

With their penchant for statistics and charts, Progressive-era investigators of commercialized sex have left convincing evidence that large numbers of middle-class men in cities and towns turned to prostitutes at least occasionally. In early-twentieth-century New York, five- and ten-dollar brothels outnumbered fifty-cent crib houses by almost two to one. The number of houses and of inmates per house, the frequency with which women in brothels turned tricks, and the prices that various houses charged suggest that many middle-class men bought sex at some time. Only the most obtuse could fail to notice its availability, while the separate spheres of the middle class provided men with the independence to partake of it without the knowledge of wives and other female family members. College students explored vice districts together; young male migrants to the city lived in rooming-house districts where prostitution was visible; men traveling on business could learn the location of brothels before they left the train station; members of social clubs visited houses of prostitution as a group. Those ubiquitous characters of the urban streets, the messenger boys and newspaper hawkers, were repositories of information about where to find what vice, and they sold their information boldly. In smaller cities close to the agricultural hinterland, the red-light districts even served the needs of that symbol of upright character, the farmer.

What it meant to patronize a prostitute, or how prominently it figured in the sexual life of middle-class men, remains sketchy. Excitement coexisted with guilt and anxiety, pleasure with disappointment. One young man, brought by his father to a fancy parlor house in New Orleans for his sexual initiation, later described the experience as a "mechanical procedure that . . . endured for perhaps a minute." Sex education surveys of the 1910s found that many younger men worried about their contacts with prostitutes, wondering whether they had contracted disease or whether their adjustment to marriage might prove more difficult because of the experience.[19] For some, buying sex was a youthful rite of passage that they quickly left behind; for others it might be an ongoing feature of their sexual lives, something that continued for years.

Just as ignorance about sexuality hampered the marital adjustment of turn-of-the-century women, regular recourse to prostitution might widen further the gulf between husband and wife that gender socialization created. As historian Ruth Rosen has pointed out, sex in the red-light districts was above all a commodity, not the stuff of romance or fantasy. The emphasis on speedy orgasm, the lack of emotional connection, and the absence of any expectation of mutuality made commercialized sex a poor training ground for middle-class bridegrooms. To the degree that young men's expectations were based on their encounters with prostitutes, they would bring to the conjugal bedroom a form of sexual expression badly out of line with what their wives might desire. On the other hand, some married men may have continued to visit the districts precisely because they could not find in their wives the kind of sexual availability, or responsiveness, they wanted. The world of commercialized prostitution may have been, as some have argued, a "necessary evil" sustaining the civilized morality of the middle class, but it did so at the price of sexual discord in marriage.

Beyond questions of emotional and sexual compatibility, the extensive patronage of prostitutes by middle-class men injected a far more serious problem into their families. In the early years of the twentieth century, as medical knowledge of venereal disease improved, doctors and social reformers directed renewed attention to it. One committee of New York doctors estimated that as many as eighty percent of men in the city had been infected with gonorrhea, and from five to eighteen percent suffered from syphilis. A Boston doctor from the same era found over a third of a sample of male hospital patients admitting gonorrheal infection.[20] Whatever the actual incidence, such reports fed a perception of an epidemic of sexually related disease. Concerning its origins, few expressed any doubts: prostitutes served as transmitting agents that spread the scourge of venereal infection from red-light districts to respectable households. As long as middle-class men patronized prostitutes, their wives and fiancées would harbor anxieties about the safety of conjugal relations. Some might wishfully exempt their husbands and brothers from the taint of such immorality, but the existence of prostitution testified to the potential of men to display uncontrollable lusts at odds with the refined, spiritualized passion that the middle classes cherished.

When middle-class men did enter the red-light district, whether as customers or as reformers, they confronted the reality of sexual values that differed from their own. Much of the commerce in sex took place in neighborhoods also populated by masses of workers who lived beyond the reach of middle-class genteel morality. A new geographic distance, born of innovations in transportation such as the streetcar, separated social groups and magnified the sense of danger with which the business and professional classes viewed the working-class majority. In their own districts, immigrants, blacks, native-born white workers, and even rural dwellers evolved marital standards that reflected the conditions in which they lived. Large families, crowded living quarters, racial and ethnic tensions, economic hardship, Old World cultural traditions, and other circumstances all conspired to shape family forms that competed with those of the more prosperous.

For middle-class Americans who did catch a glimpse into the private lives of workers, perceptions were colored by their own moral universe. Social reformers who studied tenement districts and urban slums saw families crowded into tiny apartments, with adolescent boys and girls sharing the same sleeping quarters, parents' beds in sight of their young children, and male boarders mingling with familiarity among wives and daughters. To college-educated social workers, this sort of family life did not recall the simplicity of the colonial or frontier experience, but instead seemed a source of "moral contamination," with the presence of boarders "always evil," and engendering immorality "of the grossest sort." Overcrowding forced a "crude realization of the sex relationship on young people at a very early age." Investigators in Wisconsin described a woman who took in lodgers as "practically the wife of all of them." In Philadelphia, New York, and other cities, middle-class observers commented on the presence of brothels alongside tenements that housed family groups. "At times children were playing in front of doors behind which prostitutes plied their trade," one exposé noted, and they would grin knowingly when a strange man sought admittance. Accustomed to ideals of purity, reticence, and a conjugal intimacy that rested on privacy, the middle class could see in these districts nothing but an alien, anarchic sexuality.[21]

Foreign as they appeared, the customs of the teeming working-class districts in fact pointed to a sexual morality and marital patterns of their own. For some immigrant groups, boarders might have the quality of kin, coming from their peasant villages or on the recommendation of trusted neighbors. The income they contributed to the family often provided the margin to keep a wife out of the factory, or a daughter in school. High procreation rates, common to the rural origins of many immigrants, insured additional wage earners and financial security for aging parents. The "promiscuous mingling" in apartments, hallways, and on street corners could serve as a kind of protection, keeping young girls under watchful eyes and guaranteeing that their virginity remained unviolated.

The sexual attitudes and customs of working-class groups varied according to the traditions they brought with them to urban living. Among southern black migrants, cohabitation and serial monogamy characterized the lives of many young adults. In his study of Philadelphia blacks, W. E. B. Du Bois attributed this pattern to "the difficulty of earning income enough to afford to marry." Though in some situations the practice fostered "centres of irregular sexual intercourse," with men and women changing partners after several months, in many other cases it evolved into "more or less permanent cohabitation." In time, these common-law marriages might be formalized with a wedding. For southern Italian immigrants, on the other hand, the virginity of daughters carried a high value. Unmarried females were carefully chaperoned, and even during courtship couples had little freedom to explore the erotic. As one Italian man recalled, "I used to go to her house. She sat on one side of the table, and I on the other. They afraid I touch." Three weeks before the wedding, he and his fiancée went to the theater, accompanied by a bevy of relatives. "We came to the aisles of the theatre. My mother-in-law go first, my fiancée next, my little sister, my father-in-law. I was the last one. I had two in between . . . I was next to the old man." Briefly alone with his betrothed a few days before the wedding, he tried to steal a kiss. "No, not yet!" she replied. Extraordinarily low illegitimacy rates among Italian-Americans through the 1930s testify to the success of community pressures in preserving female chastity before marriage.[22]

The hard conditions of life that they faced, and the unusual demographic patterns of the early stages of immigration, often militated against the romantic attachments or the intense, spiritualized passion that the middle class valued. With single men often in the majority, women married very young; sometimes, adolescent girls came to America from eastern and southern Europe and from Japan to marry men they had not yet met, in matches made by parents or other kin. For many immigrant daughters, marriage symbolized not romance but "a step toward freedom . . . an opportunity to be rid of disagreeable work in the factory or the home." As one young boxmaker explained, "you never rest until you die . . . I will get out by marrying somebody." Early marriage, rural traditions, and lack of information about birth control guaranteed high procreation rates. Polish women in early-twentieth-century Buffalo bore an average of eight children; Italians, eleven. One Italian husband, whose first child arrived nine months after marriage and who fathered eleven more, fatalistically explained, "we got married and they come when they come. What could I do? I can't get rid of them." Poor living conditions and inadequate medical care increased the health risks of frequent childbearing, and must have made sex a burden fraught with anxieties for many immigrant wives. One young Jewish wife in New York, desperate to avoid future pregnancies, asked a doctor for help. "You want your cake while you eat it too, do you?" he replied. "Well, it can't be done. . . . I'll tell you the only sure thing to do. Tell Jake to sleep on the roof!"[23]

Conjugal intimacy was often hard to sustain. In the Lithuanian community of Chester, Pennsylvania, children commonly slept in the same bed with their parents, who would have intercourse hurriedly after the young ones fell asleep. Husbands expected their wives to be dutiful and responsible homemakers; wives hoped for a dependable provider in their mate. Respect often took precedence over romantic affection. One autobiographical novel of an Italian immigrant family described the wife as "relieved to know" that her husband "never failed her." Thankful for what she had, she accepted that "there is nothing but this, being born and growing up, working and marrying and having a home and children. That is all there is."[24] Sex-segregated patterns of leisure kept men out of the home in the evenings, passing time with male acquaintances in neighborhood saloons. The presence of prostitutes and the absence of "respectable" women in most of these establishments testified to the double standard of morality that prevailed.

In the South of the same era, a rigid double standard also held sway among whites, a product of the racial caste system that developed in the generation after Reconstruction. The emphasis on female purity that characterized the antebellum planter class spread more widely among the white population. In large part, this ethos served as a means of both racial and gender control that allowed white men to attack their black counterparts for the flimsiest reasons and kept white women confined in their activities, with all of it resting on the access that white males had to black women. Though seldom openly acknowledged, it was widely understood that most white southern males "began their sexual experience with Negro girls, usually around the ages of fifteen or sixteen."[25] On Saturday nights throughout the South, young whites would descend on the black part of town for a quick fling. In some cases, interracial relationships might last for many years, with men fathering children and supporting mistresses, even as they seemed to lead upright lives with a white spouse and family. More often the relationships were casual and crassly exploitative.

White women, meanwhile, remained virtually untouchable, exemplifying a purity that was beyond corruption. How deeply they internalized this belief remains open to question, but one female novelist of the region, Frances Newman, wryly commented that "in Georgia a woman was not supposed to know she was a virgin until she ceased to be one." Men defended their daughters from sexual approaches. Reminiscing about turn-of-the-century Kentucky, the film director D. W. Griffith noted that "even a wink or a bashful nod towards a young lady would get one a good piece of hot lead or a kick in the pants." Among themselves, white men often joked that "until they were married, they did not know that white women were capable of sexual intercourse." Once married, men had to remain faithful, but "only after a fashion. They claimed," said Griffith, that "their wives considered it beneath them to be jealous of that sort of thing. If they had an affair with a woman of their own class, there was the devil to pay, but the other sort of thing was just a part of life." Against the backdrop of their illicit interracial liaisons, husbands might easily experience guilt at approaching their wives for sex, while women's tacit awareness of their men's hidden activities made the marriage relation in some cases a bitter one. Among themselves, white women frequently told jokes about the lasciviousness of black females, a practice that one observer called "the fleeting forms in which forbidden interests can be socially expressed." But, for the most part, they had little recourse to protest. Unlike northern wives who campaigned for social purity and a single standard, southern white women remained quiescent. Not until the 1920s and 1930s would significant numbers of them rise up in protest.[26]

Sexual exploitation by whites combined with values surviving from slavery to shape the sexual ethos of southern blacks. Except among the small black elite, female chastity before marriage was not prized. The pregnancy that might occur from premarital experimentation did not carry a stigma, and women who had given birth out of wedlock did not find their opportunities for marriage compromised. While nuclear families predominated in black rural communities, many of them evolved out of what began as simple cohabitation, with legal marriage following after a time. As one older black woman from Mississippi explained, "a man is your husband if you live with him and love each other . . . [M]arriage is something for the outside world." The improvised lyrics of songs sung by blacks suggested a relaxed attitude toward sexual matters, in contrast to the mores of whites. As one verse popular among black miners and railroad workers in turn-of-the-century Alabama proclaimed, "White folks on the sofa / Niggers on the grass / White man is talking low / Nigger is getting ass." Extramarital relations could be tolerated for men, and in some cases for women, provided certain boundaries were respected. In the 1930s one seventy-year-old widow from the Deep South remembered her husband affectionately, despite his history of sexual affairs. "I was always first," she reminisced, "and he didn't buy something for no one unless he asked me." Sometimes, though, the internalized values of a racist social structure expressed themselves in the relations of black men and women. Women might compare black men unfavorably against the favors they received from a white lover, while some blacks of both sexes expressed a preference for potential spouses of lighter skin color than themselves.[27]

While the experience of urban immigrants and the interracial South were the most visible alternatives to northern middle-class norms, other variations also existed. In the backwoods regions of the Ozarks, for instance, rural couples adopted practices that would have shocked purity reformers. Many old-time planting rituals incorporated sexual intercourse, a practice believed to guarantee fertile fields and a good crop. Along the border of Missouri and Oklahoma in the 1890s, one husband and wife walked to their newly planted field at night. Stripping their clothes off, the husband would "have at it till she squealed like a pig." In one small rural community, a naked couple planted their flax before sunrise, repeating the phrase "up to my ass, and higher too." Then, they just "laid down on the ground and had a good time." Residents claimed it was an old Indian custom, though native Americans of the area could not recall any such thing.[28]

Leisure activities in the Ozarks sustained a raucous sexuality. At country dances attended by the young and married for miles around, fiddlers improv-

ised bawdy lyrics. Popular tunes had titles such as "Grease My Pecker Sally
Ann," "Hard Pecker Reel," "Poontang on the Levee," and "Take Your Fin-
gers Out of My Pants." One man from Fayetteville, Arkansas, recalled that
at some square dances in the early twentieth century, "some of them white-
trash was plumb vulgar . . . country gals would hang every stitch of their
clothes on a nail!" One set of square dance calls went like this:

> Lead the ace and trump the king,
> Let me feel that pretty little thing,
> Up and at em, everybody dance,
> Goose that gal and watch her prance.
> Ladies do the shimmy, down goes her britches.
> In goes a little thing about six inches.

A Missouri fiddler who remembered playing a hoedown called "Fucking in the
Goober Patch" offered the opinion decades later that the dances had eventually died because "the folks that knowed 'em . . . got religion."[29]

Though Ozark ribaldry remained far beyond the ken of the genteel urban
middle class, other sets of sexual values did not. By the early twentieth century,
as Progressive reform efforts cast a spotlight on working-class life, middle-class
Americans were confronting directly these alternatives to their cherished
ways. The access that men had to women outside their social group would
come under scrutiny, exposing the tensions and fragility of civilized morality.
At the same time, the movement of middle-class women beyond their domestic
sphere would lead some of them to question the ideals of the late nineteenth
century. The marital pattern that social purity ideals encouraged would not
withstand these pressures.

Women Outside the Family: Middle-Class Professionals and Working-Class Youth

Besides the challenge that diversity posed to middle-class mores, profound
structural changes in economic life were instigating other broad shifts in sexual
values that threatened the hegemony of civilized morality. By the turn of the
century, the nation's economy was poised to move beyond the sober work ethic
that had characterized nineteenth-century capitalist development. In its stead
would come the values and institutions of a consumer society. Having built its
railroads, exploited its mines and forests, and constructed the factory complexes that produced the materials needed by heavy industry, American entrepreneurs were ready to embark upon new directions. One symbol of this
transition, the modern department store, made its debut in the 1880s and
spread quickly in the succeeding decades. These "palaces of consumption"

enticed shoppers with a glittering array of products to buy.[30] Along with consumer industries, the retail trades and the service sector would gradually become the engines propelling the economy forward. In the process, a new ethic of consumption, self-gratification, and leisure would begin to appeal to growing numbers of Americans. As one group of purity reformers mournfully expressed it, just before World War I, "the commercialization of practically every human interest in the past thirty years has completely transformed daily life. . . . Prior to 1880 the . . . main business of life was living. . . . The main business of life now is pleasure."[31]

As part and parcel of these developments, one stands out in particular as significant in the evolution of sexual behavior and values—the growing presence of women in the public sphere. Much of nineteenth-century civilized morality depended on the separation of male and female spheres, and the distinctive character structures that this division sustained. The piety, purity, and spiritual passion of the middle-class wife rested upon her domestic role; her allegiance to it motivated her activism on behalf of social purity and the single standard. After 1880, the daily stuff of many women's lives underwent a transformation. For some, particularly middle-class wives, change coexisted with the survival of domestic values. Lower fertility rates left them time for activities besides childrearing and housekeeping and helped generate a women's club movement after the 1880s; department stores drew them to downtown areas to shop. For other women, the break with the past was sharper. By the end of the century, more and more daughters of the prosperous classes were attending college and pursuing careers in the professions after graduation. Meanwhile, for young working-class women, changes in the economy were substantially altering their occupational structure. In 1870, domestic service accounted for sixty percent of female employment, thus allowing working-class daughters to earn a living, yet still confining them to a familial setting. By 1900 the proportion had declined to one-third, and by 1920 it had dropped to eighteen percent. Meanwhile, factory, office, and retail jobs grew at a rapid pace, while the number of working women expanded far faster than the growth of the female population. Most of those working outside the home for wages were young and single, with the result that the sex-segregated world of the nineteenth century became less descriptive of their experience. All of these changes were to have important consequences for sexual expression.

One set of women who were moving outside the home were the college-educated, the daughters of comfortably situated business and professional families. In many ways paragons of propriety, they were nonetheless making life choices that departed from the complex of values that had defined proper womanhood for their mothers. In doing so, their experiences helped to reveal the nature of the sexual system in which they were raised, as well as suggest the directions in which it was moving.

By 1900, a small but noticeable number of young middle-class women were enrolling in institutions of higher learning. The first generation of such women, in the 1870s and 1880s, provoked an outpouring of polemical literature about the perils intellectual work held for women. A college education would ruin a woman's health, these writers argued, and especially make her unfit for motherhood, the noblest calling of womanhood. Ignoring these warnings, the pioneers among female college students continued their education, and by the first decade of the twentieth century, their numbers were steadily increasing. Yet, their deviation from traditional female pursuits continued to evoke uneasiness. One prominent psychologist, G. Stanley Hall, wrote in 1904 that higher education threatened to produce women who were "functionally castrated . . . deplore the necessity of childbearing . . . and abhor the limitations of married life." A gynecologist of the same era simply predicted that these women would expand the ranks of the nation's "sexual incompetents."[32]

Although the development of women's intellectual powers did not result, as predicted, in shrunken wombs, nevertheless it was clear that college did seem to direct women away from marriage and motherhood. The first generation of graduates, especially, were endowed with a sense of mission. Having braved the opprobrium of society by attending college, they were not readily prepared to exchange for a life of domesticity the possibilities that an education had opened. Pioneers in the classroom, they went on to create similarly new opportunities for women in the world of work. Whether as faculty at women's colleges, residents of settlement houses, social workers, businesswomen, or journalists, they continued to make a place for themselves outside the home, beyond the boundaries of nineteenth-century domesticity. An extraordinarily high proportion of women graduates never married. Of women educated at Bryn Mawr between 1889 and 1908, for instance, fifty-three percent remained unwed. For Wellesley and the University of Michigan, the figures were forty-three percent and forty-seven percent. The proportion among those who went on for advanced degrees was even more lopsided: three-quarters of the women who received Ph.D.'s between 1877 and 1924 remained single.[33] Even among those who did marry, a significant percentage never had children. For a society that defined the female in terms of her maternal instinct, these "new women" were an anomaly, living proof of the fragility of middle-class values.

For many of these women professionals, however, remaining unmarried was not the same as being single. Among them could be commonly found pairs of women passionately attached to one another and committed to a lifetime together. Couples such as Katharine Coman and Katharine Lee Bates, Mary Woolley and Jeannette Marks, Jane Addams and Mary Rozet Smith, and

Florence Converse and Vida Scudder not only shared their lives, but moved within networks of similar women in settlement houses and women's colleges. Here was a female world of love and passion, different from the same-sex ties of the mid-nineteenth century in that its participants were freed from the bonds of matrimony, able to live and work independent of men.[34]

It is hardly surprising that many college-educated women would form relationships of passionate intensity with each other, socialized as they were into a world which valued female sensibility and female bonds. As young girls they could observe among their mothers, aunts, cousins and older sisters the importance of relationships between women. As late as the first decade of the twentieth century, magazine fiction aimed at adolescent girls and young women affirmed girlhood friendships and loyalty to one's women friends. One story in a popular magazine from 1908 described two girls in a boarding school who "had fallen in love . . . at first sight." Later in their relationship, "Carol came in, caught Jean, whirled her around, pulled her down on a cot, and gave her a warm kiss." In boarding schools and women's colleges, students developed crushes, fell madly in love, courted, wrote love notes, and exchanged presents. Although "smashing" was less common by the turn of the century, it had not yet died as a custom, and adolescent romantic love still enjoyed a lively existence in these female educational environments. Jeannette Marks, who taught at Mount Holyoke, described the women's colleges of the early twentieth century as "hotbeds of special sentimental friendships."[35] For women who now had the opportunity to earn an independent living and hence refrain from marrying, the choice to continue or pursue relationships with other women was a natural one.

Besides the pull that previous experience and socialization exerted, there were other compelling reasons that may have pushed college-educated women in the direction of a lifelong commitment to other women. As M. Carey Thomas, the president of Bryn Mawr, explained it, women scholars lived with a "cruel handicap. They have spent half a lifetime in fitting themselves for their chosen work and then may be asked to choose between it and marriage. No one can estimate the number of women who remain unmarried in revolt before such a horrible alternative."[36] Men of their class had not shared the heady intellectual atmosphere of women's colleges where students were encouraged to use their talents in the world. They had little sympathy for female aspirations and instead expected them to become dutiful wives, tending the home.

Stereotypes of the Victorian woman as sexually ignorant and passionless, as lacking in both desire and erotic interest, have obscured the nature and meaning of these middle-class female relationships. In many, many cases they were every bit as passionate, loving, and committed as our modern notions lead us to assume a heterosexual marriage would be. Unlike the hidden world of working-class female couples in which one member passed as a man, these partnerships, which were sometimes labeled "Boston marriages," were visible to the outside world, and accepted by society. Women lived together, owned property jointly, planned their travels together, shared holidays and family celebrations with one another, and slept in the same bed. The temporary separations that might normally ensue in two busy lives elicited love letters of extraordinary emotional intensity. They provide a window into the passion shared by women lovers who have been euphemistically described as close friends and devoted companions.

One such relationship was that of Rose Elizabeth Cleveland (the sister of President Grover Cleveland) and Evangeline Marrs Simpson. The two met in 1889, when Cleveland was a forty-four-year-old spinster and Simpson a widow of thirty. A powerful attraction resulted, and over the next year or so, the women interspersed time together with periods of separation in which they wrote frequently. Early on in the relationship, Simpson urged Cleveland in desperate tones to "come to see me this night—my Clevy, my Viking, my Everything—Come!" At one point Simpson sent some photographs of herself to Cleveland, and the latter wrote back as she looked at the images of her beloved:

> my Eve looks into my eyes with brief bright glances, with long raptuous embraces . . . [H]er sweet life breath and her warm enfolding arms appease my hunger, and . . . carry my body in one to the summit of joy, the end of search, the goal of love! Here is no beyond!

Sometime later, Cleveland wrote again, this time pointedly framing her words in the image of one of the world's great love affairs:

> Ah, my Cleopatra looks a very dangerous Queen, but I will look her straight in those wide open eyes that look so imperial and will crush those Antony-seeking lips, until her arms close over . . . and she becomes my prisoner because I am her captain. . . . How much kissing can Cleopatra stand?

Although many years and another marriage for Simpson were to ensue before Cleveland's passion was to be fully requited, the two women sailed for Italy together in 1910 and lived there until Cleveland's death in 1918.[37]

It would be a distortion of the historical record to attempt to homogenize relationships that were so complex. Toward the end of her life, Vida Scudder, who had enjoyed for decades a loving partnership with the writer Florence Converse, commented that "a woman's life in which sex interests have never visited, is a life neither dull nor empty nor devoid of romance." Speaking of her own experience, she wrote that "the absence of [the sex] factor need not mean dearth of romance, or of intensely emotional significant personal relations. Of these, I have had more than I care to dwell upon." Even where overtly erotic behavior was involved, it might recede into the background. As one businesswoman, born in the 1880s, explained, "I have a woman friend whom I love and admire above everyone in the world. . . . The physical factor is only one minor factor in the friendship which is based on perfect congeniality and love."[38]

On the other hand, substantial evidence exists that overtly sexual relationships among unmarried college-educated women were not at all uncommon. One study of such relationships among students found that more than "mere friendship" was involved. "The love is strong, real, and passionate," wrote the author, and has "the same characteristics of intensity and devotion that are ordinarily associated with heterosexual love." In the 1920s, when Katharine B. Davis surveyed twelve hundred unmarried college graduates, she found homoerotic relationships to be common in both women's colleges and coeducational institutions. Twenty-eight percent of the women's college graduates and twenty percent of those from coeducational schools had experienced intense ties with other women that included a physical component recognized as sexual. Almost equal numbers had enjoyed intense emotional attachments that involved kissing and hugging. Davis observed that "apparently those women who go out into the world to work, like those who go to college, are more apt to form such attachments," but she was quick to point out that "very few" could be considered "psychopathic," a term that by the 1920s was increasingly being used to stigmatize homosexual expression. In general, these women tended to see their relationships as contributing to their well-being. One thirty-eight-year-old woman with a graduate degree in nursing called her partner "as much a real mate as a husband would be. I have come to think that certain women, many, in fact, possibly most of those who are unmarried, are more attracted to women than to men . . . [T]o mate with one woman is as natural and as healthful and helpful for them as are marital relations between husband and wife. In my own case it has had a decidedly softening and sweetening effect on my temper and general attitude."[39]

The middle-class women who were coming of age in the early twentieth century were at a turning point. Forming their ties in an age when their society still validated female bonding, they also lived in an era when same-sex relationships came under sharper scrutiny. By the end of the century, European writers such as Krafft-Ebing were describing same-sex relationships in medical terms, as signs of mental and physical degeneration. After 1900, some writers used female attachments to cast stones at women's aspirations for equality. "The driving force in many agitators and militant women who are always after their rights," one commented, "is often an unsatisfied sex impulse, with a homosexual aim." By the 1920s, Freudian theories of sexual development as well as the writings of other sexologists had completed the redefinition of same-sex pairings as homosexual, and labeled them morbid and pathological. In the Davis study, evidence abounded that women were internalizing this shift in perspective. One woman wrote, for instance, that "the ethics of homosexual relationships is the most serious problem the business or professional woman has to face today. . . . In my city some business women are hesitating to take apartments together for fear of the interpretation that may be put upon it." Many women who felt their relationships had been valuable and good nevertheless defined them as "abnormal," "unnatural," or a "perversion." Davis attributed this conflict to the influence of social opinion about homosexuality. As time went on that opinion would harden and transform female couples, in the words of one of Davis's respondents, into "pariahs, dirty, evil things" in the eyes of the world.[40] In the meantime, however, these women had fully removed female sexuality from a procreative, marital context as they created lifelong partnerships that were romantic and often erotic.

While some daughters of the middle class were constructing an erotic life with other women, many more young working girls were exploring heterosexual relations beyond a marital setting as they labored in factories, offices, and retail establishments. Signs of this had already appeared in a few neighborhoods, such as New York City's Bowery, in the mid-nineteenth century, but as opportunities for employment outside the home expanded, the phenomenon gained new visibility in many more locales. Much of what we know about the premarital behavior of working-class youth comes from outside investigators, from the pens of middle-class reformers who saw only flagrant immorality in the sexually suggestive interactions of young working men and women. But used carefully, their observations help to fill out a portrait of erotic behavior that was public, nonfamilial, and part of a commercialized world of pleasure.

The novelty of young women working outside the home threw men and women together in a variety of ways. On downtown sidewalks and streetcars, in offices, department stores, restaurants, and factories, and in parks at lunch hour, young men and women mingled easily, flirted with one another, made dates, and stole time together. Freed from the protection, or restraints, of their elders' supervision, young women encountered the sexual and romantic suggestions of male admirers. In city parks, "shocking occurrences by the score are reported," wrote one reformer. "Boys and girls of sixteen and seventeen are involved in these affairs." On the shop floor, a cigarmaker observed, men will "whoop and give . . . 'cat calls' " to their favorite female co-workers. Women exchanged information with each other at work, learning from those older, and passing on to their peers advice and hints about how to comport themselves in this unsupervised heterosocial environment. At one large retail establishment, an investigator found "salacious cards, poems, etc., copied and passed from one to another." Those working in the new department stores became acquainted with a world of goods designed to arouse desire and attract the attention of admirers. Expected to dress well to impress customers, these retail clerks might "with fatal ease become involved" with male shoppers, or be "thrown with companions among her own ranks who are already committed to evil."[41]

Once the working day was done, working-class youth could take advantage of the commercialized amusements sprouting up everywhere. In cities large and small from the 1880s onward, enterprising businessmen opened dance halls, amusement parks, pleasure steamers, and nickel movie houses which offered to their patrons nighttime and Sunday diversions from the dreary world of wage labor. For young men and women, laboring at boring, monotonous jobs for fifty or more hours a week, and living in crowded tenement districts, the glitter and the glamor of the new amusements had an irresistible allure. These commercial pastimes differed from those of the middle class, and even from those of the working class of an earlier generation. Divorced for the most part from the family and neighborhood, they attracted a predominantly young, unmarried crowd of both genders, without the chaperonage of adults.

The dance hall perhaps best captures the mood and environment of this new world of commercialized pleasure. Unlike the bawdy resorts of midcentury, which no "respectable" woman would enter, these catered to mixed crowds who would arrive with groups of friends. Spreading through the downtown section of cities, in the midst of restaurants, theaters, and the workplaces where many youth passed their days, dance halls attracted the young with the sights and sounds of neon and popular music. As two social workers commented, "coming from the monotony of work, and from oftentimes dreary home surroundings, the dance-hall, with its lights, gay music, refreshments, and attractive surroundings, seems everything that is bright and beautiful." The music and dances in many of these halls owed their origins to black entertainers, whose styles had migrated north from the brothels and dives of New Orleans and Memphis where the musicians had originally found employment. Listening to the ragtime beats in one black establishment, a patron commented that "it was music that demanded a physical response." Willie Smith, a jazz pianist in pre–World War I Harlem, described the dances favored by the young. "Some of these," he said, "were pretty wild. They called them 'hug me close,' 'the shiver,' 'hump-back rag,' . . . 'the lovers' walk.' " Quickly taken up by white youth, these "tough dances" required the suggestive motion of "the pelvic portion of the body." Bodily contact was the rule. One reformer found that "couples stand very close together, the girl with her arms around the man's neck, the man with both his arms around the girl or on her hips;

their cheeks are pressed close together, their bodies touch each other." Songs with the "most blatant and vulgar" lyrics, according to Jane Addams, added to the air of sexual energy that permeated the environment.[42]

Erotic encounters were not confined to the dance floor. In one New York hall, "most of the younger couples were hugging and kissing, there was a general mingling of men and women at the different tables." At a Philadelphia locale favored by blacks, the men "slapped the girls on their bare legs, hugged some, petted others, and approached most of them in daring language." Liquor made available by neighboring taverns further weakened already loose inhibitions. One vice investigator observed that "young girls have been seen to yield themselves in wild abandon to their influence, and have been carried half fainting to dark corners of the hall, and there, almost helpless, have been subjected to the most indecent advances." By the early twentieth century these pleasure palaces had so won the allegiance of the young that commentators were referring to "dance madness." Adam Clayton Powell, a black minister in New York, deplored how "the Negro race is dancing itself to death."[43]

Nighttime dance halls were but one of a variety of institutions that sprang up in cities and that encouraged a new sexual ethic among working-class youth. By the early twentieth century, entrepreneurs were building vast amusement parks on the edges of metropolitan areas at the end of streetcar lines. The structure of these parks and the style of interaction that they encouraged mocked the genteel social rituals of middle-class America. Crowds of men and women mingled casually, while the rides and amusements encouraged spontaneous, often raucous behavior. One journalist described a day at New York's Coney Island as "a delirium of raw pleasure." The pitch for the Cannon Coaster blared, "Will she throw her arms around your neck and yell? Well, I guess, yes!" The Barrel of Love enticed patrons by proclaiming, "Talk about love in a cottage! This has it beat a mile." Little Egypt promised "one hundred and fifty Oriental beauties! . . . See her dance the Hootchy-Kootchy! Anywhere else but in the ocean breezes of Coney Island she would be consumed by her own fire!" Hidden air chutes might send the skirts of unsuspecting young women flying into the air, while rides such as the "human roulette wheel" threw men and women into each other's arms. Strangers conversed with one another. Groups of men and women made their acquaintance. Flirtations occurred, dates were made, and romances begun and ended. Meanwhile, in cities along the ocean or near lakes, steamers and excursion boats with private rooms allowed youthful lovers to escape the city for a day and indulge their romantic attachment for one another.[44]

Technological advances added to the choices awaiting working-class youth. At the turn of the century, nickelodeons displaying the newly invented motion picture—and, later on, movie houses showing feature films—quickly captured the loyalty of a working class infected by "nickel madness." Soon, in tenement districts, motion pictures had "well nigh driven other forms of entertainment from the field," according to one writer. Crowds streamed in and out of the theaters, sitting together in the dark, watching the larger-than-life images on the screen. The content was often designed to arouse the sensual. As a New York newspaper reported,

> For the first time in the history of the world it is possible to see what a kiss looks like. . . . Scientists say kisses are dangerous, but here everything is shown in startling directness. What the camera did not see did not exist. The real kiss is a revelation. The idea has unlimited possibilities.

The nature of the physical environment, as much as the content of the moving pictures, excited sexual interest. Jane Addams found that in Chicago, where many working-class youth attended the movies almost nightly, "the very darkness of the room . . . is an added attraction to many young people, for whom the space is filled with the glamor of love making." Back rows rapidly became known as "lovers' lanes," and the theater became a meeting place for acquaintances old and new.[45]

These new popular amusements created not only a heterosocial environment charged with youthful sexual energy, but also a commercial relationship between male and female that mirrored the larger social context. Although admission to some, such as the dance hall and the movie house, was often minimal, a system of "treating" developed that allowed young women to partake of a wider range of evening pleasures. In part, this reflected the less than subsistence wages that many working women received. As a Chicago waitress explained, "If I didn't have a man, I couldn't get along on my wages." But it also revealed a gender-differentiated system of roles. A young man proved his worth, and impressed the object of his affection, by being able to treat a young woman to refreshments, a night on the town, a day of rides at the amusement park, an excursion on a lake steamer, or presents. If he could not afford to do so, he might find himself without companionship. "MAN GETTING $18 A WEEK DARES NOT FALL IN LOVE," said a Chicago headline in 1919, commenting on the perils of treating. Women faced their own set of pressures. They hoarded their resources to pay for the clothes, jewelry, fancy ribbons, and cosmetics which made them attractive. "A girl who does not dress well is stuck in a corner," one New York working girl observed.[46] Embedded within the system of treating were expectations of sexual exchange—what would a young woman give, sexually, in return for the favors of a man.

These changes on the part of the young did not occur without conflict. As we will see, during the Progressive era, the world of urban commercialized amusements, along with the related problem of prostitution, became the target of middle-class reformers determined to clean up the cities and remake them to their own liking. But the behavior of young working-class women also involved a generational clash of values within their families, every bit as intense as that between classes, though without an organized, political shape to it. Parents, especially among immigrants, saw their children striking out in new directions, and were upset and confused by what they witnessed.

The conflict took many forms. For those young people living at home, their wages were often seen as part of a family economy, a contribution to the survival of the group. From daughters, especially, parents expected to have wages turned over to them, not squandered on trivial pursuits such as movies and dance halls, or on fancy store-bought clothes. Mothers watched as their daughters left home to go to work, where they learned all sorts of newfangled ideas. Daughters' behavior puzzled and disturbed older women who had come of age in an altogether different environment. Sons, too, were different. Although male youth traditionally had more freedom, the new generation of working-class men was departing from the patterns of their fathers. No longer satisfied with the sex-segregated environment of the neighborhood tavern, youth now spent their wages in the heterosocial world of commercialized leisure. "Where a man was in the habit of passing much of his time in a saloon . . . now he passes a portion, if not all of it, in the motion picture houses," claimed the Worcester *Sunday Telegram.*[47] Indeed, by the First World War, the saloon was becoming marked as the province of older men, an aging institution deserted by the young.

Observers at the time remarked on the stresses that the new world of pleasure was creating within working-class families. Acquiescence to the demands of the young provided cause for worry, as daughters, dressed in new finery, spent their evenings at dance halls and movie houses and met who-knew-what strange men. One Irish mother in New York complained about her daughter: "She stands up and answers me back. An' she's coming in at 2 o'clock, me not knowin' where she has been. Folks will talk, you know, an' it ain't right for a girl." A Mexican immigrant bemoaned the new values infiltrating the Chicano community in a ballad:

> The girls go about almost naked
> And call *la tienda* "estor" [a store]
> They go around with dirt-streaked legs
> But with those stockings of chiffon.
>
> Even my old woman has changed on me—
> She wears a bob-tailed dress of silk,
> Goes about painted like a *piñata*
> And goes at night to the dancing hall.

Insistence that wages be turned over, or that evenings be spent in a chaperoned environment, might easily provoke lies and rebellion. One immigrant father, a shopkeeper in Chicago, confessed that he dare not withhold money for the theater from his daughters for fear that "they would steal it from the till."[48] Sons might leave home, daughters might become pregnant or, worse, turn to prostitution to finance other more innocent pleasures.

Indeed, a chief source of the concern exhibited by both parents and middle-class reformers was the proximity of this nighttime world of amusements to the institutions of commercialized prostitution. Nearby saloons often sheltered prostitutes who would sometimes make their appearance at dance halls, as W. E. B. Du Bois discovered in his study of black Philadelphia. In Seattle, Japanese-American families lived alongside burlesque houses whose doors were "covered with the life-size paintings of half-naked girls." Such influences made it hard for girls to grow up as the "refined young maidens" their parents wished them to be. Innocent working girls, meanwhile, had little protection from "designing men." Many of the lodging houses in which single working men and women lived also were locales for casual prostitution. "The young man or young woman coming from the country to the city for the first time, seeking accommodations," Wisconsin investigators alleged, "is as likely to find lodging in such a disreputable house as in a safe and respectable house." Couples who met at a dance hall could retreat to one of the many cheap hotels, patronized by prostitutes, where men and women who lived with their families might rent a room to spend their evening alone together. Reformers barely distinguished these women, whom they labeled "clandestine prostitutes," from full-time sex workers. Yet, as one dance-hall habitué remarked, "some of the women . . . are out for the coin, but there is a lot that come in here that are charity." In other cases, working-class women did turn to prostitution at times, without making a permanent commitment to the trade. "The fact that she has earned money in this way does not stamp her as 'lost,' " said a 1911 federal report on working girls. "Occasional prostitution holds its place in their minds as a possible resource."[49]

It is difficult to know precisely the nature and the extent of sexual experimentation and indulgence that grew out of this youthful working-class environment. One suggestive piece of evidence is the change in the rate of premarital pregnancies. Having fallen to a low of ten percent in the mid-nineteenth century, the rate rose significantly to twenty-three percent in the decades from 1880 to 1910. Since scattered survey data from middle-class white women reveal a rate of premarital intercourse much lower than this prenuptial pregnancy rate, it is reasonable to conclude that the increase came mostly from working-class women, and that the incidence of premarital intercourse among them was naturally higher than the incidence of pregnancy.[50]

But what did this premarital experience mean? In many cases, no doubt, it reflected sexual coercion, as young women, without the protection that family and community once provided, found themselves unable to resist the demands of male suitors or workplace supervisors. In others, it evinced the desire of women for sexual pleasure and adventure outside the bonds of marriage. For some women, premarital sex may have occurred with a prospective husband only, and pregnancy may have been the desired result, a traditional way of surmounting family restraints upon marriage. But whatever the reason or the context, it seems clear that by the early twentieth century, young working-class women were engaging in a higher level of premarital sexual intercourse than had their mothers or their middle-class counterparts.

The nighttime culture of commercialized pleasure—from the dance halls and the system of treating that went with it, to the sexual liaisons of unmarried couples—was the most visible and most commented upon aspect of working-class sexuality. As such, it occupies a place of historical significance, for it represented an important shift in values and behavior. Yet, it would probably be a mistake to consider this culture typical of working-class youth, to assert that premarital experience was already the norm. Many working girls developed standards of their own that allowed for some sexual freedom but stopped short of sanctioning premarital coitus. One city missionary remarked that "young women sometimes allow young men to address them and caress them in a manner which would offend well-bred people, and yet those girls would indignantly resent any liberties which they consider dishonoring." Moreover, within the modern city, traditional values of premarital chastity for women survived, as well as courtship that took place with the knowledge and approval of parents and community, especially among immigrant groups. As Jane Addams observed of Chicago, "among the Hull House neighbors are many of the Latin races who employ a careful chaperonage over their marriageable daughters." Protection of female chastity could even coexist alongside the new world of heterosocial interaction. As one young Mexican woman who worked in a Los Angeles dance hall reported, "some men at times make propositions to me which are insulting . . . [but] my mother takes a lot of care of me so that I won't make any bad steps." Then, too, while most young working men might acquire sexual knowledge on the streets, with their peers, and through patronizing prostitutes, many of their female counterparts remained in a state of ignorance. One working woman, recalling her early years in a New England mill, told about the terror she felt when a male worker impulsively kissed her on the lips. "For two weeks I couldn't eat, I couldn't sleep—I thought I was pregnant. My mother always said, 'Don't ever let a boy touch you!' He had touched me; he kissed me." Undoubtedly, she was not the only immigrant daughter who was coming of age with less-than-extensive sexual knowledge.[51]

Disparate as the experience of young working-class women and the college-educated single woman was, the two groups shared a common characteristic: each reflected the movement of women beyond the family into the public sphere. For the working girl this might be a temporary status, cut short by marriage and motherhood; for the middle-class professional, it often proved to be a permanent life choice. In both cases, economic changes made possible the exploration of intimacy and the erotic outside the boundaries of marriage.

Both of these cultures embodied another feature that bound their experience together historically. They highlighted the shifting foundations upon which the sexual values of the middle class rested. Buffeted by the transformations in class relations and everyday life that large-scale industrial capitalism was provoking, the middle class could expect that the commercialization of sexual pleasure among working-class youth would spread outward unless vigorously resisted. With it would come the collapse of the dichotomy between private and public that was so much a part of late-nineteenth-century civilized morality. Already, the burgeoning red-light districts allowed middle-class men to purchase sexual favors with ease. The invasion of legitimate entrepreneurs into the land of Eros promised more direct upheavals.

The forms of intimacy pioneered by college-educated female couples presented a different sort of threat. Though they lived discreetly, these women nonetheless demonstrated the possibilities of love and passion entirely beyond a procreative framework. Despite the sharp decline in fertility among middle-class women, the prescriptive importance of the maternal in their world view prevented sexuality from being fully detached from reproduction. The call of feminists and social purity advocates for voluntary motherhood, while it had affirmed female passion, highlighted the extent to which procreation still figured in women's view of themselves. In constructing viable lives without motherhood, female couples offered an implicit challenge to the delicate structure of middle-class civilized morality. No wonder that apologists for marriage were beginning to attack these relationships as morbid and unnatural.

Thus, by the early twentieth century, the sexual values of the middle class were on the edge of a decisive transformation. Old and new coexisted in an uneasy balance. That tension would make the first two decades of the century a time of conflict, as defenders of the past and proponents of change contended for hegemony in sexual matters.

CHAPTER 9

Crusades for Sexual Order

FOR black Americans of the early twentieth century, Jack Johnson was a popular hero at a time when such figures were sorely needed. Denied the ballot in the South, faced with segregation in public facilities, and confronted by an epidemic of brutal lynchings, blacks could take delight in the exploits of the young fighter. Johnson triumphed over dozens of white boxers and, in 1910, was finally awarded the heavyweight crown.[1]

Unable to defeat him in the ring, proponents of white supremacy found another means of bringing his downfall. Johnson was known for his sexual relationships with white women. His second wife had been white, and he had numerous affairs with others, including a Chicago prostitute named Belle Schreiber. In October 1912 Lucille Cameron, a young woman who had left her family in Minnesota to seek employment in Chicago, visited Johnson's popular nightclub, the Cafe de Champion. After Johnson promised her employment and commenced a sexual liaison, Cameron's distraught mother had charges of abduction brought against him. The trial provoked an angry response throughout the nation's press. White southerners hinted that if Johnson visited their section of the country, they would dispense with him quickly; the black press railed against him for giving credence to white supremacist claims about black male sexuality. But Lucille adamantly refused to testify, and after the indictment was dropped, the couple married.

The authorities had one more weapon to fire against Johnson, however. In 1910, Congress passed the Mann Act, which forbade the transportation of women across state lines for "immoral" purposes. A response to the white slavery scare that was sweeping the nation, it was supposed to prevent the illicit trafficking in women for purposes of forced prostitution. When federal agents persuaded Belle Schreiber to testify that Johnson had paid for her travel from

Pittsburgh to Chicago for immoral purposes, the way was paved for an indictment. In May 1913 an all-white jury convicted Johnson, who was sentenced to one year in prison.

Johnson's trial and conviction serve as convenient symbols for the conflicts over sexuality that surfaced in the early twentieth century. The cracks in the mold of civilized morality had become so wide as to almost demand a resurgent political response. Working-class youth were eager patrons of a nighttime world of commercialized amusements that mocked middle-class sexual ideals. The educated new woman was forsaking marriage. Middle-class families had dramatically reduced their fertility, calling into question the primacy of motherhood in women's lives and smoothing the way for them to venture beyond the domestic hearth. Prostitution was running rampant in American cities, while the wages of sin seemed to be an epidemic of venereal disease. Since the 1870s, purity advocates of various stripes—Anthony Comstock and his associates, female activists of the WCTU, and zealous ministers publishing their shrill sermons—had addressed these and other issues of sexual morality. But the growth of Progressive reform after 1900 offered far more fertile soil for a sexual politics to take root and grow. In particular, white middle-class reformers targeted what they considered working-class immorality as they sought to shore up the decaying foundations of late-nineteenth-century values. Sexuality became a vehicle for exercising control over the lower classes, especially immigrants in the urbanized North and blacks in the rural South. The range of political responses that took shape—a social hygiene movement to halt the spread of venereal disease, campaigns against white slavery and prostitution, and the wave of lynching that accompanied segregation in the South—suggest the depth of concern over sexual issues at the turn of the century.

The Social Hygiene Movement

Historians have debated the meaning of Progressivism at great length. A nationwide response by the middle class to the vast changes provoked by industrial capitalism, Progressive reform called upon the state to intervene as never before in the country's economic and social life. It addressed issues that ranged from the need for playgrounds and housing codes in urban slums to checking the power of monopolistic trusts. As a number of writers have pointed out, the Progressive movement embodied sharply conflicting impulses—social order as well as social justice, efficiency along with uplift, faith in the power of education as well as a determination to coerce the recalcitrant. Issues of sexual behavior and morality easily lent themselves to these contrasting tendencies. Some reformers urged education to check the spread of vice and disease, while others organized campaigns of repression. Calls for rehabilitating the victims of commercialized prostitution coexisted with efforts to punish sexual delinquents. Sponsorship of "healthful" amusements occurred simultaneously with movements of censorship. But, however diverse the program, the Progressive era witnessed the emergence of a full-blown sexual politics. And, unlike the sexual reform efforts of the previous century, which had relied largely on moral suasion and individual self-control, early-twentieth-century crusaders unabashedly sought state regulation to achieve their goals.

Of the many issues inviting attention, venereal disease was one that especially aroused reform energies. In the late nineteenth century, advances in medical science increased knowledge of both gonorrhea and syphilis. Doctors learned more about how the diseases were transmitted, their progression, and their long-term consequences. Since improvement in treatment and cure came more slowly, it was perhaps natural that some physicians would focus on the question of prevention. Despite the efforts of nineteenth-century social purity crusaders to address the problem, reticence about sexual matters still placed major obstacles in the way of forthright discussion of venereal disease. Although the improved social stature of the medical profession in the early twentieth century made it an ideal candidate for the job, any campaign against the diseases promised to clash with key elements of middle-class moral codes.[2]

A New York physician, Prince Morrow, sounded the alarm for a "social hygiene" movement to stem the spread of syphilis and gonorrhea. Having received medical training in Europe, where venereal infection was already treated as a public health matter, he published in 1904 a medical text, *Social Diseases and Marriage,* the first comprehensive scientific treatise on the subject in English. That same year he delivered a major address before the Medical Society of the County of New York in which he issued a plea for organized action among doctors. The power of Morrow's work came in its focus on marriage. He shocked his audience with the statement that "there is more venereal infection among virtuous wives than among professional prostitutes." Morrow wrote at great length about the results: sterility among women, congenital blindness in infants, syphilitic insanity, chronic uterine inflammation, and general physical infirmity among young married women who had once been pictures of good health. All of these "innocent infections," he argued, could be traced "back to their original source in that irregular sexual commerce known as prostitution." Morrow estimated that fully sixty percent of the male population had at one time or another contracted syphilis or gonorrhea. Echoing nineteenth-century feminists, he placed the blame not on the female prostitute, but on "masculine unchastity." "The male factor," he punned, "is the chief malefactor."[3]

Although Morrow insisted that sexually transmitted diseases were medical rather than moral problems, he also recognized that social customs, institutions, and prejudices severely complicated the work of conscientious doctors. At the time Morrow wrote, some hospitals refused to accept patients with venereal disease, while many doctors were reluctant to call in the wives of infected men for treatment. "At first glance," he told his New York audience,

> it might appear that the prophylaxis of these diseases, as of other infectious diseases, dangerous to the public health, lies exclusively within the province of the medical profession. But experience has shown that this class of diseases cannot be dealt with as a purely sanitary problem. . . . In their essential nature they are not merely diseases of the human body, but diseases of the social organism. . . . To correct these evil conditions, there should be a union of all the social forces which work for good in the community.[4]

As long as shame and censure remained attached to venereal infection, Morrow argued, patients afflicted with it would avoid treatment. As long as propriety blocked open discussion of the diseases and their transmission, men would remain ignorant of the dangers of sex with prostitutes, women would enter marriage uninformed about the risks they faced, and doctors would stand by silently, refusing to intervene.

Morrow's solution was to launch a social hygiene movement. In 1905 he formed in New York City the Society of Sanitary and Moral Prophylaxis. Within a handful of years, similar groups had taken shape across the country, from Spokane to Philadelphia, and from Jacksonville to Milwaukee. Members held public meetings and conferences, published and distributed social hygiene pamphlets, and lectured widely. They spoke before local medical associations, state conferences of charities, federations of women's clubs, and professional associations. They enlisted the cooperation of the WCTU and the YMCA, state boards of health, superintendents of schools, and teachers' organizations. Their goal, as Morrow put it, was an unrelenting "campaign of education" to wipe out the ignorance and the prejudices that allowed venereal disease to infect the nation. As the movement gathered momentum, its membership as well as its aims broadened. By the time of the First World War, educators and social workers swelled the ranks of the American Social Hygiene Association, the new umbrella organization of the movement. They advocated not merely education against venereal disease, but also state-mandated blood testing before marriage, required reporting of cases of infection, and a comprehensive program of sex education that would enlist families, churches, civic institutions, and, especially, the public schools in an effort to fashion a truly hygienic code of sexual life.

The social hygiene movement mixed new and old together into a somewhat contradictory brew. In their insistence on frank and open discussion of sexual matters, reformers self-consciously placed themselves in opposition to the repressive strain of nineteenth-century politics represented by Comstock. As Maurice Bigelow, a professor of biology at Columbia University's Teachers College, put it in 1916, "we must cease to foster the secrecy created by an atmosphere of obscenity, and the study of sex must be brought into the light of day." Advocates of sex education condemned the unwillingness of parents to talk to their children about sex, arguing that the habit of silence and evasion "tends to give a wrong direction and a vicious tendency" to the sexual instinct. A number of writers went as far as to suggest that even young girls should receive instruction. Some also subscribed to a nonprocreative sexuality. Bigelow took issue with older sex-advice manuals which used "the terms 'sex' and 'reproduction' as if they were synonymous. This is no longer so in human life," he asserted, "for while reproduction is a sexual process, sexual activities and influences are often quite unrelated to reproduction." Reflecting what was already true of many middle-class marriages, Bigelow suggested that the "possibilities of affection" that physical intimacy might engender were important enough to justify contraception. The alternative, he wrote disparagingly, was "sexual asceticism between husband and wife."[5]

New as the public affirmation of separating sexuality and reproduction seemed, the social hygiene movement remained wedded to the traditions of civilized morality. Like the social purity advocates of the late nineteenth century, reformers strove hard to combat the double standard that condoned male patronage of prostitution. Morrow, for instance, was adamant that instruction about sex "should include as a cardinal feature a correction of the false impression instilled in the minds of young men that sexual indulgence is essential to health and that chastity is incompatible with full vigor." Sex might have nonprocreative purposes, but only husband and wife might properly indulge in it. Male continence before marriage and temperate sexual expression within were the highest ideals. In his *Ten Sex Talks for Boys* (1914), Irving David Steinhardt, a member of the Society of Sanitary and Moral Prophylaxis, informed his readers that sexual intercourse "should never be indulged in before marriage. . . . THE SEXUAL RELATION IS ABSOLUTELY UNNECESSARY TO YOU OR TO ANY OTHER MAN." Reminding his youthful audience that sexual relations were a synonym for "marital relations," he told them to confine it to the institution to which it belonged. Although sex education advocates dismissed the shrill pronouncements of some nineteenth-century writers that youthful masturbation led to insanity, one pamphlet cautioned that it "can never be said to be practiced moderately, and it is not to be recommended," while Bigelow claimed scientific support for the statement that "the habit may weaken the nervous system and indirectly affect general health." Boys who wished to "grow up strong in body and mind" were advised to refrain altogether. Social hygiene writers offered advice on how to avoid temptation. "The lad who plays vigorously, even violently," one author alleged, "who can 'get his second wind,' turn a handspring, do a good cross-country run, swim the river, possesses a great bulwark of defense against sexual vice, especially in its secret forms." Finally, Bigelow spoke for much of the movement in his defense of innate male and female differences. Despite his and others' advocacy of a single standard, he described men's sexual instincts as "characteristically active, aggressive, spontaneous and automatic," and alleged "physiological and psychological reasons" for "masculine aggressiveness and . . . leadership in affairs of the heart."[6]

Despite their allegiance to these older standards, social hygienists still provoked a heated response from defenders of civilized morality. One gynecologist, speaking at an American Medical Association meeting, described the topic of venereal disease as so "attendant with filth" that "we besmirch ourselves by discussing it in public." In 1906, when Edward Bok, the editor of the *Ladies Home Journal,* published a series of articles on venereal disease, he lost seventy-five thousand outraged subscribers. Later, as reformers began advocating sex instruction in the public schools, some administrators took up their pens in opposition. The superintendent of schools in New York City believed it would lead to "spiritual havoc and physical ruin," but had "too much faith in the good sense of the American people to believe that it will ever be generally and regularly taught in American schools." Even William Howard Taft, the former president, felt compelled to address the issue. In a speech delivered in Philadelphia in 1914, he described sex education as "full of danger if carried on in general public schools. . . . I deny," he continued, "that the so-called prudishness and the avoidance of nasty subjects in the last generation has ever blinded any substantial number of girls or boys to the wickedness of vice or made them easier victims of temptations."[7]

The legacy of activists was as mixed as their philosophy. During the Progressive era, they made little headway in getting sex education into the schools. But they publicized the concept widely, produced a great deal of pamphlet literature, and won important converts, such as the National Education Association, which in 1912 endorsed sex education. Not until the 1920s and beyond would they make real progress toward their goals and see some elementary sex instruction integrated into the curriculum. They were more successful in provoking government intervention, as states began to require blood tests before marriage and pass mandatory reporting laws. In the short run, however, the effort to educate the public about venereal disease led to unintended consequences. Although Morrow opposed campaigns of repression against vice, believing that they would only scatter the problem more widely, the insistent discussion by social hygienists of prostitution as the source of infection provided fuel for precisely such a response.

The Attack on Prostitution

Although organized agitation against prostitution stretched back to the 1830s, the Progressive-era crusade dwarfed all of its predecessors. No longer the province of outsiders struggling to build a constituency, the campaigns in the decade before World War I released unprecedented energies. Businessmen and male civic leaders joined feminists and ministers in an effort to eradicate commercialized vice. They gained a hearing in the halls of Congress as well as in state legislatures and municipal governments. Their efforts would permanently alter the face of prostitution in America.

The new drive against prostitution first surfaced in the form of a white slavery panic. Between 1908 and 1914, purity crusaders and others published dozens of sensationalistic tracts alleging a widespread traffic in women that sold young girls into virtual slavery. Replete with case histories, vivid illustrations, and strong advice to parents, these books described the subterfuges used by panderers to lure innocent victims to their fate. The procurer, a dark and sinister alien-looking figure, stalked the countryside in search of unsuspecting village girls. "The small towns and villages afford the most lucrative fields for men . . . engaged in the business of pandering girls," wrote Clifford Roe, a leader in the movement to expose the trade. Winning their confidence with pledges of love or the promise of employment, these pimps seduced unsuspecting women to abandon their homes and follow them to the city. Women who left the farm on their own to find employment in the city were entering, according to one tract, "a forest haunted by wolves." All of the new institutions of commercialized leisure were just so many hunting grounds where women might be snared. Migrants from the countryside received warnings against "the men who frequent dance-halls and excursion boats, ever on the alert for their prey." Movies, restaurants, and even ice-cream parlors were "dangerous places for young girls to attend unescorted." A common message echoed through the pages of most of these accounts: "Stay rather at home where all is pure, beautiful and really grand, for no artisan can build forests and mountains like the great Creator has given you; no artist can paint the growing grain and the flowers as beautiful as he. The crowded smelling [street] car can not supplant the good old horses and carriage." The paeans to rural innocence appealed to a native-born middle class distressed by the spread of an urbanized capitalist society. They ignored, however, the reality of sexual life in the hinterland. The sexual violence portrayed by Theodore Dreiser's *An American Tragedy,* for instance, belied the image of an idyllic countryside.[8]

White slave tracts, followed by novels, plays, and movies capitalizing on the same theme, attracted an avid audience. One play, *Little Lost Sister,* opened to packed houses in 1913. *Traffic in Souls,* a film, secured thirty thousand viewers for its opening week in New York. The popularity of the genre suggests that Americans were receptive to the message of the crusade. But many may also have seen the white slavery issue as an avenue for sexual titillation. Some exposés, such as H. M. Lytle's *Tragedies of the White Slaves* (1912), were graced with lurid, multicolored covers. The title page of another proclaimed, "Beautiful White Girls Sold Into Ruin . . . Illustrated with a Large Number of Startling Pictures." A third promised "Startling Revelations, Thrilling Experiences, and Life Stories" in chapters with such titles as "Adventures of a Libertine."[9] Perhaps the authors believed they needed to shock citizens into action; or perhaps the white slave panic served other, less respectable purposes, like the lurid anti-Catholic tracts of the antebellum era. In any case, the genre expanded the public discourse on sexuality even as it served more immediate, protectionist goals.

Whatever the motivation, the white slavery scare provoked a political response at the national, state, and local levels, eliciting legislative remedies. In Washington, the specter of an international traffic in women added to the current of nativist sentiment that was demanding restrictions upon immigration. Legislation of 1903 and 1907 affecting immigration had already touched upon the issue of prostitution. The former punished those who imported women for the purposes of prostitution; the latter permitted the deportation of immigrant prostitutes. But, as outrage over white slavery escalated, government studies reflected the mounting concern. They described an extensive international business in women's bodies, with immoral women as well as innocent girls being imported to the United States by the thousands every year. Foreigners became the scapegoats for the sexual anxieties of the native-born. "The vilest practices are brought here from continental Europe," a report to the Senate in 1909 warned, including "the most bestial refinements of depravity." Federal investigators claimed that "large numbers of Jews scattered throughout the United States . . . seduce and keep girls. Some of them are engaged in importation . . . [and] they prey upon young girls whom they find on the streets in dance halls, and similar places." The traffic in women, the report concluded, "has brought into the country evils even worse than those of prostitution." Diseased alien women, through their male clients, had infected "innocent wives and children" and "done more to ruin homes than any other single cause." In 1910, Congress enacted legislation that vastly widened the net into which immigrants might fall. Not merely prostitutes and procurers, but anyone "who is employed by, in, or in connection with any . . . music or dance hall or other place of amusement or resort habitually frequented by prostitutes, or where prostitutes gather," might henceforth be deported. In that same year, Congress also enacted the White Slave Traffic, or Mann, Act, which made it a federal offense to transport women across state lines for "immoral purposes." Over the next eight years, the Justice Department obtained almost twenty-two hundred convictions for trafficking in women.[10]

Most antiprostitution activity, however, occurred at the local level. Between 1910 and 1915, at least thirty-five cities and states conducted major studies of prostitution. The penchant of Progressive-era reformers to define social problems through statistical calculation makes these reports a vast compendium of detailed information about commercialized vice. Investigators roamed the red-light districts and tenement areas of cities and towns, accumulating lists of places where vice occurred, and counting the establishments. In Philadelphia, the vice commission found solicitation occurring in "saloons, cafes, restaurants, hotels, clubs, and dance halls. . . . Many public dance halls, moving picture shows, and other amusement centers are the breeding places of vice. . . . The public parks are among the worst." A statewide study by the Wisconsin legislature pinpointed parlor houses, assignation houses, roadhouses, immoral hotels, rooming and lodging houses, cafes, chop suey restaurants, saloons with bedroom connections, and dance halls. Not surprisingly, New York City captured the prize for the most numerous establishments, with over 1,800 "vice resorts" and an estimated fifteen thousand prostitutes in Manhattan in 1912. But Philadelphia could boast 372 such places, Baltimore over 300, and the small Wisconsin communities of Watertown and Janesville, 19 and 14, respectively. Prostitution appeared to exist wherever investigators chose to look.[11]

The commissions emphasized how deeply embedded commercialized vice was in contemporary America. They attacked the "Devil's Siamese Twins" of liquor and lust. Saloons competing for business would provide lewd entertainment to attract male clients, and back rooms where prostitutes could take their customers. Hotel operators and rooming-house owners found it more profitable to rent accommodations to streetwalkers by the hour or the night. In tenements, working-class families lived alongside prostitutes who consorted with customers as children played in hallways and on the streets below. Young men and women coming from the country to the city for employment might unsuspectingly find lodging in a disreputable house. In railroad stations, prostitutes boldly accosted businessmen as they arrived in the city. Everywhere apparently, prostitutes operated freely without interference from the law.

Anti-vice crusaders tried a variety of techniques to destroy the social evil. Besides the tools of investigation and publicity, they held marches and outdoor prayer meetings in the heart of the red-light districts. Female rescue workers visited brothels to persuade inmates to leave. In Baltimore, when local pressure failed to move the police to action, reformers turned to the governor's office. A few days after the release in September 1915 of a scathing report on commercialized vice in the city, police invaded the red-light district and shut it down forever. One popular method used by reformers reflected their willingness to turn to the state for more than investigation and publicity. The so-called red-light abatement law allowed private citizens to file complaints against houses of prostitution, eventually leading to permanent injunctions and the sealing of buildings found to harbor prostitutes. First enacted in Iowa in 1909, it had been copied in thirty-one other states by 1917.[12]

In attacking the social evil, the crusaders against prostitution revealed a philosophical kinship with the social hygiene movement. Again and again, the reports of vice commissions described commercialized sex as a problem spawned by men, for the profit and pleasure of men. Investigators attacked the double standard. "The present day demands chastity of men equal to that demanded of women," wrote the Wisconsin legislators. Many of the studies tried to counter the beliefs that sustained a promiscuous male sexuality. "That sexual intercourse is necessary to health," wrote the Philadelphia commissioners, "is a superstition." Men were told that continence before marriage was both possible and desirable, that nothing in "male nature" compelled them to exercise the sexual "muscle."[13] Antiprostitution forces took issue with the conspiracy of silence that left children ignorant of the ravages of venereal disease, and they urged parents to instruct their children in sexual hygiene.

The First World War brought social hygienists and anti-vice crusaders together in more than an ideological unity. As with so many other reform movements of the Progressive era, the war allowed reformers to enter the precincts of government, as they lent their energies to the Wilsonian war effort. But military mobilization bent Progressivism to its own ends, emphasizing efficiency over uplift, and social order over benevolence. Sex reformers found that only part of their agenda was implemented, and that in some respects the war provided them with the form rather than the substance of their goals.

Within days after Congress declared war in April 1917, Newton Baker, the Secretary of War, created the Committee on Training Camp Activities (CTCA) to see that the young draftees would be ready not only to fight the Germans but to resist the moral dangers that life away from home might throw in their paths. Sex reformers and purity crusaders flocked to the CTCA. Through it, they descended on military camps to provide GIs with wholesome recreation, instruct them on sexual hygiene, and clothe them, as Baker put it, with an "invisible armor" for their protection overseas. CTCA members lectured the troops on the importance of continence. "Sex organs do not have to be exercised or indulged in, in order to develop them or preserve virility," said one. "Forget them, don't think about them, or dwell upon them. Live a good vigorous life and they will take care of themselves." Posters and pamphlets distributed among the troops warned of the dangers of venereal disease and made the avoidance of prostitutes a litmus test of patriotic zeal. One poster of the U.S. Public Health Service announced that "The Government Has Declared War On Venereal Diseases." A widely circulated pamphlet, *Keeping Fit To Fight,* informed soldiers that "WOMEN WHO SOLICIT SOLDIERS FOR IMMORAL PURPOSES ARE USUALLY DISEASE SPREADERS AND FRIENDS OF THE ENEMY." It called the soldier in the hospital with venereal disease "a slacker." The CTCA combined propaganda with more tangible methods to keep soldiers from prostitutes. Pressure was placed on cities near military bases to close their red-light districts, and the army established five-mile "pure zones" to keep prostitutes away from the camps. Reformers were determined that the toleration that the military had formerly displayed toward prostitution, during the Civil War and in the West, would not be repeated.[14]

As American troops began making their way to Europe, sex reformers were heartened by the actions of the top command. General Pershing, the head of the American Expeditionary Force, had countenanced prostitution during the army's incursion into Mexico in 1916, but he took strong measures to prevent the spread of venereal disease within the AEF. Soon after his arrival in Europe, Pershing announced that "sexual continence is the plain duty of members of the AEF, both for the vigorous conduct of the war and for the clean health of the American people after the war. Sexual intercourse is not necessary for good health, and complete continence is wholly possible." Worried about the loss of manpower that VD might cause, he established early in July 1917 treatment centers in every command, and made the failure to report exposure to infection a court-martial offense. To prevent malingering, he later provided treatment at the front. In December 1917, in response to a five hundred percent increase in VD rates among soldiers stationed at St.-Nazaire, Pershing placed brothels and saloons in port cities of debarkation off limits to soldiers and stationed MPs around them.[15]

Ultimately, however, the wartime experience proved disappointing and disillusioning for reformers. The army exhibited more concern about conserving manpower than inculcating sexual purity among the troops. The first signs of conflict came over the treatment meted out to women suspected of prostitution near army bases in the states. The military suspended writs of habeas corpus, arrested women en masse, and forcibly held more than fifteen thousand in detention centers for periods averaging ten weeks. No men were arrested for patronizing prostitutes. These actions especially angered women activists involved in the war effort who viewed the prostitutes, most of whom were working-class and many of whom were unemployed, as the victims of male lust. Moreover, evidence suggests that CTCA activities in the camps never sank deeply into the psyches of most recruits, whose working-class origins placed them at a distance from the purity ideals of middle-class crusaders. As one observer noted,

> the fact is that the soldier is very much more unmoral than when he entered the army. . . . [S]horn of modesty, morals, sentiment, and subjectivity . . . men will sit til late at night . . . and talk about women—but this talk is of the physical rather than the emotional, of the types, the reactions, the temperaments, . . . the degrees of perversity, the physical reactions, the methods of approach—in fact, as if it were a problem in physics rather than morals . . . [It is] an attitude applicable not only to the public woman, but to all women in general.

Or, as labor leader Samuel Gompers more simply put it, in disparaging the work of moral reformers during the war, "real men will be men."[16]

Neither did reformers fare well in Europe. As the war progressed, it became clear that, for the army, venereal disease was a problem of physical vigor, not masculine ethics. Despite various prohibitions, soldiers on leave continued to contract VD, and so the army came to rely on chemical, rather than moral, prophylaxis. In the interests of efficiency, the army began distributing prophylactics to soldiers for self-administration. By the end of the war, the military had dispensed at least several million treatments. Reformers viewed the army's policy as pandering to the grossest forms of immorality.

When all is said and done, what had the Progressive-era sex reformers—the anti-vice investigators and the social hygienists—accomplished? On the surface, at least, their achievements seem considerable. By 1920, the red-light district had passed into history; the system of commercialized prostitution that reigned in American cities for almost half a century was destroyed. Reformers, too, had made major legislative inroads into how society dealt with the problem of venereal disease. After World War I, states began enacting mandatory reporting laws and requiring blood tests before marriage, and the U.S. Public Health Service had created a Division of Venereal Diseases. But, at a deeper level, the most cherished goals of reformers remained elusive. The red-light districts closed, but prostitution did not end. Instead, it changed its form and locale, with the streetwalker and the call girl becoming more typical. The new structure made the working-class prostitute more vulnerable to police harassment, and shifted control of her day-to-day life from the madame who ran the brothel to the male pimp who controlled her street activities with the threat, sometimes fulfilled, of violence. Ideals of male continence won little acceptance, and rather than raising male behavior to the level of a ladylike womanhood, the 1920s began initiating a revision of what was deemed proper for women.

In retrospect, the passions aroused by commercialized sex appear so intense that one wonders whether it stood for something more in the minds of the anti-vice crusaders. Indeed, although prostitution was the chief target of activists, the reports issued by vice commissions point to deeper concerns. Besides the full-time inmates of brothels, investigators waxed livid at the behavior of the much larger number of "clandestine prostitutes," or "charity girls," single women adrift in the city who worked in factories, offices, and department stores during the day and exchanged sexual favors with men at night. Newark investigators, for instance, found "a large number of girls and young women who sin sexually in return only for the pleasures given or the company of the men with whom they consort. . . . They have no ethical standards and believe . . . that they have a right to the pleasures they can gain from their bodies." Similarly, reformers in Lancaster, Pennsylvania, reported with dismay "more charity girls on the street than prostitutes. . . . They dress modestly . . . but are decidedly bold in their flirtations. There appears to be a regular lot who are well known. . . . Their conversation was often unrepeatable." Statements such as these reflect the disapproval with which proponents of sexual purity looked upon any displays of female sexual desire outside of marriage. They so little understood it that they could only define it as a point on a slippery slope of moral ruin that would descend, inevitably, to full-time prostitution. Crusaders against vice had so internalized nineteenth-century assumptions about female purity that they even discounted the testimony of prostitutes themselves about why they engaged in sex for sale. For example, when George Kneeland studied prostitution in New York City, like William Sanger in the 1850s he found woman after woman who gave plausible reasons for entering the life. A former domestic said that she was "tired of drudgery as a servant. . . . I'd rather do this than be kicked around like a dog in a kitchen by some woman who calls herself a lady." A one-time factory worker told him, "there is more money and pleasure in being a sport." In response, Kneeland wrote that "few girls ever admit that they have been forced into the life as 'white slaves.' " Apparently, it was easier for him and others to believe in a vast underground traffic in women than to accept that working-class women might choose sex either for money or the excitement it brought.[17]

This concern with female immodesty led reformers to attack not only the red-light districts, but also any other aspects of American life that seemed subversive of genteel civilized morality. They campaigned for the closing or licensing of dance halls and movie theaters, censorship of film production, and prohibition. At a rhetorical level, they urged American parents, especially those outside the major cities, to keep their daughters at home, out of the work force, and away from the big cities where temptations beckoned and procurers stalked the streets. All in all, it seems plausible to argue, as one student of these years has, that prostitution served as "a master symbol, a code word, for a wide range of anxieties."[18] The entry of women into the work force, the breakdown of the separate spheres that underlay earlier norms, and the commercialization of much of American life (including pleasure) that came with the spread of capitalist social relations, all contributed to the crisis that fed the Progressive era's sexual politics. With the boundary between pure and fallen women dissolving, crusaders desperately sought to hold the line against further change.

The twin concerns of prostitution and venereal disease also fed into the stream of American racism. By the early twentieth century, the tides of immigration had shifted decisively to southern and eastern Europe, bringing Italians, Jews, and Slavs to the United States. Much "scientific" theory at the time viewed these groups as inferior nonwhite "races." Despite the statistical evidence that most prostitutes were native-born women, reformers placed the blame for vice on alien men and women who were corrupting the nation's purity. "It was the foreigner," said Clifford Roe, "who taught the American this dastardly business."[19] Not only moral depravity but physical disease threatened the vigor of Anglo-Saxon stock. Social hygienists commented frequently on the sterility and birth deformities that venereal disease caused. At a time when the belief in the inheritability of moral character was strong in American thought, the fight against prostitution, white slavery, and venereal disease fed into eugenics campaigns to sterilize the "unfit." Between 1907 and 1917, sixteen states passed sterilization laws designed to prevent reproduction of those whom proponents viewed as undesirable. Meanwhile, alongside the movements for social hygiene and against commercialized vice, white supremacists emitted shrill cries of "race suicide," as middle-class Protestant women seemed unable, or unwilling, to match the high fertility of foreigners. Pointing to South Africa as the model of what might happen to the Caucasian race, one sociologist in 1907 wrote that whites there "stand aghast at the rabbit-like increase of the blacks." Theodore Roosevelt lambasted the Yankee middle-class woman who avoided childbearing as a "criminal against the race."[20] The sexual politics of urban Progressivism played to the fears of native-born Americans who worried about the threat that immigrants of allegedly inferior racial stock posed to their cultural hegemony.

The Southern Rape Complex: Race, Sex, and Gender in the New South

Urban Progressives were not the only Americans for whom sex and race were entwined. At the turn of the century, white southerners were joining forces to create "Jim Crow," a system of segregation that consigned blacks to an inferior caste-like status. Buttressed by law, custom, and violence, the separation of the races revolved in part around an elaborate set of sexual fears and myths that seemed to render Jim Crow immune to attack. As one outside observer described the system at its height, "sex becomes in this popular theory the principle around which the whole structure of segregation of the Negroes—down to disenfranchisement and denial of equal opportunities on the labor market—is organized. . . . Every single measure is defended as necessary to block 'social equality' which in its turn is held necessary to prevent 'intermarriage.' "[21]

By the end of the nineteenth century, it was clear that the promise of racial equality that Reconstruction seemed to offer was not to be fulfilled. As white Democratic rule returned to the South and as northern interest in the former slaves waned, blacks were left to protect their own interests. For a time an uneasy equilibrium in race relations ensued, but it was soon shattered by the discontent of farmers whose agitation in the 1880s and 1890s raised the specter of an interracial alliance of the dispossessed. Throughout the South, the white elite fomented racial hatred. Mob violence against blacks and their allies rose sharply, while Democrat-controlled state legislatures devised methods to keep blacks from voting. By the First World War, the southern states had enacted a vast array of laws that rigidly segregated the races in the public sphere.

From its start, the system of Jim Crow relied on lynching as its ultimate weapon of enforcement. Between 1889 and 1940, at least thirty-eight hundred black men and women were lynched in the former Confederacy and the border states, while many other instances likely went unreported; during the 1890s, the number of victims averaged two hundred per year. The way the act occurred marked it, in the words of one commentator, as "not merely a punishment against an individual but a disciplinary device against the Negro group."[22] An extralegal act of violence, lynching was designed to instill terror in an entire community. Rarely spontaneous, it often took the form of a public spectacle. Newspapers sometimes aroused passions against an intended victim for days in advance; sheriffs connived with mob leaders; crowds gathered to watch the execution and sometimes participated in mutilating the body; a site might be chosen that made the event visible to the local black population; and newspapers often published pictures of the corpse.

Despite the long history of violence against blacks, the epidemic of lynching might have provoked some outrage had it not been accompanied by a rationale with enough emotional power to silence white criticism. Apologists for lynching raised the specter of rape, the brutal assault of white women by sexually crazed black men. "The crime of lynching is not likely to cease until the crime of ravishing and murdering women and children is less frequent than it has been of late," one observer commented in 1904. An inflamed rhetoric fanned the fires of white animosity, rationalizing the most wanton violence.

"No law of God or man can hold back the vengeance of our white men upon such a criminal," an Atlanta journalist wrote. "We will hang two, three or four of the Negroes nearest to the crime until the crime is no longer done or even feared in all this Southern land we inhabit and love." An anonymous East Texas man declared that "God will burn . . . the Big African Brute in Hot Hell for molesting our God-like pure snowwhite angelic American Woman." The defense of white womanhood even insinuated its way into the discourse of white political leaders. Ben Tillman, a senator from South Carolina early in the twentieth century, claimed that "civilized men" were justified in the desire to "kill, kill, kill" the "creature in human form who has deflowered a white woman." As late as 1930, a southern senator shaped his reelection campaign around a defense of lynching. "Whenever the Constitution comes between me and the virtue of the white women of the South," said Senator Cole Blease, "I say to hell with the Constitution!"[23]

The rhetoric of lynching obscured the reality of the phenomenon. Besides the extralegal nature of the act, most lynchings in fact had little to do with even allegations of sexual assault; fewer than a quarter of the reported killings involved the charge of rape or other sexual offenses. In some cases, the victim was a successful black shopkeeper or businessman. His execution served as a grisly reminder to southern blacks to stay in their place. In other cases, a dispute over wages or some other kind of assertive behavior might provoke a group of whites to target a black for murder. Often, it was not the rape of a white woman, but the sexual assault of a black woman, that set a lynching in motion. In Mississippi in 1918, two young black brothers visited a white dentist who had forced himself on a pair of black teenage girls, impregnating one of them. When the dentist was murdered a few days later, a white mob lynched all four of the young blacks. The pregnant girl, sixteen-year-old Alma Howze, was so near motherhood that, according to one eyewitness, "the movements of her unborn child could be detected." The following year in Georgia, a seventy-two-year-old black man was lynched after he shot and killed a white man who was sexually attacking his black neighbor. Berry Washington was "hanged to a post, his body shot into pieces, and left hanging there." In Oklahoma, whites hung Marie Scott, whose brother had killed the white man who raped her.[24]

The fears and outrage that the rape charge elicited among whites was such that, initially, few responded to the moral challenge that lynching posed. Instead, the accusation of rape encouraged the demise of white support for racial equality. At best, white leaders shifted the onus onto blacks and urged them to stem the tide of sexual assaults. But, more often, commentators accepted the truth of the charge and sought an explanation for the propensity of black men to commit sexual offenses. Phillip Alexander Bruce, a white historian at the time, claimed that black men found "something strangely alluring and seductive . . . in the appearance of the white woman; they are aroused and stimulated by its foreignness to their experience of sexual pleasures, and it moves them to gratify their lust at any cost and in spite of every obstacle." Frances Willard, the influential leader of the Women's Christian Temperance Union, blamed "the grogshop . . . the Negro's center of power. Better whiskey and more of it," she wrote, "is the rallying cry of great, dark-faced mobs," whose drunken exploits menaced "the safety of women, of childhood, [and] the home . . . in a thousand localities." Reflecting the dominance of racial theories of heredity, some attributed the allegedly uncontrolled sexual expression of the black man to evolutionary traits initially developed as a means to offset the high death rate in Africa. In a strange twist, one medical writer enmeshed in hereditarian thought even argued against lynching because the low mentality of blacks rendered it ineffective as a deterrent. "Executed," he wrote, "they would be forgotten; castrated and free, they would be a constant warning and ever-present admonition to others of their race." But, whatever the convoluted logic or rationale, the starting point seemed to be an acceptance of the claim that southern black men were assaulting white women.[25]

Not surprisingly, some black leaders did raise their voices in protest, attempting to expose the hidden motivations behind racial violence. Frederick Douglass, the former abolitionist leader, saw the charge of rape as rooted not in fact but in the efforts of white supremacists to perpetuate Negro subordination in the face of new social conditions. After the Civil War, he wrote,

> [T]he justification for the murder of Negroes was said to be Negro conspiracies, Negro insurrections, Negro schemes to murder all the white people, Negro plots to burn the town. . . . [T]imes have changed and the Negro's accusers have found it necessary to change with them. . . . Honest men no longer believe that there is any ground to apprehend Negro supremacy. . . . [A]ltered circumstances have made necessary a sterner, stronger, and more effective justification of Southern barbarism, and hence we have . . . to look into the face of a more shocking and blasting charge.

In Douglass's view, the cry of rape was intended to paralyze the allies of blacks in the North and South, to arrest "at home and abroad, in some measure, the generous efforts that good men were wont to make for his improvement and elevation." Ida B. Wells, a black newspaper editor in Memphis, went further. Outraged by a series of lynchings that had occurred, she wrote a polemic in her paper, the Memphis *Free Speech,* in 1892. "Nobody in this section believes the old thread-bare lie that Negro men assault white women," she charged. Instead, Wells implied that the problem stemmed from the behavior of white women who enticed black men to make sexual advances. Later, she refined her argument, exposing in the process a hidden sexual dynamic of southern life:

> With the Southern man, any mesalliance existing between a white woman and a colored man is a sufficient foundation for the charge of rape. The Southern white man says that it is impossible for a voluntary alliance to exist between a white woman and a colored man, and therefore, the fact of an alliance is a proof of force. In numerous instances where colored men have been lynched on the charge of rape, it was positively known at the time of lynching, and indisputably proven after the victim's death, that the relationship sustained between the man and the woman was voluntary and clandestine, and that in no court of law could even the charge of assault have been successfully maintained.

At the time, her words so inflamed the white community in Memphis that a mob destroyed her press and offices, and Wells was forced to escape the South for her own safety.[26]

Opposition to lynching soon became a primary motive stimulating black organizational activity, especially among middle-class women. Soon after leaving Memphis, Wells began addressing groups of black women around the country. Her labors eventually sparked the formation of a Negro women's club movement. Just as white women of the era were creating new forms of voluntary association to protect themselves from male lust, their black counterparts jumped into politics to expose and resist the dual injustices of racial and sexual violence. Mary Church Terrell, the first president of the National Association of Colored Women, frequently took up her pen in response to apologists for mob violence. In 1904, when one writer in the *North American Review* used the rape charge to demonstrate the unfortunate consequences of black aspirations for "social equality," Terrell acidly replied that the "only form of social equality ever attempted between the two races, and practised to any considerable extent, is that which was originated by the white masters of slave women." She placed the blame for lynching squarely on the surviving ethos of slavery. "The white men who shoot negroes to death and flay them alive, and the white women who apply flaming torches to their oil-soaked bodies today, are the sons and daughters of women who had but little, if any, compassion on the race when it was enslaved." Meanwhile, the true victims of rape, she charged, were the "prepossessing young colored girls [who] have been considered the rightful prey of white gentlemen in the South."[27] Outrage over lynching played an important role in the formation, in 1910, of the National Association for the Advancement of Colored People. An alliance of blacks and some white reformers in the North, the NAACP targeted lynching as the most grotesque result of American racism.

Although lynching served the purpose of perpetuating black subordination in every sphere of life, the southern "rape complex," as one historian has called it, also shaped a social hierarchy of gender and a system of sexual values that lasted at least until the 1930s. Black men faced the threat of lynching; black women suffered sexual exploitation; white women lived in a state of fear and anxiety. As the assumption of black men's uncontrollable passions permeated the psyches of white women, a "nameless terror" took hold, circumscribing their freedom of movement, and foiling aspirations to break out of their domestic roles. "Nowhere in the country are we safe," wrote one. "Even on the public highways, the situation has become so serious" that "the fragile and helpless woman, innocent of any wrong," feared for her security. Meanwhile, the combination of illicit male sexual activities and suppressed female desires among southern whites added a violent erotic element to both the charge of rape and to lynching. Sexual mythology fed the fantasies of white mobs. Describing one Florida lynching, an anonymous observer wrote that "the crowds from here that went over to see [the victim] for themself said he was so large he could not assault her until he took his knife and cut her, and also had either cut or bit one of her breast [sic] off." Juxtaposed against these allegations of black sexual brutality was the reality of lynching crowds who mutilated a victim's genitals, and sometimes fought for souvenirs. The descriptions of lynchings, the way the rape charge was bandied about, and the behavior of mobs has convinced Jacquelyn Dowd Hall, a student of the phenomenon, that "rape and rumors of rape became a kind of acceptable folk pornography in the Bible Belt."[28]

By the 1920s some white southern women were rejecting the "protection" they received and abandoning the submissive roles that led them to acquiesce to mob law in the name of their purity. In large part, their campaign against lynching grew out of challenges directed at them by black women. As southern women participated in efforts at interracial understanding after World War I, blacks raised the lynching issue again and again. For instance, Charlotte Hawkins Brown, an educator from North Carolina, told a group of white women in 1920 that she and her sisters "lay everything that happens to the members of her race at the door of the Southern white woman. . . . We all feel that you can control your men. . . . [S]o far as lynching is concerned . . . if the white women take hold of the situation . . . lynching would be stopped." When critics of lynching formed the Association of Southern Women for the Prevention of Lynching, they explicitly rejected the traditional justification for it:

> Public opinion has accepted too easily the claim of lynchers and mobsters that they were acting *solely in the defense of womanhood*. Women dare no longer to permit the claim to pass unchallenged nor allow themselves to be the cloak behind which

those bent upon personal revenge and savagery commit acts of violence and lawless-ness.

Their actions dismayed many. "You may have yourself a nigger if you want one, but do not force them on others," one letter writer informed the organiza-tion. Another revealed the underlying motivation of lynching when he said, "if you want a Negro man, OK. Otherwise lay off white supremacy." Even with the campaigns against lynching, support for it died slowly. Anti-lynching bills were regularly blocked in Congress in the 1930s, and as late as 1939, sixty-four percent of the respondents in a survey of white southerners thought lynching justified in cases of sexual assault.[29]

The simultaneity of lynching in the South and the attacks on immigrants by some Progressive reformers place in bold relief the ways sexuality figured in the maintenance of social hierarchies. Southern whites justified the violent subordination of blacks as necessary to protect white womanhood. Northern-ers, fearing the growing numbers of immigrants, blamed the "enslavement" of young white girls and the infection of middle-class wives with venereal disease on alien procurers and foreign prostitutes. In both cases, the emotional power of their rhetoric came from a sexual ideology that exalted the purity and refinement of white women even as it constricted the social roles available to them. As the twentieth century wore on, changing sexual mores and new roles for women would alter the ways that the erotic served as a method of enforcing inequality.

Despite the intensity of the anti-vice campaigns of the Progressive era, it appears, in retrospect, that they represented a last gasp for nineteenth-century middle-class respectability. Even as reformers mounted their assault upon the vice districts and targeted blacks and immigrants as symbolic villains, other forces were at work pushing sexual values in a decidedly modern direction. In the years before World War I, among doctors, sexual theorists, cultural radi-cals, feminists, and others, new ideas, new social relations, and a new kind of sexual politics emerged that would help to shape in the succeeding decades a distinctively different sexual order.

CHAPTER 10

Breaking with the Past

EARLY in 1915, Anthony Comstock entered the studio of William Sanger, an architect living in lower Manhattan. The month before, an agent of Comstock's Society for the Suppression of Vice had approached Sanger in search of a copy of *Family Limitation,* a birth control pamphlet written by Sanger's wife, Margaret. The unsuspecting architect responded to the plea, only to be confronted a few weeks later by Comstock, arrest warrant in hand. The tireless obscenity foe was less interested in William than in Margaret, whose militant espousal of women's right to birth control (a phrase she herself had coined) mocked Comstock's lifelong work. Margaret Sanger had fled to Europe the year before to avoid prosecution under the federal obscenity law, and Comstock informed William that *"if I would give your whereabouts I would be acquited."* William replied that he could wait "until Hell froze over before that would occur."[1]

William's trial did not take place until September, but in the meantime, Comstock's action unleashed forces for which he was not well prepared. Throughout the country, politically radical women began agitating for open discussion of contraception, with the anarchist Emma Goldman commencing a nationwide speaking tour. Eugene Debs, the leader of the Socialist party, wrote to Sanger in Europe, encouraging her to return and promising that "we now have some means of defense and we can call a pretty good-sized bunch of revolutionists to arms." Meanwhile, William was found guilty in September and sentenced to thirty days in jail, an outcome which impelled Margaret to return to New York. Her upcoming trial stimulated further protests, including scores of letters to President Wilson from British intellectuals and a plan by Elsie Clews Parsons, a Columbia anthropologist, to have women who had practiced birth control "stand up in court" and make a public declaration. Faced with such an opposition, the federal prosecutor dropped the charges against Sanger rather than risk making her a martyr. As for Comstock, he did not live to see Sanger escape prosecution. He had caught a chill at William's trial, contracted pneumonia, and died before Margaret returned from Europe.[2]

The support that the Sangers received, as well as Comstock's passing from the scene, suggest that on the eve of World War I, America was entering a new sexual era. Margaret Sanger's fight for birth control, so different from nineteenth-century feminist advocacy of voluntary motherhood through abstinence, indicates one aspect of this reordering. At least some middle-class women were unwilling to sacrifice sexual expression in the interest of fertility control. But there were additional signs of a new sexual order as well. Among doctors and other theorists of sexuality, the shift toward a philosophy of indulgence marked the demise of nineteenth-century prescriptions about continence and self-control. New ideas about sex coincided with a new sense of sexual identity among some Americans. Finally, middle-class cultural radicals, emboldened by the critique of political and economic institutions that left-wing agitators promoted, self-consciously broke with the marital ideals of their upbringing as they sought to construct new forms of personal relationships. All of these signs of change pointed toward acceptance of a sexual ethic that encouraged expressiveness.

Ideas and Identities

The writings of Sigmund Freud perhaps best symbolize the new direction that sexual theorizing took in the twentieth century. Freud's visit to America in 1909, to lecture at Clark University, introduced his work to a number of intellectuals and professionals. Before long he was being translated and published in America; by the mid-1910s, popularizers were presenting Freudian ideas to a larger audience. Whatever subtlety or complexity his theories possessed took a backseat to the concepts that infiltrated the middle-class imagination: the notion of infantile sexuality, the drama of sexual conflict in the family, the case histories of female patients who seemed to suffer from the denial of their sexual desires, the idea that the sexual instinct permeated human life and might change the course of civilization. Above all, Americans absorbed a version of Freudianism that presented the sexual impulse as an insistent force demanding expression. "The urge is there," wrote an American analyst, A. A. Brill, "and whether the individual desires or no, it always manifests itself." The readers of *Good Housekeeping* were told that the sex instinct sought "every kind of sensory gratification. . . . If it gets its yearning it is as contented as a nursing infant. If it does not, beware! It will never be stopped except with satisfactions."[3] The implications seemed clear: better to indulge this unruly desire than to risk the consequences of suppressing it.

Although Freudianism proved more enduring in its influence, in the short run the writings of the English sexologist Havelock Ellis had a greater impact. The object of censorship in England, his *Studies in the Psychology of Sex* (six volumes of which were published between 1897 and 1910) quickly found an American readership. Described by historian Paul Robinson as the first of the sexual modernists, Ellis assaulted almost every aspect of the nineteenth-century sexual heritage. For Ellis, sexual indulgence did not pose the threat to health or character that preoccupied many earlier writers. Rather, he described it as "the chief and central function of life . . . ever wonderful, ever lovely." Ellis equated sex with "all that is most simple and natural and pure and good." He asked his readers: "Why . . . should people be afraid of rousing passions which, after all, are the great driving forces of human life?"[4] As with mass-circulation presentations of Freud, Ellis seemed to be advocating gratification rather than self-control.

Ellis did in fact seek to legitimate a broader range of sexual opportunities than the marital heterosexuality sanctioned by his nineteenth-century ancestors. He questioned the institution of marriage, calling it "essentially rather . . . a tragic condition than a happy condition." A legal document, he wrote, could not guarantee the mutual attraction and intensity of passion which alone brought contentment. Ellis advocated a period of "trial marriage" before couples made a lasting commitment, and he recognized as well that some might need variety in sexual partners. He also wrote approvingly of masturbation as an "autoerotic" form of relaxation and a method of initiating adolescents into knowledge of sex. Perhaps most daringly, Ellis wished to remove the stigma attached to homosexual behavior. "Sexual inversion," as he termed it, was a congenital condition, as natural for its practitioners as heterosexual relations were for the majority. Because he viewed it as inborn, Ellis believed that the laws criminalizing homosexual behavior were archaic and unjust, and he supported efforts to repeal them. Overall, as Robinson has noted, Ellis's defense of a variety of sexual practices reflected the belief that the world needed "not more restraint, but more passion."[5]

Even where Ellis's views seemed indebted to nineteenth-century assumptions, as in his acceptance of male and female differences and his attribution of spiritual qualities to sexual passion, he managed to draw vastly different conclusions. Though he rejected notions of female passionlessness, he did claim distinctive sexual modes for each gender. Men were characteristically active, aggressive, sexually insistent, and easily excited, while women, if not quite passive, needed the attention and stimulus of the male to be aroused.

"Modesty," Ellis wrote, "may almost be regarded as the chief secondary sexual character of women on the psychical side." He described modesty as "rooted in the sexual periodicity of the female" and "an inevitable byproduct of the naturally aggressive attitude of the male in sexual relationships."[6] But instead of marshaling these assertions in support of male sexual restraint, Ellis interpreted them as serving to encourage courtship between male and female. And, when man and woman did engage in sexual activity, Ellis saw the slower arousal of the woman as requiring extensive foreplay so that she, too, would experience satisfaction.

Ellis was not the only modern writer on sex to attract an American readership. The English utopian socialist Edward Carpenter and the Swedish theorist Ellen Key also had a devoted following. In the United States, William J. Robinson, the editor of two medical journals, penned book after book about sexuality. Robinson spoke out strongly against the nineteenth-century emphasis on continence. In a letter to a prominent supporter of the social hygiene movement, Robinson made his disagreement with its sexual philosophy abundantly clear:

> You speak the language of the tenth century; I speak the language of the 20th, or perhaps, the 25th. You speak the language of gloom and reaction; I speak the language of joy and progress. . . . You believe that the sexual instinct was given to man and should be used by him for procreation purposes only. I believe that such a belief borders on insanity. . . . You believe that extramarital relations are a sin and a crime. I believe they . . . may be unwise for many reasons, but are not more sinful or criminal per se than the gratification of any other natural instincts, such as eating or drinking.

His approach to sex logically pushed him toward support for birth control, which he viewed as the key both to a better society and to the liberation of sexuality from the shackles of prudish ignorance. In this regard, Robinson heralded the beginnings of an important shift within the medical establishment from late-nineteenth-century opinion.[7]

The significance of Freud, Ellis, and other twentieth-century theorists involved more than their advocacy of sexual expression. The shift from a philosophy of continence to one that encouraged indulgence was but one aspect of a larger reorientation that was investing sexuality with a profoundly new importance. The modern regime of sexology was taking sex beyond a procreative framework, beyond, too, its role in fostering intimacy between husband and wife. In doing so, some writers emphasized the social character of sex, as did an American doctor who said "it is sexual activity that governs life. . . . It is the basis of all society." But, more commonly, theorists attributed to sexuality the power of individual self-definition. As Ellis phrased it, "sex penetrates the whole person; a man's sexual constitution is part of his general constitution. There is considerable truth in the dictum: 'A man is what his sex is.' "[8] In these terms, sex was becoming a marker of identity, the wellspring of an individual's true nature.

Nowhere, perhaps, can this change be seen more clearly than in the new definitions and new social experiences that characterized same-sex relationships, especially among men. By the end of the nineteenth century, medical writers were turning their pens to "sodomitical behavior" and the "crime against nature" which previously had been the province of law and religion. In the process, they came to see homosexuality not as a discrete, punishable offense, but as a description of the person, encompassing emotions, dress, mannerisms, behavior, and even physical traits. As Michel Foucault has described this evolution, "the sodomite had been a temporary aberration; the homosexual was now a species."[9]

Beginning in the 1880s in the United States, and somewhat earlier in Europe, physicians began writing about the cases of "contrary sexual impulse" that came to their attention. The phenomenon appeared new and strange to them, and as they charted this unfamiliar sexual territory, they searched for words adequate to label it—*urning, tribad, invert, homosexual, third sex,* among many others. Little agreement existed about its cause or its meaning. At first, medical theorists leaned toward the hypothesis that homosexuality was a degenerative disease, an acquired form of insanity. By the early twentieth century, especially as the writings of Havelock Ellis gained wider currency, opinion had shifted toward a congenital model, and a rough consensus developed that sexual "inverts" were born that way. Not until the 1920s, when Freudianism swept competitors from the field, would the pendulum swing back to the position that homosexuality was an acquired condition. Reflecting the centrality of gender in nineteenth-century sexual arrangements, many early students of the phenomenon tended to define it not as homosexuality, but as "sexual inversion," a complete exchange of gender identity of which erotic behavior was but one small part. George Beard, an eminent American physician, wrote in 1884 that when "the sex is perverted, they hate the opposite sex and love their own; men become women and women men, in their tastes, conduct, character, feelings, and behavior." Or, as one anonymous male patient in the first decade of the twentieth century described this outlook, "my feelings are exactly those of a woman. . . . As near as I can explain it, I am a woman in every detail except external appearances."[10]

Whatever the point of view that doctors adopted, it seems clear that their writings were responding to real changes in the social organization of same-sex eroticism. By the turn of the century, the spread of a capitalist economy and the growth of huge cities were allowing diffuse homosexual desires to congeal into a personal sexual identity. Labor for wages allowed more and more men, and some women, to detach themselves from a family-based economy and strike out on their own; the anonymous social relations of the metropolis gave them the freedom to pursue their sexual yearnings. Some men and women began to interpret their homosexual desires as a characteristic that distinguished them from the majority. Slowly they elaborated an underground sexual subculture. Unlike the normative passionate friendships of the nineteenth century, or the isolated female couples in which one partner passed as a man, these women and men were self-consciously departing from the norm and creating a social milieu that nurtured their emergent sense of identity.

Abundant evidence survives from observers and participants that between the 1880s and the First World War, a sexual minority of sorts was in the making. Again and again, doctors reported the information supplied by patients that "there is in every community of any size a colony of male sexual perverts" or that "in many large cities the subjects of the contrary sexual impulse form a class by themselves." Meeting places proliferated. After a foray into the sexual underworld of New York City in 1890, a medical student from North Carolina found that "perverts of both sexes maintained a sort of social set-up in New York City, had their places of meeting, and [the] advantage of police protections." The furnished-room districts of large cities provided a setting where working women might form relationships with each other, while descriptions of the red-light districts suggest that some prostitutes formed lesbian attachments. In Harlem after the First World War, the cross-dressing lesbian Gladys Bentley performed in men's attire, and served as something of a magnet for other lesbians and male homosexuals. Several clubs along the Bowery allowed cross-dressing men and women to socialize. In many cities, men openly solicited one another on certain streets well known as "cruising" areas. In Newport, Rhode Island, "everybody who sat around [the YMCA] in the evening . . . knew" that it was a gathering spot for the sexually different. In the nation's capital, black men met "under the shadow of the White House . . . in Lafayette Square." One man wrote in 1908 that in cities such as Boston, Chicago, St. Louis, and New Orleans, "certain smart clubs are well-known for their homosexual atmospheres." He reported that "steam-baths and restaurants are plentifully known—to the initiated," and that in some places homosexual resorts were masked as literary clubs, athletic societies, and chess clubs. In San Francisco, the area surrounding the Presidio military base had become recognized by the 1890s as "a regular visiting place!"[11]

Two features of this inchoate subculture especially stand out. First, many of the pre-1920 commentaries remarked on the pervasive transvestism and other evidence of inverted gender behavior among the participants. In Chicago, for instance, in 1911, vice investigators found men who "mostly affect the carriage, mannerisms, and speech of women [and] who are fond of many articles dear to the feminine heart."[12] The frequency of such observations points to the continuing salience of gender in shaping an individual's sense of sexual meaning, and to how the erotic remained attached to conceptions of gender. Second, the meeting places tended to be sites of either moral ambiguity in American society or of transient relationships. Boardinghouses, waterfront areas where sailors congregated on leave, red-light districts, bohemian communities such as Greenwich Village, transvestite clubs paying the police for protection, military bases with soldiers far from home, YMCAs housing travelers, theaters that hosted touring companies: all of these constituted places freed from the bonds of family and community, able to tolerate deviance from the moral rules of respectable society.

Standing outside the norms of their society, these early pioneers of a homosexual identity faced enormous hurdles in creating a viable life for themselves. For one, the subculture that some were creating remained hidden and difficult to find. As a woman of twenty in the mid-1880s, Mary Casal felt that "I was the only girl who had the sex desire for woman." Years later, having stumbled upon others, she wrote, "How much suffering would have been saved me and what a different life I would have led if I had known earlier" that there were many others like herself? For some women who embraced this self-conscious sexual identity, the need to find others effected subtle changes in the older tradition of passing. Rather than try to escape detection through a successful masquerade, they only partially adopted male styles. One thirty-eight-year-old woman, according to a doctor's report, "proclaims her characteristics in the most flagrant way through her manner of dress which is always the most masculine. . . . [S]he frequents public places dressed in a manner to *attract* general notice." For most men and women, the threat of punishment and social ostracism conspired to keep their sexual proclivities a carefully guarded secret. As Francis Matthiessen, soon to become a renowned literary critic, wrote to his male lover in the early 1920s, "we would be pariahs, outlaws, degenerates," if the world were to know. "This is the price we pay for the unforgivable sin of being born different from the great run of mankind." Yet, in spite of the fears and the penalties, love could thrive. "Oh what a sweet and sacred thing it is to love and to be loved!" a Detroit man wrote soon after World War I:

> to hold within one's arms the visible representation of that beautiful spark which daily seems to grow brighter and more wondrous, to remove one's thoughts from the realm of self and let them dwell rapturously and selflessly upon some beloved companion, to press his glorious body close to one's own, to feel the warm, red blood pulsing deliciously through both, . . . to pillow one's head upon his breast, to touch one's lip to his hair, his eyes, his lips! Is Paradise more wonderful?[13]

The lyricism of his description suggests the strength of motive that led many to pursue their sexual desires even in the face of a hostile society.

Radical Lives, Radical Politics

While some Americans constructed an underground sexual subculture based upon a sense of shared identity, others departed from nineteenth-century orthodoxy in more visible, dramatic ways. In the decade before World War I, the ideas of the new sexual theorists took root among small groups of American radicals whose articulateness gave them an influence out of proportion to their numbers. Based in Greenwich Village, these homegrown bohemians self-consciously adopted a new sexual ethic and style of personal life. Their involvement in radical causes, whether as socialists, anarchists, or feminists, imparted a fervor to their erotic experimentation which they defined as an essential, innovative component of revolutionary struggle.

Central to the ideology of these cultural radicals was a belief in the necessity of a new, emancipated woman who could meet man on an equal footing in sexual, as well as in other, matters. For the men in these circles, Edward Carpenter expressed the goal well in *Love's Coming of Age* when he wrote of a future in which "marriage shall mean friendship as well as passion" and "a comradelike equality shall be included in the word love." Floyd Dell, an important figure in the bohemian world of the Village, phrased it more mundanely in an autobiographical novel. "I want a girl that can be talked to and that can be kissed," says the main character.[14] These views implied an end to the delicacy, purity, and domesticity that characterized the nineteenth-century model of femininity. Her successor would leave the private sphere of the home to fill a place in the public world of work and politics, bringing that equality to affairs of the heart.

Such an ideal assumed that women harbored strong sexual instincts and that sexual passion was as much a part of woman's nature as man's. And, indeed, the cultural radicals of the period seemed to play the part well. In recalling those days, Sherwood Anderson wrote of a "healthy new frankness . . . in the talk between men and women, at least an admission that we were all at times torn and harried by the same lusts." From women writers, too, came a more forthright portrayal of female passion. As Gladys Oaks, a socialist writer, expressed it in a poem titled "Climax":

> I had thought that I could sleep
> After I had kissed his mouth
> With its sharply haunting corners
> And its red.

> But now that he has kissed me
> A stir is in my blood,
> And I want to be awake
> Instead.

Oaks's verse had moved a long distance from the female sentimental literature of the nineteenth century.[15]

Echoing Ellis's views, these bohemian radicals also dispensed with the sanctity of marriage and the ideal of lifelong monogamy. Like earlier free lovers, they termed the marriage-based family a shackle that bound women to men in a property relationship. Unions based on sexual attraction and emotional compatibility, they argued, did not need the approval of church or state, and ought to be dissolved at the wish of either member. But unlike their predecessors, they did not believe that a coupled relationship, whether in marriage or not, demanded sexual exclusivity. Variety in partners, Ellis had suggested, might serve as fuel for the passions; psychological, or emotional, fidelity was more significant than sexual fidelity.

These beliefs led the bohemian community to engage in a good deal of self-conscious experimentation with relationships, not all of which was successful. Perceiving themselves as revolutionary innovators pioneering a new form of personal life, they tried to live true to their theories. But the ideal, in Ellen Key's words, of "a union in which neither the soul betrayed the senses, nor the senses the soul," often proved elusive. Women and men both found it difficult to discard their socialization in other than rhetorical ways. The writer Neith Boyce, in a letter to her husband, Hutchins Hapgood, detailed the pain that the new morality entailed for her:

> I have an abiding love for you—the deepest thing in me. But in a way I hate your interest in sex, because I have suffered from it. I assure you that I can never think of your physical passions for other women without pain—even though my reason doesn't find fault with you. But it's instinct and it hurts. The whole thing is sad and terrible, yet we all joke about it every day.[16]

For his part, Hapgood encapsulated the tensions in bohemian life when he titled his autobiography, *A Victorian in the Modern World.* He, along with other male radicals, discovered that sexual freedom with emancipated women carried too high a price. What he most wanted was a wife who would minister to his needs.

The failure of bohemian radicals to model their revolutionary ideals of personal life ought not obscure the critical role they played in pulling America into a modern sexual era. They were few in number, but their work as novelists, playwrights, poets, and journalists guaranteed that in some form the ideas they espoused—of Ellis, Freud, Key, and Carpenter—would reach a larger audience. If Americans were not quite ready to abandon marriage, many were prepared to accept revised notions of female sexuality and to reassess the place that sexual expression held in a happy life.

One can see evidence of the shift in white middle-class values in the patterns of nightlife that some were adopting. The heterosocial world of commercialized amusements that working-class youth enjoyed was spreading to the middle class, though in tamer, more respectable form. By the 1910s, cabarets were becoming the rage. Adapting the syncopated dance music of black entertainers to a different clientele, the cabaret allowed men and women to mingle informally outside a domestic setting. The new dance styles became so much the fashion that many of these clubs began holding afternoon "tango teas" to teach the latest steps. Under the pretext of shopping, wives and daughters would attend these daytime sessions, taught by men hired for that purpose. The atmosphere was suggestive of illicit sexuality. As *Variety* commented in 1914, "if the cabaret could talk, or the waiters tell all they know, the state would have to open a few extra courts to keep up with the rush for divorces."[17] Meanwhile, the movie industry was entering a new era as entrepreneurs constructed lavish theaters to appeal to a middle-class audience. As the motion picture traveled uptown, out of the working-class neighborhoods that first housed it, it spread its romantic sensuous imagery, and further encouraged the departure of women from a protected domestic context. By 1920, the distinctive spheres that sustained nineteenth-century sexual values were in a state of disarray. Elaine Tyler May's study of divorce cases from 1880 and 1920 confirms this assessment. In the earlier period, a woman's participation in public amusements marked her as disreputable. By 1920, many women saw such activities as part and parcel of modern life.[18]

Along with the changes in patterns of leisure, a new kind of sexual politics was taking shape. The Greenwich Village radicals wove their theories in an intense milieu of socialist agitators, labor leaders, and feminist organizers. The environment encouraged a translation from personal experimentation to social activism. Out of these circles emerged not only modern ideas but an innovative politics of sexuality far removed from the purity crusades and antiprostitution campaigns that swirled around them.

Birth control, the issue that signaled the shift, is most closely associated with the name of Margaret Sanger. As a thirty-year-old housewife and mother of three living in the suburbs of New York, she attended a socialist lecture in Manhattan in 1910 and became so excited that she persuaded her husband to move to the city. Sanger plunged rapidly into the life of New York radicals, and her apartment became a gathering place for activists and agitators such as Bill Haywood, a militant union leader; the journalist John Reed; and Alexander Berkman, a fiery anarchist agitator. Work as an organizer for

Haywood's Industrial Workers of the World led to her first arrest, while her training as a nurse put her in a critical role in the evacuation and care of children during the celebrated textile workers' strike in Lawrence, Massachusetts, in 1912 and 1913.[19]

Her experience and activities were pushing Sanger toward the issue of birth control. On one side, sexual freedom for middle-class radical women rested on their having access to contraception. On the other, Sanger was appalled by the misery of working-class women who had virtually no control over their fertility, and bore child after child despite grinding poverty. At the time, Sanger could draw on little in the way of tradition in devising a political response. For an older generation of feminists, birth control had meant not contraception but voluntary motherhood, the right to say no to a husband's sexual demands. Male radicals, wedded to a socialist tradition that exalted the working-class family and excoriated capitalism for corrupting it, by and large saw fertility control as a trivial issue, a distraction from the class struggle. Sanger was left to cut her own path.

In November 1912, Sanger began a series of articles on female sexuality for the New York *Call,* a socialist newspaper. After postal officials confiscated the paper for violating the Comstock anti-obscenity law, Sanger departed for Europe where she gathered contraceptive information and devices. Returning to New York determined to challenge the constitutionality of the Comstock statute, she began publishing her own magazine, *The Woman Rebel.* Though it ranged widely over many topics, Sanger made female autonomy, including control over one's body and the right to sexual expression, the centerpiece of the magazine. "It is none of Society's business what a woman shall do with her body," she wrote.[20] For a time, she managed to elude the postal inspectors, but when she wrote and distributed a pamphlet, *Family Limitation,* Sanger found herself charged with nine counts of violating the law, and facing forty-five years in prison. In October 1914, she fled the country, escaping to Europe where she imbibed the ideas of Havelock Ellis and other sex radicals.

Sanger's escape did not bring an end to the birth control issue; rather, in her absence, organizing efforts mushroomed. Emma Goldman, the anarchist agitator who had spoken often about sexual freedom, began to incorporate the topic of birth control into her lectures. In March 1915 in New York City, she openly discussed various methods of contraception. In August, a similar speech in Portland, Oregon, led to her arrest. Setting aside her conviction, a circuit court judge provided a harbinger of changes to come when he wrote that "the trouble with our people today is that there is too much prudery. . . . We are all shocked by many things publicly stated that we know privately to ourselves, but we haven't got the nerve to get up and admit it."[21] An arrest in New York the following year gave Goldman the opportunity to deliver in the courtroom an impassioned speech on birth control that elicited cheers and applause from the audience. Meanwhile, Sanger's work had opened the issue within the Socialist party. By early 1915, socialist women and others, had distributed over one hundred thousand copies of *Family Limitation*. Activists formed local birth control leagues around the country, raising the level of agitation considerably.[22]

Returning to the United States in October 1915, Sanger demanded a trial. Her case was now a cause célèbre, with prominent women planning to issue a mass declaration attesting to contraceptive use, and British intellectuals wiring President Wilson to intervene. When the federal prosecutor decided to drop charges, Sanger embarked on a speaking tour of 119 cities, made possible by the organizing efforts that had taken place during her exile. In October 1916 she defied the law again, this time by opening a birth control clinic in a working-class neighborhood in Brooklyn, and providing contraceptive information without a physician's presence. Arrest, trial, and jail followed, only to give the birth control controversy its greatest publicity ever. Sanger and other radical women had created an issue whose time had come.

One can hardly overestimate the importance of this emerging birth control movement. It signaled a profound shift in the sexual norms that had reigned supreme among the middle classes for half a century. To advocate fertility control for women through access to contraceptive devices rather than through abstinence implied an unequivocal acceptance of female sexual expression. It weakened the link between sexual activity and procreation, altered the meaning of the marriage bond, and opened the way for more extensive premarital sexual behavior among women. As birth control became more widely available and used, it also broadened the roles women might choose, as biology proved less and less to be destiny.

By the 1920s Americans were clearly entering a new sexual era. Many of the features that would characterize the coming system were already apparent. The new positive value attributed to the erotic, the growing autonomy of youth, the association of sex with commercialized leisure and self-expression, the pursuit of love, the visibility of the erotic in popular culture, the social interaction of men and women in public, the legitimation of female interest in the sexual: all of these were to be seen in America in the twenties.

Among the many changes during this period, two stand out as emblematic of this new sexual order: the redefinition of womanhood to include eroticism, and the decline of public reticence about sex. By 1920 the separate spheres, so critical in the construction of nineteenth-century middle-class sexual mores, had collapsed. Women were engaged in the public world, not vicariously through the moral uplift they provided for husbands and sons, but as workers, consumers, and, finally, as voters. Their participation was not equal, to be sure. But leaving the domestic hearth, even to the extent that they had, carried with it enormous implications for sexual values. Ideals of piety and purity withered as women and men met in a variety of settings. The growing autonomy of women opened up new possibilities for them to pursue the erotic; new conceptions of female sexuality both reflected and encouraged this shift. Female purity lost much of its power as an organizing principle for enforcing sexual orthodoxy as young women and men together explored the erotic. Premarital experience would alter the expectations that individuals brought to marriage, with sexual attraction becoming the bond drawing men and women to one another. Gender differences, though they persisted, would cease to be the fulcrum around which ideas about sexuality turned. Instead, sex was becoming, in the view of modern theorists, a common characteristic that motivated both men and women, and expressed one's deepest sense of self.

Alongside these changes lay the decline of reticence, another characteristic of nineteenth-century civilized morality. By comparison with the past, American society in the 1920s seemed to embrace the sexual. Sex was something to be discussed and displayed, whether through popularizations of Freud, the true-confession magazines, or the romantic imagery of Hollywood films. As one popular magazine described it just before World War I, "sex o'clock" had struck in America.[23] This new presence of the erotic in the public realm, not as an illicit underground but as an accepted feature of daily life, still lacked the explicitness and the pervasiveness that came to characterize American mores in the 1960s and 1970s. But the gulf between private expression and public silence had narrowed considerably. And, ironically, the anti-vice crusaders of the Progressive era, partisans of an older order, had contributed to the new explicitness.

To search for an explanation for this reorientation is more difficult than to describe it. Certainly, one feature that stands out is the gradual shift toward a consumer economy. One does not need to rely on conspiratorial motives nor adopt a crude determinism to say that profound economic changes were reshaping American values. An ethic that encouraged the purchase of consumer products also fostered an acceptance of pleasure, self-gratification, and personal satisfaction, a perspective that easily translated to the province of sex. Such notions would gradually replace the nineteenth-century preoccupation with the control of sexual impulses through individual self-management. Instead, expression and fulfillment became the watchwords. This emphasis on personal gratification coincided with the loss of control over most other aspects of public life. Politics seemed distant and outside the influence of most individuals; huge corporations exercised power over the business of making a living; the sprawling metropolis appeared beyond the control of its inhabitants.

The body, seemingly, remained one's own. It, at least, could be a source of fulfillment. It, at least, might remain a realm of autonomy. Although several more decades would have to pass before this perspective permeated the society, already by the 1920s circumstances were present to encourage acceptance of the modern idea that sexual expression was of overarching importance to individual happiness.

PART IV
THE RISE AND FALL
OF SEXUAL LIBERALISM,
1920 TO THE PRESENT

CHAPTER 11

Beyond Reproduction

IN the winter of 1924, the sociologists Robert and Helen Lynd arrived in Muncie, Indiana, to embark upon an intensive investigation of life in a small American city. The study that resulted, *Middletown,* became an American classic. Casting their net widely, the Lynds examined work, home, youth, leisure, religious beliefs, and civic institutions in an effort to draw a complex picture of life in the modern age. In the process, *Middletown* had much to say about the social context that was shaping sexuality in the 1920s and that would continue to affect American mores.

In order to emphasize the rapidly changing nature of social life in an industrial era, the Lynds offered 1890 as a counterpoint to the 1920s. Reflecting the small-town values that still survived at the turn of the century in parts of the country, males and females moved in different spheres; daughters remained at home with their mothers, and adolescent boys entered the public world of work which their fathers inhabited. Young men and women rarely mingled without the careful chaperonage of adults. Socializing continued to take place in public settings that brought families and community residents together. Once a couple had embarked upon a serious courtship, they gained the permission to be alone together, but most often in the family parlor or on the front porch, not far from parental supervision. A heavy taboo hung over sexual relations outside of marriage. Sex was an intensely private matter that came into public view only occasionally, when Muncie's small red-light district overstepped its boundaries, angering the citizenry.

Even as the Lynds described it, contemporary readers would have recognized this as the portrait of a world irrevocably lost. Indeed, the youth of Muncie, for whom change had been most dramatic, would not even have remembered what that earlier world was like. Instead, by the 1920s, adolescents moved in a youth-centered world, based in the high schools that most now attended. School had become, according to the Lynds, "a place from which they go home to eat and sleep."[1] Males and females met in classes, at after-school activities and evening socials. Cars provided privacy, and marked the end of the "gentleman caller" who sat in the parlor. A majority of the students went out with friends four or more evenings a week. Youth patronized movies together, drove to nearby towns for weekend dances, and parked in lovers' lanes on the way home. Almost half of Muncie's male high school students, and a third of its female students, had participated in the recent vogue of the "petting" party; girls who did not were decidedly less popular. After graduation, boys and girls alike left home to work. Increasing economic independence led to less parental supervision over premarital behavior, at the same time that work allowed the young to continue to meet away from home.

This new autonomy and mobility of youth came at a time when Muncie society, through many of the items and activities of a consumer economy, was focused more and more on sexuality. The newspaper advice columns of Dorothy Dix and other syndicated writers instructed female readers in how to catch a man, the thrill and magic of love, and the nature of modern marriage at the same time that relationships were being redefined in romantic, erotic terms. Popular songs of the decade, such as "It Had to Be You," taught that love was a mysterious experience that occurred in a flash when the "chemistry" was right. Sex adventure magazines had become big sellers with stories titled "The Primitive Lover" ("She wanted a caveman husband") and "Indolent Kisses." Muncie's nine movie theaters, open daily and offering twenty-two programs a week, filled their houses by offering such fare as *Married Flirts, Rouged Lips,* and *Alimony.* One popular film of the decade, *Flaming Youth,* attracted audiences by promising images of "neckers, petters, white kisses, red kisses, pleasure-mad daughters, sensation-craving mothers."[2]

The world that the Lynds described, of autonomous youth coming of age in a social environment where erotic images beckoned, has remained fixed in the popular view of the 1920s as a time of new sexual freedoms. Frederick Lewis Allen, in his best-selling account of the decade, *Only Yesterday,* looked at the cultural landscape and detected a "revolution in manners and morals."[3] Images from the 1920s abound to sustain his assessment—flappers and jazz babies; rumble seats and raccoon coats; F. Scott Fitzgerald novels and speakeasies; petting parties and Hollywood sex symbols. And, in fact, despite the evidence of change in sexual mores in the years before World War I, the 1920s do stand out as a time when something in the sexual landscape decisively altered and new patterns clearly emerged. The decade was recognizably modern in a way that previous ones were not. The values, attitudes, and activities of the pre-Depression years unmistakably point to the future rather than the past.

One reason, perhaps, why the twenties have loomed so large as a critical turning point is that patterns of behavior and sexual norms formerly associated with other groups in the population had, by then, spread to the white middle class. The more lavish cabaret appropriated the music and dancing of black and white working-class youth. Movie palaces replaced storefront theaters, and Hollywood directors churned out feature-length films that attracted youths and adults of every class. Bohemian radicals relinquished their proprietorship over the work of modern sexual theorists such as Ellis and Freud, whose ideas received wide currency. Purity crusaders lost the momentum of the prewar years and found themselves rapidly left behind by a culture that scoffed at the sexual prudery of its ancestors. Although each of these developments had roots in the prewar era, not until the 1920s did they experience a full flowering.

The sexual issues that preoccupied the 1920s—the freedom of middle-class youth, the continuing agitation over birth control, debates about the future of marriage, the commercial manipulation of the erotic—suggest the direction in which American values were heading. Sexual expression was moving beyond the confines of marriage, not as the deviant behavior of prostitutes and their customers, but as the normative behavior of many Americans. The heterosocial world in which youth matured encouraged the trend, and the growing availability of contraceptives removed some of the danger attached to nonmarital heterosexuality. New ideas about the essential healthfulness of sexual expression reshaped marriage, too, as couples approached conjugal life with the expectation that erotic enjoyment, and not simply spiritual union, was an integral part of a successful marital relationship. To be sure, resistance to these modern norms surfaced. Some supporters of a new "companionate" marriage advocated it as a way of containing the excesses of youthful libido, while the new visibility of the erotic in popular culture antagonized some and spawned opposition. But, in general, American society was moving by the 1920s toward a view of erotic expression that can be defined as sexual liberalism—an overlapping set of beliefs that detached sexual activity from the instrumental goal of procreation, affirmed heterosexual pleasure as a value in itself, defined sexual satisfaction as a critical component of personal happiness and successful marriage, and weakened the connections between sexual expression and marriage by providing youth with room for some experimentation as preparation for adult status.

At times during the succeeding generation, the crises that punctuated mid-twentieth-century American life seemed to obscure this trend. Under the pressure of the Depression of the 1930s, for instance, the consumerism and commercialized amusements that gave play to sexual adventure temporarily withered. Sobriety and gloom replaced the buoyant exuberance of the previous decade. Dating became a simpler affair, while the anxieties of unemployment and hard times created sexual tensions in many marriages. Birth control became less an issue of freedom for women, and more a method of regulating the poor. After World War II, the impulse to conform and settle down after years of depression, war, and cold war encouraged a rush to early marriage and saw the birth rate zoom upward. Sexual experimentation appeared lost in a maze of suburban housing developments as a new generation took on family responsibilities and raised more children than their parents had. The erotic seemed to disappear under a wave of innocent domesticity, captured in television shows like *Father Knows Best* or the Hollywood comedies of Rock Hudson and Doris Day. A resurgent purity impulse attacked symbols of sexual permissiveness such as pornography and imposed penalties on those who deviated too sharply from family values.

Despite these appearances, however, the forces that fed sexual liberalism developed apace. The availability and accessibility of reliable contraceptives highlighted the divorce of sexual activity from the procreative consequences that inhibited erotic enthusiasm. Sexual imagery gradually became an integral feature of the public realm, legitimate and aboveground. A youth culture that encouraged heterosexual expressiveness became ubiquitous. Couples looked to marriage as a source of continuing erotic pleasures. By the mid-1960s, sexual liberalism had become the dominant ethic, as powerful in its way as was the civilized morality of the late nineteenth century.

The alterations in behavior and meaning that occurred between the 1920s and the 1960s were of major proportions. To understand and appreciate them, this chapter looks first at the issue of birth control, tracing the successful efforts of reformers to have it incorporated into the life of married Americans. It then turns to the experience of youth and examines the widening sphere of sexual activity that they carved out for themselves. Finally, it explores the world of marriage, where the erotic assumed a more prominent place.

The Contraceptive Revolution

Birth control offers perhaps the most dramatic example of the change that occurred in American sexual mores during the middle of the twentieth century. At the start of the 1920s, it still bore the mark of radicalism, and the birth control movement appeared to many as a threat to moral order. The federal Comstock law, with its prohibition on the importation, mailing, and interstate shipment of contraceptive information and devices, remained in effect, and almost half of the states, including most of the populous ones of the Northeast and Midwest, had their own anti-contraceptive statutes. To agitate for birth control placed one outside the law. By the late 1960s, however, virtually all legal impediments to access had collapsed, and the federal government was actively promoting it. Advances in technology and shifts in values made reliable contraceptives an integral feature of married life as well as widely available to the unmarried.

For most of the 1920s and 1930s Margaret Sanger remained the key figure in the birth control movement and the individual most responsible for the changes that occurred. Though her leadership and visibility provided continuity with the pre–World War I agitation, the politics of the movement was undergoing an important shift. Government repression of radicalism and the decline of organized feminism after suffrage altered the context in which the fight for birth control was occurring. Sanger adapted to the new circumstances by detaching the question of contraception from larger social issues and movements. Throughout the twenties and thirties, she campaigned solely to make contraception freely available to women.[4]

Even with a narrowed focus, however, Sanger remained a militant fighter, willing to use any means necessary to achieve her goals. She continued to risk arrest, believing as she did that "agitation through violation of the law was the key to the public."[5] She also propagandized widely, through the pages of her journal (the *Birth Control Review*), through the books that she authored, and through her extensive speaking tours and public conferences. With the backing of her organization, the American Birth Control League, Sanger lobbied for legislative change and embarked once again on a venture in clinical services when she established the Clinical Research Bureau in 1923.

Sanger's lobbying efforts and the clinic that she supported point to an important way in which her strategy was evolving. In New York State in the 1920s, she campaigned for a "doctors only" bill, designed to allow physicians to provide contraceptives, but restricting that right to licensed practitioners. The Clinical Research Bureau, though it provided female clients with contraceptive devices, existed mainly to gather data that would persuade a science-conscious profession that safe, reliable methods of fertility control were available. Both initiatives aimed at enlisting the medical profession as allies in her cause, since its hostility to contraception constituted a major obstacle to success. In the process, however, the politics of birth control tilted in a more conservative direction. From a key issue in the struggle for female emancipation, contraception was gradually becoming a matter of professional health care.

As it turned out, medical support was slow to materialize. Sanger found few doctors willing to risk their professional status by an association with anything that bore her imprint. For much of the 1920s and 1930s, prominent physicians and medical organizations responded negatively to the campaign for birth control. In 1925, Morris Fishbein, the editor of the prestigious *Journal of the American Medical Association,* argued that no method of contraception existed that was "physiologically, psychologically and biologically sound in both principle and practice." A decade later, an AMA committee charged with studying the legal status of contraception reported that it was "unable to find evidence that existing laws, federal or state, have interfered with any medical advice," despite the fact that laws in a number of states were being employed against physicians.[6] When the AMA finally reversed its position in 1937, the change came largely through intensive lobbying by Sanger and her supporters of virtually every member of the AMA's House of Delegates. Even then, more time would have to elapse before American doctors were adequately trained to meet the needs of their female patients. As late as 1936, the overwhelming majority of the nation's reputable medical schools provided either no, or only incidental, training in the practice of contraception.

Sanger and other female activists, rather than the elite of the medical profession, deserve credit for making effective contraception accessible to American women. Sanger's clinic in New York served as a model for others. Local birth control leagues, staffed and run largely by women reformers, established clinics of their own. By 1930, there were fifty-five of them in twenty-three cities in fifteen states; eight years later, with the Depression having intensified the need for contraception, their numbers had grown to over three hundred. Although the clinics reached only a small proportion of American women, staff members magnified their long-term influence by the work they did with local doctors. Securing the names of physicians sympathetic to the desire of women to control their fertility, clinic personnel maintained an elaborate referral system that increased the availability of contraceptives at the same time that it performed the important task of educating the nation's doctors. Soon, private hospitals as well as some state public health services were setting up birth control facilities. By 1942, there were more than eight hundred clinics scattered across the nation.[7]

Sanger's relentless propagandizing also kept the birth control issue in the public eye. Her dogged determination encouraged her to employ any rationale that might add supporters to the cause. Believing as she did in the importance of female sexual satisfaction, she took advantage of the new emphasis on companionate marriage to attack methods such as *coitus interruptus* and urge instead the adoption of artificial contraceptives. Withdrawal, she wrote, has an "evil effect upon the woman's nervous condition. She has not completed her desire, she is under a highly nervous tension, her whole being is perhaps on the verge of satisfaction. She is then left in this dissatisfied state, which is far from humane." Sanger argued that fear of pregnancy had the unfortunate effect of making "the embraces of her husband . . . repugnant" to many wives, and led to children who were neither loved nor cared for. Birth control promised happier marriages and happier families. Regrettably, Sanger also was willing to play to nativist and middle-class fears of immigrants, blacks, and the poor. She often defined the purpose of birth control as "more children from the fit, less from the unfit." It was "nothing more or less than the facilitation of the process of weeding out the unfit, or preventing the birth of defectives."[8] Sanger's single-minded focus, though successful in making birth control a major public issue, had taken her a long distance from the radical milieu that had once nurtured her activism.

Besides making contraceptive information and techniques more widely accessible, the birth control movement campaigned steadily for law reform. In 1929, Sanger formed the National Committee on Federal Legislation for Birth Control to bring pressure to bear on Congress for revision of the Comstock law. Determined as ever to succeed, Sanger and her followers adapted their arguments to the economic crisis of the 1930s. As one female doctor argued in 1935, "the most sensitive nerve center in which to hit the public is their pocketbook. Sick poor mothers and the high mothers' death rate leaves them cold." Birth controllers trumpeted fertility limitation for the poor as an "important relief measure," and Sanger often called attention to the cost that "relief babies" and unwanted pregnancies were imposing on a shattered economy.[9] Although New Deal leaders, dependent upon the votes of a large Catholic population in the Northeast and Midwest, were unwilling to support birth control as a recovery measure, Sanger had brought the issue to the nation's capital. Between 1931 and 1934, her committee succeeded in getting five congressional hearings that generated a good deal of publicity for the cause.

Sanger's organization supplemented legislative efforts with litigation in the courts. By the early 1930s, it had sixteen cases wending their way through the judicial system. A federal court decision in 1930 permitted the shipping and advertising of birth control appliances intended for legal use. A booming business in the manufacture of contraceptive devices resulted, especially of condoms whose use could be justified for the prevention of disease. By mid-decade, the fifteen largest manufacturers of condoms were producing a million and a half per day. Drugstores, gas stations, restaurants, barbershops, and newsstands sold them, making condoms easily available to men of every class. A young Malcolm X supplemented his income shining shoes at a Boston dance hall by selling rubbers. In 1936, in a landmark decision, a federal appeals court overturned the anti-contraception provisions of the Comstock law. Writing the decision in *United States v. One Package,* Judge Augustus Hand pointed to the "weight of authority in the medical world," unavailable when the law was passed in 1873, establishing the safety and reliability of modern contraceptive practice.[10] The decision allowed doctors to prescribe contraceptives for whatever reasons they deemed appropriate. The painstaking efforts of Sanger's Clinical Research Bureau had finally borne some fruit.

Major shifts in contraceptive usage provide impressive evidence of the birth control movement's effectiveness. Interview data from the Kinsey study of female sexual behavior document the change. A comparison of white, married college-educated women born in the late nineteenth century with those born in the second decade of the twentieth reveals important differences in practice. Among the older group of women, two-fifths reported "much use" by their husbands of condoms, one-fifth of the women douched, and one-fifth often resorted to male withdrawal to limit fertility. Thirty-one percent of these women used diaphragms. By contrast, among the younger cohort, douching and withdrawal had declined almost to the point of vanishing, and the condom was slightly less commonly employed by husbands, but reliance on the diaphragm had doubled, with sixty-one percent of the respondents using it frequently.[11] Over the course of two decades, the device most espoused by birth control advocates, and the most dependable female-controlled method, had surpassed by far all other methods of fertility control among the middle class.

Although advocates of birth control might look with pride at the widespread adoption of effective contraception among the middle class, they had less reason to congratulate themselves when they surveyed the record of other social groups. In the 1920s, Sanger's Clinical Research Bureau found that its urban working-class female clientele had little access to contraceptives. Withdrawal was the method most commonly used by couples. Early motherhood, numerous pregnancies (especially among those with little education), and frequent resort to abortion provided eloquent testimony of its inadequacy. The Lynds, too, found less extensive use of contraceptives among the working class in Muncie. A sampling of middle-class wives found that all of them used birth control and took it for granted, evincing a desire for both family limitation and sexual pleasure freed from concern about pregnancy. By contrast, fewer than half of working-class wives practiced birth control, and over a third of those who did were merely "careful" in their timing of intercourse. Many knew nothing about how to control their fertility and asked for help from the interviewers. One twenty-two-year-old wife reported that "we don't use anything to prevent children. I just keep away from my husband. He don't care—only at times. He's discouraged because he's out of work." Another, who insisted that her husband stay away after the birth of a second child, found herself abandoned by her spouse.[12]

The lack of contraception was especially pronounced among whites and blacks in the rural South, where fertility rates remained the highest in the nation. One southern doctor reported that in the mountain areas of the region frequent pregnancies made marriage "nothing but a dreadful burden instead of a joyful relationship" for many women. An observer of rural white mores in the Deep South found that some men "admit using [condoms] before marriage—but almost no one, apparently, actually employs them [after marrying]." When Margaret Hagood interviewed white tenant farm women in the North Carolina Piedmont in the 1930s, she found fertility rates as high as those of the colonial era. Women expressed pride in the children they had borne, along with a desire not to have any more. "I hope you don't find me with another when you come back," was a typical farewell, yet ignorance about contraception, or insufficient cash to afford it, made the sentiment little more than wishful thinking. Among the minority of rural southerners who did strive to limit family size, some evidence suggests differences in the practices of blacks and whites. One study found that blacks were more likely to rely on the female method of douching, while whites more often depended on male withdrawal and the use of condoms.[13]

Perhaps because of the impact of the Great Depression, by the end of the 1930s evidence of more effective contraceptive use outside the white middle class was mounting. Kinsey found that among noncollege women born in the 1910s, only one out of ten relied on withdrawal, while over a third used the diaphragm, just the reverse of the pattern for women born in the late nineteenth century. When birth control advocates opened a clinic in 1936 in Logan County, West Virginia, they noted that white and black residents were eager to avail themselves of the service. Over a three-year period, clinic patients reduced their fertility a third below what it might have been. In the Piedmont, though only a tiny fraction of women used contraceptives, the vast majority favored birth control, and older women were advising their daughters to limit family size.[14]

Ironically, racial prejudice caused the South to take a leading role in the incorporation of birth control into public health services. In 1937, North Carolina became the first state to sanction the provision of contraceptives with tax dollars; it was soon followed by six other southern states. Fear of black population growth during the hard times of the Depression encouraged the move toward state-supported birth control. As an official in North Carolina explained, "on one occasion a health officer didn't think his county needed contraception. . . . When he discovered that the Negroes were accounting for 85 per cent of the births, he quickly changed his mind." In 1939, the Birth Control Federation of America, predecessor of Planned Parenthood, drew up a proposal for a special "Negro Project." Its author argued for the project because "the mass of Negroes . . . particularly in the South, still breed carelessly and disastrously." Blinded by racial stereotypes, white professionals ignored the demographic evidence that, for over a generation, black fertility had been lower than that of matched groups of whites.[15]

By the end of the 1930s, the climate of law, public attitudes, and medical opinion had altered sufficiently that birth controllers no longer felt themselves a beleaguered minority. With the formation of the Planned Parenthood Federation of America in 1942, the movement shed its outsider status and embraced a middle-of-the-road professionalism. Planned Parenthood shaped its birth control message accordingly, revealing in the process the ways that American sexual and social mores were changing. The Federation championed birth control as an essential element in family planning, a measure necessary for the health and well-being of both parents and children. With sexual satisfaction now seen as a critical feature of a happy, successful marriage, advocates of fertility control stressed the necessity of contraception as a way of dispelling fears of pregnancy that inhibited marital adjustment. The new importance ascribed to sexual compatibility can be inferred from the prominent place occupied by sex counseling for married couples in the work of Planned Parenthood clinics. The Federation also argued for the value of child spacing, so that children would get the attention they deserved, while mothers would not find their physical and emotional resources overburdened. From an issue that had once seemed to epitomize the quest for female autonomy, birth control had become a matter of insuring family stability.[16]

The loss of whatever radical intent contraception still carried should not be attributed solely to the decisions of birth control reformers. The mood of the nation made it receptive to the family planning argument. In the 1930s, for instance, though some birth controllers played upon middle-class fears of the poor to move their cause forward, hard times shaped new attitudes among working-class families too. Pregnancy now carried additional fears, as parents struggled to provide for the children they already had. As one unemployed husband expressed it,

> I could have avoided my present status if I had taken precautions to have fewer children. Before the depression I never gave a thought to birth control. Both my wife and I were against it, and let the children come as they would. Had we been able to foresee the depression, we would have felt differently about it. I'm convinced now that birth control is a good thing.

Apparently, more and more Americans agreed with him. A poll conducted by the *Ladies Home Journal* in 1938 reported that seventy-nine percent of American women approved of contraceptive practice.[17]

The relatively prosperous postwar years would bring new motives encouraging the acceptance of birth control. During the baby boom of the late 1940s and 1950s, American women were marrying younger, having children sooner, and bearing more of them than at any time in the twentieth century. Between 1940 and 1960, among women of childbearing age, the most common response to the question of how many children were "ideal" rose from two to four. Women who married in the 1950s were having a first child earlier in life than their grandmothers did.[18] Paradoxically, the baby boom made the need for contraception more pressing, precisely at a moment when its use seemed less threatening. Wives who had two, three, or four children while still in their twenties could hardly be accused of seeking contraceptive devices in order to avoid their biological destiny, or to escape the confines of the home. Yet, at the same time, few would argue with the need of postwar couples to place a limit on family size. Having accomplished their procreative duties, married couples of the 1950s had earned the right to continue their sexual relationship without doubling the size of their families.

National fertility studies conducted in 1955 and 1960 demonstrated that, the baby boom notwithstanding, most American couples had incorporated family planning into their married lives. Among wives between the ages of eighteen and forty-four, eighty-one percent had employed some form of contraception while another seven percent expected to use it. Moreover, between 1955 and 1960, a strong tendency emerged to adopt contraceptive practice at an earlier stage of marriage, for the purpose of planning first births and spacing children. The data also revealed, however, that significant differences in birth control use remained, with Catholics, blacks, and women without high school diplomas less likely to engage in contraceptive efforts, and more likely to delay use until later in marriage. In 1960, for instance, four-fifths of all whites, but only three-fifths of nonwhites, had used contraception; the proportions for college-educated and grade-school-educated women were ninety-three percent and seventy-two percent, respectively. The differences in timing were even more pronounced: eighty-six percent of grade-school women, but only thirty-nine percent of college women, did not employ birth control methods before their first pregnancy. Although in many cases the failure of Catholic women to use contraceptive methods other than rhythm coincided with religious conviction and a desire to have larger families, for blacks and for less-educated whites the absence of effective contraception sometimes led to births that were neither intended nor desired.[19]

The reasons behind these differences were complex. For blacks, residence played a great part. Southern black farm women exhibited the highest level of unwanted fertility and the lowest proportion of contraceptive use, whereas blacks without life experience in the rural South displayed no significant differences from matched groups of whites. Lack of access to doctors, who might prescribe devices such as the diaphragm, contributed to less-frequent use, while reliance on less dependable but more readily available methods, such as douching, helped account for the higher levels of unwanted fertility. Among both blacks and working-class whites, insufficient information about contraception in the early years of marriage resulted in poor efforts at fertility control. In a study of family planning practices among white working-class couples in the 1940s and 1950s, Lee Rainwater discovered that most of the women entered marriage with little or no knowledge about birth control and sex, while husbands who had used condoms before marrying saw it simply as a way of avoiding disease and shotgun weddings.[20] Parenthood loomed large in the identity of these couples, thus limiting the motivation to delay pregnancies. The poor communication between couples who adhered to rigidly defined gender roles, as well as a pervading sense that forces beyond their control shaped their fate, created barriers in the path of effective contraceptive practice.

Strong as these obstacles appeared, continuing changes in attitude, law, public policy, and contraceptive technology created in the 1960s a context in which the differences in use would narrow appreciably. Early in the decade, the National Council of Churches endorsed the practice of "mutually acceptable, non-injurious" methods of birth control in marriage. In 1965, citing the right to privacy, the Supreme Court at last eliminated any restrictions on the use of contraception by married couples when it declared unconstitutional a Connecticut law curtailing access to birth control devices. A few years later, the Court ruled that the unmarried enjoyed similar rights and protections. Several states, meanwhile, finally repealed nineteenth-century statutes that had limited the circulation of information about contraception. Concerns about overpopulation abroad and poverty at home encouraged the federal government to take a more active stance in favor of birth control. Lyndon Johnson endorsed it in his 1965 State of the Union address and in a speech before the United Nations; the War on Poverty incorporated family planning into its work; and American foreign aid programs began to include funds for contraceptive education and appliances. Throughout the 1960s, the mass media heralded birth control as the solution to the pressing danger of overpopulation.[21]

The final passing of old prohibitions on birth control coincided with revolutionary changes in contraceptive technology. In 1960, the Food and Drug Administration gave its approval to the marketing of a female oral contraceptive. "The pill," as it quickly became known, profoundly altered the relationship between erotic activity and contraceptive practice. Effective, inexpensive, and easy to use, it separated intercourse from precautionary measures to prevent pregnancy. The spontaneity of sexual passion no longer had to be interrupted by inserting a diaphragm or putting on a condom. Ironically, technology was protecting the "naturalness" of sex by interfering with its equally "natural" result. The pill became the subject of sustained speculation as journalists, social scientists, and moralists watched for its impact on the sex life of Americans. Their interest was not misplaced. By the end of the decade, married couples had made it the contraceptive of preference, a trend that was especially pronounced among wives in their twenties.[22]

The media response to the pill offers an especially dramatic example of how far American attitudes had moved since the days when Margaret Sanger was considered a dangerous radical. Here was an innovation which, as the sex educator Mary Calderone expressed it, allowed humans "to separate our sexual and reproductive lives." The pill promised to remove the inhibitions on sexual expression that fear of pregnancy imposed upon young, unmarried women. Yet, almost without exception, newspapers and mass-circulation magazines applauded its marketing and use. Journalists sought to reassure readers that American women would use their new freedom wisely and responsibly. Fears about sexual excess were misplaced. "Does the convenient contraceptive promote promiscuity?" wrote one. "In some cases, no doubt it does— as did the automobile, the drive-in movie, and the motel. But the consensus . . . is that a girl who is promiscuous on the pill would have been promiscuous without it."[23]

The 1960s represented something of a watershed in the history of birth control. The dramatic changes in both contraceptive practice and female fertility during the decade prompted some demographers to speak of a "contraceptive revolution." In 1960, virtually all contraceptive practice was coitus-related. By 1970, fifty-eight percent of married couples relied on the pill, the IUD, or sterilization—all of which provided near-perfect reliability while minimizing the vagaries of human motivation—to achieve their fertility goals. Three out of ten couples depended on the pill; twice as many had used it at one time or another. Younger wives especially turned to oral contraceptives, with a majority of those born in the 1940s adopting their use before the first pregnancy. For couples in which the wife was over thirty, voluntary sterilization emerged as the most common method of fertility control. One-quarter of the older couples in a 1970 survey had opted for surgery, with the numbers equally divided between males and females. Moreover, the trend toward sterilization seemed clearly to be accelerating. Remarkable shifts in public attitudes accompanied this change in behavior. Between 1965 and 1970, approval of both male and female sterilization became majority sentiment. Younger women exhibited the highest level of approval, suggesting that sterilization might become even more commonplace in the future. The overall result of the adoption of modern contraceptive methods was a steep decline in fertility, most of it resulting from a drop in unwanted births. By 1970, the American population was rapidly approaching, according to some demographers, a state of "reproductive rationality," as desired and actual fertility came close to converging.[24]

What most confounded demographers about contraceptive trends in the 1960s was the sudden demise of major disparities in family planning practices among various population groups. As Charles Westoff and Norman Ryder, who supervised the 1970 national fertility study, described it,

> the massive movement in the direction of reproductive rationality has carried with it both whites and blacks and, among the whites, both non-Catholics and Catholics, without major differences among these subgroups in the magnitude of change.

Low-income couples, too, had "almost caught up to the level of contraceptive protection" enjoyed by the middle class. Some differences still persisted. Among blacks, for instance, sterilization remained the province of females, as large numbers of blacks continued to be wary of the effects of surgical procedures on the male. The level of unwanted fertility was also twice as high among black women, although the absolute decline in the 1960s was greater than that for whites. But a decided trend toward earlier use of more reliable methods did emerge during the decade.[25]

Perhaps the greatest surprise to demographers came in the behavior of Catholics. In 1955, seven out of ten American Catholics conformed to church teachings on birth control, relying only on the rhythm method to achieve their fertility goals. Experts on fertility were predicting that these differences would persist. However, the ferment within Catholicism encouraged by Pope John XXIII, coupled with the introduction of the pill, provoked much speculation that the church would alter its stand. In July 1968, when Pope John's successor reaffirmed Catholic traditions and condemned oral contraceptives, American Catholics defied the predictions of demographers and church leaders alike by rejecting the papal ordinance and adopting the pill and other methods of birth control. As one Catholic mother of four explained it, "I don't confess that I take the pill, because I don't believe it is a sin." Clearly, she was not alone. By 1970, nonconformity among Catholics had jumped to sixty-eight percent; among women in their twenties the rise was even more spectacular. As the authors of the 1970 national fertility study concluded, it had become "abundantly clear that U.S. Catholics have rejected the 1968 papal encyclical's statement on birth control and that there exists a wide gulf between the behavior of most Catholic women . . . and the official stand of the Church itself."[26]

Despite the enthusiasm with which demographers described the "reproductive rationality" of Americans, contraception alone did not provide women with adequate control over their fertility. Throughout the mid-twentieth century, abortion served as a last resort for women who found themselves with an unwanted pregnancy. Its illegality makes precise figures on the number of abortions impossible to obtain, but various sources suggest that it was certainly widespread. A study of ten thousand mostly working-class clients at Margaret Sanger's clinic in the late 1920s found that one out of five pregnancies were intentionally terminated. Although half of the women had not had an abortion, those who did averaged between two and three each. Kinsey reported that twenty-two percent of his married sample had experienced an induced abortion, with most occurring either early in marriage or toward the end of the childbearing years. Among the premaritally active single women in his survey, the vast majority who became pregnant obtained an abortion. Single black women with a college education were as likely as their white counterparts to abort, while those with less education tended to carry their pregnancies to term. Even during the baby-boom years of the mid-1950s, when American culture extolled the virtues of motherhood and domesticity, the national director of Planned Parenthood privately estimated that "roughly 2,000 a day, every day—are performed in the United States. And to the best of our knowledge most of them are performed on married women with families." By the early 1960s, police experts called abortion the third-largest criminal activity in the country, surpassed only by narcotics and gambling.[27]

Interestingly, even as the legal restrictions on contraception were fading, those on abortion seemed to tighten. Many state laws allowed "therapeutic" abortions to be performed in cases where the pregnancy endangered the woman's life. Yet, in the 1940s and 1950s, the rate of therapeutic abortions performed in hospitals declined dramatically. At Kings County hospital in Brooklyn, New York, only two therapeutic abortions were authorized during these years, at a time when hospital physicians delivered over sixteen thousand babies. Women who could afford psychiatric care were best positioned to take advantage of this option, whereas impoverished nonwhite women who patronized municipal hospitals had little chance of receiving hospital-board approval. When ward patients did succeed in obtaining a therapeutic abortion, hospitals typically required that they be sterilized too. One medical advocate of abortion-law reform, in commenting on this "package" deal, considered the women who risked illegal abortions "fortunate" in comparison with their sterilized sisters.[28]

The criminality of abortion led to a complicated and variegated underground system. Prosecution remained sporadic and infrequent, with convictions difficult to obtain. New York City saw only 111 convictions between 1925 and 1950, and almost half of these resulted in a sentence of probation. In

Chicago, thirty-eight prosecutions brought but nine verdicts of guilty over a ten-year period in the 1940s and 1950s. In some places, abortionists escaped the full force of the law through a system of payoffs to lawyers, police, and judges, but in other parts of the country, especially in smaller cities and towns, practitioners operated with the knowledge of law-enforcement officials and community residents. One physician in a small town in eastern Pennsylvania estimated that he performed over twenty-eight thousand abortions in the course of a long career. A respected doctor in town, he incorporated abortion into a thriving family practice. Some doctors who refrained from offering abortions themselves nonetheless referred women to colleagues who did. One abortion specialist in Baltimore figured that he had received patients from over 350 doctors in the space of two decades. By no means, however, were most abortionists licensed physicians working in clean, antiseptic offices. Rather, a thriving underworld of "back-alley" abortionists catered to the needs of women desperate to terminate a pregnancy.[29]

Women obtained information in haphazard ways. Sisters, friends, husbands, doctors, and co-workers provided points of entry to this invisible world. Knowledge about it remained secret and unspoken, however, so that a woman faced with an unwanted pregnancy could never be assured of success in finding help. As one woman described the situation in the mid-1950s, "you had to ask around. You asked friends and they asked friends, and the ripples of asking people widened until some person whose face you might never see gave over the secret information that could save you."[30] Access to information, and to a medically safe abortion, varied according to one's social status. Older married women of comfortable means with a long-standing family doctor were most likely to receive the best services available. Younger women and poor, nonwhite women faced the most hazardous conditions.

The recollections of women who had illegal abortions testify to the humiliation and terror that the experience might entail. As a twenty-year-old in New York City in 1956, Joyce Johnson succeeded in locating an abortionist. Arriving at his office with a borrowed five hundred dollars, she readied herself for the ordeal.

"Leave on the shoes!" he barked as I climbed up on his table almost fully clothed. Was I expected to make a run for it if the police rang his doorbell in the middle of the operation? He yelled at me to do this and do that, and it sent him into a rage that my legs were shaking, so how could he do what he had to do? But if I didn't want him to do it, that was all right with him. I said I wanted him to do it. I was crying. . . . The whole thing took two hours, but it seemed much longer through the pain. . . . He gave me pills when it was over, and told me I could call him only if anything went wrong. "But don't ever let me catch you back here again, young lady!" I staggered down the cement steps of his house with my life.

Another young woman, married, found herself running a high fever and hemorrhaging a few days after an abortion. Abruptly leaving a family gathering, she took a taxi to the abortionist's home. "She let me in and I was crying and I was feverish. There was a little table there and she put me on it. . . . [S]he started working on me and I was crying and she came and I will remember this till the day I die, she came and put her arms around me on the table like that, and she said, 'Honey, did you think it was so easy to be a woman?' " That so many women braved this illegal, hazardous terrain suggests the determination with which they sought to control their fertility.[31]

The practice of sterilization also belies the notion that the "contraceptive revolution" brought full autonomy to women in matters of fertility. While demographers touted the rise in sterilization, especially in the 1960s, as an indicator that couples increasingly demanded absolute control over conception, the gross statistics hid worlds of meaning. Ever since the Progressive era, when many states enacted compulsory sterilization laws, a small number of women—generally poor, often with little education, and frequently charged with some form of delinquency—were subjected to forced surgery under legal authority. But by the 1960s, with fertility rapidly declining and family planning now universal among the white middle class, medical professionals found ways of sterilizing far larger numbers of women whose fertility patterns offended their values. In one hospital in the Southwest, a dissident doctor reported, "one staff member would lie to the patient if he felt she had too many kids and tell her her uterus needed to come out when it didn't." In a Texas hospital whose staff pushed tubal ligation, residents wore buttons saying, "Stop at two, damn it." Black, Hispanic, native American, and poor white women were generally the targets of these efforts. Analyses of sterilization incidence found that black women, whose poverty placed them in more frequent contact with a public health and welfare bureaucracy, were more than twice as likely as white women to be sterilized. Among Puerto Rican women in New York City, surgical sterilization occurred six times more frequently than among whites. In general, regardless of race, the lower the family income the more likely it was for the wife to have received a tubal ligation than for the husband to have undergone a vasectomy.[32] Without doubt, America had experienced a contraceptive revolution in the twentieth century, but for many women the revolution offered little in the way of autonomy. As voluntary family planning through contraceptive practice became the middle-class ideal, those social groups which remained outside the consensus were targeted by regulatory agencies seeking to impose the new norm.

Rituals of Youth

As one might expect, the contraceptive revolution moved hand in hand with changes in both sexual behavior and attitudes. Historians of twentieth-century mores have tended to underplay this shift, by emphasizing instead the stability of one important index of sexual behavior, the female premarital coital rate. For women coming of age in the 1920s, the incidence of premarital intercourse jumped sharply, to roughly fifty percent of the cohort, and there-after remained relatively constant until the late 1960s.[33] Yet hidden behind the stability of these figures lay a whole world of sexual change. Activity that provoked guilt in the 1920s had become integrated by the 1960s into a new code of sexual ethics that made it morally acceptable. What was daring and nonconformist in the earlier period appeared commonplace a generation later. And, as attitudes and ideals altered, so too did aspects of sexual activity. Dating, necking, and petting among peers became part and parcel of the experience of American youth, providing an initiatory stage, uncommon for their elders, leading to the coital experience of adulthood and marriage. To marriage itself, couples brought new expectations of pleasure, satisfaction, and mutual enjoyment, encouraged by a more explicit advice literature that empha-sized the sexual component of conjugal life. The integration of contraception into middle-class married life also meant that the reproductive requirement for marital intimacy had receded far into the background. Though experience might not always live up to these new standards, men and women in the mid-twentieth century were approaching marriage with heightened anticipa-tion of physical pleasure.

Evidence abounds of shifts in both standards and patterns of behavior among American youth in the decades after World War I. During the 1920s, white college youth captured the lion's share of attention of contemporaries seeking to chart the society's changing values. Although less than thirteen percent of the eighteen- to twenty-one-year-old population were enrolled in colleges at the end of the 1920s, the numbers had more than tripled since 1890. For the first time, a distinctive subculture took shape among the middle-class young, with values and activities that set them apart from their parents' generation.[34]

Sexual innovation played a key role in this new world of youth. Particularly in coeducational institutions, heterosocial mixing became the norm. Young men and women mixed casually in classes, extracurricular activities, and social spaces, with a great deal of freedom from adult supervision. Dating in pairs, unlike the informal group socializing of the nineteenth century, permitted sexual liberties that formerly were sanctioned only for couples who were courting. College youth flaunted their new freedoms. As one male editor of a campus paper provocatively expressed it, "there are only two kinds of co-eds, those who have been kissed, and those who are sorry they haven't been kissed." Magazines debated the implications of "petting parties," an increasingly common feature of college life. One study of college youth during the 1920s found that ninety-two percent of coeds had engaged in petting, and that those "rejecting all sex play feel that they are on the defensive."[35]

What a relatively small percentage of middle-class youth were experiencing in college, much larger numbers tasted in high school. By the 1920s, high school had become a mass experience, with almost three-quarters of the young enrolled. Here, too, adolescent boys and girls encountered one another daily, with casual interaction throughout the day that often continued into evening social activities. One observer of youthful mores estimated that a large majority of high school youth engaged in hugging and kissing and that a significant minority "do not restrict themselves to that, but go further, and indulge in other sex liberties which, by all the conventions, are outrageously improper." Automobiles allowed young people still living at home greater freedom of movement than ever before. Groups of teenagers might drive to the next town for a Saturday-night dance; on weeknights, too, it became easier to escape parental supervision. So quickly and widely did cars become an essential part of this heterosocial world of youth that one commentator labeled the auto "a house of prostitution on wheels." Assessing these changes, Ben Lindsey, a Colorado juvenile court judge who had dealt with the young for a generation, considered them to be reflective of a historic transformation in American life. "Not only is this revolt from the old standards of conduct taking place," he wrote, "but it is unlike any revolt that has ever taken place before. Youth has always been rebellious. . . . But this is different. It has the whole weight and momentum of a new scientific and economic order behind it."[36]

Although the innovations in sexual behavior among middle-class youth were real, they nonetheless operated within certain peer-defined limits. Young men took liberties with women of their own class that their parents would have considered improper, but the sexual freedom of the 1920s was hardly a promiscuous one. The kissing and petting that occurred among couples who dated casually did not often progress beyond that. Surveys of sexual behavior among white middle-class women revealed that the generation coming of age in the 1920s had a significantly higher incidence of premarital intercourse than women born in the preceding decades. But the evidence also suggests that, for the most part, young women generally restricted coitus to a single partner, the man they expected to marry. "Going all the way" was permissible, but only in the context of love and commitment. For men, the changes in female sexual behavior had important implications. Beginning in the 1920s, the frequency of recourse to prostitution began to decline. As Lindsey noted, "with the breaking up of those districts, [boys] turned to girls of their own class, a thing they had seldom done in the past."[37]

As young people adopted the novel practice of dating, they shaped, learned, and refashioned its rules. Newspaper advice columns in the years after World War I printed letters from confused youth who wondered whether a good-night kiss was an appropriate ending for an evening date, and who searched for words to define the feelings aroused by the dating relationship. By the 1930s, the elaboration of this teenage ritual had produced words other than "love" to describe the emotions, and had differentiated "courting" and "keeping company" from the more casual, and common, practices of "going out" and "going steady." When the Lynds returned to Muncie in the 1930s, one young man reported to them that "the fellows regard necking as a taken-for-granted part of a date. We fellows used occasionally to get slapped for doing things, but the girls don't do that much any more. . . . Our high school students of both sexes . . . know everything and do everything—openly." Although he likely exaggerated in his claims about "everything," numerous surveys of American youth confirm the widening boundaries of permissible sexual activity. The rapid acceptance of this peer-directed system of dating, as well as the quick demise of its predecessor, can be inferred from changes in that reliable arbiter of social behavior, Emily Post's *Etiquette*. A chapter which, in the 1923 edition, was titled "Chaperons and Other Conventions" became "The Vanishing Chaperon and Other New Conventions" four years later; the passing of another decade brought the wistful heading "The Vanished Chaperon and Other Lost Conventions." One study of high school students in St. Louis on the eve of World War II found dating to be ubiquitous, with most couples returning home after one in the morning. Freed from parental supervision for long hours, boys and girls alike exhibited "a fairly general acceptance of the naturalness" of kisses and light petting as part of a date. Indeed, St. Louis's high school students proved far more tolerant about sexual matters than about other kinds of behavior such as smoking and drinking.[38]

The system of dating, at least as it evolved between the two world wars, did not extend to all youth. Its adoption depended upon surplus income for clothes and entertainment, access to automobiles outside major cities, school attendance to enforce peer-based norms, and sufficient population density to sustain a range of commercialized amusements. Its contours thus mark it as a ritual of white middle-class youth in the cities and suburbs.

Among poor blacks in the rural South, for instance, older patterns of sociability persisted as young people experienced both traditional freedoms and constraints. With few sanctions against premarital intercourse, "sex play," according to one observer, "becomes matter-of-fact behavior for youth." As one young girl explained it, "I ain't never thought of there being anything wrong about it." Denied access because of segregation, poverty, and rural isolation from most of the places where formal dating took place, young rural blacks met at church, harvest festivals, picnics, and while working in the fields, much as they had in the past. Yet, an awareness of the world beyond the small rural community also generated a "longing for pleasures like those of the city." One young man expressed his discontent by telling an interviewer, "there ain't no decent place to take a girl. . . . If you ain't got a car, you just ain't nowhere." Meanwhile, black parents of moderate wealth and status, in an effort to differentiate themselves from the rural masses and to provide education and mobility for the next generation, socialized their children into strict moral codes. In his study of youth in the Black Belt before World War II, Charles Johnson found that among the elite, even young men accepted rigid standards of chastity. Parents kept close rein on their daughters, as the testimony of one North Carolina girl made clear: "Yes, I have a boy friend. He calls on me and takes me to socials. Sometimes mama lets me go to movies with him in the afternoon, but if he goes with me at night papa and mama go too."[39]

For white youth as well, rural and small-town residence affected patterns of sexual interaction. In rural communities many young people lacked mobility. "I had no car," explained one youth who bemoaned his inability to date. "We lived 20 miles from town and to get to town I had to ride with my father or some other adult." Then, too, in smaller communities adults were able to watch the behavior of the young more closely. "I'll tell you, it's really tough getting it in a small town," one young man complained. "Everyone has their eyes on you and especially on the girl. You can hardly get away with anything." A young man who moved to the city when he was seventeen noted the difference it made. He had never felt much sexual desire during his years in the country, he commented, but city life with its abundant opportunities suddenly seemed to generate "much more interest in it."[40]

Although urban working-class youth did not share in the sexual culture of the middle class, this by no means implied a sentence of chastity. In some cases it could translate into freedom from the constraints of peer-enforced norms. In cities and towns, white and black youth who dropped out of high school or who did not immediately marry after graduation found themselves earning wages, yet without the expense of maintaining a household. Removed from the web of daily gossip that shaped the behavior of high school and college students, they were more likely to move beyond petting in their sexual relationships. Dance halls, bowling alleys, skating rinks, and, after prohibition, bars provided settings for young men and women to meet; automobiles, bought with hard-earned wages, offered privacy. One high school dropout embarked upon her first sexual affair with a dance-hall partner. "I made up my mind at the dance Oscar could have it," she recalled. "Oh, it was wonderful. That night, I thought, 'I don't care if I have a baby.'" Several more relationships ensued before she married in her late teens. The thriving business in condoms that Malcolm X operated at a Boston dance hall suggests the ease with which sexual favors could be exchanged among working-class youth in the city. So, too, does evidence of prenuptial conceptions and illegitimacy among the poor and the working class. In one Illinois town, over half of the girls who did not graduate from high school gave birth within eight months of their wedding. And almost a quarter of the births in the lowest social class of whites occurred outside of marriage.[41]

By accelerating the shift to city living, and by providing youth with more economic autonomy and freedom from adult supervision, World War II brought unprecedented opportunities for premarital experience. The war released millions of youth from the social environments that inhibited erotic expression, and threw them into circumstances that opened up new sexual possibilities. Millions of young men left home to join the military, while many young women migrated in search of employment. The demands of wartime drew teenagers into the paid labor force while weakening the influence that family and community held over their behavior.

Ample testimony from the war years confirms the sexual expressiveness of youth. For many young women, men in uniform held erotic appeal. "When I was 16," one college student recalled,

> I let a sailor pick me up and go all the way with me. I had intercourse with him partly because he had a strong personal appeal for me, but mainly because I had a feeling of high adventure and because I wanted to please a member of the armed forces.

Another, rebuffed by a sailor boyfriend who felt she was too young, went on to have affairs with fifteen others by war's end. Civilian men, too, partook of the sexual freedom of the war years. One teenager described his life then as "a real sex paradise. The plant and the town were just full of working girls who were on the make. Where I was, a male war worker became the center of loose morality. It was a sex paradise." A high school student lost his virginity with a woman of thirty whose husband was overseas. "We weren't in love," he recalled, "although we were very fond of each other. The times were conducive for this sort of thing. Otherwise, nothing would ever have happened between us."[42]

The response of moral reformers points to the changes that had occurred since the previous generation. Whereas those of the First World War focused on the dangers of prostitution, by the 1940s it was the behavior of "amateur girls"—popularly known as khaki-wackies, victory girls, and good-time Charlottes—that concerned moralists. "The old time prostitute in a house or formal prostitute on the street is sinking into second place," wrote one venereal-disease expert. "The new type is the young girl in her late teens and early twenties, the young woman in every field of life who is determined to have one fling or better." Efforts to scare GIs into continence by emphasizing the danger of disease had little impact on men who, according to one officer, "think as little of a gonorrheal infection as they do of the ordinary common cold." Or, as another phrased it, "the sex act cannot be made unpopular." Local law-enforcement officials worked overtime to contain the sexual behavior of young women, yet their efforts only seemed to confirm the perception that prostitution was not the issue. Arrests for selling sexual favors rose less than twenty percent during the war years, but charges of disorderly conduct increased almost two hundred percent, and those for other morals offenses, such as promiscuous behavior or patronizing bars too frequently, increased nearly as much.[43]

After World War II, as the marriage age dropped for both men and women, the sexual norms of American teenagers continued their permissive shift. For working-class youth especially, marriage might follow soon after high school, so that their student experiences served almost as an introduction to marital life. In the postwar era, too, adolescents were more likely to have parents who themselves had dated, and who were at least somewhat more accepting of the peer-run system of dating and going steady. Writing about the immediate postwar years, Alfred Kinsey noted that on "doorsteps and on street corners, and on high school and college campuses . . . [petting] may be observed in the daytime as well as in the evening hours." He labeled petting "one of the most significant factors in the sexual lives of high school and college males and females." By the 1950s it was more common than not for high school and college students alike to have some experience going steady. The higher level of commitment implied by such a relationship granted youth the permission to explore the erotic. As one young man described it, petting was the result "of a drive that had something besides pure sex as a motivating factor. We didn't believe in petting because of the sex alone, but because we were very much in love and this was a means of expressing our love to each other." One California teenager, who admitted that she and her peers "do a lot of petting," felt that a steady relationship gave her permission for more. "Something you go all the way in should only be with someone you really love, not just any date." Where adults might see flagrantly loose behavior, young people themselves had constructed a set of norms that regulated their activity while allowing the accumulation of experience and sexual learning.[44]

Even as change occurred among youth, gender continued to give shape to the patterns of interaction. Although the boundaries of acceptable sexual behavior moved in the direction of permissiveness for both male and female youth, a double standard survived that perpetuated differences in the meaning of sexual experience. As one high school girl expressed it in the 1920s, when the system of dating was taking shape, "the girl who permits liberties is certainly popular with boys, but her popularity never lasts very long with any one boy. You know the saying 'Just a toy to play with, not the kind they choose to grow old and grey with.'" Study after study of high school and college youth from the 1930s through the 1950s confirmed the existence of a double standard. The particular issues kept shifting, from necking and light petting in the 1920s and 1930s to premarital coitus by the 1950s, but the tension between male and female remained. Boys pushed, while girls set the limit. Sometimes, boys acquiesced, but in many cases the line between subtle pressure and outright aggression was crossed, as girls found themselves forced to submit to petting or intercourse. Young women who yielded to the demands of their partners might find themselves emotionally abandoned. One sixteen-year-old, pregnant after a seduction, bitterly described the results in her case:

> How are you supposed to know what they want? You hold out for a long time and then when you do give in to them and give your body they laugh at you afterwards and say they'd never marry a slut, and that they didn't love you but were just testing because they only plan to marry a virgin and wanted to see if you'd go all the way.

In her case and others, sexual availability carried the onus of "bad girl" status, and rendered a girl someone merely "to play with."[45]

Behind this cat-and-mouse game lay the continuation of gender-based dichotomies over the significance and purpose of sexual expression. One study of college youth in the postwar decade found that the gap "between males and females in the youth culture with respect to sex and love is so marked that there are distinct male and female subcultures." College men preferred dates with sexual activity, while females favored dates free from sexual demands. College women dated more often than men, but males had far more sexual experience. The more dating partners a young man enjoyed, the more sex he was likely to have, whereas for female students, the opposite was true. For women, as the level of emotional intimacy and commitment with a partner increased, the sexual exchange grew more intense. For men, the relationship between intimacy and sex fluctuated. Among themselves, male students talked at great length about sex, and revealed "a consuming interest in the proper methods and techniques for making sexual advances to a female." Women students, on the other hand, when they did discuss sexual behavior, expressed concern about "the problems raised by the sexual aggression of the male in the dating situation, the threat of public exposure, personal regrets for sexual transgressions, or the justification of sexual activity as an expression of love."[46] As the final phrase suggests, female sexual expression continued to be deeply attached to the emotion of love and to commitment in a relationship. For a young man, sex might be an expression of love, but it could also be justified for its own sake, as a symbol of conquest, or as a badge of prestige to be sported among one's fellows.

Class differences also played an important role in the maintenance of the double standard. By pursuing sex with working-class girls, middle-class males could expect chastity from their peers without relinquishing access to intercourse themselves. One youth felt it was "all right for a boy to go as far as he wants, but not with the girl he is to marry or with a girl in his own class." College status gave young men power in their negotiations with working-class girls. Labeled as "pickups," they were sexual objects with whom one pushed "as far as you can." Within the black community, too, class shaped sexual availability. "There are some that I run around with and can do anything to," said one southern youth. "And there are some who won't let you mess with them. I don't mess with girls I go with because they are nice girls, and I don't believe it's nice to bother nice girls."[47]

Strong as it appeared, even the double standard did not remain immune to the pressures of change. For one, the very dilemma that young women faced, of how far to go with their partners, differentiated them from their mothers and grandmothers, who confronted norms that drew a sharp line against any sexual expression before marriage. Then, too, as the mores of youth moved in the direction of expressiveness, the double standard spawned tensions that made it difficult to sustain. In an era when men routinely patronized prostitutes, a strict double standard might cause little disruption in their quest for sexual release. But in a peer-constructed system of dating and courtship, it restricted the number of potential partners. As one college male explained:

> I felt that if I were sexual with someone, that indicated that I didn't respect them. I could be sexual with someone I didn't care for, but not with someone I did care for. The fact that I was never sexual with anyone is because I never dated anyone I didn't care for.[48]

Young women, meanwhile, implicitly challenged the double standard's inner logic by their pursuit of sex in the context of affection. Ira Reiss, a sociologist who surveyed the sexual mores of post–World War II youth, found that although a "recognizable double standard" existed in America, it was in a state of rapid transition. The girl remained, as Reiss put it, "the guardian of sexual limits," but she increasingly appeared to be "a half-willing" one. Chafing under the restrictions of male codes, young women found ways to pursue erotic experience shaped by an ideal that Reiss labeled "permissiveness with affection." Among teenage girls, going steady served as a means of obtaining some sexual experience while still preserving one's reputation. For working-class women who did not marry early, seeking dating partners beyond their own neighborhoods allowed them to escape the condemnatory attitudes that expressiveness closer to home would engender. For some middle-class women, the increase in autonomy that came from attending college and switching peer groups permitted "a major change in sexual standards." Surveying the social landscape at the beginning of the 1960s, Reiss confidently predicted the certain collapse of the double standard. "All the signs indicate," he wrote, "a continued trend toward equalitarian and permissive codes."[49]

Besides the tensions embedded in gender and class differences, mid-twentieth-century youth who explored the erotic encountered opposition from adults. Parents may have encouraged the elaboration of dating rituals, but they expected their children, and particularly their daughters, to observe limits. Hygiene lectures at both men's and women's colleges devoted time to the dangers of premarital indulgence. Campus administrators assumed the philosophy of *in loco parentis,* adopting rules governing visiting hours in dormitories, imposing curfews for women students, and the like. When Anne Moody enrolled in a black college in Mississippi at the end of the 1950s, she found the out-of-classroom contact between males and females carefully supervised. Advice books aimed at high school students contained strong caveats against petting. The most popular guide of the postwar years, Evelyn Duvall's *Facts of Life and Love for Teenagers,* warned that anything beyond "that goodnight kiss" could lead to trouble. The sexual instinct, she wrote, was "very strong and insistent," and once released it tended to "press for completion." Girls bemoaned the unrealistic standards of parents. "They just don't understand what kids want to do," said one, "and they think we ought to act like they acted twenty years ago." Another, who petted with her boyfriend, decided to "stop telling her [mother] everything I do. If I kept on telling her, she'd make life miserable for me." Youth faced a confusing array of messages. "Postwar America was a society with Stop-Go lights flashing everywhere we looked," one woman reminisced. "Sex, its magic spell everywhere, was accompanied by the stern warning: Don't do it."[50]

Despite the warnings, by the 1960s American youth had carved out ample space for sexual experimentation. Higher standards of wealth, the expanded opportunities that came with urban living, and the mobility provided by the automobile all pointed in the direction of more sexual experience before marriage. Gender, class, and racial identities continued to shape the form that this expressiveness took as well as the meanings it had, and adult cultural prescriptions still exercised constraints over it. But the young devised ways to create a sexual world of their own in modern America.

Reshaping Marriage

Although the middle decades of the twentieth century witnessed the diffusion of a peer-based system of premarital sexually expressive behavior, the expectation persisted that youthful experience was preparatory for marriage. This was especially true for women. American males, as Kinsey discovered, found some form of orgasmic sexual outlet early in life, but their options remained circumscribed by the constraints that still operated for their female counterparts. Not until marriage did most American women find themselves with regular access to orgasm, while many of those who had engaged in premarital coitus or petting to orgasm did so only with their future husband. Modern youth may have abandoned many of the standards of their forebears, but in the value that attached to marriage, they stood as heirs of the past.

Revised norms concerning the place of sex in marriage had accompanied the new patterns of behavior that emerged among middle-class youth in the 1920s. At the start of the decade, as one study of divorce cases revealed, nineteenth-century notions about sexual expression and gender roles, though weakening, continued to exert a powerful hold on the consciousness of husbands and wives. Partners displayed considerable ambivalence about the proper balance between duty and pleasure in marriage. Wives exhibited guilt about premarital experience and the desire for sexual gratification within marriage. Husbands, meanwhile, sometimes responded with anger to the violation of traditional standards by their wives, even as they desired sexy, youthful mates.[51] But the changes among youth during the 1920s were significant enough to provoke concern about the future of marriage and a rethinking of its purposes. When combined with the ideas of modern sex theorists and the agitation for access to contraception, the sexual expressiveness of middle-class youth sounded the death knell for an older marriage ideal. Duty, moral character, personal sacrifice, and spiritual union were fast losing their appeal as the defining characteristics of matrimony and the conjugal relationship. In response, some sociologists and advice writers mounted a campaign of their own to bring marriage into the "modern" era.

The phrase most often used to describe this new ethic was "companionate marriage," a term coined by Ben Lindsey in a book by the same name. As the concept was popularized, it redefined marriage in more egalitarian terms, consistent with the new freedoms that post-suffrage women seemed to possess. A successful relationship rested on the emotional compatibility of husband and wife, rather than the fulfillment of gender-prescribed duties and roles. Men and women sought happiness and personal satisfaction in their mates; an important component of their happiness was mutual sexual enjoyment. Although some of these features had antecedents in nineteenth-century ideals, embedded in this reconceptualization was a web of assumptions that, taken together, marked the companionate marriage as recognizably modern: a female sexual desire as strong as, even if different from, that of the male; the need to have it satisfied; the availability of birth control so that couples could enjoy sex without the worry of unwanted pregnancies; the healthiness of sexual expression apart from procreative intentions; the recognition that youth possessed sexual knowledge and experience before marriage; and easy divorce for couples without children. Although conservative critics attacked companionate marriage as encouraging loose morals, supporters saw it as a flexible response to a new social reality. As Lindsey described it, the companionate ideal "would give Marriage a chance to breathe and live; it would give it room in which to grow; it would give it soil in which to put forth roots; and it would establish it on a better basis than it has yet known."[52]

Not only the availability of birth control and the sexual freedom of youth but also a new structure and function for the family compelled a revision of marital norms. In *The Marriage Crisis,* Ernest Groves, a sociologist who pioneered in integrating courses on marriage and the family into the college curriculum, emphasized the declining economic role of the modern family. Without the common economic activity that formerly bound individuals together, he wrote,

> the desire for pleasure and the insistence upon self-expression easily become the source of discordant points of view . . . pleasure-seeking has multiplied desires . . . individual desires have been stimulated in contrast with those that used to be satisfied by the family group working together . . . family life ceases to be a means of economic production, and is an end in itself that is required to furnish individual satisfaction to outweigh the cost it imposes. This . . . has made it seem that marriage is something society imposes upon individuals as an obligation they have to accept in order to enjoy the physical pleasures of sex.[53]

Because birth control and the growing independence of women made sexual expression more easily available without marriage, Groves argued that a revision of norms concerning marriage was imperative in order to protect the institution from decay. Otherwise, the tendency toward a hedonistic pleasure-seeking ethic would proceed unchecked.

The reorientation of marriage manuals offers one important index of changing norms. In the nineteenth century, authors of prescriptive literature implicitly called attention to the importance of sex in marriage, but with a central message of control and regulation. Many writers never fully accepted the legitimacy of a nonprocreative eroticism, pointed to the dangers of sexual excess, and often displayed skepticism about the depth of female sexual needs. Though all of these prescriptions began to weaken by the turn of the century, it was not until the 1920s and 1930s that one sees a wholesale revision of norms. By then, the genre came to emphasize expression rather than control, and physical pleasures rather than more ethereal rewards. There appeared to be fairly widespread agreement among authors that the "act of sex is appropriately the central fact in the psychological situation of marriage," and that only those couples who had "cherished and refined this art" could expect to be "supremely happy."[54]

As the reference to "art" suggests, modern advice literature did more than define sex as the key to a satisfying marriage. It provided the reader with elaborate instructions, a form of teaching deemed necessary because of the contrasting nature of male and female sexuality. Male desire was active, insistent, quickly aroused, and genitally focused, whereas woman's erotic sensibility was diffuse, less conscious, and, in the words of one writer, "much more intimately interwoven with her personality." Mutual gratification, often defined as the attainment of simultaneous orgasm, required the most sensitive regard for the needs of one's partner. Men, in particular, had to control their natural impulses, while they engaged in extended foreplay and courting in order to awaken the dormant desires of their spouses. Theodore Van de Velde's *Ideal Marriage* (1930), the prototype of the explicit marriage manual, discussed at great length varieties of foreplay and coital position, from the "love bite" and "genital kiss" to the "equestrian attitude" in which the woman sat astride the male. For readers who might look askance at such experimentation, Van de Velde assured them that the Roman poet Martial considered the latter posture "so normal and obvious that he could not conceive of that paragon of married couples, Hector and Andromache, in any other attitude." One historian, in commenting on Van de Velde's book, noted that "to read its elaborate table of contents is to explore every crevice of the anatomy of sexual behavior."[55]

Van de Velde did not remain in the vanguard for long. By the end of the 1930s, more and more manuals were devoting considerable attention to technique. In the post–World War II era the preoccupation with the search for the best method to achieve simultaneous climaxes had become so pronounced that one commentator ruefully bemoaned the new "sex-as-work" ethic. One popular advice book, Eustace Chesser's *Love Without Fear,* informed readers that "success comes to those who consciously and deliberately will to achieve. . . . Both partners should, in coitus, concentrate their full attention on one thing: the attainment of simultaneous orgasm." The prescription may have been an ideal almost impossible to achieve, yet underlying the emphasis on perfecting the art of eroticism was the assumption that sex in marriage was meant to be mutually fun, that it ought to provide couples with sublime physical pleasures.[56]

Whether American couples worked as hard at sex as they were advised is open to doubt, but substantial evidence exists to warrant the conclusion that middle-class attitudes toward sex in marriage, as well as actual behavior, did change in important ways. Ernest Burgess and Paul Wallin's study of college-educated couples from the Chicago area who were wedded in the early 1940s offers a revealing counterpoint to earlier research by Mosher and Davis. In contrast to the Davis study, for instance, four-fifths of the men and three-quarters of the women believed that they had adequate information about sex prior to their wedding night and looked forward to conjugal relations with interest and anticipation. Seventy-three percent of the women reached orgasm all or most of the time, and only five percent reported never experiencing a climax. In comparing their survey with earlier ones, the authors concluded that the younger generation attached considerably greater value to sex. Partners viewed the marital bond as a pleasure-yielding relationship; an awareness of Freudian theory led couples to associate sexual expression with general well-being; and the availability of contraception had separated the procreative functions of sex from its physically pleasurable ones. "The great majority of men and women," they wrote, "enter married life with expectations of the positive significance of sex relations."[57]

A more detailed portrait of the sexual side of marriage emerges from the Kinsey reports, whose much larger number of respondents, with a wide range in ages, made for more interesting comparisons. Perhaps the most notable shift in behavior uncovered by Kinsey involved the sexual responsiveness of women. Data from the interviews suggested a "distinct and steady increase in the number of females reaching orgasm in their marital coitus." It began with the cohort born in the first decade of the twentieth century and continued with each succeeding one. More of the women born in the late nineteenth century never reached orgasm, while more of the 1920s cohort almost always achieved it during coitus. Kinsey also found that the younger generation of husbands and wives enjoyed greater variety in their lovemaking. Substantially more of them participated in oral sex, touched each other's genitals, and used a variety of coital positions. Even simple nudity had become more commonplace. Fully a third of the women born before 1900 usually remained clothed during sex, in contrast to only eight percent of the 1920s cohort.[58]

Although Kinsey was unwilling to equate female orgasm with a happy sex life, he nonetheless labeled it a "considerable achievement" attributable to franker attitudes, freer discussion, and the more extensive premarital erotic experience of younger women. "There were wives and husbands in the older generation," he wrote,

> who did not even know that orgasm was possible for a female; or if they knew it was possible, they did not comprehend that it could be pleasurable, or believe it proper for a well-bred female to respond even in her marital relationships. The average male and female today are more often aware of the significance of mutual relationships in marriage and increasingly desirous of making such relationships satisfactory.

The mutuality extended not only to concern for the woman's pleasure in sex, but also to the frequency of intercourse. "Many of the males of the older generation," Kinsey noted, "were less often inclined to consider the wife's desires in regard to the frequencies of coitus. . . . It is our impression that males of the younger generation more often limit their contacts to the frequencies which their wives desire."[59] Put more bluntly, American couples of the current generation were having sex less often than their parents.

Neither Kinsey nor others were so reckless as to claim that the weakening of taboos and the move toward mutuality had made the American marriage an erotic paradise. The modern marriage credo, which stressed equal satisfaction for husband and wife, sometimes ran aground because of the different expectations of men and women. Displays of affection loomed larger in the thinking of wives than of husbands, who attached greater importance to intercourse. Women preferred intercourse less frequently than men, and were far more likely to refuse to have sex. Men much more often acknowledged a desire for extramarital affairs than did their wives. Gender-based differences in communication hampered the ability of some couples to achieve mutually satisfying relations. Husbands expressed dissatisfaction when their wives failed to reach orgasm. As one man phrased it, "I have a sense of guilt when I have relations with her and feel she does not enjoy them as much as I do. The fact that she's not getting orgasm takes the pleasure of intercourse away from me." On their part, some wives often chose to lie about their physical response rather than hurt their husbands' feelings. One woman, who had never had an orgasm, nevertheless reported that she tried to be "as active in intercourse as I can. . . . My husband is so considerate and doesn't want to hurt me, so I couldn't hurt him." Interestingly, men in the Burgess and Wallin study displayed more discontent than did their wives. Whether the results were due to lower expectations on the part of women, or to the ability of women to shape the conjugal relationship, remained undetermined. But, in any event, a number of husbands acknowledged that they had learned to compromise by having sex less often than they would have liked. "I don't importune her for intercourse when I know she doesn't want it," said one. Kinsey, meanwhile, found that a small portion of wives in his study still remained sexually unresponsive, while on average, women achieved orgasm only about three-quarters of the time. On the male side, husbands were having intercourse less frequently than they desired. But, on balance, the authors of these studies suggested that the potential for sexual satisfaction was greater than it had been earlier in the century.[60]

Useful as these surveys are in painting a picture of middle-class marriage, they may tell us more about the ideology of sexual liberalism than about the actual meanings of marital sex. Certain assumptions, often implicit, shaped the presentation of data. Kinsey, for instance, tended to equate more sex with better as he seemed to relish the performance of the male "sexual athlete." In identifying problems in marriage, women's desire for less sex, rather than men's desire for more, appeared as the culprit. Throughout the literature on marital adjustment, one rarely finds questioned the belief that sexual satisfaction lay at the heart of a successful marriage. The conjugal pair appears in isolation, devoid of other relationships and removed from a larger social context that might affect its happiness. Turning inward and focused on each other, the white middle-class couples who served as the raw material for these studies were expected to create a utopia of mutual pleasure.

The class-bound nature of companionate ideals of marriage and sexuality becomes apparent if one turns to the experience of working-class couples. When the Lynds visited Muncie in the 1920s, for instance, they found that social class bifurcated the daily experience of Americans, including in the supposedly "natural" realm of sexual relations. Not only were patterns of contraceptive use and fertility sharply different, but the time available for relaxing in bed, the privacy that couples enjoyed, and the prior socialization that men and women brought to sex diverged according to one's class background. Kinsey's work was especially telling in its comments on the class nature of sexual behavior. Despite the hidden biases in his work, he did note the critical role that class played in shaping sexual patterns. Working-class men avoided extended foreplay. For many, "the more quickly [orgasm] is attained, the more effective the performance is judged to be." The missionary position was their preferred method. Far fewer men among the lower social groupings engaged in deep kissing, or oral contact with their partner's breasts or genitals, acts which were deemed a "perversion." Surprisingly, in view of the stereotype of working-class male prowess, considerably fewer grade-school-educated couples than college pairs displayed high levels of frequency in their marital relations. Only half as many had intercourse more than seven times a week. Among women, an added difference appeared in orgasmic experience. College women were more likely to achieve orgasm during the first year of marriage, and although the gap between educational levels narrowed as the years of marriage lengthened, it never vanished. Although Kinsey tried not to render judgment on the contrasting patterns of working-class and middle-class Americans, occasionally his bias crept through. Among less-educated Americans, he wrote at one point, "a basic biologic urge . . . is being repressed." Kinsey's preference for more and varied sex rendered working-class marriages inadequate.[61]

Gender differences regarding access to sexual information and experience before marriage as well as the absence of effective contraceptive practice shaped sexual meanings in many white working-class marriages. Males generally entered marriage with considerably more sexual experience than their wives. Although many used condoms in their premarital encounters, they saw marriage as the opportunity to discard a device that interfered with their pleasure. Their spouses, young and uninitiated, knew little. As late as the 1940s and 1950s, many working-class women approached their wedding night with little sexual experience and virtually no awareness of contraception. Time and again, in Lee Rainwater's study of couples in Cincinnati and Chicago, wives repeated the refrain, "I knew nothing when I got married." Some lacked even the most basic understanding of reproductive processes. As one woman explained, "I knew nothing about babies or how to have or not have them before I was married. . . . I always thought you had to see a doctor before you got pregnant. . . . I didn't know the act led to pregnancy."[62]

Scarce economic resources made the consequences of unplanned fertility a source of sexual tension in many marriages. One husband acknowledged that sexual relations would be better "if she didn't have to worry and was more relaxed." But he was unwilling to use condoms and his wife was too embarrassed to be fitted for a diaphragm. For one woman married nineteen years, and burdened by dangerous pregnancies, sex held no satisfactions at all:

> He wouldn't care if there was one every time we went to bed; he don't do nothing to keep them from coming. The satisfaction is all on his part. I've never felt any pleasure from being with a man, but he sure must get something, as often as he wants me! I've almost died every time I've been pregnant.

In other cases, sex became a battleground with husbands and wives matching wits over the issue of contraception. Recalcitrant husbands sought ways to have intercourse without using condoms, while their wives struggled to make their needs respected. "My husband says he has a rubber on and don't, and bang, I'm knocked up," reported one woman with five children. Another proved more successful in conjugal combat. "I don't let him stick it in me unless he has the rubber on. . . . In the beginning he used to try to fool me and say he put it on when he didn't, but I can tell the difference . . . I don't let him get away with that." In some marriages, resolution came by sharply reducing the frequency of intercourse, but in others, sex always remained a duty wives could not escape. Still having intercourse two or three times a week after nineteen years of marriage, one woman confessed that "it does nothing for me except disgust me. . . . He calls it pleasure, but I'd rather be with friends on a picnic or something."[63]

Despite the pressures they faced, many working-class couples found in sex one of the great pleasures in otherwise difficult lives. Thoughtful husbands taught their less experienced spouses, showed sensitivity to their sexual needs, and cooperated in family planning. As one wife explained, "I'll take it any time I can get it; I like it. . . . My husband really enjoys it if I make it; he always waits for me. . . . Hell, everybody else is going to the moon, I might as well go to Heaven!" Sometimes, erotic pleasure compensated for other problems. One mother of five, who said that in most respects "my husband stinks," nevertheless reported that sex had gotten better over sixteen years of marriage. "I'm satisfied most of the time," she commented. "I get all wet; I guess I come like a man does. . . . When it's best, I get crazy." For others, the effects of good sex permeated the entire relationship. "If God made anything better," one wife enthusiastically remarked, "he kept it to himself. It's wonderful. . . . We both come every time. It's the most important thing in the world. It just seems like we're happy all the time; it keeps us both happy."[64]

Among the black population, class also shaped marital norms. Studies of black families found that those of comfortable means adhered to strict notions of fidelity. Distancing themselves from the image of immorality that white culture projected onto the black lower class, husbands and wives placed special emphasis on stable relationships and marital intimacy, including the adoption of a single standard of behavior for men and women. One Chicago professional, for instance, described himself and his friends as "gentlemen all the way through" who respected the needs of their spouses. In his massive study of race relations, *An American Dilemma* (1944), Gunnar Myrdal observed that well-to-do blacks had "fewer extra-marital relations and less divorce" than whites of similar status."[65]

For the mass of lower-class blacks, sexual patterns exhibited continuity with past traditions even as new circumstances were reshaping their meaning. In rural areas as well as in cities, premarital experience was taken for granted, while the acceptance of out-of-wedlock births reduced the pressure for early marriage. Illegitimate births among blacks tended to occur within the context of a steady affair and a network of familial and friendship relationships. Hence, the line separating single status from marriage was not so sharply drawn. As one young mother, still living with her tenant-farm parents, described the relationship with the father of her child:

We was in love and just couldn't wait to get married [before having sex]. . . . He's living out here in the county now, working with his papa . . . I still loves Connie. He comes over to see me and treats me and the baby nice. We wants to get married soon's he can make a little more money.

In urban areas, a double standard shaped expectations in relationships. Although women looked for sexual satisfaction from their partners, they also knew that their mates might "run with other women." But a "good old man" at least avoided emotional attachments and did not spend his money on another. On their part, men assumed that a spouse would be "loyal to her old man . . . [and] keep other men out of the house."[66]

The hard conditions of life that poor urban blacks faced shaped patterns of sexual relations that bore little resemblance to companionate ideals of the privatized couple. Widespread unemployment and low-paying jobs made it difficult for many black men to support an independent household; the requirements of welfare agencies often made it necessary for men and women to live apart. A young woman who gave birth to a child before marriage could count on her own kin to provide for her, while the family of her mate might not be able to manage without his continuing contribution to its survival. Thus conjugal relationships, whether formalized by marriage or not, were embedded in a complex network of extended kinship ties. Those who sought middle-class ideals of domesticity had to contend with the demands for loyalty from their families of birth. As one young woman commented, "You have to get along the best you know how, and forget about your people. . . . If I ever get married, I'm leaving town!" The harsh reality of poverty, as Carol Stack has observed, created "strong conflict between kin-based domestic units and lasting ties between husbands and wives."[67]

As the experience of black and white working-class couples suggests, sexual liberalism spoke most directly to the middle class, whose incomes, socialization, and style of living made possible the intense focus on the privatized couple of the companionate ideal. For blacks struggling against the burden of poverty and unemployment, sexual relations and intimacy developed within a wider network of kinship obligations. The nucleated couple often had to compete with these other relationships. Within the white working class, gender differences remained more pronounced, while the pattern of earlier childbearing diffused the emotional intimacy of marriage. It also injected stress into marriages where the effort to support a family absorbed the attention of husbands and wives. In sum, sex still served to differentiate Americans as the cultural dominance of the companionate marriage gave to the white middle class a marker of identity.

To look at the sexual contours of middle-class youthful dating and adult marriage in the mid-twentieth century is to encounter a world that resonated with the past even as it articulated something decidedly new and modern. In unexpected ways, the gender stereotypes of the late nineteenth century each contributed an element to the ideal modern marriage: the nineteenth-century male's preoccupation with sex was reflected in the central place ascribed to sex in modern marriage, while the female's quest for spiritual communion found expression in the normative expectation that conjugal eroticism would be mutually gratifying. Gender differences in the meaning and experience of eroticism that nineteenth-century Americans would have found familiar still survived—men want more, women desire less; men seek sex, women crave love; both groups condemn women for behavior that they tolerate in men. And yet those differences no longer were so all-encompassing. As American society came to valorize the erotic, sexuality partly freed itself from a gendered framework. More and more middle-class women entered marriage with sexual information and experience, so that the gulf that once separated husbands and wives had narrowed. The contraceptive revolution diminished the anxieties about unwanted pregnancies that gave sex such different implications for males and females. In an important sense, the disengagement of sexuality from polarized gender definitions weakened certain barriers to sexual expression in marriage. Increasingly, sex appeared as the great unifier, a passion and a need common to all.

The assumptions of sexual liberalism diverged enough from those of the nineteenth century to provoke a redrawing of sexual boundaries. Old ones collapsed, while others were constructed, revealing in the process areas of tension and contradiction. The affirmation of sexual pleasure and the acceptance of a public world of youthful dating made the extreme reticence of the nineteenth century obsolete. At the same time, the attentuated link between procreation and erotic expression could call into question not only the primacy of marital sex but also the primacy of heterosexuality itself. Between the 1920s and 1960s, American society responded to these dilemmas as sex invaded the public realm and new definitions of deviance took hold.

35 and 36. By the early twentieth century, prostitution was a thriving enterprise in red-light districts throughout America. Above, one young prostitute poses alluringly for the camera as the madame stands by. Below, Madame Sperber, a black brothel keeper, poses with some of her girls. (Above, Courtesy of the Rhode Island Collection, Providence Public Library; below, Courtesy of the Joseph J. Pennell Collection, University of Kansas.)

37. The Progressive-era campaign against child labor used these photographs by Lewis Hine to protest the role errand boys played in directing men to prostitutes. (Courtesy of the Print Division, Library of Congress.)

38. Hine also captured this scene of Chicago workingmen entering and leaving a brothel during their lunch hour. (Courtesy of Walter Rosenblum.)

39. The Social Purity movement adopted this "White Cross Pledge" in an effort to make men adhere to a single standard of morality.

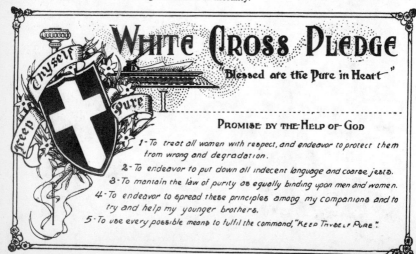

40–42. In 1922, the American Social Hygiene Association launched a sex education campaign to prevent the spread of venereal disease. Separate sets of posters for boys and girls, and for blacks and whites, were exhibited in public buildings throughout the country in an effort to channel sexuality into marriage and reproduction. (Courtesy of the Social Welfare History Archives, University of Minnesota Libraries.)

The Sex Impulse and Achievement

The sex instinct in a boy or man makes him want to act, dare, possess, strive

When controlled and directed, it gives

ENERGY, ENDURANCE, FITNESS

What Sex Brings To The Race

The creative force underlies the attractions and comradeships between boys and girls, as well as courtship, love, marriage, and family life

It makes manliness, womanliness, motherhood and fatherhood

To both boy and girl, sex gives a new joy in living, a desire for a career, a longing to do great things for the race

It inspires the arts, the sciences, and the culture of civilization

Beware of Chance Acquaintances

"Pick-up" acquaintances often take girls autoriding, to cafés, and to theatres with the intention of leading them into sex relations. Disease or child-birth may follow

Avoid the man who tries to take liberties with you He is selfishly thoughtless and inconsiderate of you

Believe no one who says it is necessary to indulge sex desire

Know the men you associate with

43. The acceptance of female sexuality in the world of the theatre is evident in the success of *The Black Crook,* an 1867 musical drama featuring scantily clad women in flesh colored tights. Despite condemnation by the respectable press, the show drew record crowds and paved the way for burlesque theatre.

44. By the turn of the century, more graphic sexual advertising announced entertainment at numerous urban music halls, such as this 1896 poster from New York City. (Courtesy of the Print Division, Library of Congress.)

45. In the twentieth century, burlesque and sexually explicit advertisement spread to the hinterland. This sign appeared in Aledo, Illinois, in 1936. (Photo by Russell Lee, Courtesy of the Print Division, Library of Congress.)

46. Moving pictures expanded the terrain of sexual commerce beyond the music hall, cabaret, and burlesque show. Despite the Hays code, which regulated Hollywood productions, on the eve of World War II "adult only" films could be viewed in the sex districts of most cities. (Photo by John Vachon, Courtesy of the Print Division, Library of Congress.)

THE BREAKDOWN

47–50. These illustrations of dancing suggest ways that sexual meanings have changed. The two from the mid-nineteenth century depict dancing in a context of intergenerational, familial sociability. By the 1930s, dancing had become an activity charged with erotic meaning for dating couples. (Opposite page above, Courtesy of the New-York Historical Society; opposite page below and this page right, Courtesy of the Schomburg Collection, New York Public Library; this page above, Courtesy of the Bettmann Archives,)

51.　During the Harlem Renaissance and the era of nightclub entertainment, whites visited cabarets, like this one in Chicago in 1941, to watch "exotic" dancers—black, mulatto and Asian women—display their sexuality. (Photo by Russell Lee, Courtesy of the Print Division, Library of Congress.)

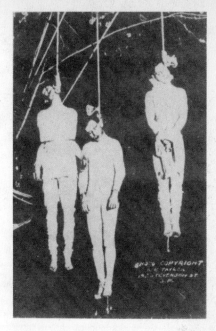

52. Three Mexicans, accused of raping a white girl in California in the 1930s, were lynched without trial.

53. White Southerners often justified lynching by claiming that black men threatened to rape innocent white women. Lynchings became public spectacles, as in this 1935 photograph from Florida. (Courtesy of the Schomburg Collection, New York Public Library.)

54. Before the adoption of the Hays Code in 1934, Hollywood films displayed open sensuality. Here Conrad Nagel kisses Greta Garbo in "The Mysterious Lady." (Courtesy of the Museum of Modern Art, Film Stills Archive.)

55. In the 1930s, the Catholic inspired National Organization for Decent Literature campaigned against the spread of sexually titillating magazines and books. Their intensive lobbying of publishers encouraged self-censorship by the industry.

56. The nightclubs of Harlem in the 1920s provided space for an inchoate homosexual subculture to grow. Gladys Bentley was a cross-dressing lesbian entertainer of the era who was open about her loves.

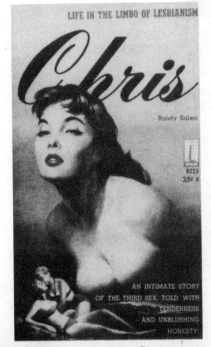

57. The "pulp" paperback genre that appeared after World War II often used sexually titillating cover pictures and copy to attract readers. Many of the lesbian pulp novels appealed to male voyeurs as well as to lesbians.

58. Artist Paul Cadmus captured the sensuality of working class dating in public space in his 1933 painting, *Shore Leave*. An example of covert gay art, the sailor in the left background cruises a young man while his shipmates frolic with women. (Courtesy of the Whitney Museum of American Art, New York.)

59. An irreverent amateur cartoonist made wartime scarcity the subject of sexual humor. (Courtesy of the Kinsey Institute for Research in Sex, Gender and Reproduction.)

SPRING PLOWING IN KANSAS AS RESULT OF W.P.B. RESTRICTIONS ON FARM MACHINERY

60. During World War II, the U.S. Navy sanctioned the use of female nudes in decorating fighter planes. Like the pictures of pin-up girls lining men's lockers, this "nose art" was supposed to boost morale and encourage heterosexual fantasy in the sex-segregated military. (Official U.S. Navy Photograph, Courtesy of the National Archives.)

61. Alfred Kinsey interviewing one of the thousands of informants for his pathbreaking studies of male and female sexuality. (Photo by Dellenback, Courtesy of the Kinsey Institute for Research in Sex, Gender and Reproduction.)

62 and 64. The 1973 Supreme Court decision of Roe v. Wade, which legalized most abortions, sparked intense political controversy. By the early 1980s, prochoice and right-to-life advocates were marching, petitioning and lobbying on the issue of abortion. (Photos courtesy of Ellen Shub, © 1987.)

63. Since 1970, lesbians and gay men have marched every year to commemorate the Stonewall Riots of June 1969, which gave birth to the gay liberation movement. Marchers in the 1977 San Francisco Gay and Lesbian Freedom Day Parade protested Anita Bryant's campaign against the Dade County, Florida, gay rights ordinance. (Courtesy of Cathy Cade.)

65. The AIDS epidemic forced an unprecedented scrutiny of sexual practices. The gay community pioneered in publicizing the need to reshape sexual behavior. (Courtesy of Ellen Shub © 1987.)

They did it 20,000 times on television last year.

Teenage pregnancy in the U.S. has reached epidemic proportions, shattering hundreds of thousands of lives and costing taxpayers $16 billion per year. Instead of helping to solve this problem, the TV networks have virtually banned any mention of birth control in programs and advertising. We need to turn this policy around. You can help.

I. On television, sex is good, contraception is taboo.

There's a lot of sex on television. We all know that. What most people don't realize is that while the networks have been hyping sex, they've banned all mention of birth control in advertising, and censor information about it in programming. (It is permitted in the news.) Millions of dollars in sexually alluring ads are okay. Ads for vaginal sprays and hemorrhoidal products are okay. So are the ads which use nudity here and there to sell products. And characters like J.R. Ewing have been seducing women a few times an hour for eight years.

In 1978, researchers counted 20,000 sexual scenes on prime-time network television (which does not even include soap operas), with nary a mention of consequences or protection. It's even higher today. The only sexual mystery left seems to be how all these people keep doing it without contraception while nobody gets pregnant.

With all that worry-free hot action on television, it's no wonder American youngsters are having sex earlier and more often.

How come nobody got pregnant?

Finally, after long negotiations, the three networks agreed to let the spots run. But only after the dreaded "C-word" — "contraception"—was censored. Instead, the networks substituted this dynamic phrase: "There are many ways to prevent unintended pregnancy."

As for network policies censoring "birth control" within programs? No change. As for the rejection of commercials for contraceptive products like condoms, foams, the pill? No change. As for the reduction of irresponsible sexual imagery? No change. As for a sense of balance between sexual hype and realistic useful information? No change.

III. Blaming the public tastes

Network executives argue that they've a responsibility to uphold high standards of public taste. The mention of birth control (except in the news) would somehow violate that. Is that true? Does the public really want uneducated pregnant teenagers? And a tax bill for $16 billion?

A recent Louis Harris Poll showed exactly what the public wants. Most Americans believe that television portrays an unrealistic and irresponsible view of sex. And 78% would like to see messages about contraception on TV. A similar percentage wants more sex education in schools. So it's not the public which resists more responsible sexual imagery. It's the television executives who resist it. Why? Maybe it's just a creative problem for them. We think they can solve it. Right now they don't even mention birth control when it's exactly appropriate. Why can't J.R. ask his latest conquest if she is prepared?

66. Despite the trend toward the open depiction of sexuality in the media, some topics remained proscribed by the television networks. In 1986, concern over teenage pregnancy impelled the Planned Parenthood Federation to attack censorship of contraceptive ads. (Courtesy of the Planned Parenthood Federation of America.)

67. The separation of sexuality, reproduction, and parenting in the late twentieth century resulted in intricate new social and legal relations. (Copyright 1986, Tom Meyer/San Francisco *Chronicle*.)

CHAPTER 12

Redrawing the Boundaries

ON June 3, 1957, San Francisco police officer William Hanrahan walked into City Lights Bookstore, a small avant-garde establishment in the North Beach section of the city. The proprietor of the store, Lawrence Ferlinghetti, had opened it to cater to the reading tastes of a motley collection of artists and bohemians who made North Beach their home. He had recently published a collection of poems by a young, unknown writer named Allen Ginsberg. Hanrahan seized copies of *Howl* on the grounds that it was "not fit for children to read," arrested the store's clerk, and had a warrant issued for Ferlinghetti.[1]

Ginsberg had arrived in San Francisco a few years earlier to join the ranks of poets and artists who had made the city their home. Self-styling themselves as Beats, they broke sharply with the values of Cold War America by rejecting the ethos of career, marriage, and suburban consumerism that the postwar middle class embraced. Until the *Howl* obscenity case, Ginsberg and his associates were unknown to the masses of Americans. But the notoriety that the trial brought, followed by the publication of Jack Kerouac's novel *On the Road,* catapulted the Beat Generation into the consciousness of the nation.

What Americans found when they looked at the Beats could not have been comforting. As Norman Mailer later noted, the Beats drew inspiration of sorts from the black hipster of the northern ghettos who moved in a world of jazz, drugs, and sex unconstrained by marriage. To these young white rebels, the black hipster appeared as a "sexual outlaw . . . exploring all those moral wildernesses of civilized life." Excluded from the secure existence of a white, middle-class consumer society, he

lived in the enormous present, he subsisted for Saturday night kicks, relinquishing the pleasures of the mind for the more obligatory pleasures of the body, and in his music he gave voice to the character and quality of his existence, to his rage and the infinite variations of joy, lust, languor, growl, cramp, pinch, scream and despair of his orgasm. For jazz is orgasm, it is the music of orgasm.

The hipster, according to Mailer, had made the decision to "encourage the psychopath in oneself." Whatever the accuracy of the description, Ginsberg seemed to acknowledge his debt to this milieu in the opening lines of *Howl:* "I saw the best minds of my generation destroyed by madness, starving hysterical naked / dragging themselves through the negro streets at dawn looking for an angry fix."[2]

Ginsberg's poem was targeted by censors in large part because of its open acknowledgment of homosexual desire. In the words of the poem, among his generation were those

> who let themselves be fucked in the ass by saintly motorcyclists,
> and screamed with joy,
> who blew and were blown by those human seraphim, the sailors,
> caresses of Atlantic and Caribbean love,
> who balled in the morning in the evenings in rosegardens and the
> grass of public parks and cemeteries scattering their semen
> freely to whomever come who may . . .

Ginsberg later reminisced that *Howl* represented for him "a crucial moment of breakthrough . . . an acknowledgment of the basic reality of homosexual joy . . . a breakthrough in the sense of a public statement of feeling and emotions and attitudes." Inspired by one kind of outlaw, the hipster, Ginsberg was proclaiming his identity as another.[3]

Howl, and the context and controversy that surrounded it, highlight points of both tension and change in mid-twentieth-century sexual norms. As it turned out, Captain Hanrahan's efforts to censor the poem failed. The judge in the case, reflecting the direction in which standards of obscenity were moving, rejected the opinion of the police and found that the poem had "social importance." Moreover, he commented that "life is not encased in one formula where everybody acts the same or conforms to a particular pattern." In the aftermath of the trial, Americans discovered the Beat Generation. The media descended on North Beach, exposing these "fugitives from the American middle class" who celebrated "booze, dope, sex, and despair" and were "overrun with homosexuals." Foiled on the obscenity front, the San Francisco police commenced a campaign of harassment against the Beat subculture and the gay world with which it overlapped.[4]

This chapter examines the contradictory patterns of expression and constraints shaped by American sexual liberalism. On the one hand, as the publication of Ginsberg's poems suggests, the discourse on sexuality expanded enormously, blurring the distinction between private and public that characterized middle-class life in the previous century. Through literature, movies, magazines, popular fiction, and pornography, sex unconstrained by marriage was put on display. On the other hand, even as the erotic seemed to permeate American life, white middle-class America struggled to maintain sexual boundaries. Some forms of behavior, such as homosexuality, remained beyond the pale; other forms, such as the mores of black urban communities, became symbols of social pathology. The sexual liberalism of midcentury perpetuated notions of good and bad, and drew a sharp line between what was judged acceptable and what was labeled deviant.

Sex on Display

Along with the removal of nineteenth-century restrictions on the availability of birth control information, mid-twentieth-century America witnessed the collapse of most prohibitions on the public portrayal of sexuality. The Comstock law of 1873, with its proscription against the mailing of contraceptive information and devices, had also included stringent provisions about obscenity. From the 1930s onward, however, the courts in the United States steadily narrowed the definition of obscenity until, by the mid-1960s, they had virtually removed the barriers against the forthright presentation of sexual matters in literature and other media. The veil of nineteenth-century reticence was torn away, as sex was put on display.

Until the 1930s, American judges had applied the broadest possible interpretation to the obscenity provisions of the Comstock Act. The courts adopted the standard enunciated in a nineteenth-century English case, *Queen v. Hicklin:* "The test of obscenity is this, whether the tendency of the matter . . . is to deprave and corrupt those whose minds are open to such immoral influences."[5] Isolated passages became the criteria for censorship, while the innocence of youth served as the yardstick for determining a work's potential to corrupt. With state laws and local purity societies buttressing the Comstock statute, censorship forces exerted a chilling effect on publishers and bookdealers well into the 1920s. Self-policing became common practice, as editors and retailers struggled to avoid costly legal entanglements. The activity of censors extended not only to contemporary writing but also to classics; customs officials regularly seized shipments of books, from Petronius to Boccaccio, deemed dangerous to the nation's morals.

Throughout this period, however, a double standard reigned in the definition of obscenity. Law-enforcement officials selectively applied the law. Antivice crusaders of the Progressive era had little trouble in publishing tracts that exposed the existence of commercialized prostitution or the horrors of white slavery, even though many of these works had all the trappings of soft-core pornography and undoubtedly titillated quite a number of readers. Similarly, social hygienists, who wrote about sexual matters for the purpose of shoring up the decaying civilized morality of the middle class, escaped legal difficulties. But where writers sought to promote change deemed radical, as in the birth control tracts of Margaret Sanger and Mary Ware Dennett or the free-love literature of anarchists, censors rushed into battle.

One important force promoting the integration of the erotic into the public realm was the reorientation of economic life. By the 1920s, it was clear to most observers that the economy had entered a new era. American capitalism no longer required an insistent ethic of work and asceticism in order to accumulate the capital to build an industrial infrastructure. Instead, corporate leaders needed consumers, men and women who were ready to spend their earnings to purchase a growing array of goods designed for personal use. By the 1920s, the leading edge of industrial activity was the manufacture of consumer items—radios, telephones, automobiles, home appliances, ready-made clothing, and processed foods. Many of these were hardly available before World War I. Moreover, for middle-class men especially, changes in work propelled them in the direction of consumption. Declining hours of labor made more leisure time available, while the loss of independence and control that came with the growth of corporate employment decreased the satisfactions that work formerly brought. Work was no longer an end in itself, but a means to something else.

The new economic order impinged upon sexual norms in a number of ways. Americans did not automatically respond to factory output by multiplying their desires for material goods; an ethic of consumption had to be sold. Advertising came into its own as an industry in the 1920s, as executives consciously strove to incite desire. In the process, they helped shape a new conception of womanhood. Advertisements aimed to persuade women to spend by emphasizing the personal allure which consumer items would obtain for them. As one advertisement pointedly claimed, *"The first duty of woman is to attract."* The makers of Lysol disinfectant promoted their product with the slogan "She looks old enough to be his mother." The manufacturer assured wives that Lysol would protect their "health and youthfulness and charm." The Lambert Pharmaceutical Company made Listerine antiseptic a common household product by inventing a new disease, halitosis, and then playing upon the romantic fears and desires of female readers. One of its ads, depicting a woman staring into a mirror, told the tragic story of an unmarried woman:

> Night after night she would peer questioningly into her mirror. . . . She *was* a beautiful girl and talented, too. She had the advantages of education and better

clothes than most girls in her set. . . . Yet in the one pursuit that stands foremost in the mind of every girl and woman—marriage—she was a failure. Many men came and went in her life. She was often a bridesmaid but never a bride.

The terrible secret that "her mirror held back," and that "even your closest friend won't tell you," was bad breath; Listerine offered a cure.[6]

Some forms of consumption, meanwhile, in themselves rested upon sexual desire. The cosmetics industry, whose sales grew from $17 million in 1914 to $141 million in 1925, depended upon women choosing to make themselves attractive to men. The plots of many Hollywood films revolved around romantic pursuit, and projected vivid images of passion into theaters throughout America. Provocative titles—*A Shocking Night, Luring Lips, Red Hot Romance, Her Purchase Price*—blazed across the marquees of movie houses. Stories of seduction and betrayal filled the pages of mass-circulation true confession magazines. Metropolitan newspapers contained advice columns about love and romance. By using veiled nudes and seductive poses, advertising also spread throughout the culture images designed to stimulate male erotic fantasies. More and more of life, it seemed, was intent on keeping Americans in a state of constant sexual excitement. And, as mainstream businesses and entrepreneurs routinely employed a sexual sell, they weakened the hold of nineteenth-century obscenity codes.[7]

Changes in literary standards after World War I also struck at the heart of older definitions of the obscene. At one time or another, many of the rising stars of American literature in the 1920s and 1930s—Ernest Hemingway, John Dos Passos, William Faulkner, Sinclair Lewis, Lillian Hellman, Erskine Caldwell, and James Farrell, among others—found themselves the target of censors. Novels of the period used street language to describe body parts and sexual acts, portrayed extramarital affairs with sympathy, presented sexual violence openly, and brought homosexuality out of hiding. The trend toward frankness was pronounced enough for Cole Porter to parody it in his Broadway musical of 1934, *Anything Goes:* "Good authors too who once knew better words / Now only use four-letter words / Writing prose / Anything Goes." Occurring in tandem with similar developments in popular culture, the integration of the erotic into literary works of obvious quality posed a serious challenge to the legal structure that still supported reticence.[8]

The first important court decision to revise the definition of obscenity came in 1934. In a case involving James Joyce's novel *Ulysses,* Judge Augustus Hand of the Second Circuit Court of Appeals rejected the *Hicklin* test of obscenity. Ruling for the defendant, Hand wrote that "the proper test of whether a given book is obscene is its dominant effect." Although not always accepted by lower courts, the ruling served as a significant precedent allowing judges to evaluate the impact of a work as a whole, rather than isolated passages. The result was a weakening of self-censorship by publishers, and some revision of law-enforcement practices. The Bureau of Customs, for instance, virtually abandoned the confiscation of classics imported into the country. The efforts of the Post Office to deny mailing privileges to *Esquire,* a slick men's magazine, failed when the Supreme Court in 1946 overturned the postmaster's action. Thereafter both the demand and the accessibility of erotically explicit material seemed to increase steadily.[9]

After World War II, pornography, as well as other media products that titillated males by sexually objectifying women's bodies, moved beyond their customary place in a marginal underground world. Soldiers who had graced their barracks and even their planes with photos and drawings of "pin-up" girls returned from Europe and Asia laden with pornography obtained abroad. They soon found a new genre of magazine available to fill their acquired tastes, as *Playboy* and a host of imitators saturated the nation's newsstands. Physique pictorials, masquerading as physical fitness magazines, filled a male homosexual market, while scandal magazines such as *Confidential* and *Keyhole* catered to a female audience. The "paperback revolution," initiated by Pocket Books in 1939, placed easily affordable books in drugstores, newsstands, and other retail outlets throughout America. By the late 1940s, publishers had discovered that sex sells, and were redesigning their covers accordingly. Bantam issued its first "beefcake" cover in 1948, promoting *The African Queen* with a naked man emerging from the water. In the same year, Popular Library produced its famous "nipple cover" to entice readers to purchase *The Private Life of Helen of Troy.* By the early 1950s, lurid designs and suggestive copy dominated the paperback field. Before long the lists of many houses would be dominated by the so-called pulp novels (named for the cheap paper on which they were printed) whose content delivered what the cover promised. Meanwhile, fly-by-night producers and distributors of erotica, working out of basements and garages, churned out playing cards, slides, photos, homemade movies, and even phonograph records of pornographic content. The minimal capital that the business required and the small size of the operations made it relatively easy to enter the field and virtually impossible for law-enforcement officials to suppress it. By the mid-1950s, estimates of the dollar volume of this sexual industry ranged from a few hundred million to a billion dollars a year.[10]

The trend toward frankness about sexual matters did not please everyone. From the mid-1930s through the 1950s a reinvigorated purity movement battled against the public display of sexuality. Every step toward greater openness was matched by renewed efforts to hold the line against "filth" and maintain standards of decency. Churches, citizens groups, and congressional investigators joined forces to uphold the collapsing barriers to sex in print and

film. In this new purity crusade, the Roman Catholic church played an initiating role. At one time a persecuted faith ministering largely to immigrants, it
had in the nineteenth century refrained from civic campaigns out of fear of
retaliation from a Protestant majority. Now, in the 1930s, it emerged as a
defender of traditional sexual morality, rousing Catholics and Protestants alike
to the cause.

Hollywood provoked the first assault from purity forces. Ever since the
birth of the motion picture early in the century, the content of films had
engendered moral controversy. In 1907, Chicago had enacted the nation's first
law to censor films. The next two decades witnessed a series of efforts to censor
followed by attempts at self-regulation that inevitably broke down. In 1927 the
Hays office, created by producers to establish industry-wide moral standards,
released its guidelines. "Don'ts" included licentious or suggestive nudity, sex
perversion, white slavery, and miscegenation; a longer list of "be carefuls"
advised caution in the depiction of first-night scenes, lustful kissing, and men
and women in bed together. But the guidelines lacked an enforcement mechanism, and Hollywood responded by merely tacking moral endings onto its
features. On the way to a conclusion, however, many a film portrayed sexual
profligacy in various forms. When another attempt at self-policing, the production code of 1930, achieved only minimal effects in altering the content of
movies, the Catholic hierarchy decided to intervene. In 1934, it formed the
Legion of Decency.[11]

The Legion of Decency adopted a twofold approach in its campaign to
clean up the nation's movie fare. It created a board that evaluated cinema
content, with an "A" awarded to acceptable features, "B" to those judged
"morally objectionable in part for all," and a "C" to those whose viewing it
condemned. Although the portrayal of crime and violence constituted one
measure of a film's moral standing, the chief criterion for a rating was its sexual
content. Fully ninety-five percent of the statements issued by Catholic bishops
focused on sex. The Legion also sought to mobilize the Catholic population
behind its ratings by encouraging a personal refusal to patronize morally
objectionable films. A survey of thirty-two dioceses in 1934 revealed that more
than three million Catholics, or two-fifths of the population in those dioceses,
had signed pledges to boycott immoral movies. Many churches prominently
displayed the Legion's list of endorsed and objectionable features, and in
succeeding years, congregations at Sunday Mass around the country were
asked to recite the pledge.

The film industry could hardly ignore the warnings. The launching of the
Legion of Decency received prominent newspaper coverage, and prompted
major press stories about morality in movies throughout the summer of 1934.
Hollywood moguls adopted a tougher production code in 1934, banning

among other things the portrayal of adultery, lustful embraces, undressing scenes, and dances suggestive of "indecent passion." Between 1936 and 1943, only one Hollywood film, Howard Hughes's *The Outlaw,* received a "C" rating, and less than ten percent were judged "objectionable in part for all." The production code remained unchanged for over two decades, sharply restricting what American moviegoers viewed in the nation's theaters.[12]

Emboldened by their success in dealing with the film industry, Catholic bishops next turned their attention to print media. The National Organization for Decent Literature (NODL), formed in 1938, targeted publishers, bookdealers, drugstores, and newsstands. It attacked the content of the new genres of comic books and mass-market paperbacks, aimed at a youthful audience, as well as more respectable literary efforts. Clerics organized delegations to boycott and picket local newsstands, to visit police and city officials, and to inundate publishers with letters of protest. They lobbied at state and national conventions of retail druggists. Especially angered by publishing companies which, it alleged, "have taken advantage of the leisure time of unemployed youths to feed them with religious and moral poison," NODL officers met with executives to demand corrective action.[13] At least two major publishers of paperbacks and magazines, Fawcett and Dell, promised to remove the objectionable contents of blacklisted periodicals.

Although World War II temporarily diverted the attention of purity crusaders, the resistance to sexual frankness was gathering momentum again by the early 1950s. New circumstances and new concerns propelled it forward. Pornography was becoming more visible in the postwar era, at the same time that Cold War politics encouraged a heightened preoccupation with family stability. Worries about internal subversion took on a moral coloration as anticommunist ideologues searched for signs of decaying values, or the corruption of youth. Pornography became associated with juvenile delinquency, which in turn threatened the nation's future. As one congressional report concluded, the "loose portrayal of sex" that characterized pornography "serves to weaken the moral fiber of the future leaders of our country." It went on to hint at "a connection between pornographic literature and subversive elements."[14] Thus did the anxieties of the Cold War find expression in sexual politics.

Congress played an important role in the postwar campaigns against sexual explicitness in the public domain. In 1952, the House authorized an investigation of paperbacks, magazines, and comic books to expose the extent of "immoral, obscene, or otherwise offensive matter." A Senate committee probing the sources of juvenile delinquency toured the country, collecting samples of obscene materials in place after place. Although it refrained from attributing delinquency solely to an acquaintance with pornography, it did conclude that children were among "the prime targets of those who distributed these filthy materials." The industry's profits depended, the committee alleged, upon "the lunch money and allowance of school children," who were receiving "sexual knowledge unfit and harmful for sexually immature boys and girls." Through the medium of comic books, pre-pubescent youngsters received "short courses in . . . rape, cannibalism, carnage, necrophilia, sex, sadism, masochism, and virtually every other form of crime, degeneracy, bestiality, and horror." The committee deplored the extent to which pornography was reaching "even our very young children, and the terrible influence such filth was having on their conduct." By the decade's end, concern about the corruption of youth was generating a shrill rhetoric reminiscent of Anthony Comstock. "The billion-dollar business in obscene and pornographic material," a House committee reported, "has become the 'golden calf' of our times—the sacrificial lambs, our youth."[15]

Congressional investigations fed into citizens' campaigns and local law-enforcement drives. The Senate subcommittee on delinquency compiled lists of pornographers discovered through their hearings and pointedly sent them to local police departments. In Houston, Minneapolis, and several other cities, law-enforcement officials responded with major raids. New York City launched an all-out drive against distributors of girlie magazines and pulp novels, as well as against retail outlets in Times Square. In one month, they seized 276,000 copies of pornographic paperbacks. The chief of police in Youngstown, Ohio, banned over four hundred paperbacks from newsstands in the city. By the end of the 1950s, fourteen states had tightened their obscenity laws to prohibit the sale and distribution of sexually suggestive comic books. In Cincinnati, an outraged young lawyer, Charles Keating, mounted a drive to eliminate smut from newsstands and drugstores. As a sign of the discontent that sexually objectifying pornography could arouse in women, nine thousand of them rang doorbells throughout the city, amassing signatures on petitions that they delivered to city officials. Galvanized into action, the vice squad raided neighborhood candy stores and arrested the proprietors whose trials were then closely monitored by concerned citizens. Out of "Operation News-stand" came Citizens for Decent Literature, which soon established chapters throughout the country. Vigilante actions took place in Chattanooga, Akron, and Scranton, among other places. Meanwhile, older groups, such as NODL, remained active. By the mid-1950s NODL had succeeded in mobilizing Protes-tant and secular proponents of censorship into an effective alliance that one critic described as a system of interlocking directorates in the anti-obscenity field. No longer content with attacks on sleazy paperbacks and cheap pornog-raphy, it also targeted works with literary merit that it judged obscene. In the 1950s, NODL's list of condemned literature included *The Catcher in the Rye,*

From Here to Eternity, The Naked and the Dead, The Well of Loneliness, and *Tea and Sympathy.* [16]

The rhetoric of the purity campaigns of the 1950s reveal both continuity and change in America's sexual history. Like the anti-vice crusaders at the turn of the century, opponents of pornography tended to ascribe all manner of evil to sex. In the words of one Philadelphia spokesman,

> girls run away from their homes and become entangled in prostitution. Boys and young men who have difficulty resisting the undue sexual stimulation become sexually aggressive and generally incorrigible. The more vicious . . . may become an exhibitionist, a rapist, a sadist, a fetishist. He may commit such antisocial acts as arson, pyromania, and kleptomania, which are often symbolic sexual acts.

Sex appeared as an uncontrollable force that spawned social chaos when its power was let loose. On the other hand, midcentury purity advocates recognized that they were no longer dealing with a hidden, marginal phenomenon. As a report to the House of Representatives noted, the availability of pornography had "moved from a dark side street into the most respectable neighborhoods and establishments in the community."[17] Notions of victims and perpetrators had also shifted. Children of both sexes, rather than young women, were the objects of concern. In contrast to the stark image of the menacing immigrant procurer or the black rapist, the postwar pornographer was rather characterless. If anything, he appeared simply as the latest variety of profit-seeking entrepreneur, a white male who might very well conform outwardly to the social mores of the suburbs.

Notwithstanding these short-term victories, a changed social context would ultimately deny these mid-twentieth-century purity crusaders the level of success attained by Comstock. For one, Comstock had represented the dominant middle-class view in the late nineteenth century. By the 1950s, the mores of the middle class had shifted profoundly, while purity crusaders acted from outside the mainstream. Then, too, zealous law-enforcement efforts to suppress pornography provoked wave after wave of litigation. By the late 1950s, obscenity cases were reaching the Supreme Court in such large numbers that the justices were forced to examine carefully the complicated constitutional issues that changing sexual mores posed. Finally, purity advocates themselves recognized that the material they targeted no longer stood so obviously outside the realm of the permissible. Analyses of the content of postwar pornography discovered that its themes were not far removed from the mainstream values embodied in popular culture. Much pornography, congressional investigators noted, portrayed sex as a source of "personal enjoyment, a biological necessity." Love was presented as a passion that "cannot be restrained, only surrendered to." Sexual liaisons took place in a world of leisure time, automobiles, nightlife, alcohol, and consumer luxuries—the very stuff of modern advertising. Good looks and attractive bodies were "idolized," much as they were in Hollywood.[18] In attacking pornography, purity advocates may have been tackling more than they had bargained for.

Ironically, the strongest assault on sexual reticence in the public realm emerged not from the pornographic fringe, nor from popular culture, but from the respectable domain of science. The publication of Alfred Kinsey's studies of male and female sexual behavior, in 1948 and 1953 respectively, propelled sex into the public eye in a way unlike any previous book or event had done. Whether bought, read, debated, or attacked, the Kinsey reports stimulated a nationwide examination of America's sexual habits and values.[19]

Kinsey was an unlikely candidate to instigate such a furor. A professor of zoology at Indiana University, he had built his professional reputation with a meticulous study of the North American gall wasp. An interest in human sexuality grew out of his experience of team-teaching a course on marriage and the family for undergraduates in the late 1930s. Students were hungry for accurate, unbiased information about sex, and as a scientist, Kinsey was appalled by the absence of reliable nonmoralistic data concerning human sexual behavior. Although some surveys of sexual behavior had appeared in the 1920s and 1930s, thus smoothing the way for Kinsey's own work, they lacked the scientific rigor that he sought. In response, he began to collect his own data by recording the sexual case histories of undergraduates and others. Before long, he had assembled a small research team and trained them in interviewing methods and note-taking techniques that allowed them to cover a subject's sex life in a couple of hours. Over the next decade, Kinsey and his associates obtained case histories of eighteen thousand men and women.

Kinsey was undoubtedly as surprised as anyone that his study of the male, the first one published, attracted so much notoriety. The 804-page tome had all the trappings of a scientific treatise. Written in a dry, almost boring style, the volume contained hundreds of elaborate charts and graphs, methodological discussions of the interviewing process and the validity of the data, and a comprehensive review of the literature. On the basis of a marketing survey of the book's potential readership, its staid medical publisher issued a first run of only five thousand copies. But even before its official release date in January 1948, demand for *Sexual Behavior in the Human Male* had far surpassed the original expectations. Almost 250,000 copies were eventually sold, and the book spent twenty-seven weeks on the New York *Times* best-seller list. Five years later, when the companion volume on the female was issued, it too became a publishing sensation.

Behind the scientific prose lay the most elaborate description of the sexual habits of ordinary white Americans ever assembled. In great detail, Kinsey calculated the frequency and incidence of masturbation, premarital petting and coitus, marital intercourse, extramarital sex, homosexuality, and animal contacts. Avoiding as far as possible the moralistic comments that often accompanied writing about sex, Kinsey adopted a "count-and-catalogue" approach: how many respondents had done what, how many times, and at what ages. The large number of cases allowed him to construct a wide spectrum of human variation. Among males, for instance, he found one who had ejaculated only once in thirty years, while another had averaged thirty orgasms a week over a thirty-year period.

Kinsey's findings proved shocking to traditional moralists. The study of the male revealed that masturbation and heterosexual petting were nearly universal, that almost ninety percent had engaged in premarital intercourse and half in extramarital sex, and that over a third of adult males had had homosexual experience. Virtually all males had established a regular sexual outlet by the age of fifteen, and fully ninety-five percent had violated the law at least once on the way to orgasm. Although the accumulative incidence figures for females were lower, they nonetheless demonstrated that American women were not models of sexual propriety. Over three-fifths had engaged in masturbation, ninety percent had participated in petting, half in premarital intercourse, and a quarter in extramarital relations. Taken together, Kinsey's statistics pointed to a vast hidden world of sexual experience sharply at odds with publicly espoused norms. And, by choosing to present his findings in dry, unsensationalistic prose, bereft of moral disapproval, Kinsey implied that cultural values surrounding sex needed revision to match the actual practices of Americans.

The aura of science that surrounded the studies made it safe for the press to give them ample publicity. A month before the male study was available in bookstores, *Look* magazine gave an indication of the way many would approach the book. "What they have learned and will learn," it editorialized,

> may have a tremendous effect on the future social history of mankind. For they are presenting facts. They are revealing not what *should* be, but what *is*. For the first time data on human sex behavior is entirely separated from questions of philosophy, moral values, and social customs.[20]

The reports became cultural landmarks, and Kinsey a household word. Professionals in a wide range of fields organized over two hundred major symposia on the male study, more than fifty books were published that capitalized on the attention the studies were attracting, and newspapers made headlines out of the release of critiques of Kinsey's work. Popular writers and columnists quickly incorporated his findings into discussions of America's sexual habits. The Indiana zoologist appeared on the cover of *Time,* while Hollywood producers scrambled to obtain movie rights to the volumes. All in all, newspaper editors discovered that articles about sex in the daily press did not elicit a horrified response from the mass of readers. Instead, opinion polls suggested that a large majority of the public approved of scientific research on sexuality and were eager to learn more. Undoubtedly, the revelation of a wide divergence between ideals and actual behavior alleviated the anxiety of many Americans about whether their own private habits set them apart from others. And the scientific credentials of the author gave legitimacy to the curiosity many Americans had about sexual subjects as well as to their presentation in the media.

The Kinsey studies, as much as pornography, shaped the context in which the Supreme Court responded to the obscenity issue. Between 1957 and 1967, the justices heard a series of obscenity cases. Though rarely achieving unanimity, the Warren Court progressively contracted the domain of obscenity, in large part by affirming the appropriateness of sex as a matter for public consumption. In 1957, in the *Roth* decision, the Court sustained the conviction of a bookdealer accused of selling pornography while also observing that "sex and obscenity are not synonymous." Only material "which deals with sex in a manner appealing to prurient interest" could be prosecuted under the obscenity statutes. That same year, the justices declared a Michigan obscenity law unconstitutional because its stringent provisions would "reduce the adult population of Michigan to reading only what is fit for children. . . . This is to burn the house to roast the pig." As other litigation involving films, photo magazines, pornographic classics, male homosexual erotica, and pulp novels reached the Court, new criteria were added to the prurience test. Finally, in 1966, in the celebrated Fanny Hill case, Justice Brennan wove together the various strands of the Court's thinking:

> A book cannot be proscribed unless it is found to be *utterly* without redeeming social value. This is so even though the book is found to possess the requisite prurient appeal and to be patently offensive. Each of the three federal constitutional criteria is to be applied independently; the social value of the book can neither be weighed against nor canceled by its prurient appeal or patent offensiveness.[21]

For the next several years, the Court cleared every book that passed before it, suggesting that nothing warranted the label *obscene*.

Although the Court neither caused the spread of sexually explicit material nor created the demand for it, its rulings did sweep away the remnants of Comstockery. The impact was almost immediate. At one extreme, pornographic books, magazines, and films proliferated, with their sexual content growing "progressively stronger," as the President's Commission on Obscenity and Pornography noted in 1970.[22] Of greater import, perhaps, was the effect of these decisions on mainstream media. Popular novels, mass-circulation magazines, metropolitan newspapers, Hollywood films, and even television, the family's entertainer, rushed to take advantage of the new liberal climate sanctioned by the courts. Hollywood adopted a much looser production code in the early 1960s; sexually explicit novels such as *City of Night* and *Naked Lunch* became best-sellers. The slow movement, evident since World War I, toward the inclusion of the erotic in the public sphere, suddenly rushed ahead, as sex became a daily staple of American popular culture. Rather than effecting a revolution in sexual standards, the Supreme Court had placed its imprimatur on tendencies inherent in the logic of sexual liberalism. Sex was now on display, for all to see.

The Homosexual Menace

Even as some sexual boundaries were dissolving, others grew tighter. Hand in hand with the more permissive attitudes of sexual liberalism toward most forms of heterosexual expression went an effort to label homosexual behavior as deviant. In the middle decades of the twentieth century, a gay subculture took root in American cities. As men and women constructed new opportunities for meeting one another, sustaining their relationships, and deepening their sense of sexual difference, American society responded fiercely by raising the penalties that lesbians and gay men faced. Especially in the 1950s and 1960s, federal, state, and local governments mobilized their resources against this underground sexual world.

During the 1920s and 1930s, the resources for naming homosexual desire slowly expanded. A Broadway play such as *The Captive,* which dealt with lesbian relationships, not only generated controversy but also brought female couples to the theater to view it. Novels such as *The Well of Loneliness* and *Strange Brother* created fictional characters that gay readers could identify with. In Harlem and other black urban enclaves, entertainers addressed the issue of same-sex attractions in their music. Songs like "Sissy Man," "Fairey Blues," and "Bull Dagger Woman" were popular tunes on the so-called race records of the interwar years. The infiltration of psychiatric and psychoanalytic concepts into popular culture contributed to this process of labeling homosexual desire even as they cast the shadow of morbidity over gay relationships. A friendship circle of lesbians in Salt Lake City in the 1920s and 1930s read and discussed together essays of Freud in an effort to understand their way of life. With the onset of World War II, psychiatrists were incorporated into the nation's military effort, screening inductees for evidence of mental instability and, in the process, asking millions of young men about homosexuality.[23]

World War II did more than propagate psychiatric definitions of homosexuality; it also created substantially new erotic opportunities that promoted the articulation of a gay identity and the rapid growth of a gay subculture.[24] The war years pulled millions of American men and women away from their families, small towns, and the ethnic neighborhoods of large cities, and deposited them in a variety of sex-segregated, nonfamilial institutions. For men, this meant service in the armed forces; for large numbers of women, it meant migrating to cities for war jobs, and often working, lodging, and socializing in virtually all-female environments. Men and women who, in normal times, might have moved directly from their parents' home into one with their spouses, experienced years of living away from kin, and away from the intimate company of the opposite sex. For a generation of young Americans, the war created a setting in which to experience same-sex love, affection, and sexuality, and to participate in the group life of gay men and women. It offered a dramatic, unexpected alternative to the years of isolation and searching for others that had characterized gay life in the previous half century. For some, their wartime careers simply made more accessible a way of living and loving they had already chosen. For others, it gave meaning to little-understood desires, introduced them for the first time to men and women with similar feelings, and allowed them to embark upon a new sexual road. Truly, World War II was something of a nationwide "coming out" experience.

Testimony from gay men and lesbians confirms the encouragement that wartime conditions gave to the formation of sexual liaisons as well as friendships. In a letter to a friend, one twenty-year-old gay draftee described how the war had unexpectedly improved his life. "You see," he wrote,

> the Army is an utterly simplified existence for me. I have no one to answer to as long as I behave during the week and stay out of the way of the MPs on weekends. If I go home, how can I stay out all night or promote any serious affair? My parents would simply consider me something perverted and keep me in the house.

Bob Ruffing, a chief petty officer in the navy, recalled the "eye contact" that first alerted him to the presence of other gay men in the service. "Pretty soon you'd get to know one or two people and kept branching out. All of a sudden you had a vast network of friends." Ironically, cultural stereotypes about male homosexuality provided a measure of protection for those in the service. Military psychiatrists trying to screen the "unfit" searched for "effeminate looks and behavior" as telltale signs. Although far fewer women served in the armed forces, for some lesbians the military also provided entry into a world dense with same-sex relationships. Pat Bond, who as a teenager in Davenport, Iowa, thought her attraction to women condemned her to a life "forever alone," received a pleasant surprise when she entered the Women's Army Corps. "Everybody was going with someone or had a crush on someone.

Always the straight women I ran into tended to ignore us, tended to say, 'Who cares? It leaves all the men for us.' " Another Iowa woman who joined the navy embarked upon her first lesbian relationship when a fellow recruit whom she "admired greatly" made discreet physical advances. "We didn't talk about what we were doing, we just did it and felt good about it. I just thought, 'Well, this is the way it's going to be forever.' "[25]

Civilians, too, participated in the heady freedom of the war years. Leaving home to find employment in a labor market desperate for workers, men and women escaped the watchful eyes of family and neighbors, and carved out a space for sexual exploration. Donald Vining was a young man living in southern New Jersey when the war began. Aware of his homosexual desires, he had had few opportunities to act on them. Moving to New York City, he lived in a men's residence club and worked in a YMCA. The latter, especially, was replete with military men on leave, and Vining found it to be a sexual wonderland. "The war is a tragedy to my mind and soul," he wrote in his diary, "but to my physical being, it is a memorable experience." By 1945, Vining had accumulated not only sexual experience, but a circle of gay friends and an extensive knowledge of homosexual meeting places. "Lisa Ben," who was raised on a ranch in northern California, sought work in Los Angeles where she lived in a rooming house filled with unmarried young women. Knowing that she was attracted to women, but having little idea of how to find others like herself, she overheard her neighbors talking one afternoon: "I thought, 'Gee, I wonder if these are some of the girls I would very dearly love to meet' . . . I started talking and finally they asked me, 'Do you like boys, or do you go out strictly with girls?' . . . It was like a Victorian melodrama!" Her newfound friends introduced her to other lesbians as well to the lesbian bars that had sprung up in Los Angeles.[26]

The changes set in motion by wartime continued after demobilization. Many gay men and lesbians, having experienced so great a transformation in their sexual and emotional lives, did not return to prewar patterns. Donald Vining, for instance, stayed in New York after the war and continued to participate in the gay life of the city. In a similar fashion, Pat Bond, when she returned from the Pacific theater after demobilization, settled in San Francisco, maintaining her ties to many of her wartime acquaintances and patronizing the lesbian bars of postwar San Francisco. Lisa Ben, too, remained in Los Angeles. Taken together, and along with the countless anonymous others whose lives were similarly affected, these changes added up to more than the sum of the individual biographies.

As male homosexuals and lesbians came to associate more freely, they created institutions to bolster their sense of identity. In this respect the gay bar played a pivotal role. Places as diverse as San Jose, Denver, Kansas City,

Buffalo, and Worcester, Massachusetts, had their first gay bars in the 1940s. These night spots offered something of a haven where gay men and lesbians could meet, form friendships, and initiate sexual relationships. Throughout the postwar era, the bar subculture spread and stabilized, relieving somewhat the isolation that had so characterized homosexual experience earlier in the century.

The subculture that evolved in the postwar years took somewhat different shape for men and women. Reflecting a long historical tradition of greater access to public space as well as a gender socialization that encouraged sexual expression, gay men sought partners in a variety of settings besides bars. In most cities, certain streets and parks, along with bus and train depots, became favored sites where men "cruised" in search of others. Larger cities also offered the option of bathhouses for gay men to exchange sexual favors. Although men and women both patronized bars, the lesbian bar subculture was considerably smaller than its male counterpart. Boston, for instance, sustained almost two dozen gay male bars in the 1950s, but only one that served an exclusively female clientele. With fewer women than men possessing the economic autonomy to live outside the family, and with bars still carrying an aura of danger and taboo, lesbians could not maintain many commercial establishments to satisfy their social needs. Moreover, for many middle-class lesbians, the erotic energy that was so close to the surface of bar life may have been threatening, clashing as it did with female norms that attached sex to idealized romantic settings. Many of them relied on other options, turning to organizations of business and professional women as the place to find female companionship, even as they remained discreet about their sexual preferences. Friendship networks also served as ways of sustaining a lesbian identity. For a female doctor in New York in the 1950s, "wonderful parties where we could be ourselves" composed the substance of her gay social life. "For the rest of the world it might have been a sub-culture," she recalled, "but my experience was that it gave me an identity, a self-identity and for the first time a community identity."[27]

As the gay subculture evolved, its members benefited from the more open public discourse about sexuality which at times, as in the case of *Howl*, presented affirming images of homosexual love. Kinsey's study of male sexual behavior was especially significant in this regard. Unsettling as many of his findings were, none proved more shocking to conventional values than the incidence figures for homosexual behavior. Kinsey's estimates dwarfed all previous calculations. Among males he found that fifty percent acknowledged erotic responses to their own sex, over one-third had had a postadolescent homosexual experience that resulted in orgasm, four percent were exclusively homosexual as adults, and one out of eight respondents were predominantly homosexual for at least a three-year period. Kinsey claimed that homosexuals were scattered throughout the population. "Persons with homosexual histories," he wrote, "are to be found in every age group, in every social level, in every conceivable occupation, in cities and on farms, and in the most remote areas of the country. . . . In large city communities . . . an experienced observer may identify hundreds of persons in a day whose homosexual interests are certain." What had once appeared as a deviant form of sexual behavior on the fringe of society now seemed to permeate American life. In 1951, Donald Webster Cory's *The Homosexual in America* combined the changes in gay life in the 1940s with the findings of the Kinsey study to argue that homosexuals were an oppressed minority. In a more popular vein, the semi-pornographic genre of paperback pulp fiction, exemplified by the novels of Ann Bannon and Paula Christian, offered easily available images of self-affirming lesbian love.[28]

The expanding possibilities for gay men and lesbians to meet did not pass without a response. The postwar years bred fears about the ability of American institutions to withstand subversion from real and imagined enemies. Political leaders mobilized the public to support a global commitment to contain Communism. The ensuing Cold War left Americans prone to hunt for scapegoats to explain how the fruits of victory in World War II could so quickly turn sour. In an atmosphere of such anxiety, homosexuals suddenly found themselves labeled a threat to national security and the target of widespread witchhunts.

Politicians first latched onto the issue of homosexuality in February 1950, the same month that Senator Joseph McCarthy initially charged that the Department of State was riddled with Communists. When a State Department official testified in Congress that several dozen employees had been dismissed because of homosexual activity, Republican leaders jumped on the revelation. Several senators charged that homosexuals had infiltrated the executive branch of government and that the Truman administration had failed to take corrective action. Guy Gabrielson, the Republican national chairman, sent a letter to seven thousand party workers warning them that "sexual perverts . . . have infiltrated our Government," and that they were "perhaps as dangerous as the actual Communists." After a District of Columbia vice-squad officer told a congressional hearing that thousands of "sexual deviates" worked for the government, pressure for an investigation built.[29] In June 1950 the Senate authorized a formal inquiry into the employment of "homosexuals and other moral perverts" in government.

The report that the Senate released in December painted a threatening picture of gay civil servants. The committee alleged that homosexuals lacked "emotional stability" and that their "moral fiber" had been weakened by sexual indulgence. Homosexuality took on the form of a contagious disease imperiling the health of anyone who came near it. Even one "sex pervert in a Government agency," the committee warned,

> tends to have a corrosive influence upon his fellow employees. These perverts will frequently attempt to entice normal individuals to engage in perverted practices. This is particularly true in the case of young and impressionable people who might come under the influence of a pervert. . . . One homosexual can pollute a Government office.

The Cold War against Communism made the problem of homosexuality especially menacing. "The social stigma attached to sex perversion is so great," the committee noted, that blackmailers made "a regular practice of preying upon the homosexual."[30] Already believed to be morally enfeebled by sexual indulgence, homosexuals would readily succumb to the blandishments of the spy and betray their country rather than risk exposure of their sexual identity.

The response to the panic over homosexuals in government was immediate and far-reaching. Dismissals from civilian posts increased twelvefold over the pre-1950 rate. In April 1953, just weeks after Eisenhower was inaugurated, the new president issued an executive order barring gay men and lesbians from all federal jobs. The FBI, charged with investigating the loyalty of all current and prospective government employees, initiated a widespread system of surveillance to keep homosexuals off the federal payroll. In an era when the military's role in American life was growing rapidly, the armed forces sharply stepped up its purges of homosexual men and women from the ranks. Yearly discharges doubled in the 1950s, and rose another fifty percent in the early 1960s. Even homosexual "tendencies" became grounds for separation from service. States and municipalities, meanwhile, followed the lead of the federal government in demanding moral probity from their personnel, while also enforcing rigorous behavioral standards in the licensing of many professions. Corporations under government contract applied to their workers the security provisions of the Eisenhower administration. One study in the mid-1950s estimated that over 12.6 million workers—more than twenty percent of the labor force—faced loyalty-security investigations as a condition of employment.[31] For lesbians, especially, who faced the constricted employment opportunities that all women confronted, the workplace discrimination of Cold War America imposed serious hardships.

The labeling of homosexuals as moral perverts and national security risks, along with the repressive policies of the federal government, encouraged local police forces across the country to harass them with impunity. The presence of bars and the stability of cruising areas in parks and on certain streets made the gay population more vulnerable to attack. Throughout the 1950s, and well into the 1960s, gay men and lesbians suffered from unpredictable, brutal

crackdowns. Arrests were substantial in many cities. In the District of Columbia, they topped one thousand per year during the early 1950s; in
Philadelphia, misdemeanor charges averaged one hundred per month. Arrests
fluctuated enormously as unexpected sweeps of gay bars could lead to scores
of victims in a single night. New York, New Orleans, Miami, San Francisco,
Baltimore, and Dallas were among the cities that experienced sudden upsurges
in police action against homosexuals and lesbians in the 1950s. Newspaper
headlines would strike fear into the hearts of gay men and lesbians by announcing that the police were combing the city for nests of deviates. Editors often
printed the names, addresses, and places of employment of those arrested in
bar raids. A survey of male homosexuals conducted by the Kinsey Institute
revealed how deeply police action extended into the gay world: twenty percent
of the respondents reported encountering trouble with law-enforcement officers.[32]

In some localities, the concern with homosexuality approached an obses-
sion. In Boise, Idaho, after the arrest of three men in November 1955 on
charges of sexual activity with teenagers, a fifteen-month-long investigation of
the city's male homosexual subculture ensued. The town fathers imposed a
curfew on Boise's youth and hired an outside investigator with experience in
ferreting out homosexuals. Over 150 news stories appeared in the local press,
and newspapers in neighboring states gave prominent coverage to the witch-
hunt. Gay men fled Boise by the score as the police called in fourteen hundred
residents for questioning and pressured homosexuals into naming friends.[33]

That a nation would mobilize such great resources against an imaginary
threat to its security suggests profound tensions in postwar American society.
At one level, Cold War politics seem sufficient to explain the irrational preoccupation with an alleged homosexual menace. A nation at the height of its
power searched for answers about why the world was exploding with danger.
Just as hidden traitors were undermining the nation's physical security, so too
did sexual deviates deplete its moral resources. But the growth of a gay
subculture also called into question the strength of another prop of Cold War
society, the family. Having been buffeted by the Depression-era and wartime
shocks to family life, Americans after World War II were returning to domesticity with renewed fervor as the foundation for social stability. In the baby-
boom years of the 1950s, with their paeans to domestic togetherness, visible
gay men and lesbians suggested the potential fragility of heterosexual familial
norms.

Male and female homosexuality played to a variety of sexual fears just at
a time when an ethic of sexual liberalism had sunk roots into the middle class.
The contraceptive revolution, along with legitimation of women's erotic

desires, had already weakened the constraints on sexual activity outside of marriage. Would women abandon their domestic and maternal duties altogether? Midcentury sexual ideology emphasized that female desire depended on men for its arousal and satisfaction, yet Kinsey found that women involved in homosexual relations were more likely to reach orgasm. Nineteenth-century feminists had worried that contraception might release men from their familial responsibilities. Now, instead, gay men were forsaking heterosexuality itself. In response, the homosexual, rather than the man who patronized prostitutes in the red-light district, became the marker that divided good men from bad. As Barbara Ehrenreich phrased it in her study of postwar masculinity, "fear of homosexuality kept heterosexual men in line as husbands and breadwinners. . . . The ultimate reason why a man would not just 'walk out the door' was the taint of homosexuality which was likely to follow him."[34]

Sexuality and Racial Control

Not only homosexuality, but race, too, served as a dividing line separating "good" sexual mores from "bad" in mid-twentieth-century America. Beginning in the 1910s, blacks began migrating from the South in large numbers, settling in what became huge urban ghettos where they were segregated largely because of racial prejudice. Though the hard times of the Depression temporarily slowed this population shift, in the decades after 1940 more blacks than ever before moved into cities of the North. As they did so, northern white society reshaped the sexual mythology of the South to its own ends. Blacks found themselves again labeled as promiscuous and dangerous, their sexual mores categorized as symbols of immorality.

In the 1920s, as blacks in New York City's Harlem and other urban ghettos sustained a vibrant nightlife, some northern whites had their first introduction to black culture. In some ways, the entertainments of these communities, and the sexual ethos that surrounded them, bore a resemblance to the experience of white working-class youth of the Progressive era. But there were differences, too. Prohibition contributed an aura of criminality to some of the proceedings, as white-controlled organized crime infiltrated the environment. Law-enforcement agencies often looked the other way, caring less about some forms of black behavior than they would if it were white. During the "roaring" twenties, places such as Harlem acted as a magnet for whites who traveled uptown to attend clubs, listen to music, and watch dancing they considered uninhibited and natural. The lyrics of much black music were far more sexually suggestive than what could be found in the tunes of white performers. In one popular song, Bo Carter crooned,

> I came over here, sweet baby, just to get my
>   ashes hauled,
> Lord, the women at the other place goin' to let
>   my ashes spoil,
> Won't you draw on my cigaret, smoke it there
>   all night long,
> Just draw on my cigaret, baby, until you make my
>   good ashes come.

One white New Yorker who participated in Harlem's nightlife described it as "an emotional holiday. Then, when the last ambiguously worded song is done, one puts on again one's hat, coat, and niceties, and once again is staid, proper, and a community pillar."[35] The explicit sensuality to be found in Harlem allowed "sophisticated" whites to see the black as a sexual "other."

White men also experienced black sensuality at closer quarters. The coincidence of the black migration north with the closing of the red-light districts had implications for the structure of prostitution. White prostitution became largely hidden, while black women found themselves on the streets. One observer of commercialized sex in Chicago in the 1930s described the significance of this difference:

> Since it is easier to observe immoral conditions among a poor and unprotected people, colored prostitutes are much more liable to arrest than white prostitutes. White women may use the big hotels or private apartments for their illicit trade, but the colored women are more commonly forced to walk the streets.

During the Depression, large numbers of poor black women who were "out of a job and can't make it any other way . . . will take a chance and 'turn a trick,' " a Chicago police captain commented.[36] But even during more prosperous times, high unemployment bred by racial discrimination led many women to resort to sex for sale.

Arrest statistics suggest the degree to which visible prostitution became largely identified with blacks. In Chicago in 1914, sixteen percent of the prostitutes appearing in court were black; by 1929, the proportion had jumped to seventy percent. Black women accounted for over half of the arrests for prostitution in New York City in the 1930s; the arrest rate among blacks was over ten times that for whites. Moreover, black women were doubly vulnerable. Gunnar Myrdal, in his study of American race relations, noted that "officers often tend to arrest Negro girls solely because they find them in company with white men, whereas white women can approach white men without being conspicuous."[37]

Although some of the prostitution among blacks served men of their own race, much of it met the needs of white men who expected black women to be sexually freer than their white counterparts. Commenting on her white customers' erotic tastes, one prostitute in the 1950s echoed a longstanding theme of white perceptions about black sexuality: "they seem to feel that, because some of us have remote ancestors who lived in Africa once, we are primitives at heart when it comes to sex." For wealthier white men, elaborate brothels offered sexual services they either could not find, or were too ashamed to seek, among women of their own race. During the 1940s, a young Malcolm X was introduced to "a special facet of the Harlem night world . . . [where] Negroes catered to monied white people's weird sexual tastes." The customers were

> rich men, middle-aged men and beyond, men well past their prime: these weren't college boys, these were their Ivy League fathers. Even grandfathers, I guess. . . . Harlem was their sin-den, their fleshpot. They stole off among taboo black people, and took off whatever antiseptic, important, dignified masks they wore in their white world. These were men who could afford to spend large amounts of money for two, three, or four hours indulging their strange tastes.

Meanwhile, for the streetwalker enmeshed in what Myrdal called "an unprotected, economically disadvantaged and overcrowded occupation," customers might come from the ranks of white laborers or office workers who drove through the black district or roamed central city neighborhoods filled with seedy hotels, in search of quick sexual release.[38] What white southerners had once taken from the black women they owned as slaves, northerners now bought in a sexual marketplace.

While the reality of prostitution provided a convenient vehicle for preserving the image of black women as symbols of promiscuous sexuality, the mythology of rape marked black men as dangerous sexual aggressors. When blacks traveled north, the image of the rapist followed them, though the criminal justice system of northern cities operated differently. Rather than face the lynch mob, black men now confronted the police and the courts. Arrests for rape were disproportionately directed against blacks, while the punishments they received were far more severe. Between 1930 and 1964, ninety percent of the men executed in the United States for rape were black. One study of sentencing found that black men convicted of raping white women received prison terms three to five times longer than those handed down in any other rape cases. Yet, at the same time that black-on-white rape evoked the most horror and outrage, it was by far the least common form of violent sexual assault. An investigation of rape cases in Philadelphia in the late 1950s found that only three percent of them involved attacks on white women by black men.[39] Infrequent though black-on-white rape was, the image of the black rapist could serve not only to control the behavior of black men in the North, but also to instill fear into white women who moved too freely in the public world.

Although prostitution and the accusation of rape offer the most extreme forms of sexual exploitation and racial control, the everyday sexual mores of the black urban underclass were used to mark the boundary between moral and immoral. As sexual liberalism took hold among the white middle class, it raised new issues for the maintenance of sexual order. In particular, how could the legitimation of heterosexual eroticism remain within "responsible" limits? How could a society that celebrated sex within marriage, and allowed youth some opportunities for exploring the erotic, prevent that freedom from turning into license? The dilemma had no easy resolution. But as black urban communities grew, the black family and black sexual mores appeared as a convenient counterpoint, identifying the line between what was permissible and what was not.

The charged meaning of black family life and sexual values emerged most clearly in the controversy surrounding the Moynihan report on the Negro family. By 1965, the movement for racial equality in the United States had reached its apogee. Years of sit-ins, freedom rides, marches, and lobbying had affected the conscience of many whites, won enactment of a comprehensive federal civil rights statute, and was leading toward passage of historic legislation to guarantee the voting rights of blacks. Black leaders, as well as government officials, were debating what these successes meant for the next stage of the black freedom struggle. It was in this context that Daniel Patrick Moynihan, then an assistant secretary in the Labor Department, prepared a study entitled *The Negro Family: The Case for National Action.* In it, he argued that the legal and judicial revolution in race relations would come to naught if certain alleged structural weaknesses in black family life were not addressed. Among the large underclass in the urban ghetto, Moynihan pointed to a series of phenomena which, he argued, would keep blacks from reaping the benefits of legal equality: serious unemployment among black men; male desertion of families; one-fourth of black households headed by women; children growing up on welfare; and almost a quarter of black births occurring outside of marriage. The result, he said, was a "tangle of pathology" that would keep many blacks trapped in a vicious cycle of poverty.[40]

Moynihan was careful to qualify his analysis in a number of ways. He attributed the weakness of the family to the historical legacy of slavery, when family ties were difficult to maintain, and to discrimination in employment, which denied many blacks the resources that would keep families together. "During times when jobs were reasonably plentiful," he stated, "the Negro family became stronger and more stable." He acknowledged, too, that "the middle-class Negro family puts a higher premium on family stability and the conserving of family resources than does the white middle-class family." Moynihan even went so far as to admit that a system in which males were dominant in the family structure was not inherently superior to one in which women's authority was greater. But, in practical terms, it was clearly a disadvantage, he said, "for a minority group to be operating on one principle, while the great majority of the population, and the one with the most advantages to begin with, is operating on another. . . . Ours is a society which presumes male leadership in private and public affairs . . . and reward[s] it. A subculture, such as that of the Negro American, in which this is not the pattern, is placed at a distinct disadvantage."[41]

No amount of qualification, however, could quiet the furor that an emotion-laden phrase such as "tangle of pathology" unleashed. From across the political spectrum, black leaders saw the report as a way of shifting the burden for being poor onto the very victims of institutionalized racism, rather than viewing poverty as rooted in entrenched racial inequality. And, in fact, many received the report in precisely that way. One influential Washington columnist interpreted the Moynihan study as a call for "self-improvement" rather than for "new demands for help from the federal government," while the *Wall Street Journal* was pleased to note that, at last, "promoting self-help" had emerged as "a large part of the ultimate answer" to black deprivation. The paper urged civil rights leaders to work to "enlighten even the most downtrodden Negro to the middle class outlook."[42] Those who were looking for ways to sidetrack concerns about structural unemployment, decaying housing, and inadequate schooling could bend the report to their own ends. They could blame the problems of ghetto life on the sexual mores of black women who bore children out of wedlock and then allegedly raised them on tax-supported welfare programs.

The controversy concerning the black family had meanings beyond the debate over the sources of racial inequality and how to eliminate it. After all, high rates of premarital sexual experience and out-of-wedlock births among Afro-Americans were of long duration and had received attention from sociologists such as E. Franklin Frazier, Charles Johnson, and Gunnar Myrdal for a generation before the Moynihan report. Moreover, it was not even clear that the rate had risen recently. The increase that Moynihan reported, from seventeen percent in 1940 to twenty-four percent in 1963, might easily have been accounted for by the growing percentage of black women who gave birth in hospitals. Admittedly, the significance of out-of-wedlock births had changed with the migration from the rural South. Blacks in northern cities more frequently came into contact with white-run institutions such as schools and the welfare bureaucracy, which labeled their cultural patterns as disorganized. For teenage girls, as Myrdal pointed out, the "sex contacts of the rural areas are classified as juvenile delinquency in the city." But Moynihan was hardly commenting on something new. What had changed over the previous generation were the sexual mores of white youth. Their behavior seemed to be moving in the direction of greater sexual permissiveness. White illegitimacy and premarital pregnancy rates *were* rising sharply, and the divorce rate was beginning a new upward climb.[43] Aiming the spotlight at illegitimacy and female-headed households among blacks served to mark these phenomena as dangerous and immoral. The image of the young black mother on welfare relayed a message: sexual freedom extracted a high personal price.

By the 1960s the nation had traveled a long way from the sexual values and practices of its nineteenth-century ancestors. Efforts to subsume the erotic into a gentle spiritualized passion and to keep it contained within the private sphere had given way as sex became an integral part of the public domain. Sexual imagery abounded in the culture. The erotic loomed large in the expectations of married couples. Youth had created a social world in which males and females shaped their own standards for what was permissible and what was not. The diffusion of contraception and technological improvements in its reliability allowed couples to separate sharply their reproductive intentions from their desire for physical pleasure. All of these tendencies had been visible in the 1920s, but by the mid-1960s they had been consolidated and had become the accepted values of mainstream culture. American society seemed to have reached a new accommodation with the erotic.

Sexual systems are not static structures, and the liberalism of midcentury was no exception. In the boundaries that the society drew between good and bad, one can see the forces that sexual liberalism sought to contain and control. It celebrated the erotic, but tried to keep it within a heterosexual framework of long-term, monogamous relationships. Sex need not be confined to marriage, but it was expected to lead in that direction. Homosexual men and women, and young black mothers who failed to marry, violated that requirement, as did the rapist and the prostitute. Thus they received public censure and served as deviants whose behavior helped identify acceptable norms.

Until the 1960s, the points of tension in sexual liberalism had proven manageable. Contraception had not led to promiscuity; white youth did not seem to be abusing their freedom; the public display of sexuality mostly remained within reasonable bounds; the domesticity of postwar Americans affirmed the importance of marriage; deviants received punishment. But the 1960s was a decade of tremendous political and social upheaval. In a variety of ways, standards of appropriate behavior and middle-class cultural values came under attack. As one might expect, sexuality would not remain immune to this process.

CHAPTER 13

Sexual Revolutions

THE year 1968 was a traumatic one for Americans. Mired in a seemingly endless war, the nation coped with the discontent that it provoked at home. A once popular president was driven from office, and two charismatic leaders, Martin Luther King and Robert F. Kennedy, were assassinated. The nation's black ghettos exploded with riots while white college students occupied campus buildings, marched in protest against the war, and rejected the values of middle America. In August, the whole world watched on television as Chicago police brutally attacked anti-war protesters outside the Democratic party's national convention.

In the midst of these conflicts, many Americans looked for reassuring signs of stability. If there was one cultural symbol of tranquil, happy times, surely the Miss America pageant would qualify. Initiated in 1921 to bolster the Atlantic City tourist trade, it had over the years come to blend a variety of elements into a popular ritual of modern life. Young, attractive women displayed the curves of their bodies, but in modest, tasteful swimsuits that contained their erotic powers. They demonstrated appropriately feminine skills—hospitality, sociability, musical talent, poise—that marked them as future wives rather than loose women. Corporations scrambled to sponsor these events and, with the advent of television, spawned new contests to provide more opportunities for advertising their products alongside American beauties. By the mid-1960s, the Miss America pageant faced competition from Miss USA, Miss Universe, Miss Teen International pageant, and the Junior Miss pageant, among others. In an era when sex sold, the duties of a beauty queen might include perching for photographs on the fender of a new Oldsmobile, or presiding at the opening of a new soft-drink bottling plant. Meanwhile, millions of male television viewers enjoyed the parade of female bodies while women vicariously experienced the pain and happiness of contestants as the winner and runners-up were announced.[1]

But by 1968 even the Miss America pageant had to contend with protest. Outside the convention hall in Atlantic City, over a hundred noisy demonstrators, all women, expressed their discontent with the "degrading mindless-boob girlie symbol" that the contest represented. They dumped objects of female "enslavement" into a giant "freedom trash can": girdles, bras, high-heeled shoes, false eyelashes, and hair curlers. Attacking the corporate commercialism as well as the sexual objectification that the contest endorsed, one poster announced, "Miss America Sells It." As a culmination of their action, these self-styled women's liberationists draped a sheep in yellow and blue ribbons, crowned it queen, and paraded it along the boardwalk while they sang, "There she is, Miss America!"[2]

The Miss America protest helped put the women's liberation movement on the map. It also suggested that beneath the surface of a sexually liberal ethic lay serious discontent. By the end of the 1960s, young radical feminists and gay militants would be mounting political challenges to the liberal consensus on sex, while disaffected middle-class youth would simply turn away from it. In the process they initiated a new era of contention and change in the realm of sex.

Singles Life and Rebellious Youth

Paradoxically, the first major challenge to the marriage-oriented ethic of sexual liberalism came neither from political nor cultural radicals but rather from entrepreneurs who extended the logic of consumer capitalism to the realm of sex. In December 1953, Hugh Hefner published the first issue of *Playboy,* a glossy monthly which made its mark through color centerfolds of nude young women. Although other magazines aiming at a male audience had titillated readers with female flesh, the overtness of *Playboy,* according to one reviewer, "makes old issues of *Esquire,* in its most uninhibited days, look like trade bulletins from the W.C.T.U." Along with the pictures came an evolving philosophy that rejected any limits on sexual expression and reserved for marriage the harshest of criticism. *Playboy* encouraged its readers to "enjoy the pleasures the female has to offer without becoming emotionally involved." Appealing to men who were upwardly mobile, the magazine saw marriage as a financial trap. Better to spend one's money on self-indulgence and luxurious living, it proclaimed, than to become one of the "sorry, regimented husbands trudging down every woman-dominated street in this woman-dominated land."[3]

Hefner parlayed his ability to arouse male fantasies into a financial and sexual empire. The circulation of his magazine rose rapidly, passing the million mark before the end of the 1950s, and peaking at six million in the early 1970s. Almost half the readers were single men. A quarter of the copies were sold on college campuses, suggesting a potentially affluent market with appeal for advertisers. By the mid-1960s, Hefner's personal fortune was estimated at $100 million. He had built a thirty-seven-story skyscraper in Chicago, owned a $6 million jet, and lived in a forty-eight-room mansion on Chicago's Gold Coast, along with thirty of his Playboy "bunnies."

In some ways, Hefner's style of actively propagating a philosophy of sexual libertinism seemed to confirm the worst predictions of nineteenth-century moralists who believed that sanctioning sex without marriage would lead to unbridled promiscuity. Hefner made himself available for magazine interviews and television appearances, where he attacked "our ferocious antisexuality, our dark antieroticism in America." The naked women of *Playboy,* he told his fascinated audiences, were "a symbol of disobedience, a triumph of sexuality, an end of Puritanism." The "Playmates of the Month" toured the country promoting the magazine, appearing at sporting events, business conventions, state fairs, and colleges. Dartmouth College hosted one as a weekend guest on the campus. To men skeptical of their ability to find such beauties for themselves, Hefner spoke in reassuring phrases:

> We suppose it's natural to think of the pulchritudinous Playmates as existing in a world apart. Actually, potential Playmates are all around you: the new secretary at your office, the doe-eyed beauty who sat opposite you at lunch yesterday, the girl who sells you shirts and ties at your favorite store. We found Miss July in our circulation department, processing subscriptions, renewals, and back copy orders.[4]

For would-be imitators of Hefner, the *Playboy* approach to sex had one obvious flaw: where were the women who would cooperate? Hefner's assurances notwithstanding, most observers of the postwar sexual scene emphasized the relational aspects of female sexuality. Women's interest in the erotic appeared strongly attached to love and romance, to seriousness of purpose. Especially in an era that celebrated family domesticity, most young women might reasonably be assumed to see sex as a prelude to marriage.

Men in search of sex free of the obligations of matrimony found a welcome ally in Helen Gurley Brown. A career woman who would make her mark in publishing by transforming *Cosmopolitan* into a top-selling magazine, she initially won notoriety by writing *Sex and the Single Girl,* a runaway best-seller of the early 1960s. Intending it as a guidebook for the unwed working woman, Brown seemed to have as little use for marriage as Hefner did. Marriage, she wrote, "is insurance for the *worst* years of your life. During your best years you don't need a husband." Echoing *Playboy,* she told her readers that men were "cheaper emotionally and a lot more fun by the dozen." They were everywhere to be found, and easily obtainable. Since a wedding was not the object, Brown encouraged single women to play the field with married men. "It's a question of taking married men, but not taking them seriously," she wrote. "Use them in a perfectly nice way just as they use you. . . . One married man is dangerous. . . . A potpourri can be fun."[5]

Brown was shrewd enough to recognize that many American women might harbor inhibitions about the cavalier sex life she was trumpeting. *Sex and the Single Girl* tackled the problem head-on. Brown urged her readers to "reconsider the idea that sex without marriage is dirty. . . . [S]ex was here a long time before marriage. You inherited your proclivity for it." Girls can say "yes," she suggested, even "nice, single girls." The pleasures were intoxicating: "an affair between a single woman and her lover can be unadulterated, cliff-hanging sex." Brown advised women to enjoy the propositions that would come their way and to use sex as the "powerful weapon" it was.[6]

Brown's manifesto for the single woman shared more with *Playboy* than sexual libertinism. It, too, was premised on an ethic of success, prosperity, and consumption. The single woman was measured "by what she does rather than whom she belongs to." She had to live by her wits and sharpen her skills in order to make it in a competitive world. Brown offered pointers for "Squirming, Worming, Inching, and Pinching Your Way to the Top."[7] Moreover, money was a prerequisite to the successful single life, and it would come not from the largess of a male admirer, but through hard work. Money bought the clothes, the cosmetics, the home furnishings, the catered parties, the vacations, and the other leisure activities that made the single girl attractive and envied.

Brown and Hefner, each in their own way, seemed to speak to the desires of at least some of America's unmarried. In the prosperous sixties, a portion of young urbanites participated in the creation of a new singles culture. Initially structured through informal institutions, singles life revolved around the parties and weekend clubs that energetic young men and women created in order to fill a social vacuum. Friday editions of city newspapers were sprinkled with classified ads announcing the upcoming events. But, before long, the market for heterosexual gathering places was invaded by enterprising businessmen. Throughout the country, singles bars began to populate the urban landscape, providing a setting for men and women to meet and form liaisons. Publishers threw together guidebooks for the unattached, computer dating services sprang into existence, and builders constructed youth-oriented apartment complexes so that the modern singles could party without the complaints of concerned parents or older Americans. Although for some this new singles culture served to facilitate the quest for a spouse, its contours made it more of a sexual, than a marriage, market. As one young man described the New

York scene, "New York is a single man's paradise. It doesn't pay to get married. . . . I am looking for a temporary companion, not a mate." The bars sustained casual contacts, not permanent relationships; the promise of excitement and adventure kept patrons returning. Women as well as men seemed to initiate encounters. One observer noted the "casual boy-meets-girl atmosphere" of singles meeting places. "A girl thinks nothing of dropping down at a table if she sees a man sitting alone—or of excusing herself if she spots someone more attractive."[8] Having reached maturity in an era where sexual information and sexual experience were more easily accessible for the young, the singles generation of the 1960s pursued these paths into adulthood.

At first glance one might reasonably wonder what was new or distinctive about this world of urban nightlife and sexual encounters. After all, working-class youth at the turn of the century had sustained a sexual subculture rooted in commercialized amusements. But the unmarried youth of that era had elicited pity, scorn, or fear from the middle class who sought to control their behavior and made them the object of reformation efforts. Now, in the 1960s, young adults of the middle class were glamorized; they embodied the unspoken fantasies of a consumer society extended to the sphere of sex. These young singles very quickly became, in the opinion of one commentator, "a new, privileged, spotlighted, envied group." The singles label seemed to connote, "as in tennis, an endeavor more vigorous, more skilled, and more fun than mere doubles."[9]

One reason, perhaps, for the shift in values was that the singles culture of the 1960s was moving with the stream of American life. In the Progressive era, the working girl raised the specter of social disorder and gender upheaval. In the postwar period, the single working woman was not only an accepted but also a necessary feature of economic life. The expansion of the retail and service sector of the labor force, the so-called pink-collar economy, drew women into the job market, married as well as single. Moreover, economic prosperity rested squarely upon an ethic of consumption, as business needed buyers for an endless array of consumer items. As one motivational psychologist told an audience of businessmen, "we are now confronted with the problem of permitting the average American to feel moral . . . even when he is spending, even when he is not saving. . . . One of the basic problems of prosperity, then, is to demonstrate that the hedonistic approach to his life is a moral, not an immoral one."[10]

Sex and the single American offered one promising avenue for achieving this goal. Young, unmarried professionals had enormous discretionary buying power, comprising even in the 1960s a $60 billion market for sellers. As the barriers against sensual imagery fell, advertisers could shape their messages around appeals to the erotic and by glamorizing the lifestyle of the unmarried.

In some instances, sexual meanings were not at all disguised. Mary Quant, the designer of the miniskirt, put bluntly the message behind her fashions. "Am I the only woman who has ever wanted to go to bed with a man in the afternoon?" she asked. "Any law-abiding female, it used to be thought, waits until dark. Well, there are lots of girls who don't want to wait. Mini-clothes are symbolic of them."[11] Not only clothes and cosmetics, but cigarettes, soft drinks, cars, liquor, stereos, and a host of other unerotic products became vehicles for a sexual sell. The consumer economy of the sixties helps explain how the singles culture could emerge from a period seemingly rooted in a marital sexual ethic and why it won such ready acceptance.

While one segment of the middle-class young pursued sexual pleasure in the name of consumerist values, another broke with the tenets of sexual liberalism by rejecting the materialistic bias of modern capitalism. By the mid-1960s, white American college students were rousing themselves from a generation-long political stupor. Their numbers swelled by the first baby boomers, and inspired by the civil rights struggle of their black counterparts in the South, white students in growing numbers set themselves firmly against the "establishment." The Vietnam War, the draft, and charges of university complicity in the military effort propelled them to take political action on and off campus. With each passing year, the volume and intensity of youth protest escalated.

Part of what gave the rebellion of the sixties so much energy was its heady mix of politics and culture. More than a response to particular government policies, the student movement generated a complex critique of American social life. The acquiescence to racial inequality in a democracy, to poverty in the world's richest nation, and to a technologically sophisticated military struggle against a peasant population seemed a damning indictment of middle-class values. As Herbert Marcuse, the Marxist philosopher whose writings appealed to radical student leaders, put it,

> This society is obscene in producing and indecently exposing a stifling abundance of wares while depriving its victims abroad of the necessities of life; obscene in stuffing itself and its garbage cans while poisoning and burning the scarce foodstuffs in the fields of its aggression; obscene in the words and smiles of its politicians and entertainers. . . . Obscene is not the picture of a naked woman who exposes her pubic hair but that of a fully clad general who exposes his medals rewarded in a war of aggression; obscene is not the ritual of the Hippies but the declaration of a high dignitary of the Church that war is necessary for peace.

For some, protest against the war coincided with a rejection of the competitive values that bred success, and the materialism that sustained a consumer economy. Music, drugs, the symbolic adoption of different modes of dress and hairstyle, all combined to fuel the sense of breaking sharply from the culture in which the young had been reared.[12]

Sexual issues were part and parcel of the decade's youth upheavals. On a number of campuses sexual freedom leagues shared attention with anti-war organizations. Students campaigned for an end to campus regulations governing visiting hours in the dorms. University health services found themselves targeted for denying oral contraceptives to the unmarried. Female students defied rules that prohibited them from living off-campus with their boyfriends. Some colleges broke sharply with tradition by acquiescing to demands for coed dorms. Alongside political buttons with the message "end the war" were those proclaiming "take it off" and "I'm willing if you are." By the end of the sixties, concerned parents and troubled administrators no doubt yearned for the days when students contented themselves with the ritualistic "panty raids" that marked the onset of spring.

Although cultural radicalism and political protest coincided for many college students, the hippie counterculture fully absorbed the energies of others. Surfacing in San Francisco, hippies first attracted media attention with their "Human Be-in" in Golden Gate Park in early 1967. Soon, hippie colonies were flourishing in most large cities and on the fringes of university towns. The "flower children," as the media dubbed them, ostentatiously mocked the values of the comfortable middle-class families from which they came. "Turn on, tune in, drop out," intoned by one of their gurus, Timothy Leary, symbolized the drug-oriented lifestyle and anti-materialistic ethic of the movement. To mainstream America, the hippies epitomized moral decay and sexual anarchy. Unlike nineteenth-century sex radicals who sought a sexual love based on spiritual values, hippie codes emphasized a freedom that was more overtly physical. As *Newsweek* reported:

> For the hippies, sex is not a matter of great debate, because as far as they are concerned the sexual revolution is accomplished. There are no hippies who believe in chastity, or look askance at marital infidelity, or see even marriage itself as a virtue. Physical love is a delight—to be chewed upon as often and as freely as a handful of sesame seeds.[13]

Living in communes in the city and in rural areas, hippies allegedly abandoned, along with sexual restraint, allegiance to the nuclear family. The media reported children being raised in common, in an atmosphere of sexual freedom, in loose extended "families." Perhaps because they rejected so directly the institutions of family and marriage, the hippies elicited the strenuous condemnation of middle America.

By the late 1960s, the sexual iconoclasm of the counterculture appeared to reach beyond the confines of small enclaves of disaffected youth. In the summer of 1969, hundreds of thousands of the young converged on Woodstock, New York, for a rock festival in which drugs, nudity, and sexual encounters abounded. On Broadway, audiences gasped at the nudity displayed in the rock musical *Hair,* and at the defiance of taboos on sexually explicit language in *Oh! Calcutta!* whose title was a thinly veiled verbal play on the French "oh, quelle cunt tu as." Tabloids such as *Screw* began publication, devoting themselves entirely to sex and intent on shocking middle-class sensibilities. Clearly, the consensus that the tenets of sexual liberalism represented was shattering, as both the counterculture and the consumer culture broke with its emphasis on stable, marriage-centered sexual relationships. "The old taboos are dead or dying. A new, more permissive society is taking shape," one magazine observed. "The crucial question" was "where the new permissiveness is leading, whether the breakdown of the old order is going to lead to some new moral system, or whether it is simply going to lead to the progressive discarding of all social restraint."[14]

The Second Wave of Feminism

Before that question could be answered, there arose challenges of a different sort to the sexual status quo. By the end of the 1960s the radicalism of American youth had given birth to two social movements which spoke directly to sexual matters. Women's liberation and gay liberation each presented a wide-ranging critique of deeply held assumptions about human sexual desire, its place in social life, and the hidden purposes it served. In particular, both movements analyzed the erotic as a vehicle for domination which, in complex ways, kept certain social groups in a subordinate place in society. No longer a natural "instinct" or "drive," sexuality emerged more clearly than ever as an issue of power and politics.

The postwar generation of American women had faced a set of conflicting role expectations that would have tested the sturdiest. On the one hand, a resurgence of domestic ideology exalted the roles of housewife and especially mother. "Anatomy decrees the life of a woman," one Harvard psychiatrist wrote, while Erik Erikson proclaimed that female "somatic design harbors an 'inner space' destined to bear the offspring of chosen men." Woman was defined by the man she married and the children she nurtured. In the baby-boom years of the 1940s and 1950s, American women seemed to live out these expectations as many married at younger-than-ever ages and bore as many children as their grandmothers had. The accelerating migration of the white middle-class population away from the central city placed added demands upon the suburban housewife whose tasks grew to fill the expanded floor plan. Besides their domestic duties, many of these housewives had to seek employment outside the home to maintain the family's economic status. Between 1940 and 1960, the proportion of married women in the labor force doubled from fifteen to thirty percent. Forced to shape their employment experience around the demands of their domestic duties, many of these women labored part-time, left and reentered the labor market, and worked at jobs with little prospect of advancement. Small wonder, then, that when Betty Friedan published *The Feminine Mystique* in 1963, she reported deep reservoirs of discontent among American housewives, a predicament she labeled "the problem that has no name."[15]

On the other hand, American women were also expected to be more than mothers and housekeepers. Marital ideals prescribed that she be an erotic companion to her husband, that the happiness of marriage would grow in proportion to the sexual magic generated between husband and wife. By the 1960s, Playboy Playmates and sexy single girls added another, more troubling ingredient to this sexual stew. Wives could look with concern at the sexual competition they faced from women who did not have to change diapers or cook for a family. For her part, the single woman might forever question her own femininity, lacking as she was the central attribute of motherhood. Whether dutiful wife or alluring single, the American woman was left to wonder whether she made the grade.

Some of the conflicts that American women faced were embedded within the system of sexual liberalism. Modern marriage was a sexual partnership, yet husbands and wives often approached the conjugal bed with widely divergent expectations about the meaning of sex. Many women hoped for love and affection; their partners sought orgasmic relief. The companionate ideal posited equality between spouses, yet wives remained economically dependent, aware that failure in marriage spelled disaster. As the birth control pill lessened the dangers of pregnancy, and the media portrayed the glamor of the single life, young women who had helped shape an ethic of "permissiveness with affection" found the rules suddenly altered. Placed on the defensive, they were rapidly losing the right to say no that nineteenth-century feminists had struggled to obtain.

Meanwhile, the conditions of life for American women were changing, promoting a rise in expectations. During the 1960s, the college population grew considerably and with it came a female cohort who might see work as more than a way station on the road to marriage. Problematic as the image of the single girl was, it did validate the choices of women who postponed marriage and sought fulfillment in a career. The birth control pill, too, though it magnified the sexual pressures that women faced, promised, in the words of one journalist, "a new kind of life," offering women "new freedom and new responsibilities."[16] The proportion of women in the labor force continued to rise steadily during the 1960s, especially drawing in married women who had completed their families, whose children were in school, and who could look forward to uninterrupted employment. In 1964, Congress passed the Civil Rights Act, aimed at correcting racial inequality but including in its provisions gender-based discrimination. Soon, the federal government was flooded with complaints from women charging sex-bias in employment. By the mid-1960s one might almost say that American women were in search of a feminist movement.

Although women's rights advocates initiated the second wave of feminism when they founded the National Organization for Women in 1966, the energy that put feminism on the map came from another group of younger, radical women. Women's liberationists, as they labeled themselves, emerged from the ranks of the civil rights movement and the New Left. Motivated by lofty ideals of social equality, genuine democracy, and the dignity of the individual, they threw themselves into the struggle for social justice. Whether teaching in freedom schools in the South, organizing the poor in northern cities, or planning demonstrations against the war in Vietnam, these young women were taking their public roles seriously, acquiring leadership skills, and experiencing a sense of empowerment at odds with the prescriptive roles embodied in the feminine mystique.[17]

The reality of life in "The Movement," however, departed dramatically from its rhetoric. Despite the nods in the direction of human liberation, male leaders in the New Left often exploited the labor of female members, devalued women's contributions to the cause, and kept leadership roles to themselves. All of this coexisted, moreover, in a climate hostile to middle-class notions of sexual morality. Women were expected to demonstrate their revolutionary fervor by breaking with conventional mores, yet sex became just another tool in the degradation of women. In an early feminist essay Marge Piercy, whose novels later chronicled the struggles of this generation, portrayed the dynamic:

> Fucking a staff into existence is only the extreme form of what passes for common practice in many places. A man can bring a woman into an organization by sleeping with her and remove her by ceasing to do so. A man can purge a woman for no other reason than that he has tired of her, knocked her up, or is after someone else. . . . There are cases of a woman excluded from a group for no other reason than that one of its leaders proved impotent with her.

For some male radicals, sex served as a vehicle to build solidarity with working-class youth. One leader of Students for a Democratic Society at the University of Washington described how men would share time "balling a chick together" before going on a demonstration. Organizers against the war popularized the slogan "girls say yes to guys who say no" in their efforts to build resistance to the draft.[18]

Such behavior and attitudes could not help but provoke a response. By the mid-1960s some movement women were beginning to speak out against the "gender caste system" that was developing. The reactions they elicited seemed to confirm their status as sexual objects. When the question of gender was raised in the Student Nonviolent Coordinating Committee, Stokely Carmichael allegedly remarked that "the only position for women in SNCC is prone." Female SDSers fared no better. During a discussion of the "women's issue" at the organization's 1965 convention, a female speaker confronted catcalls from the audience. "She just needs a good screw," one male participant shouted. Similarly, at the counter-inaugural rally sponsored by a coalition of radical groups in January 1969, Shulamith Firestone, an early organizer of women's liberation, faced cries of "take her off the stage and fuck her!" as she tried to address the topic of women's oppression.[19] Assaulted by such implacable hostility, women began abandoning New Left, gender-mixed organizations in droves, forming instead a loosely structured autonomous women's liberation movement. The first such group appeared in Chicago in 1967, but the network of relationships for sharing information among radicals was so elaborate that the impulse spread like wildfire. By the beginning of the 1970s, literally hundreds of local women's groups had taken root across the country.

The women who banded together moved quickly into the sphere of political action, but they also produced in short order a fairly elaborate body of theory that described and defined a system of gender oppression. Confronted with the paucity of radical analysis of woman's place in society, they relied on a process of "consciousness-raising" that generated both an individual understanding of their condition and the raw material from which to fashion a feminist world view. Exchanging experiences on a wide range of topics, these women discovered that their problems were not idiosyncratic, the peculiar outcome of unique relationships or family upbringing. Rather, their situations were widely shared. Out of this came the perception that "the personal is political," that the dilemmas women encountered came from a socially constructed and enforced system of gender roles that consigned women to an inferior position in society. In reaching these conclusions, radical women's liberationists laid the foundation for a vastly expanded terrain of politics. Marriage, the family, and motherhood were reinterpreted as institutions that maintained the oppression of women.[20]

Although the women's liberation movement addressed a broad set of concerns, sexuality loomed especially large in its thinking. In their consciousness-raising groups, women discussed their feelings about their bodies and about sex, commenting on, "above all, the lack of ownership. . . . We realized," wrote one, that "married or not, our bodies had ownership by many: men, doctors, clothes and cosmetic manufacturers, advertisers, churches, schools—everyone but ourselves." Maturing as they had in the post-pill, sexually permissive climate of the 1960s, most had experienced firsthand the "sexual revolution" and found it wanting. For women, sexual freedom in contemporary America had become "the right that is a duty." As Dana Densmore described it in her "declaration of independence" from the sexual revolution:

> Under the banner of "not denying our sexuality" and pointing to repression in the past . . . many of us now embrace sexuality and its expression completely uncritically. As if present excess could make up for past deprivation. . . . Sexual relations in the world today are oppressive. . . . Sex is everywhere. It's forced down our throats. It's the great sop. . . . It makes us look as if we're free and active . . . and people seem to *believe* that sexual freedom is freedom.

"Everywhere," she wrote, women were seen as "sexual objects." Advertisers projected a sexual definition of the female, informing her that "blondes have more fun" or that a certain brand of toothpaste would give her mouth "sex appeal," advising her to "wear a Playtex bra if you have an average figure but don't want to look average." Bombarded with such messages, one feminist essay proclaimed, "ninety percent of the women in this country have an inferiority complex because they do not have turned-up noses, wear a size ten or under dress, have 'good legs,' flat stomachs, and fall within a certain age bracket." The reduction of women's bodies to erotic objects had debilitating effects. Women walking down the street were the targets of stares, catcalls, and whistles. Men would "use her body with their eyes," wrote Meredith Tax, a Boston feminist. "They will evaluate her market price. . . . They will make her a participant in their fantasies. . . . Any man has this power as *man,* the dominant sex, to dehumanize woman, even to herself. No woman can have an autonomous self unaffected by such encounters."[21]

Theorists in the women's liberation movement cast a skeptical look at the sex act itself. A generation earlier, Kinsey had disputed the Freudian emphasis on the vaginal orgasm, but his argument was lost among the many other reactions his studies elicited. By the late 1960s, the social context had changed. The findings of William Masters and Virginia Johnson, sex researchers at Washington University in St. Louis, had received wide circulation. Although their conclusions could be shaped to various ends, the two sexologists had studied in detail the biological bases of human sexual responsiveness. Like Kinsey, they too broke sharply with Freudian theory by identifying stimulation of the clitoris, rather than the vagina, as the source of the female orgasm. But now, a nascent women's movement could take up the issue. Anne Koedt, in a classic and much reprinted essay, "The Myth of the Vaginal Orgasm"

(1969), articulated the feminist implications of these findings. "Women have thus been defined sexually in terms of what pleases men," she wrote. The sexually mature female who reached orgasm through vaginal penetration was the creation of male sexual preferences. Women were kept in a state of sexual confusion, labeled frigid for failing to achieve "an orgasm which in fact does not exist," and led to feign sexual satisfaction in order to keep their partners content. Demolishing the myth had significance beyond the matter of erotic pleasure. "The recognition of clitoral orgasm," Koedt concluded, "would threaten the heterosexual *institution.* For it would indicate that sexual pleasure was obtainable from either men *or* women, thus making heterosexuality not an absolute, but an option. It would thus open up the whole question of *human* sexual relationships beyond the confines of the present male-female role system." Sex thus was reinterpreted as either a mechanism for maintaining female dependence or a vehicle for breaking free. Or, as Kate Millett, the author of a best-selling feminist manifesto, succinctly described it, the act of coitus was "a charged microcosm" of sexual politics.[22]

The importance attached to sexual issues emerges most clearly when one looks at the early targets of feminist political energy. In an action that received widespread media coverage and brought women's liberation before the nation's eyes, radical feminists traveled to Atlantic City to protest the 1968 Miss America beauty pageant. In San Francisco, militant feminists disrupted the annual bridal fair sponsored by apparel manufacturers. Students at Grinnell College in Iowa staged a "nude-in" to protest the presence of a *Playboy* representative on campus. In New York City, women conducted a "whistle-in" on Wall Street during the lunch hour. Others leafleted the city's marriage bureau, informing women seeking licenses that "rape is legal in marriage," and that, "according to the United Nations, marriage is a 'slavery-like practice.' "[23] Throughout the country, young feminists held speak-outs on rape, and invaded the hearings of state legislatures debating the reform of abortion laws. In Boston, one consciousness-raising group transformed itself into a publishing collective that wrote a feminist health and sex manual, *Our Bodies, Ourselves* (1973).

As the title of the popular volume suggested, this new generation of feminists, not unlike their nineteenth-century predecessors, saw control of their bodies as a key piece in their quest for liberation. Despite the negative sexual epithets that were often thrown at them—frigid, castrating, dyke, frustrated, or, simply, ugly—women's liberation was not "antisexual." Rather, the movement was attacking the sexual objectification of women, the reduction of women by the media and by men to little more than their sex appeal or their reproductive organs. Feminists disputed the possibility of equality in marriage or in other sexual relationships when women were economically dependent on men or had internalized values that made them doubt their self-worth. To them, the oppression of women had contaminated the sex act itself, while the sexual ideology of modern America reinforced female inequality. Women's liberationists expected that only a revolutionary transformation of society could remove the corruption that attached to sex. When women achieved full autonomy, then and only then would "sexual freedom" have real meaning.

Though the revolution did not come, this modern brand of feminism did make its mark upon the consciousness of America, affecting attitudes, custom, and law. In many ways, feminism initiated a reshaping of the nation's understanding of sexuality. For instance, when the movement began, the penal codes of most states demanded corroborating evidence in rape cases, permitted questions about the victim's sexual history, and required judges to repeat to the jury the seventeenth-century dictum that "rape is the easiest charge to make and the most difficult to prove." In North Carolina only a virgin could claim rape. The women's liberation movement popularized the idea that rape was not a crime of sexual passion. Rather, it was a case of violent assault, perpetrated not only by deranged strangers, but by male relatives, boyfriends, and husbands. In the course of the 1970s, most states rewrote their rape statutes, and in twenty-five of them a complete restructuring of the offense occurred along feminist lines, largely because of the lobbying of women's groups. Colleges instituted programs to advise female students about "acquaintance rape," and in some states husbands found themselves facing indictments for "marital rape." The women's movement also invented the phrase "sexual harassment" to describe the repeated and unwanted sexual advances that generations of female workers had faced on the job. Before long, judges were recognizing the problem as an illegal condition of employment prohibited by the Civil Rights Act of 1964, women were filing suits and winning, and major corporations were hiring feminists to run seminars designed to raise the consciousness of their employees. By no means did feminism effect an end either to sexual harassment or violent assault. But it did identify sexual violence as a key element maintaining the subordination of women, provided women with new ways of understanding their situation, and expanded the resources that women had for fighting back.[24]

Perhaps the most dramatic change provoked by the women's movement came in the area of reproductive rights. Both the radicals in the women's liberation movement and more moderate feminists in organizations such as NOW recognized the pivotal position that woman's reproductive role occupied in the structure of gender oppression. Absolute control of fertility was critical if women were to attain full equality. Though advances in contraceptive technology and the removal of most barriers to access were sharply reducing the level of unwanted fertility, nineteenth-century statutes still criminalized abortion, thus placing a barrier between women and full control of their bodies. Meanwhile, the underground world of abortion, to which hundreds of thousands of women resorted every year, only reinforced a sense of helplessness and powerlessness before the workings of their own bodies. When feminism took root in the late sixties, a movement was already afoot in a number of states to reform abortion laws by giving doctors more room to recommend abortion. But feminists quickly transformed the debate, recasting the issue as one of "rights" over one's own body, and using militant tactics to achieve their goals. In New York City in 1969, radical feminists disrupted a state legislative hearing on abortion law reform; members of the Detroit Women's Liberation Coalition invaded the office of the county attorney who prosecuted abortionists; and Chicago feminists staged guerrilla theater performances at a convention of the American Medical Association. Responding to the pressure, a few states soon revised their statutes along lines closer to feminist models. Then, in January 1973, in the case of *Roe v. Wade*, the Supreme Court acted. Though it did not eliminate all restrictions on the performance of abortions, it declared unconstitutional any prohibitions on abortion in the first trimester, and made second-trimester abortions easily available. Feminists, caught unawares by this unexpected boon, hailed the decision as a major victory.[25]

Although feminists made access to abortion a key measure of female autonomy, some women faced restrictions on their ability to have children. A few months after the *Roe* decision, the press focused national attention on the issue of sterilization abuse. In Alabama, Minnie Lee and Mary Alice Relf, two young black sisters aged twelve and fourteen, had been forcibly sterilized at a government-funded family planning clinic. Meanwhile, it came to light that in Aiken, South Carolina, the only doctor willing to deliver the babies of welfare recipients required that mothers of more than two children first agree to sterilization. In 1973, the National Abortion Action Coalition revealed that fourteen states were debating legislation designed to coerce women on welfare to undergo sterilization. As the sponsor of one such bill declared, "People who live like animals should be treated as such." It soon became clear that the forced sterilization of poor women of color was far more extensive than had previously been believed. One government official estimated that federal money funded between 100,000 and 200,000 operations per year. Reliable estimates of the sterilization rate among native American and Puerto Rican women ranged between one-quarter and two-fifths of the women of childbearing age. White feminists were slower to organize around the issue than were minority communities, which saw sterilization as a means of racial control. Though the federal government released stringent regulations in 1978 to limit the practice, the lack of effective enforcement mechanisms made it difficult to eliminate.[26]

Feminists did not always find themselves in agreement over sexual matters, as their debates over lesbianism demonstrated. As militant feminists began attacking male supremacy, opponents countered by accusing feminists of sexual deviance. "Dyke-baiting" became a vehicle for impugning the movement and trivializing female political grievances. Given the condemnation that attached to lesbianism, many feminists hastily denied the charges, accepting the verdict that it was an issue of no significance. Betty Friedan called it "a lavender herring." Yet lesbians were involved in building the feminist movement from the outset and they responded to the hostility of heterosexual feminists by constructing a sexual politics of their own.[27]

With the revival of feminism in the late 1960s, lesbians flocked to the cause of women's emancipation. In many ways they were a natural constituency for the movement. Closeted though they might be, they still had to move in the public world of work to support themselves and thus encountered directly the barriers women faced in the economic sphere. Without husbands to provide them a legitimate status, and uninterested in playing the part of the sexy single girl who chased men, lesbians confronted squarely the limited options available to women. At the same time, the feminist movement was offering a setting and a climate that encouraged previously heterosexual women to come out, to explore the liberating possibilities of loving other women. As Coletta Reid, an early recruit to women's liberation in Washington, D.C., explained it,

> Almost everything I was reading at the time led me toward lesbianism. If "The Myth of the Vaginal Orgasm" was true, then intercourse was not necessary or even relevant to *my* sexual satisfaction. If "Sexual Politics" was right that male sexuality was an expression of power and dominance, then I was choosing my own oppression to stay in a relationship with a man. If sex roles were an invention of society, then women—not just men—were possible people to love, in the fullest sense of that word. If I could hug and kiss a woman I loved, why couldn't I touch all of her body? Since my husband really thought men were superior, then wasn't my needing to be in a relationship with someone superior to me, self-hating and woman-hating? The conclusion seemed inescapable.[28]

Reid was not the only one to pursue the logic of her intellectual environment. The annals of the early women's movement were filled with the stories of others who used it to move from a life as a heterosexual to lesbianism.

Their choices, and the presence of lesbians of long standing in women's organizations, did not always please their compatriots. Products of their culture, feminists were no less likely than other Americans to view lesbians with disdain, to see their sexuality as a pathological aberration at worst, or a private matter of no political consequence at best. Sensitive to the reaction that the movement was eliciting in the minds of Americans, many feminists sought to keep the issue quiet, to push lesbians out of sight. Sometimes, the results were nasty. In the New York City chapter of NOW, the energy and talent of Rita Mae Brown, a young lesbian soon to achieve fame as a novelist, lifted her to a position of influence in the organization. Her insistence that lesbianism was a key feminist issue antagonized many of her associates. Although Brown left NOW of her own choosing, others were not so fortunate, as the chapter engaged in a purge of lesbian officers. Late in 1970, the worst fears of some heterosexual feminists seemed confirmed when the media picked up Kate Millett's acknowledgment of bisexuality. *Time,* hardly a friend of the movement, gave it prominent play. "Kate Millett herself contributed," the magazine commented,

> to the growing skepticism about the movement by acknowledging at a recent meeting that she is bisexual. The disclosure is bound to discredit her as a spokeswoman for her cause, cast further doubt on her theories, and reinforce the views of those skeptics who routinely dismiss all liberationists as lesbians.[29]

Throughout the period from 1969 to 1971, women's organizations across the country were wracked by a "gay-straight" split, as tensions reached the boiling point.

Some lesbians responded to the antagonism of other feminists by leaving mixed organizations. Along with women from the nascent gay liberation movement, they formed lesbian-feminist groups of their own, fashioning in the process both a political agenda and a theory to sustain their efforts. During the early seventies, radicalized lesbians produced a body of writing that sought to reshape the contemporary understanding of same-sex relations between women and the larger issue of human sexual relations. "As the question of homosexuality has become public," wrote Charlotte Bunch, a member of the Furies collective in Washington, D.C., "reformists define it as a private question of who you sleep with in order to sidetrack our understanding of the politics of sex. For the Lesbian-Feminist, it is not private; it is a political matter of oppression, domination, and power." Heterosexuality was removed from the realm of the "natural," and reinterpreted as an ideology and an institution that kept women bound to men and blocked their struggle for full liberation. Seen from this vantage point, lesbianism became a form of political rebellion. "The Lesbian rejects male sexual/political domination; she defies his world, his social organization, his ideology, and his definition of her as inferior. Lesbianism puts women first while the society declares the male supreme. Lesbianism," Bunch continued, "threatens male supremacy at its core." Pushed to its logical conclusion this outlook implied that "feminists must become Lesbians if they hope to end male supremacy."[30]

Not all feminists became lesbians, of course, and not all lesbians left the

women's movement. Nor, for that matter, did all lesbians identify with feminism. But, as the political passions of the early seventies cooled, the goal of
ending the oppression of lesbians became integrated into the agenda of mainstream feminism. Despite the resistance of liberals such as Friedan, organizations such as NOW eventually incorporated lesbian rights into their list of
goals. As the gay movement of the 1970s grew and brought the issue of
homosexuality into the open, a gradual healing of conflict allowed some lesbians and heterosexuals to work side by side, even as other lesbians continued
to staff their own organizations and sustain an autonomous lesbian-feminist
movement.

In the long run, perhaps the signal achievement of this first generation of
self-conscious lesbian feminists was to put into bold relief the part that sexuality played in the subordination of women. In identifying female sexual expression so closely with the institution of marriage, modern sexual liberalism
sustained an ideological construct that kept women in a domestic role, while
reinforcing her inequality in the public sphere. To challenge the inevitability
or naturalness of heterosexuality was to open new realms of freedom for
females. As such, acceptance of lesbianism could serve as a benchmark for the
whole panoply of sexual questions that the second wave of feminism raised.
Whether the issue was reproductive control, rape, sexual harassment, medical
authority, prostitutes' rights, or lesbianism, feminists sought an authentic
autonomy in sexual matters and an end to the gender inequality that prevented
its achievement.

Gay Liberation

Lesbians also served as a bridge between feminism and the other sexual
liberation movement that arose in the late 1960s. One of the last of the radical
causes to spring from the youth rebellion of the decade, gay liberation, like
feminism, took issue with some core assumptions of sexual liberalism. Rejecting the notion that marriage was the appropriate site for adult eroticism, or
that heterosexuality deserved its favored status in law and custom, gay activists
assaulted the structures that relegated homosexuals to an underground, hidden
existence.

Few social movements can trace their birth to an event as unexpected and
dramatic as the one which gave life to gay liberation. On Friday, June 27, 1969,
a group of Manhattan police officers set off to close the Stonewall Inn, a gay
bar in the heart of Greenwich Village. Raids of gay bars were common enough
occurrences in the 1960s, and the police must have viewed their mission as a
routine part of their weekend duties. But the patrons of the Stonewall Inn
refused to behave according to script. As the officers hauled them one by one

into police vans, a crowd of onlookers assembled on the street, taunting the cops. When a lesbian in the bar put up a struggle, the *Village Voice* reported,

> the scene became explosive. Limp wrists were forgotten. Beer cans and bottles were heaved at the windows and a rain of coins descended on the cops. . . . Almost by signal the crowd erupted into cobblestone and bottle heaving. . . . From nowhere came an uprooted parking meter—used as a battering ram on the Stonewall door. I heard several cries of "let's get some gas," but the blaze of flame which soon appeared in the window of the Stonewall was still a shock.

Although the police officers were rescued from the torched bar, their work had just begun. Rioting continued far into the night, as crowds of angry homosexuals battled the police up and down the streets of Greenwich Village. The following day, graffiti proclaiming "Gay Power" was scribbled on walls and pavements in the area. The rioting that lasted throughout the weekend signaled the start of a major social movement. Within weeks, gay men and lesbians in New York had formed the Gay Liberation Front (GLF), a self-proclaimed revolutionary organization in the style of the New Left, seeking justice for homosexuals. As word of the Stonewall riots circulated among radical gay youth and other disaffected homosexuals, the gay liberation impulse took root across the country, spawning scores of similar groups.[31]

Dramatic as the rioting was, it was not sufficient to spark a nationwide grass-roots movement. The speed with which gay liberation grew testified to equally profound changes in the structure of gay life and the consciousness of homosexuals in the preceding years. Throughout the 1950s and 1960s, a gay subculture had been growing, providing the setting in which homosexuals might develop a group consciousness. The weakening of taboos against the public discussion of homosexuality, the pervasive police harassment of the era, and the persistent work of a small coterie of pre-Stonewall activists combined to make many lesbians and gay men receptive to the message of "gay power."

The collapse in the 1960s of strictures against the portrayal of sexual matters gave the media license to turn its attention to homosexuality. Though much of the information presented was negative—highlighting medical theories that emphasized pathology, reporting police campaigns against "deviants," or casting pitying glances at the lives of sexual outlaws—the articles in newspapers and magazines also provided welcome clues to the existence of a gay world. Magazines such as *Life* and *Look* printed photo essays of the gay subculture, alerting their audience to the concentration of homosexuals in cities such as New York, Los Angeles, and San Francisco. Series in local newspapers served much the same function as they unwittingly instructed isolated gay readers about where they might find others. A spate of Hollywood movies in the 1960s—*The Children's Hour, Advise and Consent, Walk on the*

Wild Side, among others—treated gay themes. Many writers included homosexual characters and subplots in their novels, and a number of journalists published exposés of gay life in modern America. Taken together, these forays into the world of homosexuals served as mapping expeditions that made exploration and discovery easier for countless numbers of gay men and lesbians.[32]

Meanwhile, some gay men and women were mounting a response to the repressive public policies that had characterized the Cold War era. In Los Angeles, in 1950, a group of gay men associated with the Communist party founded the Mattachine Society, a gay rights organization. A few years later, they were joined by a lesbian counterpart, the Daughters of Bilitis. During the fifties, these groups struggled to exist, as they operated with scanty resources, no models for how to proceed, and the ever-present threat of police harassment. But they did survive, establishing chapters in several cities, publishing their own magazines, and projecting, however faintly, a point of view about same-gender relationships that departed from the consensus of sin, sickness, and criminality.

During the 1960s, this pre-Stonewall generation of "homophile" leaders, as they called themselves, became bolder. Inspired by the model of the civil rights movement, activists such as Frank Kameny in New York and Barbara Gittings in Philadelphia moved beyond the task of education and shaped a more direct challenge to the laws and public policies that denied gays equality. Homophile organizations staffed picket lines around government buildings in the nation's capital to protest the ban on federal employment and the exclusion from military service. They initiated court cases to challenge discriminatory statutes, lobbied successfully to win the support of the American Civil Liberties Union, and monitored police practices. A dialogue was opened with liberal Protestant clergy, and a campaign begun within the medical establishment to have homosexuality removed from the list of mental disorders. Perhaps most importantly, these ventures made the movement newsworthy. Television cameras filmed the picketing in front of the White House, while print journalists incorporated the views of activists into their articles on gay life. By the end of the 1960s, this pioneering band had succeeded in disseminating widely a point of view that diverged sharply from the dominant consensus about homosexuality.

As consciousness within the gay subculture slowly altered, the protests of the 1960s were creating another—radicalized—gay cohort. When black power advocates proclaimed that "black is beautiful," they provided the model of an oppressed group that inverted the negative values of the society. The student movement spread skepticism toward middle-class values among white college youth and led to an alienation from mainstream America that encouraged a cavalier disregard for social respectability. The hippie counterculture urged the young to drop out and "do your own thing." Finally, the women's liberation movement launched an ideological attack on sex-role constructs while popularizing the slogan "the personal is political." Taken together, these movements offered another lens through which radical gay youth, who were keeping their homosexuality secret, might view their sexual preferences. After the Stonewall riot of 1969, when some of them gathered to form the Gay Liberation Front in New York City, they were well situated to launch a major social movement.

The culture of protest that existed at the time provided opportunities to spread the gay liberation impulse widely. Activists appeared with gay banners at the many anti-war demonstrations that erupted during the fall of 1969. At colleges and universities, gay students rallied openly alongside other campus radicals. Soon, these young gay militants were taking the message of their movement into the heart of the gay subculture. Seeing the Mafia-run bars as oppressive institutions that reinforced self-hatred and encouraged a dehumanizing sexual objectification, gay activists in many cities "liberated" the bars for an evening, and urged patrons to join the struggle for freedom.

Appearing as it did at the end of the 1960s, gay liberation adopted much of the revolutionary rhetoric of the New Left. GLF's statement of purpose announced that "we are a revolutionary homosexual group of men and women formed with the realization that complete sexual liberation for all people cannot come about unless existing social institutions are abolished. We reject society's attempt to impose sexual roles and definitions of our nature. . . . Babylon has forced us to commit ourselves to one thing . . . revolution!"[33] Rather than fight the ban on homosexuals in the military, radical gays urged resistance to the Vietnam War. They marched in solidarity with groups such as the Black Panther party, and saw themselves as an integral part of the larger movement of oppressed minorities seeking the overthrow of a destructive social order.

In articulating a critique of America's sexual mores, gay liberation borrowed heavily from the new literature of radical feminists. It argued that the oppression of homosexuals stemmed from a rigidly enforced system of heterosexual supremacy that supported the primacy of the nuclear family and the dichotomous sex roles within it. Sex was just one more vehicle used to enforce subordination and keep the system functioning. For some, gayness itself symbolized an act of political resistance to conventional roles. "We are women and men who, from the time of our earliest memories, have been in revolt against the sex-role structure and nuclear family structure," wrote Martha Shelley of GLF. Rather than being abnormal, homosexuality was seen as a natural capacity in everyone, suppressed by family and society. Gay liberation promised an end to all that. "Gay is good for all of us," proclaimed Allen Young, a former SDS member who joined GLF in 1970.

> The artificial categories "heterosexual" and "homosexual" have been laid on us by a sexist society. . . . As gays, we demand an end to the gender programming which starts when we are born. . . . The family . . . is the primary means by which this restricted sexuality is created and enforced . . . [O]ur understanding of sexism is premised on the idea that in a free society everyone will be gay.

For Young and his associates, gayness became the sign of a sexuality freed from the hierarchical assumptions of male supremacy, and from the manipulative imagery of consumer capitalism. A sensuality based on human equality would liberate the creative potential that inhered in the erotic. In leading the way toward this utopian sexual vision, gay liberationists expected that "we are going to transform society."[34]

As one of its chief tactics for accomplishing its goals, gay liberation adopted the notion of "coming out." In its older, original meaning, "coming out" referred to the acknowledgment of one's homosexuality to oneself and other gay people. Gay liberationists transformed it into a public avowal. A critical step on the road to freedom, coming out implied a rejection of the negative social meaning attached to homosexuality in favor of pride and self-acceptance. The men and women who took the plunge had to overcome the fear of punishment and be willing to brave the ostracism of society that might result. In the process, they would also shed much of the self-hatred that they had internalized. Thus, the act became both a marker of liberation and an act of resistance against an oppressive society. As the banner of New York GLF's newspaper exhorted, "Come Out For Freedom! Come Out Now! . . . Come Out of the Closet Before the Door Is Nailed Shut!"[35]

This deceptively simple proposition was both a unique product of its time and an important roadmark in the history of sexuality. At a moment when the hippie counterculture was urging the young to "do your own thing," and feminists were redefining the personal as political, coming out seemed perfectly to embody both. Moreover, it was precisely adapted to the immediate constituency and needs of the movement. With the range of penalties that exposure promised to homosexuals, it was radical youth, contemptuous of the rewards that American society offered for conformity, who were most likely to rally to the banner of gay liberation. Exclusion from the military or a civil service career, ostracism by society, and the threat of arrest held little power over these self-styled revolutionaries. And, coming out promised the movement an army of permanent recruits. By discarding the protection that came from hiding, gay men and lesbians invested heavily in the successful outcome of their struggle.

But coming out signified something more. As the gay movement grew and gathered strength in the 1970s, the example of radical activists proved infectious, and many conventional homosexuals imitated this simple act of pride. Coming out of the closet was incorporated into the basic assumptions of what it meant to be gay. As such, it came to represent not simply a single act, but the adoption of an identity in which the erotic played a central role. Sexuality became emblematic of the person, not as an imposed medical label connoting deviance, but as a form of self-affirmation. No longer merely something you did in bed, sex served to define a mode of living, both private and public, that encompassed a wide range of activities and relationships. The phenomenon of coming out highlighted just how far the erotic had moved from the previous century when it was still embedded in a web of marital duties and procreative responsibilities. And the concept of gay identity placed in sharper relief alternative self-conceptions: heterosexuality or bisexuality, "straight" or "swinger." Thus gay liberation confirmed the growing significance of the erotic in modern life, even as it seemed to break with the assumptions of sexual liberalism.

As with feminism, the revolutionary expectations of the early gay liberation movement never materialized. For one, the rebellious milieu that spawned it had lost its vigor by the mid-1970s, and the nation entered a more conservative political era. Then, too, the gay movement adapted to the times, for the most part pulling back from its radical critique of the effects of sexual repression and instead recasting itself as a movement in the long tradition of American reform. Proponents spoke of fixed sexual orientation rather than polymorphous desires; they campaigned for civil rights legislation rather than a restructuring of family life and sexual socialization. Moreover, though few activists seemed aware of it, the gay movement in important ways was moving in the same direction as mainstream sexual culture. By emphasizing the centrality of sexual expression for their own well-being, they were echoing themes that the ideologues of sexual liberalism had applied to heterosexuals in marriage. And, the commercialism that came to characterize the gay male subculture of the 1970s was not different in kind from the consumerist values that had already made sex a marketable commodity.

Nonetheless, throughout the 1970s the gay movement continued to grow, sinking deeper roots into society. By 1973, almost eight hundred gay and lesbian organizations had formed; by the end of the decade their numbers reached into the thousands. Alongside the proliferating bars sprang churches, synagogues, health clinics, community centers, law offices, travel agencies, restaurants, and a host of other businesses and nonprofit services. Lesbians formed record companies to market the music they were creating; gay men formed choruses that sang in some of the most prominent performance halls in the country. In many large cities, gay men and lesbians supported their own newspapers. Gays formed Democratic and Republican clubs, and ran for office. In Massachusetts Elaine Noble was elected to the state assembly; in Minnesota, Karen Clark and Allen Spear had similar successes; and in San Francisco, Harvey Milk became the city's first openly gay supervisor. Various constituencies within the gay population—blacks, Hispanics, Asians, youth, elders—staffed their own organizations. Gay teachers, nurses, doctors, bankers, and others created caucuses within their professions. In less than a decade, American society had witnessed, in the words of one commentator, "an explosion of things gay."[36] What had been an underground sexual subculture increasingly came to resemble an urban community.

The gay movement also made some progress in chipping away at the institutional structures, public policies, and cultural attitudes that sustained a system of oppression. In the course of the 1970s, half the states eliminated the sodomy statute from the penal code. In 1974, the American Psychiatric Association removed homosexuality from its list of mental disorders, and the following year the U.S. Civil Service Commission lifted its ban on the employment of gay men and lesbians. Several dozen cities, including populous ones such as Detroit, Boston, Los Angeles, San Francisco, Houston, and Washington, D.C., incorporated sexual preference into their municipal civil rights laws. Gay activists lobbied in many legislatures for similar statewide protections, and in Congress the movement found sponsors for a federal civil rights law. Candidates for elective office sought the endorsement of gay organizations; the national Democratic party, at its 1980 convention, for the first time included a gay rights plank in its platform. A number of liberal Protestant denominations created task forces on homosexuality, initiating the revision of Christian teachings that had remained fixed since the thirteenth century. In most large cities, police harassment, though not eliminated, declined sharply, allowing many gay men and lesbians greater freedom from fear than they had ever enjoyed. Newspapers, magazines, book publishers, and television offered positive portrayals of gay life. Perhaps most importantly, countless numbers of lesbians and gay men were coming out to their families, friends, co-workers, and neighbors, defusing the fear that attached to popular conceptions of homosexuality, humanizing the stereotypical images that most Americans held, and making possible a permanent alteration of attitudes. Equality had not been achieved. Indeed, by the late 1970s a vocal, well-organized resistance to gay liberation had emerged, demonstrating how deeply rooted in American culture the fear of homosexuality was. But the gay movement had set in motion profound changes in America's sexual mores.

In just a few short years, the system of sexual liberalism had come apart. The premium that it placed upon fulfillment and pleasure compromised its ability to point sexual desire toward the institution of marriage. The logic of consumer capitalism pushed the erotic beyond the boundaries of the monogamous couple as entrepreneurs played with erotic impulses and affluent youth pursued their pleasures outside the marital bond. Women's liberation attacked modern marriage as an oppressive institution, while gay liberation challenged the supremacy of heterosexual expression. A construct of the white middle class, sexual liberalism could not withstand the assaults that came from disaffected segments of its own constituency.

Although feminism and gay liberation presented radical critiques of sexual liberalism, neither movement had the strength in the short run to remake thoroughly the mores of the nation. Effective enough to challenge the hegemony of mid-twentieth-century orthodoxy, they succeeded in removing some constraints on sexual expression and refashioning how many Americans looked upon sex. Sexual behavior and meanings would change in the 1970s, though not always in the ways that these sexual revolutionaries envisioned.

CHAPTER 14

The Sexualized Society

TOWARD the end of the 1960s John Williamson, a successful engineer in southern California, purchased a fifteen-acre retreat in the Santa Monica mountains. Graced with a view of the ocean, the secluded site sported a two-story mansion, several smaller houses, and a building that contained an Olympic-sized pool. Williamson intended to make the property the setting in which to implement an experiment in sexual freedom. For years, a group of people "had met regularly at his house to discuss and explore ways of achieving greater fulfillment in marriage." They were all "middle-class people," many of them prosperous professionals like himself, "who held responsible jobs in the community [and] were integrated in the social system."[1] Over time, the discussions led to action, including the swapping of marital partners for sexual excitement and group sex. Williamson's newly acquired property, Sandstone, would give the venture institutional expression.

In the succeeding years, Sandstone became something of an underground tourist attraction, bringing through its doors upper-middle-class adventurers in search of new kinds of personal fulfillment and erotic delights. Those who made the trek could take off their clothes or leave them on. They could sip wine, smoke marijuana, and converse by the fireplace upstairs, or wander downstairs where they would find, in the words of one visitor, "a parlor for pleasure-seekers, providing sights and sounds that . . . [they] had never imagined they would ever encounter under one roof during a single evening." They would see

> shadows and faces and interlocking limbs, rounded breasts and reaching fingers, moving buttocks, glistening backs, shoulders, nipples, navels, long blond hair spread across pillows, thick dark arms holding soft white hips, a woman's head

hovering over an erect penis. Sighs, cries of ecstasy could be heard, the slap and suction of copulating flesh, laughter, murmuring, music from the stereo, crackling black burning wood.

Perhaps the only thing more surprising than Sandstone itself was the fact that a prominent journalist would write about it. Gay Talese's *Thy Neighbor's Wife*, from which this description is taken, became a widely reviewed, much discussed best-seller.[2]

Although Sandstone was unusual, the attraction of successful professionals to it and the marketing of it by Talese suggest that the liberal consensus about sex had dissolved. Feminists and gay liberationists were not the only ones challenging its assumptions. By the late 1960s the belief in sex as the source of personal meaning had permeated American society. The expectation that marriage would fulfill the quest could no longer be sustained. Aided by the values of a consumer culture and encouraged by the growing visibility of sex in the public realm, many Americans came to accept sexual pleasure as a legitimate, necessary component of their lives, unbound by older ideals of marital fidelity and permanence. Society was indeed becoming sexualized. From the mid-1960s to the 1980s, as the liberal consensus disintegrated, the nation experienced perhaps the greatest transformation in sexuality it had ever witnessed. The marketing of sex, important shifts in attitudes, and major changes in the life cycle of Americans all encouraged alterations in patterns of sexual behavior.

The Business of Sex

One unmistakable sign of the reorganization of sexuality came through the large-scale invasion by entrepreneurs into the field of sex. The tension in sexual liberalism, between the celebration of the erotic as the peak experience in marriage and the effort to contain its expression elsewhere, made sex ripe for commercial exploitation. Since the mid-nineteenth century, the erotic had attracted entrepreneurs. But, as we have seen, it mostly remained a marginal, illicit industry. As the Supreme Court in the 1950s and 1960s shook the legal edifice that kept sexual imagery within certain limits, the capitalist impulse seized upon sexual desire as an unmet need that the marketplace could fill. Wherever Americans looked, it seemed, the erotic beckoned in the guise of a commodity.

Pornography provides one convenient measure of the dynamic that was underway. Long confined to a shadowy underground, and formerly taking the shape of a home industry, it became in the 1970s highly visible. Thousands of movie houses featuring triple-"X"-rated films dotted the country, ranging from drive-ins on the outskirts of towns, and theaters in the central city, to fancy establishments in modern shopping malls. North Carolina and South Carolina boasted the largest concentration of adult theaters, belying the notion that pornography was the product of big-city decadence. Some of the films, such as *Deep Throat* and *The Devil in Miss Jones,* achieved respectability of sorts, becoming cult favorites that attracted large audiences. In most cities, adult bookstores sold hard-core sex magazines and paperbacks without the literary pretensions or journalistic substance to which *Playboy* and its competitors aspired. A substantial portion of newsstand sales came from publications that the police would have seized a decade earlier. Technological advances offered new opportunities and new audiences for the distribution of pornography. The introduction of video-cassette recorders in the late 1970s opened the door to a booming business in sex films for home consumption. As one maker of pornographic videos remarked, "there are some people who would like to frequent sex theaters, but for various reasons they don't. They're either ashamed to be seen going in, they don't want to take their wives with them, or whatever. This way, they're able to see the X material in the privacy of their own home, and it doesn't seem so distasteful to them." Men brought their wives or girlfriends to help them select the evening's viewing fare. Soon, the rental of pornographic movies was providing the essential margin of profit for many video stores. The spread of cable television, meanwhile, allowed producers to avoid the constraints of the federally regulated networks. A subsidiary of Time, Inc., for instance, used cable television to distribute a weekly program, *Midnight Blue,* that featured couples having sex.[3]

By the 1980s, economic analysts were referring to the "sex industry." A multi-billion-dollar endeavor, it featured high-salaried executives, a large work force, brisk competition, board meetings, and sales conventions. Al Goldstein, the publisher of *Screw* who "diversified" in the 1970s, remarked on the contrast between the sleazy image of the industry and its more prosaic—and profitable—reality. "People come into my office," he said, "and they think there are supposed to be 12 women under my desk. If there is anybody under there, it's 12 tax accountants. Or 12 attorneys. I'm a capitalist. I'm good at what I do." Industry boosters promoted the field as they would any other. Dennis Sobin, who edited *The Adult Business Report,* the chief trade magazine of the industry, commented that "the sex business has the same potential for sales and profits as the food industry. It is a growth industry that cannot go backwards."[4]

One reason, perhaps, for the confidence of this new breed of entrepreneur was that they could arguably see themselves as simply the least hypocritical of an entire spectrum of marketers of sexuality. Not only had pornography moved into the light of day, but sexual imagery had become incorporated into the mainstream of American life. Advertisers broke new ground in their use of the erotic to excite consumers. In newspaper ads, clothing manufacturers and department stores featured pre-pubescent girls in flirtatious poses. Record companies enticed buyers with sexually suggestive album covers. Calvin Klein commissioned billboards with models naked from the waist up, their buttocks snugly fitted into his designer jeans. "The tighter they are, the better they sell," he commented.[5] By the 1980s, male bodies, too, were being used to promote sales. On television, commercials for any number of products projected the message that consumption promised the fulfillment of erotic fantasies and appetites.

The visual entertainment media also made sex a staple of their shows. An evening of television might begin with game shows in which attractive female models draped themselves over prizes representing a consumer's dreams, progress to situation comedies where the plot revolved around the titillating possibilities of sexual encounters, and end with steamy adult dramas. Instead of *I Love Lucy,* viewers laughed at the innuendo of *Three's Company,* in which a man and two women cohabited, or they might wonder when Sam and Diane, the main characters in *Cheers,* would make it into bed. Rather than the simple cops-and-robbers plots of *The Untouchables,* the award-winning *Hill Street Blues* closed many episodes in the bedroom of its chief protagonists. Popular nighttime soap operas combined the themes of money, power, and sex into high Nielsen ratings. Potboiler novels became mini-series, with titles such as *Sin,* or *Hollywood Wives,* in which the characters trotted around the globe in search of sexual adventure. Multi-million-dollar budgets and the absence of frontal nudity were about the only differences between these network specials and their prodigal pornographic cousins.

The permeation of sex throughout the culture made itself felt in other ways. In the morning newspapers, "Dear Abby" and Ann Landers found themselves addressing more and more explicit sexual scenarios. A series of articles in one midwestern daily advised single men and women that "there is nothing wrong with sharing physical pleasure with somebody else. Sure, old moralistic rules flash by, but for a growing number of us they can satisfactorily be put aside. For once, it's exhilarating to be the 'bad' kid. . . . By having a variety of partners we learn there are interesting variations on the theme."[6] In the early 1980s, Dr. Ruth Westheimer, a radio personality with a grandmotherly wholesomeness, became something of a national hero, as well as a highly paid lecturer, through her enthusiastic prescriptions for sexual happiness. Magazines made space for pages of personal ads where a "DWM" (divorced white male) might seek "SF" (single female) for walks, talks, and an afternoon affair. Cars sported bumper stickers ("firemen have long hoses," "elevator operators like to go down," "teachers do it with class") that jocularly associated occupational identity with sexual prowess.

So much openness about sexuality had an impact on the prescriptive literature to which Americans were so partial. By the 1970s, marital advice books were fast losing their audience to popular sex manuals. Many of them— *Everything You Always Wanted to Know about Sex, The Sensuous Man, The Sensuous Woman*—became runaway best-sellers. Dispensing with the genteel language and scientific descriptions characteristic of midcentury books for the married, they endorsed sexual experimentation in language that twenty years earlier had been the province of pornography. "Put your girl in a soft, upholstered chair," the author of *The Sensuous Man* advised,

> and kneel in front of her so your head comes about to the level of her breasts. ... Now slide her off the chair and right onto that beautiful erect shaft. The feeling is dizzying. She is wet and very, very hot; you are face to face and in about as deep as you can be. ... [It's] an exciting way to come. When you do explode, you'll find yourself in each other's arms—exhausted, wet, beautiful—a total state of A.F.O.— all fucked out.[7]

Alex Comfort's *The Joy of Sex* played on the theme of a popular cookbook by offering menus of its own for the sexual gourmet. Liberally illustrated with erotic drawings, it depicted naked men and women in an endless variety of sexual positions. Comfort's success propelled publishers to commission companion volumes for gay men and lesbians. Even books aimed at supposedly traditional Americans dispensed with reticence. Marabel Morgan's *The Total Woman* may have held that woman's place was in the home, but it also instructed housewives to greet their husbands at the end of the day dressed in a transparent nightgown.[8]

Changing Life Cycles and New Sexual Patterns

As entrepreneurs were weaving sexuality into the fabric of public life, Americans were simultaneously experiencing dramatic demographic changes. Between the 1960s and the 1980s, the life cycle of many Americans became considerably more complex and unpredictable. The timing of marriage and childbearing, control over fertility, the instability of the traditional nuclear family, and innovations in living arrangements all encouraged a reorganization of sexual standards.

The unusual demographic patterns of the baby-boom era reversed themselves with startling rapidity in the 1970s. Between 1960 and 1980, the marriage rate declined by a quarter. By 1985, the median age of marriage for men had risen to 25.5 years, while for women it jumped to 23.2. Along with later marriage came an overall decline in fertility. Beginning in the mid-1970s, the fertility of American women hovered at the replacement level, far below the peaks reached in the late 1950s. The accessibility of legal abortions, the accelerating trend toward sterilization, and the availability of reliable contraceptives put absolute control of fertility within reach for the married. Especially within the middle class, childlessness emerged as a serious option to consider. As one couple noted, "we are the only people we know who have a child, or at least the only people we know well. . . . Some [of our friends] are married, a few might as well be, others aren't totally opposed to the idea—and they have all either ruled out families entirely or postponed them until the very distant future." By the end of the 1970s more than a quarter of married women in their late twenties remained childless.[9]

Not only were Americans marrying later and having fewer children, but families were much less likely to remain intact. Aided by the liberalization of state laws, the divorce rate began a steep climb in the mid-1960s. Between 1960 and 1980, the number of divorced men and women rose by almost two hundred percent; the divorce rate itself jumped ninety percent. For blacks, the impact of divorce was even more widely felt. In 1980, over a quarter of black men and women between the ages of twenty-five and fifty-four were divorced, in comparison to less than ten percent of whites. Many of the divorced remarried eventually, yet second marriages had even less chance of surviving. Although the rush to divorce had slowed somewhat by 1980, marriages of the late seventies had only a one-in-two chance of surviving.

All of these shifts affected the size and structure of American households, which tended to grow smaller and become more diversified in composition. During the 1970s, over half of the new households created were nonfamily ones. The traditional two-parent family with children accounted for only three-fifths of all living arrangements by 1980. Even that figure tended to overstate its predominance, since many of those families would experience dissolution, and most Americans could expect to spend a portion of their childhood and adult years in "nontraditional" situations.

One widely touted demographic innovation of the 1970s was the rise of cohabitation among men and women. Hardly noted by 1960 census-takers, it became a highly visible phenomenon in the 1970s, tripling in frequency. Although cohabiting couples constituted only three percent of American households, the chances of an individual participating in such an arrangement were much higher. One study found that almost one in five American men had lived for at least six months with a woman other than their spouse. The phenomenon was more common among blacks than whites, and a majority of the men had been previously married. Surveying the changing nature of American lifestyles, the sociologists Philip Blumstein and Pepper Schwartz confidently predicted that cohabitation "will probably become more visible and more common."[10]

In the midst of this reorganization of household and family structure, one element of change elicited special comment—the rise of the working mother. White married women had been steadily entering the labor force since World War II, and for black wives work outside the home had always been a common experience. But the rapid movement of mothers into paid employment surprised most observers. By the early 1980s a majority of mothers, including those with children of preschool age, were working for wages. Some of this change owed its origin to feminism, which validated the choices of mothers who sought employment. Some of it was due to financial necessity. As inflation escalated in the 1970s, and the changing structure of economic and social life raised the consumption needs of many families, the pressure for mothers to work mounted. Among married couples in 1980, wives with family incomes between twenty-five thousand and fifty thousand dollars were most likely to be employed. The absence of female employment consigned many families to subsistence living. Moreover, as the divorce rate mounted and more women found themselves heading households, many mothers had no choice but to work.

Whatever the motives, the high proportion of women in the work force promised upheavals in the realm of personal life and heterosexual relations. Working women were both cause and effect of many demographic changes— the rising age of marriage, later childbearing, the decline in fertility, the spread of single-person households, and cohabitation. Unhappy marriages, in which spouses felt compelled out of duty or desperation to remain together, might more readily dissolve. As Paul Glick, a Census Bureau demographer who had studied marriage and divorce for a generation, commented, "women who enter the marketplace gain greater confidence, expand their social circles independent of their husbands' friends, taste independence and are less easy to satisfy, and more likely to divorce." Or, as one Indiana wife put it, "women don't have to put up with [men's] crap—they can support themselves."[11] Working women brought greater confidence and more power to their relationships with men. Although conflict might ensue as couples readjusted their expectations, surveys indicated nevertheless that younger males in particular preferred the more egalitarian results that came with the modification of traditional sex roles.

These demographic shifts hit the black community with special force. Although black-white differentials in family structure actually narrowed in the 1970s, nontraditional living arrangements still appeared with much greater frequency among blacks. Overall incidence rates of divorce, female-headed households, and out-of-wedlock births remained higher. By 1980 almost half of black households were female-headed, a majority of black infants were born to unmarried women, and only a minority of black children were being raised in two-parent households. Approximately half of black adults were not married and living with their spouse. In assessing these statistics, one sociologist was moved to comment that "all is not well between black men and women." In contrast to the mid-1960s, when the Moynihan report provoked so much controversy within the civil rights movement, black leaders in the eighties felt freer to air their own concerns. By the early 1980s, many were rating the issue of family life equally with jobs and education as a critical concern of the community. Eleanor Holmes Norton, who served in the Carter administration, called it "the most serious long-term crisis in the black community."[12]

When combined with the invasion of sexuality into so much of the public realm, these new demographic patterns among Americans presaged a major shift in sexual behavior and attitudes. The later age of marriage increased the likelihood that women as well as men would enter the institution sexually experienced. The rise in divorce meant that more and more Americans would be searching for new sexual partners as mature adults. Children and adolescents would know that their parents were having sex outside of marriage; the openness with which heterosexual cohabitation, lesbianism, and male homosexuality were discussed provided visible alternatives to marriage. Postponed childbearing and low fertility made obvious the distinction between sex for procreation and for pleasure. Women who worked and had more sexual experience were better placed to negotiate the terms of a sexual relationship with a partner. The new explicitness of so much popular literature about the erotic almost guaranteed that many Americans would have their sexual repertoires greatly enhanced. Perhaps most significantly, the growing complexity of the American life cycle substantially weakened the hegemony of marriage as the privileged site for sexual expression. As one longitudinal study of families in Detroit concluded, "the decision to marry or remain single is now considered a real and legitimate choice between acceptable alternatives, marking a distinct shift in attitude from that held by Americans in the past."[13]

Survey data from a variety of sources confirm a striking shift in sexual values toward approval of nonmarital sexuality. As late as the 1950s, for instance, polls suggested that fewer than a quarter of Americans endorsed premarital sex for men and women. By the 1970s, these figures had been reversed. Especially among the young, substantial majorities registered their approval. Although males, blacks, the college-educated and higher-income families were more likely to accept premarital sexuality, the differences between groups were disappearing. Only older Americans and religiously devout whites tended to maintain a stance of moral disapproval. The generation gap was especially pronounced over some of the more radical departures from past orthodoxy. One study found that three-quarters of Americans over sixty-five opposed the practice of cohabitation, while the figures were reversed for the under-thirty population. Similarly, when confronted with the contemporary openness of the gay community, younger Americans proved more than three times as likely as their seniors to display tolerance for homosexuality. In their study of American couples, Blumstein and Schwartz found that among married couples, cohabiting heterosexuals, gay men, and lesbians, majorities of everyone except wives expressed approval for sexual relationships devoid of love.[14]

One important ideological source for the revamping of sexual beliefs was feminism. Particularly among younger heterosexuals, traditional notions of male and female differences weakened in the 1970s. Most looked forward to marriages in which roles blurred. Many younger males abandoned the allegiance to a double standard of behavior for their female peers. For both men and women, expectations about sexuality and intimacy changed. As Sophie Freud Loewenstein, a Boston social worker, explained it,

> Women who have taken it for granted that their sexual satisfaction was unimportant are now reading about women having multiple orgasms. Many men realize that they've been ripped off by being programmed to deny their expressive aspects. It becomes a possibility to throw out some of the old sex roles and change drastically. That change can be very frightening, but the atmosphere makes it more permissible.[15]

As its critique of sex-role conditioning spread throughout the culture, feminism altered the attitudes of Americans about the proper behavior of men and women.

Demographic change, shifts in attitudes, and the eroticism that so much of the public realm displayed contributed to a major alteration in the sexual life of many Americans. Unmarried youth as well as conjugal pairs, urban male homosexuals as well as heterosexual couples, experienced important modifications in their patterns of sexual behavior. Among other things, sexual experience was beginning at a younger age, acts once considered deviant were more widely incorporated into heterosexual relations, and the gap between the sex lives of men and women was narrowing.

The behavior of the young and the unmarried dramatically illustrates the extent of change. From the mid-1960s onward the incidence of premarital intercourse among white females zoomed upward, narrowing substantially the disparity in experience between them and their male peers. Survey after survey of white college students in every part of the country confirmed this shift. By 1980 large majorities of female students were engaging in coitus, often in relationships that held no expectation of marriage. Among black women, too, there was evidence of change, though primarily in the age at which coitus began. Between 1971 and 1976, fifteen- and sixteen-year-olds were half again as likely to have engaged in intercourse. In the early 1970s, a much broader survey that included men and women of varying educational levels also documented the rise in premarital coitus among women. By then young women were as likely to have sex as were the men in Kinsey's study a generation earlier. Morton Hunt, the author, also confirmed a greater variety in practices. Where Kinsey had found few heterosexuals who had tried fellatio or cunnilingus, by the 1970s it was a commonplace experience among those in their twenties. The frequency of intercourse for young men and women was also substantially higher, while masturbation, especially among women, was starting earlier and had become more widespread.[16]

Evidence of other sorts substantiates these survey findings. On college campuses, health services routinely distributed contraceptive information and devices to students. For those who began having intercourse earlier, or who did not attend college, Planned Parenthood clinics offered an alternative source of assistance. In Muncie, Indiana, for example, a third of teenage girls used the services of Planned Parenthood in 1979. The rise in births to unmarried teenagers, as well as the large number who sought abortions, also suggest that a growing proportion of the young were sexually active.[17]

These changes in patterns of behavior took place in a social context different from that which had shaped the behavior of youth between the 1920s and the 1960s. For one, formal dating evinced a sharp decline. Teenage youth socialized casually in groups without pairing off; friendships between males and females were more common. As one high school boy described it, in drawing a contrast between himself and his father:

> Once he told me that he wasn't brought up to think about women the way guys like me do, and it was vice versa back then. 'We were scared of each other; we didn't really have *friends* of the opposite sex' is the way he said it to me. Now that's changed! I can talk with girls I'm not dating—I mean, be real friendly with them. There's one girl at school who's the person I feel easiest with there. We're pals, but I've never wanted to make out with her!

This ease of interaction had implications for the progress of sexual experience. When the young did pair off, it tended to signal an already serious relationship. They were less likely to move gradually through the stages of kissing, necking, and petting before deciding to have intercourse. In fact, one observer of the young concluded that petting, so important in the sexual initiation of midcentury adolescents, "seems destined to take its place as a historical curiosity."[18]

The demographic patterns of the late 1960s and 1970s, as well as the less measurable effects of feminist ideology, also contributed to the shape of change. As women became sexually active earlier in life, as the age of marriage rose, and their participation in the labor force promised greater autonomy, more of them could approach sexual experience with different expectations. One twenty-eight-year-old blue-collar female, cohabiting with a male partner, firmly expressed her right to an erotic life. "I may have had an unusual upbringing, but it never occurred to me that a man wouldn't let me be sexy," she said. "I have the same needs and moods as a man, and I am not going to let some chauvinist pig stifle them." Another single woman, also in her twenties, justified nonmonogamy on the basis of her strong sexual desires. "I have a roving eye and sometimes I give in to it. . . . I consider myself a very sexual person and I need an adventure from time to time. And I think [my cohabiting partner] does too. But that's all it is—fun and a little bit of an ego thrill."[19] Their comments suggest that at least some women had moved a long distance from the 1950s, when sexual intercourse had to be justified as a sign of an abiding romantic attachment.

Not surprisingly, the erotic dimension of marriage also changed profoundly during these years. Although some elements of the past persisted, especially concerning gender differences in initiating sex, the conjugal relationship was moving rapidly in the direction of greater variety, higher levels of satisfaction, and more frequent intercourse. For instance, a study comparing the sexual practices of married couples in the early 1970s with those in the Kinsey reports found twice as many couples departing from the missionary position. Except among black couples, oral sex—both cunnilingus and fellatio—had been incorporated into the sexual repertoire of husbands and wives to such an extent that the author of the study, Morton Hunt, called the change an "increase . . . of major and historic proportions." Among whites, the move toward variety in technique and position extended across the social spectrum, narrowing considerably the class differences that Kinsey had noted. The frequency of intercourse had also risen, in a reverse of the trend displayed by Kinsey's respondents. As Hunt explained,

> Although in [Kinsey's] time the frequency of marital coitus was declining due to the wife's rising status and her growing right to have a voice in sexual matters, the regularity of her orgasm in marital intercourse was rising. . . . This increase in orgiastic reliability and overall sexual satisfaction eventually offset the forces that caused the initial drop in coital activity.

Only ten percent of the wives in Hunt's survey described their sexual relations of the preceding year as unpleasant or of no interest to them. Of the ninety percent claiming satisfaction, three-quarters were content with the frequency while one-quarter wished for more.[20]

The visibility of sex in the culture certainly contributed to these trends. Not only did it encourage an interest in the erotic, but it also made information much more readily available to adults. Particularly among working-class wives, who as late as the 1940s and 1950s were often dependent on their husbands to lead the way, the barriers to active sexual agency were dropping. A waitress in her mid-thirties described the initiative she took:

> What changed our sex life was that a bunch of us girls on the same block started reading books and passing them around—everything from how-to-do-it sex books to real porno paperbacks. Some of the men said that the stuff was garbage, but I can tell you that my husband was always ready to try out anything. . . . Some of it was great, some was awful . . . and some was just funny, like the honey business.

Another woman, married to a blue-collar worker, had him buy sex manuals to spice up their love life. "We found all different ways of caressing and different positions, and it was very nice because we realized that these things weren't dirty," she explained. "Like I could say to my husband 'Around the world in eighty days!' and he'd laugh and we'd really go at it." Moreover, much of the literature written in the 1970s, such as *The Hite Report* and Nancy Friday's *My Secret Garden,* presented sex from women's vantage point. The emphasis in these works shifted from simultaneous orgasm through intercourse to forms of pleasuring suitable for women, or what one commentator called "separate but equal orgasms." Thus, even the supposedly immutable "sex act" underwent redefinition in ways that weakened a male monopoly over the nature of sex.[21]

As couples experimented with different techniques of lovemaking, the erotic became a vehicle for exploring new realms of intimacy and power. Some men enjoyed the sensation that came from knowing they were satisfying their partners. "The whole process [of oral sex] makes me feel good about myself," said one husband. "I take serious pride in being a good lover and satisfying my partner, giving her pleasure." A businesswoman remarked that "I like oral sex very much because it is extremely intimate and I'm moved by it as an act of intimacy." For some women, oral sex evoked feelings of power. "I do feel powerful when he does it. I feel quite powerful," said one. "Sort of the Amazon mentality—all-powerful woman." Another experienced similar emotions when performing fellatio. "I'm exerting power. I'm rewarding him," she commented. "The giving of pleasure is a powerful position, and the giving of oral sex is a real, real gift of pleasure."[22]

The cultural validation of erotic pleasure also contributed to a historic shift in expectations. Among earlier generations, men and women had found themselves at odds about the frequency of sex in marriage. At the turn of the century, at least among the white middle class, many women submitted to their husbands' desires; by midcentury, many men felt themselves sexually deprived. But a survey of couples conducted in the late 1970s found virtual agreement among men and women about sexual satisfaction and frequency. Eighty-nine percent of married men and women who had sex three or more times a week expressed contentment with their sex life; among those who had sex once a week or less, the figure dropped to fifty-three percent for each gender. The responses of unmarried cohabiting couples provided roughly similar findings. Not only were most men and women indicating similar preferences, but they expected relatively high frequencies of sex. According to Blumstein and Schwartz, among all the couples they studied—heterosexual, gay male, and lesbian—"a good sex life is central to a good overall relationship," and infrequent sex provoked discontent with all aspects of the relationship. Even the readers of a mainstream women's magazine such as *Redbook* had incorporated high expectations about sex into their lives. After polling 100,000 women, the editors found that "women are becoming increasingly active sexually and are less likely to accept an unsatisfactory sex life as part of the price to be paid for marriage."[23]

One reason, undoubtedly, for the shifts in heterosexual relationships was the availability of birth control. The dramatic move in the 1960s toward effective contraception continued into the 1970s. By mid-decade three out of four married couples relied on the pill, the IUD, or sterilization.[24] Then, too, the legalization of first-trimester abortions provided a measure of last resort for wives whose contraceptive efforts failed. Though it is difficult to know how great an increase in the incidence of abortion took place in the seventies, the fact that it was medically safe and legal at least removed the dangers that formerly attached to it. The near universality of birth control practices had virtually eliminated the constraints that fears about pregnancy had imposed on the sex life of married women. It also highlighted the degree to which the erotic had been divorced from procreation.

The separation of sex from reproduction also emerged from another quarter. Not only could couples safely have sex without the expectation of conception, but technological innovations were making it possible to have babies without sex. Science was upsetting age-old certainties about the natural connection between sex and procreation. "Remember when there was only one way to make a baby?" an advertisement for a 1979 CBS special report asked. "That was yesterday. Today, nature's role is being challenged by science. Conception without sex. Egg fertilization outside the womb. 'Surrogate' mothers who can bear other couples' children. Frozen embryos stored in 'supermarkets' for future implantation."[25] Among other things, scientific change was allowing lesbian couples to have children, without choosing marriage, through the cooperation of male sperm donors. Public policy added another dimension to technological change, as welfare agencies allowed single women and single men to adopt children, thus emphasizing the distinction between biological and social parenting. Though the new technology would raise some vexing problems of its own, as the controversy over Baby M revealed, people were nonetheless making choices that seemed to confirm that making love and making babies were not the same.

The new visibility that gay life achieved in the 1970s also emphasized the weakened link between procreation and the erotic. Although it is difficult to measure change in this area with any degree of precision, certainly the social life of gay men and lesbians had altered considerably. The many organizations that existed throughout the country allowed greater ease in making friends and acquaintances, and in embarking upon relationships. Less police harassment made it safer for bars to open and stay in operation. Regional music festivals brought thousands of lesbians together for several days of companionship; annual rituals such as the gay pride marches each June became celebrations of community cohesiveness even as they made a political statement. Church attendance, political club membership, and professional caucuses all contributed to a broadening of an identity in which the erotic played a prominent role. But the historic invisibility of gay male and lesbian life makes it impossible to compare the erotic dimension of gay experience from one generation to another. Even in the 1970s there were few studies that moved beyond the impressionism of journalistic observations.

A study that did, the work of Philip Blumstein and Pepper Schwartz, is interesting in part because of the comparison it allows between men and women, and between heterosexuals and homosexuals. The researchers found that a good sexual adjustment was as important to a successful relationship among gay male and lesbian respondents as among heterosexuals, and that the higher the frequency of sex the greater the sense of satisfaction. But lesbians seemed content to have sex less often, and after two years in a relationship, the lesbian couples tended to see a significant decline in the frequency of sex. Young lesbians were more likely to engage in oral sex than were older women, and among all the couples, gay men placed the greatest stock in variety in sexual technique. Lesbians proved very similar to heterosexual men and women in the extent of nonmonogamy—twenty-eight percent of lesbians, twenty-five percent of husbands, and twenty-one percent of wives—whereas for gay men, nonmonogamy was a way of life. Furthermore, among couples that did not practice monogamy male homosexuals tended to have sex with a far larger number of partners. One percent of the lesbians, seven percent of the husbands, but more than two-fifths of the gay men, had sex with more than twenty partners while living with a mate.[26]

Even in an era that witnessed an expansion of erotic opportunities, the experience of some urban gay men appeared to stand outside the norm. When Kinsey undertook his study in the 1940s he found that although male homosexuals on average had sex less frequently than heterosexual men, some of them had far more partners in the course of a lifetime. In the 1970s, as the urban gay subculture became larger and more accessible, the chances for sexual encounters multiplied. Heterosexuals may have had their singles bars where they could meet a partner for an evening of sex, but in large cities, gay bathhouses, bars with back rooms, and stores showing pornographic films allowed gay male patrons to have sex with a series of men in rapid succession. For many, sexual promiscuity became part of the fabric of gay life, an essential element holding the community together. Yet the fact that such sex businesses could operate in the 1970s relatively free of police harassment and that the media could spotlight them in discussions of gay life says as much about heterosexual norms as about those of gay men. In the larger metropolitan areas, male homosexuals were no longer serving as symbols of sexual deviance; their eroticism no longer divided the good from the bad. Heterosexuals sustained a vigorous singles nightlife, and advertised in magazines for partners; suburban couples engaged in mate-swapping; sex clubs were featuring male strippers, with women in the role of voyeur. By the end of the decade, some "straight" men and women were even patronizing a heterosexual equivalent of the gay bathhouse, as the success of places like Plato's Retreat in New York demonstrated. The experience of the urban gay subculture stood as one point along a widened spectrum of sexual possibilities that modern America now offered.

Although it would be foolhardy to deny the depth and breadth of the changes that had occurred by the end of the 1970s, one must also acknowledge the continuities with the past. Blumstein and Schwartz, for instance, found that "there *are* new men and new women, among both heterosexual and homosexual couples, who are dealing with sexual responsibilities in new ways and trying to modify the traditions that their maleness and femaleness bring to their relationships." But they were fewer in number than the pair of sociologists expected to find, and the persistence of tradition was particularly hard for some heterosexual women whose partners proved "less 'liberated' than she—or he—thought he was."[27] Marriages were happier and more intimate than a generation earlier, but partly because so many unhappy ones ended in divorce. In a culture that was coming to identify frequent, pleasurable, varied, and ecstatically satisfying sex as a preeminent sign of personal happiness, the high rate of marital dissolution could easily mean that large numbers of Americans were failing to reach these standards. The differences in the patterns of behavior of gay men and lesbians also pointed to the continuing salience of gender in shaping sexual meanings. Moreover, while lesbians and male homosexuals had carved out some space for themselves in society, the frequency of physical assaults upon visibly gay men and women suggested that their form of nonprocreative sex still provoked outrage. Feminism, too, may have opened new realms of sexual expressiveness for women, but the extent of rape and other forms of male sexual violence still made sex an arena of danger for them. The much-vaunted "sexual revolution," though real in many ways, was hardly complete.

Two issues, in particular, were emerging by the end of the 1970s to suggest the contradictory emotions that still enshrouded sex. Since the advent of penicillin in the 1940s, the threat of venereal disease had, to a significant degree, faded as an inhibitor of nonmonogamous sexual expression. But, in the midst of Americans' recently acquired sexual "freedom," the media spotlighted a new venereal scourge. Herpes, which *Time* magazine labeled "today's scarlet letter" and the "new leprosy," was reaching epidemic proportions among young urban heterosexuals. Though the condition posed far less physical danger than syphilis, it provoked guilt and panic as well as a pulling back from erotic encounters for some. A medical professional reported that "we hear it over and over: I won't have sex again." Among victims, the disease elicited feelings of self-pollution—"you never think you're clean enough," said one. The *Soho Weekly News,* a New York paper popular among young professionals in the city, was moved to proclaim "current sexual practice" as "the real epidemic." For many, the spread of herpes came to symbolize the inherent flaws in an ethic of sexual permissiveness. Pleasure brought retribution; disease became a marker of weak moral character.[28]

Another "epidemic," that of teenage pregnancy, also highlighted ambivalence about the erotic. Although most Americans tended to look benignly upon sex between unmarried adults, the spread of sexual experience among teenagers troubled them. To a large extent, adolescents were pursuing the erotic without the approval or the guidance of their elders. Despite the visibility of sex in the culture, the acquisition of knowledge by the young remained sporadic and haphazard, largely "a private, individually motivated and covert affair," in the opinion of one sex researcher. Some parents felt it was simply wrong, despite their own experience. As one middle-class mother in Muncie had phrased it, "just because it was right for me doesn't make it okay for my kids." A survey of high school youth in the early 1980s found that almost half had learned nothing about sex from their parents. Nor were schools rushing to fill the gap. By the late 1970s only half a dozen states mandated sex education; in most places, curriculum remained up to the local school districts, which generally displayed the same caution or disregard that occurred in the home. In one New York City suburb, a high school principal refused to let the editor of the school paper print an article about birth control methods. A California school district provided sex instruction in conjunction with drivers education, indicating how marginal it was to the academic curriculum. "In order to avoid controversy," according to the authors of *Sex and the American Teenager,* "schools embrace boredom."[29]

The result of this abdication of responsibility by schools and parents was that the young were often left to drift into sexual activity without guidance and with little knowledge. Teenagers whose parents were unwilling to talk with them about sex, or who did not receive sex education in school, were more prone to engage in intercourse. Yet they were also likely to be ignorant of how conception occurred or how to prevent it. Even when schools did provide instruction, they often acted too late. One North Carolina fifteen-year-old learned about condoms in a junior high school class, after he had been having intercourse for two years. "And then I realized, man, I've been taking a lot of chances. Thirteen, fourteen, fifteen . . . Lord's been good to me," he said. Others were not so lucky, as the incidence of teenage pregnancy revealed. In 1976, among the premaritally sexually active, twenty-seven percent of white girls and forty-five percent of blacks had become pregnant by the age of eighteen. Ironically, in view of the laissez-faire stance that adults seemed to take, the young were looking for advice. As Robert Coles and Geoffrey Stokes concluded on the basis of their work with high school students,

> it seems clear from our interviews that some kids who are planning to enter sexual relationships *want* to be told to wait. But those who can't talk to their parents hear either nothing or a ritualized naysaying that has no bearing on their *immediate* situation—and those who can may find their parents unwilling to take the responsibility for saying anything more than "Be careful."[30]

Meanwhile, for those who had made their choice to have sex, accurate information about reproduction, conception, and birth control might at least save them from the tragedy of unwanted pregnancies.

That so many teenage girls were becoming pregnant in an age when reliable contraception was available says much about the contradictions within the sexually permissive culture of the 1960s and 1970s. From everywhere sex beckoned, inciting desire, yet rarely did one find reasoned presentations of the most elementary consequences and responsibilities that sexual activity entailed. Youth had more autonomy from adult supervision than ever before, allowing them to explore the erotic at a time of profound physiological changes, but adults seemed to respond by implicitly drawing a boundary at sexual activity during adolescence. Perhaps one could not stop the young from experimenting, but neither would society endorse their behavior. The result was a social problem of tragic dimensions, one that placed in bold relief the ambivalence of American society toward sex. And, the fact that young girls were left to pay a higher price for sexual activity served as a poignant commentary on the persistence of gender in the structuring of sexuality in the post-liberal era.

The reshaping of sexuality in the 1960s and 1970s was of major proportions. The marketing of sex, new demographic patterns, and the movements of women and homosexuals for equality all fostered a substantial revision in attitudes and behavior. In some ways, the process of sexualization represented pushing the logic of sexual liberalism to its extreme: once sex had been identified as a critical aspect of happiness, how could one justify containing it in marriage? Even before the 1960s, the behavior of youth and the commercial manipulation of the erotic had suggested the vulnerability of the liberal consensus. By the end of the 1970s, it was obvious that the consensus had dissolved. As Americans married later, postponed childbearing, and divorced more often, and as feminists and gay liberationists questioned heterosexual orthodoxy, nonmarital sexuality became commonplace and open. And, all of this took place in a social environment in which erotic imagery was ubiquitous.

The collapse of sexual liberalism did not, however, lead to a new, stable consensus. By the end of the 1970s, conservative proponents of an older sexual order had appeared. Their efforts to stem the tide of change and, indeed, to restore sexuality to a reproductive marital context would demonstrate the continuing power of sex to generate controversy.

CHAPTER 15

The Contemporary Political Crisis

FOR political commentators accustomed to following the byways of post–World War II presidential politics, the 1984 campaign offered an interesting spectacle. Certainly many time-tested issues made their appearance in the course of the year—the strength of the military establishment; the struggle against Communism; taxes and the economy; the continuing fight for racial equality. But there were new dimensions, too. The day before the Democratic convention opened in San Francisco, tens of thousands of homosexuals and lesbians marched through the city to the convention site, with several dozen openly gay delegates to the convention leading the way. When the party adopted its platform later in the week, it condemned the "violent acts of bigotry, hatred, and extremism" aimed at gay men and lesbians, a phenomenon the platform labeled "alarmingly common." Another plank put the party on record as recognizing "reproductive freedom as a fundamental human right." It opposed "government interference in the reproductive decisions of Americans" and declared that "a woman has a right to choose whether and when to have a child."[1] Though the platform avoided any mention of abortion, Geraldine Ferraro, the Democratic nominee for vice president, spent much of the campaign verbally dueling with the Roman Catholic hierarchy which condemned her defense of women's right to have abortion as an option.

Meanwhile, Ronald Reagan, who was running for reelection, returned to issues of sexuality again and again. During the spring primary season, he told the National Association of Evangelicals that America was losing "her religious and moral bearings." Pornography, once hidden, was now available "in virtually every drugstore in the land." Liberals, he charged, "viewed promiscuity as acceptable, even stylish. Indeed, the word itself was replaced by the term 'sexually active.' " In the liberal-dominated media, sex was everywhere. What was once "a sacred expression of love" had now become "casual and cheap." Reagan and the Republicans returned to these themes again and again. In August, he assured the publisher of the *Presidential Biblical Scorecard* that he would "resist the efforts of some to obtain government endorsement of homosexuality," and identified the sex act as "the means by which husband and wife participate with God in the creation of a new human life." As if to affirm these views, and in order to position itself against the Democratic call for reproductive freedom, the Republican party adopted a platform plank opposing abortion and endorsing legislation to make clear that "the 14th Amendment's protections apply to unborn children."[2]

For any who doubted, the 1984 presidential season made clear that whatever consensus existed in the mid-twentieth century about sexuality had dissolved by the 1980s. The debates about sex, rather than remaining the province of feminists and gay liberationists, were polarizing the nation's politics. The contentious quality of the debates stemmed not only from the demands of radicals, but also from the response of conservatives distressed by the reorientation of sexual values that had occurred since the 1960s. The sexual politics of the New Right, as well as the more recent controversies generated by the AIDS epidemic, attest to how deeply sexuality had infiltrated national politics by the 1980s.

Sexual Politics and the New Right

The rapid pace of change and the dissolution of the liberal consensus about sexuality encouraged a political response from the right. As the 1970s ended, the latest in a long line of purity movements took shape. Reacting to the gains of both feminism and gay liberation, and distressed by the visibility of the erotic in American culture, sexual conservatives sought the restoration of "traditional" values. In its rhetoric, this contemporary breed of purity advocates echoed its predecessors by attributing to sex the power to corrupt, even to weaken fatally, American society. But in other important ways, its efforts departed from the past. It plunged directly into politics, as religious fundamentalists joined forces with political conservatives to make the Republican party the vehicle for a powerful moral crusade. Availing themselves of modern technology, these New Right proponents used computerized mailing lists, direct-mail fundraising, and telephone banks to reach deeply into the population and mobilize a constituency. By the early 1980s, journalists and political analysts were giving them credit for the turn to conservatism in American life.

Although feminism and gay liberation seemed to spark the resurgence of the purity impulse, the conservative sexual politics of the 1950s had never fully died. Placed on the defensive by the decisions of the liberal Warren Court, groups such as Citizens for Decent Literature struggled on. In the 1960s, much of the battle focused on the issue of sex education in the public schools. Distressed by the court-decreed elimination of school prayer, some conservatives banded together in an effort to draw the line at sex instruction. Toward the end of the decade, the John Birch Society began targeting Mary Calderone, the renowned sex educator. In Racine, Wisconsin; Anaheim, California; Minneapolis, and other places, parents fought to keep discussions of sex out of the classroom. Ronald Reagan, then governor of California, pushed legislation prohibiting required attendance in sex education classes. Calderone's organization, the Sex Information and Education Council of the United States (SIECUS), counted over three hundred organizations opposing sex instruction in the public schools.[3] By the early 1970s, the victories of feminism and gay liberation, the Supreme Court decision on abortion, and the new visibility of pornography were fueling the fears of moral conservatives. From every side, traditional family values and sexual ethics seemed threatened.

Two events in 1977 provided the opportunity to weld scattered efforts around diverse issues into a more militant, cooperative national effort. In Dade County, Florida, passage of a gay rights ordinance led the entertainer Anita Bryant to spearhead a repeal campaign. Bryant's celebrity status propelled this local event into the national spotlight. In the same month as the Florida vote, the Supreme Court ruled that though abortion could not be prohibited, government had no constitutional obligation to fund the medical procedure. The decision gave abortion foes hope, as well as a tactic they could use to chip away at the availability of abortion.

Since the early 1970s, an important item on the gay movement's agenda had been the extension of civil rights statutes to include provisions prohibiting discrimination on the basis of sexual orientation. Activists devoted much of their energy to securing passage of municipal and county ordinances as a foundation for later efforts at the state and national level. By 1977, they had achieved upward of three dozen victories, of which the law in populous Dade County was one. But, for the first time, they encountered an outspoken opposition, ready to fight back, in Florida. Anita Bryant, who led the campaign to repeal the law, was a foe to reckon with. A former Miss Oklahoma and a popular singer in middle America, she remained in the public eye through her commercials for Minute Maid orange juice, where she projected an attractive, motherly wholesomeness. Bryant was outraged that local legislators had seemed to endorse the lifestyle of homosexuals, whom she described as "human garbage."[4] With the aid of her business-manager husband, she formed Save Our Children, Inc., and succeeded in placing a repeal initiative on the ballot.

From the start, the rhetoric of the campaign was overblown and appealed to people's most irrational fears. Bryant and her cohorts made the safety of children the centerpiece of the campaign. "They can only recruit children, and this is what they want to do," she warned Dade County parents. "Some of the stories I could tell you of child recruitment and child abuse by homosexuals would turn your stomach." George Will, the conservative columnist, saw the Miami ordinance as one more step in "the moral disarmament of society," with the right of homosexuals to marry coming next. In a foreshadowing of the direction the purity movement would take, Protestant fundamentalist ministers assumed a highly visible role. A local evangelist told reporters that "homosexuality is a sin so rotten, so low, so dirty that even cats and dogs don't practice it." Jerry Falwell, a Baptist preacher from Lynchburg, Virginia, and soon to become a national figure, flew in to help the repeal forces. "So-called gay folks," he intoned, would "just as soon kill you as look at you." Backed by the Catholic hierarchy, conservative rabbis, and Miami's daily newspapers, the Bryant campaign won a resounding victory as voters rejected the ordinance by a two-to-one majority.[5]

The media publicity that the Dade County battle received guaranteed that its influence would extend beyond its locale. Over the next year, conservatives mounted similar campaigns in St. Paul, Wichita, and Eugene, Oregon; in each case, citizens defeated gay rights in overwhelming proportions. In California, lesbians and gay men faced an even more serious threat. There, inspired by Bryant's success, an ultraconservative state senator from the Los Angeles suburbs, John Briggs, succeeded in placing an anti-gay measure on the state ballot. The Briggs initiative authorized school systems to fire gay employees, as well as anyone who publicly or privately advocated or encouraged homosexual conduct. Throughout 1978, the gay communities in San Francisco, Los Angeles, and other cities put together a well-organized grass-roots campaign against the measure. Winning the support of labor unions protective of their members' jobs, large-circulation newspapers in the state, and even conservative politicians like Ronald Reagan, who objected to the constraints on free speech, gay activists succeeded in defeating the initiative. Yet even this victory turned sour. Less than three weeks after the November vote, Dan White, a local San Francisco politician, assassinated George Moscone, the mayor, and Harvey Milk, the city's only openly gay supervisor. Milk had assumed a highly visible role in the anti-Briggs campaign. His murder, at the hands of a man who was a veteran, ex-cop, and former firefighter, who had espoused traditional family values and a conservative moral politics, seemed to symbolize the fragility of the gay community's gains.[6]

Meanwhile, a movement to curtail the right of women to choose abortion was developing. For Americans who objected to abortion, the Supreme Court's *Roe* decision in 1973 had appeared as a "bolt from the blue," catching them off-guard and unprepared. Though local anti-abortion groups formed almost immediately, the Court's ruling seemed clear and incontrovertible, leaving little room for action. Then, in 1976, Representative Henry Hyde of Illinois succeeded in attaching a rider to an appropriations bill, prohibiting the use of federal dollars to fund abortions. The next year, the Supreme Court ruled that government had the authority to bar the financing of abortion with tax dollars. Congress responded with alacrity, and by 1978, the number of federally funded abortions had fallen from 295,000 to 3,000. States, too, cut back on their coverage; by the summer of 1979, only nine states still paid for abortions. Though the constitutional right to abortion remained intact, anti-abortion forces had succeeded in sharply restricting the access that poor women had to it.[7]

The victory over funding also spurred the movement forward. Local groups became part of national organizations such as March for Life and the National Right-to-Life Committee. They registered voters and made abortion the litmus test of political acceptability, campaigning against candidates based on the single issue of abortion. As Nellie Grey, of March for Life, explained, "on a fundamental issue, you can't strike a bargain. You are either for killing babies or you're not. You can't be for a little bit of killing babies."[8] Anti-abortionists such as Dr. C. Everett Koop, who later became the Surgeon General under Reagan, toured the country with films that likened abortion to the Holocaust. Soon the inflamed passions of the anti-abortion movement were having more than rhetorical expression. By the end of the 1970s, clinics performing abortions were being torched and bombed across the country.

The involvement of purity advocates in politics, whether to defeat gay rights, restrict abortion, or curtail the spread of pornography, held an irresistible allure for traditional conservatives. During the 1970s, a new set of right-wing organizations came into existence, determined to turn back the liberal social-welfare policies of the 1960s and to reverse the retrenchment of America's role in the world. Groups such as the Conservative Caucus, headed by Howard Phillips, the Committee for the Survival of a Free Congress, led by Paul Weyrich, and the National Conservative Political Action Committee, chaired by Terry Dolan, saw the discontent spawned by sexual issues as a force that could propel their politics into power. In commenting on the potential of the alliance, Richard Viguerie, the editor of the *Conservative Digest* and a pioneer in direct-mail fundraising techniques, noted that "if abortion remains an issue, and we keep picking liberals off, this movement could completely change the face of Congress." Paul Weyrich, too, saw issues of sexuality and family life as "the Achilles' heel of the liberal Democrats." In 1979, Phillips and Weyrich helped persuade Jerry Falwell, whose television program *The Old Time Gospel Hour* reached 18 million viewers weekly, to form the Moral

Majority as a vehicle to mobilize the fundamentalist population. They also established the Religious Roundtable to bring together conservative politicians and influential television preachers such as Falwell, Pat Robertson, Jim Bakker, James Robison, and others.[9]

This religion-based New Right exploded into the nation's consciousness during the 1980 presidential campaign. While Jimmy Carter, a self-avowed born-again Christian, remained aloof from it, Ronald Reagan actively courted the fundamentalist vote, and appeared openly sympathetic to the New Right's position on abortion, school prayer, and pornography. His fervid Cold War rhetoric also appealed to preachers who feared a "godless" Communism. Reagan addressed a national convention of religious broadcasters. In return, evangelists appealed to their congregations and their television viewers to vote for righteousness. Falwell, whose Moral Majority had already enrolled seventy-two thousand ministers and four million lay members, castigated the "minority of secular humanists and amoralists [who] are running this country and taking it straight to hell." He warned the nation's liberals that "the moralists in America have had enough. [We] are joining hands together for the changing, the rejuvenating of a nation." James Robison, a Fort Worth television preacher, even appropriated the language of gay liberation in his appeals. "It's time for God's people to come out of the closet and the churches—and change America."[10] After Reagan won by a landslide and Republicans captured control of the Senate, many political commentators were quick to attribute an almost invincible power to the moralistic politics of the New Right.

When the new Congress reconvened in 1981, the assessment of the media and the worst fears of feminists and gay liberationists seemed ready to be confirmed. Despite their rhetorical opposition to big government, conservatives were prepared to sanction state intervention in issues of sexual morality and family life. In short order, Senator Jesse Helms of North Carolina and Representative Hyde introduced a bill that defined life as beginning at conception, and hence made abortion equivalent to murder. Another anti-abortion politician, Representative Robert Dornan of California, presented to the House a constitutional amendment that identified life as beginning when the sperm fertilizes the ovum, thus including the birth control pill and the IUD as potential abortifacients. Republican conservatives also resurrected the Family Protection Act, which had died an unceremonious death during the Carter presidency. Its thirty-six provisions included one that prohibited federal funds for schools whose curriculum "would tend to denigrate, diminish or deny the role differences between the sexes as they have been historically understood in the United States," and another that denied government benefits, including social security, to anyone who presented homosexuality "as an acceptable alternative life style or suggests that it can be an acceptable life style." Meanwhile, religious leaders kept up the impassioned rhetoric. Falwell aroused his supporters by declaring, "we are fighting a holy war and this time we are going to win." His frequent appeals for funds—by 1981 he was raising over a million dollars a week—enticed contributions with questions such as, "Do you approve of known practicing homosexuals teaching in public schools?" Through its political agenda, the New Right appeared intent on restoring sex to its reproductive moorings and safely confining it to the family.[11]

Despite their apparent power, the purity crusaders of the 1980s made only limited gains at the national level. Although abortion debates proved rancorous, consuming much of the time of Congress, no further restrictions were passed into law. Issues such as abortion or school prayer were too unpredictable, and too threatening to Republican unity, for the Reagan administration to pay much more than lip service to them. Instead, Reagan devoted his energy to expanding the nation's military establishment and dismantling liberal social-welfare programs. Some sops were thrown to the New Right. In 1985, Attorney General Edwin Meese established a commission on pornography that toured the country intent on exposing the social harm allegedly caused by explicit sexual materials. Its 1,960-page report, replete with an alphabetical listing of magazines, films, and books ranging from *A Cock Between Friends* to *69 Munching Lesbians,* reached the conclusion that pornography caused violence and irreparable damage to society. Its exclusion of social scientific evidence to the contrary, and the fact that law-enforcement agents and vice-squad officers comprised the largest group of witnesses, probably made the outcome foreordained.[12] Of greater significance, Reagan also tended to appoint to the federal judiciary men and women sympathetic to the New Right. The five-to-four 1986 Supreme Court decision in *Bowers v. Hardwick* that sustained the constitutionality of sodomy laws directed against homosexuals was, perhaps, a harbinger of things to come.

On a local level, meanwhile, purity crusaders more easily flexed their political muscles. School districts throughout the nation faced increasing surveillance from parents angry over sex education classes or the novels that students were asked to read. In Chicago in 1986, the actions of the Roman Catholic hierarchy succeeded in defeating a gay rights ordinance, the passage of which had seemed certain until church leaders spoke up. An Atlanta campaign against adult theaters and bookstores reduced the numbers of such establishments from forty-four in the late seventies to a mere handful by 1981. North Carolina legislators enacted a new, tougher pornography law that allowed police to seize materials and make arrests without a prior order from the courts. When the law went into effect in October 1985, legitimate bookstores and convenience markets quickly pulled *Playboy* and *Penthouse* from the shelves. Though New Right forces could not apparently return the nation to an earlier era of sexual reticence, they did seem to be setting outer limits for sexual permissiveness.

The effort to contain pornography reveals how complex the alignments over sexual issues had become. A major focus of feminist energy in the 1970s had been efforts to combat sexual violence—rape, harassment, wife battering, and incest. Whether these phenomena had increased in scope, or feminist campaigns had simply brought them to light, is impossible to determine. But, the eruption of pornographic imagery into the public sphere seemed like the last straw for activists who daily encountered the victims of violence. In Los Angeles, feminists protested the display of a billboard for a record album that depicted a woman bound by ropes alongside the slogan "I'm 'Black and Blue' for the Rolling Stones." In a number of cities local feminists picked up the cue. At first the issue they dramatized was the association of sex with violence, whether in pornography or the mainstream media. But, before long, they telescoped the problem into a single-minded preoccupation with pornography. Organizations such as Women Against Pornography put together slide shows aimed at exposing the brutalizing fantasies that some hard-core materials purveyed, and their members conducted tours of the porn districts that had sprung up in the early 1970s. Anti-porn feminists subscribed to the dictum "pornography is the theory, rape is the practice." Andrea Dworkin, a leading theorist of the cause, attributed the explosion of pornography to fears of feminist power. "All over this country," she said, "a new campaign of terrorism and vilification is being waged against us. Fascist propaganda celebrating sexual violence against women is sweeping this land. . . . Pornography is the propaganda of sexual terrorism." By the early 1980s Dworkin and feminist lawyer Catharine MacKinnon were drafting their own model obscenity statutes, which defined pornography as a violation of women's civil rights, and they found themselves in political alliance with the New Right in Indianapolis and Suffolk County, New York, and other places where the anti-pornography impulse was strong. Some anti-porn feminists were also witnesses before the Meese commission, urging it to take a tough stand against sexually explicit materials.[13]

Other feminists, meanwhile, bristled at the potential for censorship contained in the anti-porn movement and at the dangers that this unexpected alliance posed to women's exploration of the erotic. Ellen Willis, who had helped launch women's liberation in New York City, acknowledged that pornography could be a "psychic assault," but that "for women as for men it can also be a source of erotic pleasure." For a woman to enjoy pornography, she wrote, "is less to collaborate in her oppression than to defy it, to insist on an aspect of her sexuality that has been defined as a male preserve. . . . [I]n rejecting sexual repression and hypocrisy—which have inflicted even more damage on women than on men—[pornography] expresses a radical impulse." Willis attacked the "goody-goody" concept of sexuality that anti-porn activists espoused as "not feminist but feminine." It preserved, she argued, the old "good girl–bad girl" dichotomy that denied most women access to erotic pleasure and adventure. Dismayed by the political alliance that anti-porn feminists seemed to be making with right-wing purity crusaders, some women formed groups such as the Feminist Anti-Censorship Task Force to resist any move toward stricter obscenity laws. Within feminist circles, the 1980s witnessed renewed debates over the meaning of sexuality. Activists dissected its dual nature as a source, in the words of one feminist anthology, of both "pleasure and danger" to women.[14]

Despite the strange alliance over pornography, most ideologues of the Christian-based purity crusade identified feminism and gay liberation as the evils they were organizing against. Yet the reasons for the New Right's rapid growth was both more and less than the existence of radical movements for sexual liberation. Much of the strength of the New Right came from communities that had never encountered an open homosexual and certainly never sheltered a gay bathhouse. Many fundamentalists also moved in a relatively self-contained social milieu in which women remained housewives and mothers, and youth socialized at church-sponsored events. Yet, they could not stay unaware of the vast social changes that were sweeping the nation—the rise in divorce, the entry of women into the work force, the openness of urban gay male subcultures, the commercialization of sex, and the sexualization of commerce. Especially for some women—those for whom mothering was a central task, who did not work for wages, and who remained religiously devout—the values of the post-liberal era seemed to attack the very source of their self-worth. At times, New Right leaders acknowledged that they were attacking not merely a clearly delineated opposition such as gay liberation, but something more amorphous and widespread. Falwell, for instance, in lambasting pornography, called network television "the greatest vehicle being used to indoctrinate us slowly to accept a pornographic view of life. Pornography is more than a nudey magazine," he said. "It is a prevailing atmosphere of sexual license."[15] In an era when much of mainstream culture was promoting the erotic, little wonder that moral conservatives responded with fury.

At the same time, the New Right also had its own well-defined symbolic concern that brought its diffuse anxieties together. Whatever the issue—abortion or the Equal Rights Amendment, gay liberation or pornography, sex education or the lyrics of rock music—the sexuality of youth served as the unifying element in its campaigns. Opponents of the purity forces often missed this, instead seeing the New Right through the issues they felt most passionate about, such as gender equality, the dismantling of homosexual oppression, or the protection of civil liberties. But beneath the specific campaigns, the behavior of youth emerged again and again as the central focus of the New Right. Its attacks on pornography, for instance, first took shape around the issue of "kiddie-porn," which easily became the object of new legislation. In mobilizing their forces, Anita Bryant and other gay rights antagonists repeatedly raised the phantom of child recruitment. Faced with an epidemic of pregnant teenagers, parents targeted the schools, not because of a failure to provide the instruction that might allow the young to have sex safely, but because the schools were allegedly giving adolescents too much information. Even issues such as abortion and the ERA, so central to the feminist agenda for women's equality, resonated with concerns about the young. A right-to-life activist in California, for example, saw abortion as one part of a larger problem of youthful sexual expression:

> I don't think we would have as many sexually active teenagers, first of all, if contraception weren't readily available and acceptable. . . . There's more of a temptation to participate in sex than we had when we were young . . . because you just knew that if you were sexually active you might well get pregnant.

A leader of the anti-ERA forces in New York State also turned to the young in explaining her involvement in politics. "For one thing, it would allow gays to marry and adopt children," she said. "If anything ever happened to me, I don't want to think that gays could adopt my children."[16]

Fears about the sexual behavior of youth give the contemporary purity crusade the historical specificity one would expect to find in a social movement. For of all the changes in sexual mores that occurred in the 1960s and 1970s, the spread of sexual activity among the young marked the sharpest break with the past. Certainly some male youth had found sexual release in earlier eras, whether through masturbation or with prostitutes. And, in the mid-twentieth century, young women found sexual expressiveness open to them in the context of romance and approaching marriage. But the values and patterns of behavior that had emerged by the 1970s were different. Youth engaged not just in occasional experimentation, nor did they have sex only in the context of a marriage-oriented relationship. The erotic became incorporated as a regular, ongoing feature of their maturation. The visibility of sex in American culture gave them a familiarity with sex and an interest in it regardless of their parents' wishes. The lyrics of the songs they listened to and danced to—"Let's spend the night together" or "I want a man with a slow hand," to name just two—incited desire as well as suggested possibilities. That many of them would not marry until well into their twenties, and that cohabitation was an acceptable option, made the marriage-oriented ethic of sexual liberalism increasingly irrelevant to their lives. It was the ability and willingness of youth to explore the erotic that most signaled the passing of sexual liberalism. It also imparted emotional power to a purity crusade that attacked all the manifestations of the post-liberal era and that sought the restoration of a marriage-based sexual system replete with gendered and reproductive meanings.

The AIDS Crisis

While the New Right vigorously pursued political solutions to the new sexual permissiveness, an argument for retrenchment came from another, unexpected quarter. In 1980 and 1981, a few doctors in Los Angeles, San Francisco, and New York began encountering puzzling medical phenomena. Young homosexual men in the prime of life were dying suddenly from a rare pneumonia, pneumocystis carinii, or wasting away from an unusual cancer, Kaposi's sarcoma, that normally attacked older men of Mediterranean ancestry who recovered from the disease. By the summer of 1981 it became clear to these doctors, as well as to the Centers for Disease Control in Atlanta, that a devastating new disease syndrome had entered the annals of medicine. Acquired Immune Deficiency Syndrome (AIDS), as it was labeled, destroyed the body's natural defenses against infection, making the victim susceptible to a host of opportunistic infections which the body seemed incapable of resisting. Unlike other recent new illnesses, such as Legionnaire's Disease or Toxic Shock Syndrome, from which most patients recovered, AIDS had no cure. The immune system did not return to normal, and the mortality rate was frighteningly high. Moreover, the case load grew at an alarming pace: 225 at the end of 1981, 1,400 by the spring of 1983, 15,000 in the summer of 1985, and 40,000 two years later.

AIDS revealed how tenuous the progress of gay liberation had been. Because the initial victims in the United States were gay men, and because a majority of the total cases remained within the male homosexual population, AIDS gave those who were hostile, or even ambivalent, toward homosexuality the opportunity to vent their spleen. The New Right quickly recognized AIDS as a vehicle to whip up hysteria and move its political agenda forward. Evangelists proclaimed the disease a just retribution from God. Falwell piously announced that "a man reaps what he sows. If he sows seed in the field of his lower nature, he will reap from it a harvest of corruption." One cover of his *Moral Majority Report* pictured a white family wearing masks under the headline "Homosexual Diseases Threaten American Families."[17] In Dallas, a group of physicians formed Dallas Doctors Against AIDS and filed a brief on behalf of a court appeal to restore the state's sodomy statute. In Washington, New Right politicians floated proposals to quarantine carriers and high-risk groups, raising the specter of concentration camps for gay men. The military imposed mandatory testing for the presence of antibodies to the virus believed to induce AIDS, while Congress enacted legislation requiring the test for all immigrants. Both measures involved areas where gay activists had sought relief from discriminatory policies, and thus they transformed the disease into a new weapon to preserve inequality. Even liberal magazines ran stories titled "The Gay Plague." Profiles of the initial victims led doctors to speculate that AIDS was a by-product of contemporary gay male life, a result of sexual promiscuity and "fast-lane" living.

As the medical establishment searched for explanations, some of the mystery dissolved. In France in 1983, and in the United States soon thereafter, researchers isolated a virus that was apparently the culprit. AIDS was infectious rather than contagious. The virus could not be transmitted casually, but seemed to require the exchange of bodily fluids—blood or semen—between one person and another. Rather than a "homosexual disease," it was apparently a quirk that in the United States AIDS first manifested itself among gay men. But once present in that population, it could be passed from partner to partner through anal or oral sex, with the dense web of sexual relationships in the gay male subculture allowing for its rapid spread. Moreover it soon became clear that gay men were not the only high-risk group. Intravenous drug users, whose sharing of needles allowed blood to pass from one to another, accounted for a significant minority of AIDS cases. The virus could also be transmitted through sexual contact from men to women, and from pregnant mothers infected with the virus to their newborn infants. Indeed, by 1986, much media coverage focused on the alleged dangers of the disease spreading quickly through the heterosexual population.

For the gay male community, AIDS provoked fear, anguish, and soul-searching, as well as an upsurge of organization and political involvement. As the case load mounted, the disease moved beyond large gay centers such as New York, San Francisco, and Los Angeles, to cities and towns throughout the nation. Death and dying became endemic, as young men found friends and lovers taken ill, with no prospect of recovery. Initial lack of knowledge about how the disease was transmitted, and the mounting evidence of a long incubation period, made many wonder if they were already harboring the condition in a latent stage. Gay men woke in the morning to check their bodies for the appearance of lesions that signaled Kaposi's sarcoma. The common cold or flu triggered worries about the onset of pneumonia. For some, the fact of AIDS called into question the viability of a nonmonogamous gay male life. As one person with AIDS ruefully commented, "the belief that was handed to me was that sex was liberating and more sex was more liberating." AIDS seemed to be a cruel outcome of the freedom that gay liberation promised. It also shook the pride and confidence that the 1970s had gradually built. "The psychologi-

cal impact of AIDS on the gay community is tremendous," said Richard
Failla, an openly gay judge in New York City. "It has done more to undermine
the feelings of self-esteem than anything Anita Bryant could have ever done.
Some people are saying 'Maybe we *are* wrong—maybe this is a punishment.'"[18]
In some cities, activists bitterly fought among themselves over whether gay
bathhouses should be closed as a threat to survival or kept open as a hard-won
community institution. As with herpes a few years earlier, a dread disease
brought an undercurrent of guilt to the surface, transforming a medical condition into a moral commentary.

On the other hand, the gay community also responded to the AIDS crisis
with an enormous outpouring of energy and determination. In New York City,
the Gay Men's Health Crisis formed in 1981, at the very start of the epidemic.
It drew in thousands of volunteers to help care for the sick and dying, raised
millions of dollars for education and research, and lobbied for state and federal
research money to unravel the mystery of the disease and find a cure. In city
after city where cases appeared, the gay community mounted similar efforts.
Formerly apolitical gay men found themselves furious at the callousness of the
Reagan administration, whose tepid response to the epidemic suggested a
cavalier disregard for the lives of homosexuals. For some, the mobilization of
the community in the face of the AIDS crisis promised a return of sorts to the
idealism and solidarity of the Stonewall era. "I haven't experienced this kind
of caring since the early days of gay liberation," said one GLF activist from
the early seventies.[19] It also led to a profound re-examination of issues of sexual
behavior and intimacy. AIDS organizations widely publicized "safe-sex"
guidelines to cut the risk of transmission. In New York and San Francisco,
where AIDS hit first and ravaged the community most severely, the impact
of the campaigns in reshaping gay male sexuality could be seen in the large
decline in the incidence of other sexually transmitted diseases such as syphilis
and gonorrhea. Men used condoms for anal sex, reduced sharply the number
of sexual partners they had, and learned to enjoy practices such as mutual
masturbation. Business at gay bathhouses that did remain open fell dramatically. Observers within the community pointed to a new emphasis on dating,
romance, and monogamous relationships. One study of urban gay males found
that between 1984 and 1987 the proportion who were celibate rose from two
to twelve percent, while those in a monogamous partnership jumped from
twelve to twenty-eight percent.[20] The group in the population that had most
symbolized the new sexual contours of the post-liberal era was cutting another
path.

By the mid-1980s it was also evident that the fear of AIDS was beginning
to reach into the heterosexual population. For a generation raised with penicillin and antibiotics, the long historical association of sexual promiscuity with

disease had faded as an inhibitor of behavior. Then, at the start of the 1980s, the media gave play to the prevalence of genital herpes. AIDS added a lethal dimension to the disease problem. Especially as it became clear that AIDS could be transmitted through heterosexual intercourse, and after the death of Rock Hudson made AIDS a household word, many heterosexuals took stock of their own sexual habits. On college campuses, health administrators made AIDS a prime focus of their educational efforts. The director of the health service at the University of Southern California thought that students seemed "less willing to have casual encounters than they were four or five years ago." Many universities reported a sharp decline in the cases of venereal disease on campus. Trust and intimacy loomed larger as factors in a sexual relationship, particularly perhaps for women. As one female graduate student phrased her concerns, "it is no longer a question of just you yourself. It's now a question of the commitment of the person with whom you're involved. If he switch-hits, or if he ever has in the last three or four years, it could be a real problem."[21]

As the case load mounted, the potential ramifications of AIDS for reshaping American sexuality spread. Issues as diverse as teenage pregnancy, sex education, and the presentation of sexual behavior in the media were swept up in the vortex created by AIDS. New, and sometimes unexpected, political alignments formed. The Reagan administration, led by Secretary of Education William Bennett, latched onto the crisis as an opportunity to promulgate a new chastity message among the nation's youth. One federally financed pamphlet, *Sex Respect,* encouraged teenagers to "just say no." But Reagan's Surgeon General, Everett Koop, who a few years earlier had been a prominent anti-abortion activist, dissented vigorously and urged comprehensive sex education in the schools, including the information that condoms were effective in fore-stalling the spread of the virus. Organizations working on the issue of teenage pregnancy found that AIDS was opening doors previously closed to them. Marian Wright Edelman, founder and president of the Children's Defense Fund, reported that the new sense of urgency created by the epidemic was accomplishing "what one million teenage pregnancies couldn't do: get us talking about sex. . . . People who were tongue-tied realize that they must address something that is lethal."[22] On some campuses students campaigned to have condom vending machines installed in dormitories. Remaining taboos in the media fell. Some network affiliates began accepting ads for condoms, prime-time series addressed the issues of birth control and "safe sex," and news anchors found themselves speaking of anal intercourse before millions of viewers.

Although the political activity of the New Right and the threat of AIDS seemed to augur a retrenchment in the behavior of many Americans, as the

1980s drew to a close it was not at all clear what the future would bring. Certainly the outcome of current controversies about sex would have to build upon the complicated set of sexual meanings that had evolved over generations. For instance, in seeking a restoration of sexuality to marriage, replete with reproductive consequences, advocates of the new chastity had to contend with the permeation of the erotic throughout American culture, the expansive and varied roles available to American women, and a contraceptive technology that sustained the nonprocreative meanings of sexual behavior. A new sexual system that harkened back to a vanished world could not simply be wished into existence.

What the current crisis over AIDS and the new conservatism does allow us to do, however, is to take stock of some of the recurring themes that have emerged in the history of sexuality we have surveyed in these chapters. For almost two centuries sexuality had been moving into the marketplace. At first largely restricted to prostitution and located in a marginal urban underworld out of view of the middle class, sex gradually became the province of big-time entrepreneurs and pervaded the entire culture. The concert saloons of the nineteenth century and the dance halls of the Progressive era were the prototypes of the elaborate high-tech disco; the titillating postcards and one-reelers of the turn of the century were but pale forerunners of the glossy sex magazines and feature-length video cassettes of the 1980s. However, not only did modern capitalism sell sexual fantasies and pleasures as commodities, but the dynamics of a consumer-oriented economy had also packaged many products in sexual wrappings. The commercialization of sex and the sexualization of commerce placed the weight of capitalist institutions on the side of a visible public presence for the erotic. Political movements based on sexual issues alone, whether of the right or the left, faced huge obstacles in their efforts to alter this trend, unless they tackled other issues as well. Sex was too deeply embedded in the fabric of economic life for a purity movement to reshape its meaning in fundamental ways. Exploitable as it was for profit, sex had become resistant to efforts at containment that failed to address this larger economic matrix. And, for movements such as feminism and gay liberation that attacked the manipulation of sexuality to sustain social inequality, systems of gender relations as well as economic structures required revision if activists were to achieve their goals.

The contemporary debates over sex also highlight the continuing efforts of Americans to define a place for sex in their lives. The colonial era was the least problematic, with its clear meanings and boundaries and its pervasive methods of regulation. But, at least since the early nineteenth century, when the reproductive moorings of sexual relations came loose for the urban middle class, many Americans have had to grapple, in a self-conscious way, with the meaning and purpose of sexual relations. Spiritual union, emotional satisfaction, individual identity: these and other definitions have competed for hegemony. For much of the nineteenth and twentieth centuries, the values of the white, native-born urban middle class placed a premium on sexual expression within the context of marriage, even as working-class youth, blacks, an emergent gay community, and others pursued alternative sexual ethics. As the dominant middle-class culture has come to attach more value to sexual fulfillment and pleasure, preserving marriage as a privileged site for sexual expression has proven more difficult. Then, too, the easy availability of effective methods of birth control has removed much of the danger that once attached to nonmarital heterosexuality. And, as women have moved out of the home and into the labor market, their interest in keeping sex within a marital context has declined. The contrast between feminists of the nineteenth and twentieth centuries is instructive in this regard. Whereas the former saw contraception as encouraging male sexual license and therefore opposed it, contemporary feminists have championed a full range of reproductive choice for women so that they might have autonomy in sexual matters.

The search for meaning has itself been shaped by the changing forms of economic life and social institutions. The once self-contained farming communities of the colonial era, in which parents maintained control over youth and families existed within a dense web of community ties, have long given way to a complex mass society. Families are left to fend for themselves and, increasingly, the individual has become the economic and social unit of society. Though not free of agencies of regulation, the individual has more autonomy than ever before to make choices about "personal life." And the range of choices is wider than in the past. A permanent monogamous partnership is one, but so is serial monogamy, homosexual identity, singles life, cohabitation, and unmarried motherhood. Were the choices not so varied, the possibility of AIDS spreading through the population would be too remote to evoke such deep concern.

Contemporary events also illustrate the continuing power of sex as a symbol capable of arousing deep, irrational fears. In the nineteenth and early twentieth centuries, female purity most often served as the symbol that mobilized social anxieties, as campaigns against prostitution and the hysteria over white slavery demonstrated. In the South it combined with fears about racial amalgamation to maintain a rigid caste system of race relations. Today, female purity has lost much of its symbolic force. But the response to AIDS certainly proves the ease with which sexual issues can unleash the irrational. And, despite the openness of nonmarital sex in contemporary culture, a public sexual misstep by a political leader can provoke outrage and lead to one's downfall. Gary Hart's fortunes fell much more quickly than did Nixon's in the face of Watergate or Reagan's in the wake of the Iran-Contra scandal.

Finally, the AIDS epidemic and the politics it spawned emphasize the persistence of sexuality as a vehicle for social control. The mythology about blacks propagated by slave owners, the nineteenth-century medical campaigns against abortion, the nativist implications of the white slavery scare, the wave of lynchings in the South, the Cold War preoccupation with homosexuality: these and other episodes demonstrate how commonly sexuality has fostered the maintenance of social hierarchies. The response to AIDS continued this long historical tradition. Gay activists attacked the slow response of the Reagan administration as a sign of how little value it placed on gay lives. The reluctance of government agencies to fund safe-sex campaigns and to provide intravenous drug users with sterilized needles as parts of a comprehensive prevention program allowed the disease to keep spreading not only through the gay male community but also among inner-city black and Hispanic populations where drug use is a serious problem. As in the past, state legislatures targeted prostitutes rather than male customers even though female-to-male transmission of AIDS is much less likely than the reverse. The unwillingness of conservative moralists to make birth control and safe-sex information available to sexually active youth not only perpetuated teenage pregnancy but now threatened the lives of some of the young. Power over sex is the power to affect the life and death of Americans.

Whatever the outcome of the current crisis over sexuality, Americans will have to take account of the legacy of three centuries of sexual change. Birth control is so embedded in social life that a purely reproductive matrix for sex is no longer even remotely possible. Women's role in the family and the public realm has altered so profoundly that a gender-based system resting on female purity is not likely to be resurrected. The capitalist seizure of sexuality has destroyed the division between public reticence and private actions that the nineteenth-century middle class sought to maintain. Perhaps what the study of America's history allows us to say with assurance is that sexuality has become central to our economy, our psyches, and our politics. For this reason, it is likely to stay vulnerable to manipulation as a symbol of social problems and the subject of efforts to maintain social hierarchies. As in the past, sex will remain a source of both deep personal meaning and heated political controversy.

Notes

Introduction

1. John Gagnon and William Simon, *Sexual Conduct: The Social Sources of Human Sexuality* (Chicago, 1973).

2. For reviews of earlier literature, see Estelle B. Freedman, "Sexuality in Nineteenth-Century America: Behavior, Ideology and Politics," *Reviews in American History* 10 (December 1982), pp. 196–215.

3. Edmund S. Morgan, "The Puritans and Sex," *New England Quarterly* 25 (December 1942), pp. 591–607; Stephen Marcus, *The Other Victorians: A Study of Sexuality and Pornography in Mid-Nineteenth-Century England* (New York, 1966); Carl Degler, "What Ought to Be and What Was: Women's Sexuality in the Nineteenth Century," *American Historical Review* 79 (December 1974), pp. 1467–90, and *At Odds: Women and the Family in America from the Revolution to the Present* (New York, 1980); Peter Gay, *The Bourgeois Experience, Victoria to Freud* (New York, 1984), vol. 1, *The Education of the Senses;* Michael Foucault, *The History of Sexuality,* trans. Robert Hurley (New York, 1978), vol. 1, *An Introduction;* Daniel Scott Smith, "The Dating of the American Sexual Revolution: Evidence and Interpretation," in Michael Gordon, ed., *The American Family in Social-Historical Perspective* (New York, 1973), pp. 321–35; Linda Gordon, *Woman's Body, Woman's Right: A Social History of Birth Control in America* (New York, 1976).

4. Gordon, *Woman's Body;* Carroll Smith-Rosenberg, *Disorderly Conduct: Visions of Gender in Victorian America* (New York, 1985); Judith Walkowitz, *Prostitution and Victorian Society: Women, Class, and the State* (New York, 1980).

5. For examples of the efforts of scholars to decode the hidden sexual content of diaries, see Janet Farrell Brodie, "Family Limitation in American Culture, 1830–1900," Ph.D. dissertation, University of Chicago, 1982 (Mary Pierce Poor diary); Gay, *The Bourgeois Experience,* vol. 1 (Mabel Loomis Todd diary); and Marion S. Goldman, *Gold Diggers and Silver Miners: Prostitution and Social Life on the Comstock Lode* (Ann Arbor, 1981) (Alf Doten diary). On family censorship and efforts to restore original documents, see Lillian Faderman, "Emily Dickinson's Letters to Sue Gilbert," *Massa-*

chusetts Review 18 (September 1977), pp. 19–27; Blanche Cooke, "The Historical Denial of Lesbianism," *Radical History Review* 20 (Spring–Summer 1979), pp. 60–65; and Martin Bauml Duberman, "Uncensoring the Mountain Chant," in *About Time: Exploring the Gay Past* (New York, 1986), pp. 33–36.

6. There are intriguing parallels here with the history of economic regulation. The mercantilism of an organic, preindustrial society gave way to laissez-faire self-regulation in the nineteenth century. Since the late nineteenth century, interest groups have competed over the ways that the liberal state should legitimately regulate economic life.

Chapter 1. Cultural Diversity in the Era of Settlement

1. Michael Zuckerman, "Pilgrims in the Wilderness: Community, Modernity, and the Maypole at Merry Mount," *New England Quarterly* 50 (June 1977), pp. 255–77.

2. Antonia Fraser, *The Weaker Vessel: Woman's Lot in Seventeenth-Century England* (London, 1984), p. 32; Alan MacFarlane, *Marriage and Love in England: Modes of Reproduction, 1300–1840* (New York, 1986), pp. 179, 205.

3. On early modern sexual values, see Steven Ozment, *When Fathers Ruled Family Life in Reformation Europe* (Cambridge, Mass., 1983), pp. 99–101, and Lawrence Stone, *The Family, Sex and Marriage in England, 1500–1800* (London, 1977).

4. Thomas Laqueur, "Orgasm, Generation, and the Politics of Reproductive Biology," *Representations* 14 (Spring 1986), p. 1; Angus McLaren, *Reproductive Rituals: The Perception of Fertility in England from the Sixteenth to the Nineteenth Century* (London, 1984), pp. 14–20; Fraser, *Weaker Vessel,* p. 50.

5. Peter Laslett, *The World We Have Lost,* 3d ed. (New York, 1984), pp. 155, 158; Geoffrey Robert Quaife, *Wanton Wenches and Wayward Wives: Peasants and Illicit Sex in Early Seventeenth-Century England* (New Brunswick, N.J., 1979), pp. 59, 179, 245; Keith Wrightson, *English Society, 1580–1680* (New Brunswick, N.J., 1982), p. 85; MacFarlane, *Marriage and Love in England,* p. 305.

6. Laslett, *World,* pp. 116–18; Fraser, *Weaker Vessel,* pp. 66–68; Robert V. Schnucker, "Elizabethan Birth Control and Puritan Attitudes," *Journal of Interdisciplinary History* 5 (Spring 1975), pp. 655–67; MacFarlane, *Marriage and Love in England,* pp. 240–41; Wrightson, *English Society,* p. 105.

7. Jonathan Ned Katz, *Gay/Lesbian Almanac: A New Documentary* (New York, 1983), pp. 26–27; Ramón Arturo Gutiérrez, "Marriage, Sex and the Family: Social Change in Colonial New Mexico, 1690–1846," Ph.D. dissertation, University of Wisconsin, Madison, 1980, p. 26.

8. Alden T. Vaughan, *New England Frontier,* rev. ed. (New York, 1979), pp. 260–63; Neal Salisbury, *Manitou and Providence: Indians, Europeans, and the Making of New England, 1500–1643* (New York, 1982), pp. 132–33; Zuckerman, "Pilgrims in the Wilderness," pp. 266–67.

9. Walter L. Williams, *The Spirit and the Flesh: Sexual Diversity in American Indian Culture* (Boston, 1986), pp. 17, 87–90; Evelyn Blackwood, "Sexuality and Gender in Certain Native American Tribes: The Case of Cross-Gender Females," *Signs* 10 (Autumn 1984), pp. 27–42.

10. Karen Kupperman, *Settling with the Indians* (Totowa, N.J., 1980), p. 59; James Axtell, ed., *The Indian Peoples of Eastern America: A Documentary History of the Sexes*

(New York, 1981), p. 90; Axtell, *The Invasion Within: The Contest of Culture in North America* (New York, 1985), pp. 169–70. See also Salisbury, *Manitou,* pp. 136, 294, and William G. McLoughlin, *Cherokees and Missionaries, 1787–1839* (New Haven, 1984), pp. 78, 181, 204.

11. Eleanor Leacock, "Montagnais Women and the Jesuit Program for Colonization," in Mona Etienne and Eleanor Leacock, eds., *Women and Colonization: Anthropological Perspectives* (New York, 1980), p. 31.

12. Axtell, *Indian Peoples,* pp. 88, 71–72. See also John Upton Terrell and Donna M. Terrell, *Indian Women of the Western Morning: Their Life in Early America* (New York, 1974).

13. Axtell, *Indian Peoples,* pp. 71–72; Alden T. Vaughan and Edward W. Clark, eds., *Puritans Among the Indians: Accounts of Captivity and Redemption, 1676–1724* (Cambridge, Mass., 1981), p. 70; Gutierrez, "Marriage, Sex and the Family," pp. 118–19; McLoughlin, *Cherokees,* p. 218.

14. Mary Beth Norton, "The Evolution of White Women's Experience in Early America," *American Historical Review* 89:3 (June 1984), pp. 593–619.

15. Lorena S. Walsh, " 'Till Death Do Us Part': Marriage and Family in Seventeenth-Century Maryland," in Thad W. Tate and David L. Ammerman, eds., *The Chesapeake in the Seventeenth Century: Essays in Anglo-American Society* (Chapel Hill, 1979), pp. 126–52.

16. Mary Beth Norton, "Gender and Defamation in Seventeenth-Century Maryland," *William and Mary Quarterly* 44 (January 1987), p. 38; William Hand Browne et al., eds., *Archives of Maryland, Judicial and Testamentary Business of the Provincial Court* (Baltimore, 1891–1936), 10:516, 41:432–33 and 291–94. (Hereafter cited as *Arch. Md.*)

17. *Arch. Md.* 10:109–12; Norton, "Gender and Defamation," cites *ménage à trois* in the Chesapeake. For similar cases in an area of New England with a high sex ratio, see Christine Heyrman, *Commerce and Culture: The Maritime Communities of Colonial Massachusetts* (New York, 1984), pp. 215–16.

18. Kathleen Verduin, " 'Our Cursed Natures': Sexuality and the Puritan Conscience," *New England Quarterly* 56: (June 1983), pp. 228–29; Mary Latham, vol. 38B, pp. 39, 42a [1645?] Massachusetts State Archives, Boston, Mass. (Hereafter cited as Mass. Arch.)

19. Donna J. Spindel and Stuart W. Thomas, Jr., "Crime and Society in North Carolina, 1663–1740," *Journal of Southern History* 49:2 (May 1983), pp. 222–44. For examples of what Peter Laslett (*World,* p. 155) calls a "bastardy prone sub-society" see *Arch. Md.* 53:599, and Herbert G. Gutman, *The Black Family in Slavery and Freedom, 1750–1925* (New York, 1976), p. 339.

20. *Arch. Md.* 41:270–72, 10:170–86.

21. Lyle Koehler, *A Search for Power: The "Weaker Sex" in Seventeenth-Century New England* (Champaign, Ill., 1980), pp. 91ff.

22. Peter C. Hoffer and William B. Scott, eds., *Criminal Proceedings in Colonial Virginia* (Athens, Ga., 1984), p. 70; *The Secret Diary of William Byrd of Westover, 1709–1712,* ed. Louis B. Wright and Marian Tingling, (Richmond, Va., 1941), p. 90.

23. Mary P. Ryan, *Womanhood in America: From Colonial Times to the Present* (New York, 1983), p. 33; Raphael Semmes, *Crime and Punishment in Early Maryland* (Baltimore, 1938), p. 188; Mary Sumner Benson, *Women in Eighteenth-Century Amer-*

ica: Study of Opinion and Social Usage (New York, 1935), p. 229. Cases of impregnated servants appear in *Arch. Md.* 5:337, 525–26, 41:14, 53:xxix, 54:518.

24. Allan Kulikoff, "A 'Prolifick' People: Black Population Growth in the Chesapeake Colonies, 1700–1790," *Southern Studies* 16:4 (Winter 1977), pp. 391–428; Herbert S. Klein and Stanley L. Engerman, "Fertility Differentials Between Slaves in the United States and the British West Indies: A Note on Lactation Practices and Their Possible Implications," *William and Mary Quarterly* 35 (April 1978), pp. 356–74; Peter H. Wood, *Black Majority: Negroes in Colonial South Carolina, from 1670 to the Stono Rebellion* (New York, 1974) pp. 144–45, 161–65; Daniel Scott Smith, "The Long Cycle in American Illegitimacy and Prenuptial Pregnancy," in Peter Laslett, Karla Oosterveen, and Richard M. Smith, eds. *Bastardy and Its Comparative History* (Cambridge, Mass., 1980), p. 376; Gutman, *Black Family,* p. 331; Winthrop Jordan, *White over Black: American Attitudes Toward the Negro, 1550–1812* (Baltimore, 1969), pp. 160–61.

25. Edmund S. Morgan, *American Slavery, American Freedom* (New York, 1975), p. 336. See Chapter 2 on the regulation of miscegenation.

26. Norton, "Evolution"; Daniel Blake Smith, *Inside the Great House: Planter Life in Eighteenth Century Chesapeake Society* (Ithaca, 1980), p. 128; Morgan, *American Slavery,* p. 335.

27. Kulikoff, " 'Prolifick' People," p. 408; Klein and Engerman, "Fertility Differentials"; Gutman, *Black Family,* pp. 344–46.

28. Robert V. Wells, "Illegitimacy and Bridal Pregnancy in Colonial America," in Laslett, *Bastardy,* pp. 356–57.

Chapter 2. Family Life and the Regulation of Deviance

1. Stephen Innes, *Labor in a New Land: Economy and Society in Seventeenth-Century Springfield* (Princeton, 1983), pp. 132–33.

2. Laurel Thatcher Ulrich, *Goodwives: Image and Reality in the Lives of Women in Northern New England, 1650–1750* (New York, 1983), p. 95.

3. Robert Oaks, " 'Things Fearful to Name': Sodomy and Buggery in Seventeenth-Century New England," in Joseph Pleck and Elizabeth Pleck, eds. *The American Man,* (Englewood Cliffs, N.J., 1980), pp. 66–69. See also Jonathan Ned Katz, ed., *Gay/Lesbian Almanac: A New Documentary* (New York: Harper and Row, 1983), pp. 87, 111. Bestiality persisted in rural areas long after the colonial period. In 1867, for example, a sixteen-year-old white boy had "carnal intercourse with one of his ewes" (Herbert G. Gutman, *The Black Family in Slavery and Freedom, 1750–1925* [New York, 1976], p. 394).

4. David H. Flaherty, *Privacy in Colonial New England* (Charlottesville, 1972), esp. pp. 42–43, 76, and 78; Nancy Cott, "Eighteenth-Century Family and Social Life Revealed in Massachusetts Divorce Records," in Nancy F. Cott and Elizabeth H. Pleck, eds., *A Heritage of Her Own* (New York, 1979), p. 119; Linda K. Kerber, *Women of the Republic: Intellect and Ideology in Revolutionary America* (Chapel Hill, 1980), p. 166; and vol. 7, p. 225 (1683) Manuscript Court Records, New Hampshire State Archives, Concord, N.H.

5. Roger Thompson, *Women in Stuart England and America* (London, 1974), p. 244; Mary Beth Norton, "Gender and Defamation in Seventeenth-Century Maryland," *William and Mary Quarterly* 44 (January 1987), pp. 3–39; Roger Thompson, *Sex in*

Middlesex: Popular Mores in a Massachusetts County, 1649–1699 (Amherst, 1986), pp. 180–81. See also Ulrich, *Goodwives,* p. 96, and Robert B. St. George, "Heated Speech and Literacy in Seventeenth-Century New England," in *Seventeenth-Century New England* (Publications of the Colonial Society of Massachusetts Collections, 1984), pp. lxiii, 275–322.

6. Katz, *Gay/Lesbian Almanac,* p. 83; Lyle Koehler, *A Search for Power: The "Weaker Sex" in Seventeenth-Century New England* (Champaign, Ill., 1980), pp. 73, 76. See also Kathleen Verduin, " 'Our Cursed Natures': Sexuality and the Puritan Conscience," *New England Quarterly* 56 (June 1983). On women, see Barbara Epstein, *The Politics of Domesticity: Women, Evangelism, and Temperance in Nineteenth-Century America* (Middletown, Conn., 1981), pp. 42–43.

7. Philip Greven, *The Protestant Temperament: Patterns of Child-Rearing, Religious Experience, and Self in Early America* (New York, 1977), esp. pp. 248, 314, 316.

8. Otto T. Beall, "Aristotle's Master Piece in America: A Landmark in the Folklore of Medicine," *William and Mary Quarterly,* 3d ser., 20:2 (April 1963), pp. 208–10; Steven Nissenbaum, *Sex, Diet, and Debility in Jacksonian America: Sylvester Graham and Health Reform* (Westport, Conn., 1980), chap. 2.

9. *Aristotle's Compleat Masterpiece* (New York, 1788), p. 58.

10. Edmund S. Morgan, ed., *The Diary of Michael Wigglesworth, 1653–1657: The Conscience of a Puritan* (reprint, New York, 1965), pp. 4, 30–31, 50, 80; Verduin, " 'Cursed Natures,' " p. 225. On women's conversions, see Epstein, *Politics of Domesticity,* p. 42.

11. Franklin B. Dexter, ed., *Ancient Town Records* (New Haven, 1917), vol. 1, *New Haven Town Records, 1649–1662,* pp. 178–79; Thompson, *Sex in Middlesex,* pp. 72–73, 87–88; Susie M. Ames, ed., *Country Court Record of Accomack-Northampton, Virginia, 1640–1645* (Charlottesville, 1973), p. 117; Edmund S. Morgan, *The Puritan Family: Religion and Domestic Relations in Seventeenth-Century New England* (New York, 1944), pp. 128–29; Eli Faber, "Puritan Criminals: The Economic, Social and Intellectual Background to Crime in Seventeenth-Century Massachusetts," *Perspectives in American History* 11: (1977–78), pp. 101, 116–17.

12. Daniel Blake Smith, *Inside the Great House: Planter Life in Eighteenth-Century Chesapeake Society* (Ithaca, 1980), pp. 140–41.

13. *Ibid.,* pp. 130–34; Morgan, *Puritan Family,* pp. 54–57.

14. Koehler, *Search,* p. 424; Flaherty, *Privacy,* pp. 82, 156, 73; William Hand Browne et al., eds., *Archives of Maryland,* (Baltimore, 1891–1936), 10:499 (hereafter *Arch. Md.*).

15. Henry Reed Stiles, *Bundling: Its Origins, Progress and Decline in America* (Albany, 1869), pp. 13, 66; Dana Doten, *The Art of Bundling* (New York, 1938), p. 66; Flaherty, *Privacy,* p. 78.

16. Koehler, *Search,* pp. 80, 434; Morgan, *Puritan Family,* p. 33; John Demos, *A Little Commonwealth: Family Life in Plymouth Colony* (New York, 1970), p. 158n35.

17. Ralph Semmes, *Crime and Punishment in Early Maryland* (Baltimore, 1938), pp. 182–83; Demos, *Little Commonwealth,* 152–58; Ulrich, *Goodwives,* p. 31; Mary Woodin, vol. 9, p. 104a, Sept. 25, 1677, Mass. Arch. (see also 9:378, March 13, 1749).

18. Lorena S. Walsh, " 'Till Death Do Us Part': Marriage and Family in Seventeenth-Century Maryland," in Thad W. Tate and David L. Ammerman, eds., *The Chesapeake in the Seventeenth Century: Essays in Anglo-American Society* (Chapel Hill,

1979) pp. 126–52; Stephanie Grauman Wolf, *Urban Village: Population, Community, and Family Structure in Germantown, Pennsylvania, 1683–1800* (Princeton, 1976), p. 259; Daniel Scott Smith, "The Long Cycle in American Illegitimacy and Prenuptial Pregnancy," in Peter Laslett et al., eds., *Bastardy and Its Comparative History* (Cambridge, Mass., 1980), p. 369; Daniel Scott Smith and Michael Hindus, "Premarital Pregnancy in America, 1640–1971: An Overview and an Interpretation," *Journal of Interdisciplinary History* 5:4 (July 1975), pp. 537–70.

19. On New England, see Flaherty, *Privacy,* p. 160. See also Emil Oberholzer, Jr., *Delinquent Saints: Disciplinary Actions in the Early Congregational Churches of Massachusetts* (New York, 1956), chap. 8, and *Arch. Md.* 54:366, 371.

20. Faber, "Puritan Criminals," p. 140–43.

21. Morgan, *Wigglesworth,* p. 88. See also Ulrich, *Goodwives,* p. 109, and Morgan, *Puritan Family,* p. 141.

22. Koehler, *Search,* pp. 78–79.

23. *Ibid.,* p. 37; D. B. Smith, *Great House,* pp. 155–56, 162.

24. Cott, "Massachusetts Divorce," p. 126.

25. William Byrd, *The Secret Diary of William Byrd of Westover, 1709–1712,* Louis B. Wright and Marion Tinling, eds. (Richmond, Va., 1941), p. 337. See also D. B. Smith, *Great House,* p. 162, and Catherine M. Scholten, *Childrearing in American Society: 1650–1850* (New York, 1985), p. 19.

26. Ulrich, *Goodwives,* p. 112; Ethan Smith, ed. *Memoirs of Mrs. Abigail Bailey,* (reprint, New York, 1980); Cott, "Massachusetts Divorce," pp. 119–20.

27. Demos, *Commonwealth,* p. 95. See also Kerber, *Women of the Republic,* p. 172.

28. Koehler, *Search,* pp. 78–79.

29. Mary Beth Norton, *Liberty's Daughters: The Revolutionary Experience of American Women, 1750–1800* (Boston, 1980), p. 77. See also Mary P. Ryan, *Womanhood in America, from Colonial Times to the Present* (New York, 1975), pp. 54, 57, and Demos, *Commonwealth,* p. 66.

30. Scholten, *Childrearing,* p. 13. On Bradstreet, see Koehler, *Search,* p. 56, and Jeannine Hensley, ed., *The Works of Anne Bradstreet* (Cambridge, Mass., 1967), pp. 236ff.

31. Daniel Scott Smith, "The Demographic History of Colonial New England," in *The American Family in Social-Historical Perspective,* ed. Michael Gordon (New York, 1973), p. 410; Wolf, *Urban Village,* p. 262; Scholten, *Childrearing,* pp. 72–73; Koehler, *Search,* pp. 56–57.

32. Cott, "Massachusetts Divorce," p. 119; Michael Zuckerman, "Pilgrims in the Wilderness: Community, Modernity, and the Maypole at Merry Mount," *New England Quarterly* 50 (June 1977), p. 266; Carol F. Karlsen, "The Devil in the Shape of a Woman: The Witch in Seventeenth-Century New England," Ph.D. dissertation, Yale University, 1980, p. 218; *Arch. Md.* 10:503–4, 41:20.

33. Wilson H. Grabill, Clyde V. Kiser, and Pascal K. Whelpton, "A Long View," in Gordon, ed., *American Family* pp. 377–78; Norton, *Liberty's Daughters,* pp. 72–75; Nancy Osterud and J. Fulton, "Family Limitation and Age at Marriage: Fertility Decline in Sturbridge, Massachusetts, 1730–1850," *Population Studies* 30 (November 1976), p. 483.

34. D. B. Smith, *Great House,* pp. 27–28; Allan Kulikoff, "A 'Prolifick' People: Black Population Growth in the Chesapeake Colonies, 1700–1790," *Southern Studies* 16:4 (Winter 1977), p. 408.

35. *Arch Md.* 53:xxix, 54:518, 30:560; Edmund S. Morgan, *American Slavery, American Freedom* (New York, 1975), p. 333.

36. Donna J. Spindel and Stuart W. Thomas, Jr., "Crime and Society in North Carolina, 1633–1740," *Journal of Southern History* 49:2 (May 1983), pp. 223–44. Witchcraft was one offense in which women predominated—up to eighty percent of accused witches were women—but it is not clear that American witchcraft charges had much to do with sexuality, as opposed to gender. According to John Demos, colonial women accused as witches were less likely to have had a prior record of sexual offenses than were other women. Property relations seem to have been more important than sexual behavior in determining witchcraft accusations in seventeenth-century New England. Demos, *Entertaining Satan: Witchcraft and the Culture of Early New England* (New York, 1982), pp. 77–78; Karlsen, "The Devil," pp. 214–19, 333–34.

37. Peter C. Hoffer and William B. Scott, eds., *Criminal Proceedings in Colonial Virginia* (Athens, Ga., 1984), pp. 19–20, 71, 77; e.g., *Arch. Md.* 10:112; Betty B. Rosenbaum, "The Sociological Bases of the Laws Relating to Women Sex Offenders in Massachusetts, 1620–1860," *Journal of Criminal Law and Criminology* 27 (March–April 1938), pp. 820–21; Thomas Clarke, 9:221–22 (January 31, 1736) Mass. Arch. (see also 9:265 [July 16, 1742]).

38. Cott, "Massachusetts Divorce," p. 126. On the seventeenth century, see Koehler, *Search,* pp. 147–52.

39. Manuscript Court Records, vol. 7 (1683), pp. 225, 233, 241, 245, *New Hampshire State Archives,* Concord, N.H.; Semmes, *Crime,* pp. 178–79, cites attacks on men.

40. Flaherty, *Privacy,* p. 176.

41. Christine Heyrman, *Commerce and Culture: The Maritime Communities of Colonial Massachusetts* (New York, 1984), pp. 49–50; Flaherty, *Privacy,* p. 207.

42. Semmes, *Crime,* pp. 182–83; Ames, *Accomack* (record for July 4, 1643), p. 290; Flaherty, *Privacy,* p. 43.

43. Cott, "Massachusetts Divorce," p. 110 (see also Mass. Arch. 9:265); *Arch. Md.* 54:55 (see also 53:225); Heyrman, *Commerce,* p. 216.

44. Katz, *Gay/Lesbian Almanac,* pp. 90–91, 111–18, and Katz, *Gay American History,* (New York, 1976), pp. 12–13; Robert S. Oaks, "Defining Sodomy in Seventeenth-Century Massachusetts," *Journal of Homosexuality* 6:1–2 (Fall–Winter 1980–81), p. 82. Katz has found twenty legal cases concerning homosexual relations in the period 1607 to 1740. See also Mass. Arch. 38b:41, 41a (n.d.).

45. Semmes, *Crime,* p. 204; Katz, *Gay/Lesbian Almanac,* pp. 54–55 and 84–85; Koehler, *Search,* p. 82.

46. Heyrman, *Commerce,* p. 286.

47. Thompson, *Sex in Middlesex,* p. 75; Koehler, *Search,* p. 95; Barbara S. Lindemann, "'To Ravish and Carnally Know': Rape in Eighteenth-Century Massachusetts," *Signs* 10:1 (Autumn 1984), p. 80.

48. Lindemann, "'To Ravish,'" p. 80.

49. Winthrop D. Jordan, *White over Black: American Attitudes Towards the Negro, 1550–1812* (Baltimore, 1969), pp. 157 and n44. See this book for discussion of interracial sex.

50. Lindemann, "'To Ravish,'" p. 68; Ulrich *Goodwives,* pp. 99–102; 38B:189 (September–October 1654) Mass. Arch.

51. Flaherty, *Privacy,* p. 207; Ulrich, *Goodwives,* pp. 90–92. For examples of mid-

wives' role, see Elizabeth Taylor's affidavit in James Otis Papers, Aug. 18, 1681, Massachusetts Historical Society, Boston, and *Arch. Md.* 41:20.

52. Robert V. Wells, "Illegitimacy and Bridal Pregnancy in Colonial America," in Peter Laslett, Karla Oosterveen, and Richard M. Smith, eds., *Bastardy and Its Comparative History* (Cambridge, Mass., 1980), p. 358; Morgan, *Puritan Family,* pp. 130–31; Ulrich, *Goodwives,* pp. 102–3; Koehler, *Search,* p. 354.

53. Morgan, *Puritan Family,* pp. 130–31. On Quakers, see Jack Donald Marietta, "Ecclesiastical Discipline in the Society of Friends, 1662–1776," Ph.D. dissertation, Stanford University 1968.

54. Neal W. Allen, Jr., ed., *Province and Court Records of Maine,* vol. 7 (Portland, Maine, 1975), pp. 121–23 (April 2, 1723). Berthold Fernow, ed., *The Records of New Amsterdam, 1653 to 1674, Anno Domini,* vol. 3 (Baltimore, 1976), p. 370.

55. Quoted in Wells, "Illegitimacy," p. 361.

56. *Arch. Md.* 41:14–16. See also Wolf, *Urban Village,* p. 298.

57. Robert V. Wells, *Revolutions in Americans' Lives: A Demographic Perspective on the History of Americans, Their Families, and Their Society* (Westport, Conn., 1982), p. 59.

58. Wells, *Revolutions,* p. 40, and "Illegitimacy," pp. 354ff; Wolf, *Urban Village,* p. 261.

59. Misc. bound ms., April 25, 1693, Massachusetts Historical Society, Boston; Ulrich, *Goodwives,* p. 198; Semmes, *Crime,* p. 195.

60. Wells, "Illegitimacy," p. 360; Koehler, *Search,* pp. 200–201; Peter C. Hoffer and N. E. H. Hull, *Murdering Mothers: Infanticide in England and New England, 1558–1803* (New York, 1981), pp. 45–48, 53, 58, 63.

61. Verduin, " 'Cursed Natures,' " p. 227.

62. Jordan, *White over Black,* p. 78.

63. *Ibid.,* pp. 30–32, 196–97, 459; David Brian Davis, *The Problem of Slavery in Western Culture* (Ithaca, 1966), pp. 468–70.

64. Morgan, *American Slavery,* pp. 335–36; Letitia Woods Brown, *Free Negroes in the District of Columbia, 1790–1846* (New York, 1972), pp. 25–29; Jordan, *White over Black,* pp. 77–80, 139–41, 164; Wells, "Illegitimacy," p. 358; Peter H. Wood, *Black Majority: Negroes in Colonial South Carolina, from 1670 to the Stono Rebellion* (New York, 1974), pp. 233–35.

65. Jordan, *White over Black,* pp. 137–38, 473n80; Davis, *Problem of Slavery,* p. 281.

66. Jordan, *White over Black,* pp. 139, 145, and 473, note 81.

67. When Pennsylvania lawmakers substituted life imprisonment for the death penalty from 1700–1718, they did so only for whites. For blacks, rape of a white (but not black) woman—along with buggery, burglary, and murder—remained capital offenses (Katz, *Gay/Lesbian Almanac,* p. 61).

68. Jordan, *White over Black,* pp. 158, 398.

69. Davis, *Problem of Slavery,* pp. 274–75; Carl N. Degler, *Neither Black nor White: Slavery and Race Relations in Brazil and the United States* (New York, 1971).

70. Jordan, *White over Black,* p. 178.

Chapter 3. Seeds of Change

1. Christine Stansell, *City of Women: Sex and Class in New York, 1789–1860* (New York, 1986), pp. 24–26.

2. Roy Porter, "Mixed Feelings: The Enlightenment and Sexuality in Eighteenth-Century Britain," in Paul-Gabriel Bouce, ed., *Sexuality in Britain in the Eighteenth Century* (London, 1985), pp. 1–27; *Dr. Benjamin Franklin and the Ladies: Being Various Letters, Essays, Bagatelles and Satires to and About the Fair Sex* (Mt. Vernon, 1939), pp. 67–69. See also Peter Cominos, "Late Victorian Sexual Respectability and the Social System," *International Review of Social History* 8, Pt. 1 (1963), pp. 224ff.

3. Angus McLaren, *Reproductive Rituals: The Perception of Fertility in England from the Sixteenth to the Nineteenth Century* (London, 1984), pp. 13–14, 26–28.

4. Lawrence Stone, *Family, Sex and Marriage in England, 1500–1800* (London, 1977), chap. 10.

5. Stone, *Family,* esp. p. 261.

6. Daniel Blake Smith, *Inside the Great House: Planter Life in Eighteenth-Century Chesapeake Society* (Ithaca, 1980), p. 138 (see also pp. 135–40); Mary Beth Norton, *Liberty's Daughters: The Revolutionary Experience of American Women, 1775–1800* (Boston, 1980), p. 60; Ellen K. Rothman, *Hands and Hearts* (New York, 1984), p. 11. See also Mary Beth Norton, "The Evolution of White Women's Experience in Early America," *American Historical Review* 89:3 (June 1984), pp. 593–619; and Laurel Thatcher Ulrich, *Goodwives: Image and Reality in the Lives of Women in Northern New England, 1650–1750* (New York, 1983).

7. Adams to Smith, February 14, 1763, in L. H. Butterfield and Marc Friedlander, eds., *Adams Family Correspondence,* vol. 1 (Cambridge, 1963), p. 3; Norton, *Liberty's Daughters,* p. 53; Philip L. White, *Beckmantown, New York: Forest Frontier to Farm Community* (Austin, 1979), p. 108.

8. Ulrich, *Goodwives,* pp. 115–16

9. D. B. Smith, *Great House,* pp. 143–44.

10. Joan Hoff-Wilson, "The Illusion of Change: Women and the American Revolution," in Alfred Young, ed., *The American Revolution: Explorations in the History of American Radicalism* (DeKalb, Ill., 1976), p. 404.

11. Daniel Scott Smith, "The Dating of the American Sexual Revolution," in Michael Gordon, ed., *The American Family in Social-Historical Perspective* (New York, 1973), 323.

12. Robert V. Wells, "Illegitimacy and Bridal Pregnancy in Colonial America," in Peter Laslett, Karla Oosterveen and Richard M. Smith, eds., *Bastardy and Its Comparative History* (Cambridge, Mass., 1980), pp. 354–55.

13. Stansell, *City of Women,* pp. 27, 24.

14. Nancy F. Cott, "Passionlessness: An Interpretation of Victorian Sexual Ideology, 1790–1850," in Nancy F. Cott and Elizabeth H. Pleck, eds., *A Heritage of Her Own* (New York, 1979), p. 170; Joan Jensen, *Loosening the Bonds: Mid-Atlantic Farm Women, 1750–1850* (New Haven, 1986), pp. 117–18.

15. Cott, "Passionlessness," pp. 169ff; Norton, *Liberty's Daughters,* pp. 51–53; Ronald T. Takaki, *Iron Cages: Race and Culture in Nineteenth-Century America* (Seattle, 1982), pp. 40, 20–21.

16. Cott, "Passionlessness," pp. 165–68.

17. [John Adams], *Sketches of the Fair Sex* (Boston, 1807), pp. 94–95, 192.

18. *The Works of Aristotle the Famous Philosopher, in Four Parts* (New England, 1831), pp. 17, 6–9.

19. Henry Reed Stiles, *Bundling: Its Origins, Progress and Decline in America* (Albany, 1869), pp. 54–55.

20. Stiles, *Bundling,* pp. 87, 97.

21. For nineteenth-century examples of bundling, see Daniel Scott Smith, "The Long Cycle in American Illegitimacy and Prenuptial Pregnancy," in Laslett, et al., *Bastardy*, p. 371; and Dana Doten, *The Art of Bundling* (New York, 1938), p. 66.

22. Robert V. Wells, "Family Size and Fertility Control in Eighteenth-Century America: A Study of Quaker Families," *Population Studies* 25:1 (1971), esp. pp. 76–79; Jensen, *Loosening the Bonds*, pp. 29, 119; Norton, *Liberty's Daughters*, pp. 232–34.

23. Nancy F. Cott, "Eighteenth-Century Family and Social Life Revealed in Massachusetts Divorce Records," in Cott and Pleck, *Heritage*, p. 123; Linda K. Kerber, *Women of the Republic: Intellect and Ideology in Revolutionary America* (Chapel Hill, 1980), pp. 166–75; Norton, *Liberty's Daughters*, p. 234; Jay Fliegelman, *Prodigals and Pilgrims: The American Revolution Against Patriarchal Authority* (New York, 1982), chap. 5.

24. Susan Dion, "Women in the *Boston Gazette*, 1755–1775," *Historical Journal of Massachusetts* 14:2 (June 1986), p. 91.

25. Wells, "Illegitimacy," p. 356; Barbara S. Lindemann, " 'To Ravish and Carnally Know': Rape in Eighteenth-Century Massachusetts," *Signs* 10:1 (Autumn 1984), p. 75; Elizabeth Pleck, *Domestic Tyranny: The Making of American Social Policy Against Family Violence from Colonial Times to the Present* (New York, 1987), p. 31; Peter C. Hoffer and N. E. H. Hull, *Murdering Mothers: Infanticide in England and New England, 1558–1803* (New York, 1981), pp. 65ff; Sharon Ann Burnston, "Babies in the Well: An Underground Insight into Deviant Behavior in Eighteenth-Century Philadelphia," *The Pennsylvania Magazine of History and Biography* 106:2 (April 1982), pp. 151–86.

26. Robert V. Wells, *Revolutions in Americans' Lives: A Demographic Perspective in the History of Americans, Their Families, and Their Society* (Westport, Conn., 1982), p. 64; David H. Flaherty, *Privacy in Colonial New England* (Charlottesville, 1972), p. 160.

27. Carl Bridenbaugh, *Cities in the Wilderness: The First Century of Urban Life in America, 1625–1742* (New York, 1968), pp. 71–73; Lyle Koehler, *A Search for Power: The "Weaker Sex" in Seventeenth-Century New England* (Champaign, Ill., 1980), p. 208; Flaherty, *Privacy*, p. 212; Roger Thompson, *Women in Stuart England and America* (London, 1974), p. 42.

28. Carl Bridenbaugh, *Cities in Revolt* (New York, 1955), pp. 160, 121; Philip Greven, *The Protestant Temperament: Patterns of Child-Rearing, Religious Experience, and Self in Early America* (New York, 1977), p. 249; Dilley, vol. 43, p. 864, May 16, 1754, Mass, Arch., Stansell, *City of Women*, pp. 14–15.

29. Benjamin Franklin, *The Autobiography of Benjamin Franklin: A Genetic Text*, ed. J. A. Leo Lemay and P. M. Zall (Knoxville, Tenn., 1981), p. 70.

30. Stansell, *City of Women*, pp. 25–26; Bridenbaugh, *Cities in Revolt*, pp. 122, 316–18.

Chapter 4. Within the Family

1. Clelia Duel Mosher, *The Mosher Survey: Sexual Attitudes of Forty-five Victorian Women*, ed. James Mahood and Christine Wenburg (New York, 1980), pp. 375–86, 128–39 (Cases 35 and 12).

2. Estelle B. Freedman, *Their Sisters' Keepers: Women's Prison Reform in America, 1830–1930* (Ann Arbor, 1981), pp. 14, 83–85.

3. Daniel Scott Smith, "Family Limitation, Sexual Control, and Domestic Feminism," in Mary S. Hartman and Lois Banner, eds., *Clio's Consciousness Raised* (New York, 1974), table 3.1, p. 123.

4. John Modell, "Family and Fertility on the Indiana Frontier, 1820," *American Quarterly* 23:5 (December 1971), pp. 615–34; Maris A. Vinovskis, "Socioeconomic Determinants of Interstate Fertility Differentials in the United States," *Journal of Interdisciplinary History* 6:3 (Winter 1976), pp. 375–96; Richard A. Easterlin, "Factors in the Decline of Farm Fertility in the United States: Some Preliminary Research Results," *Journal of American History* 63:3 (December 1976), pp. 600–614; Richard H. Steckel, "Antebellum Southern White Fertility: A Demographic and Economic Analysis," *Journal of Economic History* 40:2 (June 1980), pp. 331–50; Catherine Clinton, *The Plantation Mistress: Women's World in the Old South* (New York, 1982), pp. 60–61, 152–56; Michael Haines, "Fertility and Marriage in a Nineteenth-Century Industrial City: Philadelphia, 1850–1880," *Journal of Economic History* 40:1 (March 1980), pp. 151–58; Tamara K. Hareven and Maris A. Vinovskis, "Marital Fertility, Ethnicity, and Occupation in Urban Families: An Analysis of South Boston and the South End in 1880," *Journal of Social History* 8:3 (Spring 1975), pp. 464–77; Lawrence A. Glasco, "The Life Cycles and Household Structure of American Ethnic Groups: Irish, Germans, and Native-born Whites in Buffalo, New York, 1855," in Nancy F. Cott and Elizabeth H. Pleck, eds., *A Heritage of Her Own* (New York, 1979), pp. 268–89; Hasia R. Diner, *Erin's Daughters in America: Irish Immigrant Women in the Nineteenth Century* (Baltimore, 1983), p. 54.

5. Easterlin, "Farm Fertility"; Yasukichi Yasuba, *Birth Rates of the White Population in the United States, 1800–1860: An Economic Study* (Baltimore, 1962); Vinovskis, "Fertility Differentials"; D. S. Smith, "Family Limitation". See also Patricia Branca, *Silent Sisterhood: Middle-Class Women in the Victorian Home* (London, 1975), chap. 7, and, for a useful summary of interpretations, Carl N. Degler, *At Odds: Women and the Family in America from the Revolution to the Present* (New York, 1980), chap. 9.

6. The terms *contraception* and *family limitation* are used interchangeably here. The term *birth control* is reserved for the modern movement in which it was coined (see Chapter 10).

7. [Nicholas Francis Cooke], *Satan in Society, By a Physician* (Cincinnati, 1871), pp. 150–51; Marion Goldman, *Gold Diggers and Silver Miners: Prostitution and Social Life on the Comstock Lode* (Ann Arbor, 1981), p. 53. See also Henry J. Warner, *The Magic Monitor and Medical Intelligencer* (New York, 1859), pp. 133–35. For a survey of methods, see Janet Farrell Brodie, "Family Limitation in American Culture, 1830–1900," Ph.D. dissertation, University of Chicago, 1982, chap. 11.

8. Wilson Yates, "Birth Control Literature and the Medical Profession," *Journal of the History of Medicine* 31:1 (January 1976), pp. 42–54; Michael A. La Sorte, "Nineteenth-Century Family Planning Practices," *Journal of Psychohistory* 4:2 (Fall 1976), pp. 163–83; Brodie, "Family Limitation," pp. 23–25, 365–66; David M. Kennedy, *Birth Control in America: The Career of Margaret Sanger* (New Haven, 1970), p. 45.

9. La Sorte, "Practices," esp. pp. 175–78; John Paul Harper, "Be Fruitful and Multiply: Origins of Legal Restrictions on Planned Parenthood in Nineteenth-Century America," in Carol Ruth Berkin and Mary Beth Norton, eds., *Women of America: A History* (Boston, 1979), pp. 245–65; Brodie, "Family Limitation," part I. For an example of the range of methods advised, see *Dr. Groves' New Marriage Guide and Book of Nature*, rev. ed. (New York, 1869), chaps. 7 and 8.

10. La Sorte, "Practices," p. 173; Brodie, "Family Limitation," p. 471.

11. Yates, "Birth Control," p. 44; *Police Gazette,* January 4, 1890, p. 15. See Chap. 7 of this book on the Comstock law.

12. John Mack Faragher, *Women and Men on the Overland Trail* (New Haven, 1979), p. 123; Foote to Gilder, Dec. 21, 1876, Mary Hallock Foote Papers, Special Collections, Green Library, Stanford University.

13. Elizabeth Hampsten, *Read This Only to Yourself: The Private Writings of Midwestern Women, 1880–1910* (Bloomington, Ind., 1981), p. 104.

14. Sandra L. Myres, *Westering Women and the Frontier Experience, 1800–1915* (Albuquerque, 1982), pp. 154–55; Peter Gay, *The Bourgeois Experience, Victoria to Freud* (New York, 1984), vol. 1 *Education of the Senses,* pp. 257–58.

15. Ellen K. Rothman, *Hands and Hearts: A History of Courtship in America* (New York, 1984), p. 141; James C. Mohr, ed., and Richard E. Winslow III, associate ed., *The Cormany Diaries: A Northern Family in the Civil War* (Pittsburgh, 1982), p. 131 and n. 14; Myres, *Westering Women,* pp. 154–55.

16. Brodie, "Family Limitation," pp. 432–36; Mosher, *Mosher Survey,* cases 35, 28, and 47; Gay, *Bourgeois Experience,* p. 85.

17. Myres, *Westering Women,* p. 155; Faragher, *Overland Trail,* p. 123; James C. Mohr, *Abortion in America: The Origins and Evolution of National Policy, 1800–1900* (New York, 1978), p. 7; Michael Grossberg, *Governing the Hearth: Law and Family in Nineteenth-Century America* (Chapel Hill, 1985), p. 181; La Sorte, "Practices," p. 169; Darlis Miller, "Foragers, Army Women and Prostitutes," in Joan M. Jensen and Darlis Miller, eds., *New Mexico Women: Intercultural Perspectives* (Albuquerque, 1986): pp. 155–66.

18. Miller, "Foragers," p. 156; La Sorte, "Practices," pp. 167–72; John S. Haller, Jr., and Robin M. Haller, *The Physician and Sexuality in Victorian America* (Urbana, Ill., 1974), p. 117.

19. La Sorte, "Practices," pp. 167–69; Harper, "Be Fruitful," p. 250. See also Mohr, *Abortion,* chap. 3.

20. Gerda Lerner, *The Female Experience: An American Documentary* (Indianapolis, 1977) pp. 426–27. See also Linda Gordon, *Woman's Body, Woman's Right: A Social History of Birth Control in America* (New York, 1976).

21. Roger Lane, *Violent Death in the City: Suicide, Accident and Murder in Nineteenth-Century Philadelphia* (Cambridge, Mass. 1979), pp. 54–55; Erna Olafson Hellerstein et al., eds., *Victorian Women: A Documentary Account of Women's Lives in Nineteenth-Century England, France, and the United States* (Stanford, 1981), pp. 201–2; Edward Van Every, *Sins of America, as "Exposed" by the Police Gazette* (New York, 1931), pp. 14–22.; Grossberg, *Governing the Hearth,* p. 181.

22. Gay, *Bourgeois Experience,* p. 97; Robert L. Griswold, *Family and Divorce in California, 1850–1890: Victorian Illusions and Everyday Realities* (Albany, 1982), pp. 136–37; Helen Olson Halversen and Lorraine Fletcher, "Nineteenth-Century Midwife: Some Recollections," *Oregon Historical Quarterly* 70:1 (March–December 1969), p. 48.

23. Ann Firor Scott, *The Southern Lady: From Pedestal to Politics, 1830–1930* (Chicago, 1970), p. 38. The rarity of southern personal sources on contraception and abortion is noted in Sally McMillen, "Mother's Sacred Duty: Breast Feeding Patterns Among Middle and Upper Class Women in the Antebellum South," *Journal of Southern History* 51:3 (August 1985), p. 348, and Clinton, *Plantation Mistress,* p. 206.

24. Eugene D. Genovese, *Roll, Jordan, Roll: The World the Slaves Made* (New York, 1974), pp. 465–66; Dorothy Sterling, ed., *We Are Your Sisters: Black Women in the Nineteenth Century* (New York, 1984), pp. 32, 40.

25. Mohr, *Abortion,* p. 50; La Sorte, "Practices," p. 172; Lane, *Violent Death,* p. 99.

26. Mohr, *Abortion,* p. 88.

27. Ibid., chap. 2; Grossberg, *Governing the Hearth,* pp. 161–66. On criminalization, see chap. 7 of this book.

28. Grossberg, *Governing the Hearth,* pp. 179–81; La Sorte, "Practices," p. 171.

29. Grossberg, *Governing the Hearth,* pp. 70–77, 218.

30. Ronald T. Takaki, *Iron Cages: Race and Culture in Nineteenth-Century America* (Seattle, 1982), p. 24.

31. Jayme Socolow, *Eros and Modernization: Sylvester Graham, Health Reform, and the Origins of Victorian Sexuality in America* (Rutherford, N.J., 1983), p. 167. On medical advice, see, e.g., Haller and Haller, *Physician,* and Ronald G. Walters, ed., *Primers for Purity: Sexual Advice to Victorian America* (Englewood Cliffs, N.J., 1974).

32. Haller and Haller, *Physician,* pp. 260–61; Charles Rosenberg, *The Cholera Years: The United States in 1832, 1849 and 1866* (Chicago, 1962).

33. Carroll Smith-Rosenberg, "Sex As Symbol in Victorian Purity: An Ethnohistorical Analysis of Jacksonian America," *American Journal of Sociology* 84, supplement (1978), pp. S212–S247; Walters, *Primers,* p. 116.

34. Takaki, *Iron Cages,* p. 24.

35. Stephen Nissenbaum, *Sex, Diet and Debility in Jacksonian America: Sylvester Graham and Health Reform* (Westport, Conn., 1980), pp. 30, 110; Walters, *Primers,* pp. 149–50; G. J. Barker-Benfield, *The Horrors of the Half-Known Life: Male Attitudes Toward Women and Sexuality in Nineteenth-Century America* (New York, 1976), chap. 14; *Dr. Groves' New Marriage Guide,* chap. 5; *Facts and Important Information for Young Men Showing the Awful Effects of Masturbation* (Boston, 1844), pp. 10–11.

36. Nissenbaum, *Sex, Diet and Debility,* chap. 2; R. P. Neuman, "Masturbation, Madness, and the Modern Concepts of Childhood and Adolescence," *Journal of Social History* 8 (Spring 1975), pp. 1–27; R. H. MacDonald, "The Frightful Consequences of Onanism: Notes on the History of a Delusion," *Journal of the History of Ideas* 28:3 (July–Sept. 1967), pp. 423–31.

37. Barker-Benfield, *Horrors,* p. 179; Walters, *Primers,* pp. 34–46.

38. John Ware, *Hints to Young Men, on the Relations of the Sexes* (1850; reprint, Boston, 1866), pp. 30–33; Peter Gardella, *Innocent Ecstasy: How Christianity Gave America an Ethic of Sexual Pleasure* (New York, 1985), pp. 69–73; Henry Guernsey, *Plain Talk on Avoided Subjects* (1882), cited in Degler, *At Odds,* p. 259.

39. Hellerstein et al., *Victorian Women,* 177–79; [Cooke], *Satan,* 143; Eliza Duffey, *What Women Should Know* (Philadelphia, 1873) and *The Relations of the Sexes* (1876; reprint, New York, 1889), p. 313; Barbara Welter, "The Cult of True Womanhood, 1820–1860," in Michael Gordon, ed., *The American Family in Social-Historical Perspective* (New York, 1973), p. 228.

40. Regina G. Kunzel, " 'Fair and Tender Ladies': Conceptions of Women in Nineteenth-Century New England Balladry," Senior honors thesis, Stanford University Department of History, 1981, p. 40; Faragher, *Overland Trail,* pp. 151–55.

41. David Brian Davis, *Homicide in American Fiction, 1798–1860: A Study in Social Values* (Ithaca, 1957), p. 212.

42. Nancy F. Cott, "Passionlessness: An Interpretation of Victorian Sexual Ideology, 1790–1850," in Cott and Pleck, *Heritage*, pp. 162–81; D. S. Smith, "Family Limitation"; Degler, *At Odds*, pp. 257–59.

43. P. C. Dunne and A. F. Dubois, *Young Married Lady's Private Medical Guide*, trans. F. Harrison Doane (Boston, 1853), p. 16; [Cooke] *Satan*, pp. 143, 146–47; Jean DuBois, *The Secret Habits of the Female Sex*, English translation (New York, 1848); [Cooke], *Satan*, p. 106; Mary Gove Nichols, *Lectures to Ladies on Anatomy and Physiology* (Boston, 1842). See also Haller and Haller, *Physician*, pp. 105–6.

44. Gay, *Bourgeois Experience*, pp. 159–60; Charles A. Green, *Build Well: The Bases of Individual, Home, and National Elevation* (Boston, 1885), p. 76.

45. Hellerstein, *Victorian Women*, pp. 179–80.

46. Journal 4, January 13, 1840, Caroline Healey Dall Papers, Massachusetts Historical Society, Boston, Mass. We thank Gary Sue Goodman for this reference.

47. Rothman, *Hands and Hearts*, chap. 1.

48. Bell Wiley, *The Plain People of the Confederacy* (Baton Rouge, La., 1944), p. 61; Faragher, *Overland Trail*, pp. 144–45, 155–56; Goldman, *Gold Diggers*, p. 40.

49. Lois Banner, *American Beauty* (New York, 1983), pp. 80–82; Christine Stansell, *City of Women: Sex and Class in New York 1789–1860* (New York, 1986), pp. 83, 90, 93, 254n35.

50. Frank C. Tilley and Jean La Croix, "Only in Fun" (songsheet), No. 0615-17, Print Division, Library of Congress, Washington, D.C.

51. Stansell, *City of Women*, pp. 83, 86–90, 97.

52. Grossberg, *Governing the Hearth*, pp. 35, 39; Rothman, *Hands and Hearts*, pp. 103–10.

53. Mohr, *Cormany Diaries*, Dec. 12, 1860, and April 14, 1860, pp. 64, 80.

54. Gerda Lerner, *The Grimke Sisters from South Carolina* (New York, 1971), pp. 216–30; Gay, *Bourgeois Experience*, pp. 456–57.

55. Gay, *Bourgeois Experience*, pp. 129, 79.

56. Degler, *At Odds*, p. 32; Grossberg, *Governing the Hearth*, pp. 41–42; Elaine Tyler May, *Great Expectations: Marriage and Divorce in Post-Victorian America* (Chicago, 1980), p. 43; Mohr, *Cormany Diaries*, July 7, 1860, pp. 109–10.

57. Ellen K. Rothman, "Sex and Self-Control: Middle-Class Courtship in America, 1770–1870," in Michael Gordon, ed., *The American Family in Social-Historical Perspective* (New York, 1983), pp. 402–6; Rothman, *Hands and Hearts*, pp. 136–37.

58. Stansell, *City of Women*, pp. 77, 83.

59. For example, Mary Pierce Poor's diary records marital intercourse on an average of 1.12 times per week; in Dr. Clelia Mosher's survey, the seven women born in the first half of the nineteenth century had sex with their husbands on an average of 1.35 times per month; the Abigail English divorce case, cited below, claimed intercourse six times per week (Brodie, "Family Limitation," chap. 12; Mosher, *Mosher Survey*, cases 19, 14, 12, 35, and 47; Robert L. Griswold, "Sexual Cruelty and the Case for Divorce in Victorian America," *Signs* 11:3 [Spring 1986], pp. 529–41).

60. Glenda Riley, *Frontierswomen: The Iowa Experience* (Ames, Iowa, 1981), p. 127; Mohr, *Cormany Diaries*, Nov. 23, 1862, p. 251.

61. Clinton, *Plantation Mistress*, p. 207; Gay, *Bourgeois Experience*, pp. 125–26, 84.

62. Elizabeth Pleck, *Domestic Tyranny: The Making of American Social Policy Against Family Violence from Colonial Times to the Present* (New York: Oxford University Press, 1987), p. 94; Peter Bardaglio, "Families, Sex and the Law: the Legal

Transformation of the Nineteenth-Century Southern Household," Ph.D. dissertation, Stanford University, 1987, p. 224–25; Brodie, "Family Limitation," pp. 447–48.

63. Mosher, *Mosher Survey,* cases 19, 14, 12, 28, 35, and 47.

64. Several states expanded the grounds for divorce to include impotence, including Pennsylvania (1815) and Michigan (1832) (Grossberg, *Governing the Hearth,* pp. 109–10); Marilyn Ferris Motz, *True Sisterhood: Michigan Women and Their Kin, 1820–1920* [Albany, N.Y., 1983], pp. 122–24).

65. May, *Expectations,* pp. 34–38; Griswold, *Family and Divorce,* p. 115.

66. Susan L. Johnson, "Women's Households and Relationships in the Mining West: Central Arizona, 1863–73" Master's thesis, Arizona State University, 1984, p. 90; Griswold, "Sexual Cruelty," p. 538.

67. Johnson, "Women's Households," p. 103; May, *Expectations,* pp. 34–38.

68. Harriette A. Andreadis, "The Women's Commonwealth: A Study in the Coalescence of Social Forms," *Frontiers* 7:3 (1984), p. 80; Kathryn Kish Sklar, *Catharine Beecher: A Study in American Domesticity* (New Haven, 1973), pp. 206–9; Diner, *Erin's Daughters,* p. 58.

69. Mohr, *Cormany Diaries,* Aug. 22, 27, Sept. 1, 1865, pp. 510, 580, 581, xxx.

70. Stansell, *City of Women,* p. 78; Bardaglio, "Families," 188–89; Griswold, *Family and Divorce,* pp. 73–76; Jane Turner Censer, "Smiling Through Her Tears: Ante-Bellum Southern Women and Divorce," *American Journal of Legal History* 25:1 (January 1981), pp. 32–33.

71. Stansell, *City of Women,* p. 61; Gay, *Bourgeois Experience,* pp. 90–95.

72. Griswold, *Family and Divorce,* pp. 88–89; Goldman, *Gold Diggers,* p. 53; Bonnie L. Ford, "Women's Sexuality in California, 1840–72: A Matter of Class," Paper presented at the Western Association of Women Historians, May 1986, pp. 7, 12.

Chapter 5. Race and Sexuality

1. "Case of Eliza Grayson, No. 236, 596," Widow's Pension of the United States Colored Troops, Record Group 15, Records of the Veterans Administration, National Archives and Records Administration, Washington, D.C.

2. Ronald T. Takaki, *Iron Cages: Race and Culture in Nineteenth-Century America* (Seattle, 1982), pp. 50, 115, 217.

3. Walter L. Williams, *The Spirit and the Flesh: Sexual Diversity in American Indian Culture* (Boston, 1986), p. 167; Katherine Weist, "Beasts of Burden and Menial Slaves: Nineteenth-Century Observations of Northern Plains Indian Women," in Patricia Albers and Beatrice Medicine, eds., *The Hidden Half: Studies of Plains Indian Women* (Washington, D.C., 1983); Raymond DeMallie, "Male and Female in Traditional Lakota Culture," in *The Hidden Half,* p. 256; William G. McLoughlin, *Cherokees and Missionaries, 1789–1839,* (New Haven, 1984), pp. 204–5.

4. Rayna Green, "The Pocahontas Perplex: The Image of Indian Women in American Culture," *Massachusetts Review* 16 (Autumn 1975), p. 711; Glenda Riley, *Women and Indians on the Frontier, 1825–1915* (Albuquerque, 1984), pp. 74–75, 132.

5. Deena Gonzales, "The Spanish-Mexican Women of Santa Fe: Patterns of Their Resistance and Accommodation, 1820–1880," Ph.D. dissertation University of California, Berkeley, 1985, pp. 86–87; Antonia Castañeda, "The Political Economy of Nineteenth-Century Stereotypes of Californianas," Paper presented at the Pacific Coast Branch, American Historical Association, August 12–14, 1982, p. 4.

6. Rebecca McDowell Craver, *The Impact of Intimacy: Mexican-Anglo Intermarriage in New Mexico, 1821–1846,* in Southwestern Studies Monograph no. 66 (El Paso, 1982), p. 4; Darlis Miller, "Cross-Cultural Marriages in the Southwest: The New Mexico Experience, 1846–1900," *New Mexico Historical Review* 57:4 (October 1982), pp. 335–60; Janet LeCompte, "The Independent Women of Hispanic New Mexico, 1821–1846," *Western Historical Quarterly* 12:1 (January 1981), pp. 29, 32.

7. Gonzalez, "Spanish-Mexican Women," p. 32; Ramón Arturo Gutiérrez, "Marriage, Sex and the Family: Social Change in Colonial New Mexico, 1690–1846," Ph.D. dissertation, University of Wisconsin, Madison, 1980, pp. 31ff, 58, 350; LeCompte, "Independent Women," pp. 29, 32.

8. Richard Griswold del Castillo, *La Familia: Chicano Families in the Urban Southwest, 1848 to the Present* (Notre Dame, 1984), p. 79.

9. Gonzales, "Spanish-Mexican Women," p. 30.

10. del Castillo, *La Familia,* pp. 84, 88–91; Gonzalez, "Spanish-Mexican Women," p. 144; Susan L. Johnson, "Women's Households and Relationships in the Mining West: Central Arizona, 1863–1873," Master's thesis, Arizona State University, 1984, pp. 81–82.

11. Craver, *Impact of Intimacy,* pp. 17–20, 25–32; Gonzalez, "Spanish-Mexican Women," p. 115.

12. Gonzalez, "Spanish-Mexican Women," pp. 118–19; Albert Hurtado, "Ranchos, Gold Mines and Rancherias: A Socioeconomic History of Indians and Whites in Northern California, 1821–1860," Ph.D. dissertation, University of California, Santa Barbara, 1981, p. 263; Riley, *Women and Indians,* pp. 131, 181–83.

13. McLoughlin, *Cherokees and Missionaries,* pp. 25–26, 68–69, 187–88; del Castillo, *La Familia,* pp. 66–67. Where sex ratios remained high, in towns such as Santa Fe and Tucson, intermarriage persisted (del Castillo, n25–27).

14. Castañeda, "Political Economy," pp. 17–19; Ralph Mann, *After the Gold Rush: Society in Grass Valley and Nevada City, California, 1849–1870* (Stanford: Stanford University Press, 1982), pp. 50, 62.

15. Gutiérrez, "Marriage, Sex and the Family, pp. 118–19, 208; Cheryl J. Foote and Sandra K. Schackel, "Indian Women of New Mexico, 1535–1680," in Joan M. Jensen and Darlis Miller, eds., *New Mexico Women: Intercultural Perspectives* (Albuquerque, 1986), pp. 27–29; Williams, *Spirit and the Flesh,* p. 139.

16. Castañeda, "Political Economy," pp. 17–18; Riley, *Women and Indians,* pp. 69–70.

17. Hurtado, "Ranchos, Gold Mines and Rancherias," pp. 273–81; Mann, *After the Gold Rush,* p. 51.

18. Peggy Pascoe, "Gender and the Search for Moral Authority: Protestant Women and Rescue Homes in the American West, 1870–1930," Ph.D. dissertation, Stanford University, 1986, pp. 102–7; Martin Bauml Duberman, Fred Eggan, and Richard O. Clemmer, "Documents in Hopi Indian Sexuality: Imperialism, Culture, and Resistance," *Radical History Review* 20 (Spring–Summer 1979), esp. pp. 106–7; McLoughlin, *Cherokees and Missionaries,* pp. 78, 204–5; Joan M. Jensen, "Native American Women and Agriculture: A Seneca Case Study," *Sex Roles* 3:5 (1977), pp. 423–39.

19. Takaki, *Iron Cages,* p. 40.

20. Jane Turner Censer, *North Carolina Planters and Their Children, 1800–1860* (Baton Rouge, 1984), pp. 24–26, 70.

21. Winthrop D. Jordan, *White over Black: American Attitudes Towards the Negro, 1550–1812* (Baltimore, 1969), p. 474; Deborah Gray White, *Ain't I a Woman? Female Slaves in the Plantation South* (New York, 1985), p. 41.

22. Bertram Wyatt-Brown, *Southern Honor: Ethics and Behavior in the Old South* (New York, 1982), pp. 210–11, 293; Catherine Clinton, *The Plantation Mistress: Woman's World in the Old South* (New York, 1982), p. 113.

23. Ann Firor Scott, *The Southern Lady: From Pedestal to Politics* (Chicago, 1970), pp. 24, 37–42; Wyatt-Brown, *Southern Honor*, pp. 304–6; Clinton, *Plantation Mistress*, pp. 78–85; Censer, *North Carolina Planters*, p. 24.

24. Clinton, *Plantation Mistress*, pp. 104, 204; Wyatt-Brown, *Southern Honor*, p. 295.

25. White, *Female Slaves*, p. 43; Clinton, *Plantation Mistress*, p. 105.

26. Drew Faust, *James Henry Hammond and the Old South: A Design for Mastery* (Baton Rouge, 1982), pp. 241–43, 290, 314–15.

27. Wyatt-Brown, *Southern Honor*, pp. 299, 315–16.

28. Herbert G. Gutman, *The Black Family in Slavery and Freedom, 1750–1925* (New York, 1976), pp. 295–97.

29. Gutman, *Black Family*, pp. 63–64, 73–74, 117–18; Herbert Gutman and Richard Sutch, "Victorians All? The Sexual Mores and Conduct of Slaves and Their Masters," in Paul A. David et al., eds., *Reckoning With Slavery: A Critical Study of the Quantitative History of American Negro Slavery* (New York, 1976), p. 142; Dorothy Sterling, ed., *We Are Your Sisters: Black Women in the Nineteenth Century* (New York, 1984), pp. 34–35; Jacqueline Jones, *Labor of Love, Labor of Sorrow: Black Women, Work, and the Family from Slavery to the Present* (New York, 1985), p. 33.

30. Gutman, *Black Family*, pp. 60–66; Sterling, *Sisters*, p. 32; Letitia Woods Brown, *Free Negroes in the District of Columbia, 1790–1846* (New York, 1972), p. 3; Eugene D. Genovese, *Roll, Jordan, Roll: The World the Slaves Made* (New York, 1976), pp. 460–61; Eliza Grayson deposition, October 28, 1893.

31. Sterling, *Sisters*, p. 33.

32. White, *Female Slaves*, p. 150.

33. George P. Rawick, ed., *The American Slave: A Composite Autobiography* (Westport, Conn., 1972), vol. 12 (Georgia), pt. 2, p. 296, pt. 1, p. 228; Sterling, *Sisters*, pp. 34–35.

34. Gutman, *Black Family*, pp. 270–75, 83, 137; John W. Blassingame, *The Slave Community: Plantation Life in the Antebellum South* (New York, 1972), p. 86.

35. Rawick, *American Slave*, vol. 3 (South Carolina), pt. 3, p. 209; vol. 7 (Mississippi), p. 151; and vol. 12 (Georgia), pt. 2, pp. 268–69.

36. Blassingame, *Slave Community*, p. 81. Masters occasionally defended female slaves from unwanted sexual advances or tried to prevent the separation of families by sale. See, e.g., Rawick, *American Slave*, vol. 17 (Florida), p. 90, and Helen Tunnicliff Catterall, ed., *Judicial Cases Concerning American Slavery and the Negro* (1929–1937; reprint, New York, 1968), p. 423.

37. Gutman, *Black Family*, pp. 70, 67–68; White, *Female Slaves*, p. 156–57.

38. Peter Laslett, *Family Life and Illicit Love in Earlier Generations: Essays in Historical Sociology* (New York, 1977), p. 254; Herman Lantz and Lewellyn Hendrix, "Black Fertility and Black Family in Nineteenth-Century America," *Journal of Family History* 3:3 (Fall 1978), p. 255. A slight decline in black fertility at midcentury is noted

in Melvin Zelnick, "Fertility of American Negro in 1830 and 1850," *Population Studies* 20:1 (July 1966), pp. 77–83.

39. Rawick, *American Slave*, vol. 12 (Georgia), pt. 1, pp. 228 and 89; vol. 17 (Florida), p. 87; Gutman, *Black Family*, p. 77.

40. Angela Davis, "The Black Woman's Role in the Community of Slaves," *Black Scholar* 3 (December 1971); On fertility control see White, *Female Slaves*, pp. 84–88; Gutman, *Black Family*, pp. 80–81, 85; Rawick, *American Slave*, vol. 18 (Florida), p. 116.

41. Robert William Fogel and Stanley L. Engerman, *Time on the Cross The Economics of American Negro Slavery* (Boston, 1974) p. 132.

42. White, *Female Slaves*, pp. 152, 29–31; Sterling, *Sisters*, p. 25; Gutman, *Black Family*, p. 80; Rawick, *American Slave*, vol. 3 (South Carolina), pp. 194–95; Jones, *Labor of Love*, p. 37.

43. Rawick, *American Slave*, vol. 6 (Alabama), p. 46; Sterling, *Sisters*, pp. 26–27; Leon F. Litwak, *Been in the Storm So Long: The Aftermath of Slavery* (New York, 1979), p. 239.

44. Clinton, *Plantation Mistress*, pp. 216, 211; Sterling, *Sisters*, p. 24; Wyatt-Brown, *Southern Honor*, pp. 311, 314, 318; Suzanne Lebsock, *The Free Women of Petersburg: Status and Culture in a Southern Town, 1784–1860* (New York, 1984), p. 96.

45. White, *Female Slaves*, p. 37; Sterling, *Sisters*, p. 27.

46. Nancy F. Cott, ed., *Root of Bitterness: Documents of the Social History of American Women* (New York, 1972), p. 204.

47. Blassingame, *Slave Community*, p. 83; Catterall, *Judicial Cases*, pp. 451, 470, 320, 307. See also Joel Williamson, *Crucible of Race* (New York, 1984), p. 41, and Gutman, *Black Family*, p. 389. In Petersburg, Virginia, manumissions declined from the late eighteenth to the mid-nineteenth century (Lebsock, *Free Women of Petersburg*, pp. 95–96).

48. Catterall, *Judicial Cases*, p. 470; Gerda Lerner, *The Grimke Sisters from South Carolina* (New York, 1971) pp. 359–60.

49. Blassingame, *Slave Community*, p. 84.

50. Gary B. Mills, "Miscegenation and the Free Negro in Antebellum 'Anglo' Alabama: A Reexamination of Southern Race Relations," *Journal of American History* 68 (January 1981), pp. 22–23; John Blassingame, *Black New Orleans* (Chicago, 1973), p. 19; Blassingame, *Slave Community*, p. 84; Gutman, *Black Family*, 614n13.

51. Gutman, *Black Family*, pp. 424, 418–19; Grossberg, *Governing the Hearth*, pp. 133–34.

52. Elizabeth Pleck, "The Two-Parent Household: Black Family Structure in Late Nineteenth Century Boston," in Michael Gordon, ed., *The American Family in Social Historical Perspective* (New York, 1973), pp. 152–78; Litwak, *Been in the Storm*, pp. 243–44; Daniel Scott Smith, "The Long Cycle in American Illegitimacy and Prenuptial Pregnancy," in Peter Laslett, Karla Oosterveen, and Richard M. Smith, eds., *Bastardy and Its Comparative History* (Cambridge, Mass., 1980), p. 376; Gutman, *Black Family*, pp. 64–65.

53. Gutman, *Black Family*, pp. 394–99, 24–26; Sterling, *Sisters*, p. 341; Lerner, *Grimke Sisters*, pp. 172–88.

54. Litwak, *Been in the Storm*, pp. 265–66; Blassingame, *New Orleans*, pp. 203–5; Grossberg, *Governing the Hearth*, p. 136.

55. Gutman, *Black Family*, pp. 393, 400; Litwak, *Been in the Storm*, p. 243; Blassingame, *New Orleans*, p. 206; Sterling *Sisters*, pp. 341–42.

56. Grossberg, *Governing the Hearth*, p. 138; Gutman, *Black Family*, pp. 400, 389; Rawick, *American Slave*, vol. 7 (Mississippi), pp. 109–10.

Chapter 6. Outside the Family

1. "Notes & Notions," vol. 7, 1884–1885, pp. 478–81, 494–95, 100–108, 158, in the Frederick Shelley Ryman Papers, Massachusetts Historical Society, Boston, Massachusetts; Martin Bauml Duberman, *About Time: Exploring the Gay Past* (New York, 1986), p. 42.

2. Celia Morris Eckhardt, *Fanny Wright: Rebel in America* (Cambridge, Mass., 1984), p. 156.

3. Amanda Porterfield, *Feminine Spirituality in America: From Sarah Edwards to Martha Graham* (Philadelphia, 1980), p. 99; Eckhardt, *Fanny Wright*, p. 187.

4. Members of the women's rights movement that originated in the 1840s concentrated on reforming marriage rather than sex. Even their mild efforts at dress reform—adoption of the "bloomer" pantaloons for women—evoked such strong fears of gender disorder that feminists dropped their crusade for more practical clothing. Late-nineteenth-century feminists tried to raise the problem of marital sexuality, but they continued to risk condemnation for doing so.

5. Taylor Stoehr, *Free Love in America: A Documentary History* (New York, 1979), pp. 8, 278.

6. Dolores Hayden, *The Grand Domestic Revolution: A History of Feminist Design for American Homes, Neighborhoods and Cities* (Boston, 1981), p. 93; Stoehr, *Free Love in America*, pp. 12, 23.

7. Jayme Sokolow, *Eros and Modernization: Sylvester Graham, Health Reform, and the Origins of Victorian Sexuality in America* (Rutherford, N.J., 1983), pp. 130–31; Stephen Nissenbaum, *Sex, Diet, and Debility in Jacksonian America: Sylvester Graham and Health Reform* (Westport, Conn., 1980), pp. 158–70.

8. Thomas Low Nichols and Mary Gove Nichols, *Marriage: Its History, Character and Results* (Cincinnati, 1854), pp. 220–24, and *Esoteric Anthropology* (New York, 1853), pp. 153ff.

9. Lawrence Foster, *Religion and Sexuality: Three American Communal Experiments of the Nineteenth Century* (New York, 1981), pp. 46–47.

10. Louis J. Kern, *An Ordered Love: Sex Roles and Sexuality in Victorian Utopias: the Shakers, the Mormons, and the Oneida Community* (Chapel Hill, 1981), pp. 83, 93–97.

11. *Ibid.*, pp. 97–98, 100, 107–8.

12. *Ibid.*, p. 153.

13. Emily M. Austin, *Mormonism: or Life Among the Mormons* (Madison, Wis., 1882; reprint, New York, 1971), pp. 208, 216. We are grateful to Peggy Pascoe for this source.

14. Donald M. Scott and Bernard Wishy, eds., *America's Families: A Documentary History* (New York, 1982), pp. 336–37, 342–44.

15. Kern, *Ordered Love*, pp. 162–63, 150–53.

16. Foster, *Religion and Sexuality*, p. 94; Kern, *Ordered Love*, p. 242.

17. Kern, *Ordered Love,* p. 244.

18. *Ibid.,* pp. 203, 238–41, 250–55.

19. In *Truth About Love,* cited in Nancy Sahli, *Women and Sexuality in America: A Bibliography* (Boston, 1984), pp. 36–37.

20. Carroll Smith-Rosenberg, "The Female World of Love and Ritual: Relations Between Women in Nineteenth-Century America," in Nancy F. Cott and Elizabeth H. Pleck, eds., *A Heritage of Her Own* (New York, 1979), pp. 311–42.

21. On censorship, see Lillian Faderman, "Emily Dickinson's Letters to Sue Gilbert," *Massachusetts Review* 18 (September 1977), pp. 19–27; Robert K. Martin, *The Homosexual Tradition in American Poetry* (Austin, 1979); and Blanche Cook, "The Historical Denial of Lesbianism," *Radical History Review* 20 (Spring–Summer 1979), pp. 60–65.

22. Jonathan Ned Katz, ed., *Gay/Lesbian Almanac: A New Documentary* (New York, 1983), p. 39; Vern L. Bullough and Martha Voght, "Homosexuality and Its Confusion with the Secret Sin in Pre-Freudian America," *Journal of the History of Medicine and Allied Sciences* 28:2 (April 1973), pp. 143–55; Jonathan Katz, ed., *Gay American History,* (New York, 1976), p. 26; Lillian Faderman, *Surpassing the Love of Men: Romantic Friendship and Love Between Women from the Renaissance to the Present* (New York, 1981), p. 291. On the shift from homosexual acts to the homosexual role, see Mary McIntosh, "The Homosexual Role," *Social Problems* 16 (Fall 1968), pp. 182–92.

23. Michael Lynch, "New York City Sodomy, 1796–1873," Paper presented at the Institute for the Humanities, New York University, February 1, 1985, pp. 1–2.

24. Charley Shively, ed., *Calamus Lovers: Walt Whitman's Working Class Camerados* (San Francisco, 1987), pp. 56–58.

25. Katz, *Gay American History,* pp. 33–34.

26. Lynch, "New York City Sodomy," pp. 3, 10, 17; John Burnham, "Early References to Homosexual Communities in American Medical Writings," *Medical Aspects of Human Sexuality* 7:8 (August 1973), pp. 34, 40–41, 46–49.

27. Shively, *Calamus Lovers,* p. 99; Katz, *Gay American History,* pp. 655n35, 470, 27–28.

28. Walter L. Williams, *The Spirit and the Flesh: Sexual Diversity in American Indian Culture* (Boston, 1986), p. 159; Katz, ed., *Gay American History,* pp. 508–12; Ann M. Butler, *Daughters of Joy, Sisters of Misery: Prostitutes in the American West, 1865–1890* (Urbana, Ill., 1985), p. 144.

29. Katz, *Gay American History,* pp. 211, 214–25, 235, 253; Erna Hellerstein et al., *Victorian Women: A Documentary Account of Women's Lives in Nineteenth-Century England, France and the United States* (Stanford, 1981), pp. 186–87; Allan Berube, "Lesbian Masquerade," *Gay Community News* 7 (November 17, 1979), pp. 8–9.

30. Smith-Rosenberg, "Female World of Love and Ritual," p. 314; Nancy F. Cott, *The Bonds of Womanhood: "Woman's Sphere" in New England, 1780–1835* (New Haven, 1977), especially chap. 5.

31. Margaret J. M. Sweat, *Ethel's Love-Life: A Novel* (New York, 1859), pp. 82, 86. We are grateful to Eric Garber for calling our attention to this novel. See also Faderman, *Surpassing the Love of Men,* chap. 2.

32. Letter 96, in *The Letters of Emily Dickinson,* vol. 1, edited by Thomas H. Johnson (Cambridge, Mass., 1965), p. 215; Faderman, "Emily Dickinson's Letters," p. 214.

33. Nancy Sahli, "Smashing: Women's Relationships Before the Fall," *Chrysalis* 8 (Summer 1979), p.21.

34. John S. Haller and Robin M. Haller, *The Physician and Sexuality in Victorian America* (Urbana, Ill., 1974), p. 106; [Nicholas Francis Cooke], *Satan in Society, By a Physician* (Cincinnati, 1871), p. 107.

35. Sahli, "Smashing," p. 18, and "Changing Patterns of Sexuality and Female Interaction in Late Nineteenth-Century America: Some Case Studies from the Feminist Movement," Paper presented at the Berkshire Conference on the History of Women, Bryn Mawr College, June 11, 1976, pp. 3–4.

36. Katz, *Gay American History,* pp. 456–61, 467–80, and (on Henry David Thoreau and Charles Warren Stoddard, who shared these concerns) 456–61); Walt Whitman, *Democratic Vistas and Other Papers* (reprint, St. Clair Shores, Mich., 1970), pp. 67–68; Martin, *Homosexual Tradition,* p. 33.

37. Shively, *Calamus Lovers,* pp. 39, 43.

38. *Ibid.,* pp. 71, 110, 116; Justin Kaplan, *Walt Whitman: A Life* (New York, 1980), p. 314.

39. Shively, *Calamus Lovers,* p. 113; Katz, *Gay American History,* p. 350.

40. Duberman, *About Time,* pp. 41–48.

41. Katz, *Gay American History,* pp. 221–23. On the medicalization of deviance, see Chap. 10, this book.

42. Adrienne Siegel, "Brothels, Bets and Bars: Popular Literature Guidebooks to the Urban Underground, 1840–1870," *North Dakota Quarterly* 44:2 (Spring 1976), pp. 5–22; [Gustav Lening], *The Dark Side of New York and Its Criminal Classes* (New York, 1873), pp. 372, 387–88, 394; Christine Stansell, *City of Women: Sex and Class in New York, 1789–1860* (New York, 1986), p. 95.

43. George Ellington, *The Women of New York* (New York, 1850), p. 163; Edward Crapsey, *Nether Side of New York, or The Vice, Crime, and Poverty of the Great Metropolis* (New York, 1872), p. 143; [Lening], *Dark Side of New York,* pp. 360–61.

44. Peter Gardella, *Innocent Ecstasy: How Christianity Gave America an Ethic of Sexual Pleasure* (New York, 1985), p. 25; Ralph Ginzburg, *An Unhurried View of Erotica* (New York, 1958), p. 74; Felice Flanery Lewis, *Literature, Obscenity, and Law* (Carbondale, Ill., 1976), p. 524.

45. "Satanic Literature," *The National Magazine* 2 (January 1853), pp. 25–28.

46. Capt. M. G. Tousley to Abraham Lincoln, March 23, 1864, copy of typescript in Vertical File, Institute for the Study of Sex, Gender, and Reproduction, Indiana University, Bloomington, Indiana (hereafter Kinsey Institute); Robert W. Waitt, Jr., "A Kinsey Report on the Civil War," Speech given at the Kentucky Civil War Round Table, Fall 1963, typescript, Vertical File, Kinsey Institute), p. 5; Ginzburg, *Unhurried View,* p. 74.

47. William H. Gerdts, *The Great American Nude: A History in Art* (New York, 1974), p. 103.

48. *Police Gazette,* May 28 and November 12, 1892. On saloons, see Leonard Ellis, "Men Among Men: An Exploration of All-Male Relationships in Victorian America," Ph.D. dissertation, Columbia University, 1982, pp. 117, 150–52. At this time the term *gay* referred to those who did not adhere to strict moral standards, and the gay life meant prostitution or dissipation, not homosexuality.

49. Stansell, *City of Women,* pp. 181–84, 188.

50. Lois Banner, *American Beauty* (New York, 1983), pp. 42, 75–76; *Dark Side,* p. 366; William Sanger, *The History of Prostitution* (1858; reprint, New York, 1895), pp. 575–80; Jacqueline Baker Barnhart, "Working Women: Prostitution in San Francisco from the Gold Rush to 1900," Ph.D. dissertation, University of California, Santa Cruz, 1976, pp. 82–83; Roger Lane, *Violent Death in the City: Suicide, Accident and Murder in Nineteenth-Century Philadelphia* (Cambridge, Mass., 1986), pp. 123–25, 175.

51. Catherine Clinton, *The Plantation Mistress: Woman's World in the Old South* (New York, 1982), p. 104; Bertram Wyatt-Brown, *Southern Honor: Ethics and Behavior in the Old South* (New York, 1982), p. 293; Suzanne Lebsock, *The Free Women of Petersburg: Status and Culture in a Southern Town, 1784–1860* (New York, 1984), p. 179; Richard Tansey, "Prostitution and Politics in Antebellum New Orleans," *Southern Studies* 18 (Winter 1979), pp. 451–60.

52. Herbert G. Gutman, *The Black Family in Slavery and Freedom, 1750–1925* (New York, 1976), p. 613; Waitt, "Kinsey Report on the Civil War," pp. 3–5; Jacqueline Jones, *Labor of Love, Labor of Sorrow: Black Women, Work, and the Family from Slavery to the Present* (New York, 1985), p. 270; Lawrence Murphy, "The Enemy Among Us: Venereal Disease Among Union Soldiers in the Far West, 1861–1865," *Civil War History* 31:3 (September 1985), p. 259.

53. Waitt, "Kinsey Report on the Civil War," pp. 3–6; Paul Boyer, *Urban Masses and Moral Order in America, 1820–1920* (Cambridge, Mass., 1978), p. 192.

54. Marion S. Goldman, *Gold Diggers and Silver Miners: Prostitution and Social Life on the Comstock Lode* (Ann Arbor, 1981), pp. 1, 61–63.

55. Butler, *Daughters of Joy,* pp. 9–11, 36.

56. Lucie Cheng Hirata, "Free, Indentured, Enslaved: Chinese Prostitutes in Nineteenth-Century America," *Signs* 5 (Autumn 1979), pp. 3–29; Yuji Ichioka, "Ameyuki-San: Japanese Prostitutes in Nineteenth-Century America," *Amerasia Journal* 4:1 (1977), pp. 1–21.

57. Goldman, *Gold Diggers,* p. 102; Joseph F. Kett, *Rites of Passage: Adolescence in America, 1790 to the Present* (New York, 1977), p. 89.

58. Sanger, *History of Prostitution,* pp. 488–522.

59. Estelle B. Freedman, *Their Sisters' Keepers: Women's Prison Reform in America, 1830–1930* (Ann Arbor, 1981), pp. 84–85; Goldman, *Gold Diggers,* pp. 67–71; Butler, *Daughters of Joy,* pp. 5, 15; Hasia R. Diner, *Erin's Daughters in America* (Baltimore, 1983), pp. 114–17; James Oliver Horton and Lois E. Horton, *Black Bostonians: Family Life and Community Struggle in the Antebellum North* (New York, 1979), p. 35.

60. Julie Roy Jeffrey, *Frontier Women: The Trans-Mississippi West, 1840–1880* (New York, 1979), p. 121.

61. Ralph Mann, *After the Gold Rush: Society in Grass Valley and Nevada City, California, 1849–1970* (Stanford, 1982), p. 37; Deena Gonzalez, "The Spanish-Mexican Women of Santa Fe: Patterns of Their Resistance and Accommodation, 1820–1880," Ph.D. dissertation, University of California, Berkeley, 1985, p. 79; Sandra L. Myres, *Westering Women and the Frontier Experience, 1800–1915* (Albuquerque, 1982), pp. 255–56; Waitt, "Kinsey Report on the Civil War," p. 3; Butler, *Daughters of Joy,* pp. 74–76; Goldman, *Gold Diggers,* p. 134; Jeffrey, *Frontier Women,* pp. 123–24.

62. Clinton, *Plantation Mistress,* p. 104; Ryman Papers, Mass. Hist. Soc.; Robert L. Griswold, *Family and Divorce in California, 1850–1890: Victorian Illusions and Everyday Realities* (Albany, N.Y., 1982), p. 118; Goldman, *Gold Diggers,* pp. 51–54.

Chapter 7. Sexual Politics

1. William W. Sanger, *The History of Prostitution: Its Extent, Causes, and Effects Throughout the World* (orig. 1858; reprint New York, 1895), Appendix, pp. 694–95; "The Shame of St. Louis," *The Woman's Journal* May 3, 1873, p. 1.

2. Ruth Rosen, *The Lost Sisterhood: Prostitution in America, 1900–1918* (Baltimore, 1982), p. 4; Joan M. Jensen, *Loosening the Bonds: Mid-Atlantic Farm Women, 1750–1850* (New Haven, 1986), p. 71; Christine Stansell, *City of Women: Sex and Class in New York, 1789–1860* (New York, 1986), p. 61.

3. Ronald G. Walters, "The Erotic South: Civilization and Sexuality in American Abolitionism," *American Quarterly* 25 (May 1973), pp. 177–201; Paul G. Faler, *Mechanics and Manufacturers in the Early Industrial Revolution* (Albany, N.Y., 1981), pp. 123–37; Paul Johnson, *A Shopkeeper's Millennium: Society and Revivals in Rochester, New York, 1815–1837* (New York, 1978), p. 58; Allan Dawley, *Class and Community: The Industrial Revolution in Lynn* (Cambridge, Mass., 1976), p. 116; Paul S. Boyer, *Urban Masses and Moral Order in America, 1820–1920,* (Cambridge, Mass., 1978), pp. 8, 12.

4. Mary P. Ryan, *Cradle of the Middle Class: The Family in Oneida County, New York, 1790–1865* (New York, 1981), p. 116; Barbara Berg, *The Remembered Gate: Origins of American Feminism* (New York, 1978), p. 181.

5. Estelle B. Freedman, *Their Sisters' Keepers: Women's Prison Reform in America, 1830–1930* (Ann Arbor, 1981), p. 33; Berg, *Remembered Gate,* p. 181.

6. Carroll Smith-Rosenberg, *Disorderly Conduct: Visions of Gender in Victorian America* (New York, 1985), pp. 109–28.

7. Freedman, *Sisters' Keepers,* chap. 2; Barbara Hobson, "Seduced and Abandoned, A Tale of a Wicked City: The Response to Prostitution in Boston, 1820–1860," Paper presented at the Berkshire Conference on the History of Women, Mt. Holyoke College, August 23, 1978, p. 4; Smith-Rosenberg *Disorderly Conduct,* pp. 109–28.

8. Berg, *Remembered Gate,* p. 184.

9. Ryan, *Cradle of the Middle Class,* pp. 119–22.

10. Michael Grossberg, *Governing the Hearth: Law and the Family in Nineteenth-Century America* (Chapel Hill, 1985), pp. 47–48; Taylor Stoehr, *Free Love in America: A Documentary History* (New York, 1979), p. 24; Berg, *Remembered Gate,* p. 211.

11. G. J. Barker-Benfield, *The Horrors of the Half-Known Life: Male Attitudes Toward Women and Sexuality in Nineteenth-Century America* (New York, 1976), pp. 88–89, 97, and chap. 11; Ann Douglass Wood, "The Fashionable Diseases: Women's Complaints and Their Treatment in Nineteenth-Century America," in *Clio's Consciousness Raised,* ed. Mary S. Hartman and Lois Banner (New York, 1974), pp. 3–8.

12. David M. Kennedy, *Birth Control in America: The Career of Margaret Sanger* (New Haven, 1970), p. 45.

13. James C. Mohr, *Abortion in America: The Origins and Evolution of National Policy, 1800–1900* (New York, 1978); Grossberg, *Governing the Hearth,* especially p. 161; Smith-Rosenberg, *Disorderly Conduct,* pp. 217–41.

14. James Boyd Jones, "A Tale of Two Cities: The Hidden Battle Against Venereal Disease in Civil War Nashville and Memphis," *Civil War History* 31:3 (September 1985), p. 275.

15. David J. Pivar, *Purity Crusade: Sexual Morality and Social Control, 1868–1900* (Westport, Conn., 1973), p. 95; John C. Burnham, "Medical Inspection of Prostitutes

in America in the Nineteenth Century: The St. Louis Experiment and its Sequel," *Bulletin of the History of Medicine* 45:3 (May–June 1971), pp. 203–18.

16. Judith R. Walkowitz, *Prostitution and Victorian Society: Women, Class, and the State* (New York, 1980), part II.

17. Susan B. Anthony, "Social Purity" (1875), in Aileen S. Kraditor, ed., *Up from the Pedestal: Selected Writings in the History of American Feminism* (Chicago, 1968), pp. 159–67. On the origins of social purity, see Pivar, *Purity Crusade,* chaps. 1–3.

18. Burnham, "Medical Inspection," pp. 203–218; Pivar, *Purity Crusade,* chap. 2. Pivar identifies two women's groups that favored the licensing of prostitutes in the 1890s, one in Boston and one in Illinois (p. 119).

19. On rescue homes, see Pivar, *Purity Crusade,* pp. 95, 107–10, and Freedman, *Sisters' Keepers,* chap. 7; also on homes, including Cameron House, see Peggy Pascoe, "Gender and the Search for Moral Authority: Protestant Women and Rescue Homes in the American West, 1870–1930," Ph.D. dissertation, Stanford University, 1986.

20. *Report of the International Council of Women* (Washington, D.C., 1888), p. 274; Ellen Battelle Dietrick, "Rescuing Fallen Woman," *Woman's Journal,* May 27, 1893, p. 162; Elizabeth Pleck, "Feminist Responses to 'Crimes Against Women,' 1800–1896," *Signs* 8:3 (Spring 1983), p. 459.

21. Barbara Epstein, *The Politics of Domesticity: Women, Evangelism, and Temperance in Nineteenth-Century America* (Middletown, Conn., 1981), pp. 125–28; Pivar, *Purity Crusade,* pp. 111–14.

22. Ruth Bordin, *Women and Temperance: The Quest for Power and Liberty, 1873–1900* (Philadelphia, 1981), pp. 110–11; Pivar, *Purity Crusade,* p. 140.

23. Pleck, "Feminist Responses," p. 459.

24. Harriet Stanton Blatch, "Voluntary Motherhood" (1891), in Kraditor, *Up from the Pedestal,* pp. 167–75; Linda Gordon, *Woman's Body, Woman's Right: A Social History of Birth Control in America* (New York, 1976), chaps. 5–6. For an example of the theme of race progress through willing mothers, see John Cowan, *The Science of a New Life* (New York, 1880).

25. Elizabeth Blackwell, "On the Abuses of Sex-II. Fornication," in Erna Olafson Hellerstein et al., eds., *Victorian Women: A Documentary Account of Women's Lives in Nineteenth Century England, France, and the United States* (Stanford, Ca, 1981), pp. 179–180; see also Blackwell, *The Human Element in Sex: A Medical Inquiry into the Relation of Sexual Physiology to Christian Morality* (London, 1884); Ida Craddock, "Right Marital Living" (1899), in Stoehr, *Free Love,* p. 631.

26. Gordon, *Woman's Body,* chap. 5.

27. Elizabeth Lisle Saxon, in *Report of the International Council of Women,* p. 251; William Leach, *True Love and Perfect Union: The Feminist Reform of Sex and Society* (New York, 1980), p. 51 and chap. 2; Pivar, *Purity Crusade,* p. 131.

28. Milton Rugoff, *Prudery and Passion: Sexuality in Victorian America* (New York, 1971), pp. 121–22; Wayne E. Fuller, *The American Mail: Enlarger of the Common Life* (Chicago, 1972), p. 251.

29. Felice Flanery Lewis, *Literature, Obscenity, and Law* (Carbondale, Ill., 1976), pp. 5–7; Ralph Ginzburg, *An Unhurried View of Erotica* (New York, 1958), p. 73.

30. William H. Gerdts, *The Great American Nude: A History in Art* (New York, 1974), pp. 36, 46.

31. Joshua C. Taylor, *William Page, The American Titian* (Chicago, 1957), pp. 47–48; Gerdts, *Great American Nude,* pp. 78, 80.

32. Robert Bremner, introduction to *Traps for the Young,* by Anthony Comstock, (Cambridge, Mass., 1967), p. xx.

33. [YMCA], *A Memorandum Respecting New York as a Field for Moral and Christian Effort among Young Men: Its Neglected Condition; and the Fitness of the New York Young Men's Christian Association as a Principal Agency for its Due* (New York, 1866), pp. 3–6.

34. Comstock, *Traps for the Young,* pp. 25, 42.

35. Bremner, introduction to Comstock, *Traps for the Young,* p. xi.

36. New York Society for the Suppression of Vice, *Second Annual Report* (January 27, 1876), p. 11; Fuller, *American Mail,* pp. 252–55, 267–68; Paul S. Boyer, *Purity in Print: The Vice-Society Movement and Book Censorship in America* (New York, 1968), p. 10.

37. Gerdts, *Great American Nude,* pp. 110, 148.

38. Boyer, *Purity in Print,* pp. 12, 17–19; New England Watch and Ward Society, *Quarter of a Century and Twenty-Fifth Annual Report* (Boston, 1903), pp. 6–7; Pivar, *Purity Crusade,* pp. 182–84; Rugoff, *Prudery and Passion,* pp. 128, 132–33; Hal D. Sears, *The Sex Radicals: Free Love in High Victorian America* (Lawrence, Kans., 1977), p. 115; Bremner, introduction to Comstock, *Traps for the Young,* pp. xxvi–xxviii.

39. Stoehr, *Free Love,* pp. 48, 63, 67 (Craddock letter, pp. 311–13). See below in present chapter for discussion of Heywood and Harmon.

40. *Ibid.,* pp. 39–45; M. M. Marberry, *Vicky: A Biography of Victoria C. Woodhull* (New York, 1967).

41. Stoehr, *Free Love,* pp. 42, 364–66.

42. *Ibid.,* pp. 41–44; Mary S. Marsh, *Anarchist Women, 1870–1920* (Philadelphia, 1981), pp. 72ff; Sears, *Sex Radicals,* pp. 158, 177–79.

43. Sears, *Sex Radicals,* pp. 68–85; Marsh, *Anarchist Women,* p. 90.

44. Stoehr, *Free Love,* p. 59; Sears, *Sex Radicals,* p. 226.

45. Sears, *Sex Radicals,* p. 120.

Chapter 8. "Civilized Morality" Under Stress

1. Katharine B. Davis, *Factors in the Sex Life of Twenty-Two Hundred Women* (New York, 1929).

2. The phrase comes from Freud's article " 'Civilized' Sexual Morality and Modern Nervous Disorder," published in 1908. For a discussion of it in an American context see Nathan G. Hale, *Freud and the Americans: The Beginnings of Psychoanalysis in the United States, 1876–1917* (New York, 1971).

3. Paula S. Fass, *The Damned and the Beautiful: American Youth in the 1920s* (New York, 1977), pp. 60–61.

4. *Ibid.,* pp. 66–67.

5. Davis, *Factors in the Sex Life;* Clelia Mosher, *The Mosher Survey: Sexual Attitudes of Forty-five Victorian Women,* ed. James Mahood and Kristine Wenburg (New York, 1980).

6. Paul Robinson has coined the phrase "sexual enthusiast" to describe the modern reaction against Victorianism. See Paul Robinson, *The Modernization of Sex: Havelock Ellis, Alfred Kinsey, William Masters, and Virginia Johnson* (New York, 1976), p. 3.

7. *The Mosher Survey,* cases 30, 33, 19, 32.

8. Davis, *Factors in the Sex Life,* p. 67; Alice B. Stockham, *Tokology: A Book for Every Woman* (Chicago: Alice B. Stockham and Co., 1883).

9. Davis, *Factors in the Sex Life,* pp. 344–45, 64, 67.

10. *The Mosher Survey,* cases 14, 17, 33, 47; Davis, *Factors in the Sex Life,* p. 168.

11. Davis, *Factors in the Sex Life,* pp. 69–71.

12. *The Mosher Survey,* cases 40, 44, 10, 12.

13. Ellen K. Rothman, *Hands and Hearts: A History of Courtship in America* (New York, 1984), p. 239.

14. *Ibid.,* pp. 200, 255, 240, 228, 238.

15. *Ibid.,* pp. 220, 236, 187.

16. Max J. Exner, *Problems and Principles of Sex Education: A Study of 948 College Men* (New York, 1915), pp. 4–6, 20, 15–17.

17. *Ibid.,* pp. 9–11.

18. *G. A. R. Souvenir Sporting Guide* (New Orleans, 1895) and *The "Blue Book"* (privately printed, 1936), copies in Institute for the Study of Sex, Gender, and Reproduction, Bloomington, Indiana (hereafter Kinsey Institute); George Kneeland, *Commercialized Prostitution in New York,* rev. ed. (New York, 1917), p. 11. For other sources from which this discussion of the red-light district is drawn see Ruth Rosen, *The Lost Sisterhood: Prostitution in America, 1900–1918* (Baltimore, 1982); Syracuse Moral Survey Committee, *The Social Evil in Syracuse* (Syracuse, 1913); *Report of the Vice Commission of Philadelphia* (Philadelphia, 1913); American Vigilance Association, *A Report on Vice in the City of Lancaster, Pa.* (1913).

19. Rosen, *The Lost Sisterhood,* p. 95. For the fears of younger men see Exner, *Problems and Principles,* and Paul Strong, *The Effectiveness of Certain Social Hygiene Literature* (New York, 1923).

20. Allan M. Brandt, *No Magic Bullet: A Social History of Venereal Disease in the United States Since 1880* (New York, 1985), pp. 12–13.

21. Robert A. Woods and Albert J. Kennedy, eds., *Young Working Girls: A Summary of Evidence from Two Thousand Social Workers* (Boston, 1913), pp. 66, 54, 104; *Report and Recommendations for the Wisconsin Legislative Committee to Investigate the White Slave Traffic and Kindred Subjects* (Madison, 1914), p. 44; Kneeland, *Commercialized Prostitution,* p. 27.

22. W. E. B. Du Bois, *The Philadelphia Negro: A Social Study* (1899; reprint, New York: Schocken Books, 1967), p. 166; Virginia Yans-McLaughlin, *Family and Community: Italian Immigrants in Buffalo, 1880–1930* (Urbana, Ill., 1982), p. 93.

23. Woods and Kennedy, *Young Working Girls,* p. 161; Kathy Peiss, *Cheap Amusements: Working Women and Leisure in Turn-of-the-Century New York* (Philadelphia, 1986), p. 45; Yans-McLaughlin, *Family and Community,* p. 105; Margaret Sanger, *My Fight for Birth Control,* excerpted in Linda K. Kerber and Jane De Hart Mathews, *Women's America: Refocusing the Past* (New York, 1982), p. 313. On Japanese women see Yuji Ichioka, "*Amerika Nadeshiko:* Japanese Immigrant Women in the United States, 1900–1924," *Pacific Historical Review* 49 (1980), pp. 339–57.

24. Peter Paul Jonitis, *The Acculturation of the Lithuanians of Chester, Pennsylvania* (reprint, New York, 1985), p. 404; Yans-McLaughlin, *Family and Community,* p. 95.

25. John Dollard, *Caste and Class in a Southern Town* (New Haven, 1937), p. 139.

26. Anne Firor Scott, *The Southern Lady: From Pedestal to Politics* (Chicago, 1970), p. 217; Lary May, *Screening Out the Past: The Birth of Mass Culture and the Motion Picture Industry* (New York, 1980), p. 69; Dollard, *Caste and Class,* pp. 139, 168.

27. Hortense Powdermaker, *After Freedom: A Cultural Study in the Deep South* (New York, 1939), pp. 152, 160; Lawrence Levine, *Black Culture and Black Consciousness* (New York, 1977), p. 279.

28. Vance Rudolph, " 'Unprintable' Ozark Folk Beliefs," typescript, 1954, Kinsey Institute, Bloomington, Indiana, pp. 34–35.

29. Vance Rudolph, "Ribaldry at Ozark Dances," typescript, 1954, Kinsey Institute, Bloomington, Indiana, pp. 2, 11–12, 16–17.

30. For the rise of the department store see Susan Porter Benson, *Counter Cultures: Saleswomen, Managers, and Customers in American Department Stores, 1890–1940* (Urbana, Ill., 1986).

31. Syracuse Moral Survey Committee, *The Social Evil in Syracuse,* p. 81.

32. Roberta Frankfort, *Collegiate Women: Domesticity and Career in Turn-of-the-Century America* (New York, 1977), p. 88; Carroll Smith-Rosenberg, *Disorderly Conduct: Visions of Gender in Victorian America* (New York, 1985), p. 259.

33. For the propensity of college-educated women to remain single see Frankfort, *Collegiate Women,* pp. 58–59, 73–75, 112–13; Mabel Newcomer, *A Century of Higher Education for American Women* (New York, 1959), p. 212; and Lillian Faderman, *Surpassing the Love of Men: Romantic Friendship and Love between Women from the Renaissance to the Present* (New York, 1981), p. 186.

34. See, for instance, Blanche Wiesen Cook, "Female Support Networks and Political Activism: Lillian Wald, Crystal Eastman, Emma Goldman," in Nancy F. Cott and Elizabeth H. Pleck, eds., *A Heritage of Her Own* (New York, 1979), pp. 412–44; Nan Bauer Maglin, "Vida to Florence: 'Comrade and Companion,' " *Frontiers* 4:3 (Fall 1979), pp. 13–20; Judith Schwarz, *"Yellow Clover:* Katharine Lee Bates and Katharine Coman," *Frontiers* 4:1 (Spring 1979), pp. 59–67; and Anna Mary Wells, *Miss Marks and Miss Woolley* (Boston, 1978).

35. Faderman, *Surpassing the Love of Men,* pp. 302–3; Wells, *Miss Marks and Miss Woolley,* p. 110.

36. Frankfort, *Collegiate Women,* p. 33.

37. Paula Petrik, "Rose Elizabeth Cleveland and Evangeline Marrs Simpson Whipple," unpublished paper, 1978. We wish to thank the author for permission to quote from her paper.

38. Faderman, *Surpassing the Love of Men,* p. 251; Nan Bauer Maglin, "Vida to Florence," p. 18; and Davis, *Factors in the Sex Life,* p. 282.

39. Faderman, *Surpassing the Love of Men,* p. 251; Davis, *Factors in the Sex Life,* pp. 312, 295, 280.

40. Smith-Rosenberg, *Disorderly Conduct,* p. 283; Davis, *Factors in the Sex Life,* pp. 263, 290.

41. Kneeland, *Commercialized Prostitution,* p. 76; Peiss, *Cheap Amusements,* pp. 50–51; Woods and Kennedy, *Young Working Girls,* pp. 26–27.

42. Woods and Kennedy, *Young Working Girls,* p. 108; Jervis Anderson, *This Was Harlem: A Cultural Portrait, 1900–1950* (New York, 1982), pp. 18, 72; Peiss, *Cheap Amusements,* p. 102; Jane Addams, *The Spirit of Youth and the City Streets* (New York, 1909), p. 18.

43. Kathy Peiss, " 'Charity Girls' and City Pleasures: Historical Notes on Working-Class Sexuality, 1880–1920," in Ann Snitow, Christine Stansell, and Sharon Thompson, eds., *Powers of Desire: The Politics of Sexuality* (New York, 1983), p. 76; T. J.

Woofter, *Negro Problems in Cities* (Garden City, N.Y., 1928), p. 273; Kneeland, *Commercialized Prostitution,* pp. 70, 74.

44. Peiss, *Cheap Amusements,* p. 125; John F. Kasson, *Amusing the Million: Coney Island at the Turn of the Century* (New York, 1978), pp. 43, 53.

45. Stuart Ewen and Elizabeth Ewen, *Channels of Desire: Mass Images and the Shaping of American Consciousness* (New York, 1982), p. 87; Lewis A. Erenberg, *Steppin' Out: New York Nightlife and the Transformation of American Culture, 1890–1930* (Westport, Conn, 1981), p. 70; Addams, *The Spirit of Youth,* p. 86. For the rise of movies as mass entertainment see May, *Screening Out the Past.*

46. Joanne Meyerowitz, "Holding Their Own: Working Women Apart from Family in Chicago, 1880–1930," Ph.D. dissertation, Stanford University, 1983, pp. 158–59; Peiss, *Cheap Amusements,* p. 64.

47. Roy Rosenzweig, *Eight Hours for What We Will: Workers and Leisure in an Industrial City, 1870–1920* (New York, 1983), p. 214.

48. Peiss, *Cheap Amusements,* p. 70; Addams, *The Spirit of Youth,* pp. 91–92; Paul S. Taylor, *Mexican Labor in the United States: Chicago and the Calumet Region* (Berkeley, 1932), pp. vi–vii.

49. Monica Sone, *Nisei Daughter* (Boston, 1953), pp. 6, 28; Du Bois, *Black Philadelphia,* pp. 320–21; Wisconsin Vice Report, p. 43; Peiss, *Cheap Amusements,* p. 111.

50. For premarital pregnancy rates see Daniel Scott Smith and Michael Hindus, "Premarital Pregnancy in America, 1640–1971: An Overview and an Interpretation," *Journal of Interdisciplinary History* 5 (1975), pp. 537–70; and Daniel Scott Smith, "The Dating of the American Sexual Revolution: Evidence and Interpretation," in Michael Gordon, ed., *The American Family in Social-Historical Perspective* (New York, 1973), pp. 321–35.

51. Peiss, "Charity Girls," p. 75; Addams, *The Spirit of Youth,* p. 43; Manuel Gamio, *The Mexican Immigrant* (Chicago, 1931), p. 161; Tamara Hareven, *Family Time and Industrial Time* (New York, 1982), p. 76.

Chapter 9: Crusades for Sexual Order

1. Information on Johnson can be found in Al-Tony Gilmore, "Jack Johnson and White Women: The National Impact," *Journal of Negro History* 58 (1973), 18–38. See also Finis Farr, *Black Champion* (New York, 1964).

2. The best account of venereal disease and its treatment in this era is Allan M. Brandt, *No Magic Bullet: A Social History of Venereal Disease in the United States Since 1880* (New York, 1985), pp. 7–51.

3. Prince A. Morrow, "A Plea for the Organization of a Society of Sanitary and Moral Prophylaxis," in *Transactions of the American Society of Sanitary and Moral Prophylaxis,* vol. 1 (1906), p. 21; and Morrow, *Social Diseases and Marriage* (New York, 1904), pp. 332, 340.

4. Morrow, "A Plea," p. 17.

5. Maurice A. Bigelow, *Sex-Education* (New York, 1916), pp. 5, 22, 220; and Max J. Exner, *Problems and Principles of Sex Education: A Study of 948 College Men* (New York, 1915), p. 15.

6. Morrow, *Social Diseases,* p. 355; Patricia J. Campbell, *Sex Education Books for Young Adults, 1892–1979* (New York, 1979), pp. 35, 44; American Society for Sanitary

and Moral Prophylaxis, *The Young Man's Problem* (New York, 1912), p. 15; Bigelow, *Sex-Education,* pp. 143–44, 177, 188.

7. Mark Thomas Connelly, *The Response to Prostitution in the Progressive Era* (Chapel Hill, N.C., 1980), p. 72; Bigelow, *Sex-Education,* pp. 222–25.

8. Clifford G. Roe, *The Prodigal Daughter: The White Slave Evil and the Remedy* (Chicago, 1911), pp. 156, 162; Connelly, *The Response to Prostitution,* p. 123; O. Edward Janney, *The White Slave Traffic in America* (New York, 1911), pp. 30, 98.

9. Rev. F. G. Terrell, *The Shame of the Human Race* (1908); Rev. F. M. Lehman, *The White Slave Hell, or With Christ at Midnight in the Slums of Chicago* (Chicago, 1910). For more on white slavery see Connelly, *The Response to Prostitution,* pp. 114–35; and Ruth Rosen, *The Lost Sisterhood: Prostitution in America, 1900–1918* (Baltimore, 1982), pp. 112–36.

10. Francesco Cordasco, *The White Slave Trade and the Immigrant* (Detroit, 1981), pp. 80, 71–72, 58; Connelly, *The Response to Prostitution,* p. 56.

11. *Report of the Vice Commission of Philadelphia* (Philadelphia, 1913), p. 21; *Report and Recommendations for the Wisconsin Legislative Committee to Investigate the White Slave Traffic and Kindred Subjects* (Madison, 1914), p. 38. For other discussions of prostitution see George Kneeland, *Commercialized Prostitution in New York,* rev. ed. (New York, 1917); and Baltimore Vice Commission, *Baltimore Vice Report* (Baltimore, 1916).

12. Society for the Suppression of Vice of Baltimore City, *The Abolition of the Red-Light Districts in Baltimore* (Baltimore, 1916), p. 4; Rosen, *The Lost Sisterhood,* p. 29.

13. *Report and Recommendations for the Wisconsin Legislative Committee,* pp. 116–17; *Report of the Vice Commission of Philadelphia,* p. 5.

14. Brandt, *No Magic Bullet,* pp. 64–67; David J. Pivar, "Cleansing the Nation: The War on Prostitution, 1917–1921," *Prologue* 12 (Spring 1980), p. 37.

15. Donald Smythe, "Venereal Disease: The AEF's Experience," *Prologue* 9 (Summer 1977), p. 65; see also Brandt, *No Magic Bullet,* pp. 96–121.

16. Connelly, *The Response to Prostitution,* p. 147; Brandt, *No Magic Bullet,* p. 67.

17. Connelly, *The Response to Prostitution,* p. 40; American Vigilance Association, *A Report on Vice in the City of Lancaster, Pa.* (1913), p. 44; Kneeland, *Commercialized Prostitution,* pp. 104–5.

18. Connelly, *The Response to Prostitution,* p. 6.

19. Cordasco, *The White Slave Trade,* p. 34.

20. Linda Gordon, *Woman's Body, Woman's Right: Birth Control in America* (New York, 1977), pp. 139, 136. For eugenics and sterilization in this era see Mark Haller, *Eugenics: Hereditarian Attitudes in American Thought* (New Brunswick, N.J., 1963), and Donald Pickens, *Eugenics and the Progressives* (Nashville, 1968).

21. Gunnar Myrdal, *An American Dilemma* (New York, 1944), pp. 586–87.

22. *Ibid.,* p. 560.

23. Angela Y. Davis, *Women, Race, and Class* (New York, 1981), pp. 190, 170; Jacquelyn Dowd Hall, *Revolt Against Chivalry* (New York, 1979), pp. 147, 112, 170.

24. Gerda Lerner, ed., *Black Women in White America* (New York, 1972), pp. 162–63, 189.

25. Hall, *Revolt Against Chivalry,* p. 146; Davis, *Women, Race, and Class,* p. 188; *Sexual Crimes Among the Southern Negroes Scientifically Considered: A Correspondence* (1893), p. 22.

26. Davis, *Women, Race, and Class,* pp. 185–86, 188; Lerner, *Black Women in White America,* pp. 202–3.

27. Lerner, *Black Women in White America,* pp. 208–10.

28. Hall, *Revolt Against Chivalry,* pp. 150–53.

29. *Ibid.,* pp. 93, 194, 154; Hortense Powdermaker, *After Freedom: A Cultural Study in the Deep South* (New York, 1939), p. 389.

Chapter 10. Breaking with the Past

1. Margaret Sanger, *My Fight for Birth Control* (New York, 1931), pp. 120–21; David M. Kennedy, *Birth Control in America: The Career of Margaret Sanger* (New Haven, 1970), pp. 72–73.

2. Kennedy, *Birth Control in America,* pp. 72–74; James Reed, *From Private Vice to Public Virtue: The Birth Control Movement and American Society Since 1830* (New York, 1978), p. 97.

3. Nathan G. Hale, Jr., *Freud and the Americans: The Beginnings of Psychoanalysis in the United States, 1876–1917* (New York, 1971), pp. 342, 405.

4. Paul Robinson, *The Modernization of Sex: Havelock Ellis, Alfred Kinsey, William Masters, and Virginia Johnson* (New York, 1976), p. 27; Hale, *Freud and the Americans,* pp. 265–66.

5. Robinson, *The Modernization of Sex,* pp. 31, 28.

6. Havelock Ellis, "The Evolution of Modesty," in *Studies in the Psychology of Sex* (New York, 1936), pp. 1, 40.

7. Allan M. Brandt, *No Magic Bullet: A Social History of Venereal Disease in the United States Since 1880* (New York, 1985), p. 49. For an extended discussion of the shift in medical thinking see Linda Gordon, *Woman's Body, Woman's Right: Birth Control in America* (New York, 1977), pp. 159–85.

8. Jonathan Ned Katz, *Gay/Lesbian Almanac* (New York, 1983), p. 312; Jeffrey Weeks, *Sexuality and Its Discontents: Meanings, Myths and Modern Sexualities* (London, 1985), p. 62

9. Michel Foucault, *The History of Sexuality,* trans. Robert Hurley (New York, 1978), vol. 1, *An Introduction,* p. 43.

10. George Chauncey, Jr., "From Sexual Inversion to Homosexuality: Medicine and the Changing Conceptualization of Female Deviance," *Salmagundi* 58–59 (Fall–Winter 1983), p. 119; Katz, *Gay/Lesbian Almanac,* p. 311.

11. George Chauncey, Jr., "Christian Brotherhood or Sexual Perversion? Homosexual Identities and the Construction of Sexual Boundaries in the World War One Era," *Journal of Social History* 9 (Winter 1985), pp. 190, 204; Katz, *Gay/Lesbian Almanac,* pp. 218–19, 234, 258, 328–29; Joanne Meyerowitz, "Sexuality in the Furnished Room Districts: Working-Class Women, 1890–1930," Paper presented at the 1986 annual meeting of the Organization of American Historians; Ruth Rosen, *The Lost Sisterhood: Prostitution in America, 1900–1918* (Baltimore, 1982), p. 82; Eric Garber, "T'Ain't Nobody's Bizness: Homosexuality in 1920s Harlem," in Michael J. Smith, ed., *Black Men/White Men* (San Francisco, 1983), p. 11.

12. Katz, *Gay/Lesbian Almanac,* p. 335.

13. *Ibid.,* pp. 304–5, 339 (emphasis added), 413, 397; Louis Hyde, ed., *Rat and the Devil: Journal Letters of F. O. Matthiessen and Russell Cheney* (Hamden, Conn., 1978), p. 29.

14. Ellen Kay Trimberger, "Feminism, Men, and Modern Love: Greenwich Village, 1900–1925," in Ann Snitow, Christine Stansell, and Sharon Thompson, eds., *Powers of Desire: The Politics of Sexuality* (New York, 1983), pp. 133, 136.

15. Leslie Fishbein, *Rebels in Bohemia: The Radicals of "The Masses," 1911–1917* (Chapel Hill, N.C., 1982), p. 74; Mari Jo Buhle, *Women and American Socialism, 1870–1920* (Urbana, Ill., 1981), p. 263.

16. Trimberger, "Feminism, Men, and Modern Love," pp. 133, 142.

17. Lewis A. Erenberg, *Steppin' Out: New York Night Life and the Transformation of American Culture, 1890–1930* (Westport, Conn., 1981), p. 85.

18. Elaine Tyler May, *Great Expectations: Marriage and Divorce in Post-Victorian America* (Chicago, 1980).

19. The discussion of Sanger is taken from Gordon, *Woman's Body, Woman's Right;* Kennedy, *Birth Control in America;* and Reed, *From Private Vice to Public Virtue.*

20. Reed, *From Private Vice to Public Virtue,* p. 87.

21. Richard Drinnon, *Rebel in Paradise* (Boston, 1961; paperback, 1970), p. 167.

22. For the role of socialist women see Buhle, *Women and American Socialism,* pp. 276–79.

23. "Sex O'Clock in America," *Current Opinion* 55 (1913), 113–14.

Chapter 11. Beyond Reproduction

1. Robert S. Lynd and Helen Merrell Lynd, *Middletown* (New York, 1929), p. 121.

2. *Ibid.,* pp. 242, 266.

3. Frederick Lewis Allen, *Only Yesterday: An Informal History of the 1920s* (New York, 1931).

4. The discussion of Sanger's work is drawn from Linda Gordon, *Woman's Body, Woman's Right: Birth Control in America* (New York, 1977); David M. Kennedy, *Birth Control in America: The Career of Margaret Sanger* (New Haven, 1970); and James Reed, *From Private Vice to Public Virtue: The Birth Control Movement and American Society Since 1830* (New York, 1978).

5. Reed, *From Private Vice to Public Virtue,* p. 102.

6. *Ibid.,* pp. 144, 187.

7. Estimates of the number of birth control clinics may be found in Gordon, *Woman's Body, Woman's Right,* p. 270; Reed, *From Private Vice to Public Virtue,* p. 117; and Gunnar Myrdal, *An American Dilemma* (New York, 1944), p. 178.

8. Kennedy, *Birth Control in America,* pp. 130, 109, 115.

9. Gordon, *Woman's Body, Woman's Right,* pp. 304, 314.

10. Malcolm X, *The Autobiography of Malcolm X* (New York, 1965; paperback 1973), p. 48; Kennedy, *Birth Control in America,* p. 250.

11. Reed, *From Private Vice to Public Virtue,* p. 124.

12. Marie Kopp, *Birth Control in Practice: An Analysis of Ten Thousand Case Histories* (New York, 1934); Lynd and Lynd, *Middletown,* p. 123.

13. Reed, *From Private Vice to Public Virtue,* p. 248; John Dollard, *Caste and Class in a Southern Town* (New Haven, 1937), p. 478; Margaret Jarman Hagood, *Mothers of the South: Portraiture of the White Tenant Farm Woman* (Chapel Hill, N.C.: 1939), pp. 118–21, 127; Gilbert H. Beebe, *Contraception and Fertility in the Southern Appalachians* (Baltimore, 1942), p. 97.

14. Reed, *From Private Vice to Public Virtue,* p. 124; Beebe, *Contraception and Fertility,* p. 132; Hagood, *Mothers of the South,* p. 124.

15. Reed, *From Private Vice to Public Virtue,* p. 255; Gordon, *Woman's Body, Woman's Right,* p. 332. For black fertility rates see Reynolds Farley, *Growth of the Black Population* (Chicago, 1970).

16. For a discussion of Planned Parenthood see Gordon, *Woman's Body, Woman's Right,* pp. 341–90.

17. Mira Komarovsky, *The Unemployed Man and His Family* (New York, 1940), p. 132; Reed, *From Private Vice to Public Virtue,* p. 240.

18. Pascal Whelpton et al., *Fertility and Family Planning in the United States* (Princeton, N.J., 1966), pp. 34, 303–4.

19. *Ibid.,* pp. 350, 183, 191, 71–72.

20. *Ibid.,* pp. 338–63; Lee Rainwater, *And the Poor Get Children: Sex, Contraception, and Family Planning in the Working Class* (Chicago, 1960, 1967).

21. Whelpton et al., *Fertility and Family Planning,* p. 70; Reed, *From Private Vice to Public Virtue,* pp. 378–79. The Supreme Court cases are *Griswold v. Connecticut* (1965) and *Eisenstadt v. Baird* (1972).

22. For the development of oral contraceptives see Reed, *From Private Vice to Public Virtue,* pp. 311–66.

23. *Saturday Evening Post,* January 15, 1966, p. 22; *Time,* April 7, 1967, p. 80.

24. Charles Westoff and Norman Ryder, *The Contraceptive Revolution* (Princeton, N.J., 1977), pp. 18–22, 29–32, 42, 71–72, 82, 219.

25. *Ibid.,* pp. 219, 30, 71–72, 96, 107.

26. *Newsweek,* July 6, 1964, p. 52; Westoff and Ryder, *The Contraceptive Revolution,* pp. 23–24, 30.

27. Kopp, *Birth Control in Practice,* pp. 206–8; Alfred Kinsey, "Illegal Abortion in the United States," in Robert W. Roberts, ed., *The Unwed Mother* (New York, 1966), pp. 196–97; Paul Gebhard et al., *Pregnancy, Birth, and Abortion* (New York, 1958), pp. 119, 162; William Vogt to Susan Hatt, August 22, 1957, box 2, file 8, Mary Calderone Papers, Schlesinger Library, Radcliffe College, Cambridge, Massachusetts; Edwin M. Schur, *Crimes Without Victims* (Englewood Cliffs, N.J., 1965), p. 25.

28. Schur, *Crimes Without Victims,* pp. 14, 22; Mary S. Calderone, ed., *Abortion in the United States* (New York, 1958).

29. Kristen Luker, *Abortion and the Politics of Motherhood* (Berkeley, 1984), p. 53; Lawrence Lader, *Abortion* (Indianapolis, 1966), pp. 44–48, 70.

30. Joyce Johnson, *Minor Characters* (Boston, 1983), p. 107.

31. *Ibid.,* p. 110; Luker, *Abortion and the Politics of Motherhood,* p. 105.

32. Boston *Globe,* December 4, 1974, p. 2; Ad Hoc Women's Studies Committee Against Sterilization Abuse, *Workbook on Sterilization* (1978), pp. 12–14.

33. For the change in premarital coitus see Daniel Scott Smith, "The Dating of the American Sexual Revolution: Evidence and Interpretation," in Michael Gordon, ed., *The American Family in Social-Historical Perspective* (New York, 1973), pp. 321–35, and Ernest W. Burgess and Paul Wallin, *Engagement and Marriage* (Philadelphia, 1953), pp. 319–33.

34. For school attendance and youth behavior see Ellen K. Rothman, *Hands and Hearts: A History of Courtship in America* (New York, 1984), pp. 210, 346; and Christina Simmons, "Marriage in the Modern Manner: Sexual Radicalism and Reform in America, 1914–1941," Ph.D. dissertation, Brown University, 1982, pp. 105–7.

35. Paula Fass, *The Damned and the Beautiful: American Youth in the 1920s* (New York, 1977), pp. 264–66.

36. Ben Lindsey and Wainwright Evans, *The Revolt of Modern Youth* (Garden City, N.Y., 1925), pp. 54, 59; Lynd and Lynd, *Middletown,* p. 114.

37. Lindsey and Evans, *Revolt of Modern Youth,* p. 67; Burgess and Wallin, *Engagement and Marriage,* pp. 324, 332–33.

38. Rothman, *Hands and Hearts,* p. 298; Helen Moore Priester, "The Reported Dating Practices of One Hundred and Six High School Seniors in an Urban Community," Master's thesis, Cornell University, 1941, p. 112. See also John Modell, "Dating Becomes the Way of American Youth," in David Levine et al., eds., *Essays on the Family and Historical Change* (Arlington, Tex., 1983), pp. 91–126.

39. Charles S. Johnson, *Growing Up in the Black Belt: Negro Youth in the Rural South* (Washington, D.C., 1941), pp. 226, 231; Carter G. Woodson, *The Rural Negro* (Washington, D.C., 1930), p. 133; Hylan Lewis, *Blackways of Kent* (Chapel Hill, N.C., 1955), p. 93.

40. Winston Ehrmann, *Premarital Dating Behavior* (New York, 1959), pp. 87, 104.

41. August B. Hollingshead, *Elmtown's Youth: The Impact of Social Classes on Adolescents* (New York, 1949), pp. 163, 420, 429; Malcolm X, *Autobiography,* p. 48.

42. Ehrmann, *Premarital Dating Behavior,* pp. 73–74.

43. Allan M. Brandt, *No Magic Bullet: A Social History of Venereal Disease in the United States Since 1880* (New York, 1985), pp. 164, 167–68; Karen Anderson, *Wartime Women: Sex Roles, Family Relations, and the Status of Women during World War II* (Westport, Conn., 1981), pp. 106–7.

44. Rothman, *Hands and Hearts,* pp. 300, 305; Clark Vincent, *Unmarried Mothers* (New York, 1961), pp. 40–41.

45. Modell, "Dating Becomes the Way," p. 95; Vincent, *Unmarried Mothers,* p. 46.

46. Ehrmann, *Premarital Dating Behavior,* pp. 270–71.

47. *Ibid.,* p. 166; Johnson, *Black Belt,* p. 229.

48. Benita Eisler, *Private Lives: Men and Women of the Fifties* (New York, 1986), p. 130.

49. Ira Reiss, *Premarital Sexual Standards in America* (Glencoe, Ill., 1960), p. 91, and "Sexual Codes in Teen-Age Culture," *Annals of the American Academy of Political and Social Science* 338 (1961), pp. 58, 62.

50. Eisler, *Private Lives,* pp. 128, 110; Anne Moody, *Coming of Age in Mississippi* (New York, 1965), pp. 217–28; Patricia J. Campbell, *Sex Education Books for Young Adults, 1892–1979* (New York, 1979), p. 93; Hollingshead, *Elmtown's Youth,* p. 209; Ehrmann, *Premarital Dating Behavior,* p. 106.

51. See Elaine Tyler May, *Great Expectations: Marriage and Divorce in Post-Victorian America* (Chicago, 1980).

52. Ben Lindsey and Wainwright Evans, *The Companionate Marriage* (New York, 1927), pp. vii–viii.

53. Ernest Groves, *The Marriage Crisis* (New York, 1928), pp. 48–51.

54. Michael Gordon, "From an Unfortunate Necessity to a Cult of Mutual Orgasm: Sex in American Marital Education Literature, 1830–1940," in James Henslin and Edward Sagarin, eds., *The Sociology of Sex,* rev. ed. (New York, 1978), p. 74.

55. *Ibid.,* pp. 73, 77; Theodore Van de Velde, *Ideal Marriage* (New York, 1930), p. 221.

56. Dennis Brissett and Lionel Lewis, "Guidelines for Marital Sex: An Analysis of

Fifteen Popular Marriage Manuals," *Family Coordinator* 19 (January 1970), pp. 41–48; Chesser quoted in Eisler, *Private Lives,* p. 147.

57. Burgess and Wallin, *Engagement and Marriage,* p. 498.

58. Alfred C. Kinsey et al., *Sexual Behavior in the Human Female* (Philadelphia, 1953), pp. 356, 362–65.

59. *Ibid.,* pp. 358–59.

60. Burgess and Wallin, *Engagement and Marriage,* pp. 668, 671–72; Kinsey, *Female,* pp. 352–53, 375; Alfred C. Kinsey et al., *Sexual Behavior in the Human Male* (Philadelphia, 1948), p. 571.

61. Lynd and Lynd, *Middletown,* pp. 110–30; Kinsey, *Male,* pp. 572–74.

62. Rainwater, *And the Poor Get Children,* p. 65.

63. *Ibid.,* pp. 18, 85–86, 37, 21, 114.

64. *Ibid.,* pp. 99–100, 97.

65. St. Clair Drake and Horace Cayton, *Black Metropolis* (New York, 1945), p. 533; Myrdal, *An American Dilemma,* pp. 932–33.

66. Johnson, *Black Belt,* p. 227; Drake and Cayton, *Black Metropolis,* pp. 586–87.

67. Carol Stack, *All Our Kin: Strategies for Survival in a Black Community* (New York, 1974), pp. 108–15.

Chapter 12. Redrawing the Boundaries

1. San Francisco *Chronicle,* June 4, 1957, p. 3.

2. Norman Mailer, *Advertisements for Myself* (New York, 1966; Berkley-Medallion ed.), pp. 312, 314, 321; Allen Ginsberg, *Howl and Other Poems* (San Francisco, 1956), p. 9.

3. *Allen Ginsberg: Gay Sunshine Interview with Allen Young* (Bolinas, Calif., 1974), pp. 11–12; Ginsberg, *Howl,* p. 12.

4. San Francisco *Chronicle,* October 4, 1957, p. 1; *Look,* August 19, 1958, pp. 64ff; *Time* quoted in Morris Dickstein, *Gates of Eden: American Culture in the Sixties* (New York, 1977), p. 12; *Nation,* November 1, 1958, pp. 316–22.

5. Robert Haney, *Comstockery in America: Patterns of Censorship and Control* (Boston, 1960), p. 16.

6. Stuart Ewen, *Captains of Consciousness: Advertising and the Social Roots of the Consumer Culture* (New York, 1976), p. 182; Roland Marchand, *Advertising and the American Dream: Making Way for Modernity, 1920–1940* (Berkeley, 1985), pp. 15, 19.

7. Raymond Moley, *The Hays Office* (Indianapolis, 1945), p. 26. For discussions of consumerism and sexuality see also Elaine Tyler May, *Great Expectations: Marriage and Divorce in Post-Victorian America* (Chicago, 1980), pp. 60–72; and Robert S. Lynd and Helen Merrell Lynd, *Middletown* (New York, 1929), pp. 251–71.

8. For changing standards in literature in the 1920s and 1930s see Felice Flanery Lewis, *Literature, Obscenity, and Law* (Carbondale, Ill., 1976), pp. 103–45.

9. Hand quoted in Haney, *Comstockery in America,* p. 28; *Hannegan v. Esquire* (1946).

10. See, especially, Kenneth Davis, *Two-Bit Culture: The Paperbacking of America* (Boston, 1984), pp. 135–41; Gay Talese, *Thy Neighbor's Wife* (Garden City, N.Y., 1980; paperback, 1981), pp. 58–62, 88–101.

11. Moley, *The Hays Office,* pp. 240–41; Paul Facey, S.J., "The Legion of Decency:

A Sociological Analysis of the Emergence and Development of a Social Pressure Group," Ph.D. dissertation, Fordham University, 1945. The discussion of the Legion of Decency is taken from Facey.

12. Moley, *The Hays Office,* pp. 106–9.

13. National Organization for Decent Literature, *The Drive for Decency in Print* (Huntington, Ind.: 1939?), pp. 38, 44.

14. U.S. House of Representatives, 86th Cong., 1st sess., Committee on Post Office and Civil Service, Subcommittee on Postal Operations, *Obscene Matter Sent Through the Mails* (Washington, 1959), pp. 1, 14.

15. Davis, *Two-Bit Culture,* p. 219; U.S. Senate, 84th Cong., 1st sess., Committee on the Judiciary, *Juvenile Delinquency* (Washington, 1955), pp. 9, 49–50, and *Comic Books and Juvenile Delinquency* (Washington, 1955), p. 7; House of Representatives, *Obscene Matter,* p. 1.

16. Davis, *Two-Bit Culture,* pp. 237–39; House of Representatives, *Obscene Matter,* pp. 48–54; Lewis, *Literature, Obscenity, and Law,* pp. 161–84.

17. Maryland Crime Investigating Committee, *Youth, Obscene Materials, and the United States Mails* (Baltimore, 1963), p. 12; House of Representatives, *Obscene Matter,* p. 15.

18. House of Representatives, *Obscene Matter,* pp. 42–43.

19. Alfred Kinsey et al., *Sexual Behavior in the Human Male* (Philadelphia, 1948), and *Sexual Behavior in the Human Female* (Philadelphia, 1953). The discussion of Kinsey is drawn from Paul Robinson, *The Modernization of Sex: Havelock Ellis, Alfred Kinsey, William Masters, and Virginia Johnson* (New York, 1976), pp. 42–119; Wardell B. Pomeroy, *Dr. Kinsey and the Institute for Sex Research* (New York, 1972); and Regina Markell Morantz, "The Scientist as Sex Crusader: Alfred C. Kinsey and American Culture," *American Quarterly* 29 (Winter 1979), pp. 563–89.

20. *Look,* December 7, 1947, pp. 106–7.

21. Haney, *Comstockery in America,* pp. 40–41; Richard Kuh, *Foolish Figleaves? Pornography in—and Out of—Court* (New York, 1967), p. 18; and *A Book Named "John Cleland's Memoirs of a Woman of Pleasure" v. Massachusetts,* 383 U.S. 413 (1966).

22. Commission on Obscenity and Pornography, *Report* (New York, 1970), p. 112.

23. See Jonathan Katz, *Gay American History* (New York, 1976), pp. 82–91; Eric Garber, " 'T'Ain't Nobody's Bizness': Homosexuality in 1920s Harlem," in Michael J. Smith, ed., *Black Men/White Men* (San Francisco, 1983), pp. 11–14; Vern Bullough and Bonnie Bullough, "Lesbianism in the 1920s and 1930s: A Newfound Study," *Signs* 2 (1977), pp. 895–904.

24. Unless otherwise noted, the discussion of gay life is taken from John D'Emilio, *Sexual Politics, Sexual Communities: The Making of a Homosexual Minority in the United States, 1940–1970* (Chicago, 1983).

25. Allan Berube, "Marching to a Different Drummer," *The Advocate,* October 15, 1981, p. 21; D'Emilio, *Sexual Politics, Sexual Communities,* p. 26; *Newsweek,* June 9, 1947, p. 54; Allan Bérubé, "Coming Out Under Fire," *Mother Jones,* February–March 1983, p. 28.

26. Donald Vining, *A Gay Diary, 1933–1946* (New York, 1979), p. 220; D'Emilio, *Sexual Politics, Sexual Communities,* p. 30.

27. D'Emilio, *Sexual Politics, Sexual Communities,* p. 98; Leila J. Rupp and Verta Taylor, *Survival in the Doldrums: The American Women's Rights Movement, 1945 to*

the 1960s (New York, 1987), pp. 97–108, 121–24; Marcy Adelman, ed., *Long Time Passing: Lives of Older Lesbians* (Boston, 1986), pp. 116–17.

28. Kinsey, *Male,* p. 627; Donald Webster Cory [pseud.], *The Homosexual in America* (New York, 1951); Fran Koski and Maida Tilchen, "Some Pulp Sappho," in Karla Jay and Allen Young, eds., *Lavender Culture* (New York, 1979), pp. 262–74.

29. Katz, *Gay American History,* pp. 91–92.

30. U.S. Senate, 81st Cong., 2d sess., Committee on Expenditures in Executive Departments, *Employment of Homosexuals and Other Sex Perverts in Government* (Washington, 1950), pp. 3–4.

31. See Ralph S. Brown, Jr., "Loyalty-Security Measures and Employment Opportunities," *Bulletin of the Atomic Scientists,* April 1955, pp. 113–17.

32. John Gagnon and William Simon, *Sexual Conduct* (Chicago, 1973), pp. 138–39.

33. See John Gerassi, *The Boys of Boise* (New York, 1966), and Katz, *Gay American History,* pp. 109–19.

34. Barbara Ehrenreich, *The Hearts of Men: American Dreams and the Flight from Commitment* (Garden City, N.Y., 1983), pp. 26, 34.

35. Lawrence Levine, *Black Culture and Black Consciousness* (New York, 1977), p. 242; Jervis Anderson, *This Was Harlem: A Cultural Portrait, 1900–1950* (New York, 1982), p. 168.

36. Harold Gosnell, *Negro Politicians* (Chicago, 1933), p. 120; St. Clair Drake and Horace Cayton, *Black Metropolis* (New York, 1945), p. 597.

37. Gunnar Myrdal, *An American Dilemma* (New York, 1944), p. 1268.

38. Robert Staples, ed., *The Black Family* (Belmont, Calif., 1971), p. 372; Malcolm X, *The Autobiography of Malcolm X* (New York, 1965; paperback 1973), pp. 117, 119; Myrdal, *An American Dilemma,* p. 332.

39. See Angela Y. Davis, *Women, Race, and Class* (New York, 1981), p. 172; Susan Brownmiller, *Against Our Will* (New York, 1975), p. 216; Robert Staples, *The Black Woman in America* (Chicago, 1973), p. 65.

40. U.S. Department of Labor, *The Negro Family: The Case for National Action* (Washington, 1965), pp. 8, 29.

41. *Ibid.,* pp. 21, 6, 29.

42. Lee Rainwater and William Yancey, *The Moynihan Report and the Politics of Controversy* (Cambridge, 1967), pp. 135, 138.

43. *The Negro Family,* p. 8; Myrdal, *An American Dilemma,* p. 984. For older, classic studies of the black family see E. Franklin Frazier, *The Negro Family in Chicago* (Chicago, 1932), and *The Negro Family in the United States* (Chicago, 1939). For illegitimacy rates see Clark E. Vincent, "Teen-Age Unwed Mothers in American Society," *Journal of Social Issues* 22:2 (April 1966), pp. 22–33, and Lynn K. White, "The Correlates of Urban Illegitimacy in the United States, 1960–1970," *Journal of Marriage and the Family* 41 (1979), pp. 715–26.

Chapter 13. Sexual Revolutions

1. *Time,* June 28, 1968, pp. 55–56.

2. New York *Times,* September 8, 1968, p. 81; *Life,* September 20, 1968, p. 92.

3. Gay Talese, *Thy Neighbor's Wife* (Garden City, N.Y., 1980; paperback 1981), p. 101; Barbara Ehrenreich, *The Hearts of Men: American Dreams and the Flight from Commitment* (Garden City, N.Y., 1983), p. 47.

4. *Look,* January 10, 1967, p. 56; Talese, *Thy Neighbor's Wife,* p. 106.

5. Helen Gurley Brown, *Sex and the Single Girl* (New York, 1962), pp. 4, 28, 34.

6. *Ibid.,* pp. 257, 226.

7. *Ibid.,* pp. 89, 94.

8. *Look,* August 23, 1966, pp. 93–94. See also Barbara Ehrenreich and Deidre English, *For Her Own Good: 150 Years of the Experts' Advice to Women* (Garden City, N.Y., 1978), pp. 258–68.

9. *Time,* September 15, 1967, p. 26.

10. Ehrenreich, *The Hearts of Men,* p. 45.

11. *Newsweek,* November 13, 1967, p. 67.

13. Herbert Marcuse, *An Essay on Liberation* (Boston, 1969), pp. 7–8. For the counterculture see Theodore Roszak, *The Making of a Counterculture* (Garden City, N.Y., 1969).

13. *Newsweek,* February 6, 1967, p. 92.

14. *Newsweek,* November 13, 1967, pp. 74, 78.

15. Judith Hole and Ellen Levine, *Rebirth of Feminism* (New York, 1971), p. 186; Anne Koedt, Ellen Levine, and Anita Rapone, *Radical Feminism* (New York, 1973), p. 179; Betty Friedan, *The Feminine Mystique* (New York, 1963).

16. *Saturday Evening Post,* January 15, 1966, pp. 21–22.

17. The best account of the origins of the women's liberation movement is Sara Evans, *Personal Politics: The Roots of Women's Liberation in the Civil Rights Movement and the New Left* (New York, 1979). See also Jo Freeman, *The Politics of Women's Liberation* (New York, 1975).

18. Robin Morgan, ed., *Sisterhood Is Powerful* (New York, 1970), p. 430; Hole and Levine, *Rebirth of Feminism,* p. 120.

19. Hole and Levine, *Rebirth of Feminism,* pp. 112, 134.

20. See, for example, Shulamith Firestone, *The Dialectics of Sex: The Case for Feminist Revolution* (New York, 1970); Kate Millett, *Sexual Politics* (Garden City, N.Y., 1970); and Juliet Mitchell, *Women's Estate* (New York, 1971).

21. Hole and Levine, *Rebirth of Feminism,* pp. 121, 202; Koedt, Levine, and Rapone, *Radical Feminism,* pp. 108–11, 28.

22. Koedt, Levine and Rapone, *Radical Feminism,* pp. 199, 206; Kate Millett, *Sexual Politics.* For Masters and Johnson see William H. Masters and Virginia E. Johnson, *Human Sexual Response* (Boston, 1966) and *Human Sexual Inadequacy* (Boston, 1970), and Paul Robinson, *The Modernization of Sex: Havelock Ellis, Alfred Kinsey, William Masters, and Virginia Johnson* (New York, 1976), pp. 120–90.

23. Hole and Levine, *Rebirth of Feminism,* p. 144.

24. Jennifer Temkin, "Women, Rape and Law Reform," in Sylvana Tomaselli and Roy Porter, eds., *Rape* (London, 1986), pp. 16–40; Susan Brownmiller, *Against Our Will: Men, Women, and Rape* (New York, 1975); Mary Bularzik, "Sexual Harassment at the Work Place: Historical Notes," *Radical America,* 12:4 (July–August 1978), pp. 25–43; New York *Times,* December 23, 1979, section 3, p. 7.

25. Hole and Levine, *Rebirth of Feminism,* p. 298; Kristen Luker, *Abortion and the Politics of Motherhood* (Berkeley, 1984), pp. 66–125.

26. New York *Times,* July 2, 1973, p. 10, and August 1, 1973, p. 27; National Abortion Action Committee, press release, July 12, 1973, in Vertical Files, Schlesinger Library, Radcliffe College, Cambridge, Mass.; Angela Y. Davis, *Women, Race, and Class* (New York, 1981), pp. 215–21; Rosalind P. Petchesky, *Abortion and Woman's*

Choice: The State, Sexuality, and the Conditions of Reproductive Freedom (New York, 1984), pp. 179–80.

27. See Robin Morgan, *Going Too Far* (New York, 1977), p. 175.

28. Nancy Myron and Charlotte Bunch, eds., *Lesbianism and the Women's Movement* (Baltimore, 1975), p. 93.

29. *Time,* December 14, 1970, p. 50. See also Sydney Abbott and Barbara Love, *Sappho Was a Right-On Woman* (New York, 1972), pp. 107–34.

30. Myron and Bunch, *Lesbianism and the Women's Movement,* pp. 29, 31–32.

31. *Village Voice,* July 3, 1969, p. 18; John D'Emilio, *Sexual Politics, Sexual Communities: The Making of a Homosexual Minority in the United States, 1940–1970* (Chicago, 1983), pp. 231–37.

32. The discussion of pre-Stonewall gay activism comes from D'Emilio, *Sexual Politics, Sexual Communities.*

33. *Ibid.,* p. 234.

34. Karla Jay and Allen Young, *Out of the Closets: Voices of Gay Liberation* (New York, 1972), pp. 32, 29; Toby Marotta, *The Politics of Homosexuality* (Boston, 1981), p. 101.

35. Donn Teal, *The Gay Militants* (New York, 1971), p. 61.

36. The phrase is used by Marotta in *The Politics of Homosexuality.*

Chapter 14. The Sexualized Society

1. Gay Talese, *Thy Neighbor's Wife* (Garden City, N.Y., 1980; paperback, 1981), p. 188.

2. *Ibid.,* p. 398.

3. New York *Times,* April 5, 1979, p. B15.

4. New York *Times,* February 10, 1981, p. B6, and February 9, 1981, p. B6.

5. New York *Times,* February 9, 1981, p. B6.

6. Theodore Caplow et al., *Middletown Families* (Minneapolis, 1982), pp. 173–74.

7. Quoted in Morton Hunt, *Sexual Behavior in the 1970s* (New York, 1974), p. 9.

8. Alex Comfort, ed., *The Joy of Sex: A Gourmet Guide to Love Making* (New York, 1972); Marabel Morgan, *The Total Woman* (Old Tappan, N.J., 1975).

9. *New York Times Sunday Magazine,* May 25, 1975, p. 10. Unless otherwise noted, the demographic information in this and the following paragraphs is from Andrew Hacker, ed., *U/S: A Statistical Portrait of the American People* (New York, 1983).

10. Richard R. Clayton and Harwin L. Voss, "Shacking Up: Cohabitation in the 1970s," *Journal of Marriage and the Family* 39 (1977), pp. 273–83; Philip Blumstein and Pepper Schwartz, *American Couples: Money, Work, Sex* (New York, 1983; paperback, 1985), p. 36.

11. New York *Times,* November 27, 1977, p. 74; Caplow et al., *Middletown Families,* p. 131.

12. Robert Staples, *Black Masculinity* (San Francisco, 1982), p. 115; New York *Times,* August 13, 1984, p. B4.

13. New York *Times,* December 23, 1982, p. C5.

14. See Hunt, *Sexual Behavior in the 1970s,* p. 21; B. K. Singh, "Trends in Attitudes toward Premarital Sexual Relations," *Journal of Marriage and the Family* 42 (1980), pp. 387–93; New York *Times,* November 27, 1977, p. 75; Norval D. Glenn and Charles

N. Weaver, "Attitudes Toward Premarital, Extramarital, and Homosexual Relations in the U.S. in the 1970s," *Journal of Sex Research* 15 (1978), pp. 108–18; Blumstein and Schwartz, *American Couples,* pp. 255, 272.

15. New York *Times,* November 28, 1977, p. 36.

16. Ira E. Robinson and Davor Jedlicka, "Change in Sexual Attitudes and Behavior of College Students from 1965 to 1980: A Research Note," *Journal of Marriage and the Family* 44 (1982), pp. 237–40; Robert R. Bell and Kathleen Coughey, "Premarital Sexual Experience Among College Females, 1958, 1968, and 1978," *Family Relations* 29 (1980), pp. 353–57; Melvin Zelnick, Young J. Kim, and John F. Kanter, "Probabilities of Intercourse and Conception Among Teenage Women, 1971 and 1976," *Family Planning Perspectives* 11 (1979), pp. 177–83; Hunt, *Sexual Behavior in the 1970s,* pp. 150, 166, 77, 87.

17. Caplow et al., *Middletown Families,* pp. 169–70, 185.

18. Robert Coles and Geoffrey Stokes, *Sex and the American Teenager* (New York, 1985), p. 7; Hunt, *Sexual Behavior in the 1970s,* p. 142.

19. Blumstein and Schwartz, *American Couples,* pp. 208, 282.

20. Hunt, *Sexual Behavior in the 1970s,* pp. 202, 198, 187, 192.

21. *Ibid.,* pp. 183–84; Barbara Ehrenreich, Elizabeth Hess, and Gloria Jacobs, *Re-Making Love: The Feminization of Sex* (Garden City, N.Y., 1986), p. 100.

22. Blumstein and Schwartz, *American Couples,* pp. 232, 236.

23. *Ibid.,* pp. 201–3; Ehrenreich et al., *Re-Making Love,* p. 164.

24. New York *Times,* July 22, 1977, p. 1.

25. New York *Times,* October 31, 1979, p. C19.

26. Blumstein and Schwartz, *American Couples,* pp. 202–3, 236, 273. For another study see Karla Jay and Allen Young, *The Gay Report: Lesbians and Gay Men Speak Out About Sexual Experiences and Life Styles* (New York, 1979).

27. Blumstein and Schwartz, *American Couples,* p. 305.

28. Allan M. Brandt, *No Magic Bullet: A Social History of Venereal Disease in the United States Since 1880* (New York, 1985), pp. 170–74, 179–82.

29. Hunt, *Sexual Behavior in the 1970s,* p. 130; Caplow et al., *Middletown Families,* p. 171; Coles and Stokes, *Sex and the American Teenager,* p. 38.

30. Coles and Stokes, *Sex and the American Teenager,* pp. 37, 99.

Chapter 15. The Contemporary Political Crisis

1. New York *Times,* July 19, 1984, p. 21.

2. New York *Times,* March 7, 1984, p. 20; August 18, 1984, p. 8; August 22, 1984, p. 18.

3. See files 234 and 235, box 14, Mary Calderone Papers, Schlesinger Library, Radcliffe College, Cambridge, Massachusetts.

4. *Newsweek,* June 6, 1977, p. 22.

5. *New Republic,* May 7, 1977, p. 14; *Newsweek,* May 30, 1977, p. 92, and June 6, 1977, p. 22.

6. For the events in California see Randy Shilts, *The Mayor of Castro Street: The Life and Times of Harvey Milk* (New York, 1982); and John D'Emilio, "Gay Politics, Gay Community: San Francisco's Experience," *Socialist Review* 55 (January–February 1981), pp. 77–104.

7. Kristen Luker, *Abortion and the Politics of Motherhood* (Berkeley, 1984), p. 137; Andrew Hacker, "Of Two Minds About Abortion," *Harper's,* September 1979, pp. 16–22.

8. *Newsweek,* June 5, 1978, p. 47.

9. *Time,* April 6, 1981, p. 26, and August 20, 1979, pp. 20–21.

10. *Time,* October 13, 1980, p. 35; *Newsweek,* September 15, 1980, pp. 28, 36.

11. *New Republic,* May 23, 1981, pp. 630–32; *New Yorker,* May 18, 1981, pp. 60, 122.

12. U.S. Department of Justice, Attorney General's Commission on Pornography, *Final Report,* 2 vol. (Washington, 1986). For a trenchant critique of the commission see Carole S. Vance, "Porn in the U.S.A.: The Meese Commission on the Road," *Nation,* August 2–9, 1986, pp. 76–82.

13. New York *Times,* December 4, 1978, p. D10. See also Laura Lederer, *Take Back the Night* (New York, 1980), and Lisa Duggan, "Censorship in the Name of Feminism," *Village Voice,* October 16, 1984, pp. 11–12ff.

14. *Village Voice,* November 12, 1979, p. 8; Carole S. Vance, *Pleasure and Danger: Exploring Female Sexuality* (Boston, 1984).

15. Jerry Falwell, *Listen, America!* (Garden City, N.Y., 1980), p. 201. See also Luker, *Abortion and the Politics of Motherhood,* pp. 159–75, 194–97.

16. Luker, *Abortion and the Politics of Motherhood,* p. 172; New York *Times,* November 15, 1977, p. 46.

17. *Newsweek,* August 8, 1983, p. 33; *New Republic,* August 1, 1983, p. 19.

18. *Newsweek,* August 8, 1983, p. 30.

19. *Ibid.,* p. 40.

20. Study results are reported in the Greensboro *News and Record,* June 7, 1987.

21. *Newsweek,* October 28, 1985, pp. 81–82.

22. San Francisco *Chronicle, Sunday Punch Magazine,* December 14, 1986, p. 3; New York *Times,* March 14, 1987, p. 56.

Selected Bibliography

Achilles, Paul Strong. *The Effectiveness of Certain Social Hygiene Literature.* New York: American Social Hygiene Association, 1923.

Adair, Nancy, and Adair, Casey. *Word Is Out: Stories of Some of Our Lives.* San Francisco: New Glide Publications, 1978.

Axtell, James, ed. *The Indian Peoples of Eastern America: A Documentary History of the Sexes.* New York: Oxford University Press, 1981.

Barker-Benfield, G. J. *The Horrors of the Half-Known Life: Male Attitudes Toward Women and Sexuality in Nineteenth-Century America.* New York: Harper and Row, 1976.

Bayer, Ronald. *Homosexuality and American Psychiatry: The Politics of Diagnosis.* New York: Basic Books, 1981.

Bell, Robert R. *Premarital Sex in a Changing Society.* Englewood Cliffs, N.J.: Prentice-Hall, 1966.

Berg, Barbara. *The Remembered Gate: Origins of American Feminism.* New York: Oxford University Press, 1978.

Blassingame, John W. *The Slave Community: Plantation Life in the Antebellum South.* New York: Oxford University Press, 1972.

Blumstein, Phillip, and Schwartz, Pepper. *American Couples: Money, Work, Sex.* New York: William Morrow, 1983.

Boyer, Paul S. *Purity in Print: The Vice-Society Movement and Book Censorship in America.* New York: Charles Scribner's Sons, 1968.

———. *Urban Masses and Moral Order in America, 1820–1920.* Cambridge: Harvard University Press, 1978.

Brandt, Allan M. *No Magic Bullet: A Social History of Venereal Disease in the United States Since 1880.* New York: Oxford University Press, 1985.

Brissett, Dennis, and Lewis, Lionel. "Guidelines for Marital Sex: An Analysis of Fifteen Popular Marriage Manuals." *Family Coordinator* 19 (January 1970): 41–48.

Brodie, Janet Farrell. "Family Limitation in American Culture, 1830–1900." Ph.D. dissertation, University of Chicago, 1982.

Brown, Helen Gurley. *Sex and the Single Girl.* New York: Bernard Geis Associates, 1962.

Brown, Steven E. "Sexuality and the Slave Community." *Phylon* 42 (Spring 1981): 1–10.

Browne, William Hand, et al., eds. *Archives of Maryland, Judicial and Testamentary Business of the Provincial Court.* Baltimore: Maryland Historical Society, 1891–1936.

Brownmiller, Susan. *Against Our Will: Men, Women, and Rape.* New York: Simon and Schuster, 1975.

Burgess, Ernest W., and Wallin, Paul. *Engagement and Marriage.* Philadelphia: J. B. Lippincott, 1953.

Burnham, John C. "American Historians and the Subject of Sex." *Societas* 2 (Autumn 1972): 307–16.

―――. "Medical Inspection of Prostitutes in America in the Nineteenth Century: The St. Louis Experiment and Its Sequel." *Bulletin of the History of Medicine* 45:3 (May–June 1971): 203–18.

Butler, Ann M. *Daughters of Joy, Sisters of Misery: Prostitutes in the American West, 1865–1890.* Urbana: University of Illinois Press, 1985.

Byrd, William. *Another Secret Diary of William Byrd of Westover, 1739–1741.* Ed. Maude H. Woodfin. Richmond, Va.: Dietz Press, 1942.

―――. *The Secret Diary of William Byrd of Westover, 1709–1712.* Ed. Louis B. Wright and Marion Tinling. Richmond, Va.: Dietz Press, 1941.

Calderone, Mary, ed. *Abortion in America: Proceedings of a Conference Sponsored by the Planned Parenthood Federation of America, 1955.* New York: Paul Hoeber, 1958.

Campbell, Patricia J. *Sex Education Books for Young Adults, 1892–1979.* New York: R. R. Bowker, 1979.

Castañeda, Antonia. "The Political Economy of Nineteenth-Century Stereotypes of Californianas." Paper presented at the Pacific Coast Branch, American Historical Association, San Francisco August 12–14, 1982.

Catterall, Helen Tunnicliff, ed. *Judicial Cases Concerning American Slavery and the Negro.* 1929–1937. Reprint. New York: Octagon Books, 1968.

Censer, Jane Turner. *North Carolina Planters and Their Children, 1800–1860.* Baton Rouge: Louisiana State University Press, 1984.

Chauncey, George, Jr. "Christian Brotherhood or Sexual Perversion? Homosexual Identities and the Construction of Sexual Boundaries in the World War One Era." *Journal of Social History* 9 (Winter 1985): 189–211.

―――. "From Sexual Inversion to Homosexuality: Medicine and the Changing Conceptualization of Female Deviance." *Salmagundi* 58–59 (Fall–Winter 1983): 114–46.

Clayton, Richard R., and Voss, Harwin L. "Shacking Up: Cohabitation in the 1970s." *Journal of Marriage and the Family* 39 (May 1977): 273–83.

Clinton, Catherine. *The Plantation Mistress: Woman's World in the Old South.* New York: Pantheon Books, 1982.

Cody, Cheryll Ann. "A Note on Changing Patterns of Slave Fertility in the South Carolina Rice District, 1735–1865." *Southern Studies* 16 (Winter 1977): 457–63.

Coles, Robert, and Stokes, Geoffrey. *Sex and the American Teenager.* New York: Harper and Row, 1985.

Comstock, Anthony. *Traps for the Young.* Ed. and intro. Robert Bremner. Cambridge, Mass., Belknap Press, 1967.

Cook, Blanche Wiesen. "Female Support Networks and Political Activism: Lillian Wald, Crystal Eastman, Emma Goldman." In *A Heritage of Her Own,* ed. Nancy F. Cott and Elizabeth H. Pleck, pp. 412–44. New York: Simon and Schuster, Touchstone, 1979.

Cordasco, Francesco. *The White Slave Trade and the Immigrant.* Detroit: Blaine Ethridge Books, 1981.

Cott, Nancy F. "Eighteenth-Century Family and Social Life Revealed in Massachusetts Divorce Records." In *A Heritage of Her Own,* ed. Nancy F. Cott and Elizabeth H. Pleck, pp. 107–35. New York: Simon and Schuster, Touchstone, 1979.

———. "Passionlessness: An Interpretation of Victorian Sexual Ideology, 1790–1850." In *A Heritage of Her Own,* ed. Nancy F. Cott and Elizabeth H. Pleck, pp. 162–81. New York: Simon and Schuster, Touchstone, 1979.

Davis, Angela Y. *Women, Race, and Class.* New York: Random House, 1981.

Davis, Katharine B. *Factors in the Sex Life of Twenty-Two Hundred Women.* New York: Harper and Row, 1929.

Davis, Madeline, and Kennedy, Elizabeth Lapovsky. "Oral History and the Study of Sexuality in the Lesbian Community: Buffalo, New York, 1940–1960." *Feminist Studies* 12 (Spring 1986): 7–26.

Degler, Carl N. *At Odds: Women and the Family in America from the Revolution to the Present.* New York: Oxford University Press, 1980.

———. "What Ought to Be and What Was: Women's Sexuality in the Nineteenth Century." *American Historical Review* 79 (December 1974): 1467–90.

del Castillo, Richard Griswold. *La Familia: Chicano Families in the Urban Southwest, 1848 to the Present.* Notre Dame: University of Notre Dame Press, 1984.

D'Emilio, John. "Capitalism and Gay Identity." In *Powers of Desire: The Politics of Sexuality,* ed. Ann Snitow, Christine Stansell, and Sharon Thompson, pp. 100–13. New York: Monthly Review Press, 1983.

———. "Gay Politics, Gay Community: San Francisco's Experience." *Socialist Review* 55 (January–February 1981): 77–104.

———. *Sexual Politics, Sexual Communities: The Making of a Homosexual Minority in the United States, 1940–1970.* Chicago: University of Chicago Press, 1983.

Demos, John. *A Little Commonwealth: Family Life in Plymouth Colony.* New York: Oxford University Press, 1970.

Dexter, Franklin B., ed. *Ancient Town Records.* Vol. 1, *New Haven Town Records, 1649–1662.* New Haven: New Haven Colony Historical Society, 1917.

Ditzion, Sidney. *Marriage, Morals and Sex in America: A History of Ideas.* New York: Bookman Associates, 1953.

Dollard, John. *Caste and Class in a Southern Town.* New Haven: Yale University Press, 1937.

Drake, St. Clair, and Cayton, Horace. *Black Metropolis.* New York: Harcourt, Brace, 1945.

Duberman, Martin Bauml. *About Time: Exploring the Gay Past.* New York: Gay Presses of New York, 1986.

———; Eggan, Fred; and Clemmer, Richard. "Documents in Hopi Indian Sexuality:

Imperialism, Culture, and Resistance." *Radical History Review* 20 (Spring–Summer 1979): 99–130.

Du Bois, W. E. B. *The Philadelphia Negro.* Reprint. Milwood, New York: Kraus-Thompson Organization, 1973.

Easterlin, Richard A. "Factors in the Decline of Farm Fertility in the United States: Some Preliminary Research Results." *Journal of American History* 63 (December 1976): 600–614.

Eckhardt, Celia Morris. *Fanny Wright: Rebel in America.* Cambridge: Harvard University Press, 1984.

Ehrenreich, Barbara. *The Hearts of Men: American Dreams and the Flight from Commitment.* Garden City, N.Y.: Anchor/Doubleday, 1983.

———; Hess, Elizabeth; and Jacobs, Gloria. *Re-Making Love: The Feminization of Sex.* Garden City, N.Y.: Anchor, 1986.

Ehrmann, Winston. *Premarital Dating Behavior.* New York: Henry Holt, 1959.

Ellis, Havelock. *Studies in the Psychology of Sex.* New York: Random House, 1936.

Epstein, Barbara. *The Politics of Domesticity: Women, Evangelism, and Temperance in Nineteenth-Century America.* Middletown, Conn.: Wesleyan University Press, 1981.

Erenberg, Lewis A. "Everybody's Doin' It: The Pre–World War I Dance Craze, the Castles and the Modern American Girl." *Feminist Studies* 3 (Fall 1975): 155–70.

———. *Steppin' Out: New York Night Life and the Transformation of American Culture, 1890–1930.* Westport, Conn.: Greenwood Press, 1981.

Ewen, Elizabeth. "City Lights: Immigrant Women and the Rise of the Movies." *Signs* 5 (Spring 1980): 45–65.

Exner, M[ax]. J. *Problems and Principles of Sex Education: A Study of 948 College Men.* New York: Association Press, 1915.

Facey, Paul, S. J. "The Legion of Decency: A Sociological Analysis of the Emergence and Development of a Social Pressure Group." Ph.D. dissertation, Fordham University, 1945.

Faderman, Lillian. *Surpassing the Love of Men: Romantic Friendship and Love Between Women from the Renaissance to the Present.* New York: William Morrow and Co., 1981.

Farley, Reynolds. *Growth of the Black Population.* Chicago: Markham Publishers, 1970.

Fass, Paula S. *The Damned and the Beautiful: American Youth in the 1920s.* New York: Oxford University Press, 1977.

Flaherty, David H. *Privacy in Colonial New England.* Charlottesville: University of Virginia Press, 1972.

Foster, Lawrence. *Religion and Sexuality: Three American Communal Experiments of the Nineteenth Century.* New York: Oxford University Press, 1981.

Foucault, Michel. *The History of Sexuality.* Trans. Robert Hurley. Vol. 1, *An Introduction.* New York: Pantheon, 1978.

Frankfort, Roberta. *Collegiate Women: Domesticity and Career in Turn-of-the-Century America.* New York: New York University Press, 1977.

Fraser, Antonia. *The Weaker Vessel: Woman's Lot in Seventeenth-Century England.* London: Weidenfeld and Nicholson, 1984.

Frazier, E. Franklin. *The Negro Family in Chicago.* Chicago: University of Chicago Press, 1932.

Freedman, Estelle. "Sexuality in Nineteenth-Century America: Behavior, Ideology and Politics." *Reviews in American History* 10 (December 1982): 196–215.

———. " 'Uncontrolled Desires': The Response to the Sexual Psychopath, 1920–1960." *Journal of American History* 74 (June 1987): 83–106.

———. *Their Sisters' Keepers: Women's Prison Reform in America, 1830–1930.* Ann Arbor: University of Michigan Press, 1981.

Friedman, Lawrence M., and Percival, Robert V. *The Roots of Justice: Crime and Punishment in Alameda County, California, 1870–1910.* Chapel Hill: University of North Carolina Press, 1981.

Gardella, Peter. *Innocent Ecstasy: How Christianity Gave America an Ethic of Sexual Pleasure.* New York: Oxford University Press, 1985.

Gay, Peter. *The Bourgeois Experience, Victoria to Freud.* Vol. 1, *Education of the Senses.* New York: Oxford University Press, 1984.

———. *The Bourgeois Experience, Victoria to Freud.* Vol. 2, *The Tender Passion.* New York: Oxford University Press, 1986.

Gebhard, Paul H., et al. *Pregnancy, Birth, and Abortion.* New York: Harper and Brothers, 1958.

Gerdts, William H. *The Great American Nude: A History in Art.* New York: Praeger, 1974.

Ginzburg, Ralph. *An Unhurried View of Erotica.* New York: Helmsman Press, 1958.

Goldman, Marion S. *Gold Diggers and Silver Miners: Prostitution and Social Life on the Comstock Lode.* Ann Arbor: University of Michigan Press, 1981.

Gonzalez, Deena. "The Spanish-Mexican Women of Sante Fe: Patterns of Their Resistance and Accommodation, 1820–1880." Ph.D. dissertation, University of California, Berkeley, 1985.

Gordon, Linda. *Woman's Body, Woman's Right: A Social History of Birth Control in America.* New York: Grossman, 1976.

Gordon, Michael. "From Unfortunate Necessity to a Cult of Mutual Orgasm: Sex in American Marital Education Literature, 1830–1940." In *The Sociology of Sex,* ed. James M. Henslin and Edward Sagarin, pp. 53–77. Rev. ed. New York: Schocken Books, 1978.

———., and Shunkweeler, Penelope J. "Different Equals Less: Female Sexuality in Recent Marriage Manuals." *Journal of Marriage and the Family* 33 (November 1977): 459–66.

Grabill, Wilson; Kiser, Clyde, and Whelpton, Pascal. *The Fertility of American Women.* New York: John Wiley, 1958.

Greven, Philip. *The Protestant Temperament: Patterns of Child-Rearing, Religious Experience, and Self in Early America.* New York: Alfred A. Knopf, 1977.

Griswold, Robert L. *Family and Divorce in California, 1850–1890: Victorian Illusions and Everyday Realities.* Albany: State University of New York Press, 1982.

Grossberg, Michael. *Governing the Hearth: Law and the Family in Nineteenth-Century America.* Chapel Hill; University of North Carolina Press, 1985.

Groves, Ernest. *The Marriage Crisis.* New York: Longmans, Green, 1928.

Gutiérrez, Ramón. "Honor Ideology, Marriage Negotiation, and Class-Gender Domination in New Mexico, 1670–1846." *Latin American Perspectives* 12 (Winter 1985): 81–104.

————. "Marriage, Sex and the Family: Social Change in Colonial New Mexico, 1690–1846." Ph.D. dissertation, University of Wisconsin, Madison, 1980.

Gutman, Herbert G. *The Black Family in Slavery and Freedom, 1750–1925.* New York: Pantheon Books, 1976.

Hagood, Margaret Jarman. *Mothers of the South: Portraiture of the White Tenant Farm Woman.* Chapel Hill: University of North Carolina Press, 1939.

Hale, Nathan G. *Freud and the Americans: The Beginnings of Psychoanalysis in the United States, 1876–1917.* New York: Oxford University Press, 1971.

Hall, Jacquelyn Dowd. *Revolt Against Chivalry: Jessie Daniel Ames and the Women's Campaign Against Lynching.* New York: Columbia University Press, 1979.

Haller, John S., Jr., and Haller, Robin M. *The Physician and Sexuality in Victorian America.* Urbana: University of Illinois Press, 1974.

Haney, Robert. *Comstockery in America: Patterns of Censorship and Control.* Boston: Beacon Press, 1960.

Hill, Adelaide Cromwell, and Jaffe, Frederick S. "Negro Fertility and Family Size Preferences: Implications for Programming of Health and Social Services." In *The Negro American,* ed. Talcott Parsons and Kenneth Clark, pp. 205–24. Boston: Beacon Press, 1966.

Hirata, Lucie Cheng. "Free, Indentured, Enslaved: Chinese Prostitutes in Nineteenth-Century America." *Signs* 5 (Autumn 1979): 3–29.

Hite, Shere. *The Hite Report.* New York: Macmillan, 1976.

————. *The Hite Report on Male Sexuality.* New York: Knopf, 1981.

Hoffer, Peter C., and Scott, William B., eds. *Criminal Proceedings in Colonial Virginia.* Athens, Ga.: University of Georgia Press, 1984.

Hoffer, Peter C., and Hull, N. E. H. *Murdering Mothers: Infanticide in England and New England, 1558–1803.* New York: New York University Press, 1981.

Hole, Judith, and Levine, Ellen. *Rebirth of Feminism.* New York: Quadrangle, 1971.

Hollingshead, A. B. *Elmtown's Youth.* New York: John Wiley, 1949.

Hunt, Morton. *Sexual Behavior in the 1970s.* New York: Dell, 1974.

Hurtado, Albert. "Ranchos, Gold Mines and Rancherias: A Socioeconomic History of Indians and Whites in Northern California, 1821–1860." Ph.D. dissertation, University of California, Santa Barbara, 1981.

Jay, Karla, and Young, Allen. *After You're Out: Personal Experiences of Gay Men and Lesbian Women.* New York: Douglass Links, 1975.

————. *The Gay Report: Lesbians and Gay Men Speak Out About Sexual Experiences and Life Styles.* New York: Summit Books, 1979.

————. *Out of the Closets: Voices of Gay Liberation.* New York: Douglass Links, 1972.

Jeffrey, Julie Roy. *Frontier Women: The Trans-Mississippi West, 1840–1880.* New York: Hill and Wang, 1979.

Johnson, Charles S. *Growing Up in the Black Belt: Negro Youth in the Rural South.* Washington, D.C.: American Council on Education, 1941.

Johnson, Susan L. "Sharing Bed and Board: Cohabitation and Cultural Difference in Central Arizona Mining Towns." *Frontiers* 7 (1984): 36–42.

Jones, Jacqueline. *Labor of Love, Labor of Sorrow: Black Women, Work, and the Family from Slavery to the Present.* New York: Basic Books, 1985.

Jones, James Boyd, Jr. "A Tale of Two Cities: The Hidden Battle Against Venereal Disease in Civil War Nashville and Memphis." *Civil War History* 31 (September 1985): 270–76.

Jones, James H. *Bad Blood: The Tuskegee Syphilis Experiment.* New York: Free Press, 1981.

Jordan, Winthrop D. *White over Black: American Attitudes Towards the Negro, 1550–1812.* Baltimore: Penguin Books, 1969.

Katz, Jonathan, ed. *Gay American History: Lesbians and Gay Men in the U.S.A.* New York: Thomas Crowell, 1976.

Katz, Jonathan Ned, ed. *Gay/Lesbian Almanac: A New Documentary.* New York: Harper and Row, 1983.

Katz, Michael B., and Stern, Mark J. "Fertility, Class, and Industrial Capitalism: Erie County, New York, 1855–1915." *American Quarterly* 33 (Spring 1981): 63–92.

Kennedy, David M. *Birth Control in America: The Career of Margaret Sanger.* New Haven: Yale University Press, 1970.

Kerber, Linda K. *Women of the Republic: Intellect and Ideology in Revolutionary America.* Chapel Hill: University of North Carolina Press, 1980.

Kern, Louis J. *An Ordered Love: Sex Roles and Sexuality in Victorian Utopias.* Chapel Hill: University of North Carolina Press, 1981.

Kett, Joseph F. *Rites of Passage: Adolescence in America, 1790 to the Present.* New York: Basic Books, 1977.

Kinsey, Alfred, et al. *Sexual Behavior in the Human Female.* Philadelphia: W. B. Saunders, 1953.

———. *Sexual Behavior in the Human Male.* Philadelphia: W. B. Saunders, 1948.

Kneeland, George. *Commercialized Prostitution in New York.* Rev. ed. New York: Century Co., 1917.

Koedt, Anne; Levine, Ellen; and Rapone, Anita. *Radical Feminism.* New York: Quadrangle Books, 1973.

Koehler, Lyle. *A Search for Power: The "Weaker Sex" in Seventeenth-Century New England.* Champaign: University of Illinois Press, 1980.

Komarovsky, Mira. *Blue-Collar Marriage.* New York: Random House, 1964.

———. *The Unemployed Man and His Family.* New York: Social Studies Association, 1940.

Kopp, Marie. *Birth Control in Practice: An Analysis of Ten Thousand Case Histories.* New York: McBride, 1934.

Kuh, Richard. *Foolish Figleaves? Pornography in—and out of—Court.* New York: Macmillan, 1967.

Kulikoff, Allan. "A 'Prolifick' People: Black Population Growth in the Chesapeake Colonies, 1700–1790." *Southern Studies* 16 (Winter 1977): 391–428.

Ladner, Joyce. *Tomorrow's Tomorrow.* Garden City, N.Y.: Doubleday, 1971.

Laslett, Peter. *Family Life and Illicit Love in Earlier Generations: Essays in Historical Sociology.* New York: Cambridge University Press, 1977.

———. *The World We Have Lost.* New York: Charles Scribners, 1984, 3rd. ed.

———; Oosterveen, Karla; and Smith, Richard M. *Bastardy and Its Comparative History.* Cambridge: Harvard University Press, 1980.

La Sorte, Michael A. "Nineteenth-Century Family Planning Practices." *Journal of Psychohistory* 4 (Fall 1976): 163–83.

LeCompte, Janet. "The Independent Women of Hispanic New Mexico, 1821–1846." *Western Historical Quarterly* 12 (January 1981): 17–35.

Lederer, Laura. *Take Back the Night.* New York: William Morrow, 1980.

Levine, Lawrence W. *Black Culture and Black Consciousness: Afro-American*

Folk Thought from Slavery to Freedom. New York: Oxford University Press, 1977.

Lewis, Felice Flanery. *Literature, Obscenity, and Law.* Carbondale, Ill.: Southern Illinois University Press, 1976.

Lindemann, Barbara S. " 'To Ravish and Carnally Know': Rape in Eighteenth-Century Massachusetts." *Signs* 10 (Autumn 1984): 63–82.

Lindsey, Ben, and Evans, Wainwright. *The Companionate Marriage.* New York: Boni and Liveright, 1927.

————. *The Revolt of Modern Youth.* Garden City, N.Y.: Garden City Publishing, 1925.

Litwack, Leon F. *Been in the Storm So Long: The Aftermath of Slavery.* New York: Vintage Books, 1979.

Luker, Kristen. *Abortion and the Politics of Motherhood.* Berkeley: University of California Press, 1984.

Lynch, Michael. "New York City Sodomy, 1796–1873." Paper presented at the Institute for the Humanities, New York University, February 1, 1985.

Lynd, Robert S., and Lynd, Helen Merrell. *Middletown: A Study in Contemporary American Culture.* New York: Harcourt, Brace, and World, 1929.

————. *Middletown in Transition.* New York: Harcourt, Brace, Jovanovich, 1937.

MacFarlane, Alan. *Marriage and Love in England: Modes of Reproduction, 1300–1840.* New York: Oxford University Press, 1986.

McLoughlin, William G. *Cherokees and Missionaries, 1789–1839.* New Haven: Yale University Press, 1984.

Marcus, Steven. *The Other Victorians: A Study of Sexuality and Pornography in Mid-Nineteenth-Century England.* New York: Basic Books, 1966.

Marotta, Toby. *The Politics of Homosexuality.* Boston: Houghton Mifflin, 1981.

May, Elaine Tyler. *Great Expectations: Marriage and Divorce in Post-Victorian America.* Chicago: University of Chicago Press, 1980.

May, Lary. *Screening Out the Past: The Birth of Mass Culture and the Motion Picture Industry.* New York: Oxford University Press, 1980.

Millett, Kate. *Sexual Politics.* Garden City, N.Y.: Doubleday, 1970.

Modell, John. "Dating Becomes the Way of American Youth." In *Essays on the Family and Social Change,* ed. David Levine et al., pp. 91–126. Arlington, Tex.: University of Texas Press, 1983.

Mohr, James C. *Abortion in America: The Origins and Evolution of National Policy, 1800–1900.* New York: Oxford University Press, 1978.

————, ed. and Winslow, Richard E., III, assoc. ed. *The Cormany Diaries: A Northern Family in the Civil War.* Pittsburgh: University of Pittsburgh Press, 1982.

Morantz, Regina Markell. "The Scientist as Sex Crusader: Alfred C. Kinsey and American Culture." *American Quarterly* 29 (Winter 1979): 563–89.

Morgan, Edmund S. *American Slavery, American Freedom.* New York: W. W. Norton and Company, 1975.

————, ed. *The Diary of Michael Wigglesworth 1653–1657: The Conscience of a Puritan.* New York: Harper and Row, 1946, 1965.

————. "The Puritans and Sex." *New England Quarterly* 25 (December 1942): 591–607.

————. *The Puritan Family: Religion and Domestic Relations in Seventeenth-Century New England.* 1944. Reprint. New York: Harper and Row, 1966.

Morgan, Robin, ed. *Sisterhood Is Powerful: An Anthology of Writings from the Women's Liberation Movement.* New York: Vintage, 1970.

Mosher, Clelia Duel. *The Mosher Survey: Sexual Attitudes of Forty-five Victorian Women.* Edited by James Mahood and Kristine Wenburg. New York: Àrno Press, 1980.

Murphy, Lawrence R. "The Enemy Among Us: Venereal Disease Among Union Soldiers in the Far West." *Civil War History* 31 (September 1985): 257–69.

———. "The House on Pacific Street: Homosexuality, Intrigue and Politics During World War II." *Journal of Homosexuality* 12 (Fall 1985): 27–49.

Myrdal, Gunnar. *An American Dilemma.* New York: Harper and Row, 1944.

Myres, Sandra L. *Westering Women and the Frontier Experience, 1800–1915.* Albuquerque: University of New Mexico Press, 1982.

Myron, Nancy, and Bunch, Charlotte, eds. *Lesbianism and the Women's Movement.* Baltimore: Diana Press, 1975.

Neuman, R. P. "Masturbation, Madness, and the Modern Concepts of Childhood and Adolescence." *Journal of Social History* 8 (Spring 1976): 1–27.

Nissenbaum, Stephen. *Sex, Diet, and Debility in Jacksonian America: Sylvester Graham and Health Reform.* Westport, Conn.: Greenwood Press, 1980.

Norton, Mary Beth. "The Evolution of White Women's Experience in Early America." *American Historical Review* 89 (June 1984): 593–619.

———. "Gender and Defamation in Seventeenth-Century Maryland." *William and Mary Quarterly* 44 (January 1987): 3–39.

O'Neill, William L. *Divorce in the Progressive Era.* New Haven: Yale University Press, 1967.

Oaks, Robert. " 'Things Fearful to Name': Sodomy and Buggery in Seventeenth-Century New England." In *The American Man,* ed. Joseph Pleck and Elizabeth Pleck, pp. 53–76. Englewood Cliffs, N.J., Prentice-Hall, 1980.

Oaks, Robert S. "Defining Sodomy in Seventeenth-Century Massachusetts." *Journal of Homosexuality* 6 (Fall–Winter 1980–81): 79–83.

Osterud, Nancy, and Fulton, J. "Family Limitation and Age at Marriage: Fertility Decline in Sturbridge, Massachusetts, 1730–1850." *Population Studies* 30 (November 1976): 481–94.

Padgug, Robert A. "Sexual Matters: On Conceptualizing Sexuality in History." *Radical History Review* (Spring–Summer 1979): 3–23.

Peiss, Kathy. *Cheap Amusements: Working Women and Leisure in Turn-of-the-Century New York.* Philadelphia: Temple University Press, 1986.

Petchesky, Rosalind P. *Abortion and Woman's Choice: The State, Sexuality, and the Conditions of Reproductive Freedom.* New York: Longman, 1984.

Pivar, David J. "Cleansing the Nation: The War on Prostitution, 1917–1921." *Prologue* 12 (Spring 1980): 29–40.

Pleck, Elizabeth. *Domestic Tyranny: The Making of American Social Policy Against Family Violence from Colonial Times to the Present.* New York: Oxford University Press, 1987.

Powdermaker, Hortense. *After Freedom.* New York: Viking, 1939.

Rainwater, Lee. *And the Poor Get Children: Sex, Contraception, and Family Planning in the Working Class.* Chicago: Quadrangle, 1960.

———. "Crucible of Identity: The Negro Lower-Class Family." *Dædalus* 95 (1966): 172–216.

———, and Yancey, William. *The Moynihan Report and the Politics of Controversy.* Cambridge: MIT Press, 1967.

Rawick, George P., ed. *The American Slave: A Composite Autobiography.* Westport, Conn.: Greenwood Press, 1972.

Reed, James. *From Private Vice to Public Virtue: The Birth Control Movement and American Society Since 1830.* New York: Basic Books, 1978.

Reiss, Ira. *Premarital Sexual Standards in America.* Glencoe, Ill.: Free Press, 1960.

———. *The Social Context of Premarital Sexual Permissiveness.* New York: Holt, Rinehart and Winston, 1967.

Riley, Glenda. *Women and Indians on the Frontier, 1825–1915.* Albuquerque: University of New Mexico Press, 1984.

Robinson, Paul. *The Modernization of Sex: Havelock Ellis, Alfred Kinsey, William Masters, and Virginia Johnson.* New York: Harper and Row, 1976.

Rosen, Ruth. *The Lost Sisterhood: Prostitution in America, 1900–1918.* Baltimore: Johns Hopkins University Press, 1982.

———, ed. *The Maimie Papers.* Textual editor, Sue Davidson. Old Westbury, New York: Feminist Press, 1977.

Rosenberg, Charles E. "Sexuality, Class, and Role in Nineteenth-Century America." *American Quarterly* 25 (May 1973): 131–53.

Rosenzweig, Roy. *Eight Hours for What We Will: Workers and Leisure in an Industrial City, 1870–1920.* New York: Cambridge University Press, 1983.

Rothman, Ellen K. *Hands and Hearts: A History of Courtship in America.* New York: Basic Books, 1984.

Rubin, Lillian. *Intimate Strangers: Men and Women Together.* New York: Harper and Row, 1983.

———. *Worlds of Pain: Life in the Working-Class Family.* New York: Basic Books, 1976.

Rupp, Leila J. " 'Imagine My Surprise': Women's Relationships in Historical Perspective." *Frontiers* 5 (Fall 1980): 61–70.

Ryan, Mary P. *Cradle of the Middle Class: The Family in Oneida County, New York, 1790–1865.* New York: Cambridge University Press, 1981.

———. "The Power of Women's Networks: A Case Study of Female Moral Reform in Antebellum America." *Feminist Studies* 5 (Spring 1979): 66–86.

Sahli, Nancy. "Smashing: Women's Relationships Before the Fall." *Chrysalis* 8 (Summer 1979): 17–27.

———. *Women and Sexuality in America: A Bibliography.* Boston: G. K. Hall and Co., 1984.

Sanger, William W. *The History of Prostitution; Its Extent, Causes and Effects throughout the World.* 1858. Reprint. New York: American Medical Press, 1895.

Schlossman, Stephen, and Wallach, Stephanie. "The Crime of Precocious Sexuality: Female Juvenile Delinquency in the Progressive Era." *Harvard Educational Review* 48 (February 1978): 65–94.

Scholten, Catherine M. *Childrearing in American Society: 1650–1850.* New York: New York University Press, 1985.

Scott, Anne Firor. *The Southern Lady: From Pedestal to Politics.* Chicago: University of Chicago Press, 1970.

Sears, Hal D. *The Sex Radicals: Free Love in High Victorian America.* Lawrence, Kans.: Regents Press, 1977.

Shively, Charley, ed. *Calamus Lovers: Walt Whitman's Working Class Camerados.* San Francisco: Gay Sunshine Press, 1987.

Shorter, Edward. "Illegitimacy, Sexual Revolution, and Social Change in Modern Europe." In *The American Family in Social-Historical Perspective,* edited by Michael Gordon, pp. 296–320. New York: St. Martin's, 1973.

Simmons, Christina. "Marriage in the Modern Manner: Sexual Radicalism and Reform in America, 1914–1941." Ph.D. dissertation, Brown University, 1982.

Simon, William, and Gagnon, John H. *Sexual Conduct: The Social Sources of Human Sexuality.* Chicago: Aldine Publishing Company, 1973.

Smith, Daniel Blake. *Inside the Great House: Planter Life in Eighteenth-Century Chesapeake Society.* Ithaca: Cornell University Press, 1980.

Smith, Daniel Scott. "The Dating of the American Sexual Revolution: Evidence and Interpretation." In *The American Family in Social-Historical Perspective,* ed. Michael Gordon, pp. 321–35. New York: St. Martin's Press, 1973.

———. "The Demographic History of Colonial New England." In *The American Family in Social-Historical Perspective,* ed. Michael Gordon, pp. 397–415. New York: St. Martin's Press, 1973.

———. "Family Limitation, Sexual Control, and Domestic Feminism in Victorian America." In *Clio's Consciousness Raised,* ed. Mary S. Hartman and Lois Banner, pp. 119–36. New York: Harper and Row, 1974.

———. "The Long Cycle in American Illegitimacy and Prenuptial Pregnancy." In *Bastardy and Its Comparative History,* ed. Peter Laslett, Karla Oosterveen, and Richard M. Smith, pp. 362–78. Cambridge: Harvard University Press, 1980.

———, and Hindus, Michael. "Premarital Pregnancy in America, 1640–1971: An Overview and an Interpretation." *Journal of Interdisciplinary History* 5 (July 1975): 537–70.

Smith-Rosenberg, Carroll. *Disorderly Conduct: Visions of Gender in Victorian America.* New York: Alfred A. Knopf, 1985.

———. "The Female World of Love and Ritual: Relations Between Women in Nineteenth-Century America." In *A Heritage of Her Own,* ed. Nancy F. Cott and Elizabeth H. Pleck, pp. 311–42. New York: Simon and Schuster, Touchstone, 1979.

———. "Sex as Symbol in Victorian Purity: An Ethnohistorical Analysis of Jacksonian America." *American Journal of Sociology* 84, supplement (1978): S212–S247.

———, and Rosenberg, Charles. "The Female Animal: Medical and Biological Views of Woman and Her Role in Nineteenth-Century America." *Journal of American History* 60 (September 1973): 332–56.

Sokolow, Jayme. *Eros and Modernization: Sylvester Graham, Health Reform, and the Origins of Victorian Sexuality in America.* Rutherford, N.J.: Farleigh Dickenson University Press, 1983.

Spindel, Donna J., and Thomas, Stuart W., Jr. "Crime and Society in North Carolina, 1663–1740." *Journal of Southern History* 49 (May 1983): 222–44.

Stack, Carol. *All Our Kin: Strategies for Survival in a Black Community.* New York: Harper and Row, 1974.

Stansell, Christine. *City of Women: Sex and Class in New York, 1789–1860.* New York: Alfred A. Knopf, 1986.

Staples, Robert. *The Black Family: Essays and Studies.* Belmont, Calif.: Wadsworth Publishing Co., 1971.

————. *The World of Black Singles.* Westport, Conn.: Greenwood Press, 1981.

Steckel, Richard H. "Antebellum Southern White Fertility: A Demographic and Economic Analysis." *Journal of Economic History* 40 (June 1980): 331–50.

Sterling, Dorothy, ed. *We Are Your Sisters: Black Women in the Nineteenth Century.* New York: W. W. Norton and Co., 1984.

Stiles, Henry Reed. *Bundling: Its Origins, Progress and Decline in America.* Albany: Joel Munsell, 1869.

Stoehr, Taylor. *Free Love in America: A Documentary History.* New York: AMS Press, 1979.

Stone, Lawrence. *Family, Sex and Marriage in England, 1500–1800.* New York: Harper and Row, 1979.

Strong, Bryan. "Ideas of the Early Sex Education Movement in America, 1890–1920." *History of Education Quarterly* 12 (Summer 1972): 129–61.

Stycos, Joseph Mayone. *Family and Fertility in Puerto Rico.* New York: Columbia University Press, 1955.

Takaki, Ronald T. *Iron Cages: Race and Culture in Nineteenth-Century America.* Seattle: University of Washington Press, 1982.

Talese, Gay. *Thy Neighbor's Wife.* Garden City, N.Y.: Doubleday, 1980.

Teal, Donn. *The Gay Militants.* New York: Stein and Day, 1971.

Thompson, Roger. *Sex in Middlesex: Popular Mores in a Massachusetts County, 1649–1699.* Amherst: University of Massachusetts Press, 1986.

————. *Women in Stuart England and America.* London: Routledge and Kegan Paul, 1974.

Trimberger, Ellen Kay. "Feminism, Men, and Modern Love: Greenwich Village, 1900–1925." In *Powers of Desire: The Politics of Sexuality,* ed. Ann Snitow, Christine Stansell, and Sharon Thompson, pp. 131–52. New York: Monthly Review Press, 1983.

Verduin, Kathleen. " 'Our Cursed Natures': Sexuality and the Puritan Conscience." *New England Quarterly* 56 (June 1983): 220–37.

Vice Commission of Chicago. *The Social Evil in Chicago.* New York: Arno Press, 1970.

Vincent, Clark. *Unmarried Mothers.* New York: Free Press, 1961.

Vining, Donald. *A Gay Diary, 1933–1946.* New York: Pepys Press, 1979.

Vinovskis, Maris A. "Socioeconomic Determinants of Interstate Fertility Differentials in the United States." *Journal of Interdisciplinary History* 6 (Winter 1976): 375–96.

Walkowitz, Judith R. *Prostitution and Victorian Society: Women, Class, and the State.* New York: Cambridge University Press, 1980.

Walsh, Lorena S. " 'Till Death Do Us Part': Marriage and Family in Seventeenth-Century Maryland." In *The Chesapeake in the Seventeenth Century: Essays in Anglo-American Society,* ed. Thad W. Tate and David L. Ammerman, pp. 126–52. Chapel Hill: University of North Carolina Press, 1979.

Walters, Ronald G. "The Erotic South: Civilization and Sexuality in American Abolitionism." *American Quarterly* 25 (May 1973): 177–201.

————, ed. *Primers for Purity: Sexual Advice to Victorian America.* Englewood Cliffs, N.J.: Prentice-Hall, 1974.

Weeks, Jeffrey. *Coming Out: Homosexual Politics in Britain from the Nineteenth Century to the Present.* London: Quartet Books, 1977.

———. *Sex, Politics, and Society: The Regulation of Sexuality Since 1800.* London: Longman, 1981.

———. *Sexuality and Its Discontents: Meanings, Myths and Modern Sexualities.* London: Routledge and Kegan Paul, 1985.

Wells, Anna Mary. *Miss Marks and Miss Woolley.* Boston: Houghton Mifflin, 1978.

Wells, Robert V. "Demographic Change and the Life Cycle of American Families." *Journal of Interdisciplinary History* 2 (1971–72): 273–82.

———. "Family Size and Fertility Control in Eighteenth-Century America: A Study of Quaker Families." *Population Studies* 25 (1971): 73–82.

———. "Illegitimacy and Bridal Pregnancy in Colonial America." In *Bastardy and Its Comparative History,* ed. Peter Laslett, Karla Oosterveen, and Richard M. Smith, pp. 349–61. Cambridge: Harvard University Press, 1980.

———. "Quaker Marriage Patterns in a Colonial Perspective." *William and Mary Quarterly,* 3d ser., vol. XXIX (July 1972): 415–42.

———. *Revolutions in Americans' Lives: A Demographic Perspective on the History of Americans, Their Families, and Their Society.* Westport, Conn.: Greenwood Press, 1982.

Westoff, Charles F., and Ryder, Norman B. *The Contraceptive Revolution.* Princeton, N.J.: Princeton University Press: 1977.

Whelpton, Pascal, et al. *Fertility and Family Planning in the United States.* Princeton, N.J.: Princeton University Press, 1966.

White, Deborah Gray. *Ain't I a Woman? Female Slaves in the Plantation South.* New York: W. W. Norton and Co., 1985.

Williamson, Joel. *New People: Miscegenation and Mulattoes in the United States.* New York: The Free Press, 1980.

Williams, Walter L. *The Spirit and the Flesh: Sexual Diversity in American Indian Culture.* Boston: Beacon Press, 1986.

Woods, Robert A., and Kennedy, Albert J., eds. *Young Working Girls: A Summary of Evidence from Two Thousand Social Workers.* Boston: Houghton Mifflin, 1913.

Wrightson, Keith. *English Society, 1580–1680.* New Brunswick, N.J.: Rutgers University Press, 1982.

Wyatt-Brown, Bertram. *Southern Honor: Ethics and Behavior in the Old South.* New York: Oxford University Press, 1982.

Yates, Wilson. "Birth Control Literature and the Medical Profession in Nineteenth-Century America." *Journal of the History of Medicine* 31 (January 1976): 42–54.

Yellis, Kenneth. "Prosperity's Child: Some Thoughts on the Flapper." *American Quarterly* 21 (1969): 44–64.

Zelnick, Melvin. "Fertility of the American Negro in 1830 and 1850." *Population Studies* 20 (July 1966): 77–83.

Index